ASPIRATION AND REALITY IN LEGAL EDUCATION

Aspiration and Reality in Legal Education

DAVID SANDOMIERSKI

UNIVERSITY OF TORONTO PRESS
Toronto Buffalo London

Toronto Buffalo London
utorontopress.com

ISBN 978-1-4875-0594-3 (cloth)
ISBN 978-1-4875-3300-7 (EPUB)
ISBN 978-1-4875-3299-4 (PDF)

Library and Archives Canada Cataloguing in Publication

Title: Aspiration and reality in legal education / David Sandomierski.
Names: Sandomierski, David, author.
Description: Includes bibliographical references and index.
Identifiers: Canadiana (print) 20190223677 | Canadiana (ebook) 20190223782 | ISBN 9781487505943 (cloth) | ISBN 9781487533007 (EPUB) | ISBN 9781487532994 (PDF)
Subjects: LCSH: Law – Study and teaching – Canada. | LCSH: Law – Philosophy.
Classification: LCC KE289 .S26 2020 | LCC KF272 .S26 2020 kfmod | DDC 340.071/071–dc23

Cover art: An Emptying of the Canvas: The Metaphorical Blank Slate, by Zao Wou-Ki (1959).

This book has been published with the help of a grant from the Federation for the Humanities and Social Sciences, through the Awards to Scholarly Publications Program, using funds provided by the Social Sciences and Humanities Research Council of Canada.

University of Toronto Press acknowledges the financial assistance to its publishing program of the Canada Council for the Arts and the Ontario Arts Council, an agency of the Government of Ontario.

Canada Council for the Arts
Conseil des Arts du Canada

Funded by the Government of Canada
Financé par le gouvernement du Canada

Canada

Even a blank slate imposes its limits – you need a slate and you need chalk; you have limited space before you have to erase and start over; and your primary mode of communication will be words, not pictures or actions.

– Rod Macdonald

Contents

Acknowledgments ix

1 The Lawyer as Citizen: Integrating Theory and Practice in Legal Education 3

2 Contracts and the Eclectic Toolkit of Legal Reasoning 40

3 Promise and Performance in Canadian Common Law Contracts Casebooks 78

4 Making Better Lawyers: The Aspiration to Translate Theory into Practice 152

5 The Failure to Operationalize: Realism and Formalism in Canadian Common Law Contracts Teaching 178

6 Transcending Langdell: Agency, Structure, and Transformation in Contemporary Legal Education 291

Works Cited 341

Index 365

Acknowledgments

This book began at the University of Toronto Faculty of Law, an intellectually supportive environment that made possible this empirical and theoretically informed study. I am incredibly grateful to Jennifer Nedelsky for her sublime alchemy of unconditional support and intellectual challenge. Angela Fernandez and David Schneiderman provided exceptionally helpful guidance, suggestions, and critique. Jutta Brunnée and Mariana Mota Prado championed this project at all stages. Comments by Kerry Rittich and Bob Gordon were extremely helpful in refining the final manuscript.

I have benefited from mentorship and intellectual guidance from many generous interlocutors over the years. These include Rod Macdonald, Blaine Baker, Shauna Van Praagh, Joel Bakan, Robert Leckey, Harry Arthurs, Nicholas Kasirer, Philip Girard, and Evan Fox-Decent. I would like to thank Thomas McMorrow for reading numerous drafts and for his generous conversations. Kate and Ben Berger provided sage advice on the final stages of the manuscript, including on the title. Joshua Karton and John Enman-Beech provided helpful feedback on early drafts of Chapter 3. I have also learned a great deal from conversations with Eric Adams, Wendy Adams, Mark Antaki, Roxana Banu, Susan Bartie, Faisal Bhabha, John Bliss, Annie Bunting, Joseph Carens, Erika Chamberlain, Eddie Clark, David Dyzenhaus, Trevor Farrow, Adrien Habermacher, Claire Houston, Daniel Huizenga, Daniel Jutras, Lisa Kelly, Howie Kislowicz, Hoi Kong, Rande Kostal, Joanna Langille, Sonia Lawrence, Ryan Liss, Paul Maharg, Derek McKee, Janet Mosher, Palma Paciocco, Mike Pal, Melanie Randall, Jen Raso, Sean Rehaag, Bruce Ryder, Nick Sage, Noel Semple, Jacob Shelley, Lorne Sossin, Anna Su, Michael Trebilcock, Stephen Waddams, David Wiseman, Robert Wai, Alice Woolley, and Albert Yoon.

I have benefited greatly from presenting elements of this project at multiple venues. These include the University of Alberta's centenary conference on legal education, a joint conference of the American Bar Foundation and the National Science Foundation, and annual meetings of the Canadian Association of Law Teachers, the Canadian and American Law and Society Associations, and the American Society for Legal History. Faculty workshops at the University of Toronto Faculty of Law, the Allard School of Law at UBC, Osgoode Hall Law School, and Western University Faculty of Law have also been instrumental in refining my ideas. I am particularly grateful to Hoi Kong, Virginia Torrie, and Richard Devlin for participating in an early Author-Meets-Reader event, and to David Wiseman, President of CALT, for facilitating it.

This research was supported by the Social Sciences and Humanities Research Council of Canada through a Vanier Canada Graduate Scholarship, the Faculty of Law and School of Graduate Studies at the University of Toronto, and the Faculty of Law and Work Study Program at Western University. I am grateful to Canadian publishers Thomson Reuters Canada, Emond, and LexisNexis Canada for complimentary review copies and for sharing confidential sales data. I am also grateful to the National Committee of Accreditation of the Federation of Law Societies of Canada for providing confidential numbers of examination sittings for Contract Law, and to the American Association of Law Schools for providing data on the number of US Contracts professors. Meera Deo and Chad Christensen at the Law School Survey of Student Engagement generously provided raw data and research support. Professor Alan Hanna at the University of Victoria helpfully shared his reading materials for Transsystemic Contracts at the very last hour. I would like to thank the staff at the Clara Thomas Archives & Special Collections at York University, the University of Toronto Archives, and the Harvard Law School's Historical and Special Collections.

Chapter 3 served as the basis for a substantially revised publication, David Sandomierski, "Tension and Reconciliation in Canadian Contracts Casebooks" (2017) 54 Osgoode Hall LJ 1183. Certain material from Chapters 1 and 4 appears in David Sandomierski, "Theory and Practice, Together at Last: A Heretical, Empirical Account of Canadian Legal Education," in Meera Deo, Mindie Lazarus-Black & Elizabeth Mertz, eds, *Power, Legal Education, and Law School Cultures* (Routledge, 2019). Some material from Chapter 1 appears in David Sandomierski, "Training Lawyers, Cultivating Citizens, and Re-Enchanting the Legal Professional" (2014) 51 Alta L Rev 739. This research was conducted under a Research Ethics Board protocol at the University of Toronto. Certain interviews and email correspondence have been attributed with permission.

This study would not have been possible without the generous involvement of my participants, who trusted me with their materials and words, and who gave up their precious time to meet and correspond with me. I am grateful for the fastidious and professional transcription services of Jen Bodmer (English) and Pénélope Maheu-Tessier (French), for administrative support from Rachel Kim, and for the superb editorial and research assistance of Emily Denomme and Tyler Mäkinen. Daniel Quinlan at the University of Toronto Press has been extremely supportive in shepherding the book manuscript through the review and revision process. I owe a special debt of gratitude to my copy editor, Barry Norris, for his close eye and inspired suggestions, and to Judy Dunlop for having produced a meticulous and illuminating index.

Finally, this work would never have been completed without the support of my family. I would like to thank my mom for her love and care over the years, and her partner James for instilling in me a love of writing at a young age. I am indebted to my sister Megan for helping me find the time and space to work on this project with a busy young family. I will forever associate this project with the birth and early years of my three children, Eve, Aila, and Amy. They have taught me more about life, law, and learning than I could have ever imagined. Sarah, my partner throughout this adventure, has made it all possible. I learn from her every day, and am inexpressibly grateful.

ASPIRATION AND REALITY IN LEGAL EDUCATION

Chapter One

The Lawyer as Citizen: Integrating Theory and Practice in Legal Education

Whether we experience law as a benign facilitator of our goals, a manifestation of systemic unfairness, an imposition of power and violence, or, indeed, even in instances when we do not "see" it at all, law nevertheless serves the social role of helping us govern ourselves according to rules and principles. Law is, among many other things, a tool for achieving human purposes. That tool can be used in infinitely different contexts, deployed in innumerable ways. We all live law, and learn about law, from the day we are born. But only some of us take on the vocation of practising law in a formal sense. And the vast majority of those who do, at least in Canada and the United States, prepare to do so by going to law school.

Law schools are a key place where lay people are initiated into the intellectual and professional world of law – where students learn to think like a lawyer and where, crucially, they begin to imagine how they might tangibly contribute to society through law. Lawyers take on many different roles in both the public and private realms: they advocate to legal officials, political bodies, and the media; they negotiate and facilitate deals and structure transactions; they counsel clients about strategy and provide life advice; they help navigate the complexity of the administrative state and defend against state power; they adjudicate disputes; they advise governments – and this is just a partial list. Moreover, many legally educated graduates do not formally practise law but engage with law to advance other social goals. They serve as journalists, activists, politicians, entrepreneurs, non-profit leaders, academics – again, the list of vocations through which a legal education can valuably advance collective or individual goals is almost infinite.

It might therefore be considered a happy accident, therefore, that modern legal education is largely administered within universities. Universities are places where the broadest of horizons can be imagined – where one can seek to understand the "universe" or aspire to "universal" understanding. A chief aim of the university is the pursuit of greater understanding through critical enquiry. Many universities – and all Canadian ones that currently house a law school – are, moreover, publicly funded, and thereby take on an even greater public mandate.[1] Given this liberal and civic institutional footing and the extensive reach of law throughout society, one might optimistically predict that going to law school constitutes not only an intellectually transformative experience, but also one that exposes students to the widest range of visions for contributing to society through law.

This book asks whether Canadian law schools – those that teach in the common law tradition – are living up to this potential. It does so by exploring the attitudes and practices of teachers of one course that all law students must take as part of their first year of legal study:

---

1 The only possible exception in Canada is the proposed law school at Trinity Western University, a private university. The Supreme Court of Canada has upheld the denial of accreditation of this law school by the Law Societies of British Columbia and Ontario. See *Law Society of British Columbia v Trinity Western University and Brayden Volkenant*, 2018 SCC 32, [2018] 2 SCR 293 [*Trinity* BC]; *Trinity Western University and Brayden Volkenant v Law Society of Upper Canada*, 2018 SCC 33, [2018] 2 SCR 453 [*Trinity* Ontario]. This has prompted Trinity Western to withdraw its proposal. That proposal, however, arguably could be revived given the school's subsequent decision to remove the offending mandatory covenant. See Wendy Stueck & Sunny Dhillon, "B.C.'s Trinity Western University drops mandatory covenant forbidding sex outside heterosexual marriage", *Globe and Mail* (14 August 2018), online: https://www.theglobeandmail.com/canada/british-columbia/article-bcs-trinity-western-university-drops-mandatory-covenant-forbidding/. For a further discussion of the case, see *infra* notes 22–5 and accompanying text.

At the time of writing, the Ontario government had refused to provide Ryerson University with additional funding for its law school. However, the university remains publicly funded and, to the extent that it will allocate a portion of its funding envelope to the law school, and given that law students will be eligible for government student loans, the law school will benefit from public support. See Kristin Rushowy, "Ryerson's law school gets some provincial support, students now eligible for OSAP", *Toronto Star* (6 September 2019), online: https://www.thestar.com/politics/provincial/2019/09/06/ryersons-law-school-gets-some-provincial-support-students-now-eligible-for-osap.html.

The proposed new law school at Memorial University of Newfoundland currently is contemplated being run without provincial financial support at the otherwise publicly funded university, this assumption serving as a "starting point for a conversation with the province about its potential investment interest" (Anita Balakrishnan, "Memorial University senate approves law school proposal", *Canadian Lawyer* (27 November 2018), online: https://www.canadianlawyermag.com/legalfeeds/author/anita-balakrishnan/memorial-university-senate-approves-law-school-proposal-16547/, quoting Noreen Golfman, Provost and Vice-President (Academic).

Contracts. By exploring what Canadian common law Contracts professors believe about law, how they describe the activity of "thinking like a lawyer," and by studying their teaching philosophies, practices, and materials, we can learn something about how beginning students are acculturated into the discipline and profession of law. What does training students to think like lawyers include and exclude? What intellectual and other skills are students encouraged to develop, and for what are they rewarded? How do professors' theoretical beliefs about law become translated into a vision of what law graduates have to offer society? In other words, how does the rite of passage that is first-year Contracts participate in the development of legal and professional consciousness?[2]

This book is part of a broader project of teasing out the immanent potential of legal education to model the legal professional as a steward of law as a public resource. This model legal professional deploys a holistic catalogue of skills and perspectives, whose wide variety is commensurate with the many and varied instantiations of law, to make diverse social contributions in the private and public spheres. He or she integrates the notion of being a public official with the provision of legal services, and inhabits numerous roles according to various situations: this legal professional might function as a problem solver, activist, advocate, counsellor, policy thinker, and architect of social structures. This chapter's title uses the shorthand "citizen" to capture this aspiration. That is not an ideal term – it has connotations of elitism, exclusion, and inequality.[3] Nevertheless, it is the connotations of civic engagement, versatility, and public-spiritedness that I mean to invoke here.[4] The lawyer *as* citizen integrates the technical, cognitive, epistemic, and practical

2 On Contracts as a rite of passage, see e.g. *The Paper Chase*, 1973, DVD (Beverly Hills, CA: 20th Century Fox Home Entertainment, 2003).

3 See Ayelet Shachar, *The Birthright Lottery: Citizenship and Global Inequality* (Cambridge, MA: Harvard University Press, 2009); W Wesley Pue, "Educating the Total Jurist?" (2005) 8 Legal Ethics 208 at 220.

4 The ideas of participation, deliberation, and service derive from the tradition of civic republicanism, with its origins in Aristotelian conceptions of civic virtue. See generally Iseult Honohan, *Civic Republicanism* (New York; London: Routledge, 2002) at 5 ("[c]itizens must be active, accepting duties and performing public service both military and political ... [T]hey must cultivate civic virtue, or a commitment to the common good"), 23–7; Aristotle, *Politics*, translated by CDC Reeve (Indianapolis, IN; Cambridge: Hackett, 2017) III.1, 1275a22–3 (The citizen "is defined ... by his participation in judgment and office"), III.4, 1277a27–9 ("even though they are dissimilar, [citizens] have the preservation of the community as their function"). I mean to emphasize these elements of participation and service without the corresponding delimiting questions of who is "qualified" or "authorized" to become a citizen (III.1, 1275b17–19).

tasks of the legal professional with the facilitative work of advancing human purposes in diverse sites of private associational life and social organization, along with the civic-mindedness of the social actor in the public realm. The composite term "lawyer *as* citizen" reminds us that the legal professional's work is at once concerned with public and private ends, and that the cultivation of versatility is a manifestation of the diverse roles and responsibilities of the legal professional. It signals the idea that, just as law extends its reach into every corner of society, legal education should prepare its graduates to make contributions in every corner by deploying the full range of their intellectual and affective capabilities, which their legal education in turn has portrayed as relevant to law.

This book makes a modest but particular contribution to this broader project. It is an empirical study – and thus largely descriptive, not normative or prescriptive – of the present state of law teaching. My goal is not to develop a full theorization of the lawyer-as-citizen idea – although I take inspiration from leading theoretical thinkers, as outlined below – but rather to study one particular element of it. The subset of the lawyer-as-citizen vision that I focus on is the idea that legal education can cultivate an eclectic toolkit of skills for the lawyer to deploy in a wide range of contexts, and thereby model an image of the legal professional as one able to engage with law in diverse sites across the social order. The distinctly public or civic components of the idea, while extremely important, do not figure as prominently in this study, largely because these themes did not emerge in an extensive way in the data I have collected and analysed.

The subject of my analysis is the attitudes and teaching practices of Canadian common law Contracts professors. I focus on what these teachers expressed to me in interviews and in their published and in-course teaching materials. Despite the specificity of this information, the observations and insights derived from the study have broad implications for legal education – not just for the teaching of Contracts, and not just in Canada. Contracts is a particularly good case study because, as I expand upon in detail in Chapter 2, the mainstream contract law scholarship of the twentieth century provides the foundation for exposing students to a wide variety of legal theories: it is a perfect candidate for equipping students with an eclectic toolkit and modelling a broad vision of legal practice. And yet, as I will also detail, the teaching of Contracts is both the source and product of a powerful inherited tradition, one that models a much narrower vision of the lawyer than is natural to the subject matter. Like legal education generally, in Contracts it is possible to translate a diverse range of theories about law into an ambitious vision of the lawyer as citizen; but at the same time, as might be observed across different courses, jurisdictions, and facets of the law school environment, in Contracts this possibility is not entirely realized. This study elucidates some of the barriers to translating the ideals of law into a workably broad vision of what it means to think like, and work as, a lawyer.

As an empirical project, this book generates two distinct insights. First, it demonstrates that there actually is, among contemporary Canadian common law Contracts professors, a broad aspiration consistent with the vision of cultivating the lawyer as citizen. Professors ascribe to a wide range of theories about law, many of them heavily influenced by the realist and critical schools of twentieth-century American legal thought. These theories, if put into practice, would equip students with an eclectic set of tools and an understanding of how to engage with law broadly in pursuit of diverse public and private ends. What is more, the vast majority of professors, when asked why theory is important, say that it is so *primarily* in order to produce better lawyers – to translate theory into practice.

At the same time, when we look at how professors model "practice," we discover that this aspiration is imperfectly realized. Diverse theories *do not* appear to be directly translated into practice, at least in two senses of the word *practice*. First, most Contracts professors understand the practice of legal reasoning ("thinking like a lawyer") in a way that does not reflect the diverse range of theories they hold. The attitudes of law reflected in the way professors describe this core professional competency do not map onto the range of theories these professors appear to believe in. Second, when we look at some elements of their teaching – their descriptions of their practices and philosophy, their teaching materials, and their evaluation methods – the practice of educating, likewise, reflects a much narrower range of theories about law than those they say they believe in. Thus, this study suggests that in large part the aspiration to translate theory into practice – and hence to accomplish one element of the lawyer-as-citizen goal – is not being realized.

The next section explores how the idea of the lawyer as citizen grows out of an intellectual tradition in which theory and practice are conceived of as mutually reinforcing concepts that can be integrated in a public-spirited vision of legal education. That integrative view is in large part a reaction against the dominant discourse, in which theory and practice are placed in opposition via a story of jurisdictional tussle between universities and law societies. The aspiration on behalf of the participants in my study to translate theory into practice should be understood in light of these debates.

THEORY AND PRACTICE IN LEGAL EDUCATION

Theory and Practice in Opposition

A primary trope in legal education, in Canada and abroad, is that there is a fierce debate between law societies and universities about jurisdiction over and control of legal education. Contemporary debates manifest the tension in particularly sharp terms: commentators demand that law schools produce "practice ready" lawyers; law societies demand that law schools deliver students with defined "competencies."[5] These demands, while precipitated by contemporary disruptions to the market for legal services, are not new. In Ontario they manifested in the dramatic resignation of the Osgoode Hall Law School faculty in 1949 to form the University of Toronto Faculty of Law in 1957, and ultimately in the decision to move Osgoode Hall Law School to York University.[6] As Harry Arthurs describes, what began as debates over who should control admission to practice developed into wide-ranging debates about the means and ends of legal education. These included questions of "whether law faculties ought to provide a liberal education in law or occupational training for legal practice; about competing theories of pedagogy and how to implement them; about the critical challenge posed by legal scholarship to conventional views of law and legal institutions; and ultimately about whether replication of existing models of legal professionalism was in the best interests of the bar and public."[7]

The conventional narrative, at least in Ontario, is that the universities' victory over jurisdiction has permitted law faculties to pursue liberal, critical, and public-interested ends freed from the narrow demands of

---

5 See e.g. David Segal, "What they don't teach law students: lawyering", *New York Times* (19 November 2011), online: http://www.nytimes.com/2011/11/20/business/after-law-school-associates-learn-to-be-lawyers.html; American Bar Association, Task Force on the Future of Legal Education, "Working Paper" (1 August 2013), online: http://www.americanbar.org/content/dam/aba/administrative/professional_responsibility/taskforcecomments/aba_task_force_working_paper_august_2013.authcheckdam.pdf) [*ABA Report*]; Brian Z Tamanaha, *Failing Law Schools* (Chicago: University of Chicago Press, 2012); Federation of Law Societies of Canada, Common Law Degree Implementation Committee, *Final Report*, August 2011, online: http://docs.flsc.ca/Implementation-Report-ECC-Aug-2011-R.pdf [*FLSC Report*]; HW Arthurs, "The Tree of Knowledge, The Axe of Power: Le Dain and the Transformation of Canadian Legal Education" in G Blaine Baker & Richard Janda, eds, *Tracings of Gerald Le Dain's Life in the Law* (Montreal; Kingston, ON: McGill-Queen's University Press, 2019) 106.

6 C Ian Kyer & Jerome E Bickenbach, *The Fiercest Debate: Cecil A Wright, the Benchers, and Legal Education in Ontario* (Toronto: Osgoode Society, 1987).

7 Arthurs, "Tree of Knowledge", *supra* note 5 at 108.

producing technically competent ("practice-ready") lawyers. Recent requirements imposed on the curriculum by the Federation of Law Societies can be considered, in this regard, to "repudiate the decades-long truce between the profession and the academy."[8]

Beyond Ontario, the theory/practice debate seems apt to characterize major developments in the common law world. To take a historical example, William Blackstone's inauguration as Vinerian Chair at Oxford in 1758 enabled him to centre legal education in a university. As Kyer and Bickenbach write, "Blackstone's views on the nature and aims of legal education formed the basic creed of those who were to argue for the university law school for the next three centuries: law can be systematically taught, not merely as a body of practical rules but as a science; as a science, law can be taught only in a university setting surrounded by teachers and students of the other sciences ... [And] legal education needed a literature, the product of specialized legal scholars able to assess and recommend changes in the law."[9] Similarly, in the United States, the founding of Harvard Law School "reflected the novel notion that institutions of higher learning had a role to play in the education of American lawyers."[10] The "English root" – Blackstone's idea of university education – had been transplanted and would flourish in the United States, taking firm hold with the widespread adoption of Christopher Columbus Langdell's case method. Like Blackstone, Langdell argued that, "[s]ince law is a science, and since cases are the experimental data of the science, legal education must be limited to the university."[11] The end of the nineteenth and beginning of the twentieth centuries were characterized by a conflict between university law schools and proprietary night schools run largely by practitioners; the

8 *Ibid* at 121. For a recent example of Canadian law professors' resisting pressure to produce "practice-ready" graduates, see Benjamin Berger et al, "A Submission to the LSUC Dialogue on Licensing: A Response from Some Ontario Law Professors" (2017), online: https://lsodialogue.ca/wp-content/uploads/2018/07/Written-Submissions-Dialogue-on-Licensing-D2_2018jul6-red.pdf at Part V ("Our key concerns are to protect our law schools from being converted into practical legal training programs and to resist the notion that our mission should be to create so-called 'practice-ready' graduates"). *Cf* Ian Holloway & Steven I Friedland, "The Double Life of Law Schools" (2017) 68 Case Western Reserve L Rev 397 at 398 ("we are living in a time of struggle – struggle for the control of the soul of legal education").

9 *Supra* note 6 at 8–9 (citations omitted).

10 Andrew Porwancher, Book Review of *On the Battlefield of Merit: Harvard Law School, the First Century* by Daniel R Coquillette & Bruce A Kimball, (2016) 34 Law & Hist Rev 819 at 819.

11 Kyer & Bickenbach, *supra* note 6 at 16.

former eventually triumphed, and university legal education became, and remains, the predominant form of law study today.[12]

Theory and Practice as Mutually Reinforcing

Despite this dominant narrative of debate and opposition, however, there is another, secondary narrative that acknowledges cooperation between the legal profession and the university, and that conceives of theory and practice as mutually reinforcing. At one level, this narrative is grounded in historical fact. Not every Canadian law school was born of conflict. The Manitoba Law School, for example, was founded in 1914 "as a joint undertaking of the University and Law Society," its curriculum jointly agreed upon by faculty members and members of the profession, and jointly financed. As one of its founding members stated, "We have always felt particularly happy about the cordial and close relationship between the University and Law Society, bodies which we believe should share in the responsibility for legal education – each having a different, but equally important function to fulfil."[13] Such an attitude of cooperation persisted into the 1960s, when a law society report described legal education as "an ideal blending of the vocational and academic."[14] To this day, a seat on the Robson Hall Faculty Council is reserved for a member of the Law Society of Manitoba.

At another, more conceptual level, more recent writings on legal education express the aspiration that a liberal, academic study of law can make more effective and creative legal professionals and, correlatively, that empirical examples from practice can enrich theoretical enquiry. The flagship 1983 *Law and Learning* report is one example. In it, Harry Arthurs characterizes Canadian legal education as aspiring to "humane professionalism," a term that itself integrates the goals of the university and the profession. Arthurs describes the relationship in the following way:

> [W]hile the cultivated ability to stand at a distance from conventional wisdom, to view it critically, must be defended on its intrinsic merits as being the essence of education, it also has at least three important "practical"

12 See generally *ibid*, c 1; Daniel R Coquillette & Bruce A Kimball, "The Republic of Merit: Harvard Law School, the First Century (1817–1910)" in *The Bicentennial History of the Harvard Law School* (Cambridge, MA: Harvard University Press, 2015), vol 1.

13 EK Williams, "Legal Education in Manitoba: 1913–1950" (1950) 28 Can Bar Rev 759 at 760; EK Williams, "Legal Education in Manitoba: 1913–1950" (1950) 28 Can Bar Rev 880 at 882, 884, 891. See also W Wesley Pue, "Common Law Legal Education in Canada's Age of Light, Soap and Water" (1995) 23 Man LJ 654 at 665–74.

14 Quoted in GPR Tallin, "Legal Education in Manitoba" (1964) 15 UTLJ 433 at 434.

> benefits. It enables lawyers to adapt to changes when they occur, to assist in bringing about such changes through law reform and other public activities, and to accomplish change themselves in the limited context of serving individual clients whose interests do not coincide with accepted solutions. From the student's perspective, having to deal with both the intellectual and the practical at once generates a dialectic which ... contributes to the student's tough-mindedness. This could help to explain why law schools, in their humane intellectual activities, might make a contribution to preparation for professional practice that is both vitally important and easily overlooked.[15]

Another way that the compatibility between theory and practice manifests is in attempts to integrate the public mission of university education with the professional training objectives of law schools. Anthony Kronman effects such an integration through his ideal of the "lawyer-statesman," developed at length in *The Lost Lawyer: Failing Ideals of the Legal Profession*. Kronman argues how an education that trains lawyers well also cultivates the ideals of deliberative wisdom and civic-mindedness – key traits of the statesman. Correlatively the statesman's virtues make excellent lawyers. Great advocates and counsellors require deliberative wisdom to assist their clients in deliberating about ends, and require civic-minded commitment to the intrinsic goods of the legal system to predict judicial outcomes effectively.[16] Kronman's vision thus integrates high public ideals with the legal professional role:

> The outstanding lawyer ... is, to begin with, a devoted citizen. He cares about the public good and is prepared to sacrifice his own well-being for it ... He is distinguished ... by his special talent for discovering where the public good lies and for fashioning those arrangements needed to secure it. The lawyer-statesman is a leader in the realm of public life, and other citizens look to him for guidance and advice, as do his private clients ...
>
> The good lawyer does care about the soundness of the legal order ... [H]e shares the judge's public-spirited devotion to it. This is in fact a condition for his being successful at his work. The good lawyer's public-spiritedness is not, moreover, something tacked onto his professional

15 Consultative Group on Research and Education in Law, *Law and Learning* (Report to the Social Sciences and Humanities Research Council of Canada, Chairman Harry Arthurs) (Ottawa: Social Sciences and Humanities Research Council of Canada, 1983) at 49–50 [*Arthurs Report*].

16 Anthony T Kronman, *The Lost Lawyer: Failing Ideals of the Legal Profession* (Cambridge, MA: Belknap Press, 1993) at 14–15, 118–20, 72, 98, 113.

> skills, a kind of moralistic addendum to his craft. Rather, it is an essential component of that craft and cannot be separated from it.[17]

Like Kronman and Arthurs, each of whose integrative vision arguably contributes to the "redemption of legal professionalism,"[18] the *Carnegie Report* of 2007 advocates an integration of the cognitive, practical, and professional-identity "apprenticeships" under the aegis of "civic professionalism."[19] As with the other two accounts, civic professionalism integrates the liberal, critical, and public-spirited values of the academy with the demands of the profession in a reciprocal fashion. Professionalism is directed not simply towards individual or client-focused ends, but rather to collective, public service:

> To be a professional in the full sense is to understand oneself as claimed by a craft and a purpose in whose service to use that craft. Yet precisely because that purpose is a public one, directed toward others, professionals can also be conscious of the limits and specificity of their domain. With this awareness, professionals can appreciate other ways of living and contributing to the larger life of their times. They can be citizens as well as experts ...
>
> It is because of their sense of who they are and how they understand themselves in the world that these professional skills become assets for everyone.[20]

Accordingly, major debates about legal education tend to focus not only on the jurisdictional relationship between two key institutions – the academy and the profession – but also on the relationship between the ideals for which these institutions stand as proxy. These are, on the one hand, the virtue of theoretical and critical enquiry and the goal of producing broad-minded, public-spirited citizens; and, on the other, the virtue of effective service to clients and the legal system. Although the conventional story places these two sets of ideals in opposition, a significant secondary narrative aspirationally suggests that the intellectual and social enquiry of university study can support and cultivate a broad and effective vision of legal practice (and, correlatively, that training for the practice of law can cultivate broader public and

---

17 *Ibid* at 14–15, 145.

18 Julian Webb, "The 'Ambitious Modesty' of Harry Arthurs' Humane Professionalism" (2006) 44 Osgoode Hall LJ 119 at 127.

19 William M Sullivan et al, *Educating Lawyers: Preparation for the Profession of Law* (San Francisco: Jossey-Bass, 2007) [*Carnegie Report*] at 28, 13 ("we propose an integration of student learning of theoretical and practical legal knowledge and practical identity").

20 *Ibid* at 30–1 [emphasis added].

civic virtues).[21] In this second narrative we see the possibility of educating the lawyer *as* citizen: the integration of the professional and public-service objectives serves to broaden the sense of what qualifies as lawyerly work, and it equips that professional with a diverse series of skills and abilities to accomplish various ends, many of which are public facing.

The Supreme Court of Canada recently lent its pedigree to the idea that legal education exists to serve the public interest. The majority of the Court upheld the decisions of both the Law Society of British Columbia (LSBC) and the Law Society of Upper Canada (LSUC) to deny accreditation of Trinity Western University's proposed law school on the grounds that it required students to sign a covenant in which they undertook to refrain from "sexual intimacy that violates the sacredness of marriage between a man and a woman." The majority found that the law societies acted reasonably in exercising their statutory duty to regulate the profession in the public interest in denying accreditation due to the discriminatory effect of the covenant on prospective LGBTQ students.

At a very basic level, the majority's comments that "the public interest is a broad concept" would seem to imply that legal education, to the extent it prepares students for the profession, is one that should engage with the public interest in a broad way.[22] If the legal profession exists to serve the public interest, then legal education ought to prepare students to accomplish this task. The cases can therefore be read as high authority for the normative claim that legal education *ought* to aspire to educate the lawyer as citizen.

The decisions can also, however, be read as a reflecting the sense that the lawyer-as-citizen idea is one potentially shared by both "opposing" camps of academics and practitioners. Whereas the public interest character of legal education might be thought an extension of the university's public mandate, *Trinity Western* suggests that it might be equally acceptable to representatives of the profession – both judges and law society regulators.

At the same time, the cases also reflect and arguably reinforce the oppositional narrative. An important issue in the case was the extent to which law societies were permitted to consider factors other than competence in assessing law school programs. The majority held that law societies were entitled to consider more than a law school's academic program (in this case, the discriminatory effect of a criterion of

21 I expand on the preceding analysis and literature in David Sandomierski, "Training Lawyers, Cultivating Citizens, and Re-Enchanting the Legal Professional" (2014) 51 Alta L Rev 739.

22 *Trinity* BC, *supra* note 1 at para 34.

admission relating to personal characteristics).[23] The dissenting justices vehemently disagreed, arguing that law societies had no mandate to encroach on the jurisdiction of law schools over legal education. The dissent by Justices Brown and Côté allude to the "fiercest debate":

> The LSBC's mandate is limited to the governance of "the society, lawyers, law firms, articled students and applicants" (s.11). *It does not extend to the governance of law schools,* which lie outside its statutory authority ... The only proper purpose of an approval decision by the LSBC is to ensure that individual licensing applicants are fit for licensing.
>
> ...
>
> Though the majority denies it, by allowing the LSBC to refuse to accredit a law school solely on the basis of its admissions policies – and in the absence of any concerns relating to the fitness of that school's graduates – it allows the LSBC to do that which it is not statutorily empowered to do – govern law schools by regulating their admissions policies. It does, in effect, tell law schools "how [they] should operate."[24]

In the companion Ontario appeal, Brown and Côté further upheld the barrier between law societies and law schools: "The [*Law Society Act*] does not grant the LSUC the power to regulate law schools, including their admissions policies. *Nor does it state that law schools provide legal education on the LSUC's behalf.* Again, the LSUC's functions, duties, and powers start at the licensing process – that is, at the doorway to the legal profession, and *not at the doorway to the law school.* This restriction applies to *any* law school, whether private and denominational, or not."[25] The image here is one in which law schools and the profession inhabit mutually exclusive domains of control and authority – reflecting the perennial debate over "jurisdiction" in legal education.

How these comments will be interpreted and taken up remains to be seen. Perhaps the dissent will be treated benignly as yet another instantiation of a familiar debate. Or perhaps, to the extent that Justice Brown and Côté were writing in *dissent*, the *Trinity Western* cases might be considered to support an *expanded* authority of law societies over law schools, and might provide authority for a more extensive "encroachment" on the domain of the academic law school.

23 *Ibid* at paras 37–40.

24 *Ibid* at paras 273, 290 [emphasis added].

25 *Trinity* Ontario, *supra* note 1 at para 68.

THE "ECLECTIC TOOLKIT" AS ONE ELEMENT OF THE LAWYER AS CITIZEN

To fully realize the capacious visions of humane professionalism, civic professionalism, the lawyer-statesman, or the lawyer as citizen, one no doubt would require interventions across the curriculum and, indeed, the political economies of legal education and the legal services market. To truly integrate theory and practice, one could imagine, for example, wholesale experiments in pedagogical reform along experiential or problem-based lines; a revisiting of law school rankings, given their effects on curricular design; a reorganization of law school financing to address the effect that debt load might have on career choice; or a project of rapprochement between conventionally opposed camps in licensing conversations.[26] Moreover, in order to understand more fully the relationship between theory and practice in legal education, one could study how professors describe or model the daily tasks of lawyers; investigate how professors come to know what they think they know about legal practice; study law students' reflective essays on their clinic assignments; or study the process of co-teaching between academics and practitioners. The levers and subjects of study are as broad and far-reaching as is the lawyer-as-citizen aspiration.

This study investigates one subset of this field, focusing on one specific instantiation of the relationship between theory and practice in legal education. I am interested in how specific theories about law get translated into visions of what it means to think like a lawyer. This question is significant because legal reasoning is capable of being conceived of as an "eclectic toolkit" of various analytical moves, derived from a diverse series of beliefs about law.[27] This eclectic toolkit would be an essential element of the legal professional who can deploy a diverse range of skills and attributes to a wide range of public and private

26 See e.g. Lorne Sossin, "Experience the Future of Legal Education" (2014) 51 Alta L Rev 849; Faisal Bhabha, "Towards a Pedagogy of Diversity in Legal Education" (2015) 52 Osgoode Hall LJ 59; Paul Maharg, *Transforming Legal Education: Learning and Teaching Law in the Early Twenty-First Century* (Burlington, VT: Ashgate, 2007); Wendy Nelson Espeland & Michael Sauder, *Engines of Anxiety: Academic Rankings, Reputation, and Accountability* (New York: Russell Sage Foundation, 2016); Law Society of Upper Canada, *Dialogue on Licensing: Discussing the Realities, Challenges and Opportunities of Lawyer Licensing in Ontario* (Law Society of Upper Canada, 2017), online: https://lsodialogue.ca/wp-content/uploads/2017/03/Dialogue-Topic-1-EN.pdf.

27 David Kennedy & William W Fisher III, "Introduction" in David Kennedy & William W Fisher III, *The Canon of American Legal Thought* (Princeton, NJ: Princeton University Press, 2006) 1 at 3.

problems. Determining the extent to which legal reasoning – as Canadian common law Contracts professors describe and teach it – reflects a wide range of attitudes about law can indicate the extent to which the aspiration to translate theory into practice (and the related ideal of educating the lawyer as citizen) is being realized.

Legal Reasoning as a Practice

Legal reasoning is useful for understanding the relationship between theory and practice for a few reasons. Most simply, we can speak sensibly about a *practice* of legal reasoning: thinking like a lawyer is a mental "action" or "undertaking."[28] In a deeper sense, legal reasoning – with its implication that there might, empirically, be something distinctively "legal" about it – is a term that describes the argumentative and discursive practices that all legal professionals share.[29] It "provides students with a sense of self-identity as a lawyer which cannot be unlearned."[30]

---

28 *The Oxford English Dictionary* (online), *sub vero* "practice," 2b ("[a]n action, a deed; an undertaking, a proceeding"). It also seems to fit the definition of practice as a "habitual" or "customary" action: 3a ("[t]he habitual doing or carrying on *of* something; usually, customary, or constant action or performance; conduct").

29 In using legal reasoning as a central subject of analysis, it is important to distinguish between two different ways in which legal reasoning might be conceived of as distinctive. The "stronger" form of distinctiveness aligns with the idea that law is an autonomous form of discourse, and thus that legal reasoning really is a special form of reasoning. For a seminal example, see Ernest J Weinrib, "Can Law Survive Legal Education?" (2007) 60 Vanderbilt L Rev 401 at 419–20, 425–6. As I expand upon in Chapter 5, some professors do indeed talk about legal reasoning's distinctiveness in a way that evokes formalist values of coherence and autonomy. But, separate and apart from this particular attitude, there is a more common way in which "legal reasoning" is often understood. This is the almost universal reference to the idea that there is a lingua franca, or common set of professional tools, that lawyers share. One may thus speak intelligibly of a "legal" reasoning even while believing that "legal reasoning is ordinary reasoning applied to legal problems" (Larry Alexander & Emily Sherwin, *Demystifying Legal Reasoning* (New York: Cambridge University Press, 2008)) at 3. For an elaboration of the "empirical" understanding of legal reasoning's distinctiveness, see Frederick Schauer, *Thinking Like a Lawyer: A New Introduction to Legal Reasoning* (Cambridge, MA: Harvard University Press, 2009) at 8, 11.

30 Fiona Donson & Catherine O'Sullivan, "Building Block or Stumbling Block? Teaching *Actus Reus* and *Mens Rea* in Criminal Law" in Kris Gledhill & Ben Livings, eds, *The Teaching of Criminal Law: The Pedagogical Imperatives* (Milton Park, UK: Routledge, 2017) 21 at 23–4, citing G Åkerlind et al, "A Threshold Concepts Focus to First Year Law Curriculum Design: Supporting Student Learning Using Variation Theory" in *13th Pacific Rim First Year in Higher Education Conference* (Adelaide, Australia, June 2010), and MH Weresh, "Stargate: Malleability as a Threshold Concept in Legal Education" (2014) 63 J Legal Ed 689) [references and quotation marks omitted].

Legal reasoning is the lingua franca needed to participate effectively in the legal profession, and thus may be considered the foundational source of expertise and authority for conducting a wide range of legal professional tasks. Although not as concrete a task as, say, drafting a document or filing a statement of claim, legal reasoning can be considered a sort of proto-practice, an epistemological foundation on which all other elements of legal practice are built.

But the most important sense, for present purposes, is the idea that legal reasoning may be thought to *put into practice*, or operationalize, particular theoretical ideas about law. This third sense accords with the Oxford English Dictionary's second meaning of *practice* – the "actual application or use of an idea, belief, or method, as opposed to the theory or principles of it."[31] It suggests that a given view of law, if "applied," generates a distinct vision of legal reasoning and, correlatively, that one may infer an underlying attitude about law from a given description of legal reasoning.

For example, if one believes that law should treat everyone equally, then legal reasoning might involve developing rational ways of distinguishing cases when arriving at different legal results in similar circumstances. If one believes that law should take into account individual circumstances in order to be fair and compassionate, then legal reasoning might involve a careful determination of facts and situating events in their broader social context. If one believes that law should strive to distribute resources fairly, then legal reasoning might involve thinking about winners and losers and identifying distributive consequences of rules. If one believes that law is an instrument for achieving social ends, then legal reasoning might involve anticipating and comparing the consequences of different rules, and experimenting with different policy means to achieve a given end. If one believes that law is a manifestation of political preferences, then legal reasoning might involve thinking about the links between legal interpretation and the relative desirability of contested political visions, and arguing in favour of a particular end (and thus a particular interpretation).

---

31 *Oxford English Dictionary* (online), *sub vero* "practice," 2a. The definition continues: "performance, execution, achievement; working; operation; activity or action considered as being the realization of or in contrast to theory. *Cf. Praxis.*" *Praxis*, in turn, receives its first definition as "the practice or exercise of a technical subject or art, as distinct from the theory of it; (also) accepted or habitual practice or custom," and its second definition (in relation to Marxist and neo-Marxist thought) as "conscious, willed action ... that through which theory or philosophy is transformed into practical social activity") (*ibid*, *sub vero* "praxis").

Legal Reasoning: An Eclectic Toolkit

As these examples show, a diverse series of beliefs about law corresponds – at least in principle – with a diverse range of skills and activities. Incorporating into legal reasoning the insights of diverse theories of law thus represents one example of a successful translation of theory into practice. A major question posed in this study is whether, in fact, Canadian common law Contracts professors do provide a diverse range of descriptions of legal reasoning, consistent with their diverse theoretical beliefs.

This question is pertinent not only because it helps answer whether one element of the lawyer-as-citizen vision is being realized, but also because the scope and breadth of legal reasoning is a question that transcends jurisdictions. In the United States, for example, there are competing characterizations of legal reasoning. On the one hand, as David Kennedy and William Fisher argue in the Introduction to their *Canon of American Legal Thought*, American legal reasoning is "an eclectic practice built from the methodological sediment laid down in successive projects of wholesale criticism and reform." In drawing together into their canon the various leading schools of thought in twentieth-century scholarship – legal realism's "wholesale assault on [classical legal thought's] jurisprudence of forms, concepts, and rules," legal process, and the "emergence of an array of methodologies associated variously with economics, sociology, liberal theory, and the work of critical studies scholars" – Kennedy and Fisher argue that the theoretical ideas from those schools have generated an "eclectic toolkit of contemporary legal reasoning."[32] In fleshing out this idea, they suggest that contemporary legal reasoning is a composite of the various critical schools, that the ideas of each have "found [their] way into the background consciousness of the legal professional":

> Fuller, Hart and Sacks, Coase, Calabresi, Galanter each proposed specific types of policy argument that have become routine methods of judicial reasoning. Law students are drilled in making Fullerian arguments about the "functions" of formal rules, and Hart and Sacksian arguments about "institutional competence." They learn from Coase to attend to the reactions of market actors to background rules, which may well affect, even reverse, their impact. They learn to argue, alongside Macaulay and Galanter, in ways that foreground the gap between "law in the books and law in

32 Kennedy & Fisher, "Introduction", *supra* note 27 at 3, 10.

action," and the different impact of legal norms on differently situated parties. And so on. Each new method of professional policy argument ... resolves the tension between deduction and policy reasoning differently – and *each of their resolutions has found its way into the background consciousness of today's legal professional.*[33]

The Kennedy & Fisher account is a perfect example of the claim that attitudes about law become operationalized into legal reasoning, a process that exemplifies the translation of theory into practice. One of the purposes of compiling their canon is to exemplify how the insights of the realist and post-realist schools have become internalized into the core professional activity of legal reasoning. In their formulation, the seminal articles they compile "clarify and reform the way ... lawyers interpret legal rules and decisions when advising clients, the way judges reason about cases, the way legal professionals in a wide variety of settings – civil servants, administrators, judges, legislators, teachers, businesspeople, humanitarian advocates, and more – think about the policy objectives and implications of legal rules, and the way legal scholars understand the workings of the legal system."[34] In this vision, legal reasoning is an eclectic toolkit composed of the methodological sediment of these schools, but it is also the intellectual substructure for a practical activity to be deployed in a wide range of pursuits by the legal professional. It is this type of broad, and broadly applicable, legal professional activity that, in my view, successfully translates theory into practice and serves as one key element of the education of the lawyer as citizen.[35]

But *is* such a vision of legal reasoning actually being taught in law schools? Kennedy and Fisher appear to believe that it is: they intend their canon to serve, for law students, "as a kind of decoder ring for the modes of reasoning their professors *are urging* to adopt in law school."[36] There is reason to believe, however, that this assertion might be more

33 *Ibid* at 4 [emphasis added].

34 *Ibid* at 1.

35 "Eclecticism" is not the only possible means by which attitudes about law may be put into practice in the service of the lawyer as citizen. It is entirely possible that one particular theory alone can generate a capacious understanding of legal reasoning and the lawyer's role, and thus that the lawyer-as-citizen vision could be realized not by recourse to an available toolkit, but rather through one overarching philosophy. For example, a "critical legal pedagogy" might aim to "persuade students that legal discourses and practices comprise a medium ... in which they can pursue moral and political projects and articulate alternative visions of social organization and social justice" (Karl E Klare, "Teaching *Local 1330* – Reflections on Critical Pedagogy" (2001) 7 Unbound: Harvard Journal of the Legal Left 58 at 77–8).

36 Kennedy & Fisher, "Introduction", *supra* note 27 at ix [emphasis added].

aspirational – or, at the very least, partial to their own experiences – than grounded in empirical fact. For, as one recent study on the teaching of legal reasoning in US Contracts classes has shown, a much narrower vision might be on offer.

Legal Reasoning and the Marginalization of Policy and Context

In a study that has been described as representing the "best of research in legal education,"[37] Elizabeth Mertz's close linguistic analysis of eight first-year Contracts classrooms in a diverse range of US law schools appears to show that Kennedy and Fisher's vision is not reflected in the way that US Contracts teachers train their students to think like lawyers.[38]

Contrary to the claim that legal reasoning is an "eclectic toolkit" of argumentative strategies inherited from the various realist and critical schools, Mertz demonstrates that the process of initiating students into the "particular linguistic and textual tradition" of law actually *marginalizes* considerations of morality, policy, and social context. "Legal training," she writes, "focuses students' attention away from a systematic or comprehensive consideration of social context and specificity." With its focus on textual analysis, the legal reading taught in Contracts classes conceals "the social roots of legal doctrines," the "injustices and power inequalities that are enacted in the system," and "avoid[s] examination of the ways that abstract categories, as they develop, privilege some aspects of conflicts and events over others."[39]

This "erasure of context" occurs largely through the emphasis placed on certain features of legal reading: discerning the appropriate hierarchy of legal authority, recontextualizing cases as precedents, delimiting what constitute the "facts" of a case, and applying law to facts in a process of "analogical parsing." Together these habits generate standards for "correct legal readings" and determine the "tight, technical center" of legal reasoning. The method conveys a conception of justice as one defined largely by the resolution of a duel between two opposing positions, and emphasizes "layers of textual authority as neutral sources for legal decision making."[40]

---

37 Fiona Cownie, "Legal Education and the Legal Academy" in Peter Crane & Herbert M Kritzer, eds, *Oxford Handbook of Empirical Legal Research* (Oxford: Oxford University Press, 2010) 854 at 859.

38 Elizabeth Mertz, *The Language of Law School: Learning to "Think Like a Lawyer"* (New York: Oxford University Press, 2007).

39 *Ibid* at 4–5, 212–13.

40 *Ibid* at 212, 61–4, 67, 72, 76, 77, 5.

At the same time, Contracts teaching casts to the periphery broader questions about justice, grouping them into a catch-all category of "policy." These policy discussions, in contrast to the "carefully disciplined core focus" of legal reasoning, usually proceed on "anecdotal or speculative" grounds. They are used to retain the credibility of legal discussion by admitting some "flexibility and openness," but the "broadly painted backgrounds ... stand in marked contrast to the central legal discussion, marginal not only in terms of discursive structure, but also because these policy discussions never impart any real analytic standards for assessing one story against another ... When social context comes in the door, structure, standards, and rigor exit."[41] Mertz's account suggests that the teachers of contract law in her study have failed to operationalize realist ideas into a vision of legal reasoning that they communicate to their students. As I expand upon in Chapters 2, 3, and 5, the schools of legal realism and its intellectual heirs are typified by their commitment to the importance of policy and context – two features that Mertz describes as being marginalized by the linguistic and discursive practices that condition students to think like lawyers. Indeed, Mertz's catch-all category of policy questions that are treated *unseriously* in classroom discussions – "whether law operates in a just manner, whether certain legal decisions were motivated by class interests or other extralegal concerns, whether particular social conditions caused or resulted from specific legal decisions" – closely resembles the considerations of justice, class, politics, and social effects that, according to Kennedy and Fisher, characterize the realist and critical schools of thought.[42] Legal reasoning, as Mertz portrays it as being taught, looks much less like the "methodological sediment" of the various critical schools than it does the distillate of "pure" legal reason.[43]

This restrained vision of legal reasoning also communicates to the law student a diminished vision of legal judgment: "From a world in which normative judgment is circumscribed by a rich sense of social context – who someone was, the full depth of feelings and motives that inspired

41 *Ibid* at 77–9.

42 *Ibid* at 77.

43 "Pure" legal reasoning would entail disciplinary distinctive reasoning that scrupulously avoids consideration of "extraneous" social context or normative influences. *Cf* Hans Kelsen, *Introduction to the Problems of Legal Theory: A Translation of the First Edition of the Reine Rechtslehre or Pure Theory of Law*, translated by Bonnie Litschewski Paulson & Stanley I Paulson (New York: Oxford University Press, 1997), c 2 (upholding the distinction between law and justice and between law and morality); Lawrence Friedman, *Contract Law in America* (New Orleans: Quid Pro Books, 2011) at 14–15 ("'Pure' contract doctrine is blind to details of subject matter and person").

certain actions, the circumstances that conspired to push events in one way or another, personal histories, social inequalities, and more – law students are moved into a new world, in which legal judgment is circumscribed by linguistic norms, texts and the arguments they permit, and layers of authoritative language."[44] By constraining what it means to think like a lawyer, teaching law can also therefore have a funnelling effect, redirecting students' expansive understandings of law and justice to a much narrower conception of what constitutes legal reasoning and activity. When law is remote from social context, legal decision making becomes "alienat[ed]" from ethics, and lawyers become alienated from "socially shared values."[45] It is not a far cry to imagine the law student becoming alienated from his or her convictions, intuitions, and values. The legal self the law student gradually inhabits is, in this vision, a partial version of him- or herself, constrained and bound by adherence to established patterns of thinking, reading, writing, and relating with authority.[46]

It is, moreover, reasonable to think that this transformation affects the ways in which students conceive of their role as legal professionals. The epistemological transformation that first-year students experience might coincide and intermingle with other transformations, such as the tendency for students to transition from a more symbolic or ethical vision of law towards an instrumental one, and from a vocational understanding of career to a professional one.[47] Mertz's discoveries and analysis evoke other empirical studies that have explored how the development of students' legal consciousness has contributed to cynicism and a narrowing of professional aspirations captured by the term "public interest drift."[48] The Mertz study thus shows how some US Contracts professors operationalize a much narrower set of attitudes about law in how they teach legal reasoning than the eclectic series of ideas that Kennedy and Fisher identify. Moreover, the study also suggests

44 Mertz, *supra* note 38 at 216.

45 *Ibid* at 220.

46 *Cf* James Boyd White, *Living Speech* (Princeton, NJ: Princeton University Press, 2006); James Boyd White, *Acts of Hope: Creating Authority in Literature, Law, and Politics* (Chicago: University of Chicago Press, 1994).

47 See Pierre Noreau & Pierre-Olivier Bonin, "Faire droit ... devenir juriste: trajectoire des étudiants en faculté: une étude en contexte québécois" (2017) 22 Lex Electronica 169.

48 See John Bliss, "Divided Selves: Professional Role Distancing among Law Students and New Lawyers in a Period of Market Crisis" (2017) 42 Law & Soc Inq 855; Robert Granfield, "Cynicism and the Law: The Emergence of Legal Consciousness in Law School" (1994) 25 J Soc Phil 188 at 205; Howard S Erlanger et al, "Law Student Idealism and Job Choice: Some New Data On an Old Question" (1996) 30 Law & Soc Rev 851.

how such a constrained image of legal reasoning might inhibit the ability of first-year law school to educate the lawyer as citizen.

THEORY AND PRACTICE IN CANADIAN COMMON LAW CONTRACTS TEACHING

It is against this backdrop that this empirical study of Canadian common law Contracts professors lies. I examine which vision – Kennedy and Fisher's incorporation of eclecticism, or Mertz's portrayal of marginalization – best captures the attitudes and practices of Canadian common law Contracts teachers. But my reason for investigating this question is not to construct or create a distilled image of what legal reasoning looks like in common law Canada. Instead, I compare the ways that professors *themselves* understand and characterize legal reasoning with the ways that they understand and characterize law. The vast majority of Canadian common law Contracts professors do happen to espouse beliefs consistent with the realist and critical schools identified in Kennedy and Fisher's canon: they emphasize the indeterminacy of law and the importance of policy and politics, and they consider granular social context to be essential to understanding law and contractual relations. If these attitudes about law were to be operationalized into corresponding visions of legal reasoning, we would expect to see professors describe legal reasoning in the eclectic manner that Kennedy and Fisher do. The major, and perhaps surprising, discovery is that by and large they do not.

Most professors, when they describe what legal reasoning is, do not indicate that a series of arguments derived from diverse schools of thought is part of the "legal professional's background consciousness" or "toolkit." Instead, while speaking generally about law, many professors emphasize the contingent and changeable nature of rules; when they describe legal reasoning, they portray rules as more fixed than mutable. Although many admit that law derives from various sources, including legislatures and the "private law of the parties," in describing legal reasoning many portray courts as the dominant source of authority, and adjudication as the dominant legal process. Whereas many of the theories to which professors ascribe emphasize the importance of understanding the underlying policy or political rationales for the outcomes of cases, legal reasoning is primarily portrayed as the manipulation of the facial terms of judicial reasoning. Instead of a collection of eclectic intellectual and argumentative techniques, the overwhelming main activity of legal reasoning is presented as "determining relevance" – an activity that often takes the content of rules as a given, and relies on an image of law as an internally coherent system. These contrasts, taken together, suggest that there is a significant gap between the theories professors ascribe to and the vision of legal reasoning they aim to communicate to their students. This represents a failure to translate theory fully into practice.

I also compare professors' avowed attitudes about law with the attitudes about law reflected in their teaching. Teaching is another manifestation of the idea of "practice": choices about teaching methods, materials, and evaluations put into practice certain beliefs about law. Just as I do with professors' descriptions of legal reasoning, I analyse what professors tell me about their teaching, as well as their written course materials and evaluations, for the implicit, underlying attitudes about law they reveal. And just as with the first comparison, I discover a similar indication that many professors' theoretical commitments are not being translated into practice.

Again, notwithstanding a stated commitment to the mutability of legal rules, professors often describe (in both interviews and syllabi) the objective of their course as being for students to "master" a knowledge of rules – as if rules were fixed data points, not the product of contingent social, political, or historical circumstances. Many of the teaching methods described indicate a similar desire to "deliver" a fixed content. The standard form of evaluation – a hypothetical fact pattern – appears to test for the skill of determining relevance, reinforcing the relatively narrow conception of legal reasoning that most professors describe. Despite the highly sceptical tradition of the realist and critical schools to which most professors pledge allegiance, critique is often relegated to a tertiary concern (after mastering knowledge and legal reasoning), and sometimes avoided altogether. The overwhelming image is that the *teaching* of Contracts tends to emphasize and require the mastery of a core doctrinal knowledge. This nearly ubiquitous emphasis appears to presuppose that the "basics" of law are to be found in judicial formulation of rules.

It is somewhat surprising to observe this attitude so frequently, especially among the many professors who express a commitment to the realist and critical schools. Those schools offer up alternative accounts of what is "basic" or foundational to law, including the importance of policy rationales (such as efficiency or distributive justice), the political combat of opposing ideologies, historical factors, the desire to sustain contractual relations, or factual or social "context" generally. The importance of these underlying factors and professors' sceptical posture vis-à-vis judicial reasoning do not seem to translate into how law and legal reasoning are taught in first-year Contracts.

This book develops these points in some detail and also renders them somewhat more nuanced. As I detail, not all professors espouse realist and critical beliefs about law, and not all attitudes about legal reasoning, or teaching methods, convey an attitude about law that appears to contradict the professed beliefs. Nevertheless one overall trend is consistent with the sketch just provided: there is an aspiration to translate theory into practice, but there is also, simultaneously, a gap between professors' theoretical commitments and the vision of law manifested both in how they describe legal reasoning and in their teaching. By scrutinizing the substantive content of their views about law and legal reasoning, and ascribing, provisionally, the labels of realism and formalism to illuminate the gap, this book reveals how the translation of theory into practice is imperfect and, as a result, educating the lawyer as citizen remains, at this juncture, an unrealized aspiration.

METHODOLOGY

The main subject of analysis in this study are the words spoken or written by instructors who teach common law Contracts at Canadian law faculties. Some of these instructors also edit the commercial casebooks. Unlike Mertz, I have not conducted classroom observations, and unlike other leading recent empirical projects on professional consciousness development in legal education, I did not speak with students.[49] This choice of methodology naturally generates some caveats. I have no way of knowing, for example, what professors actually do in class. Professors could be doing less, or more, than what they describe. To the extent that I relied on written course materials such as syllabi, lecture notes, and examination scripts as an indication of actual teaching practices, these documents were largely not created with the intention of reflecting the classroom reality to a third-party observer. And even to the extent that they might reflect what goes on in the classroom, they are imperfect guides; "the map is not the territory."[50] One's classroom teaching might be entirely different from what a syllabus or examination script suggests. And just as my study can say little reliably about what actually goes on in the classroom, it also says very little about what messages concerning law, legal reasoning, and legal practice students *actually* receive. For all these reasons, this study should be thought of as part of a broader project for which additional empirical studies would be beneficial.

49 See e.g. Bliss, *supra* note 48.

50 Alfred Korzybski, *Science and Sanity: An Introduction to Non-Aristotelian Systems and General Semantics*, 5th ed (Brooklyn, NY: Institute of General Semantics, 1994) at 58.

At the same time, reliance on professors' words has its advantages. I was able to access what professors *aspire* to do, and what they *believe* – phenomena that are well captured by their subjective descriptions. Professors were free to tell me in their own words what their ideals are about law and legal education, and this had the benefit of capturing, one hopes, the most ambitious formulations possible. A project that aims to tease out the immanent potential of legal education benefits greatly from the aspirational nature of this discourse, because it sets the outside limits of what might be possible.

Moreover, by treating professors' words as texts, I was able to interpret them alongside legal scholarship, so that the substance of the ideas in my data was informed by, and cast light on, themes in the scholarship. This enabled me to perform the key analytic move of this book, which is to identify the gap between professors' stated theoretical commitments and the ideas of law "put into practice" in their understandings of legal reasoning and in their teaching. Law professors are well spoken and knowledgeable, the subject matter of the interviews was deeply familiar to them, and they were in control of the interview environment. So the interview transcripts lent themselves well to being treated as texts: they provided articulate and well-elaborated answers, many of which made direct reference to scholarly thinkers or specific events. This is not to say that I took everything said at face value. Some of the most interesting moments were when a professor's words in one part of the interview appeared to lie in tension with what he or she said in another part. But the point is that I took the spoken words seriously and could compare them on the same plane with words in their documentary sources and in the scholarship. That these texts spoke together so well is highlighted by the fact that many of my participants had actually published in the fields of contract law and legal education from whose literature I drew.

I also interpreted documentary sources – course syllabi, exam questions, slides, and other teaching materials – for the implicit and explicit attitudes about law they reveal. This exercise finds its greatest expression in Chapter 3, where I conduct a comprehensive analysis of the commercial Canadian common law Contracts casebooks. Casebooks play four notionally different roles: they are artefacts produced by my participants, some of whom are the casebook editors themselves; they are published, scholarly texts amenable to interpretation, analysis, and critique; they are tools used in the classroom; and they are historical documents that change over time according to events, intellectual currents, and the identities of their editors. As I do when I analyse my interview data, I weave into my analysis of the casebooks substantive ideas from the literature on contract law, legal thought, and legal education.

Unlike another doctoral work that focuses on teaching methods in Canadian legal education, my study focuses very much on the "what" of legal education, and to the extent that I discusses the "how," I do so primarily to explore what the teaching methods say about substantive attitudes about law, legal reasoning, and legal practice.[51] This book focuses, therefore, neither on language or pedagogy per se, but explores both pedagogical choices and spoken and written language to discern the substantive ideas communicated about law, legal reasoning, and the relationship between theory and practice.

Why Contracts?

This project is situated within an emerging international interest in empirical studies in legal education, adding to the relatively sparse, but growing, collection of Canadian contributions to the field.[52] It is distinctive in that, in addition to being empirical, it simultaneously engages with the ideas contained in substantive law.[53] In this approach, the book

---

51 Annie Rochette, *Teaching and Learning in Canadian Legal Education: An Empirical Exploration* (DCL Thesis, McGill University Faculty of Law, 2010) [unpublished].

52 In a 2010 entry in the *Oxford Handbook of Empirical Legal Research*, Fiona Cownie identifies only two Canadian contributions, and compares these to the "large quantity of empirical research focused on legal pedagogy in the United States" (*supra* note 37 at 858). Although this list was underinclusive at the time, and there is a growing collection of such studies, the numerical comparison is probably still apt. Nevertheless, it is worth signalling the two studies Cownie cites, the ones she missed at the time of writing, and projects undertaken since then to signal the emergence of the field in Canada. See *Arthurs Report*, *supra* note 15; Annie Rochette & W Wesley Pue, "'Back to Basics'? University Legal Education and 21st Century Professionalism" (2001) 20 Windsor YB Access Just 167 (cited by Cownie); Natasha Bakht et al, "Counting Outsiders: A Critical Exploration of Outsider Course Enrollment in Canadian Legal Education" (2007) 45 Osgoode Hall LJ 667 (missed by Cownie); Desmond Manderson & Sarah Turner, "Coffee House: *Habitus* and Performance among Law Students" (2006) 31 L & Soc Inq 649 (missed); Rochette, *Teaching and Learning in Canadian Legal Education*", *supra* note 51 (missed); Harry Arthurs & Annie Bunting, "Socio-legal Scholarship in Canada: A Review of the Field" (2014) 41 JL & Soc'y 487; Craig Forcese, "The Law Professor as Public Citizen: Measuring Public Engagement in Canadian Common Law Schools" (2016) 36 Windsor YB Access Just 66. Two in-progress doctoral projects promise to expand the field even further. See Michelle Leering, "Conceptualizing Reflective Practice for Legal Professionals" (2014) 23 J L Soc Policy 1 (theoretical foundations of a doctoral project on reflective practice at Queen's University Faculty of Law); Adrien Habermacher, *Institutional Cultures and Legal Education at Select Canadian Law Faculties* (DCL Thesis, McGill University Faculty of Law, 2019) [unpublished].

53 Despite the breadth of studies cited in the previous footnote, much legal education research in Canada has tended to consist largely of critical commentary, literature reviews, or first-person accounts of actual experience. See e.g. Harry W Arthurs,

seeks to break down the dichotomy between legal scholarship and the scholarship on legal education. It strives to elucidate the intimate connection between the construction of legal and professional consciousness that occurs in law school and the substantive attitudes about law that are taught there. By focusing on a course that is part of the putative core curriculum, it also permits two additional reflections. On the one hand, it enables us to imagine how significant change within legal education is possible while retaining its existing structure. On the other, it invites us to question the premises on which our understandings of "core" courses are based, and to imagine new structures and possibilities.

Contracts is an ideal course to study for a number of reasons. It is a mandatory element of almost every first-year law program throughout the common law world, and has been for a very long time.[54] The course figures prominently in law school lore.[55] Contracts was the subject of the seminal casebook, Christopher Columbus Langdell's *A Selection of Cases on the Law of Contracts*, and is thus perennially associated with the case method and thinking like a lawyer.[56] It is also the focus of Mertz's study,[57] and there is a significant literature (largely American) on the teaching of Contracts.[58]

"Poor Canadian Legal Education: So Near to Wall Street, So Far from God" (2000) 38 Osgoode Hall LJ 381; Stephanie Ben-Ishai, "Thinking about Technology in Canadian Law Schools: A Literature Review" (2007) 1 Canadian Legal Education Annual Review 37; Richard Devlin, Anthony Duggan & Louise Langevin, "Doing Theory in First Year Contracts: The Iceberg Method" (2007) 1 Canadian Legal Education Annual Review 1; Jennifer Koshan et al, "Rewriting Equality: The Pedagogical Use of Women's Court of Canada Judgments" (2010) 4 Canadian Legal Education Annual Review 1.

54 For example, in Alfred Reed's empirical study of Canadian and US law schools in the 1920s, Contracts was the only course that *every single* school offered in first year (Alfred Z Reed, *Present-Day Law Schools in the United States and Canada*, Carnegie Foundation Bulletin 21 (Boston: Merrymount Press, 1928) at 256)). In the United States, Contracts is an "immutable pillar of the first-year curriculum of every law school" (Friedman, *supra* note 43 at 18).

55 See e.g. *The Paper Chase*, *supra* note 2; Scott Turow, *One L: The Turbulent True Story of a First Year at Harvard Law School* (New York: Penguin, 1978).

56 See Christopher Columbus Langdell, *A Selection of Cases on the Law of Contracts: With a Summary of the Topics Covered by the Cases: Prepared for Use as a Text-Book in Harvard Law*, 2d ed (Boston: Little, Brown, 1879).

57 Mertz does not directly attribute the subject matter of Contracts to her decision to choose that course, except that, as a mandatory course taught in the first semester of first year, it enabled her to "avoid possible variation by subject matter" and "to catch the socialization process at a critical moment; it is during this first semester that students receive their primary initiation into distinctively legal language and thought" (*supra* note 38 at 34).

58 See e.g. Lawrence M Friedman & Stewart Macaulay, "Contract Law and Contract Teaching: Past, Present, and Future" [1967] Wisc L Rev 805; Klare, "Teaching *Local 1330*", *supra* note 35.

But most important, the subject directly engages with diverse messages about law and legal reasoning. Contract law is amenable to a wide range of philosophies about law. To cite just one example, its philosophical foundations can be said to track a transformation from Aristotelian virtues of promise keeping, liberality, and commutative justice to liberal values of autonomy, freedom, and individualism.[59] Moreover, while contract law is amenable to diverse *theories* about law, it has also been a vehicle by which eclectic visions of *legal reasoning* have been developed and advanced. Most of the major schools that Kennedy and Fisher identify as constituting the major developments in American legal thought have important instantiations in contract law scholarship.[60] One goal of Chapter 2 is to illustrate how the development of American legal thought could be told using examples from contract law scholarship. As representative of these schools of thought, mainstream contract law scholarship exemplifies the eclectic series of ideas that are said by Kennedy and Fisher to constitute contemporary legal reasoning. Contracts thus would seem to be a natural course in which to introduce students to these diverse attitudes about law and to present legal reasoning as an eclectic and broad practice.

Finally, focusing on discrete attitudes about contract law and the teaching practices of Contracts professors permits an analysis at a different scale than is adopted elsewhere. Much scholarship analyses legal education from a macro perspective. This is true of structural scholarship that attempts to identify broad trends in legal education, of normative scholarship that attempts to defend the academic vision of legal education, of reports emphasizing the role of market forces, and of interventions from the profession, the academy, and third-party research institutes on the topic of curricular reform and design. Theoretical or

---

59 See generally James Gordley, *Philosophical Origins of Modern Contract Doctrine* (Oxford: Oxford University Press, 2011). See also Charles Fried, *Contract as Promise: A Theory of Contractual Obligation* (Cambridge, MA: Harvard University Press, 1981). Contract law is also the subject matter of extensive historical studies that seek to understand the broad sweep of the development of legal thought and the common law. See e.g. PS Atiyah, *The Rise and Fall of Freedom of Contract* (Oxford: Clarendon Press, 1979); AWB Simpson, *A History of the Common Law of Contract: The Rise of the Action of Assumpsit* (Oxford: Clarendon Press, 1975).

60 Four articles in Kennedy & Fisher's *Canon of American Legal Thought* (*supra* note 27) are taken directly from contract law scholarship: Robert L Hale, "Coercion and Distribution in a Supposedly Noncoercive State" (1923) 38 Political Science Quarterly 470; Lon L Fuller, "Consideration and Form" (1941) 41 Colum L Rev 799; Stewart Macaulay, "Non-Contractual Relations in Business: A Preliminary Study" (1963) 28 Am Soc Rev 55 [Macaulay, "Non-Contractual Relations"]; Duncan Kennedy, "Form and Substance in Private Law Adjudication" (1976) 88 Harv L Rev 1685 [Kennedy, "Form and Substance"].

polemic interventions about legal education's mission also tend to be pitched at a higher level of generality.[61] These bird's-eye views can produce an image of legal education akin to a territorial map, on which borders are clearly defined factions, coloured in and homogeneous. But just as in research about *law*, where "scale functions so that a specific perspective becomes embedded in forms of regulation and governance," the focus on the macro scale in legal education might predispose researchers and commentators to focus on categories that might not *necessarily* be determinative of lived experience.[62] Getting many individual professors to speak freely in their own words opened up insights that might not obtain with a focus on institutions, curricula, or markets. The methodology also permitted me to hear from professors other than the self-selected subset who write and publish on legal education.

That said, while operating at a more individual and granular scale, a focus on professors' accounts of their own teaching is also quite abstract, in the same way that scholarly arguments are. The professors in my study describe an activity, law teaching, which itself is a marriage of two highly abstract endeavours, law and education. The information revealed are not discrete data points as in other major investigations, but rather rich, thick, and layered testimonies.[63] These accounts directly inform the themes about legal education, but they are also subject to further meta-analysis and amenable to broader generalizations. In the same vein, the review of the casebooks permitted me to conduct an in-depth analysis of the books most professors use in their class in order to analyse closely and probe

---

61 See e.g. HW Arthurs, "The Political Economy of Canadian Legal Education" (1998) 25 JL & Soc 14; Arthurs, "Tree of Knowledge", *supra* note 5; Tamanaha, *Failing Law Schools*, *supra* note 5; *ABA Report*, *supra* note 5; *FLSC Report*, *supra* note 5; Roderick A Macdonald, "Curricular Development in the 1980s: A Perspective" (1982) 32 J Legal Ed 569 at 585; *Carnegie Report*, *supra* note 19; Kronman, *Lost Lawyer*, *supra* note 16; Duncan Kennedy, "Legal Education and the Reproduction of Hierarchy" (1982) 32 J Legal Ed 591.

62 Jennifer Raso, "Unity in the Eye of the Beholder? Reasons for Decision in Theory and Practice in the Ontario Works Program" (2020) 70 UTLJ 1 at 6. For the concept of scale, Raso draws productively on Mariana Valverde, "Jurisdiction and Scale: Legal 'Technicalities' as Resources for Theory" (2009) 18 Social & Legal Studies 139; Mariana Valverde, *Chronotopes of Law: Jurisdiction, Scale and Governance* (Abingdon, UK: Routledge, 2015); and Boaventura de Sousa Santos, "Law: A Map of Misreading: Toward a Post-modern Conception of Law" (1987) 14 J Law and Society 279.

63 Compare Robert Nelson et al, *After the JD, Wave 3: A Longitudinal Study of Careers in Transition, 2012–2013, United States (ICPSR 35480)*, online: http://doi.org/10.3886/ICPSR35480.v1; Law Student Survey of Student Engagement, online: http://lssse.indiana.edu/.

their implicit and explicit attitudes about law. As it happens, my analysis of these books reveals a tension between the introductory expressions about law and the attitudes about law reflected in the more granular treatment of substance in the remedies chapter that parallels the observations made about individual Contracts teachers. This parallel reinforces the broad, thematic claims about Canadian legal thought that a close look at individual attitudes (interviewees or editors) makes possible.

Participants

My study focuses on instructors at Canadian law schools where a significant part of the first-year Contracts course in the main program (JD or LLB) is taught in the common law tradition. In effect, this includes all Canadian common law faculties operating at the time of study, plus the Faculty of Law at McGill University, for a total of eighteen institutions.[64] I approached all professors who were teaching first-year Contracts at these institutions in the academic years 2013–14, 2014–15, 2015–16, some teaching in 2016–17, and selected former teachers of Contracts, including retired and working professors who were no longer teaching the course. The relatively small size of the professoriate in Canada enabled me to aspire to such a comprehensive list, which would not be remotely attainable in the United States.[65] In total, I conducted sixty-seven interviews with Canadian common law Contracts professors, fifty-four of whom shared written course materials, and received written materials from an additional eight non-interview participants.[66]

64 The eighteen are the Schulich School of Law at Dalhousie University; the University of New Brunswick Faculty of Law; the University of Moncton Faculty of Law; the McGill University Faculty of Law; the Faculty of Law – Common Law Section, University of Ottawa; the Faculty of Law, Queen's University; the University of Toronto Faculty of Law; Osgoode Hall Law School; the Faculty of Law, Western University; the Faculty of Law, University of Windsor; the Bora Laskin Faculty of Law at Lakehead University; Robson Hall, Faculty of Law, University of Manitoba; the College of Law, University of Saskatchewan; the Faculty of Law, University of Alberta; the Faculty of Law, University of Calgary; the Faculty of Law, Thompson Rivers University; the Peter A Allard School of Law, University of British Columbia; and the Faculty of Law, University of Victoria.

65 As of 15 June 2017, the "dynamic database" of the American Association of Law Schools listed 1,180 "tenured, tenure-track, long-term contract, deans, and emeritus faculty" as teaching Contract Law (Keeley Kerrins, American Association of Law Schools, email correspondence with author, 15 June 2017).

66 I invited one hundred people to participate in an interview and conducted sixty-eight interviews. I excluded one interview and participant from my sample set, generating a participation rate of 68 per cent (sixty-seven out of ninety-nine) for

Among those interviewed, forty-eight presented as male and eighteen as female (one preferred not to disclose gender information). Professors had diverse levels of teaching experience, as indicated by Figure 1, and held positions as varied as tenured or tenure-track professors (of all rank), sessional lecturers or adjunct professors, visiting scholars, fellows, and professors emeriti.[67] For simplicity, I refer to each participant in this study as a "professor."

Aside from gender information, I did not collect information about participants' markers of personal identity such as race, sexual orientation, First Nations status, socio-economic background, or disability. Moreover, in reporting on my findings I have decided to conceal the gender information of my participants. Accordingly, I do not attempt to draw parallels between the attitudes and practices of professors, on the one hand, and their personal identity characteristics. Granular information about how these personal identity characteristics might inform or determine the substance of participants' views and practices is not, therefore, a contribution this study makes – although drawing such parallels would be a fruitful avenue for future studies, given the burgeoning diversity within Canadian legal education and the important questions of how personal identity characteristics might affect both students' and teachers' professional and intellectual development.[68] In designing this study, I deliberately chose not to focus on these factors, but instead on the stated attitudes and aspirations of law professors and on accounts and evidence of their practices. To the extent that I was interested in their identities, it was their intellectual and professional identities, which I discerned both in the interview process and by gathering such professionally relevant information as institution, position, research areas, courses taught, and level of experience teaching.

---

interview participants. I invited nine people to submit materials only (with no interview request), and invited all interviewees to submit written interviews, for an overall participation rate of 58 per cent (sixty-two out of one hundred and eight).

67 Calculated as the difference in years between the date of the interview and the first year of full-time teaching (not counting sessional lecturing or fellowships).

68 Survey data suggest that the student bodies of Canadian law schools are characterized by diversity across a number of dimensions. For example, at ten Canadian law schools (all of which are represented in this study), in 2017 almost a third of students identified as non-white and almost 10 per cent identified as non-heterosexual. See e.g. Law Student Survey of Student Engagement, *supra* note 63 (data on file with author). Many Canadian law schools publicly disclose detailed diversity data of their student bodies. See e.g. Osgoode Hall Law School, "Admissions Survey: Fall Call of 2021 Entering Class", online: https://www.osgoode.yorku.ca/admissions-survey/; University of Windsor, Windsor Law, *Summary Report: Diversity Survey 2017*, online: https://www.uwindsor.ca/law/sites/uwindsor.ca.law/files/diversity_summary_report_2017.pdf.

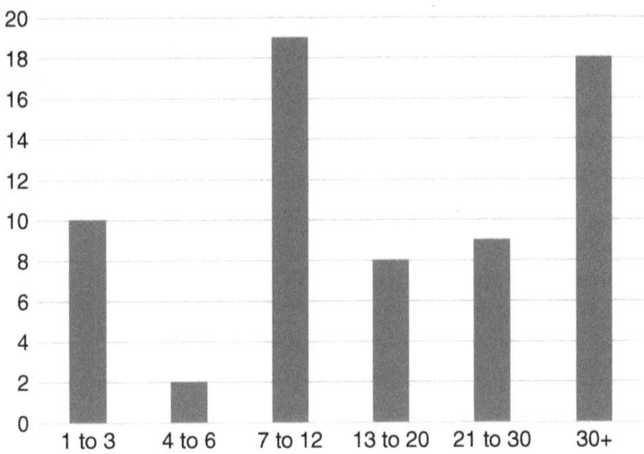

Figure 1: Interview Participants: Number of Years of Teaching Experience

Data Collection and Analysis

This study adopts the interpretive paradigm of qualitative research, whose goals "involve empathetic understanding of participants' day-to-day experiences and an increased awareness of the multiple meanings given to the routine and problematic events by those in the setting."[69] I used the grounded theory approach, which entails both an open-ended approach to data collection and analysing the data by coding for themes and relating these codes at increasingly higher levels of abstraction until a theory emerges.[70] The insights I generated about the relationship between theory and practice, between attitudes about law and legal reasoning, and about Canadian legal thought were therefore not predetermined, but "grounded in" the data – the words of the professors in interview and in their written materials.

In grounded theory, "data gathering and data analysis are simultaneous."[71] This philosophy informed my intuitive and organic approach to the semi-structured interviews, which lasted on average an hour. My

69 Carol A Bailey, *A Guide to Qualitative Field Research*, 2d ed (Thousand Oaks, CA: Pine Forge Press, 2007) at 53.

70 See generally Anselm Strauss & Juliet Corbin, *Basics of Qualitative Research: Techniques and Procedures for Developing Grounded Theory* (Thousand Oaks, CA: Sage, 1998); J Morse et al, *Developing Grounded Theory: The Second Generation* (Walnut Creek, CA: Left Coast Press, 2009) at 18, reproduced in Julianne S Oktay, *Grounded Theory* (New York: Oxford University Press, 2012) at 14.

71 Morse et al, *supra* note 70 at 14.

questions were informed by an *in situ* analysis of the present conversation and by preliminary analysis of previous interviews. Nevertheless, I would often use specific questions about pedagogy to kick things off. Common questions that arose were:

- How long have you been teaching Contracts?
- Do you like teaching the course? What do you like about it?
- What are your goals in teaching the course?
- Why are those goals important?
- How do you structure the course?
- What reading materials do you assign?
- How do you evaluate your students?
- What do the best exam answers do?
- Where did you study law?
- How do you prepare for your class?
- Are there any particular influences on your approach to the subject matter or the course?

These questions inevitably led to answers that included references to scholarly authors, mentors, specific cases or other examples from the course, philosophical ideas, and so on. I pursued and expanded on these references, and conversations gradually transitioned into a more probing and intellectually demanding discussion about the nature of law, legal reasoning, and legal education. I then would either pick up on a theme or word from that answer or return to another of the questions above. I also used the interviews to gather information about law professors' intellectual development, including where they studied, the mentors they had, relevant professional experiences, and other stories from their lives. Of the sixty-seven interviews, I conducted fifty-four in person and thirteen by phone or videoconference, between February 2013 and February 2017. I interviewed most participants in their university office, but occasionally met in other places, such as a professional office, a restaurant, hotel lobby, or other venue, to accommodate each participant in an environment in which he or she felt most comfortable.

Sixty-six of sixty-seven interview participants agreed to having their interviews audio recorded. A professional transcriber transcribed all audio recordings except one, generating approximately 1,500 single-spaced pages of transcript data. Professors also emailed copies of their course materials, and occasionally provided hard copies during our interview or by mail. I wrote to some participants several times to get updated versions of course syllabi. In total, I received 263 written materials, including a course syllabus from 60 individual participants and 24 examination scripts.[72]

I did the bulk of my theory building through manual coding of hard copies, using a highlighter to mark relevant passages on the transcripts, and index cards to record line number references according to different themes (codes). I "constantly compar[ed]" and iteratively developed these codes.[73] I also periodically wrote down emerging thoughts and ideas about the bigger picture in memos, and coded these memos.[74] This stage of open coding was the most time intensive, taking approximately three months of full-time work.

I then grouped collections of codes onto broader "composites" containing several codes and their pinpoints. This manual and paper method provided intimate engagement with the material and made the theory-building exercise more manageable and robust. I used computer software for qualitative analysis (NVivo Pro for Windows), largely for its retrieval and search functions – to supplement examples in Chapters 4, 5, and 6, and to find what my participants said about the casebooks for inclusion in Chapter 3. All of the substantive analysis, however, relied on the manual and paper method – as has been the case in two major recent empirical studies in legal education.[75]

My process of analysing the casebooks in Chapter 3 conceptually resembled grounded theory in the sense that I set out to generate insights about the casebooks with an open mind. It differed in that I was able to draw on considerable secondary material, and so the themes and theories in Chapter 3 are informed not only by the interplay between researcher

---

72 In total, I received eighty-six course syllabi, forty-seven slides or handouts, twenty-four final examination scripts, eleven assignments, thirty-four reading lists, eight instructions, criteria, or grading memos for assignments or examinations, eight problem exercises, three sample examinations or assignments completed by students, nine practice examinations, nine sample or complete course readings, twenty class notes, course notes, or annotated syllabi, and four miscellaneous documents.

73 See Morse et al, *supra* note 70 at 16.

74 The process of including my own notes and memos as part of the data to be analysed at the composite-producing stage reflects the collapsing, in grounded theory, of data analysis and data gathering. The idea that a researcher's own notes can serve as material to be analysed is also the key idea of "system closure," around which one leading qualitative software program (the one I happened to use), NVivo, was designed. See Tom Richards, "An Intellectual History of NUD*IST and NVivo" (2002) 5 J Social Research Methodology 199 at 201, 203.

75 See Michael Hunter Schwartz, Gerald F Hess & Sophie M Sparrow, *What the Best Law Teachers Do* (Cambridge, MA: Harvard University Press, 2013), conversation with Gerald Hess, 28 September 2013; Espeland & Sauder, *supra* note 26, conversation with Michael Sauder, 3 March 2017.

and the subject of analysis, but also by the insights of third-party commentators. I focus, in that chapter, on the three major commercial casebooks in Canada, *Swan*, *Waddams*, and *Ben-Ishai & Percy*, and one historical predecessor to *Waddams*, *Milner*.[76] I analyse the introductions and prefaces of each edition of all four books, as well as the remedies chapters in the newest edition of the three contemporary books. I do so in the context of having reviewed all published reviews of the books I could find, and selected writings (and reviews thereof) by casebook editors. I obtained confidential sales data from the three publishers and confidential data from the National Committee of Accreditation about the number of annual contract law examinations. I incorporated perspectives on the casebooks by my participants, and also reviewed syllabi in order to determine adoption rates.

A Note on Quotations and Citations

References to the participants' words are, with the exception of Professors 67 and 71, to the professionally produced transcripts of my interviews. The English transcriber indicated verbal emphasis using italics in the transcription. Therefore, italics that appear, unless otherwise noted, represent this verbal emphasis. Occasionally I removed the transcriber's italicization. Where I add emphasis, I use italics if there are no other italics in the quotation, and indicate in the footnote that emphasis has been added. If there are italics in the transcription, I add emphasis by underlining.

I removed one-word linguistic fillers (e.g., "uh," "like," "um") for ease of reading. Linguistic fillers of two or more words (e.g., "sort of," "kind of," "you know") were removed and replaced with an ellipsis. I also deleted the transcriber's notation of wordless speech acts (e.g., "laughs," "coughs," "chuckles," "sighs") and pauses, except in rare instances where I felt they were relevant. I also changed certain common linguistic reductions to their proper written form (e.g., "gonna" becomes "going to," "wanna" becomes "want to"). When I quote an exchange between myself and a participant, my words are preceded by "[R]" (for Researcher). When I cite course syllabi, I use the term "Syllabus" uniformly in the footnote citation, regardless of the title of the original document (e.g., "course outline," "course syllabus," "syllabus"). Other teaching materials reproduce the title of the original (e.g., "reading list," "A Note on the Course," etc.).

---

76 Detailed citations for the casebooks appear in Chapter 3.

OVERVIEW OF THE BOOK

In Chapter 2, I explore how contract law scholarship serves to develop some of the major schools of thought identified in Kennedy and Fisher's canon. The purpose is to show how the Contracts course, to the extent that it incorporates mainstream scholarship in the area, is naturally predisposed to model the substantive and methodological insights of American legal realism and its intellectual heirs – critical legal studies, law and economics, and socio-legal studies. This detail illustrates how contract law scholarship gives rise to an eclectic picture of legal reasoning and, by extension, a broad vision of legal practice.

In Chapter 3, I conduct a comprehensive, historical, and comparative review of the Canadian commercial common law Contracts casebooks. I show how the ideas about law from American legal realism and its heirs have figured prominently in Canadian casebooks over the course of their history. The ideas that law is contingent on social and historical factors and that underlying factors account for judicial decisions appear to motivate the core philosophy of all the editors to some extent, and later schools of thought also figure explicitly in the books' introductory chapters.

However, despite the apparent influence of the American canonical schools and their "wholesale assault on the jurisprudence of forms, concepts, and rules," the vision of law that most editors present through their treatment of one substantive topic tells a very different story.[77] In the two most frequently used casebooks in Canada, representing approximately 90 per cent of the market, the treatment of remedies portrays a vision of law and legal reasoning that has a close kinship with the classical attitudes that their editors purportedly reject. Their focus on rules and cases reveals an underlying commitment to internal coherence, doctrinal consistency, and a view of legal reasoning that privileges analogical reasoning and marginalizes policy. The casebooks, therefore, fail to fully operationalize their realist attitudes about law into their treatment of substance and legal reasoning. Thus, editors' propositional commitments to eclecticism remain suspended at the level of theory; legal methodology is overwhelmingly homogeneous, tied up with a conventional conception of the rule of law associated with formalism. This stands in contrast to at least one recent US Contracts casebook that explicitly attempts to embody methodological pluralism.[78]

77 Kennedy & Fisher, "Introduction", *supra* note 27 at 10.

78 See Daniel Markovits, *Contract Law and Legal Methods* (New York: Foundation Press, 2012).

In Chapters 4 and 5, I delve into my participant data to explore the extent to which the disjuncture between theory and practice surfaces among Canadian common law Contracts professors. Chapter 4 treats the issue of theory and practice generally. My data reveal that the vast majority of professors, when they talk about their teaching, endeavour to incorporate theoretical and critical perspectives into their courses. When asked to explain the value of theory and critique, however, they usually do not say that theory and critique matter for their own sake. Instead, Contracts professors overwhelmingly emphasize the instrumental and practical virtues of theory and critique: they make "better lawyers."

At the same time, a near consensus about integration would be an incomplete picture, for things change when professors begin talking about their role or mission, or that of the law school, in general terms. In these instances, professors are much more likely to reproduce the oppositional construct of academy and profession. Some professors describe role or mission in terms of balance or integration, but these remain in the minority. Instead, the trend suggested by my data is that professors aspire, through their teaching, to integrate theory and practice, but they also still construct the academy and profession in tension with each other, suggesting a residual disjuncture between theory and practice.

Chapter 5 explores the extent to which professors' aspirations to integrate theory and practice in their teaching are borne out by the attitudes about law reflected in their descriptions of legal reasoning and in their teaching practices and materials. Are the gaps witnessed in the casebooks – between attitudes about law and attitudes about legal reasoning, between an embrace of eclectic theories and a monolithic conception of practice, between aspiration and reality – reproduced among Contracts professors? Or, do professors' stated aspirations to teach theory and critique *as a means* to making better lawyers result in a conception of legal reasoning and a series of teaching practices that operationalize the attitudes, theories, and beliefs about law that Contracts professors hold?

The overwhelming impression is that, by and large, the disjuncture identified in the casebooks resurfaces in the attitudes and teaching practices of Contracts professors, and that, accordingly, the desire to translate theory into practice is largely aspirational, not a demonstrated reality, in Canadian common law Contracts teaching. In Chapter 5, I detail how a series of realist ideas figures prominently in professors' expressions of their attitudes about law. Like the casebook editors, a majority of Contracts professors overwhelmingly pledge allegiance to the importance of policy, politics, and context in understanding law, and emphasize law's contingency and indeterminacy. Only a minority champion the value of coherence, the importance of rules for guiding thinking, and analogical reasoning, on which they claim the rule-of-law value of equal treatment depends. As in the casebooks, however, the majority of professors describe legal reasoning as the discernment of relevant similarities with reference to an internally coherent system of rules, treating the judicial formulation of doctrinal rules seriously in a way that fails to translate into practice the realist ideas to which they are purportedly committed. Pedagogical choices about how to teach and evaluate students, as well as the substance of course readings and explicit signals in course syllabi, reveal that professors largely operationalize these more formalist commitments in their teaching. As a result, Canadian common law Contracts teaching evidences a widespread commitment to an eclectic suite of realist and critical theories, but a largely homogeneous vision of legal reasoning that fails to put these theories into practice. The resulting picture is one closer to Mertz's than to Kennedy and Fisher's.

In Chapter 6, I explore three factors that might account for the gap between aspiration and reality in Canadian common law Contracts teaching, each through the words of my participants. The first is the possibility that the realist and formalist commitments that surface simultaneously among teachers and casebook editors might be reconciled at a conceptual level. The second factor that might explain the disjuncture is the rationale of pedagogical effectiveness. Both of these accounts have their shortcomings, and in the final section of the book I depart from the implicit premise of the entire project – that the exercise of individual agency alone (expressed, as it has been, through theoretical commitments and pedagogical choices) yields a complete understanding of Canadian common law Contracts teaching. I explore the complex interplay between structure and agency in legal education, drawing from my participants' words the various ways in which they are constrained or conditioned by structural factors such as institutional culture, incentives, administrative constraints, and pressure from colleagues and students. I suggest that, in the end, it is by understanding the interplay between structure and agency that one might begin to reimagine existing forms, categories, and concepts in legal education, and thereby forge a path towards the full realization of law professors' capacious aspirations for legal education.

Chapter Two

Contracts and the Eclectic Toolkit of Legal Reasoning

In a world completely unconstrained by past practices or tradition, a course that brings together the concepts of "contract" and "law" could lead to nearly infinite permutations of approaches. "Contract" connotes ideas as diverse as The Social Contract, complex commercial agreements, marriage, clicking "I Accept," and unspoken arrangements between family members.[79] "Law," on at least the pluralist hypothesis, inhabits multiple sites and is expressed in multiple modes through various combinations of its formal, explicit, informal, and implicit character.[80] To think about the confluence of all the ways in which human beings "project[] exchange into the future"[81] and "govern" themselves according to "rules,"[82] to select just a few examples of many possible

79 See John Locke, "An Essay Concerning the True Original, Extent and End of Civil Government," Part VIII; David Hume, "Of the Original Contract"; JJ Rousseau, "The Social Contract," Parts V and VI (reprinted in *Social Contract: Essays by Locke, Hume, and Rousseau With an Introduction by Sir Ernest Barker* (Westport, CT: Greenwood Press, 1980) at 56ff, 148ff, and 178ff, respectively); Margaret Jane Radin, *Boilerplate: The Fine Print, Vanishing Rights, and the Rule of Law* (Princeton, NJ: Princeton University Press, 2013).

80 See generally Roderick A Macdonald, "Pour la reconnaissance d'une normativité juridique implicite et inférentielle" (1986) 18 Sociologie et Sociétés 47; Roderick A Macdonald, "Les Vieilles Gardes: hypothèses sur l'émergence des normes, l'internormativité et le désordre à travers une typologie des institutions normatives" in Jean-Guy Belley, ed, *Le droit soluble: Contributions québécoises à l'étude de l'internormativité* (Paris: Librairie générale de droit et de jurisprudence, 1996) at 233.

81 Ian R Macneil, *The New Social Contract: An Inquiry into Modern Contractual Relations* (New Haven, CT: Yale University Press, 1980) at 4.

82 See Lon L Fuller, *The Morality of Law*, rev ed (New Haven, CT: Yale University Press, 1969) at 241; Roderick A Macdonald, "Here, There ... and Everywhere: Theorizing Legal Pluralism; Theorizing Jacques Vanderlinden" in N Kasirer, ed, *Étudier et enseigner le droit: hier, aujourd'hui et demain – Études offertes à Jacques Vanderlinden*

expansive formulations, is to invite an astoundingly capacious set of inquiries about the nature of law, the nature of human relations, and their interrelation.

Moreover, private law, of which contract law forms an integral part, is an important constitutive element of a society.[83] Private law determines the conditions under which the state will impose liability between parties. These conditions not only determine the rules and standards by which legal officials adjudicate disputes; they also form the background conditions against which private associational activity occurs.[84] Since the permutations of existing and prospective relationships are almost infinite, private law is potentially applicable everywhere. A private law course like Contracts could therefore be a launching pad for inquiries into the desired ends of the entire political community, in which legal reasoning is presented as an expansive toolkit of means to achieve those ends.

Of course, no Contracts teacher finds him- or herself with a tabula rasa. An old tradition conceives of contract law as the collection of mainly abstract rules, paradigmatically targeted towards discrete transactions in the commercial sphere, articulated in the decisions of appellate judges. Around these rules and decisions has grown an entire field of contract law scholarship, from treatises that purport to summarize and classify these rules, to critical scholarship that deploys judicial decisions as a means of making broader claims about society.[85] These cases and scholarship make first-year Contracts largely a slate onto which much has already been etched. This chapter details how major elements of American contract law scholarship of the twentieth century

---

(Montreal: Éditions Yvon Blais, 2006) 381 at 393. See also Roderick A Macdonald, "Custom Made – for a Non-Chirographic Critical Legal Pluralism" (2011) 27 CJLS 301 at n 38.

83 An explicit instantiation of this fact lies in the recognition that the Civil Code of Quebec "lays down the *jus commune*" (Preliminary Provision). That private law is an important element for the construction of a political community is reflected in the allocation of "property and civil rights" to provincial levels of jurisdiction. See *Constitution Act, 1867* (UK), 30 & 31 Vict, c 3, reprinted in RSC 1985, Appendix II, No 5, s. 92(13); *Quebec Act, 1774* (UK), 14 Geo III, c 83.

84 See e.g. Robert H Mnookin & Lewis Kornhauser, "Bargaining in the Shadow of the Law: The Case of Divorce" (1979) 88 Yale LJ 950 at 950.

85 I say "purport" to summarize and classify, because the act of writing a treatise might have the effect, and possibly the intention, of forming and moulding the common law by privileging certain decisions over others. See e.g. Stephen Waddams, "Nineteenth-Century Treatises on English Contract Law" in Angela Fernandez & Markus Dirk Dubber, eds, *Law Books in Action: Essays on the Anglo-American Legal Treatise* (Oxford: Hart, 2012) 127.

provide an expansive opportunity for exposing students to a wide variety of attitudes about law and, crucially, legal reasoning.

One reason Mertz's discovery of the erasure of context, marginalization of policy, and bounded notions of legal reasoning in first-year Contracts classes is so shocking is that the subject matter of the course seems so thoroughly to mitigate against such erasure. The critiques of American legal realists and their heirs – through the field of contract law scholarship – overwhelmingly emphasize the importance of policy, context, and politics for understanding judicial behaviour and for evaluating law. They systematically attack the image of law as a set of internally consistent rules, autonomous from the social phenomena to which they purportedly apply. They also demonstrate that a vision of legal reasoning that relies on judicially articulated principles as part of an internally coherent system – the "jurisprudence of forms, concepts, and rules" – is inadequate, in part because it does not take into account the "real" factors that lead to legal results. In its place, they endow legal reasoning with the eclectic methodological sediment that Kennedy and Fisher describe. This eclecticism implies that a much broader vision of legal reasoning and, by implication, a much broader sense of the range of activities and purposes of legal professional activity than Mertz describes is communicated in the Contracts classes she studied.

In this chapter, I aim to accomplish three goals. First, I illustrate how mainstream contract law scholarship tracks the development of American legal thought (as Kennedy and Fisher characterize it) and how, accordingly, a course in Contracts is a natural forum in which to expose students to the realist and critical ideas explored in that scholarship. Second, I aim to acquaint the reader with the substance and details of some of these schools of thought, whose canonical status sometimes lends their ideas to generalization and caricature.[86] As I show in Chapters 3 and 5, these American ideas figure prominently in Canadian common law Contracts casebooks and in the ideas of Canadian common law Contracts professors; a close look at the seminal works here will help the reader better understand the scholarly antecedents to the attitudes that appear to significantly inform Canadian common law Contracts teaching. Third, I hope to elucidate how mainstream contract law scholarship of the twentieth century contains a wide range of different theories about law, each of which can be translated into

86 Legal realism is the subject of both famous generalizations – "We are all realist now" – and caricatures – "what the judge ate for breakfast." See Joseph William Singer, "Legal Realism Now", Review Essay of *Legal Realism at Yale: 1927–1960* by Laura Kalman (1988) 76 Cal L Rev 465; Schauer, *supra* note 29 at 129.

a different element of the lawyer's toolkit. These elements, taken together, reflect the breadth of activities from which the legal professional in the broadest, public-spirited sense would draw. One need look no further than this scholarship to see how law *could* be taught so as to model legal reasoning as a capacious practice and, by extension, to educate the lawyer as citizen.

CLASSICAL LEGAL THOUGHT, LEGAL SCIENCE, AND LEGAL FORMALISM

The critique that legal education insufficiently incorporates considerations of morality, justice, context, politics, and policy in its portrayal of legal reasoning essentially amounts to the claim that the modes and messages of classical legal thought persist in the contemporary Contracts classroom. Classical legal thought's emphasis on abstraction and coherence and its sense that law can be explained wholly with internal reference to doctrinal rules translate into a bounded notion of legal reasoning that was common in the classrooms Mertz observes and, as we will see, surfaces in Canadian common law Contracts professors' descriptions. It was against this vision that the realists and their heirs rebelled.

The classical law of contract revelled in abstraction. It was a period in which the rules of contract law decided by courts were abstracted into "pure" contract doctrine. As Lawrence Friedman has described it, "[T]he 'pure' law of contract is an area of ... abstract relationships. 'Pure' contract doctrine is blind to details of subject matter and person. It does not ask who buys and who sells, and what is bought and sold ... Contract law is abstraction – what is left in the law relating to agreements when all particularities of person and subject-matter are removed."[87] Although numerous treatises participated in this abstracting and rationalizing process, the work that instilled this idea of abstraction into legal education more than any other was Christopher Columbus Langdell's 1870 casebook, *A Selection of Cases on the Law of Contracts* – the first such casebook ever written.[88]

Langdell is famous for inventing the case method, a method that relied on two pillars of legal science. The first pillar was inductive

87 Friedman, *supra* note 43 at 20.

88 See Bruce Kimball, "Langdell on Contracts and Legal Reasoning: Correcting the Holmesian Caricature" (2007) 25 Law & Hist Rev 345 at 348, n 8 and accompanying text. See also Karl E Klare, "Contracts Jurisprudence and the First-Year Casebook", Book Review of *Problems in Contract Law: Cases and Materials* by Charles L Knapp, (1979) 54 NYU L Rev 876 at 878.

reasoning. Langdell sought to "compel" his students to discern the relevant principles of contract law by reading the raw cases in which the doctrine was "embodied."[89] In this, his science resembled the empirical method of the natural sciences: like the "laboratories" for the chemist, the "museum of natural history" for geologists, and the "botanical garden" for botanists, the law library was the "proper workshop" of professors and students.[90] The other pillar was deductive reasoning. Having discerned the relatively few "essential doctrines" in which the law consisted, these rules could be applied to future situations to deduce results. In 1879 Langdell produced a "summary of topics covered by the cases" in which he sought to "develop fully all the important principles involved in the cases."[91] The summary was published as a stand-alone book in 1880, and has been described as the first "general theory of Contract."[92] Whether or not this claim is entirely accurate,[93] Langdell is probably unique for the "parsimony" with which he selected the principles of contract law, identifying the most "salient, abstract dimensions" of the multifarious categories that previous treatise writers had employed.[94]

This two-part process – abstraction into rules and application of abstract rules to determine future results – typified the formalist approach in classical legal thought.[95] The abstract propositions were "operative" – used to "provide solutions to problems" – as opposed to being merely

---

89 Kimball, "Langdell on Contracts", *supra* note 88 at 350, citing Note, (1891) 5 Harv L Rev 89. See also Langdell, *Selection of Cases* (1879), *supra* note 56, Preface to the First Edition at viii.

90 Christopher Columbus Langdell, speech to the Harvard Law School Association, 1886, reprinted in Grant Gilmore, *Death of Contract* (Columbus: Ohio State University Press, 1974), note 22. See also Kimball, *supra* note 88 at 348.

91 Langdell, *Selection of Cases* (1879), *supra* note 56 at viii–ix, Note to the Second Edition (unnumbered page).

92 Gilmore, *Death of Contract*, *supra* note 90 at 12.

93 See Morton Horwitz, Book Review of *Death of Contract* by Grant Gilmore, (1975) 42 U Chi L Rev 787 At 795); Kimball, *supra* note 88 at 43; Waddams, "Nineteenth-Century Treatises", *supra* note 85 at 141 (ascribing the conceptualization of contract to Langdell's contemporaries, Anson and Pollock); Gordley, *supra* note 59 at 113, 217, 227, 230.

94 Kimball, "Langdell on Contracts", *supra* note 88 at 356.

95 See Duncan Kennedy, "Toward an Historical Understanding of Legal Consciousness: The Case of Classical Legal Thought in America, 1850–1940" (1980) 3 Research in Law and Sociology 3 at 8; Kennedy, "Form and Substance", *supra* note 60 at 1729; Morton Horwitz, "The Rise of Legal Formalism" (1975) Am J Legal Hist 251; G Blaine Baker, "Introduction: Quebec and the Canadas, 1760–1867: A Legal Historiography" in G Blaine Baker & Donald Fyson, eds, *Quebec and the Canadas* (Toronto: University of Toronto Press, 2013) 3 at 36.

descriptive or classificatory. Moreover, the "rationalistic ordering" of the rules implied an internal consistency or coherence that could be used to determine the validity of other rules.[96] Just as geometrical theorems must be consistent with axioms and postulates in Euclidean geometry, so legal rules (such as the mailbox rule) could be plainly "wrong" if they were not consistent with the (relatively few) essential principles.[97] Classical contract law was to be "judged by its logical symmetry."[98] Langdell once even referred to considerations of "substantive justice and the interests of the contracting parties" as "irrelevant," leading Oliver Wendell Holmes Jr to state, famously, that "the life of law has not been logic; it has been experience."[99] And although some scholars have sought to "correct the Holmesian caricature" and see in Langdell's thinking a concern for history, context, policy, and justice,[100] nevertheless Langdellian legal science is more often considered the epitome of classical legal theory, which aspires "that the legal system be made complete through universal formality, and universally formal through conceptual order."[101]

Classical legal thought has a number of implications for legal reasoning. The focus on law as an internally self-sufficient system implies the idea that legal reasoning is a wholly internal mental process of ratiocination, which is both solitary and linear. It assumes that the words of judges can be taken at face value, and that judicially described principles of law are the determining factors in legal decision making. It makes distinguishing between similar cases an important intellectual activity on the grounds that a coherent system ought to provide rational justifications for arriving at different results in similar cases. And it suggests that the standards for determining the acceptability of law are contained within the internal system of judicial reasons and that recourse to external considerations is unnecessary.[102] It is against these ideas that the realist thinkers, of which Holmes was among the first, rebelled.

---

96 Kennedy, "Toward an Historical Understanding", *supra* note 95 at 3, 19, 21; see also Thomas C Grey, "Langdell's Orthodoxy" (1983) 45 U Pitt L Rev 1 at 9.

97 See Grey, *supra* note 96 at 3–5, 14–16; Gilmore, *Death of Contract*, *supra* note 90 at 13.

98 Friedman, *supra* note 43 at 212.

99 See Oliver Wendell Holmes Jr, Review of *A Selection of Cases on the Law of Contracts, With a Summary of the Topics Covered by the Cases* by Christopher Columbus Langdell, (1880) 14 Am L Rev 233 at 234 [Holmes, Review of Langdell].

100 See Grey, *supra* note 96 at 14; Kimball, *supra* note 88.

101 Grey, *supra* note 96 at 11.

102 *Cf* Ernest Weinrib, *The Idea of Private Law*, rev ed (Oxford: Oxford University Press, 2012) at 45–6 ("What is paramount to the formalist is not the substantive desirability of any legal arrangement, but the coherence of the justificatory considerations that support its component features").

LEGAL REALISM

As Morton Horwitz writes, "Legal Realism is the culmination of the early-twentieth-century attack on the claims of ... Classical Legal Thought to have produced an autonomous and self-executing system of legal discourse."[103] Legal realism peeled back the veil of formal rationality to reveal a series of political, psychological, policy, and contextual factors that accounted for judicial decisions. This scholarship, conducted significantly through contract law, transformed the intellectual preoccupations of legal study. In place of ratiocination within an internally consistent system came the search for extrinsic, contextual factors. Scepticism about the words and concepts of formal doctrine overtook classification. Legal realism opened the door to talking about, devising, and caring about policy, laid bare political preferences, and opened the field of legal enquiry to include social relations. The corollary of the idea that all of these elements are constitutive of law is that reasoning about policy, politics, and social context are essential elements of thinking like a lawyer.

Although legal realism is often denied the status of a cohesive movement – described as "more an intellectual mood than a clear body of tenets"[104] – its influences have left an indelible mark on contemporary legal education. As Laura Kalman writes, the phrase "We are all legal realists now" is used "so frequently that it has become a truism to refer to it as a truism."[105] Early examples of legal realism still figure prominently in legal education today, and so do legal realism's "heirs" – critical legal studies, law and economics, and socio-legal studies.[106]

Functionalism Overtakes Formalism

Legal realists attacked classical legal thought in large part by attacking formalism. They rejected the ideal of abstract legal rules – what Felix Cohen derisively referred to as "transcendental nonsense."[107] Realists

---

103 Morton Horwitz, *Transformation of American Law, 1870–1960* (New York: Oxford University Press, 1992) at 193.

104 *Ibid* at 169; Karl N Llewellyn, "Some Realism about Realism – Responding to Dean Pound" (1931) 44 Harv L Rev 1222 at 1233–4; Grant Gilmore, "Legal Realism: Its Cause and Cure" (1961) 70 Yale LJ 1037 at 1038.

105 Laura Kalman, *Legal Realism at Yale: 1927–1960* (Chapel Hill: University of North Carolina Press, 1986) at 229. See also Singer, "Legal Realism Now", *supra* note 86 at 465.

106 Singer, "Legal Realism Now", *supra* note 86 at 503.

107 Felix S Cohen, "Transcendental Nonsense and the Functional Approach" (1935) 35 Colum L Rev 809.

argued that legal outcomes could never be determined mechanistically via the process of deduction. Rather, a number of factors suggested that all legal decision making was the product of indeterminate factors: judicial psychology, competing interpretations of vague and ambiguous concepts, and discretionary interpretations of what the "holdings" of cases were.[108]

The so-called objective and abstract rules, rather, "concealed" a range of political, ethical, and moral factors that judges actually relied upon. The legal realists thus attempted to expose these factors and to demonstrate that law in reality was not divorced from policy considerations.[109] A key insight of legal realism was to show that law was not discovered, but made: "Legal principles are not inherent in some universal, timeless logical system; they are social constructs."[110] In the famous words of Karl Llewellyn, the law is not the rules, but what legal officials actually *do*. Most legal realists were thus committed to functionalism, a concern with "effects," or "actual experience."[111]

In the field of contract law, Fuller and Perdue typified this approach in their two-part exposé, in the *Yale Law Journal*, of the judicial tendency to recognize the reliance interest despite the fact that prevailing doctrine took a narrower and more categorical approach to damages.[112] Fuller and Perdue identified the "judicial impulses" that led to the awarding of the reliance interest, arguing that the bright-line rule of all-or-nothing recovery in the field of contract law was not only undesirable, but itself subject to the whims and uncertainties of judicial psychology. They conclude, exemplifying the realist predilection for functionalism, with an appeal for a more "flexible scheme of legal sanctions" that would recognize "the need for compensating reliance ... on its own account."

---

108 See Jerome Frank, *Law and the Modern Mind* (New York: Coward-McCann, 1949); Horwitz, *Transformation of American Law*, *supra* note 103 at 175–8; Cohen, "Transcendental Nonsense", *supra* note 107 at 838–40; Singer, "Legal Realism Now", *supra* note 86 at 471; Karl N Llewellyn, *The Bramble Bush: On Our Law and Its Study* (New York: Oceana, 1989).

109 Cohen, "Transcendental Nonsense", *supra* note 107 at 818, 847; Gilmore, "Legal Realism", *supra* note 104 at 1038. See also LL Fuller & William R Perdue, Jr, "The Reliance Interest in Contract Damages: 2" (1937) 46 Yale LJ 373 at 376 ["Reliance Interest 2"]; Horwitz, *Transformation of American Law*, *supra* note 103 at 170.

110 Singer, "Legal Realism Now", *supra* note 86 at 474.

111 Llewellyn, *Bramble Bush*, *supra* note 108 at 3; Kalman, *supra* note 105 at 29; Llewellyn, "Some Realism about Realism", *supra* note 104 at 1222; Cohen, "Transcendental Nonsense", *supra* note 107 at 822.

112 LL Fuller & William R Perdue, Jr, "The Reliance Interest in Contract Damages: 1" (1936) 46 Yale LJ 52 ["Reliance Interest 1"]; Fuller & Perdue, "Reliance Interest 2", *supra* note 109 at 401–6, 411, 418.

They also argued that breaking down the "ancient categories" of contract and tort would make it "possible to analyse the *general problem* of the legal sanction to be given expectancies created by words or conduct in terms of the *policies* involved."[113] Five years later, in 1941, Fuller provided an analogous analysis in "Consideration and Form." In that article, Fuller "define[s] consideration in terms of its underlying policies," underscoring both the three distinct functions (evidentiary, cautionary, and channelling) of the formal basis for consideration, and the "principle of private autonomy" as its substantive basis.[114]

The concern with policy reflected a desire that law be conceived of as a "purposive ordering of human affairs," in contrast to the mechanical, categorical, and deductive mental processes championed by legal science.[115] The Fuller & Perdue articles, which Morton Horwitz has called "perhaps the single most influential piece of Realist doctrinal work," deployed an "anti-formalist critical spirit ... against one of the dominant formalist paradigms of the old order – that remedies logically flow from the nature of rights ... [The] strategy of disaggregating and contextualizing the question of contract damages, as well as the consequentialist policy orientation, ... were part of a generational revolt against formalism."[116] This attack on formalism, in large part an attack on writers such as Williston – chief reporter of the *Restatement of Contracts*, proponent of Holmes's objective theory of contract, and admirer of Langdell – had begun several decades earlier in Arthur Corbin's law review writings. These ideas eventually received full treatment in his massive treatise on contracts – what Grant Gilmore has called "the greatest law book ever written."[117]

Corbin distrusted abstract doctrine, emphasizing that all rules of law were "working rules" – rules that "represent past human transactions and influence those that are to come." When a writer, judge, or legislator initially states a rule, he or she does so as an "experiment," to see

113 Fuller & Perdue, "Reliance Interest 2", *supra* note 109 at 376, 419–20 [emphasis added].

114 Fuller, "Consideration and Form", *supra* note 60 at 800–3, 806–10; Duncan Kennedy, "From the Will Theory to the Principle of Private Autonomy: Lon Fuller's 'Consideration and Form'" (2000) 100 Colum L Rev 94 (the Fuller article ushers in a "conflicting considerations" paradigm).

115 Fuller & Perdue, "Reliance Interest 1", *supra* note 112 at 52.

116 Horwitz, *Transformation of American Law*, *supra* note 103 at 184.

117 See Gilmore, *Death of Contract*, *supra* note 90 at 14–17, 43–4, 57–8; Horwitz, *Transformation of American Law*, *supra* note 103 at 49–50; Samuel Williston, ed, *A Selection of Cases on the Law of Contracts* (Boston: Little, Brown, 1903), vol 1 at iii–iv (describing his "indebtedness" to Langdell); Arthur Linton Corbin, *Corbin on Contracts: A Comprehensive Treatise on the Rules of Contract Law* (St Paul, MN: West, 1950).

"how it will work and whether it will work at all." If the rule has been shown to work – as scholarship and experience can determine – it can help "direct our steps, to avoid pain and loss, and to live in some degree of peace and comfort." If law and legal scholarship did not aim at discovering working rules, Corbin wrote, "it would indeed be well to hang the lawyers, close the law schools, burn the libraries, abolish the courts, and .... [e]specially ... to read no further in ... the law of contracts."[118] This pragmatic approach to understanding legal rules led Corbin to conduct careful historical reviews of cases, focusing on the "operative facts," undermining the idea that "doctrines can be used mechanically, and that there are correct and unchangeable definitions."[119] Corbin emphasized that judicial decisions in contract law "depend upon the notions of the court as to policy, welfare, justice, right and wrong, such notions often being inarticulate and subconscious."[120]

The legal realists' attack on formalism, conducted in part through the field of contract law, thus incorporated an emphasis on the actual decisions made by officials, as opposed to the rules themselves; a concern with the operative facts and judicial psychology; a focus on what the purposes of rules were and how they actually operated in practice; and an attention to the policy implications of legal decisions. With these new concerns, the legal realists rejected the abstractions of contract doctrine championed by Langdell, Williston, and the *Restatement of Contracts*, shedding a light on real life – real people, real effects, and the function of legal rules.

The Politics of Legal Realism

Whether the functionalism of the realists was designed to argue for particular social policies or, instead, was neutral is a matter of debate. Some, like Laura Kalman, argue that the functionalism that undergirded the legal realists aspired to objectivity and was relativistic in its attention to particularity; as a result, it was primarily non-normative.[121] That some legal realists conducted empirical studies of law, and that the desire to classify persisted (no longer according to principles, but according to facts or "situation types"), might suggest that legal realism turned

118 Corbin, *Corbin on Contracts*, *supra* note 117, vol 1 at IV–V.

119 *Ibid* at 346, s 109. See also Gilmore, *Death of Contract*, *supra* note 90 at 58.

120 Arthur Corbin, "Offer and Acceptance, and Some of the Resulting Legal Relations" (1917) 26 Yale LJ 169 at 206, cited in Horwitz, *Transformation of American Law*, *supra* note 103 at 50.

121 Kalman, *supra* note 105 at 36–7.

towards a value-free social science.[122] However, critical legal scholars such as Singer, Horwitz, and Schlegel argue that legal realism was anything but value neutral, that it embodied an inherent critique of market neutrality, and that legal realist writers deployed their work to advance particular political convictions.[123] Thus, in realism we see the seeds of the importance of politics in legal reasoning – a theme that would be taken up in earnest by members of the critical legal studies school.

Horwitz argues that "Realism is a continuation of the Progressive attack on the attempt of late-nineteenth-century Classical Legal Thought to create a sharp distinction between law and politics and to portray law as neutral, natural, and apolitical."[124] Singer, in turn, unpacks how the realist attack on freedom of contract deployed its market critique: "[A] major goal of the legal realists was to undermine laissez-faire ideology by attacking the idea of a self-regulating market system based on free contract, which operated largely outside state influence and control." Realist scholars argued that the state was intimately involved in the regulation of private activity: by enforcing contracts, contract law became public, not private, and the rules and conditions under which they were enforced implemented particular decisions about the "moral character of market relations and the fair distribution of power in the market."[125]

The realists underscored the various ways decisions about contracts implement the social policy of encouraging market transactions. By declaring certain contracts (such as social agreements, political arrangements, or religious matters) outside the bounds of contract law, the state is implementing social decisions about *which* contracts to enforce. The state effects this social policy even more explicitly when it regulates the substantive terms of contracts through legislation. And finally, in the interpretation of contracts, especially in gap filling, courts make

122 See John Henry Schlegel, *American Legal Realism and Empirical Social Science* (Chapel Hill: University of North Carolina Press, 1995) (describing the empirical work of Charles Clark, William Douglas, Underhill Moore, and Walter Wheeler Cook); Kalman, *supra* note 105 at 29; Singer, "Legal Realism Now", *supra* note 86 at 474; Horwitz, *Transformation of American Law*, *supra* note 103 at 181–2.

123 See Schlegel, *supra* note 122 at 8 (legal realists did "attempt to do some empirical legal research and to turn their policy preferences into law").

124 See Horwitz, *Transformation of American Law*, *supra* note 103 at 170.

125 Singer, "Legal Realism Now", *supra* note 86 at 477, 483. *Cf* Friedman, *supra* note 43 at 20 ("The abstraction of classical contract law ... is a deliberate relinquishment of the temptation to restrict untrammeled individual autonomy or the completely free market in the name of social policy. The law of contract is, therefore, roughly coextensive with the free market"). See also Horwitz, *Transformation of American Law*, *supra* note 103 at 33; Friedrich Kessler, "Contracts of Adhesion – Some Thoughts about Freedom of Contract" (1943) 43 Colum L Rev 629 at 630.

value and public policy judgments about which customary practices to refer to.[126]

The realists also critiqued the idea of market neutrality by looking at the substance of the private law rules themselves, quite apart from their argument that contract law as a whole has a public element. Contract doctrine itself, in other words, "inescapably engages courts in making moral and public policy decisions about the legitimate distribution and use of power in the market place."[127] Doctrines of duress, mistake, or undue influence could be thought of as manifestations of a deliberate decision to accept a certain degree of coercion or to resolve the inequality of bargaining power in a particular way.[128] The market could not be neutral because, according to Robert Hale, it was "permeated with coercive restrictions ... out of conformity with any formula of 'equal opportunity' or of 'preserving the equal rights of others.'"[129] Thus, the attack on formalism, on this interpretation, not only attacked a way of thinking – via categorical, deductive rationality – it also identified and subsequently attacked the political commitment to laissez-faire ideology implicit in the legal system's support of a free market economy.

Legal Realism's Legacies for Legal Reasoning: Politics, Policy, and Context

According to Singer, legal realism ushered in a "pragmatic" tradition of legal reasoning, one typified by at least four points, each of which has its implications for constructing a toolkit of reasoning techniques for judges and lawyers. First, the realists demonstrated that it is "impossible to induce a unique set of legal rules from existing precedents," and thus one must necessarily "engage in ethical inquiry" to determine which differences are relevant in translating prior cases into future outcomes. Second, the realists "hoped to lower the overall level of abstraction in legal reasoning" by focusing on the actual value choices at play.

126 Singer, "Legal Realism Now", *supra* note 86 at 483–5 (summarizing Morris R Cohen, "The Basis of Contract" (1933) 46 Harv L Rev 553 and PS Atiyah, *Essays on Contract* (Oxford: Clarendon Press, 1986) 29).

127 Singer, "Legal Realism Now", *supra* note 86 at 486.

128 See Hale, "Coercion and Distribution in a Supposedly Noncoercive State", *supra* note 60; Robert L Hale, "Bargaining, Duress, and Economic Liberty" (1943) 43 Colum L Rev 603; John P Dawson, "Economic Duress – An Essay in Perspective" (1947) 45 Mich L Rev 253. See also Clare Dalton, "An Essay in the Deconstruction of Contract Doctrine" (1985) 94 Yale LJ 997 at 1029–31.

129 Hale, "Coercion and Distribution in a Supposedly Noncoercive State", *supra* note 60 at 470.

This requires focusing on the particular facts at hand and developing an ability to "address more honestly" the values at stake in a given decision. Third, judges (and hence lawyers) should "make law based on a thorough understanding of contemporary social reality," which requires "closely examin[ing] the social context in which those affected by legal rules operate." And finally, in "applying rules in light of their purposes [and] looking to the goals of the rules and their social effects," judges need to "balance pragmatically competing interests in light of competing policies, principles, and values." This breaks down into the concrete tasks of "identify[ing] a range of alternative legal solutions to any problem; (2) predict[ing] the consequences of deciding one way rather than another; (3) articulat[ing] the competing interests, values, and policies involved ...; (4) compar[ing] the relative advantages of alternative approaches, including the social consequences ... and the values that would be protected; and finally (5) mak[ing] a choice designed, as Felix Cohen said, to 'promot[e] the good life of those whom it affects.'"[130]

This portrays a rather broad list of factors for lawyers (or judges or law students) to incorporate into their understanding of what are acceptable legal arguments. The commitments of the realists to underlying factors, particular facts, historical contingency, social outcomes, and prospective thinking transform legal reasoning away from an exercise of abstraction, deduction, and prediction into a historically, factually, and contextually grounded exercise that transparently engages with values and political preferences, and positions the lawyer to think prospectively about the design choices needed to achieve them. This adds at least three elements to the lawyer's eclectic toolkit. It trains students to speak in the language of policy, which is conceptually distinct from speaking in terms of rules and principles. It invites students to engage in analysis drawn from other disciplines, such as economics, to assess (and ultimately argue for) these policy rationales.[131] And it encourages students to deliberate about the ends themselves – to wrestle with competing visions of justice and to formulate arguments that might help attain the chosen vision. Much like Kennedy and Fisher, Singer argues

130 Singer, "Legal Realism Now", *supra* note 86 at 499–502 (citing Felix Cohen, *Ethical Systems and Legal Ideals: An Essay on the Foundations of Legal Criticisms* (New York: Harcourt, Brace, 1933) at 42).

131 The Brandeis brief is one early tangible example of the incorporation of social scientific evidence into legal argumentation. See Martha Minow, "Foreword: Justice Engendered" (1987) 101 Harv L Rev 10 at 88–9. But see Noga Morag-Levine, "Facts, Formalism, and the Brandeis Brief: The Origins of a Myth" [2013] U Ill L Rev 59.

that these elements already inform how private law is actually taught in the classroom.[132]

In the next few sections, I expand on how the schools of thought that followed the early realists – critical legal studies, law and economics, and socio-legal studies – built on the realist foundations. These examples demonstrate how contract law scholarship could provide a solid basis for incorporating concerns of politics, policy, and context into the lawyer's eclectic toolkit.

LAW IS POLITICS: CRITICAL LEGAL STUDIES

The authors and teachers who comprised the critical legal studies (CLS) movement of the 1970s and early 1980s built on many of the legal realist insights in the service of a particular political project: the desire to create a "more humane, egalitarian, and democratic society."[133] The movement's impact on legal education has been considerable, transmitting some key messages to generations of law students. Primary among these is the insistence that "law is politics." CLS authors continued the work of the legal realists in trying to uncover the political values contained within legal doctrine, highlighting ideological oppositions and identifying "conservative hegemony" in law in order to reject it. These views gave rise to an aspiration for a "utopian" reimagination of the legal order. CLS scholars assert that legal education is a key instrument for facilitating the revolutionary project implied by its critique.[134]

To the lawyer's toolkit the CLS scholars add an ability to discern the ideology underlying both the positive law and the techniques and patterns of legal reasoning. The critique that contract doctrine is indeterminate invites students (and future lawyers) to manipulate doctrinal analysis in order to change the law and attain fairer distribution. On a broader scale, the utopian premises of the school invite students to

---

132 Singer, "Legal Realism Now", *supra* note 86 at 474 (law professors use situation types to explain results in cases, "bring out the policy and moral implications of rule choices" that underlie cases; and use cases to analyse economic efficiency, "identify social problems in need of legislative or administrative regulation," or "demonstrate that the law serves the needs of the rich and powerful").

133 Duncan Kennedy & Karl E Klare, "A Bibliography of Critical Legal Studies" (1984) 94 Yale LJ 461 at 461.

134 Elizabeth Mensch, "The History of Mainstream Legal Thought" in David Kairys, ed, *The Politics of Law: A Progressive Critique*, rev ed (New York: Pantheon Books, 1990) 13 at 33; David Kairys, "Introduction" in Kairys, *Politics of Law* 1 at 3. See also Duncan Kennedy, "Politicizing the Classroom" (1995) 4 Rev L Women's Stud 81 at 84; Kennedy, "Legal Education and the Reproduction of Hierarchy", *supra* note 61 at 610.

think about the broader political project of all legal activity. Thus, in addition to adding tools to the toolkit, CLS aspires to position the lawyer's role broadly in society, contributing also to the bigger-picture image of the lawyer as citizen.

Ideology Underlies Law and Legal Reasoning

Perhaps the most common feature among CLS thinkers is the idea that two opposing value systems underlie law. Contract law is a favourite subject of this "dialectical or structural" analysis.[135] These opposing value systems – alternatively described as individualism/altruism, individualism/collectivism, or self-regarding/other-regarding – describe an underlying structure of law, both the content of rules and the process of legal reasoning itself. Acknowledging the presence of both opposing values within law serves to "break down the sense that legal argument is autonomous from moral, economic, and political discourse in general."[136]

The classic example of the idea that ideological differences can explain both positive law and legal reasoning appears in Duncan Kennedy's landmark article, "Form and Substance in Private Law Adjudication." This article, which Kennedy self-describes as an "abstract[ion] to private law" of a previous contract law article on credit cards[137] – and which itself relies heavily on analysis of contract doctrine – develops in detail the distinction between individualism and altruism. Individualism entails making a "sharp distinction between one's interests and those of

---

135 Kennedy, "Form and Substance", *supra* note 60 at 1712–13, 1723. *Cf* Jay M Feinman, "Critical Approaches to Contract Law" (1983) 30 UCLA L Rev 829 at 854 ("contract law ... actually is only a recast, idealized form of the underlying illegitimate socio-economic order"); Jay M Feinman & Peter Gabel, "Contract Law as Ideology" in Kairys, *supra* note 134 at 373.

136 Kennedy, "Form and Substance", *supra* note 60 at 1724. See also *ibid* at 1712–13, 1719–23; Feinman, "Critical Approaches to Contract Law", *supra* note 135 at 838, 839–44; Joseph Singer, "The Legal Rights Debate in Analytical Jurisprudence from Bentham to Hohfeld" [1982] Wisc L Rev 975 at 980; Dalton, *supra* note 128 at 1006, n 14. Some critics have subsequently "recanted" the idea of structural centrality, but, as Kronman writes, "many others ... have followed [Kennedy] in his original assumptions, taking the argument of 'Form and Substance'" as a model. See Peter Gabel & Duncan Kennedy, "Roll Over Beethoven" (1984) 36 Stan L Rev 1 at 15–16; Kronman, *Lost Lawyer*, *supra* note 16 at 246, n 135 (citing such authors as Allan Hutchison, Patrick Monahan, Robert Gordon, and Steven Winter).

137 Stewart Macaulay, "Private Legislation and the Duty to Read – Business Run by IBM Machine, the Law of Contracts and Credit Cards" (1966) 19 Vanderbilt L Rev 1051.

others," ignores discussions of "ends or values," places no restraint on the choice of ends, and has "no moral content whatsoever." Altruism, by contrast, rejects the distinction between self-interest and the interests of others. It enjoins individuals to sacrifice for and share with one another and to make themselves vulnerable to non-reciprocity. Altruist justice is collective: it seeks order according to "shared ends." In pursuit of this "universal ideal of human brotherhood," discussion about values is "the highest form of discourse," in which the contingency of ends "provides occasions for ingenuity but never dispute."[138]

For Kennedy, individualism and altruism do not only "manifest themselves in the debates about the content of private law rules"; the poles on the ideological spectrum also account for different styles of legal argumentation. In particular, Kennedy argues that "altruist views on substantive private law issues lead to willingness to resort to standards in administration, while individualism seems to harmonize with an insistence on rigid rules rigidly applied." He describes three ways – moral, economic, and political – in which rules correspond with individualism and standards with altruism. On a moral plane, he argues how formally realizable rules emphasize self-reliance: rules put contracting parties on notice of their obligations; any adverse effects are "deserved," and "those who suffer have no one to blame but themselves." By contrast, standards relax the rigidity of formal rules, enable particular factors to be taken into account, and thereby mitigate the perils of over- or under-inclusion. A reliance on standards might have the effect of requiring the party who would have benefited from the bright-line rule to forego his or her advantage, a result that reflects the altruist concern with mercy, sharing, and sacrifice.[139]

On an economic plane, Kennedy revisits the connection the realists had made between contract doctrine and laissez-faire capitalism. Individualism and a preference for rules enjoy an "exact correspondence." Both rules and individualism are non-interventionist, in that they both are inclined to avoid the "total" realization of legislative purpose; rules in contract doctrine, like the individualist, tend to prefer to leave people to their own devices; and "both rules and the substantive reduction of altruistic duty will encourage transaction in general." By contrast, the altruist critique of laissez-faire argues that the public interest would be better served by considering the particularities of the situation, which a reliance on standards permits. Thus, the "altruist substantive and formal arguments are identical ... The economic argument for standards

138 Kennedy, "Form and Substance", *supra* note 60 at 1768–72.

139 *Ibid* at 1713, 1685, 1738–40.

is the formal version of the ... proposition ... that we can sometimes enforce our substantive values in particular cases ... without the disastrous consequences the individualist predicts."[140]

Kennedy highlights the political correspondence by identifying and critiquing two "gambits" that have been used to argue that judges should do "nothing but formulate and apply formally realizable general rules." The "institutional competence" gambit asserts that judges, unlike legislatures, do not have the resources to conduct the wide-ranging factual inquiries they would need to do to determine the consequences of their decisions. Accordingly, they should leave result orientation to the legislature and confine themselves to general prescriptions. The "political question" gambit asserts that judges should refrain from employing standards, because standards involve "value judgments," which are legitimately engaged in only by an elected majority. Judges should restrict themselves to fact finding, a rational and objective enterprise.[141]

Kennedy argues how these arguments in favour of rules-based adjudication are "'essentially' individualist." By enjoining the judge from performing legislative functions – from considering "result[s]," "implement[ing] the community's substantive purposes," "behav[ing] politically," introducing "new principles" of law, or "creating" doctrines – those who advance these arguments compel the judge to defer to private power, to legitimate existing power disparities, and to effect a "quintessentially individualist program."[142]

Thus, for Kennedy, substance and form are intertwined, playing out a timeless structural opposition between individualism and altruism. Other CLS authors, also writing on contract law, have performed variations on this theme. Jay Feinman argues for the relationship between individualism and "formal adjudication" on the one hand, and between collectivism and "purposive adjudication" on the other.[143] Clare Dalton identifies a similar interconnectedness.[144]

The relationship of form to substance deepens the relationship between law and politics by suggesting that not only substantive rules are political, but so is legal rationality itself. Different reasoning strategies embody different ideological values. The relationship of form to substance signals to students that the choice of what type of legal argument

---

140 *Ibid* at 1745–51.
141 *Ibid* at 1752–3.
142 *Ibid* at 1753, 1760–1.
143 "Critical Approaches to Contract Law", *supra* note 135 at 847.
144 *Supra* note 128 at 1026.

to adopt entails a commitment to a particular ideology. In this way, it challenges the naturalness of legal reasoning that focuses on adjudication and disclaims responsibility for distributive effects. Moreover, by identifying moral, economic, and political implications of rules-and standards-based reasoning – by connecting legal rationality to historical, social, and cultural phenomena – CLS, like legal realism, places law on the same plane as other disciplines, breaking down the barrier between "legal" and other modes of reasoning.

Law's Indeterminacy: Deconstructing Contract Doctrine

Another critical element of the lawyer's toolkit is the ability to devise novel argumentative strategies to argue for change in the positive law. This ability depends upon at least two important insights offered by CLS scholarship. The first is the idea that contract doctrine is indeterminate: rules do not necessarily cohere, and do not on their own determine results of legal decision making. This crack in the edifice of an apparently solid doctrine opens up possibilities for advocacy and reform. Second, by showing how underlying considerations might help account for the results in decided cases, a critical analysis invites lawyers (or students) to propose alternative considerations.

Clare Dalton, in a path-breaking article for both CLS and feminism, highlights indeterminacy and its associated possibilities for advocacy. In "An Essay on the Deconstruction of Contracts Doctrine," she breaks down conventional dualities within contract doctrine and points the way to alternative formulations. Although she, like Duncan Kennedy and Jay Feinman, seeks to examine how a "split" between "self and other, subject and object ... structures our contract doctrine," she also proposes how a novel category – opinions about women – might be used to address the issues of knowledge and power that underlie the doctrine.[145]

Dalton draws on the theoretical resources of Jacques Derrida – in particular, his understanding of the "supplemental" pole in dichotomies – to problematize three dichotomies that recur throughout contract doctrine: between the public and the private, the objective and the subjective, and form and substance. She argues that, in privileging one pole of each dichotomy over the other, contract law historically has performed a disservice by displacing the real problems of power and knowledge. Moreover, this privileging is inaccurate because it ignores

---

145 *Ibid* at 1000.

the important supplemental role that the disfavoured pole plays, and fails to show how each pole is constituted and entailed by the other. As a result, the "reassurance" that contract doctrine purports to provide – that it can resolve problems of knowledge and power in "all but the 'hard case'" – is illusory. Dalton uses traditional areas of contract law – implied contracts, duress, unconscionability, intent, and consideration – as well as rules on cohabitation agreements to show the inconsistency and indeterminacy of the doctrines.[146]

Building on the old realist theme, Dalton seeks to show how contract doctrine has attempted to "suppress 'publicness'" by artificially separating public from private. She "dissolve[s]" this dichotomy by showing how the traditional distinction between quasi-contract as public and contract implied-in-fact as private "does not and cannot hold." Public concerns "necessarily inform" the finding of a contract in fact, and quasi-contract "depends on prior understandings of the private relationships of the parties." Such unsuccessful distinctions suggest that the doctrine is "wrestl[ing] with knowledge," where knowledge of public requires knowledge of private, and vice versa. Similarly, the doctrines of duress and unconscionability are "self-consciously 'public' insofar as they are designed to police the limits of a fair bargain," but the doctrinal devices "suppress the public aspect" by denying that "these questions can be answered only by recourse to non-neutral and non-consensual choices." By diverting attention from the public question of power to the private aspects of agreement, both the case law and the *Restatement of Contracts* "forestall" or "distract ... from" the overtly political question of drawing lines for the legitimate use of power.[147]

Dalton goes on to deconstruct the rules around manifestation and intent to explore the "subversive" supplementary role that subjective intent plays in contract doctrine. She argues that subjective will remained an important source of obligation even in the Holmesian objective theory of contract. She shows how the resort to formal hierarchies for determining contractual intent had to revert to subjective intent to retain legitimacy, even though the doctrine was unable to "identify intention in any reliable way." And she shows how standards of responsibility add "yet another layer of indeterminacy to the decisionmaking process" by introducing contradictory criteria for decision making.[148]

Dalton then examines consideration doctrine to demonstrate that form and substance are necessarily intertwined. She complicates the

146 *Ibid* at 1000–2, 1007.
147 *Ibid* at 1010–11, 1014–15, 1018–19, 1022, 1024, 1026, 1037–8.
148 *Ibid* at 1040–2, 1050–2, 1063.

dominant "story" that consideration is exclusively a question of form, arguing that the formal theory inevitably makes reference to two alternative notions of substance: subjective intent and objective value. She shows how substance plays an important role in both the Holmesian bargain theory and reliance theory, arguing that case law has maintained the bargain/reliance distinction only by recourse to substance. Accordingly, the "conventional" need to view consideration as form cannot stand: we are unable to "recognize form without reference to substance, or to recognize substance without its embodiment in some form." Since consideration-as-form and consideration-as-substance operate at cross-purposes, the result is indeterminacy. Moreover, the failure of the substance/form dichotomy suggests that consideration cannot avoid its status as a "mechanism for policing the adequacy of exchange," which is a question of power.[149]

Given that existing rules fail to resolve the questions of knowledge and power about which they are fundamentally concerned, doctrine is indeterminate. Dalton undertakes a similar move in her examination of cohabitation agreements: doctrine in that subject-matter area "blind[s] us to some aspects of what the disputes are actually about," "denies the complexities, and ambiguities, of human relationships," and offers "false assurance that ... public can be reconciled with private, manifestation with intent, form with substance." From here, she moves beyond the descriptive to the inventive. She proposes an alternative category to "illuminate" the process of arriving at legal decisions: the "nightmarish" images of women in the cases. She describes how alternate images of woman-as-angel/woman-as-whore "influence how judges frame rule-talk and policy-talk," and can help us "understand[] ... this particular set of cases." Since these images involve the "same perceived divide between self and other" as do the doctrinal categories, they are "as deserving of attention" as is the doctrine.[150]

Dalton's analysis suggests that indeterminacy is a plausible characterization of contract doctrine. As will become evident later, many professors aim to disabuse students of the idea that law is certain and that doctrinal rules determine outcomes; Dalton's article can be thought of in this regard as a legitimating authority for this commitment.

Moreover, by positing "knowledge and power" – two abstract and far-reaching ideas – as the fundamental interests that contract law seeks to attain, she invites the search for (and manipulation of) alternative underlying interests, in the same way that Lon Fuller posited reliance

---

149 *Ibid* at 1069–83, 1087–92, 1094, 1066.

150 *Ibid* at 1095, 1108–13.

or "private autonomy" as foundations of legal decisions.[151] Dalton's work thus might encourage those teaching legal reasoning to look for deep, structural ideas well beneath the surface of judicially formulated reasons. It also implies that these ideas – and thus legal reasoning itself – might draw from other disciplines and frameworks, such as "psychological, psychoanalytic, and feminist theory, as well as ... myth and history."[152]

Finally, Dalton's inventive move – to propose an entirely non-doctrinal category for analysing the outcome of cases – invites creativity on the part of law students and lawyers. In the same way that Dalton positions images about women and conventional doctrine as equally deserving of attention, law professors might invite students to propose other categories or lenses for making arguments about law, including "concrete aspects of social life."[153] This approach would add to the lawyer's toolkit strategies of experimentation and nonlinear thinking, broadening the range of factors available to influence legal decisions.

Critique Leads to Reimagination, Revolution, Utopia

In the CLS imaginary, politics runs throughout law: as an account of the policies motivating judicial decision making, in the form of legal reasoning itself, and as deeper issues (such as power and knowledge) that underlie the doctrine. These elements generate a series of skills for the eclectic toolkit: an ability to identify ideology in substantive law, to devise creative arguments focused on underlying considerations, and to interrogate legal reasoning techniques themselves for their ideological content. But there is an additional way in which CLS might contribute to educating the lawyer as citizen. For numerous CLS authors, critique is not just a descriptive or analytical project, but a political and social project as well. Contract law has "utopian" or "revolutionary" possibilities.[154] This adds to the toolkit a boldness in envisioning the scope and ends of legal argumentation and legal practice. CLS thinking urges students to resist and transform the socioeconomic inequities that these structures reflect and sustain – and to do so in a distinctly "lawyerly" way.

---

151 See Fuller & Perdue, "Reliance Interest 1", *supra* note 112; Fuller, "Consideration and Form", *supra* note 60.

152 Dalton, *supra* note 128 at 1112–13.

153 *Ibid* at 1003.

154 See e.g. Feinman, "Critical Approaches to Contract Law", *supra* note 135 at 857ff; Kennedy, "Legal Education and the Reproduction of Hierarchy", *supra* note 61 at 614; Karl Klare, "Teaching *Local 1330*", *supra* note 35 at 78.

CLS authors might draw on specific examples from contract law cases to illustrate these utopian possibilities. Feinman, for example, writes that "every contracts case" has the potential for lawyers to "transform ordinary situations into extraordinary occasions." As an example, he cites the suggestion by a judge in a pretrial hearing that the long-standing presence of a steel mill in the community might have created a property right in the people. Though not ultimately successful, Feinman argues that such a suggestion exemplifies that "retreat to established doctrine" is never "compelled."[155] In this way, the creativity and inventiveness observed in Dalton's article becomes a resource for legal argumentation and analysis at all stages of the judicial process. Karl Klare uses the same case – *Local 1330* – to train his students to construct novel arguments in favour of social justice.[156] His vision of "critical legal pedagogy" aims to "empower" students to participate "*as lawyers* in transformative social movements," to view their professional life as an opportunity to "infuse legal rules and practices with emancipatory and egalitarian content," and to argue "professionally and respectably for the utopian and the possible."[157]

Through critique of contract doctrine, whether by illuminating structural oppositions, deconstructing existing dualities in doctrine, or inviting students to think creatively, scholars in the critical legal studies school intimately connect the study and practice of law with politics. They do so by highlighting the political elements of doctrine and legal reasoning, by modelling new and creative ways of reimagining legal reasoning, by encouraging lawyers to deliberate about ends, and, finally, by connecting the practice of law to a political agenda and a utopian vision. Students learn that they can "pursue moral and political projects and articulate visions of social organization and social justice" through the "medium" of "legal discourse," a discourse that is infused with considerations of context.[158] This context includes both the granular appreciation of "concrete social reality" and the more general context of opposing ideologies. By emphasizing that politics is inseparable from law and that legal analysis is inseparable from context, CLS thus complicates and enriches the notion of legal reasoning and legal practice.

---

155 Feinman, "Critical Approaches to Contract Law", *supra* note 135 at 857–9.

156 *United Steel Workers, Local 1330 v US Steel Corp*, 492 F Supp 1 (ND Ohio 1980), aff'd in part, vacated and remanded in part, 631 F (2d) 1264 (6th Cir 1980) [*Local 1330*].

157 Klare, "Teaching *Local 1330*", *supra* note 35 at 77–8 [emphasis in original].

158 *Ibid.*

POLICY: LAW AND ECONOMICS

The law and economics movement, like CLS, inherited from the legal realist tradition the inclination to look beyond the words of judicial decisions to determine other factors that account for them. Like the authors studied so far, law and economics scholars argued that concepts from "outside" law are internal to, and operative on, legal reasoning. Law and economics, despite its numerous differences with CLS, likewise emphasizes social and economic context over the written text. It also continues the realist tradition of encouraging students to speak, do, and care about policy. The extensive influence that law and economics has had on contract law reinforces the idea that teaching Contracts is a natural field in which to build the lawyer's eclectic toolkit of legal reasoning.[159]

Efficiency: The Retreat from Politics

In contrast to CLS, law and economics retreats from politics in at least two ways. First, whereas CLS encourages a debate among values, law and economics forecloses any such debate by positing efficiency as the presumptive standard for analysing and understanding law. Rigorous studies about means (typified by cost-benefit analyses) eclipse political debate about desired social ends.[160]

Second, and relatedly, whereas distributional outcomes are a central preoccupation of CLS, they are often a secondary concern in the economic analysis of law. Economists are generally interested in the "size of the pie" as opposed to how it is sliced. A primary example is the powerful influence that the Coase theorem has had on the economic analysis of law. Ronald Coase demonstrated that, under certain assumptions (including zero transaction costs and wealth effects), legal liability is immaterial to the allocation of resources. An efficient result will be obtained regardless of the right conferred; the right only affects distribution of profits as between people. Since transaction costs are never zero, much subsequent analysis has focused on what conditions will maximize efficiency. The minor role that distribution plays in the

---

159 Numerous scholars have argued that it is almost impossible to teach contract law without considering law and economics. See e.g. Frank H Stephen, *The Economics of the Law* (Brighton, UK: Wheatsheaf Books, 1988).

160 See e.g. Kronman, *Lost Lawyer*, *supra* note 16 at 228; Richard A Posner, *Economic Analysis of Law*, 4th ed (Boston: Little, Brown, 1992) at 13; Duncan Kennedy, "Cost-Benefit Analysis of Entitlement Problems: A Critique" (1981) 33 Stan L Rev 387. See also C Edwin Baker, "The Ideology of the Economic Analysis of Law" (1975) 5 Phil & Pub Affairs 3 at 34–6.

Coase theorem reflects the broad tendency in economic analysis for efficiency concerns to predominate over distributional ones.[161]

Another way this preference for efficiency over distributional concerns arises is in law and economics' preference for forward-looking planning (ex ante concerns) over after-the-fact distribution (ex post). The law and economics scholar is generally concerned with how legal rules will affect future instances of initial behaviour, not with how damages will be awarded after the fact. Forward looking, guided by the measuring stick of Kaldor-Hicks efficiency (which posits only a *hypothetical* redistribution), law and economics thus self-consciously avoids the question of "politics" to the extent that politics is understood either as being a contest about ends or a concern with distributional consequences. Indeed, even when law and economics scholars consider distributional justice, they may do so using the yardstick of efficiency.[162]

The Primacy of Policy

In place of politics, law and economics emphasizes an enquiry into means. Its major influence on legal reasoning is to encourage the ability to infer the consequential effects of existing legal rules and to anticipate how different rules may be employed to effect social change – to cultivate a policy mind.[163] Like classical legal thought, legal realism,

---

161 See e.g. A Mitchell Polinsky, *An Introduction to Law and Economics* (Boston: Little, Brown, 1989) at 7; RH Coase, "The Problem of Social Cost" (1960) 3 J L & Econ 1; Stephen, *supra* note 159 at 29–32 (citing C Veljanovski, "The Coase Theorems and the Economic Theory of Markets and Law" (1982) 35 Kyklos 66); Posner, *Economic Analysis of Law*, *supra* note 160 at 22, 49–53; Robert Cooter & Thomas Ulen, *Law and Economics*, 6th ed (Boston: Pearson Education, 2012) at 1, 7–9, n 2. For a strong version of the argument that only efficiency should guide legal policy analysis, see Louis Kaplow & Steven Shavell, *Fairness Versus Welfare* (Cambridge, MA: Harvard University Press, 2002); Louis Kaplow & Steven Shavell, "Why the Legal System Is Less Efficient Than the Income Tax in Redistributing Income" (1994) 23 J Legal Studies 667. But see Chris Sanchirico, "Deconstructing the New Efficiency Rationale" (2001) Cornell L Rev 1005; Daniel A Farber, "What (If Anything) Can Economics Say about Equity?", Book Review of *Fairness Versus Welfare* by Louis Kaplow and Steven Shavell (2003) 101 Mich L Rev 1791.

162 See e.g. Richard A Posner & Andrew M Rosenfield, "Impossibility and Related Doctrines in Contract Law: An Economic Analysis" (1977) 6 J Legal Studies 83 at 113; Stephen S Ashley, "The Economic Implications of the Doctrine of Impossibility" (1975) 26 Hastings LJ 1251 at 1251; Posner, *Economic Analysis of Law*, *supra* note 160 at 24, 356, c 17; Stephen, *supra* note 159 at 57–8.

163 See e.g. Cooter & Ulen, *supra* note 161 at 9 ("Economics conceives of laws as incentives for changing behavior (implicit prices) and as instruments for policy objectives (efficiency and distribution)").

and CLS, law and economics uses doctrine as a sort of laboratory. In this case, the student seeks to understand economic policies that might have accounted for legal decisions. It is then a short step to evaluate judicial decisions on economic grounds and, ultimately, to pivot into a more creative mode in which students are asked to reflect on the efficacy of certain legal rules and to devise recommendations.

A brief selection of law and economics scholarship in contract law illustrates how economic analysis employs policy-based reasoning. Economic analysis can provide a standard for determining the choice of "instrument," suggesting, for example, that the costs of a judicial unconscionability standard outweigh the benefits and that legislative intervention would therefore be preferable.[164] Economic analysis can recommend "policy expedients" to attain, in the case of procedural unconscionability, a "socially optimal" level of information produced by the supply side of the market. It can assess the "effects" of doctrine, using the Coase theorem to determine that liability rules in the case of substantive unfairness (in a songwriter's contract) are unlikely to affect the ultimate disparity in bargaining power.[165] It can prescribe efficiency-based recommendations to courts, for example, to impose "risk on the better information-gatherer" in cases of mistake or to recommend discharge in the case of impossibility based on whether the promisee or promisor is the superior risk bearer.[166] It can measure whether cases are "correctly" decided from an economic perspective or assess – using ex ante considerations – whether a given test (such as the uniqueness requirement for awarding the remedy of specific performance) is "economically rational."[167]

All of these examples suggest that economic analysis can help students participate in the "design of optimal legal policy."[168] In most examples, the method is to assume an end goal (greater efficiency), and then assess both the substance of the rules and the appropriate rule

164 Richard A Epstein, "Unconscionability: A Critical Reappraisal" (1975) 18 J Law & Econ 293 at 303, 305; Donald N Dewees & Michael J Trebilcock, "Judicial Control of Standard Form Contracts" in Paul Burrows & Cento G Veljanovski, eds, *The Economic Approach to Law* (London: Butterworth, 1981).

165 MJ Trebilcock, "The Doctrine of Inequality of Bargaining Power: Post-Benthamite Economics in the House of Lords" (1976) 26 UTLJ 359 at 373, 382–3.

166 Anthony T Kronman, "Mistake, Disclosure, Information, and the Law of Contracts" (1978) J Legal Studies 1 at 4; Posner & Rosenfield, *supra* note 162 at 90.

167 Posner & Rosenfield, *supra* note 162 at 102, 105; Anthony T Kronman, "Specific Performance" (1978) 45 U Chi L Rev 351 at 369.

168 Anthony T Kronman & Richard A Posner, eds, *The Economics of Contract Law* (Boston: Little, Brown, 1979) at 153 (notes and questions to the chapter on Mistake and Impossibility).

maker in light of this end. The student steeped in this tradition (or taught by someone so steeped) thus might develop policy literacy, aptitude, and concern.

Efficiency and Economic Science

Law and economics also operates at a higher level of abstraction. This resides in the idea that the rules, "taken as a whole, tend to look as though they were chosen with a view to maximizing social wealth" – the claim that the common law more generally is motivated by questions of efficiency.[169] This more macro perspective provides an overarching explanatory account for the common law. In this respect, it is akin to CLS, whose individualist/collectivist lens also provides a structural explanation (the presence of the duality between individualism/altruism). This similarity led Kronman to describe both as coexisting under the broader category of "scientific realism." Both traditions seek to uncover a "latent order" beneath the chaotic surface of dispersed decisions, employ the use of abstract arguments to identify this order, and look in the direction of a "simple" or "comprehensive" account of the basic legal structure.[170]

This external perspective, as in CLS, constitutes a preoccupation with context extrinsic to law. Economic science provides a set of distinctive methods to apply to areas of public and private law. Unlike Langdellian legal science, which used empirical inductive methods to discover the principles immanent in the reported decisions, law and economics considers legal doctrine as a more pliable, less authoritative subject of analysis. Rather than viewing judicial reasoning as constitutive of the principles, the operating principle (efficiency) is derived from outside the law. Legal discourse accordingly can be discounted as "rhetoric" that "conceals, rather than illuminate[s]," the "true grounds of legal decision"; legal doctrines might be no more than "inarticulate gropings toward efficiency." Correlatively, legal education "consists primarily of learning to dig beneath the rhetorical surface to find [economic] grounds."[171]

Posner illustrates this approach in his research on contract law, distinguishing cases where legal reasoning alone is inconclusive, "explain[ing]" case outcomes and "translating" from legal into economic terms, and

169 Frank I Michelman, "A Comment on *Some Uses and Abuses of Economics in Law*" (1979) 46 U Chi L Rev 307 at 308. See also Posner, *Economic Analysis of Law*, 4th ed, *supra* note 160 at 23; Stephen, *supra* note 159 at 195ff.

170 Kronman, *Lost Lawyer*, *supra* note 16 at 245–6, 226–7.

171 Posner, *Economic Analysis of Law*, 4th ed, *supra* note 160 at 23, 17–18. See also Henry Hansmann, "The Current State of Law-and-Economics Scholarship" (1983) 33 J Legal Ed 217 at 226–7.

analysing cases to illustrate "how the courts can arrive at an economically efficient result yet disguise it as an apparently meaningless semantic distinction."[172] This approach might encourage scepticism about legal reasoning – not so much the scepticism that law conceals political bias (as realist and CLS writings encourage) or that law is primarily an instrument for a selection of policy tools (compatible with realism, CLS, and law and economics), but, rather, a deeper scepticism about whether law has a distinct reasoning method and can be treated as a stand-alone discipline. By identifying a primary scientific Archimedean point, the approach might imply that, even if *economics* were not one's chosen lens, some other lens would be needed to make sense of legal reasoning. The endeavour of understanding law, even critiquing legal reasoning, on its own terms might then seem naive without the scientific standards of a distinctive discipline.[173]

Law and economics thus might be a bridge to developing the lawyer's toolkit according to a broader ethos of interdisciplinarity. For example, the University of Chicago, the epicentre of law and economics, embodies a robustly interdisciplinary approach to the study of law, making it administratively easy for students to take courses "across the midway" from the law school, in all sorts of disciplines.[174] The emphasis on economics as a distinct discipline might have the effect of raising the esteem of other disciplines as a core part of legal study. That is, rather than emphasizing the negative – law is not a discipline; legal reasoning means nothing on its face – law and economics, as a well-developed application of an exogenous discipline to law, could encourage the embracing of other disciplines while prompting reflection about what, if anything, makes law distinctive. And this might be answered both at the level of methodology or reasoning (cutting against the law and economics scepticism) or at the level of values (such as justice, fairness, and so on) whose relationship to efficiency could then be explored.[175]

---

172 Richard A Posner, "Gratuitous Promises in Economics and Law" (1977) 6 J Legal Studies 411, reprinted in Kronman & Posner, *supra* note 168, 46 at 57, 59–60; Posner & Rosenfield, *supra* note 162 at 106.

173 *Cf* George Priest, "Social Science Theory and Legal Education: The Law School as a University" (1983) 33 J Legal Ed 437 ("As a legal scholar becomes serious about some behavioral science and sophisticated in its practice, he is pulled away from the law as a distinct subject and even as an interesting subject" at 437–8).

174 See Martha Nussbaum, "Crossing the Midway, By and By" (7 February 2013), *The Record* (Alumni Magazine of the University of Chicago Law School), online: http://www.law.uchicago.edu/alumni/magazine/spring13/crossing.

175 Posner hints at this complex relationship when he writes that "there is more to justice than economics ... Always, however, economics can provide value clarification by showing the society what it must give up to achieve a noneconomic ideal of justice" (*Economic Analysis of Law*, 4th ed, *supra* note 160 at 27).

Summary

Law and economics, a major strain of American contract law scholarship, adopts the practices and premises of economic science, positing efficiency as a primary metric against which to measure legal rules. Judicial decisions are viewed as social facts or phenomena to which extrinsic analysis is applied, suggesting that the supposed internal rationality of the common law is not only secondary but potentially mere rhetoric. Unlike CLS, however, which looks beneath the surface of judicial reasoning to lay bare ideology, law and economics tends to evade political considerations. This is evident in its emphasis on allocation over distribution and in its claim that distributional concerns are dealt with more efficiently through the tax-and-transfer system. Having posited efficiency as the social end to be determined, the enquiry becomes a means-focused exercise in policy development. The implication is to undermine the idea that there is a distinctively legal way of reasoning and instead to emphasize more functional thinking.[176] The student learns to critique judicial reasons as to whether they are "correctly" decided, inferring the effects of rules on ex ante choices, and prospectively guessing about aggregate consequential future behaviour. This process of inference invites students to suggest or prescribe alternative rules that would have optimal effects on efficiency.

Although the desired end – efficiency – is not posited as a matter of debate (in the way that CLS encourages debate over desired ends), the law student is encouraged to care about the consequences of legal rules and to venture creative, forward-looking policy solutions. By considering legal rules as instruments of a universal standard for analysing social and economic context, economic analysis inserts law into the social fabric, breaking down the barriers between law and policy, law and society. Also, by questioning whether the terms of legal discourse provide intelligible and operative standards for decision making, law and economics also encourages students to consider the methods of other disciplines, not only expanding their toolkit, but incidentally introducing them to other premises, values, and subject matters.

CONTEXT: SOCIO-LEGAL STUDIES AND RELATIONAL CONTRACT THEORY

As much as legal realism, CLS, and law and economics sought to uncover the underlying policy or politics of law, these traditions share with classical legal thought a commitment to at least two premises: that the

176 See Hansmann, *supra* note 171 at 226.

primary source of law is the state, and that the discrete contract is a sufficient starting point for analysis of contract law. The focus, in both CLS and law and economics, on judicial decisions as the primary subject of analysis illustrates these twin commitments. The work of Stewart Macaulay and Ian Macneil rejects these premises and forges radically new directions in the study of contract law, deploying empirical methods that more closely intertwine law and society. Socio-legal studies, and the theory of contractual relations they generated, radically reformulate the concepts and questions of contract law. They introduce into the lawyer's toolkit the ability to discern thick descriptions of context – factual, social, or historical – and to use this context to frame facts in a persuasive narrative for the purposes of client advocacy or law reform. Moreover, by highlighting the normative content of a given relationship beyond positive law, socio-legal studies encourage the lawyer to consider a wider swath of legal tools and levers to help achieve individual and social ends, pluralizing the sources of law to be deployed by the lawyer as citizen.

Stewart Macaulay

Stewart Macaulay's groundbreaking work, "Non-Contractual Relations in Business: A Preliminary Study," undermined one of the foundational premises of contract law: that it matters at all. The article concludes, on the basis of an empirical study of the manufacturing sector in Wisconsin in the mid-1950s, that, in business exchanges, parties seldom rely on their written contracts or on their rights afforded by the rules of contract doctrine. Contract might not be necessary because other devices, such as commercial norms, personal relationships, or a desire to continue doing business in the future, serve equivalent functions. Contract might also produce undesirable effects on business relationships or impede flexibility; costs of litigation or its threat might outweigh benefits. When businesses *do* use contract, it is when the gains exceed the costs, occasionally for "irrational" reasons, or due to the idiosyncrasy of the decision maker.[177]

Macaulay's piece is relational in the sense that it tries to understand the forces that sustain, and the role that law plays in, long-term business relationships. One underlying assumption is that ongoing relationships

177 Macaulay, *supra* note 60 at 55, 62–6. See also Robert W Gordon, "Is the World of Contracting Relations One of Spontaneous Order or Pervasive State Action? Stewart Macaulay Scrambles the Public-Private Distinction" in Jean Braucher, John Kidwell & William C Whitford, eds, *Revisiting the Contract Law Scholarship of Stewart Macaulay* (Portland, OR: Hart, 2013) 49 at 59.

are desirable – or, at minimum, are deemed by the economic actors at play to be desirable.[178] "Non-Contractual Relations in Business" led to numerous relational law and economics studies exploring how businesses "solved relational problems without the *ex post* intervention of courts" – findings that included the point that many firms often did not act opportunistically and that there was a widespread desire for reciprocity. One recent study provides some nuanced support for Macaulay's finding, showing how California businesses in a range of sectors eschew formal contract enforcement but nevertheless use formal contracts as "scaffolding to support the implementation of the informal enforcement mechanisms that underpin the efficacy of relational contracts."[179]

Macaulay's article, and his broader work, paved the way for sociological relationalism. Such scholars shifted attention away from business-business relationships and towards relationships of less equal bargaining power, including franchise relationships, adhesion contracts, consumer contracts, and bankruptcy. These scholars also emphasized the importance of context over the strict interpretation of the contract's text: given the rich informal normative forces at play between individuals, it was argued that courts should give this exogenous content force in the interpretation of formal doctrines. Whether the parol evidence rule should be strictly enforced, as in New York, or whether there should be more exceptions to enable extrinsic contextual information to be considered, as in California, is a good proxy for the debate. Llewellyn's formulation in Article 2 of the Uniform Commercial Code, in which agreement was defined as the "bargain of the parties in fact as found in their language or by implication of other circumstances" is another example of such a context-led standard.[180]

"Non-Contractual Relations in Business" has also influenced the development of legal pluralism in contract law scholarship. To the extent that actual behaviour becomes the focus of empirical study, awareness of non-state normative orders increases. Thus, the empirical work in

---

178 *Cf* Macaulay, "Private Legislation and the Duty to Read", *supra* note 137 at 1069 (expressing a preference for "transactional policy"); Stewart Macaulay, "The Real Deal and the Paper Deal: Empirical Pictures of Relationships" (2003) 66 Mod L Rev 44 at 70 (exalting the notion of settlement).

179 Robert E Scott, "The Promise and the Peril of Relational Contract Theory" in Braucher, Kidwell & Whitford, *supra* note 177, 105 at 110–13, 121–2; Gillian K Hadfield & Iva Bozovic, "Scaffolding: Using Formal Contracts to Support Informal Relations in Support of Innovation" [2016] Wisc L Rev 981 at 1018. See also Gordon, "Macaulay Scrambles the Public-Private Distinction", *supra* note 177 at 66.

180 See Scott, "Promise and Peril", *supra* note 179 at 113–14, 120, 126–35; Macaulay, "Real Deal and the Paper Deal", *supra* note 178 at 48 (quoted excerpt), 45, 79.

"Non-Contractual Relations in Business" has expanded to various other sites and relationships, leading to a larger subset of normative orders, extending, arguably, to the existence of "everyday law."[181] Macaulay, Gordon writes, "paints a richly variegated landscape of 'interpenetrated rather than distinct entities,' a variety – in ascending order of degree of formal organization – of networks, 'semi-autonomous social fields,' and private governments; all of them lawmakers in the sense of generating norms and rules and imposing sanctions on those subject to them, creating a de facto society of 'legal pluralism.'"[182] "Non-Contractual Relations in Business" was a thirteen-page article published outside the law review system, yet it became the most-cited article on contract law of the twentieth century.[183] It impugns the notion that "contract-law-as-taught-in-law-schools" is a foundational element of market behaviour and suggests that informal relationships effectively predominate. To a certain degree, the article continues the themes integral to both law and economics and CLS – cost-benefit analysis and power relationships, to name but two. But the socio-legal approach probes these questions while attacking the premises on which mainstream theory rests – that contract doctrine matters to people and that the rules of the state are the pre-eminent site of law.[184]

Ian Macneil

Informed by Macaulay's early work, Ian Macneil developed a rich theoretical construct called the relational theory of contract. Macneil deploys the term "relational" in two senses: to describe a type of contract,

181 See e.g. Jean-Guy Belley, "L'entreprise, l'approvisionnement et le droit: vers un théorie pluraliste du contract" (1991) 32 Cahiers de Droit 253. This is the first of a three-part series in which Belley studies the commercial and contracting practices of Alcan, a large aluminum manufacturer in the Saguenay-Lac-St-Jean region of Quebec. Macaulay cites Belley's work (in its later book-length form) as an example of empirical scholarship relating to the continuing business relationship ("Real Deal and the Paper Deal", *supra* note 178, n 69). Given that Belley's work is published only in French, Macaulay reproduces a summary of it from Daniel Jutras, "The Legal Dimensions of Everyday Life" (2001) 16 CJLS 45.

182 Gordon, "Macaulay Scrambles the Public-Private Distinction", *supra* note 177 at 63 [footnotes omitted] (citing S Moore, "Law and Social Change: The Semi-Autonomous Social Field as an Appropriate Object of Study" (1973) 7 Law & Soc Rev and M Galanter, "Justice in Many Rooms: Courts, Private Ordering, and Indigenous Law" (1981) 19 J Legal Pluralism & Unofficial Law 1).

183 F Shapiro, "The Most-Cited Law Review Articles Revisited" (1996) 71 Chicago-Kent L Rev 751.

184 Gordon, "Macaulay Scrambles the Public-Private Distinction", *supra* note 177 at 61–4.

the "relational contract," distinguished from the "discrete contract"; and to describe a set of properties, "relational aspects," that apply to all contracts. He rejects the classical premise that the discrete contract between economically self-maximizing individuals is an appropriate model for understanding contracting behaviour. In its place he offers an iconoclastic revisioning, reorienting the frame through which contract can be understood.[185]

Macneil argues that the two main norms of classical contract law – discreteness and presentiation (the "bringing of the future into the present") – are "impossible" to achieve.[186] In light of the "prevalence of the relation in the post-industrial world," every contract is at least in part relational; aside from the simple exchange of goods, there is almost no contract in which "no relation exists between the parties."[187]

The founding concepts of Macneil's theory differ radically from the animating concepts of will, autonomy, and economic self-interest that undergird classical (or neoclassical) contract law. Macneil's "primal roots" of contract include the specialization of labour and the broad understanding of exchange it entails, a sense of choice, and conscious awareness of the future, all of which are "embedded and intertwined in a society."[188] Contract, rather than being intimately related to the notion of promise, is defined much more broadly as "the relations among parties to the process of projecting exchange." Although promise is one of many "exchange projectors," non-promissory projectors are often more important. These include the expectation of future exchange, "future motivations arising out of dependence on ongoing relations," and "hidden" projectors such as the production or securing of goods for sale in the future.[189]

These radically different starting points in turn imply norms that are more complex and relational than those in classical contract law. The

185 David Campbell, "Ian Macneil and the Relational Theory of Contract" in Ian R Macneil, *The Relational Theory of Contract: Selected Works of Ian Macneil* (David Campbell, ed) (London: Sweet & Maxwell, 2001) 3 at 45, 9; Jay Feinman, "The Reception of Ian Macneil's Work on Contract in the USA" in Macneil, *Relational Theory of Contract* 59 at 61–2.

186 Macneil, *New Social Contract*, *supra* note 81 at 60; Ian R Macneil, "Contracts: Adjustment of Long-Term Economic Relations under Classical, Neoclassical and Relational Contract Law" (1978) 72 Nw U L Rev 854 at 883.

187 Ian R Macneil, "The Many Futures of Contract" (1974) 47 S Cal L Rev 691 at 694; Macneil, *New Social Contract*, *supra* note 81 at 10.

188 Macneil, *New Social Contract*, *supra* note 81 at 3–4, 72–3. See also Macneil, "Contracts: Adjustment of Long-Term Economic Relations", *supra* note 186 at 873–6; Macneil, "Many Futures of Contract", *supra* note 187 at 700.

189 Macneil, *New Social Contract*, *supra* note 81 at 4; Macneil, "Many Futures of Contract", *supra* note 187 at 715–16.

"especially relational" norms – role integrity, preservation of the relation, harmonization of conflict, and "supracontractual" social and political norms – contribute to Macneil's "'rich classificatory apparatus' for the analysis of contracts," but they are especially important because of the substantive messages they convey about human relations.[190] Macneil's "major achievement" is to reveal relational contracts as a class of contracts in which "conscious co-operation" predominantly guides parties' action. Wealth maximization, quite in contrast to the central role it plays in the classical conception of the discrete contract, drastically recedes in importance in the relational contract. The fact that the "common norms" include such norms as contractual solidarity and mutuality emphasizes the centrality that the notion of solidarity plays in his thinking.[191]

Relationalism and Legal Education

The paradigm of contractual relations introduces into legal education new ideas about human and economic relations and, with them, new ideas about law. It offers a fully theorized account of social and economic relations that demonstrates "how economic purposes and actions are deeply embedded in social fields, in densely woven webs of local customs, conventional morals, bonds of loyalty and entrenched hierarchies." Relationalism suggests that norms and sanctions of the state play but a marginal role in contracting behaviour, and that among the state norms that do matter, the common law rules are much less relevant than their prominent place in legal education would suggest. Moreover, a series of socio-legal studies provides empirical support for the notion that contracting parties actually *do* behave in ways consistent with these theories.[192]

A Contracts course inspired by relationalism and socio-legal studies would incorporate a number of distinctive features. As the

---

190 Macneil, *New Social Contract*, *supra* note 81 at 65, 66, 70; Feinman, "Reception of Ian Macneil's Work on Contract in the USA", *supra* note 185 at 62 (citing OE Williamson, *Economic Organization: Firms, Markets and Policy Controls* (Brighton, UK: Harvester Wheatsheaf, 1986) at 103). See also Ian R Macneil, "Economic Analysis of Contractual Relations: Its Shortfalls and Its Need for a 'Rich Classificatory Apparatus'" (1981) 75 Nw U L Rev 1018.

191 Campbell, "Ian Macneil and the Relational Theory of Contract", *supra* note 185 at 17–18; Feinman, "Reception of Ian Macneil's Work on Contract in the USA", *supra* note 185 at 62; Macneil, *New Social Contract*, *supra* note 81 at 44–7, 52.

192 Robert W Gordon, "Macaulay, Macneil, and the Discovery of Solidarity and Power in Contracts" [1985] Wisc L Rev 565 at 573–4. For a list of such empirical studies, see Macaulay, "Real Deal and the Paper Deal", *supra* note 178, n 69.

discrete transaction recedes as the subject of analysis, the doctrinal canon loses its relevance: consent becomes less important than society; the bargain theory of consideration gives way to a notion of exchange that is broader in concept and more continuous and extended in time; and the measure of damages looks less like a foundational question for the nature of contractual liability than it does a mere fillip for bargaining.[193]

As a "continuation of the [realist] project of contextualism," relationalism invites the inclusion of empirical, historical, and narrative accounts of context in the study of judicial decisions.[194] Relationalism thus provides the lawyer with new resources for making persuasive arguments. Decisions in cases – both the formulation of doctrinal rules and the bottom-line outcome – can be seen as a product of diverse contextual factors, not just the four corners of the agreement or the syllogistic processing of abstract rules. Historical case-in-context studies emphasize how a complex mix of factors led to specific decisions and how the uptake of various doctrines and rules is historically contingent; contemporary socio-legal inquiries into judicial decisions can illustrate how "judicial activity affects decisions about cooperation and readjustment."[195] An appreciation of these factors can signal to students the importance of bringing these specific contextual factors to the attention of a court. Into the toolkit come the skills of tracing a narrative and framing a case in a certain light. Applied more broadly, the emphasis on social context and power relations might cultivate the skill of deploying discrete examples when intervening in public discourse, whether in media interviews, legislative advocacy, or social activism. Contracts casebooks by both Macaulay and Macneil specifically emphasize putting contract law into its full context, signalling the

---

193 See Gordon, "Macaulay, Macneil", *supra* note 192 at 572–4; Ian R Macneil, "Whither Contracts" (1969) 21 J Legal Ed 403, n 2.

194 Feinman, "Reception of Ian Macneil's Work on Contract in the USA", *supra* note 185 at 60; Gordon, "Macaulay, Macneil", *supra* note 192 at 567–8.

195 See e.g. Richard Danzig, *The Capability Problem in Contracts* (Mineola, NY: Foundation Press, 1978); AW Brian Simpson, "Quackery and Contract Law, *Carlill v Carbolic Smoke Ball Company* (1893)" in AW Brian Simpson, *Leading Cases in the Common Law* (Oxford: Clarendon Press, 1995) 259; AW Brian Simpson, "The Beauty of Obscurity: *Raffles v Wichelhaus* and *Busch* (1864) in Simpson, *Leading Cases in the Common Law* 135; Macaulay, "Real Deal and the Paper Deal", *supra* note 178 at 78 (detailing how a judge encouraged settlement through a number of techniques – announcing on day one that he expected the case to get settled, hosting cocktail parties at his house for the lawyers and corporate executives, extending negotiation conferences, and appointing a law school dean as a special master in charge of mediation).

inherently "practical" use of a socio-legal understanding of exchange relations.[196]

Relationalism also displaces the state as the sole focus of legal enquiry, inviting legal educators to "abandon the assumptions of legal centrism" and to emphasize other modes and sites of normativity. In the words of Macneil, the "non-legal as well as legal aspects of contractual relationships should be considered."[197] A Contracts course organized around relational theory could communicate to students the primacy of lived experience, not only emphasizing contractual relations over contract doctrine, but also foregrounding the internal law of the contractual relationship – the actual operating norms and practices – over the formal contract. Focusing on the internal law of the parties might cultivate skills related to planning, including the forward-looking activity of helping parties determine their goals, ascertain costs, and communicate a mutual agreement with respect to either performance or risk. These skills include fact finding, negotiation, drafting, and applying legal knowledge. These practical activities would serve the parties' goal of maintaining their ongoing relationships.[198]

Applying these planning skills more broadly, students might also learn to pursue, through policy interventions, the norms of solidarity and mutuality associated with the work of Macneil and Macaulay. An empirical focus on context tends to shine a light on actual injustices; understanding the "dark side" of real relationships – the possibility of entrenched power relations – might draw attention to unfairness, but it also might concretize some of the more macro arguments about distributive justice encountered in other areas of the curriculum or through an exposure to CLS.[199] At the same time, the planning skills that students are developing to help individual parties navigate and protect

196 Ian R Macneil, *Contracts: Exchange Transactions and Relations*, 2d ed (Mineola, NY: Foundation Press, 1978) at xix. See also Stewart Macaulay et al, "What Contract Study Should Be" in *Contracts: Law in Action* (Charlottesville, VA: Michie, 1995), vol 1 at 29 ("We try to put contract law into its full context"); Ian R Macneil, *Cases and Materials on Contracts: Exchange Transactions and Relationships* (Mineola, NY: Foundation Press, 1971) at xv ("A considerable amount of text [tries] ... to put the legal materials into the economic, social, financial and commercial contexts in which they exist"). Subsequent citations to the Macneil casebook are to the second edition unless otherwise noted.

197 Robert E Scott, "Conflict and Cooperation in Long-Term Contracts" (1987) 75 Cal L Rev 2005 at 2053–4; Macneil, "Whither Contracts", *supra* note 193 at 415. *Cf* Roderick A Macdonald & Jason Maclean, "No Toilets in Park" (2005) 50 McGill LJ 721.

198 Macneil, *Contracts: Exchange Transactions and Relations*, *supra* note 196 at xix, 20–1, 27–43.

199 See Gordon, "Macaulay, Macneil", *supra* note 192 at 569–71.

their own relationships might be analogized to skills for social planning. Macneil hints at such a reciprocal relationship between serving the client and serving society through the planning function when he describes the goals for his students in his casebook. He wants them to develop a sense of justice and injustice in a "system based on ongoing contractual relations" and to appreciate the interplay between "exchange transactions and relations with the legal system." Practical lawyerly activity and a pursuit of social justice are to be integrated, not opposed:

> It would be easy to infer from these titles that Part I [Introduction to the Nature of Contract] is the basis for a "policy-and-justice" approach to contract study and Part II [Planning Contractual Relations] the basis for a "practical" approach ... I do not believe that policy, justice and practice can thus be separated. The deep currents both of social justice and of social injustice flowing through our exchange-oriented socioeconomic system manifest themselves in every "practical" contract question. At the same time, no one unfamiliar with the "practical" world of contracts can fully understand the exchange currents of social and economic policy flowing so strongly through our society and its legal system.[200]

Macneil's invocation that "policy-and-justice" concerns are intimately tied to the practical activities of the lawyer exemplifies the integrative notion of the lawyer as citizen. Sociological relationalism highlights the mutually reinforcing qualities of theory and practice: relational theory, derived from empirical studies of actual contracting behaviour, can generate practical insights for actual lawyerly activity, encouraging lawyers to include in their toolkit the planning functions essential to maintaining healthy relationships. A theoretical understanding of the contingency of legal results (at individual and doctrinal levels) translates into a range of advocacy skills of framing and constructing context-rich narratives for the purposes of tailored persuasion. Moreover, an empirical focus on actual contracting relationships can shed light on the broader phenomenon of inequality, and the planning skills to achieve the individual healthy relationship might be analogized to social planning, reversing the metaphor by which formal contracts are referred to as "statutes of private governments" and pursuing the health of societal bonds.[201] In these ways, sociological relationalism incorporates many of the lawyer's tools implied by legal realism, law and

200 Macneil, *Contracts: Exchange Transactions and Relations*, *supra* note 196 at xix, xvii–xviii.
201 Macaulay, "Real and Paper Deal", *supra* note 178 at 63.

economics, and CLS: a concern with context, an awareness of politics, and a forward-looking policy outlook.

THE CONTRACTS CANON, THE ECLECTIC TOOLKIT, AND THE LAWYER AS CITIZEN

The subset of contract law scholarship surveyed in this chapter paints a counterimage to the acontextual practices of Contracts teaching identified by Elizabeth Mertz. It shows how the implicit tenets of Mertz's account of legal reasoning – classical legal science's emphasis on rules, principles, courts, and the separation of law from politics, morality, and social behaviour – were systematically attacked by leading American contract law scholars over the course of the twentieth century. The realists and their heirs highlighted the indeterminacy of doctrine and autonomous legal reasoning; emphasized the importance of the underlying functional, purposive, or consequentialist rationales for the operative rules; highlighted the importance of "contextual factors" (facts, political pressures, judicial idiosyncrasy, history) in arriving at legal decisions; and focused on the "'real' factors informing and the actual social consequences resulting from those decisions in order to reform the rules, principles, and decisional practices so that the legal system will serve its valid purposes more effectively."[202]

This embrace of context, policy, and politics has generated a diverse set of tools for advocacy and planning at both the individual and societal levels. In some formulations, such as that in Macneil's casebook just cited, these perspectives can also yield a broader, integrated picture of the lawyer as citizen. A course in Contracts, by simply embracing the leading contract law scholarship of the twentieth century, therefore can quite naturally provide students with a toolkit comprised of the eclectic range of methodological commitments that, according to Kennedy and Fisher, characterize American legal thought. Mertz's account signals some failure in translation from these theories to the practical exercise of training students to think like lawyers.

The remainder of this book explores whether a similar or analogous signal failure arises in Canadian common law Contracts teaching. At first blush, this might seem like an odd question, because Canada, it hardly needs reminding, is a separate country from the United States, with a different legal system and legal culture. But, as it turns out, the

202 Robert W Gordon, "American Law through English Eyes: A Century of Nightmares and Noble Dreams", Book Review of *Patterns of American Jurisprudence* by Neil Duxbury (1996) 84 Geo LJ 2215 at 2224–5, 2232.

thinkers canvassed in this chapter have made an indelible mark on the attitudes of Canadian common law Contracts professors. In the way they formulate their beliefs about law, the majority of Canadian teachers and casebook editors disclose a sophisticated and enthusiastic commitment to the realist themes of politics, policy, and context. However, only a minority – and in some cases, a very small minority – go on to translate these theories into a more practical treatment of substance, description of legal reasoning, or teaching methods.

I explore this contrast next in the context of the casebooks. For a generation, editors of the Canadian commercial common law Contracts casebooks have pledged allegiance to realist and critical ideas about law. But throughout this time, only one book – with but 10 per cent of the market share – deliberately operationalizes these theories into a vision of the lawyer as planner, problem solver, and policy designer. The others present law and legal reasoning in a way that reveals an underlying commitment to the values of doctrinal coherence and analogical reasoning. This contrast between realist beliefs and the execution of ideas associated with formalism signals the failure to fully translate theory into practice, and is the overwhelming puzzle this study lays bare.

Chapter Three

Promise and Performance in Canadian Common Law Contracts Casebooks

In the United States, scholars have long embraced the contract law casebook as metonym for the shifting and turbulent terrain of legal thought. The attempts by Stewart Macaulay and Ian Macneil to design their casebooks around a richly contextual framework – in Macneil's case, by organizing an entire half of the book around the notion of planning (as we observed in Chapter 2) – illustrate an aspiration to operationalize a philosophy of law into a teaching text. Scholars and reviewers of casebooks in the United States have associated different casebooks with different theories of law. The first Contracts casebook, Christopher Columbus Langdell's *Selection of Cases on the Law of Contract*, has long stood as a primary illustration of classical legal thought in action.[203] Once the "age of anthology," which Langdell ushered in, ended in the mid-twentieth century, casebooks were increasingly reviewed for the way editors "wear their heart upon their sleeve."[204] Lon Fuller's "post-realist" innovation in 1947, Kessler and Sharp's "anticonceptualist" intervention in 1953, and Knapp's "humanist" take on the teaching matter in 1976 stand as three well-reviewed examples of how Contracts casebooks were received as signposts for major changes in attitude about law and legal reasoning.[205] As Janet Ainsworth writes: "Because casebooks still

203 Langdell, *Selection of Cases*, *supra* note 56. See Grey, *supra* note 96 at 11; Kennedy, "Toward an Historical Understanding", *supra* note 95 at 8; Kennedy, "Form and Substance", *supra* note 60 at 1729; Horwitz, "Rise of Legal Formalism", *supra* note 95.

204 E Allan Farnsworth, "Contracts Scholarship in the Age of the Anthology" (1987) 85 Mich L Rev 1390 at 1407; Benjamin Kaplan, Book Review of *Contracts: Cases and Materials* by Friedrich Kessler & Malcolm Pitman Sharp, (1954) 63 Yale LJ 1039 at 1039.

205 Klare, "Contracts Jurisprudence and the First-Year Casebook", *supra* note 88 at 882, 884, 895; Lon L Fuller, *Basic Contract Law* (St Paul, MN: West, 1947); Friedrich Kessler & Malcolm Pitman Sharp, *Contracts: Cases and Materials* (New York: Prentice-Hall, 1953); Charles L Knapp, *Problems in Contract Law: Cases and Materials* (Boston: Little,

maintain the center of gravity in legal education, they serve as the vehicle through which each succeeding generation of lawyers is socialized into patterns of thinking about law and legal practice."[206]

In Canada, meta-level discussion about the casebooks is less developed. Although there are numerous thoughtful reviews of selected editions of Canadian Contracts casebooks, there has been little attempt to draw high-level insights by looking at the books together and over the course of their development. This chapter does precisely that. I look at the prefaces and introductions of all editions of the four Canadian published casebooks – one historical (*Milner*),[207] and three current (*Swan*,[208] *Waddams*,[209]

Brown, 1976). See also Malcolm Sharp, Book Review of *Basic Contract Law* by Lon L Fuller (1948) 15 U Chi L Rev 79; Kaplan, *supra* note 204.

206 "Law in (Case)books, Law (School) in Action: The Case for Casebook Reviews (1997) 20 Seattle UL Rev 270 at 275. See also *ibid* at 274 ("[c]asebooks provide their authors with an opportunity to construct a thoroughly realized, if often inadequately articulated, instantiation of their own particular jurisprudential and normative belief systems").

207 JB Milner, ed, *Cases and Materials on Contracts* (Toronto: University of Toronto Press, 1963) [*Milner* 1st ed]; SM Waddams, ed, *Milner's Cases and Materials on Contracts*, 2d ed (Toronto: University of Toronto Press, 1971) [*Milner* 2d ed]; SM Waddams, ed, *Milner's Cases and Materials on Contracts*, 3d ed (Toronto: University of Toronto Press, 1977) [*Milner* 3d ed]; SM Waddams, ed, *Milner's Cases and Materials on Contracts*, 4th ed (Toronto: Emond Montgomery, 1985) [*Milner* 4th ed].

208 John Swan & Barry J Reiter, *Contracts: Cases, Notes & Materials* (Toronto: Butterworth, 1978) [*Swan* 1st ed]; John Swan & Barry J Reiter, *Contracts: Cases, Notes & Materials*, 2d ed (Toronto: Butterworth, 1982) [*Swan* 2d ed]; John Swan & Barry J Reiter, *Contracts: Cases, Notes, and Materials*, 3d ed (Toronto: Emond Montgomery, 1985) [*Swan* 3d ed]; John Swan & Barry J Reiter, *Contracts: Cases, Notes and Materials*, 4th ed (Toronto: Emond Montgomery, 1991) [*Swan* 4th ed]; John Swan, Barry J Reiter & Nicholas C Bala, *Contracts: Cases, Notes & Materials*, 5th ed (Toronto: Butterworths, 1997) [*Swan* 5th ed]; John Swan, Barry J Reiter & Nicholas C Bala, *Contracts: Cases, Notes & Materials*, 6th ed (Toronto: Butterworths, 2002) [*Swan* 6th ed]; John Swan, Barry J Reiter & Nicholas C Bala, *Contracts: Cases, Notes & Materials*, 7th ed (Toronto: LexisNexis Canada, 2006) [*Swan* 7th ed]; Angela Swan, Barry J Reiter & Nicholas C Bala, *Contracts: Cases, Notes & Materials*, 8th ed (Toronto: LexisNexis Canada, 2010) [*Swan* 8th ed]; Angela Swan, Nicholas C Bala & Jakub Adamski, *Contracts: Cases, Notes & Materials*, 9th ed (Toronto: LexisNexis Canada, 2015) [*Swan* 9th ed].

209 SM Waddams, M Trebilcock & MA Waldron, *Cases and Materials on Contracts* (Toronto: Emond Montgomery, 1994) [*Waddams* 1st ed]; SM Waddams, MJ Trebilcock & MA Waldron, *Cases and Materials on Contracts*, 2d ed (Toronto: Emond Montgomery, 2000) [*Waddams* 2d ed]; SM Waddams et al, *Cases and Materials on Contracts*, 3d ed (Toronto: Emond Montgomery, 2005) [*Waddams* 3d ed]; SM Waddams et al, *Cases and Materials on Contracts*, 4th ed (Toronto: Emond Montgomery, 2010) [*Waddams* 4th ed]; SM Waddams et al, *Cases and Materials on Contracts*, 5th ed (Toronto: Emond Montgomery, 2014) [*Waddams* 5th ed]; SM Waddams et al, *Cases and Materials on Contracts*, 6th ed (Toronto: Emond Montgomery, 2018) [*Waddams* 6th ed].

and *Ben-Ishai & Percy*)[210] – to tease out their stated and implied attitudes about law. I then compare what these casebook editors say with how the current books present legal reasoning through their treatment of substance in their chapters on remedies. To supplement this textual analysis, I draw on scholarly reviews of the casebooks, casebook editors' selected other writings, and selected reviews thereof.

All the major books in Canada owe an intellectual debt to the canonical American legal scholars explored in the previous chapter. Canadian common law Contracts casebook editors encourage students to seek the underlying values of rules and doctrines, to reason purposively and functionally, to consider social realities of contracting, and to engage in policy thinking. The influences of Corbin, Fuller, Gilmore, and Macneil figure prominently. Ideas from later schools also play a central role: CLS, law and economics, socio-legal approaches, and feminist and race critiques of contract doctrine surface in the introductory passages in each book, to different degrees. The influences manifest differently in each book – sometimes incorporated into explicit argument (*Swan*), sometimes operating implicitly in editorial choices (*Waddams*), sometimes coalescing in a critical survey (*Ben-Ishai & Percy*), sometimes appearing in a "perspectives" chapter (*Waddams*). However expressed, the dominant set of intellectual theories that explicitly frames the study of Contracts in Canada derives from these American critical traditions.

---

210 Prior to the eighth edition, the lead editors were Christine Boyle and David Percy. In the eighth and subsequent editions, Stephanie Ben-Ishai replaced Christine Boyle. In this chapter, when referring generally to the casebook, I name it by its contemporary authors, *Ben-Ishai & Percy*. When referring historically to any of the first seven editions, I use *Boyle & Percy*. See Christine Boyle & David R Percy, eds, *Contracts: Cases and Commentaries* (Toronto: Carswell, 1978) [*Boyle & Percy* 1st ed]; Christine Boyle & David R Percy, eds, *Contracts: Cases and Commentaries*, 2d ed (Toronto: Carswell, 1981) [*Boyle & Percy* 2d ed]; Christine Boyle & David R Percy, eds, *Contracts: Cases and Commentaries*, 3d ed (Toronto: Carswell, 1985) [*Boyle & Percy* 3d ed]; Christine Boyle & David R Percy, eds, *Contracts: Cases and Commentaries*, 4th ed (Toronto: Carswell, 1989) [*Boyle & Percy* 4th ed]; Christine Boyle & David R Percy, eds, *Contracts: Cases and Commentaries*, 5th ed (Toronto: Carswell, 1994) [*Boyle & Percy* 5th ed]; Christine Boyle & David R Percy, eds, *Contracts: Cases and Commentaries*, 6th ed (Toronto: Carswell, 1999) [*Boyle & Percy* 6th ed]; Christine Boyle & David R Percy, eds, *Contracts: Cases and Commentaries*, 7th ed (Toronto: Thomson Carswell, 2004) [*Boyle & Percy* 7th ed]; Stephanie Ben-Ishai & David R Percy, eds, *Contracts: Cases and Commentaries*, 8th ed (Toronto: Carswell, 2009) [*Ben-Ishai & Percy* 8th ed]; Stephanie Ben-Ishai & David R Percy, eds, *Contracts: Cases and Commentaries*, 9th ed (Toronto: Carswell, 2014) [*Ben-Ishai & Percy* 9th ed]; Stephanie Ben-Ishai & David R Percy, eds, *Contracts: Cases and Commentaries*, 10th ed (Toronto: Carswell, 2018) [*Ben-Ishai & Percy* 10th ed].

Despite this surface commitment to realist and critical approaches, however, only one of the three books (*Swan*) operationalizes these attitudes into a workable vision of legal reasoning and legal practice in the remedies chapter. The two most frequently used casebooks, *Ben-Ishai & Percy* and *Waddams*, model a vision of legal reasoning that embodies a commitment to law more kindred with the classical attitudes their editors purportedly reject than to the realist attitudes propositionally advanced in the introductions. Whether expressed as a commitment to "tradition" or simply performed without commentary, these books treat cases as the archetypical source of law and legal reasoning as predominantly the exercise of distilling rules, exploring how they interrelate, and applying them to hypothetical fact situations in search of relevant similarities. This focus on rules and cases reveals an underlying commitment to the more formalist values of internal coherence and doctrinal consistency and the related conception of legal reasoning that makes analogical reasoning central and policy thinking marginal.

The casebooks thus suggest that, although the eclecticism of American legal thought is alive and well in Canada, editors of Canadian common law Contracts casebooks largely do not translate their theoretical commitments into practice; the realist and critical ideas remain suspended at the level of theory and not incorporated into the presentation of doctrine and legal reasoning in these pedagogical texts. The overwhelming impression is of a conventional conception of legal reasoning inspired by formalist commitments to internal coherence and the rule of law, and a correspondingly bounded vision of legal practice that models the courtroom advocate, the barrister, in an emphasis on litigation and judicial reasons for decision. The vision of legal thought portrayed by the Canadian common law Contracts casebooks is closer to the picture painted by Mertz than it is to the one imagined by Kennedy and Fisher.

WHAT IS SAID: CRITICAL AND REALIST PERSPECTIVES IN CANADIAN COMMON LAW CONTRACTS CASEBOOKS

The late 1970s was a flashpoint for the emergence of American ideas in Canadian common law Contracts casebooks. In 1978 two new books, *Swan* and *Boyle & Percy*, came on the scene. Both have an extensive introductory chapter full of messages from American legal realism and subsequent critical theories of law, introductions that have been carefully edited up until their present editions. The third major casebook today, *Waddams*, traces its intellectual roots to 1977, the year that Stephen

Waddams published his realist textbook, *The Law of Contracts*,[211] and completed his first major revision of *Milner* (3d ed). In this section, I detail the messages contained in the three casebooks, and in James Milner's original Introduction.

Underlying Messages about Law in **Swan**

Swan is a good place to start for a few reasons. First, it sets out its realist messages so clearly, and provides a good intellectual basis for understanding the messages communicated in the other books. Of the books, it is the most polemical, which has the virtue for review purposes of explicitly and powerfully making claims. Where analogous claims are sketched in the other books, foregrounding *Swan* enables us to understand them in greater depth. Where the other books differ from *Swan*, this early immersion helps highlight the contrasts.

But it is also *Swan*'s outlier status that justifies a substantial focus. Unique among the books, Swan operationalizes her theoretical commitment to realism into a methodological approach – what she calls the "solicitor's perspective." But *Swan* is also by far the least-adopted commercial casebook in Canada – as noted, enjoying only about 10 per cent of market share (and used by about 15 per cent of the participants in this study).[212] It has provoked hostile scholarly reviews, including by editors of leading Canadian Contracts teaching texts.[213] To generate more majoritarian claims about the nature of Canadian legal thought on the basis of the other casebooks, *Swan*, the maverick outlier, serves as an instructive foil.

From the very first edition, Swan and her co-editors have expounded a distinctive vision of law and a self-conscious awareness of the role that Contracts teaching plays in forming the legal consciousness of

211 SM Waddams, *The Law of Contracts* (Toronto: Canada Law Book, 1977) [Waddams text 1st ed].

212 Market share is determined by the confidential sales data provided by the three publishers between 2011 and 2016, discounting the negligible number of sales attributable to the Contracts examinations for the National Committee of Accreditation. For participants in my study, I counted the casebook used at the time of the interview or, if not an interview participant, at the time a syllabus was first sent in. Fifty-eight of seventy-five participants (77 per cent) in the study used a commercial casebook.

213 See GHL Fridman, Book Review of *Studies in Contract Law* by Barry J Reiter & John Swan, eds, (1981) 26 McGill LJ 408 [Fridman, Review of Reiter & Swan]; David Percy, Book Review of *Studies in Contract Law* by Barry J Reiter & John Swan, eds, (1981) 59 Can Bar Rev 853 [Percy, Review of Reiter & Swan]; Brian Coote, Book Review of *Studies in Contract Law* by Barry J Reiter & John Swan, eds, (1981) 19 UWO L Rev 357.

students. The following statements capture central elements of this vision: law is an instrument for achieving social purposes; contract law does and should operate to satisfy the reasonable expectations of the parties, and can be evaluated according to this criterion; studying contract law requires understanding competing and contradictory values; adjudication is only one available form of social ordering among many worth understanding; social context is essential to understanding and practising contract law; relational contracts are important; "usefulness" and reality matter exceedingly more than abstractions. Increasingly with each successive edition, the "solicitor's perspective" serves to put this philosophy into practice.

Swan 1st ed

Angela (at the time John) Swan and Barry J Reiter, professors of law at the University of Toronto at the time of publication, authored the first edition of *Contracts: Cases, Notes and Materials* in 1978. The publication was based on earlier drafts of teaching materials used at the University of Toronto, and were "put together after several years of co-operation between the authors and Professor E.J. Weinrib," also of Toronto.[214] The casebook began, in other words, as a teaching document, and this pedagogical stance is retained right up to the present ninth edition.[215] In the Preface to the first edition, the authors acknowledge the close influence of Fuller and Eisenberg's *Basic Contract Law* (3d ed) and Ian Macneil's *Contracts: Exchange Transactions and Relations* (2d ed). Fuller's and Macneil's influence are indeed strongly felt throughout the book, both informing the ideas in the Introduction and in the form of excerpts throughout the book.[216]

---

214 *Swan* 1st ed, *supra* note 208 at vii. See also A Anne McLellan, Review of *Swan* 1st ed and *Ben-Ishai & Percy* 1st ed, (1979) 28 UNB LJ 257 at 259. Weinrib's participation in the textbook "antedated" his ideas on corrective justice and formalism, and so the mention of his involvement should not imply the importation of those ideas into the text. Weinrib and Swan taught a first-year course that combined contracts and torts in the mid-1970s, and shared offices beside each other for a number of years. In Weinrib's opinion, the statement referring to him in the Introduction "significantly overstates" his role (email correspondence with author, 4 June 2017).

215 See Roger Brownsword, Book Review of *Swan* 1st ed, (1979) 42 Mod L Rev 479 at 479 ("the positive criterion [for case selection] is pedagogic interest"); *Swan* 9th ed, *supra* note 208 at §1.59.

216 *Swan* 1st ed, *supra* note 208 at vii, cc 1, 9. Macneil's "Whither Contracts" (*supra* note 193) is the final excerpt in every edition.

The Introduction to the first edition represents an early articulation of the authors' commitment to four ideas (the numbers that follow track the enumeration of sections in the Introduction): (1) social context is as important as "institutional" concerns about the development of the law; (2) studying law requires confronting and balancing competing values, and asking whether cases "make sense" might require a wide range of evaluative criteria; (3) the law is about solving problems, adjudication is only one of many legal modes of problem solving, and assessing adjudication requires analysing more than simply the reasons for decision, including the role of the lawyer, judge, and jury in formulating facts; and (4) studying contracts must be done in its historical context.[217]

These ideas – the value of social and historical context, the awareness of multiple forms of social ordering, the central role of (balancing competing) values, and a focus on law as problem solving – would develop in later editions into a more fully articulated vision of law. This blossoming began quickly, with the second edition, published in 1982, again by Butterworths.

Swan 2d ed: Macneil and the Reasonable Expectations of the Parties

Two significant intellectual events occurred after the publication of the first edition, both of which made their mark on the second. One was the publication in 1980 of Ian Macneil's *The New Social Contract*. The Introduction to the second edition contains nine new pages of text, six of which are dedicated to Macneil's theories of law, from his definition of promise to the centrality of exchange to the distinction between discrete and relational contracts.[218] The other event was the crystallization of the authors' philosophy of contract law resulting from workshops on contract law in the spring of 1979. These workshops, involving Stephen Waddams, Michael Trebilcock, and other scholars, resulted in a book edited by Reiter and Swan and published by Butterworths. In the first chapter of *Studies in Contract Law*, Reiter and Swan set out what they claim is a "common assumption" of all the studies in the book: "The assumption is that the fundamental purpose of contract law is the protection and promotion of expectations reasonably created by contract. We believe that the law should and does protect such reasonable expectations and that all 'contract rules' are merely specific illustrations of this

217 *Swan* 1st ed, *supra* note 208 at xxvii–xxxi.
218 *Swan* 2d ed, *supra* note 208 at xlii–xlvi.

guiding principle."[219] The idea that contract law both *does* and *should* protect reasonable expectations implies other commitments about law, about which Reiter and Swan are fairly transparent in their essay. These include the notion that contract law, and law in general, is purposive, functional, and instrumental; that contract law can be evaluated according to its "suitability" to actual relationships; that legal institutions beyond courts, such as legislation and "administrative processes," play a role in effecting change; that it is important to look "below the surface" to "identify and assess ... principles and policies" that underlie cases and legislative instruments; and, ultimately, that the purpose of legal study can serve an "intensely practical" function – that is, to recommend more effective rules of (contract) law.[220]

Studies in Contract Law has been described as a "theoretical companion" to *Swan* and, indeed, the above commitments are reflected in references to reasonable expectations throughout the various editions.[221] The theory also surfaces for the first time more directly in the second edition: "[Law is] justified only in so far as it forwards or participates in the achievement of social values ... It makes no sense to ask whether a rule exists as a separate inquiry from a consideration of the rule's purpose and function ... [A] rule can really only be said to exist in so far as it does help to achieve some social goal."[222] Thus, Reiter and Swan signal to their students that their casebook will not teach rules for their own sake or evaluate them according to the standards of internal consistency. Instead, and in concert with the contributions of Macneil, their focus is on the *real* phenomenon of exchange, the *real* reasons behind

---

219 Barry J Reiter & John Swan, eds, *Studies in Contract Law* (Toronto: Butterworth, 1980) at 6. On the commonality of the idea, see Mary Hatherly, Book Review of *Studies in Contract Law* by Barry J Reiter & John Swan, eds (1981) 30 UNBLJ 265 at 270 (the studies "partake of a common philosophical perspective"); Fridman, Review of Reiter & Swan, *supra* note 213 at 408 (a "heavy-handed[]" endeavour "to attain some sort of internal consistency"). But see Percy, Review of Reiter & Swan, *supra* note 213 at 864 ("a collection of law review articles with only a loose connective theme").

220 Reiter & Swan, *supra* note 219 at 2–5. See also Hatherly, *supra* note 219 at 271 (the central hypothesis of the book is that "a contract is an instrumentality ... [or] purposive mechanism"); Percy, Review of Reiter & Swan, *supra* note 213 at 854 (influence of Karl Llewellyn's emphasis on what "courts, legislatures and administrative bodies do in fact").

221 Hatherly, *supra* note 219 at 270. See e.g. *Swan* 1st ed, *supra* note 208 at xxvii (reasonable expectations as one of three things the judge must consider); *Swan* 2d ed, *supra* note 208, c 6 (380 paragraphs of text under the subheading "Protection of Reasonable Expectations").

222 *Swan* 2d ed, *supra* note 208 at li.

decisions, the practical and functional role of the law to deliver *real* social results – and, by implication, the need for students to develop skills and perspectives that can make a *real* impact for their clients.[223]

Although the (mostly positive) reviews of the *Swan* casebook tended to focus largely on the novelty of the approach, it is really in the reviews of *Studies in Contract Law* that the departure becomes most apparent.[224] On the more complimentary side, Mary Hatherly emphasizes the influence of the "American perspective" – Posner, Fuller, Macneil, and Gilmore – and writes that the authors "succeeded in establishing a Canadian approach to contract analysis which is provocative, intelligent and as persuasive as the arguments advanced by exponents of the bargain theory." She writes of the "plausibility of the central hypothesis" of "contract as a purposive mechanism."[225]

By contrast, three reviewers took issue with the Reiter & Swan hypothesis. These more critical reviewers included David Percy, law professor at the University of Alberta and editor of *Boyle & Percy*, which also came out in 1978; Gerald Fridman of the University of Western Ontario, author of *The Law of Contract in Canada*; and Brian Coote, a law professor at the University of Auckland, in New Zealand.[226] Each of these is, in different form, an attack on the underlying theory of law propounded in *Studies in Contract Law*. Fridman, for example, accuses the authors of being "hypercritical[,]... tend[ing] toward the revolutionary":

> Their critical approach ... reveals an essentially antagonistic attitude to the spirit of Blackstone. They are far from being laudatory of the common law ... The "basic assumption" ... involve[s] too much psychology ... What the courts do now is combine the attempt to discover what was the true nature of the bargain between the parties ... with the application of legal

223 *Ibid* at xliv, xli, li.

224 See McLellan, *supra* note 214 ("a highly personal approach ... one that may not be readily adopted by others·in the field" at 261); Brownsword, *supra* note 215 ("a more varied, demanding and stimulating agenda than English equivalents" at 479); Linda Vincent, Book Review of *Swan* 1st ed, (1979) 9 Man LJ 347 at 347, 349 (a "lively, thought-provoking and ... rather sophisticated" book, which nevertheless needs supplement because of the authors' "selective and idiosyncratic approach"); Gordon Turriff, Book Review of *Swan* 1st ed, (1979–80) 4 Can Bus LJ 489 at 491 ("The editors deserve congratulations for taking a compendious and difficult subject which defies logic in so many ways and presenting it in a way, I am sure, that appeals to students of varying abilities and interests"). But see Rodney Brazier, Book Review of *Swan* 1st ed, (1980) 43 Mod L Rev 235 (emphasizing the book's irrelevance to a UK audience).

225 Hatherly, *supra* note 219 at 270–1.

226 GHL Fridman, *The Law of Contract in Canada*, 6th ed (Toronto: Carswell, 2011).

> policies that are intended to give effect to what the courts believe will be a reasonable, workable, and suitable law of contract ... To replace this by some more general, supposedly "people-oriented," approach to the law of contract, would ... invite perhaps a less "mythological" system of rules into the courtroom, but also a less certain, less secure system.[227]

Along similar lines, Percy and Coote also attack the realist grounding of *Studies of Contracts*. Coote attacks the theory of reasonable expectations as an uninformed attempt on behalf of ill-equipped law professors to "codify and institutionalize the 'horse-sense' of judges and legislators," an approach that hypocritically deploys a standard of consistency ("one of the very sins of which [the authors] accuse the 'positivists.'")[228] Percy criticizes the use of the concept as leading to a "dogmatic condemnation of some decisions as 'wrong' and to a lack of emphasis on other significant policies which underly the law of contracts,"[229] arguing that the "'theme' of protecting reasonable expectations and the 'purpose' of encouraging economic efficiency are often ... contradictory."[230] He calls the Reiter & Swan introductory essay "the most disappointing part of the book, because the initial promise of a useful analysis is not sustained."[231]

Swan, 3d and 4th eds: The Solicitor's Perspective and the Reduced Importance of Cases

Uncowed, Reiter and Swan would go on in subsequent editions to develop the theme of the reasonable expectations of the parties. The idea, however, would develop and evolve into an increasingly operationalized

227 Fridman, Review of Reiter & Swan, *supra* note 213 at 422–3.

228 Coote, Review of Reiter & Swan, *supra* note 213 at 358–9.

229 Percy, Review of Reiter & Swan, *supra* note 213 at 856.

230 *Ibid* at 855.

231 *Ibid* at 854. See also Patrick Atiyah's review, which calls the preliminary essay "somewhat simplistic." For Atiyah, the concept of contract has "dropped out" of the Reiter & Swan theory, producing the result that the purpose of the law is to give effect to reasonable expectations, a "vacuous" goal, "uncertain" as to its contents (Book Review of *Studies in Contract Law* by Barry J Reiter & John Swan, eds, (1981) 5 Can Bus LJ 245 at 247). Other, briefer, reviews (generally positive, but more descriptive, rather than analytical) include Dean I Scaleta, Book Review of *Studies in Contract Law* by Barry J Reiter & John Swan, eds, (1981) 11 Man LJ 117; Saul Schwartz, Book Review of *Studies in Contract Law* by Barry J Reiter & John Swan, eds, (1981) 15 UBC L Rev 519 at 519 ("Their basic premise is one with which few would disagree: that is, while judges display an uncommon degree of 'horse-sense' in reaching the 'right' decision they are much less adept at rule-making").

account, what the authors eventually called the "solicitor's" perspective. The trend begins in the third and fourth editions, whose form signals the substantive change. In the hands of a new publisher, Emond Montgomery, the third edition underwent "ruthless editing," "the elimination of many cases," and a page count shortened by about a third. Reminiscent of Ian Macneil, who divides his casebook into parts on "policy-and-justice" and "planning," Part 1 of *Swan* (3d ed) now dealt with topics "introductory to the problems of the modern law of contracts," while Part 2 explored "the problems of making the law of contracts function efficiently in the modern world." Most significantly, perhaps, by the third edition Barry Reiter was no longer a law professor, but rather a "partner in the firm of Tory, Tory, DesLauriers and Binnington." By the fourth edition (1991), Swan had left academia as well.[232]

The third and fourth editions, therefore, evince a number of substantive changes, many of them seemingly related to the editors' developing identities as practitioners. As they write in the introduction: "[W]e have been pleased to find that our ideas seem to work very well when applied to the practical problems of advising clients and helping to make contractual relations work." They retain their theoretical stance about law being about the achievement of social values, but emphasize instead the limits of studying case law and, crucially, develop the solicitor's perspective. In a "Note on the Materials," they write:

> The consequence of a focus on cases ... tends to encourage one to think that we are concerned only about what happened (or might happen) in court: that every problem and issue should be approached as if it were going to be decided by a court. We believe that this introduces an unfortunate bias in developing an understanding of the law of contracts. The law of contracts is about agreements ... Any contractual dispute should therefore be regarded not as a common or everyday event, but as an unfortunate aberration. *It is a much more important function of lawyers to keep their clients out of court* than it is to engage in the process of litigation once the parties have chosen to bring their dispute before a court.
>
> The materials we shall examine are pathological. So long as one considers only court decisions, one can get no glimpse of how healthy contracts work ...
>
> The role of the solicitor in drafting contracts and in structuring contractual arrangements will be emphasized ...

---

232 *Swan* 3d ed, *supra* note 208 at xxiv, inside cover (unnumbered); *Swan* 4th ed, *supra* note 208, inside cover (unnumbered) (identifying Swan as "a partner in the firm of Aird & Berlis").

> [In studying cases, w]e must consider how useful the [judicial] statement is, how satisfactory it is as a basis for prediction of what the courts will do in the future, and, *most important, how well the statement functions as a guide to lawyers who want to keep their clients out of trouble.*[233]

The underlying theory is the same – the fourth edition states that "almost none of the ideas that underlay the previous editions" has changed – but it is pursued through a more operationalized account: getting the student to put him- or herself into a prospective or planning state of mind, focused on keeping the client "out of trouble." The role of the solicitor is mentioned in the third edition twice, for the first time. The impression that one is moving away from the academic to the practical is further reinforced by the omission in the third edition of the three-page section on "Philosophical Ideas About Contract" that appeared in the second edition.[234]

Coupled with the rise of the desire to get students to think of themselves as lawyers is the powerful caveat that they not lose their intuitive or even childlike sense of human dignity:

> [T]he most important aspect of any study of the law of contracts (or of any area of the law, for that matter) is the ability to retain a sense that the law is part of human life and that it must always respect human dignity. We have to retain an almost childlike faith that things *must* be fair ... Without this faith in fairness, law can easily become little more than an implacable and impersonal set of rules divorced from human values and based on some abstract idea of the need for certainty and predictability. Do not become cynical: there is too much at stake to risk the dangers of an unconcern for fairness and decency. Do not fall into the trap of thinking that it is somehow "unlawyerly" to be passionately concerned for justice, or of believing that "to think like a lawyer" means that one has to forget that one person who, until law school, *did* care that results be fair and that people behave decently towards each other.[235]

This rise of a "practical" sensibility is therefore not in tension with, but directly in aid of, a view that seeks to place law, and law practice, within a broader social, indeed even moral, context.

---

233 *Swan* 3d ed, *supra* note 208 at xxviii, xxx–xxxi [emphasis added].

234 *Swan* 4th ed, *supra* note 208 at xxviii; *Swan* 3d ed, *supra* note 208 at xxxi, xxxiii; *Swan* 2d ed, *supra* note 208 at xlvii–l.

235 *Swan* 3d ed, *supra* note 208 at xxxiii.

They also begin the Introduction of the fourth edition with a discussion about the fall of the Soviet Union. In addition to using this event to reprise their point that the law of contracts is about exchange relations, whose problems "have become the stuff of philosophies and moral codes," thereby exemplifying the point that law is "permeated by ideas that express very deeply held values and moral ideas," they use the occasion to reformulate their functional approach to contract law: "We hope that these materials will not be viewed as an apology for a market economy or as accepting the social value of exchange relations as either beyond question or raising questions outside their scope ... [W]hatever view one takes of their value, *making the system work*, thinking through what fairness and justice requires, and *what are the best means* to protect those who need protection are important questions. A useful focus for lawyers is to remember that to an important extent, '*law is the science of getting from here to there.*'"[236]

The emphasized portions of the above passage illustrate the commitments the editors continue to hold that law should be instrumental to social ends and not admired or revered for its own internal coherence. "Getting from here to there" can be interpreted at two different levels of generality. In one sense, the role of the lawyer is to assist the client in getting from here to there – achieving exchange-related goals while staying out of trouble. At the same time, the legal system can be evaluated by how effectively it achieves its goals – ensuring fairness and justice, and protecting those in need of protection. The commitments are in a way distinct – the training of lawyers who can think prospectively, and the education of critics who can evaluate a legal system – but they also seem to flow from an underlying unified idea of law as an instrumentality.

Further, the emphasis on instrumentalism appears to welcome critical discussions *about* ends themselves: although the authors believe "we have to take the existence of a market economy as a fact," they assert that "we do not have to agree on its political, moral or philosophical bases."[237] Reiter and Swan appear to want to lay bare the reasons behind decisions, as the American realists did; they invite critical discussion about the ends towards which legal regulation should aim; they want students to become adept at evaluating whether legal regulation succeeds at achieving these ends; and they want students to develop a set of tools, including litigation, but extending to planning and even law reform.

---

236 *Swan* 4th ed, *supra* note 208 at xxx [emphasis added].
237 *Ibid* at xxix.

Swan 5th ed: More Solicitor, Social Context, Justice

This somewhat polymathic approach to studying contract law continues through subsequent editions. For the fifth edition (1997), the publisher has changed again, back to Butterworths, and a third editor has been added: Nicholas C Bala, professor of law at Queen's University. The structure of the Introduction remains largely the same in the fifth edition, but there are some additions and changes. The theme of the solicitor is expanded upon slightly, as seen in the claim that "most lawyers who practice ... contract law are negotiators and drafters, not litigators" and that the utility of cases lies primarily in determining "what might have been done to avoid the problem, what advice (or different advice) the parties might have been given, or how the relation between the parties might have been better structured." Also, the authors reinforce their commitment to the broad social context – updating their examples and inserting a paragraph on domestic contracts, an area in which Bala had previously published. This example serves to illustrate "how far rules developed for commercial relations can be pushed or applied in a very different context." The authors reinforce, with added text, their commitment to cultivating students' appreciation for justice and fairness, tempered with a caveat about the need for precision.[238]

Swan 6th ed: Expanding the Framework

The sixth edition (2002) elaborates on the themes of justice and fairness, continues to expand the contextual frame, and says more to students about their evolving identities as lawyers. The three editors return for this edition, though Swan is now listed as both a practising lawyer *and* as a professor of law at McGill University (a position Swan held from 1996 to 2002). This renewed academic affiliation can be felt in the Introduction. Although law is still defined as the "science of getting from here to there," "making the system work" is no longer listed as a related "important question." The emphasis is instead on "[t]hinking about what fairness, justice and efficiency demand of different types

---

238 *Ibid* at xxviii, xxv, xxx ("fairness and justice are and can properly be made central to the law. You must, however, be careful in saying that a decision is 'just' or 'fair.' These terms are usually conclusions: they are not reasons and, as conclusions, they have to be justified"). For Bala's research on the domestic contract, see e.g. Nicholas Bala, "Domestic Contracts and the Supreme Court Trilogy: A Deal Is a Deal" (1988) 13 Queen's LJ 1; Nicholas Bala, "Recognizing Spousal Contributions to the Acquisition of Degrees, Licences, and Other Career Assets towards Compensatory Support" (1989) 8 Can J Fam L 23.

of exchange relations." Also perhaps inspired by McGill, which immediately preceding and during Swan's tenure was preoccupied with reforming the curriculum to incorporate a "transsystemic" legal education, the Introduction speaks of the "broad similarities in the types of contractual problems that are faced in different countries," how a student "with a good understanding of the contract law in Canada will be well placed to begin to study contractual regulation in other legal systems," and the influence on Canadian contract law of other jurisdictions, including the United Kingdom, the United States, and "some subtle influences from the thinking of those trained in the Quebec Civil Code."[239]

This nod to transsystemic or interjurisdictional relevance can be thought of as expanding the geographic frame of reference, and the contextual frame is pushed further at other points in the Introduction. New text is added in the beginning section that expands upon the fifth edition's reference to how commercial rules should be applied to non-commercial contexts.[240] The authors then discuss another legal framework outside the conventional bounds of private law, arguing how the Canadian Charter of Rights and Freedoms "has caused judges to reconsider their role as lawmakers. Judges are now more willing to consider whether a principle of common law produces socially, economically, and legally desirable results ... [T]here is now a clear willingness to permit incremental change in the common law."[241] Contract law, in other words, is viewed not only as the product of doctrinal rules, primarily judicially made, but also as connected to the broader social and legal context. Reference at the beginning of the Introduction to "public" agreements, such as Aboriginal treaties, illustrates the very broad canvas on which the authors paint their image of contract law's relevance.[242]

The message to students in all of this is that a wide range of skills, contexts, facts, and perspectives is necessary to understand contract law. As this understanding develops with each successive edition, so too do the messages addressed directly to students about their role in approaching the study of contract law. In the sixth edition, the authors

239 *Swan* 6th ed, *supra* note 208 at xxii. On transsystemic legal education, see e.g. Harry Arthurs, "Madly Off in One Direction: McGill's New Integrated, Polyjural, Transsystemic Law Programme" (2005) 50 McGill LJ 707.

240 *Swan* 6th ed, *supra* note 208 at xxiii ("our concern is [not] only with economic interests ... Increasingly the law is struggling with questions of how to recognize non-economic interests in exchange transactions").

241 *Ibid* at xxxi.

242 *Ibid* at xxiii.

expand on the distorting effect that a focus on case law has for students – it encourages them to think "that every problem and issue should be approached as if it were going to be decided by a court" – and they further develop the message to students about the need for precision in making evaluations about the "justice" or "fairness" of legal rules.[243]

Swan 7th ed and Swan, *Canadian Contract Law*: Reigniting Controversy

The seventh edition came out in 2006, the same year that Swan published her treatise, *Canadian Contract Law*. Similar to the Reiter & Swan essay of 1980, the thesis of *Canadian Contract Law* is that contract law is designed to protect the reasonable expectation of the parties.[244] This theme drew criticism, just as the Reiter & Swan collection of essays, *Studies in Contract Law*, did. Geoff Hall, a lawyer at McCarthy Tétrault and soon-to-be author of a text on contractual interpretation, criticized the treatise for "blur[ring] the distinction between what the law is and what (in Swan's view) the law should be," arguing that Swan "gives too much credence to grand theory," that the principle does not accord with the majority of case law, and that reasonable expectations is unsuitable as an organizing principle because it is both circular (parties' expectations are created in part by judicial decisions) and indeterminate (the principle cannot yield a result in difficult cases, the ones most likely to be litigated).[245]

Reiter rose to Swan's defence, arguing that, while protecting the reasonable expectations of the parties might not appear consistently in judicial articulations of doctrine, it is not what judges "say" that matters, but rather what they do. For Reiter (and Swan), protecting reasonable

243 *Ibid* at xxix–xxx, xxxii ("To say that a decision is 'unfair' or 'unjust' is really a conclusion that needs to be explored ... [A case may fail] to protect the reasonable expectations of the parties, or ... encourage exploitative behaviour ... The result [may be] economically expensive and lead[] to the mis-allocation or waste of resources").

244 John Swan, *Canadian Contract Law* (Markham, ON: LexisNexis, 2006) at 639 ("the broad purpose of the law of contracts [is] to protect the parties' reasonable expectations"). See also Angela Swan & Jakub Adamski, *Canadian Contract Law*, 3d student ed (Toronto: LexisNexis, 2012) at §1.2 [Swan & Adamski, Student Ed].

245 Geoff R Hall, "A Study in Reasonable Expectations", Book Review of *Canadian Contract Law* by John Swan, (2007) 45 Can Bus LJ 150 at 151, 153–8, 162–4. See also Stephen A Smith, "The Reasonable Expectations of the Parties: An Unhelpful Concept" (2009) 48 Can Bus LJ 366 [Smith, "Unhelpful Concept"]. The first edition of Hall's textbook was published the same year as Hall's review of the Swan treatise. See Geoff R Hall, *Canadian Contractual Interpretation Law* (Markham, ON: LexisNexis, 2007).

expectations captures the pursuit of justice that judges engage in prior to deciding which doctrinal explanations they will use to arrive at the end result. This standard is desirable – it leads to "economic organization that is in the best interests of society" – and it also leads to a more *useful* understanding of what judges do, directing solicitors to "look to facts supportive of reasonable expectations" and litigators to "adduce supportive evidence and argue on these terms."[246]

The publication of Swan's *Canadian Contract Law* therefore reignited an old debate among contract law scholars between those focused on the "real" underlying reasons for decisions and those more inclined to take contract doctrine on its face, searching accordingly for conceptual purity. Critics like Hall, who decry the indeterminacy of the reasonable expectations account for its lack of fit with doctrine, echo the classical legal thinkers in contract law whose search for coherence gave rise to sophisticated doctrinal theories centred around the intentions of the parties. The reasonable expectations theory, by contrast, allies itself to functional, equitable, and contextual mechanisms in contract law such as detrimental reliance, estoppel, and good faith. The resistance to reasonable expectations as an organizing theory should therefore be understood as part of a perennial debate about the relationship of form and function, text and context, that runs through contract law (and legal theory generally). Understood as a manifestation of this perennial debate, a parallel can be drawn to the lifelong disagreements between Samuel Williston (reporter of the classical *Restatement on the Law of Contracts*) and Arthur Corbin (reporter of the functionalist *Restatement (Second) on the Law of Contracts*). As Stephen Smith notes in his own critique of the reasonable expectations concept, the Reiter & Swan hypothesis has a true kinship with Corbin, whose first section in his great 1950 treatise is titled "The Main Purpose of Contracts Is the Realization of Reasonable Expectations Induced by Promises."[247]

---

246 Barry J Reiter, "A Study in Reasonable Expectations: A Rebuttal to Geoff Hall" (2008) 46 Can Bus LJ 95 at 95, 97, 99.

247 See Sébastien Grammond, "Reasonable Expectations and the Interpretation of Contracts across Legal Traditions" (2010) 48 Can Bus LJ 345 at 346–7, 364–5; Smith, "Unhelpful Concept", *supra* note 245 at 366, 378–9 (demonstrating the similarity but not congruence of protecting induced reliance and protecting "expectations"). See generally Gilmore, *Death of Contract*, *supra* note 90, c 3. On Corbin as the origin of the reasonable expectations concept, see also Jay M Feinman, "Good Faith and Reasonable Expectations" (2014) 67 Ark L Rev 524 at 534. But see JH Baker, "From Sanctity of Contract to Reasonable Expectation?" (1979) 32 Current Legal Problems 17 at 22–3 (reasonable expectations can be traced back to at least as early as 1763 to Adam Smith and through to the writings of Austin and Pollock).

Despite these criticisms, the Swan treatise drew praise for its novelty and sophistication of thought. As with the casebook, no one challenges the treatise's originality; it likewise receives praise for its pedagogical value. Rick Bigfoot, professor of law at Bond University in Australia, in his review of the third edition of the treatise, describes it as "an excellent, multi-layered, educational resource for investing law students ... with comprehensive content knowledge and critical legal reasoning skills."[248]

A careful reading of the Introduction to the seventh edition of the casebook reveals the influences of the treatise. Although much of the text of the Introduction is the same as in the sixth edition, there are three significant additions. Two of these consist of themes that had been present in the second edition (the one immediately following the publication of *Studies in Contract Law*) but were removed in the third. It is almost as if the effort in crystallizing the ideas about reasonable expectations inspired reflection on once-abandoned themes.

The first of these additions is a reference to the conceptual distinction between discrete and relational contracts. The editors once again refer to Macneil's *The New Social Contract*, and announce that the book will consider "how to modify the legal regime which largely developed based on the model of the discrete contract to deal with the increasingly common relational contract."[249]

The second addition is a reference to the "growing body of theoretical literature on contracts." Unlike, however, the reference to philosophical concepts of law that appeared in the second edition, which purported to consider these concepts as central to the casebook, the reference to theory here signals a disdain for abstractions: "those wishing a sustained theoretical study of contract" are encouraged to look elsewhere, and the reader is reminded that "judges and lawyers developed the common law with only limited explicit reference to theories of law, and an understanding of what judges have done is a foundation for more advanced theoretical analysis and criticism."[250] Such veiled antipathy to theory would seem to be consistent with the claim at the beginning of Swan's treatise that "what is most important is not some abstract value like 'freedom of contract' or some economic value like efficiency, but what is a defensible

---

248 Rick Bigfoot, Book Review *Canadian Contract Law*, 3d ed by Angela Swan & Jakub Adamski, eds, (2014) 55 Can Bus LJ 313 at 313–15. See also Anne Menon, Book Review of *Canadian Contract Law* by John Swan, (2007) 32 Can L Libr Rev 33 at 34 (praising the book's "unique structure").

249 *Swan* 7th ed, *supra* note 208 at xxxi–xxxii. This distinction was present in the second edition (*supra* note 208 at xlv–xlvi) but removed in the third, when the casebook migrated to Emond Montgomery and underwent heavy pruning.

250 *Swan* 7th ed, *supra* note 208 at xxxiii. Compare *Swan* 2d ed, *supra* note 208 at xlvii–l.

result from the point of view of the parties."[251] This distancing from theory coincides with Swan's departure from academia – the seventh edition affiliates her exclusively with Aird Berlis LLP – and the specific references to Stephen Smith and Stephen Waddams in the Introduction might implicitly signal Swan's difference of opinion with her former colleagues.[252]

A third addition to the Introduction of the seventh edition is that contract law as a category for study is an "artificial construct." The editors write that grouping materials under the rubric of contract can be "misleading if it suggests that the neat boundaries fixed for a particular course or ... casebook ... really do represent neatly separated ideas or topics." Instead, the study of contracts "must be situated in a functioning society and its legal system." Such "functioning systems" are "analytically messy." A problem that can be viewed from one perspective as a contract problem can, from another point of view, be considered one of "torts, restitution, business associations or, for example, those of interest to a Competition Bureau or a provincial securities commission." Thus, while not descriptive of reality, the isolation of a body of "contract" law represents an "over-simplif[ication]," which is to be followed by seeing how things fit together. This analytical messiness is a long-standing concern of Swan's as a teacher and figures prominently in her treatise.[253]

The combined effect of these additions is to highlight the indeterminacy of contract law doctrine and to emphasize the criteria of usefulness and purposiveness. The Introduction also serves to portray the law in books as a contingent and manipulable tool to achieve social ends, ends

---

251 Swan & Adamski, Student Ed, *supra* note 244 at §1.2.

252 Both Stephen Smith's *Contract Theory* (New York: Oxford University Press, 2004) and SM Waddams's *Dimensions of Private Law: Categories and Concepts in Anglo-American Legal Reasoning* (Cambridge: Cambridge University Press, 2003) had come out in-between the sixth and seventh editions. Although Smith's critique of reasonable expectations would not come out until 2009, it is possible that, given that they were both at McGill between 1998 and 2002 (Swan was a Visiting Professor from 1996 to 2002, and Smith started at McGill in 1998), Swan might have been aware of a difference of opinion between the two at the time of writing the Introduction to the seventh edition.

253 *Swan* 7th ed, *supra* note 208 at xxxv–xxxvi. On the theme of analytical messiness in Swan & Adamski, *supra* note 248, see Bigfoot, *supra* note 248 at 319, 321. The reference in *Swan* 1st ed, *supra* note 201 to Ernest Weinrib signals this long-standing concern. As Weinrib recounts, "One year in the mid-seventies Swan and I taught a combined first year small group that covered both contracts and torts, and that reflected our belief at the time that the boundaries between contract law and tort law were more blurred than the traditional taxonomy of private law acknowledged" (email correspondence with author, 3 June 2017).

which must always be placed in their broadest possible context. Other additions to the seventh edition's Introduction further these points – reminding the reader that the casebook is merely an "*introduction* to a very broad and complex study that may consume the rest of your professional life," that the "common law is always changing," and that "these materials do not purport to resolve controversies, but rather reflect the fact that there are emerging and controversial areas of contract law."[254]

The Introduction changes little with the eighth edition (2010), although Reiter and Bala have switched places in the order of authorship – the eighth edition's editors are listed in the order of Swan, Bala, and Reiter.

Swan 9th ed: Full Chapter Status

The ninth and most recent edition (2015) witnesses some more significant changes. Reiter is replaced by Jakub Adamski, Swan's collaborator on *Canadian Contract Law*, who, in the third edition of that treatise, had been elevated to the status of co-author. Adamski "practices litigation and corporate law," and teaches selected law courses at McGill and the Université de Montréal.[255]

The main difference between the introductory sections in the eighth and ninth editions is that the introductory commentary now gains the full status of a chapter, entitled "Contracts, Their Context, and Learning the Law." Such a move suggests that these introductory statements should be considered to be equally substantive as the remainder of the book – which makes sense given the theoretical richness that underpins them and the careful way in which they have been developed over the years. All of these themes have accreted over the course of the eight preceding editions; the ninth edition reflects them all. The editors continue to update examples (exemplifying their concern with context), provide additional references to the solicitor's role, elaborate on the realist and functional theme, expand on the nature of the community of lawyers, and continue to emphasize the importance of precision.[256]

---

254 *Swan* 7th ed, *supra* note 208 at xxiii–xxxiv [emphasis in original].

255 See Swan & Adamski, Student Ed, *supra* note 244 at vii–viii; *Swan* 9th ed, *supra* note 208 at vii.

256 *Swan* 9th ed, *supra* note 208 at §§1.16, 1.31, 1.34 (updated examples); §1.41 (adding "to advise clients"); §1.49 ("reasons for judgment are always more than a story"); §1.46 ("Students are dropped into the middle of a functioning economy with real, live problems"); §1.52 (cases become "coded phrases" for lawyers); §1.74 ("The use of the plural pronoun in federal statutes when the referent is singular is horrible and to be strongly deprecated").

The result is that Chapter 1 of the ninth edition of *Swan* represents not only the editors' best attempt at presenting the material in a way that encapsulates their particular approach to the subject matter; it also reflects the gradual development of the editors' ideas and life experiences over the better part of four decades. From their genesis as academic iconoclasts – challenging prevailing attitudes among Canadian contract law scholars with realist views – to their journey away from academia into practice, albeit one never fully divorced from the university (by virtue of Swan's temporary return and Bala's participation as of the fifth edition), the *Swan* editors now present, in their first chapter, an explicit and fully conscious vision of the meaning and value of studying not just contract law, but law in general.

This view instructs students to demand justice and fairness in their evaluation of the law, to understand law not as fixed or determinate, but rather as malleable and contestable. It exhorts the student to imagine the law as a tool for achieving ends and to both debate those ends and to critique the law's success at achieving them. It presents common law decisions as the primary source material, but is self-critical about the limits of adjudication as a mode of social ordering. It highlights relational contracting as economically and socially significant, and enlists the student both in critiquing doctrine and in imagining how law can preserve or enrich existing relationships. The student is encouraged to do all this while remaining aware of the broader social context and cultivating a concern for rigour and precision. The reasonable expectations of the parties idea serves as a realist and pragmatic overarching theoretical framework.

Compared with the other casebooks, the messages in *Swan* are more unified, explicit, and polemical. But what is most distinctive about *Swan* is the attempt to operationalize these theoretical attitudes about law into a workable vision of practice under the aegis of the solicitor's approach. Swan appears to want her students to think of themselves as future solicitors, planners, and problem solvers and to break away from a vision of legal practice that emphasizes adjudication. As will be shown later in this chapter, the way she treats the remedies chapter consistently executes this vision, encouraging functional reasoning over conventional analogical reasoning focused on the judicial formulation of rules. Moreover, as the next section shows, the scepticism about judges' words and adjudication's centrality sets her apart from the two other casebooks that enjoy the majority market share.

Waddams: *Underlying Messages about Law and Legal Education*

Waddams has its origins in a casebook edited by University of Toronto professor James Bryce Milner and first published in 1963.[257] Following Milner's untimely death at the age of fifty-one in 1969, Stephen Waddams took over the casebook, editing three successive editions of *Milner's Cases and Materials on Contracts* in 1971, 1977, and 1985. In 1994, Waddams, together with Michael Trebilcock (University of Toronto) and Mary Anne Waldron (University of Victoria) brought out *Cases and Materials on Contracts*, replacing *Milner* with *Waddams*.[258] Successive editions of *Waddams* came out in 2000, 2005, 2010, 2014, and 2018. Each edition acknowledges Milner's influence, and so *Milner* is a fitting place to begin to understand the underlying attitudes – continued or abandoned – in *Waddams*.

Milner 1st ed: Multiple Legal Processes, Integration of Theory and Practice, and a Tension

Milner, like Swan would a decade and a half later, wrote a fairly long and substantive Introduction to his casebook. It is a rich source of messages about law and, like *Swan*, it conveys a "highly personal" approach: "This introduction has been deliberately written in the first person because I intend it primarily for my own classes. I should warn any other reader that the objectives of legal education and the consequent arrangement of topics in a course are highly personal, and my views may very well not be shared by other law teachers."[259] This personal approach happens to bear some similarity to that of Swan. Implicitly repudiating Langdell, Milner disabuses the student of the idea that "the cases are building blocks, that each has an understandable shape and will fit neatly into a little wall of law, snugly and certainly." Instead, for Milner, the "correct" answer is that each case stands for a "little segment of human history, history of an event or of an idea, or

257 The genealogy goes back further, by virtue of this casebook's "faint resemblance" to Dean Wright's original casebook (*Milner* 1st ed, *supra* note 207 at xx). See Angela Fernandez, "An Object Lesson in Speculation: Multiple Views of the Cathedral in *Leaf v International Galleries*" (2008) 58 UTLJ 481 at 509–10 (detailing Wright's consent to have his casebook reproduced by the University of British Columbia and the "first published casebook" in Canada by Falconbridge in 1927).

258 See *Waddams* 1st ed, *supra* note 209 at iii. The acknowledgment of Milner is retained in prefaces to all successive editions.

259 *Milner* 1st ed, *supra* note 207 at xix.

of both." The facts are primary – he cites an unnamed Supreme Court justice who claimed that "when I have mastered the facts I have done seventy-five per cent of the job" – but he cautions the students against unproblematically accepting the characterization of the facts in the appellate case reporter. The facts are not always known, witnesses are "not perfect," judges might omit facts in their retelling of the story, and lawyers might have purposely kept "background facts" out of the record. These caveats parallel Swan's admonition to students to think of how counsel "got the facts before the judge" in her discussion of the fact-finding process.[260]

Even more reminiscent of Swan's approach – Swan and Milner overlapped as faculty members at the University of Toronto for about four years, though they "never did talk much about Contracts" – is Milner's practical side.[261] Milner writes that the "important question is: What is to be done with the case?" He reminds students that the client likely will not ask what the law is, but "more commonly what can he do, or not do, in particular circumstances." Like Swan, for whom the lawyer's job is to keep the client out of trouble, for Milner, the "business man ... consult[s] his lawyer [when] he wants to avoid trouble and he is not sure what to do." Milner emphasizes the purposive nature of contract law, both making the claim explicitly ("the prediction of law becomes a complex purposive activity of man") and using purposiveness as the rationale for certain editorial choices, such as starting the book with remedies (an approach that gives "an excellent perspective of the purposes of the law in enforcing contracts"). Milner relates human purposes to the "basic problem of justice": "All of this should make apparent to you the importance to the law of human purposes. These purposes are many, varied, and conflicting; the task of the law is to sort them out and promote those that should be promoted and suppress those that should be suppressed. We might call the difficult task of selection the basic problem of justice."[262] Also like Swan, this emphasis on purpose leads Milner to point out that most contract lawyers conduct solicitor-like work, rather than barrister-like work, reflecting a "legislative" mode of ordering: "Their professional action ... may take the form

260 *Ibid* at vii–ix; *Swan* 2d ed, *supra* note 208 at liii. Both Swan and Milner use the example of *Hadley v Baxendale* (1854), 9 Ex 341, 156 ER 145 to suggest that background factors – "background facts" for Milner (1st ed, *supra* note 207 at ix), or for Swan the judge's own "perception of the propriety of one party's conduct" (2d ed, *supra* note 208 at liv) – impact the fact-finding process.

261 Angela Swan, email correspondence with author, 19 October 2016.

262 *Milner* 1st ed, *supra* note 207 at vii, xv–xix. *Cf Swan* 3d ed, *supra* note 208 at xxxi.

of, for example, drafting clauses in a contract, persuading an administrative official to vary a regulation, or a legislative committee to recommend an amendment to a statute, or organizing a new corporation. All of these activities are in a sense legislative, rather than adjudicative, and they justify, in my view, an even greater emphasis on the legislative area than our legal education presently offers."[263]

Like Swan, Milner warns students against thinking about law solely in terms of adjudication.[264] Like Swan, he emphasizes these multiple forms of social ordering as alternative modes the lawyer should develop in pursuit of justice. He describes "three basic processes" as separate branches of the legal discipline: "the contract process, of negotiation, promise and exchange;" "adjudication, of which the judicial process is an instance, but so is arbitration;" and "legislation, or the exercise of power by a body authorized to make rules for general application," including both state legislative bodies and private individuals given such power by "contract or special arrangement." This implies that legal education should, at the very least, elevate the status of "legislative" processes to that of adjudicative ones.[265]

These ideas are directly attributable to Lon Fuller. Milner generated his "great debt" to Fuller during his time at Harvard Law School, where Milner (at the age of thirty-one, after having taught law for four years at Dalhousie) studied with Fuller as a graduate student in 1949–50.[266] It was a time of ferment in legal education at Harvard, with Fuller recently having chaired the 1947 Special Committee on Legal Education. The curricular reforms that followed "stressed the importance of reducing concern with problems at the appellate level and focusing on ... trial, counseling, negotiating, drafting and the like."[267]

In the winter of 1948, Fuller published a more refined version of these ideas in an article entitled "What the Law Schools Can Contribute to

---

263 *Milner* 1st ed, *supra* note 207 at xi, xvii.

264 Compare *ibid* at xi ("First year law students can too easily get the impression that life in the law is just one continuous lawsuit. Case study falsely emphasizes this impression. The cases are almost always cases in courts, and the constant reading of cases may tend to drive out of mind the other areas in which law is equally operative"); *Swan* 3d ed, *supra* note 208 at xxx–xxxi ("The consequence of a focus on cases – that is, on the record of judicial decisions – tends to encourage one to think that we are concerned only about what happened (or might happen) in court: that every problem and issue should be approached as if it were going to be decided by a court").

265 *Milner* 1st ed, *supra* note 207 at xvii–xviii.

266 *Ibid* at xx.

267 Robert Summers, *Lon L Fuller* (Stanford, CA: Stanford University Press, 1984) at 15 (quoting Albert Sacks).

the Making of Lawyers."[268] In the essay, Fuller advocates for a new conception of legal education that views its object as giving "the student an understanding of, and an insight into, the *processes* in which a lawyer participates." Fuller divides law into two basic social processes: adjudication and legislation. Adjudication includes "all forensic methods of deciding disputes, including informal arbitration and the work of administrative tribunals as well as the traditional processes of our courts." Legislation "refers not merely to the planning and drafting of statutes, but includes the negotiation and drafting of contracts and other private documents." He argues that traditional legal education is deficient at emphasizing the legislative process, with professors operating under the false assumption that it will be sufficiently covered incidental to a focus on adjudication. Fuller recommends that legal education should teach processes in their "most elementary form," and expects that knowledge of rules and skills would emerge as a by-product of this saturation.[269]

Milner not only read this article while at Harvard, but organized a graduate student reading series at which Fuller presented it. Milner and Fuller would remain in correspondence for the subsequent two decades, and Milner would include this article in a list of recommended Fuller readings he shared with members of the Canadian judiciary. Milner also encountered a series of related legal-process ideas in the Legislation Seminar he took with Henry Hart, architect of the legal process school. Indeed, Milner's two highest grades were in Fuller's Jurisprudence seminar and in Hart's course. It is no surprise, then, that the language in Milner's casebook so closely resembles Fuller's ideas. Milner's emphasis on process, his division into legislative and adjudicative processes, his highlighting of lawyerly activities that emerge from the legislative arena, and his criticism of legal education as unequally weighted towards the adjudicative all reflect his Harvard education.[270]

---

268 Lon L Fuller, "What the Law Schools Can Contribute to the Making of Lawyers" (1948) 1 J Legal Ed 189 [Fuller, "Law Schools"].

269 *Ibid* at 189, 192–7, 199 [emphasis in original].

270 James Milner, Memorandum to "Fellow Graduate Students", 28 November 1949, York University Libraries, Clara Thomas Archives & Special Collections, James B Milner fonds, 1992–014/005(161); James Milner, Letter to Justice JL McLennan, 21 December 1956, York University Libraries, Clara Thomas Archives & Special Collections, James B Milner fonds, 1992–014/005(149). Milner received his highest grade, a 39.5 out of 50, in Fuller's Jurisprudence Seminar. His second-highest grade (39 out of 50) was in Hart's Legislation seminar. See Harvard Law School, Examination Record of James Bryce Milner, June 1950, York University Libraries, Clara Thomas Archives & Special Collections, James B Milner fonds, 1992–014/005(161). On the relationship of these ideas to the legal process writings of Hart & Sacks, see

Teaching at the University of Toronto in the 1950s and 1960s, Milner would have been in good company with other Harvard graduates. Caesar Wright (the founding dean at the Faculty of Law who hired Milner), John Willis, Bora Laskin, and Dick Risk all studied there. Both Willis and Laskin enjoyed a minor correspondence with Fuller, exchanging information about the Canadian Bill of Rights and Canadian administrative law. Milner even told Fuller about a planned project of his and Laskin's, never undertaken, to write an introductory law text using the ideas of legal process. Thus, Milner's Fuller-inspired ideas might have reflected a larger intellectual undercurrent at the University of Toronto at the time.[271]

There is another way in which the intellectual climate at the University of Toronto Faculty of Law in the 1950s and 1960s can be felt in Milner's introduction. As retold in *The Fiercest Debate*, this period followed the dramatic wresting away of control over legal education from the Law Society of Upper Canada.[272] The shadow of the fierce debate can be felt in the *Milner* introduction, but in a way that challenges the conventional narrative of opposition. Milner's approach highlights the mutually reinforcing qualities of university study and legal practice, foreshadowing the more elaborate "integrative" accounts of theory and practice in legal education in the *Arthurs Report*, *Carnegie Report*, and Kronman's *Lost Lawyer* of the subsequent generations.

Milner's support of Fuller's views reveals a commitment to the more practical sides of legal study. The focus on problem solving and the mastery of different legal processes is intimately related to a client-focused notion of legal practice: helping the client figure out what he or she can "do, or not do, in particular circumstances."[273] At

---

William N Eskridge, Jr & Philip P Frickey, "The Making of *The Legal Process*" (1994) 107 Harv L Rev 2031 at 2039–40; James Milner, Letter to Caesar Wright, 4 May 1950, York University Libraries, Clara Thomas Archives & Special Collections, James B Milner fonds, 1992–014/005(161) ("Hart's idea is that legislation is a fancy name for legal method. I thought I was back in jurisprudence for five weeks").

271 See Harvard Law School, *Alumni Directory of the Harvard Law School 1963: The Quinquennial Catalogue* (Cambridge, MA: Harvard Law School, 1963) at 832–3; John Willis, Letter to Lon L Fuller, 24 February 1961, Lon Fuller Papers, Harvard Law School Historical and Special Collections, box 8, folder 11; Bora Laskin, Letter to Lon L Fuller, 28 January 1959, Harvard Law School Historical and Special Collections, box 4, folder 16; James Milner, Letter to Lon L Fuller, 3 March 1959, York University Libraries, Clara Thomas Archives & Special Collections, James B Milner fonds, 1992–014/005(149). See also Fernandez, "Object Lesson", *supra* note 257 at 508, quoting Kyer & Bickenbach, *supra* note 6 at 236–7; Philip Girard, "Who's Afraid of Canadian Legal History?" (2007) 57 UTLJ 727 at 740.

272 Kyer & Bickenbach, *supra* note 6 at 236–7.

273 *Milner* 1st ed, *supra* note 207 at xv.

the same time, he demonstrates a genuine commitment to the academic study of law.

Milner exalts university study in his discussion of the tendency to ask whether a case is "rightly decided." At first his language suggests caution in asking this question, intimating that it might "introduce the element of ethics into the rather more precise world of legal propositions." Yet, as Milner goes on, it becomes clear that these excursions are to be embraced, not resisted. This is so not only because it prompts reflection on non-adjudicative processes, but also because of the academic nature of university legal study itself:

> What, then, is the answer to the teacher's question, "Is the case 'right'?" Can there be any less of an answer than an examination of the possible reasonable and practical alternatives? The answer to the question may be a qualified "yes, but" in some cases, because on a proper view of the problem of the case it may appear that there are other legal processes better adapted to its solution than the adjudicative. While the case as presented may be "rightly" decided, the problem of the case, which is also the law student's concern, is not satisfactorily solved. It is admittedly a dangerous question, one that opens up large and exciting vistas and yet, in a *university*, no matter how modern, can one properly refuse to consider it?[274]

The proper domain of "*university*" study is therefore not only to contain oneself within the frame of analysis (adjudication), but to look beneath the phenomenon of the case itself to consider the underlying "problem," which might not be "satisfactorily solved" by even a "rightly decided case." In this somewhat elliptical passage, therefore, Milner is affirming both the role of the traditional case method and the idea that other "large and exciting vistas" – which could be a reference to other disciplines – can be brought into the law classroom. Such an incorporation of other disciplines into legal study is precisely what Fuller had in mind in his own essay about legal education.[275]

Moreover, Milner's case study approach is far from facile or mechanical. Like Swan's, it is steeped in a nuanced concern with justice. Milner quotes Cardozo's *Nature of the Judicial Process* to the effect that "Law never *is*, but is always about to be," compares it to Lord Mansfield's aphorism that the common law "works itself pure" by drawing

---

274 *Ibid* at xiii–xiv [emphasis in original].

275 See Fuller, "Law Schools", *supra* note 268 at 201 ("It is apparent that this process of synthesizing considerations that lie in different realms of human competence is one aspect of the larger process I have called legislation").

on "fountains of justice," and calls the idea that law is "*always* about to be" a "great" one. Milner also emphasizes the "uncertainty in the law." He tries to disabuse the student of the idea that law "consist[s] of a long series of settled rules ... to memorize and to understand." He does not let the student plunge into complete relativism – he asserts that there is "accepted doctrine" – but emphasizes that the lawyer's task is not just to provide the client with the applicable doctrine. And finally, while the *Milner* Introduction is light on theory per se, it richly alludes to theory. Milner uses a meteorological metaphor to canvass the various approaches of "black letter law, functional analysis, and the law-in-action" – all references to legal scholarly traditions. And the Introduction is laced with references to legal scholars: Holmes, Cardozo, and Fuller.[276]

Thus the *Milner* Introduction communicates to students a remarkably conciliatory vision of the relationship between the academic study of law and legal practice. The articulation of what a lawyer does is assimilated to a similar type of purposive activity – helping clients stay out of trouble, or solve problems – that accounts for the nature of law itself. The vision of law as a process both feeds the academic inclination to understand law in a nuanced way and equips the future lawyer to be of use to future clients.

These reflections suggest a slight differentiation from Swan. Whereas Milner's purposive, process-centric vision of law might seem to reconcile academic and practical goals of legal education in one fell swoop, Swan's vision oscillates in its emphasis of one or the other, perhaps reflecting Swan's own move in and out of practice. Swan, while never abandoning her commitment to the idea that justice must be at the centre of legal study or that social context be held in contemplation – both ideas at home in a principle-centric academic university – nevertheless signals a type of pre-eminence to practice, both explicitly (recounting in a Preface that the editors are pleased to see their ideas being borne out in practice) and implicitly (in prioritizing "usefulness" as a standard of evaluation). Swan's stance on the academic/practical divide, of course, cannot be characterized as facile or one-sided, but hers is of a different flavour – a conciliation that happens in-between the lines as a product of accreted life experience and successive editorial revisions.

---

276 *Milner* 1st ed, *supra* note 207 at ix, xiv–xvi [emphasis in original], quoting *Omychund v Barker* (1744), 1 Atk 21 at 33, 27 ER 15 at 22–3 (Lord Mansfield), OW Holmes, "The Path of the Law" (1897) 10 Harv L Rev 457, Benjamin N Cardozo, *The Nature of the Judicial Process* (New Haven, CT: Yale University Press, 1921), and Fuller, *Basic Contract Law*, *supra* note 205.

Milner, in part because his early death halted the development of the casebook and its Introduction, demonstrates the conciliation a little more all-at-once.

A Not-So-Abject Apology

There are, of course, other differences between Milner's view and Swan's. Whereas Swan is quite emphatic in her cautions against a focus on case law, Milner, by contrast, qualifies these cautions. Thus his "apology for so many cases is not quite abject, because first year law students are expected to learn thoroughly the judicial process, how and why it works and what its limitations are."[277] As Angela Fernandez observes, "Milner seems to have been uncomfortable with something about th[e] process of canonization or codification of cases in law school casebooks."[278] Yet this did not stop him from adopting the classical form of the casebook, choosing, unlike Swan, to provide relatively sparse commentary. As the legal-historian-to-be Clifford Ian Kyer wrote in comparatively reviewing the two casebooks (*Milner* 3d ed and *Swan* 1st ed) when he was a second-year law student at the University of Toronto:

> Waddams' edition of Milner's casebook fits more comfortably into the traditional mold. The principal teaching aid is the body of cases ... [T]he cases predominate; the other materials simply supplement them.
>
> Swan and Reiter's volume ... abounds with notes by the authors and lengthy articles and excerpts from monographs. The cases are important, but they do not represent as substantial a portion of the volume as do the cases in Waddams' book. In a sense, what Swan and Reiter have produced is a combination casebook, text-book, and book of readings on the law of contracts ...
>
> Waddams' casebook is more succinct. It presents the essentials of the law of contracts in a shorter compass. As Milner thought best, the student is left to think things out largely on his own. Swan and Reiter provide the student with more direction.[279]

---

277 *Milner* 1st ed, *supra* note 207 at xi.

278 Fernandez, "Object Lesson", *supra* note 257 at 504 (citing *Milner* 1st ed, *supra* note 207 at vii).

279 Clifford Ian Kyer, Book Review of *Milner* 3d ed and *Swan* 1st ed, (1978) 37 U Toronto Fac L Rev 152 at 152, 153, 155. Although Kyer is commenting on Waddams's fairly substantial reworking of the Milner text, the above observations about style apply to all editions, even the first, of *Milner*. See e.g. Christopher Carr, Book Review of *Milner* 2d ed, (1971) 6 UBC L Rev 451 at 451 (Waddams has "steered towards updating Professor Milner's work rather than producing a new book"); C Granger, Book Review of *Milner* 2d ed, (1971) 5 Ottawa L Rev 268 at 269 (Waddams has "left the second edition substantially similar to the first").

The sparse approach to editing (providing "just the cases"), on the one hand, provides an occasion for Milner to express his pedagogical desire that students take responsibility for their own critical thinking, a decidedly academic virtue that was at the heart of early justifications of the case method.[280] For Milner, studying cases enabled students to think things out "largely on [their] own." He pleads with students to trust their own thinking. "[B]efore you have been completely brain washed," he writes, "I hope you may add to the intellectual ferment that ought to characterize any lively classroom of beginning law students." In advising students how to read a case, he tells them they have to

> [t]ry to do two rather irreconcilable things. You have to get to know the best which has been thought and said about the law of contracts, and you must turn a stream of fresh and free thought upon our stock notions and habits ... You have to know what judges and legislatures have said but you also have to know that there are other, and sometimes better, ideas that they might have expressed; and you have to know the legal system, how and why it works, or doesn't work, so that you, as future law reformers, may have some hope that your better ideas will be adopted.[281]

It is to this goal of stimulating fresh, critical insight that Milner attributes his own reticence with questions and commentary: "I have not put questions after every case because you may not bother to ask your own if you spend too much time worrying about mine. Your own efforts will be more rewarding in the long run. Take nothing for granted until you are forced to. Ask yourself whether you fully understand the judge's point of view before you attempt to criticize it, but do not hesitate to criticize it constructively."[282]

On the other hand, Milner's choice to include only cases has a thornier implication. This is the idea that, despite Milner's repeated insistence that adjudication is only one legal process among many, he nevertheless implicitly prioritizes it. *Milner*'s traditional form – a heavy collection of cases with minimal commentary – implies that there is something of great value to

---

280 See e.g. William A Keener, "The Inductive Method in Legal Education" (1894) 17 Ann Rep ABA 473 at 488–9 (the case method "is a method distinctly productive of individuality in teaching and of a scientific spirit of investigation, independence and self-reliance on the part of the student"). See generally Angela Fernandez, *Spreading the Word: From the Litchfield Law School to the Harvard Case Method* (SJD thesis, Yale University, 2007) at 331–41 (detailing the theme of inculcating independence in the early debates about the case method).

281 *Milner* 1st ed, *supra* note 207 at xi–xii.

282 *Ibid* at xii–xiii.

be discerned from the cases. The student might very well think for him- or herself, but if the primary object of reflection is the case, then it is perhaps inevitable that "the judicial process, how and why it works and what its limitations are" will remain the primary focus. This tendency might serve to reinforce the idea that law is typified by judicial reasoning, thereby endorsing the view that there is a distinct mode of legal rationality – that, for Milner, the "precise world of legal propositions" is very much real.

If this inference is correct – that a prioritization of short case excerpts with minimal commentary suggests a faith in an inherent legal rationality (recall that Milner approvingly cites Lord Mansfield's idea of the common law's working itself "pure") – then there is somewhat of a tension between the stated goals of understanding *various* legal processes and the implicit messages communicated about law through the main body of the casebook. Milner seems aware of the tension – it is "admittedly" a casebook, "there should probably be more" legislative examples, and he "apolog[izes]" (albeit not quite "abject[ly]") for too many cases. But it is an open question whether this tension is simply a result of Milner's not being able to accomplish the Fullerian goal, given limited resources and time, or whether the reproduction of Fuller's philosophy masks an unconscious preference for the case method, and with it the adjudicative process and so-called internal legal reasoning. Indeed, *unlike* in Fuller's essay, there are no specific references to the role of "external" disciplines in the *Milner* Introduction – only the cryptic reference to other "new and exciting vistas" that are the domain of the university.[283]

Milner 2d ed: The Tension Deepens

This tension appears more accentuated in the Introduction to the second edition (1971) of *Milner*. Waddams is now the editor because of Milner's death in 1969, but the Introduction remains Milner's and includes some revisions by him – it is dated "1963 and 1968."[284] The changes consist largely in a new section at the end of the Introduction entitled "Instead of a Definition." This text expands on the idea of legal process by highlighting themes of institutional competence and describing "new trends in private arrangements." Although these themes serve to deepen the connection to Fuller, they also more deeply implicate Milner in an apparent tension between Fullerian views and more conventional commitments.

Milner makes the point that, in the nineteenth century, courts performed two functions: "develop[ing] contract doctrine (a 'legislative'

283 Fuller, "Law Schools", *supra* note 268 at 199–202.

284 *Milner* 2d ed, *supra* note 207 at xxxi.

role) and settl[ing] disputes over the facts and their interpretation (an 'adjudicative' role)." As the economy became more complex in the twentieth century, however, this allocation of responsibility shifted away from the courts exclusively to other areas of the state: legislatures and administrative agencies. Milner suggests that this shift in institutional allocation of responsibility was appropriate because, for example, "[t]he social problems of our time demand a less haphazard timing of their solution ... The legislatures have been able to provide more generalized solutions and from a strategically more effective point of view." From this statement might be inferred the placing of greater importance on non-adjudicative legal processes.[285]

The need for new forms of legal regulations flows from the changes in the "character" of private arrangements, a phenomenon that urges Milner to expand on the Fuller-like prescription earlier that the lawyer must master these various modes of social ordering in order to be effective. Multiple legal processes are, in a way, tools to achieve the purpose of helping clients maintain and preserve contractual relations:

> The lawyer simply has to widen his horizon to include in his understanding of contract law, not only judge-made law but legislative and administrative controls as well. He must also know more about the changing reliance in business and domestic arrangements, on private ways of settling disputes rather than on litigation in a State court. Use of the courts for even simple settlements of disputes will be avoided where continuing business relations make resort to the emotionally charged atmosphere of courts undesirable. The lawyers will increasingly work out sensible settlements without the judges' supervision. All of this is meant to protect the reader from over-exposure to judicial opinions.[286]

Although this passage furthers the functional and process-pluralist ideas of Fuller (and reflects certain elements of socio-legal and relational theorists), it also signals a potentially countervailing preference for adjudication. From what "over-exposure" to judicial opinions are these comments meant to protect the reader? It can be none other than what follows in the remainder of the casebook: an anthology of cases of Milner's own making. This reprise of his "apology" serves to highlight the gap between the Introduction and the views of law implied by the choice to emphasize case law in the main body of the book.

---

285 *Ibid* at xxx.

286 *Ibid* at xxx–xxxi.

Such a tension appears in another added passage near the beginning of the new section, where Milner writes that a "large part of human affairs is successfully conducted by private arrangements that do not involve the State in any immediate way. It is with this area of private arrangement that this book is concerned." The very next paragraph, however, begins: "The circumstances under which the State can be and should be invoked are at the heart of contract law."[287] This juxtaposition invites the question: is "this book" concerned with non-state "private arrangements," or with the "circumstances under which the State can and should be invoked"? The former emphasizes private normativity and the functional phenomenon of contracting behaviour; the latter, state normativity and the legalistic treatment of that activity (primarily, adjudicative responses to relationship breakdown).

How to make sense of this apparent tension? One could read it away by loosening the rigours of linguistic interpretation. The book, in other words, *is* "concerned" with the underlying problem of private arrangements, but treats that problem using the best available means, which happen to be judicial decisions. On this interpretation, there is no tension in underlying philosophy, just an acknowledgment of the limited availability of subject matter to study other legal processes (legislation, administration, private arrangement) effectively. This is certainly a plausible position, but if this is the case, why then is there no specific explanation? There is no attempt to account for the reason case law is emphasized, other than to affirm the importance of adjudication for the first-year law student. This suggests, therefore, that the retention of case law is a conscious choice – the "apology is not so abject."

Summary of *Milner*

The *Milner* introduction reveals a range of related but at times apparently contradictory messages. The emphasis on multiple legal processes coincides with the idea that law is above all a purposive endeavour, a study of "means and ends," as Fuller has written elsewhere. By implication, the end goal of legal education is to produce lawyers, or "social architects," who are able to accomplish various client or social ends by using the means most appropriate to the circumstances.[288] A realist

287 *Ibid.*

288 Lon L Fuller, "American Legal Philosophy at Mid-Century", Book Review of *Jurisprudence, Men and Ideas of the Law* by Edwin W Patterson, (1954) 6 J Legal Ed 457 at 477, 478; Lon L Fuller, "Means and Ends" in Kenneth I Winston, ed, *The Principles of Social Order: Selected Essays of Lon L Fuller*, rev ed (Oxford; Portland, OR: Hart, 2001)

view of law as functional, a legal process embrace of multiple forms of social ordering, and an integrative view of theory and practice all appear in the *Milner* introduction. In these ways, it resembles the *Swan* casebook. Swan, too, acknowledges the influence of both Fuller and the legal process school, although Swan never met Fuller.[289]

At the same time, Milner appears to be conflicted about legal processes, as evidenced by his not-so-abject apology and his decision to rely on the case method so heavily. His minimalist approach to casebook writing, which takes for granted the predominance of cases, might suggest a subconscious preference for adjudication, notwithstanding the propositional claims to the contrary. This tension forecasts three related phenomena about the teaching of Contracts in Canada. First is the immediate successor to *Milner*, Waddams's editorship and eventual departure to produce his own casebook. As the next section will show, Waddams displays no similar ambivalence about the importance of adjudication. For Waddams, the importance of case law is accepted without caveat or qualification, and he even takes occasion in his textbook to argue for the importance of its centrality. What might have become a broader flourishing of Fullerian legal process ideas at the University of Toronto apparently expired with Milner's untimely death. In its place grew a sophisticated and complex exposition of contract law that, however much it continued the American legal realist tradition, cemented the dominance of the adjudicative process in Canadian common law Contracts teaching materials.

Second, the tendency to consider adjudication as the predominant mode in Contracts teaching is a more general one. It figures prominently in the best-selling casebook, *Ben-Ishai & Percy*, which contains its own version of a not-so-abject apology. This tendency to naturalize the case method is, moreover, shared by the vast majority of Canadian common law Contracts teachers. So, although American legal realism figures prominently

---

61. On "social architects," see e.g. Lon L Fuller, "The Lawyer as Architect of Social Structures" in Kenneth I Winston, ed, *The Principles of Social Order: Selected Essays of Lon L Fuller*, rev ed (Oxford; Portland, OR: Hart, 2001) 285; John MA DiPippa, "Lon Fuller, The Model Code, and the Model Rules" (1996) 37 S Tex L Rev 303; Fuller, *Morality of Law*, *supra* note 82 at 241.

289 See *Swan* 1st ed, *supra* note 208 at vii; Angela Swan, email correspondence with author, 19 October 2016 ("Another very important influence on my thinking was the "Legal Process" materials of Hart [& Sacks] ... They provided me with a vehicle for fitting my views on the substantive law, initially of Conflicts and then Contracts, into a functioning legal structure ... I never met Fuller ... I had hoped to meet him when he came to Ottawa once but family responsibilities prevented that and he died not long after").

in the other two books and in the attitudes of most Contracts teachers generally (as we will see in Chapter 5), challenges to adjudication remain more or less isolated in *Swan* and in the first two editions of *Milner*.

Third, the difference between one's propositional claims about law and the ideas of law communicated by higher-order choices about substance, structure, or method is a persistent theme of common law Contracts teaching in Canada. We see it, too, in *Waddams* and *Ben-Ishai & Percy*, and, indeed, it is the major observation made about Contracts teachers' attitudes in Chapters 4 and 5. Propositional, or aspirational, statements about law and law teaching seemed destined to lie in tension with actual practices.

Subsequent Editions of *Milner* and the Rise of *Waddams*

Major changes to *Milner* came in the third edition (1977), when Waddams's imprint became the most obvious. Significant changes included the functionalist reorganization of materials around the concept of a bargain, with a greater emphasis on reliance; a new thematic chapter on the protection of weaker parties; and revisions to reflect a "rapid and fundamental change" in the law of contracts. The third edition adds "a considerable amount of statutory material on consumer protection" and a "substantial number of questions and problems."[290]

These changes seem to take *Milner* further in the direction of Milner's Introduction and *Swan*. At the same time, however, the third edition begins to depart from those authors' Fuller-inspired writings – *Milner* remains very much in the "traditional" mould.[291] Despite the addition of new questions and problems, reviewers of the third edition considered the additions to fall short of higher standards in other casebooks. And while the reorganization of materials was generally praised, it was not perceived to be as radical as Reiter and Swan's *Studies in Contract Law*.[292] Fridman, who had so energetically attacked the "hyper-critical" and "revolutionary" approach of Reiter and Swan, is comparatively sanguine about the third edition of *Milner*. He chastises the authors for the lack of a pan-Canadian focus, but saves his most scathing critique for the choice to present remedies first. He gets in his jab ("[c]onceptually speaking, this is almost to adopt the heresy of Holmes, i.e. that a person

290 *Milner* 3d ed, *supra* note 207 at vii.

291 Kyer, Book Review of *Milner* 3d ed and *Swan* 1st ed, *supra* note 279 at 153.

292 See e.g. RS Nozick, Book Review of *Milner* 3d ed, (1978) 16 Alta L Rev 544 at 545–6; GHL Fridman, Book Review of *Milner* 3d ed, (1977) UWO L Rev 256 at 257 [Fridman, Review of *Milner* 3d ed].

'buying' a promise is really only purchasing potential damages"), but he is briefer in his critique and somewhat more conciliatory, acknowledging the academic liberty of each instructor. Combined, this suggests that even to a formalist, promise-centric doctrinalist such as Fridman, Waddams's editorial choices were perceived as a rather lesser threat than were Reiter and Swan's ideas.[293]

Although the fourth and final edition (1985) of *Milner* does not contain major substantive changes, it appears to be more distinctly the work of Waddams. The book looks different: the publisher has changed to Emond Montgomery (*Swan* also moved to Emond Montgomery in 1985, staying there for two editions). The Milner Introduction is now billed as "*Professor Milner's* Introduction to the First Edition," implying a distancing. And in the very short Preface, Waddams writes: "Cross-references to my textbook on the law of contracts have been added."[294] These short words provide a major clue as to the philosophy underlying Waddams's editorship.

The textbook to which Waddams is referring is *The Law of Contracts*, published in 1977 (the year of the third edition of *Milner*) by the Canada Law Book Company.[295] It was an innovation in Canada, introducing a legal realist approach to treatise writing that emphasized an appreciation for the underlying principles animating contract law decisions, based on an analysis of what judges do, not (only) what they say. *The Law of Contracts* was received as a "departure from the traditional approach" of the two pre-existing Anglo-Canadian treatises (Fridman's 1976 *The Law of Contract in Canada* and JE Côté's 1974 *An Introduction to the Law of Contract*). Soberman describes Waddams as a present-day Corbin, his book signalling the arrival of "substantial critical analysis" on the Canadian scene. Beale, another reviewer, comments on Waddams's concern for functionalism and policy.[296]

These observations of the realist character of the text are borne out by its Preface, written in August 1977, around the time of the Preface

293 See Fridman, Review of *Milner* 3d ed, *supra* note 292 at 256–7; Fridman, *Law of Contract in Canada*, *supra* note 226 at v, 1.

294 *Milner* 4th ed, *supra* note 207 at vii [emphasis added].

295 Waddams text 1st ed, *supra* note 211.

296 DA Soberman, Book Review of Waddams text 1st ed, (1979) 17 UWO L Rev 314 at 314–17; Hugh Beale, Book Review of Waddams text 1st ed, (1980) 15 J Soc't Pub Tchrs L ns 139 at 139–40. But see PFP Higgins, Book Review of Waddams text 1st ed, (1979) 42 Mod L Rev 239 at 239 ("The lay-out of the book appears to follow the orthodox lay-out of the established books on the subject, although somewhat different terminology is used"). See generally Fridman, *Law of Contract in Canada*, *supra* note 226; JE Côté, *An Introduction to the Law of Contract* (Edmonton: Juriliber, 1974).

to the third edition of *Milner*. It continues to be reproduced in the student edition of the textbook to this day. In it, Waddams communicates three essential features of his philosophy. First is the "aim" of the book, which is to look "beyond surface rules of contract law to the conflicting principles that lie beneath." Second is the idea that contract law is in a state of flux between rigidity and flexibility, the latter in ascendance at the time of writing. And third, Waddams expresses reverence for the role of adjudication in achieving "rational decision making," an end that is bolstered by the recognition of underlying principles:

> I do not mean at all to say that legal reasoning is of no consequence, or that cases can be determined by some intuitive apprehension of "justice" not requiring communicable reasons. So long as we value rationality in decision making we shall continue to require that like cases should be decided alike and that there should be a rational distinction between cases that are decided differently. *I do not believe that these ends can be otherwise realized than by an impartial tribunal giving reasons subject to appeal.* But rational decision making is strengthened, not weakened, by open recognition of conflicting values. It is better to recognize competing values, even if that recognition appears to involve a difficult and uncertain balance, than to pursue certainty by adopting a rule that suppresses important countervailing principles. Such pursuit is self-defeating, for important values are rarely permanently suppressed. The rule that is supposed to achieve clarity and certainty becomes riddled with exceptions, judicial and statutory, devised to avoid injustice, and leads in the end to the loss of the very certainty that was supposed to be its chief merit.[297]

In this passage we observe the seeds of a tension analogous to that in *Milner*. On the one hand, there is the commitment to the realist tradition of identifying the underlying reasons for legal phenomena. "Values" either underlie the rules or, to the extent that they appear incompatible, spring up like weeds to crack and transform them. Waddams's kinship with Swan is also apparent here – the *Swan* editors referred to the centrality of values in the Introduction to every edition of their casebook.[298] On the other hand, in his treatment of "rational decision

---

297 SM Waddams, Preface to the First Edition, reproduced in SM Waddams, *The Law of Contracts*, 6th student ed (Toronto: Canada Law Book, 2010) at vii–viii [Waddams, Preface to 1st ed text] [emphasis added].

298 See e.g. *Swan* 1st ed, *supra* note 208 at xxvii; *Swan* 2d ed, *supra* note 208 at l, li; *Swan* 3d ed, *supra* note 208 at xxxii, xxiii; *Swan* 4th ed, *supra* note 208 at xxvii, xxviii, xxx; *Swan* 5th ed, *supra* note 208 at xx, xxix; *Swan* 6th ed, *supra* note 208 at xxxii, *Swan* 7th ed, *supra* note 208 at xxiv, xxxvi; *Swan* 8th ed, *supra* note 208 at xxx, xliii, *Swan*

making," Waddams reveals other prior commitments, some of which might not be congruent with those of Fuller, Milner, or Swan. Whereas Waddams takes care to *argue for* the importance of values (their recognition strengthens rational decision making and might reduce uncertainty by exposing the source of haphazard exceptions), he merely *asserts* the importance of rational decision making. At least three fundamental assumptions underlie this approach.

First, it assumes that law is legitimized by a particular type of thinking: the articulation of "rational" grounds for drawing relevant distinctions. Second, by referring without explanation to some undefined collectivity – "[s]o long as *we* value rationality in decision making" – Waddams implies that this definition of legal reasoning is the product of a professional consensus so strong it does not need elaboration or justification. Finally, Waddams places adjudication at the centre of law and legal reasoning. Absent from Waddams's Preface to his textbook is any Milner- or Fuller-like reference to multiple forms of social ordering or diverse legal processes. Instead the contrary assumption about the importance, indeed exclusivity, of adjudication appears: "I do not believe that these ends can be *otherwise* realized than by an impartial tribunal giving reasons subject to appeal." The Preface does not preclude there being valuable skills other than "rational decision making" that might be better encouraged through different legal processes, but the absence of any such discussion, coupled with the force of argument and the implied sense of consensus, produces the distinct impression that "impartial tribunal[s] giving reasons" are the most important feature of the legal system.[299]

Therefore, we observe in the Preface to the first edition of Waddams's textbook another dual message. The surface message is the importance of underlying values and the need to look at function, not form. As Fuller & Perdue did in the case of reliance, Waddams examines what judges actually do, and uses this comparative study to argue both a descriptive and prescriptive point about a principle. This is most evident in the chapter on unconscionability, which draws heavily from Waddams's seminal realist article on the subject.[300] This mode of analysis

---

9th ed, *supra* note 208 at §§ 1.56, 1.59, 1.6. In his textbook, Waddams thanks Swan, as well as Warren Mueller and Peter Hogg, for "helpful suggestions" on the treatise (Waddams text 1st ed, *supra* note 211 at viii).

299 *Cf* Lon L Fuller, "The Forms and Limits of Adjudication" (1978) 92 Harv L Rev 353 at 374ff (discussing the multiple forms of adjudication), 366 (describing adjudication as "a device which gives formal and institutional expression to the influence of reasoned argument in human affairs, ... [and] assumes a burden of rationality not borne by any other form of social ordering").

300 SM Waddams, "Unconscionability in Contracts" (1976) 39 Mod L Rev 1 at 1 ("the law of contract, when examined for what the judges do, as well as for what they

likewise gives rise to concerns about policy: Waddams's prefatory comments – "I have attempted to assess the changes that have occurred and to analyze the reasons for them with a view to suggesting what further changes seem desirable" – are reminiscent of the common attitude that Reiter and Swan attribute to contributors (including Waddams) to the *Studies in Contract Law* collection.[301] At the same time, there lurks a deeper assertion about the nature of law: there is a distinctive legal reasoning, legitimate by virtue of a rationality that consists in the ability to draw "rational distinction[s] between cases that are decided differently." Judicial decisions are not only key illustrations of such legal reasoning, but the end cannot be realized "otherwise." Implicitly, Waddams also suggests that the mastery of this distinctive type of rationality is a precondition to being part of an undefined legal community.

A couple of paragraphs in a Preface to a treatise should not, however, serve as fodder for too vast an inference. Other authors, including Swan and Milner, make reference to the type of legal reasoning to which Waddams refers, and so it would be unfair to give the impression that Waddams is alone in its articulation.[302] Also, to reduce Waddams's philosophy to a mere focus on legal rationality would misrepresent his contributions to a nuanced understanding of the common law tradition.[303] However, if the goal is to understand the messages communicated to first-year students, then what is stated or not stated in the rare moments

---

say, shows that relief from contractual obligations is in fact widely and frequently given on the ground of unfairness, and that general recognition of this ground of relief is an essential step in the development of the law"). *Cf* Fuller & Perdue, "Reliance Interest 2", *supra* note 109 at 373 ("We have attempted to bring together for comparative study a series of situations in which judicial intervention has been (or in our opinion, should be) limited to a protection of what we have called the reliance interest"), 418 ("the contractual reliance interest receives a much wider (though often covert) recognition in the decisions than it does in the textbooks").

301 Waddams, Preface to 1st ed text, *supra* note 297 at viii. *Cf* Reiter & Swan, *supra* note 219 at 2 ("the law attempts to support particular principles and to promote particular policies, and this purposive aspect of the law is both desirable and inevitable").

302 See e.g. *Swan* 9th ed, *supra* note 208 at §1.62 ("The law must operate in a way that permits decisions to be made on clearly articulated and appropriate bases. Judicial decisions have to be rationally defended. The legal process must be carried out in a way that permits such a defense"); *Milner* 2d ed, *supra* note 207 at xxii ("Are the reasons consistent with other judgments you have read? Do you agree with the judge's interpretation of earlier decisions or statutes? Are his reasons consistent with themselves? Has the judge used words ambiguously? Has he disclosed an attitude inconsistent with the ideal detachment of a judge?").

303 See e.g. SM Waddams, *Principle and Policy in Contract Law: Competing or Complementary Concepts?* (Cambridge: Cambridge University Press, 2011) at 227–8; Waddams, *Dimensions*, *supra* note 252.

when the author speaks directly to them ought to be taken seriously. It is in these moments, as in Prefaces, that an author attempts to bring to consciousness (or indeed, to argue for) his or her commitments about law.

Waddams as a general rule is quite sparing in his introductory or prefatory comments in the casebooks he has edited – the three *Milner* versions contained short, half- or quarter-page Prefaces, a practice continued in all editions of *Waddams*. None of the *Waddams* editions contains a significant introductory passage in the vein of *Swan* or *Milner*. Thus, there are few occasions where Waddams speaks directly to students – which is why the Preface to the first edition of his textbook is such a helpful aid. Waddams did, however, write an entire book directed to beginning law students. Examining the messages communicated by that book can serve to reinforce some of the observations made above.[304]

The Editor's Underlying Philosophy: Introduction to the Study of Law

Waddams's *Introduction to the Study of Law* came out in 1979, two years after his treatise and the third edition of *Milner*.[305] It was the first Canadian book addressed to intending law students, and received some early favourable reviews for its "economy and wit," its "style and manner," and for "adequately circumnavigat[ing] the world of what law is, who lawyers are, how they think, and why law teachers behave as they do." These short reviews emphasized Waddams's ability to captivate his readers, the book's "currency and pertinence," and his provision of a "concise and complete picture of how Canada's legal system operates."[306]

In a much longer and more critical review in the *University of Toronto Law Journal*, Roderick A Macdonald examines some of the implicit messages communicated by Waddams's book. Macdonald critiques Waddams for communicating a positivist, adjudication-centric, deterministic,

304 The potential influence of such introductory texts should not be underestimated. For example, HLA Hart's *The Concept of Law*, "one of the most influential works in modern legal philosophy," is "based on introductory lectures in jurisprudence" given to law students at the University of Oxford (Leslie Green, "Introduction" in HLA Hart, *The Concept of Law*, 3d ed (Oxford: Oxford University Press, 2012) xv at xv; Leslie Green, "Preface to the Third Edition" in Hart, *ibid* xi at xi.

305 SM Waddams, *Introduction to the Study of Law* (Toronto: Carswell, 1979).

306 Alan Pratt, Book Review of *Introduction to the Study of Law* by SM Waddams, (1979) 37 U Toronto Fac L Rev 270 at 270; Ken Norman, Book Review of *Introduction to the Study of Law* by SM Waddams, (1980) 45 Sask L Rev 171 at 172–3; Roger Bilodeau, Book Review of *Introduction to the Study of Law*, 3d ed by SM Waddams, (1988) 67 Can Bar Rev 394 at 394.

and insular vision of law. Although Macdonald's analysis at times provides a caricatured impression of the book (and is decidedly hostile in tone), his efforts to render explicit the philosophy of law communicated to incoming students are useful for understanding the range of possible messages in the casebook, also intended for first-year students.

Macdonald's review contains two parts. First, he examines the text to discern the attitudes about law, legal education, and the role of the lawyer that are "implicit" in the materials. The "fundamental orientation" of the book, he writes, conveys the idea "that law and justice are separate concerns, that justice is relative and often not capable of rational discovery, and that equity, fairness, and justice militate against a law which is stable, certain, and predictable ... Waddams appears to suggest that it is not only desirable, but also possible, for judges simply to apply the law, ... justifying their judgments by an appeal to a pre-existing law which can be objectively determined." Critiques of the remainder of the text include the point that Waddams adopts a "traditional view of law, legal problems, and the lawyer's role," that he fails to elucidate or justify his "epistemological and semantic assumptions," and that he unduly emphasizes the adjudicative mode for dispute settlement.[307]

In the second part of his review, Macdonald reports on the "explicit and implicit views picked up by students" on the basis of his own "canvass [of] the reactions of those who have read it as a preparation for law school." In this analysis, Macdonald is even more emphatic. He describes "a series of four propositions about law, complemented by several corollaries":

1 All law happens in courts: a/ the adversarial, adjudicative processes of the common law are the best, if not the only way for a legal system to operate; b/ all other societal decision-making agencies, including legislatures, perform a minor role in the Canadian legal system; c/ hence, the lawyer's principal preoccupation is with reading and analysing cases and in preparing for court.
2 Law can be certain, objective and authoritative: a/ it is a one-way projection of authority from official state organs; b/ the concept of precedent and the principles of statutory interpretation always give one right answer to any question; c/ the "law in books" is a lawyer's main concern.
3 Law is a distinct discipline with its own internal logic: a/ concerns such as justice, morality, economic efficiency, and social practice are

307 RA Macdonald, Book Review of *Introduction to the Study of Law* by SM Waddams, (1981) 31 UTLJ 436 [Macdonald, Review of Waddams] at 437–43.

only marginally related to the business of determining the law; b/ law can be compartmentalized, and legal practice is largely a matter of finding the correct rule to apply; c/ legal training should be restricted to professional lawyers, who will uphold its conservative values.
4 There is little, even today, that can be called an indigenous Canadian law; a/ most law in Canada is pure English common law; b/ American law and developments are of little significance; c/ understanding Canadian legislation and the peculiarities of Canadian society is not of great importance for lawyers.[308]

Having stated these views in brief compass, Macdonald goes on to find passages from the primer that "generate these impressions" on behalf of the reader. What follows are five and a half pages of textual analysis coupled with further articulations of these themes.[309]

Macdonald's critique portrays a great distance between the view of law communicated by the Waddams primer and the Fullerian view of law as process, and lawyer as social architect. When Macdonald writes, for example, that "law is seen to be about resolving disputes and therefore none of its planning or facilitating functions are emphasized" and that the "student is likely to develop an unbalanced appreciation of the law and the lawyer's role," he is almost perfectly describing values opposite to those identified by Milner or Fuller in their discussions of the need to teach different legal processes equally.[310]

That Macdonald would have had Fuller in mind is likely, given that he completed his master's thesis, a review of Fuller's complete works, under Swan's supervision in 1975. So Macdonald was perhaps keen to see in a book that focused on cases, and that espoused a traditional view of legal reasoning, a very partial and "troubling" image of law.[311] However, although the review might be particularly astringent, his analysis is well supported by textual references. No doubt, some, if not all, of the messages that Macdonald identifies represent a reasonable (if contestable) interpretation. This being the case, two observations arise.

First, his review might signal an increasing philosophical distance between Fullerian casebook editors such as Swan and Milner, on the one hand, and Waddams, on the other. Although Waddams diligently remounted *Milner* three times, his eventual break to produce his own

308 *Ibid* at 444–5.
309 *Ibid* at 445–9.
310 *Ibid* at 447, 446.
311 *Ibid* at 444. See Roderick Alexander Macdonald, *Prolegomena to a Theory of Legal Relevance* (LLM Thesis, Faculty of Law, University of Toronto, 1975) [unpublished].

casebook might have flowed from such a philosophical departure. One might also suspect that any intellectual kinship with Swan (the supposed shared "fundamental premise" from *Studies in Contract Law*) was either not as robust as Reiter and Swan originally claimed, or had declined over time.

At the same time, it is also apparent that many of the messages about law identified by Macdonald patently contradict Waddams's own stated views. For example, the idea that law can be "certain, objective and authoritative" and that the "law in books" is a lawyer's main concern seem to run precisely counter to Waddams's views that the underlying values of doctrine need to examined, that "the foundations of even the most firmly established rules are being undermined," and that it is what judges *do*, in addition to what they say, that matters.[312] The idea that Macdonald ascribes to the primer that "justice, morality, economic efficiency, and social practice are only marginally related to the business of determining the law" seem to expressly contradict the instrumental and purposive philosophy of law ascribed to Waddams by Reiter and Swan and to Waddams's own work in his seminal article on unconscionability and in *Principle and Policy in Contract Law*.[313]

The Macdonald critique therefore brings to light the possibility that the messages communicated by the substance of a text might differ from the author's own beliefs, attitudes, or commitments about law. Indeed, Macdonald signals this very point when he writes, "It is nowhere suggested that the author himself would subscribe to any of these views implicit in his manual. He might, in fact, reject them all. Nevertheless, they are all perspectives that intending law students who read the book gained from it. They are all perspectives which, one suspects, any reader of *Introduction to the Study of Law* would develop."[314] This insight is relevant at this juncture for two reasons. First, it recommends caution when drawing on exogenous evidence (such as other writings or biographical details) to infer the messages conveyed by a given text. Although such materials can help one understand an author's intellectual development and commitments about law and legal education, one should not blindly assume a one-to-one correspondence between these and the messages conveyed by a particular casebook. The need for such caution is reinforced when one recalls that a casebook, as an artefact, can be emphasized, presented, or framed in various ways by

312 Waddams, Preface to 1st ed text, *supra* note 297 at viii; Waddams, "Unconscionability in Contracts", *supra* note 300 at 1.

313 Macdonald, Review of Waddams, *supra* note 307 at 445.

314 *Ibid* at 450.

different teachers. One must look not only at the casebooks themselves, but also at how they are used.[315]

Second, the possibility of distance between an author's commitments and those communicated by his or her work can be understood as a manifestation of a tension that arises more ubiquitously in legal education. This is the tension between one's stated commitments about law, on the one hand, and the ideas about law communicated implicitly through teaching, on the other. As we will see in Chapters 4 and 5, these commitments often diverge. What law professors say they believe about law (and legal education) is often more diverse and wide-ranging than the set of messages communicated by their teaching, which tends to coalesce around a more monolithic understanding of legal reasoning and legal practice.

Waddams

The *Waddams* casebook is – as has already been mentioned, but bears repeating – predominantly free of explicit messages about legal education. There is no substantive Introduction, as there is in the Waddams textbook on contract law, or in the *Swan* casebook, or indeed – as will be discussed – in the third major Canadian common law Contracts casebook, *Ben-Ishai & Percy*. In fact, the minimalist Preface seems to disclaim any idiosyncrasy: the casebook is presented as a seemingly neutral "collection of materials suitable for the basic course in the subject" to be adaptable to individual instructors' purposes. Although the casebook makes one potentially controversial editorial decision – it places remedies at the beginning of the book – even here the editors disclaim any intention to prescribe: "We do not expect that all users of the book will proceed through it sequentially, and we have designed it to be suitable for dealing with the material in several different orders. Some users will wish to start with contract formation. Others will wish to start with remedies. Others might prefer to start with the theoretical perspectives. We hope that all will find the book equally suitable for their purposes."[316] Thus the editors offer little explicit theoretical or perspectival guidance

315 *Cf.* Fernandez & Dubber, *Law Books in Action*, *supra* note 85.

316 *Waddams* 1st ed, *supra* note 209 at iii. This Preface is largely unchanged in subsequent editions. The third edition adds a short paragraph on the "growing importance of the law of restitution" (*supra* note 209 at iii), the fourth edition acknowledges the contributions of Michael Trebilcock (who ceased to be an editor after the third edition) (*supra* note 209 at iii), and the sixth edition acknowledges the contributions of Mary Anne Waldron (who ceased to be an editor after the fifth edition) (*supra* note 209 at iii).

to the teacher. Nor is Waddams's own purposive approach to contract law (presumably still alive, as he continues to reproduce the Preface to the first edition of his textbook in all successive editions) given an airing. This editorial choice suggests two features of *Waddams*. First, the messages about law and what it means to be a lawyer are largely implicit, and might require an exegesis analogous to the one Macdonald conducted of the implicit messages of *Introduction to the Study of Law*. Second, this choice to let the materials speak for themselves *itself* might communicate a message about law and legal reasoning.

I discuss these implicit messages in the second part of this chapter, which consists of a closer reading of the remedies chapter of each of the casebooks. However, a brief word on Chapter 1 of *Waddams* is relevant here. Chapter 1 is an innovation with the move from *Milner*. It contains a series of theoretical pieces on the rationale, as stated in the Preface, that "[t]here has been a lively interest, during the past ten years, in the theory of contract law."[317] The chapter reproduces scholarly articles without any interspersed commentary; the first edition features philosophical, promise-based, economic, critical, feminist, and socio-legal perspectives, and the selection is modified and added to in the third, fourth, fifth, and sixth editions, with an increasing diversity of perspectives. This format reveals several salient features. First, there is the strong presence of American legal scholars representing American canonical schools of thought; in the sixth edition, for example, seven out of the eleven authors excerpted spent most of their careers at American law schools. Second, the theories are presented neutrally, as an eclectic offering of ideas without evaluative commentary by the editors. And third, this strategy physically separates these theories from the remainder of the book. As I discuss further below, these theories seem not to be operationalized into the vision of substance and legal reasoning that appears in the remedies chapter. Accordingly, the first chapter of *Waddams* illustrates the tendency to separate the eclectic range of ideas in American legal thought from the substantive presentation of contract doctrine and legal reasoning in the remainder of the book. These ideas, privileged in one sense by being placed first, can also be hived off as "purely" theoretical and dispensed with if desired.[318]

In summary, there is an apparent tension in the philosophy underlying *Waddams*. On the one hand, we have ample evidence in Waddams's

317 *Waddams* 1st ed, *supra* note 209 at iii.

318 As it turns out, a number of instructors do not assign this chapter at all. See e.g. [048], Interview, lines 393–413; [025], Interview, lines 443–5. See also *infra* note 390.

contract treatise, his contributions to the Reiter and Swan collection, and his early writings on unconscionability that he adopts a purposive and functional approach to the study of law, and considers it essential to understanding the values underlying judicial reasons for decision. On the other hand, the implicit messages in *An Introduction to the Study of Law* and his textbook Preface suggest a view that privileges adjudication, that takes judicial reasoning seriously, and that considers legal reasoning to consist primarily of discerning relevant differences in pursuit of rationality – for which judicial decisions are the best resource.

The big-picture editorial choices in *Waddams* reinforce this tension. On the one hand, the failure to replace the *Milner* Introduction with a new substantive introductory text might suggest a conscious distancing from Milner's Fullerian views. The absence of commentary also might suggest a prioritization of the adjudicative method – presenting cases as the default primary source of law, "speaking for themselves." On the other hand, the inclusion of American realist and critical schools of thought in the introductory chapter, the functional organization in certain chapters (for example, Protection of Weaker Parties, Public Policy), the increased presence of restitution, the attempt (though perhaps not fully realized) to add in questions and commentary, the placement of remedies at the beginning of the book, the explicit referencing throughout the text to Waddams's textbook – might all be said to convey a more functional, purposive, or realist image of law.

As I show in the second part of this chapter, the impression is a lot less ambiguous when one considers the actual treatment of substance. In the chapter on remedies, the realist and critical inclinations are largely not translated into the presentation of substantive law. The stated philosophy from the Preface to the textbook, emphasizing rationality and judicial reasons, appears very much to motivate the treatment of substance, and structures the dominant image of legal reasoning and legal practice. Before proceeding to that discussion, however, an exploration of the explicit messages of the most widely assigned Canadian common law Contracts casebook, *Ben-Ishai & Percy*, is in order.

Ben-Ishai & Percy: Underlying Messages about Law and Legal Education

On its face, *Ben-Ishai & Percy* differs from *Swan* and *Waddams* in at least two ways. It is more self-consciously a collaboration – a collection of chapters by various contributors throughout the years. The book is also more national in character. Its genesis, as a collaborative project begun in the mid-1970s through the Canadian Association of Law Teachers, reflects these features.[319]

Accordingly, *Ben-Ishai & Percy* should be understood differently than *Swan* or *Waddams* where, despite acknowledgment of collaboration, one lead voice (Swan) or one lead editor (Waddams) clearly predominates. The editors' goal in *Ben-Ishai & Percy* consistently has been to "expose students to slightly different approaches to contracts problems," and to provide some "degree of uniformity to the various sections of the book without affecting the flavour of each individual contribution." Indeed, appearing before the Preface in every edition is a list of the contributors – with their institutional affiliation – identified with each chapter.[320] A quick look at the list communicates that each chapter is the individual work of one subeditor, representing regions across the country. This contrasts with *Swan*, with fewer editors all speaking with one voice, and with *Waddams*, where the editorship of different chapters is not identified and whose predecessor, *Milner*, had been criticized for its Ontario-centrism.[321]

The collaborative nature of the casebook, however, does not imply a lack of personal touch by the lead editors. In fact, in contrast with *Waddams*, and more reminiscent of *Milner* and *Swan*, *Ben-Ishai & Percy* contains a lengthy introductory chapter that canvasses a wide set of views about contract law and law in general, heavily influenced by American legal realism and its heirs. This Introduction suggests that the teaching of first-year Contracts is fertile ground in which to cultivate a nuanced and critical understanding of law and an eclectic vision of legal reasoning and legal practice. At the same time, however, other aspects of the Introduction reveal a complicated relationship with this critical view. As with *Milner*, lurking behind the realist and critical presentation are clues that the traditional approach predominates.

The Boyle Introduction

The introductory comments in *Ben-Ishai & Percy* have been carefully tended, permitting growth and evolution over the years. A major leap forward occurred in the sixth edition, when the introductory comments

319 See *Ben-Ishai & Percy* 10th ed, *supra* note 210 at v.

320 *Ibid* at iii. The first edition lists fifteen different chapter editors from eight Canadian law schools and one Canadian Department of Law (*Boyle & Percy* 1st ed, *supra* note 210 at iii); the tenth edition lists nine different chapter editors from six different Canadian law schools. The University of Toronto, where both Swan's and Waddams's academic careers were headquartered, is not represented in any of the nine editions.

321 *Waddams* 6th ed, *supra* note 209 at iii (Preface signed by "The Editors"). See Fridman, Review of *Milner* 3d ed, *supra* note 292 at 256–7; Nozick, *supra* note 292 at 546.

received billing as a full chapter (Chapter 1) and their authorship was attributed solely to Christine Boyle. In the eighth edition, Stephanie Ben-Ishai and David Percy took over the chapter. Here, the discussion begins with an analysis of Boyle's comments, focusing on the last edition (the seventh) in which Boyle participated, and proceeds with amendments made by Ben-Ishai and Percy.[322]

Chapter 1 begins with a kind of see-saw between critical and traditional justifications for the study of contract law. The very first sentence is a quotation from Macneil, that memorable recast that the law of contracts is "an affirmation of the human will to affect the future" through the projection of exchange.[323] Immediately thereafter, a host of traditional rationales for studying contract law follows. Substantive law is billed as relevant in itself and as a "stepping" stone to upper-year courses. The casebook is said to "equip" students to reflect on values, starting with freedom of contract. Skills figure predominately: the course will teach them the "analysis and use of case law and, to a lesser extent, legislation," with emphasis on applying rules and principles to hypothetical fact situations and questions that prompt reflection on law reform.[324]

But quickly, students are told that this is not all that is important: "The law should not be studied in a philosophical vacuum, without consideration of its function in society and without discussion of the value judgments inherent in any judicial discussion or legislative rule ... [T]he law ... is not made up of a static body of rules, simply awaiting discovery by the conscientious student."[325] What follows is a series of sections, each of which introduces a different theoretical or critical perspective, largely drawn from the American canonical schools.

First, Boyle debunks the "Classical Theory of Contract." After suggesting that ideas of laissez-faire economic liberalism still "retain great power," Boyle reproduces an excerpt from Grant Gilmore's *The Death of Contract* to disrupt the idea of a stable body of doctrine. Students are encouraged to look for classicism and romanticism in the judgments

---

322 See *Boyle & Percy* 6th ed, *supra* note 210 at v–vi. In the sixth edition, in addition to Chapter 1, the editors also added Chapter 11, which reflects David Percy's reflections on the interrelation of contract with tort and fiduciary law and the evolution of various doctrines.

323 *Boyle & Percy* 7th ed, *supra* note 210 at 1. All editions, up to the present (10th ed, *supra* note 210 at 1), commit the typographical error of writing "protecting exchange," instead of "projecting exchange," Macneil's actual formulation (Macneil, *New Social Contract*, *supra* note 81 at 4).

324 *Boyle & Percy* 7th ed, *supra* note 210 at 1.

325 *Ibid.*

they will read and are told that "law is a social construct and so ... must change and adapt over time." The advent of the Internet serves as example.[326]

The next section, "The Intersection of 'Private' and 'Public Law,'" makes the realist point that "the free market is a form of government regulation in itself," citing both law and economics scholar Michael Trebilcock and critical scholar Allan Hutchison to this effect. Boyle also underscores how "democratic decisions about how to promote such things as equality, a healthy environment, safe and fair working and housing conditions, and the public welfare in general" operate to constrain freedom of contract.[327]

"Freedom of Contract" is the title of the third section, which asks the student to reflect on his or her own experience to assess "the degree to which freedom of contract is a reality." Boyle references Ayres's work on gender and race discrimination in car sales, and provides a statutory example prohibiting the sale of body parts to demonstrate "legal" limits on freedom of contract. She discusses the doctrine of good faith to show how the common law "has become more activist in protecting vulnerable people." The section concludes with the suggestion from the critical legal studies scholar Jay Feinman that modern contract law is "neoclassical" in that it "attempts to balance the individualist ideals of classical contract with communal standards of responsibility to others."[328]

The following section, "What Promises Are Enforceable," encourages the student to think critically – one could say realistically – about the rule requiring consideration: "You will start to develop your own ideas soon about which obligations are (and should be) legally enforceable ... In doing this it will be necessary to look behind the words of the judges who decide cases." The fifth section, on remedies, provides a mini-introduction to the measure of remedies, making the additional point, with reference to Stuart Macaulay, that law might not be a significant mechanism for dispute settlement.[329]

The next section, "Theories of Contracts," provides a brief introduction to diverse theories of contract law, including law and economics and

---

326 *Ibid* at 2.

327 *Ibid* at 3–4.

328 *Ibid* at 4–5, citing Ian Ayres, "Fair Driving: Gender and Race Discrimination in Retail Car Negotiations" (1991) 104 Harv L Rev 817.

329 *Boyle & Percy* 7th ed, *supra* note 210 at 6, citing Stewart Macaulay, "Elegant Models, Empirical Pictures and the Complexities of Contract" (1977) 11 Law & Soc Rev 507 at 510). The Macaulay piece has been cited since the second edition (*supra* note 210 at lvi).

critical legal studies.[330] The brief reference to these theories is eclipsed, however, by Boyle's discussion of feminism, by far the most significant examination of that topic of the three commercial casebooks. The seventh edition of *Boyle & Percy* contains a full two pages of synthesized text surveying a wide range of feminist thought, a text that had been built upon gradually since the fourth edition.[331]

The next section, "Relational Contracts," not only introduces students to Macneil's concept of relational contracts ("that there is an unwarranted focus on one-time exchanges rather than ongoing relationships," in Boyle's paraphrased words); it also connects the concept to later chapters and considers several counterpoints. Boyle also cites studies that relate relational theory to feminism and references a "gay-friendly" approach.[332]

---

330 *Boyle & Percy* 7th ed, *supra* note 210 at 7–9, citing Richard A Posner, *Economic Analysis of Law*, 6th ed (Boston: Little, Brown, 2003), Michael J Trebilcock, *The Common Law of Restraint of Trade: A Legal and Economic Analysis* (Toronto: Carswell, 1986), Patrick Atiyah, "Executory Contracts, Expectation Damages, and the Economic Analysis of Contract" in Patrick Atiyah, *Essays on Contract*, *supra* note 126, 150), and Jay Feinman, "The Significance of Contract Theory" (1990) 58 U Cinn L Rev 1283 at 1287–8.

331 The first reference to feminism appeared in the fourth edition, where Boyle included just one short paragraph on Dalton's work on deconstruction (*supra* note 210 at lxv, referring to Dalton, "Essay in the Deconstruction of Contract Doctrine", *supra* note 128). In the fifth edition, two paragraphs were added, largely highlighting feminist critiques of preconception contracts, cohabitation agreements, pay equity, domestic work, and affirmative action (*supra* note 210 at lxxxii). The sixth edition adds a paragraph on feminist analyses that "have tended to be critical of contract law's emphasis on the notion of exchange" (*supra* note 210 at 6–7). The seventh edition adds three paragraphs, including long quotes totalling almost a page (*supra* note 210 at 8–9). By contrast, *Swan* has a short paragraph referring to Mary Joe Frug, "Re-Reading Contracts: A Feminist Analysis of a Contracts Casebook" (1985) 34 Am U L Rev 1065, and Barbara Sullivan, "It's All in the Contract: Rethinking Feminist Critiques of Contract" (2001) 18 Law in Context 112 (9th ed, *supra* note 208 at §2.253). *Waddams* reproduces an excerpt from Gillian K Hadfield, "An Expressive Theory of Contract: From Feminist Dilemmas to a Reconceptualization of Rational Choice in Contract Law" (1998) 146 U Pa L Rev 1235 (5th ed, *supra* note 209 at 16).

332 *Boyle & Percy* 7th ed, *supra* note 210 at 10–11, citing Macneil, *New Social Contract*, *supra* note 81, Ian R Macneil, "Relational Contract Theory: Challenges and Queries" (2000) 94 Nw UL Rev 877, Melvin A Eisenberg, "Why There Is No Law of Relational Contracts" (2000) 94 Nw UL Rev 805, Patricia J Williams, "Alchemical Notes: Reconstructing Ideals from Deconstructed Rights" (1987) 22 Harv CR-CL L Rev 401, Patricia A Tidwell & Peter Linzer, "The Flesh-Colored Band Aid – Contracts, Feminism, Dialogue, and Norms" (1991) 28 Hous L Rev 791, and Craig W Christensen, "Legal Ordering of Family Values: The Case of Gay and Lesbian Families" (1997) 18 Cardozo L Rev 1299.

In a section unique among the Canadian common law Contracts casebooks, a little over a page is dedicated to "First Nations and Treaties" (the section was developed between the fifth and seventh editions). Boyle argues that, although treaties differ from conventional contracts in that they "could be seen as resembling international agreements and as having a constitutional quality," and whereas treaties do not yet have "the status of contract, with the connotations of sanctity that implies," a study of contract law nevertheless can inform the student's understanding of the fiduciary obligation of the Crown and other issues of interpretation: "For instance, is there an obligation to negotiate in good faith? Is there ... a difference between treaties and modern commercial transactions between two parties of relative equal bargaining power? Is interpretation strict or generous, and how do the courts reconcile different perspectives? When can terms be implied?"[333]

The penultimate section highlights the importance of "transcending conceptual boundaries": "It may be helpful to ... avoid thinking of contracts, or any of your courses, in 'pigeonholes.'" Students are encouraged to rethink the contract/tort divide, reminded of the overlap between "the law relating to aboriginal rights, treaties and contracts," and given restitution as an example of the overlap between contract, tort, and unjust enrichment.[334]

The final section provides "A Final Word of Caution." In text that has remained substantially unchanged since the second edition, Boyle introduces a major warning to keep the materials "in perspective," signalling their limitations and alternative possibilities:

> The student should realize that the emphasis on case law, especially appellate case law, is not the only way to study "law" and represents a particular focus which not all would accept as useful. One alternative would be to discover empirically-recurring problems for contracting parties and examine the impact of the law on these problems, rather than allowing the choice of appropriate areas of study to be dictated by the lottery of litigation. Such an approach would concentrate on the total functioning of the law, that is, on the sociology of the law as a means of social control and as a mechanism for dispute settlement.[335]

This caveat about the use of appellate case materials very closely resembles that of both *Swan* and *Milner*. And, similar to Milner's

---

333 *Boyle & Percy* 7th ed, *supra* note 210 at 11–12.
334 *Ibid* at 12.
335 *Ibid* at 13, originally appearing in *Boyle & Percy* 2d ed, *supra* note 210 at lviii.

not-so-abject apology (and to a lesser extent Swan's acknowledgment of the importance of courts), it is followed by an explanation of why, notwithstanding this "word of caution," a departure from case law is a path not taken: "Although this approach is not adopted here, our contributors preferring to concentrate on the inculcation of skills associated with more traditional materials, it is important to remember that this has significant limitations, dictated by the objective chosen."[336]

Up until this caveat, the messages of the Boyle Introduction are complex and rich, but consistent in their realist bent. The Introduction draws from a range of realist and critical schools and perspectives – legal realism, feminism, law and economics, CLS, and socio-legal studies – largely featuring American writers, to challenge the classical vision of law. Boyle invites the student to reflect on how law, including both common law and legislation, might be reformed to achieve social purposes. The chapter models and invites self-criticism, encouraging students to question the materials and, by extension, their own presuppositions.

The Influence of Ben-Ishai and Percy

For the most part, Stephanie Ben-Ishai and David Percy continue to celebrate critical and realist messages in the introductory chapter of the eighth, ninth, and tenth editions. There are, however, a number of noteworthy changes. Ben-Ishai and Percy remove the sections on First Nations and Treaties and Feminism, reducing the commentary on feminism to just two paragraphs and, after completely removing references to First Nations issues in the eighth and ninth editions, insert one paragraph on Indigenous perspectives in the tenth.[337] They add, on the other hand, extended commentary pertaining to the role of the common law in policing freedom of contract, provide new examples that focus on financial transactions, refer to novel issues arising from the "use of technology and electronic communications ... algorithms and AI, FinTech, and digital currencies," and elaborate on the function of critical theory – all while preserving and carefully editing the Boyle text.[338] The general orientation is the same, but one can observe two

336 *Boyle & Percy* 7th ed, *supra* note 210 at 13. *Cf Swan* 9th ed, *supra* note 208 at §§1.38–1.41; *Milner* 1st ed, *supra* note 207 at xi.

337 *Ben-Ishai & Percy* 8th ed, *supra* note 210 at 11–13. The new paragraph on Indigenous issues refers to the "renewed interest and urgency around exploring the continuing legacy of settler colonial structures in both the oppression of Canadian Indigenous peoples and the suppression of their laws" (*Ben-Ishai &* Percy 10th ed, *supra* note 210 at 12). See the discussion in Chapter 5 below under "Indigenous Perspectives," pages 213–18.

338 *Ben-Ishai & Percy* 10th ed, *supra* note 210 at 3.

subtle shifts: a greater concern for substantive equality, and a greater value placed on cases.

The best example of the shift towards substantive equality is the significant development of the "Freedom of Contract" theme, which Ben-Ishai and Percy divide into two sections: Reality and Regulatory Response (comprising the Boyle text) and Common Law Response (new text). In the new section, Ben-Ishai and Percy provide almost three new pages of analysis that expands on how judicial interventions have ensured that freedom of contract "was never perfectly realized." This has occurred "within the traditional categories of contract law" and in the creation of "general principles that transcend" the law of contract, such as the fiduciary principle and the doctrine of good faith. A realistic attitude animates the discussion: "A failure by judges to openly discuss the real reasons for their decisions" might mislead courts and commentators, distort rules, or "lead to arbitrary or unfair results." About half of this text appears to have been taken directly from Chapter 11 of the seventh edition, written by David Percy, and about half consists of new material.[339]

This commentary can be seen as emphasizing the ways in which common law judges ensure greater substantive equality among the parties to the contract. A similar concern is revealed by the choice of examples that Ben-Ishai and Percy insert into other parts of the text. For example, they highlight the work of Bridgeman and Sandrik on "bullshit" credit card agreements to introduce the need for regulatory intervention into markets. They supplement the example of racial discrimination in car sales with a study demonstrating racial discrimination in mortgage lending. They also, new in the tenth edition, refer to the "significant financial innovation that ... has been the domain of specific statutory regulation but creates new forms and content for contract law." These examples might reflect Ben-Ishai's own scholarly concerns with substantive equality in the financial sector.[340]

---

339 *Ibid* at 7–8, citing *Hodgkinson v Simms*, [1994] 3 SCR 377, 117 DLR (4th) 161. The tenth edition also briefly mentions *Bhasin v Hrynew*, 2014 SCC 71, [2014] 3 SCR 494, and reproduces the case in the chapter entitled "Representations and Terms; Classifications and Consequences" (*supra* note 210 at 6, 462). Compare *Swan* 9th ed, *supra* note 208 at §§2.256–2.259 (reproducing *Bhasin v Hrynew* in the remedies chapter). See also *Boyle & Percy* 7th ed, *supra* note 210 at vi (describing Chapter 11 as Percy's "personal" contribution to the casebook).

340 *Ben-Ishai & Percy* 10th ed, *supra* note 210 at 4–5, citing Curtis Bridgeman & Karen Sandrik, "Bullshit Promises" (2008), FSU College of Law, Public Law Research Paper No 314, and Richard D Marisco, "The Higher Cost of Being African-American or Latino: Subprime Home Mortgage Lending in New York City 2004–2005" (2007), NYLS Legal Studies Research Paper No 07/08–12; *Ben-Ishai & Percy* 10th ed, *supra*

The addition of a new section on "common law responses" is revealing not only for its concern for substantive equality, but also for its fidelity to case law as an important source of information. Although Ben-Ishai and Percy make plenty of references to sources other than cases – legislative or regulatory responses and academic argument – they add a significant number of cases to illustrate or extend points made by Boyle. A new section on "Common Law Responses" to freedom of contract is the best and longest example of this, but we see it also in the section on Transcending Conceptual Boundaries, where they cite two cases in support of Boyle's idea that students should not think of their courses as "pigeonholes."[341]

The editorial decision to preserve Boyle's points but also, presumably, to improve on them by adding judges' words might indicate a certain commitment to the adjudicative process. Despite the editors' clear commitment to critique ("keep in mind that the law is merely a consensus reached at one point in time by the individuals who were at the table ... [N]otions about 'justice,' 'truth,' 'right' and 'wrong' are fluid and intangible"), they demonstrate commitments to more conventional understandings of law.[342]

Ben-Ishai & Percy: The Traditional Flip Side

The caveat to the Word of Caution – "our contributors preferring to concentrate on the inculcation of skills associated with the more traditional materials" – signals the flip side to the carefully crafted critical commentary.[343] This flip side is a commitment to adjudication, the inculcation of conventional legal reasoning skills, a marginalization of policy, and an uncritical acceptance of the notion of a "core" of doctrinal substance. Such views surface explicitly in the text: the authors describe their materials as "somewhat traditional, for they are designed to constitute the basis of a core course in Contracts"; the book is "intended to contain what the contributors feel to be core materials for a basic course in the principles of contract law."[344] These themes have

---

note 210 at 3. See Stephanie Ben-Ishai & Saul Schwartz, "The Role of Governments in the Overindebtedness of the Economically Disadvantaged" (2010) 35 Queen's LJ 539.

341 See *Ben-Ishai & Percy* 10th ed, *supra* note 210 at 3, 6 (referring to consumer protection legislation and to Richard H Thaler & Cass R Sunstein, *Nudge: Improving Decisions about Health, Wealth, and Happiness* (New Haven, CT: Yale University Press, 2008)); *ibid* at 13–14 (citing *J Nunes Diamonds v Dominion Electric Protection Company*, [1972] SCR 769 and *Central Trust Co v Rafuse*, [1986] 2 SCR 147, 31 DLR (4th) 481).

342 *Ben-Ishai & Percy* 10th ed, *supra* note 210 at 12.

343 *Ibid* at 15.

344 *Boyle & Percy* 1st ed, *supra* note 210 at v, 1.

also been identified in scholarly reviews of the casebook ever since the first edition.

In a review of the first edition, David Vaver suggests that the editors "correctly" say that their approach is traditional. Vaver, after some praise and critique, declares the "real difficulty" of the book to be its philosophy:

> The impression I got is that contract law is a relatively static subject which looks for its solutions to an internally generated logic ... This book does not systematically examine where the law of contract came from and where it is going ... [Almost no scholarly article] is considered worthy of extensive quotation. Such quotation would put a subject or an area as a whole in some sort of philosophical, economic, or social context ... The format of case followed by notes and questions repeated *ad nauseam* is good as far as it goes, but gives the erroneous impression that contract law is a purely deductive art with the occasional statutory incursion to mar its inexorable internal logic.[345]

In a similar vein, writing about the second edition, John Manwaring, then of the Université de Moncton, reinforces the traditional character of the book: "[I]t reminds me of those severely traditional black shoes with sensible heels and strong laces that my grandmother used to wear – solid, well-made, very comfortable and unlikely to irritate."[346] Manwaring elaborates on the advantages and disadvantages of the "traditional design." On the plus side, he lauds the authors for having placed remedies at the back of the book. For Manwaring, this signals a "return" to the "formal logic of the law of contracts as the organizing principle." Offering his own take on the timeless theme of whether remedies should go first or last in a Contracts course, he argues that placing remedies first gives a false impression that the "conception of the law as primarily functional or instrumental" is the dominant form of legal consciousness in Canada today. The *Boyle & Percy* structure is superior, he argues, because it does not "obscur[e] the contradictions within the dominant legal consciousness," but rather permits students to "investigate the formal logic of the law of contracts and the evolution of Canadian legal consciousness while building into the

345 David Vaver, Book Review of *Boyle & Percy* 1st ed, *supra* note 210, (1979) 17 Alta L Rev 567 at 567, 570–2.

346 JA Manwaring, Book Review of *Boyle & Percy* 2d ed, *supra* note 210, (1982) Can Bar Rev 781 at 783.

discussion examples of principle and counter-principle which show that the final categories are extremely problematic in light of actual exchanges."[347]

However, he writes, the book does not succeed at this goal of foregrounding formalism in order to debunk it. It fails to avoid the danger that "the law of contracts will be presented as a system of scientific rules to be deduced from certain basic principles or premises." Although the Introduction acknowledges this danger by raising questions that can help "avoid this return to formalism":

> [t]he weakness of the book is precisely that the issues are raised in the introduction and not adequately integrated into the discussion of doctrine ... After the introduction, these issues are either never mentioned again, or mentioned in a perfunctory note. The student will quickly get the message: the study of law involves the study of cases. The rest is just gloss. It is not really law but merely policy ...
>
> Thus, the decision to structure the book according to the categories of the formal logic of contract law gives the impression that formalism is still tenable after all these years ... [W]hat would have been an important step forward in Canadian casebook design if done with the requisite sophistication becomes a step backwards into history.[348]

In addition to this critique that the body of the casebook betrays the commitments espoused in the Introduction, Manwaring argues that the book insufficiently highlights legislation and ignores the "realities of the exchange relation," citing Lawrence Friedman, Stewart Macaulay, and a related comment in an essay by Rod Macdonald.[349]

These critiques – a marginalization of policy and politics, a failure to disrupt the classical, formalist image of law, and insufficient attention paid to exchange realities – surface again in Richard Devlin's review of the fifth edition of *Boyle & Percy*. In that article, Devlin offers a number of comments in the spirit of "critical affirmation." Despite the casebook's virtues, he writes, "there is something missing. Each chapter tends to focus on the micro details of its particular subject area with

---

347 *Ibid* at 783–5.

348 *Ibid* at 785.

349 *Ibid* at 786, citing Friedman, *supra* note 43, Macaulay, "Non-Contractual Relations", *supra* note 60, Friedman & Macaulay, *supra* note 58, and Rod Macdonald, "Legal Education on the Threshold of the 1980s: Whatever Happened to the Great Ideas of the 60s" (1979) 44 Sask L Rev 39 at 43 (classic contract law imagines "the private sale of used typewriters and bicycles").

little effort to locate these issues within the larger context of the contemporary debates around contract law."[350]

In particular, Devlin bemoans the "decontextualizing (and depoliticizing) tendency" in a number of chapters – a tendency that effaces "ideological predispositions" in the chapters on Certainty of Terms and Representations, and "constrain[s] the opportunity for students to critically analyze" materials on Frustration. Issues of race and gender fare better, representing "significant progress in the process of modernizing and contextualizing contract law," but these issues are ultimately "ghettoized" by being characterized, for example, "as 'women's issues' and therefore marginal." Later on, Devlin recommends that greater use be made of "sociolegal studies of the operation of contracts," and suggests that "critical empiricism" can "enrich and destabilize" understanding, bolstering what he suggests is an insufficiently detailed allusion to thinkers such as Ian Macneil.[351]

Like Manwaring, Devlin critiques the disjuncture between the Introduction – which he qualifiedly endorses for presenting "issues of competing theoretical perspectives, identity, and ideology" – and the rest of the book. He urges the editors to "encourage their contributors to attempt to incorporate these larger debates explicitly into their chapters" with the aim of providing "greater intellectual depth and stronger thematic coherence, thereby enabling teachers and students to escape the dull compulsion of the doctrinal." He specifically singles out the final paragraph of the Introduction, in which the editors explicitly abandon the socio-legal approach to contracts in favour of the "inculcation of skills associated with more traditional materials." For Devlin, this is a "curious surrender of editorial influence."[352]

Devlin acknowledges that practical challenges might preclude covering all critical perspectives in a casebook. He acknowledges that his critiques, if taken seriously, would result in a "somewhat" longer book, but he rejects the idea that the alternative – treating the casebook as a

---

350 Richard F Devlin, Book Review of *Boyle & Percy* 5th ed, *supra* note 210, (1996) 27 Can Bus LJ 144 [Devlin, Review of *Boyle & Percy* 5th ed] at 145–6 (virtues include the selection of cases, use of law reform commission proposals, the sense that there is "an increasing Canadianization of contract law," pithy introductions, informative notes and commentaries, and appropriate emphasis on the more problematic elements of contract law).

351 *Ibid* at 147, 148, 150. As of the sixth edition, Devlin has served as editor of the Frustration chapter in *Ben-Ishai & Percy*. He takes the opportunity to remedy the critiques he levels, adding in an extended introduction to the chapter and an entire section on "Social Force Majeure."

352 *Ibid* at 148–9; *Boyle & Percy* 5th ed, *supra* note 210 at lxxxvii.

source of "core" contract doctrine and resorting to instructors' supplements to provide additional perspectives – is either straightforward or unproblematic: "[T]here is a legitimacy and hierarchy problem. When one attempts to raise issues of, for example, gender, class, race or sexual orientation in a contracts course there are some students who resist on the basis that it is not real law and they are only being forced to study these issues because of the subjective preferences of the individual teacher ... [W]hat constitutes the core of a contracts course is contestable and contingent upon certain material and ideological presumptions; if we want our supplements to problematize and endanger the conventional structure and practices of contracts pedagogy we need to be more inclusive."[353] Accordingly, the failure to integrate such critical perspectives thoroughly into the core of the Contracts casebooks can be seen as marginalizing these perspectives.

Devlin appears to have held this critique of *Boyle & Percy* even after he became a contributing editor (in the sixth edition, immediately following his critical review). In an article co-written by Anthony Duggan and Louise Langevin in which the authors argue for integrating theory into the teaching of first-year Contracts, Devlin includes the seventh edition of *Boyle & Percy* in a footnote for the following proposition: "[T]he leading Canadian textbooks and teaching materials on contracts are somewhat thin when it comes to the theoretical dimensions of contract law ... [T]he overwhelming emphasis is on relatively traditional doctrinal discussion and analysis."[354] Judging from his publicly available syllabus, Devlin continues to supplement *Ben-Ishai & Percy* heavily with his own custom reading list.[355]

The overwhelming impression of the *Ben-Ishai & Percy* casebook gleaned from the Introduction and reviews is of a series of contradictory messages. On the one hand, the significant intellectual accomplishment of the Introduction to synthesize a range of critical and external perspectives on contract law – coupled with its status as the first chapter of the book – signals a genuine commitment by the editors to foreground realist and critical perspectives. The introductory chapter could function to disabuse students of the idea that law is a series of internally

353 Devlin, Review of *Boyle & Percy* 5th ed, *supra* note 350 at 151, 149.

354 Devlin, Duggan & Langevin, *supra* note 53 at 1.

355 Richard Devlin & Sarah Berger Richardson, Syllabus (Schulich School of Law at Dalhousie University, 2018–19), online: https://cdn.dal.ca/content/dam/dalhousie/pdf/law/Academic%20Information%20Syllabi%20Moots%20Regulations/Syllabi/LAWS%201000%20Contracts%20Syllabus%202018-2019%20Devlin.pdf [Devlin Syllabus].

consistent abstract rules. The reader is invited to take into account context, human behaviour, values, political preferences, and policy desiderata when analysing or practising law.

These explicit messages are contradicted, however, by the apparent sense that another attitude – the "traditional" one, in which law is presented as a formalist system of rules in the Langdellian mould and the adjudicative process as archetypal – predominates. Among all the casebooks, *Ben-Ishai & Percy*'s Introduction canvasses the broadest range of perspectives with the greatest degree of synthesis and the most explicit commitment to realist and critical ideas. It is also the most explicit in its deliberate choice to emphasize a "traditional" thrust. The influence of tradition and convention seem to exert a gravitational pull on editorial choices, drawing them back to an ostensible "core" to propagate mainstream methods of teaching and conventional doctrinal categories despite the editors' critical awareness of their limitations. Like *Milner*, the acknowledgment of these limitations does not translate into any significant action to reform the conventional approach. As the next section shows, the force of the gravitational field is indeed strong, and affects the way the editors of *Waddams* and *Ben-Ishai & Percy* treat their substantive material.

WHAT IS DONE: MESSAGES COMMUNICATED BY SUBSTANCE

As we have seen, the introductory and prefatory comments of the casebooks – in which editors have the opportunity to say what they are attempting to do and what they believe – reveal both the influence of American realist and critical schools of thought and a commitment to a traditional core of legal knowledge and legal reasoning that reflects the formalist attitudes reminiscent of Langdell. Here, I explore the extent to which the editors' treatment of one substantive subject area – remedies – reveals a similar tension. Although *Swan* carries forward the solicitor's approach into the treatment of remedies, evidencing a good degree of fit between the editors' propositional statements about law and their treatment of substance and legal reasoning, the image of legal reasoning and legal practice conveyed by both *Waddams* and *Ben-Ishai & Percy* coincides much more closely with the formalist and classical commitments in their introductions than to the critical and realist ones.

I chose to analyse the remedies chapter for a number of reasons. First, the subject matter is perhaps most naturally suited to an approach that challenges formalist understandings of law. Ever since Fuller and Perdue's seminal articles on the reliance interest, a functional approach – a focus on the underlying interests – has framed the introductory study of remedies. Thus, if the realist attitude is to be present anywhere in the first-year course, it is very likely to be here; conversely, were more formalist attitudes to predominate in the teaching of remedies, this would be evidence of a powerful formalist underlying commitment.

Second, the role of remedies in the first-year course has been a long-standing matter of debate, reflecting a deeper debate about the nature of law. The traditional order of teaching Contracts is to begin with formation and proceed somewhat chronologically through the life of the contract. Indeed, fully half of Langdell's casebook focuses on the formation stage and the book includes no section on remedies, an approach that can be seen as embodying the abstraction of classical legal thought.[356]

By contrast, ever since Holmes's review of Langdell's casebook, in which he famously wrote that "the life of the law has not been logic: it has been experience," the realist emphasis on purposes and effects has translated into the view that remedies should be considered a foundational starting point. As Stanley Handerson, an editor of the "leading [American] contemporary example of the remedies-first approach," writes, "contract law is best understood ... if it is approached through a remedy-centred study. The underlying purposes of contract law (what it seeks to protect, and how it hopes to accomplish its aims) are revealed most clearly when problems are looked at from a perspective of taking care of harms or losses, or gains held unjustly."[357]

The innovation to put remedies first is attributed to Fuller, who did so in the first edition of his own contract law casebook in 1947. Although Fuller did not articulate why he did so in that edition, correspondence between him and Corbin about a planned (but ultimately aborted) jointly authored casebook reveals some of his reasons. In proposing the new order to Corbin, Fuller wanted to "bring home to the student the fact that back of the question, 'Is there a contract?' there always lies a

356 Langdell, *Selection of Cases* (1879), *supra* note 56 at xi–xiii (Table of Contents). See Klare, "Contracts Jurisprudence and the First-Year Casebook", *supra* note 88 at 877–8 (Langdell's casebook, "in its emphasis on problems of offer and acceptance, exemplified a way of thinking about contracts as abstract relationships, analysable apart from their social context"). See also *infra* notes 667, 669 and accompanying text.

357 Holmes, "Review of *A Selection of Cases on the Law of Contracts*", *supra* note 99 at 234; John P Dawson, William Burnett Harvey & Stanley D Henderson, *Contracts: Cases and Comment*, 8th ed (Mineola, NY: Foundation Press, 2003) at iii, cited in Scott D Gerber, "*Corbin and Fuller's Cases on Contracts* (1942?): The Casebook That Never Was" (2003) 72 Fordham L Rev 595 at 596.

more specific problem of enforcement." He wanted to make the student "remedy-minded," to ensure that contract law is analysed in the terms of the "hierarchy of interests" from his "Yale article." He was modelling this approach after his own experiment of having reversed the traditional order of teaching in the Property course, in which he placed the consequences of legal possession before a definition of possession – which had the virtue of "imparting a functional conception of legal rules."[358]

Placing remedies first thus can be understood as communicating the "central realist message" that "it is impossible to understand the nature of legal rights and relationships or to logically deduce remedial conclusions from them without knowing what courts can and actually will do to and for litigants."[359] However, although some editors in the United States have adopted the remedies-first approach, the traditional approach remains prevalent. Even later editions of Fuller's book have abandoned the remedies-first approach (although the rationale for this is often described as "pedagogical," not philosophical).[360]

Swan: The Remedies Chapter

Of the three books, *Swan* demonstrates the closest correspondence between the messages communicated in Chapter 1 and the remedies chapter. As in Chapter 1, the remedies chapter emphasizes a functional approach to law, the solicitor's perspective, and an appreciation for context. The editors communicate these messages through their ample commentary, which they intersperse between almost every excerpt.

Explicit references to the role of remedies play an important role in the chapter in arguing for a particular vision of law. The chapter opens

358 Fuller, *Basic Contract Law*, *supra* note 205; Lon L Fuller, Letters to Arthur L Corbin (7 October 1940, 10 November 1941, 24 November 1941), reproduced in Gerber, *supra* note 357 at 604, 615, 617, 620. On Fuller's book as an "innovation," see Gerber, *ibid* at 625; Farnsworth, *supra* note 204 at 1436.

359 Klare, "Contracts Jurisprudence and the First-Year Casebook", *supra* note 88 at 882.

360 See Farnsworth, *supra* note 204, n 167 (identifying three US casebooks presenting remedies first); Gerber, *supra* note 357 at 597 (distinguishing remedies-first approaches from "hybrid" approaches that briefly present remedies prior to formation); Gerber, *ibid* at 626 (the fourth and sixth editions of *Basic Contract Law*, under the editorship of Melvin Eisenberg, returned to the remedies-last approach, on the rationale that "policy issues raised by consideration" are more accessible to first-year students), 615 (Corbin tells Fuller that he might be "asking too much of beginners" by starting with remedies).

with an argument for why remedies is best studied first, using the conventional "formation-first" approach as a foil:

> One difficulty that a [formation-first approach] creates is that it distorts the relative importance of the topics that make up what is called the "Law of Contracts." Lawyers spend comparatively little time worrying about the process of contract creation. They spend much more of their time worrying either about the risks that the deal creates for their clients and the ways by which those risks may be avoided, controlled or allocated, or in negotiating the deal and keeping the arrangements working smoothly when the parties are in the deal or relation and need to co-operate.
>
> It makes more sense to start the study of contract law by considering what might happen when things go wrong, what the risks of non-performance might be, where they come from and what one can do about them. Once one understands the rights that a party may have if a contract is not performed and the consequences of non-performance of a contract, one has a better grasp of the problems that making a deal might create.[361]

With its focus on risk, negotiation, "keeping the arrangements working smoothly," "deals," and solving "problems," the editors signal that the subject matter of remedies reinforces the importance of relational contracts and the solicitor's role in prospective planning and avoiding litigation.

The introduction to this chapter goes on to place the question of remedies in its broadest possible ambit, surveying a range of possible remedies for breach, spanning criminal sanctions, formal and informal exclusion from a business or trade, being "publicly labelled as one who did not keep promises," a court declaration that a contract has been breached, orders of specific performance and, finally, damages. It ends with an elaboration of the pedagogical justification for beginning with remedies: asking what the law will do if it decides to enforce a promise "make[s] more intelligible the inquiry ... into the kinds of promises the law will enforce," encourages lawyers and clients "to have a general idea of the risks and consequences of what they are doing," and empowers the lawyer to determine whether "the amount likely to be recovered makes it worth starting or defending an action." The first words of the first substantive chapter of the book, then, decentre courts and their remedies from an understanding of law, invite the student to adopt a pragmatic and practical state of mind, and emphasize function over form.[362]

---

361 *Swan* 9th ed, *supra* note 208 at §§2.1–2.2.

362 *Ibid* at §§2.3, 2.8.

Elsewhere in the chapter, the subject matter of remedies serves as a departure point for commentary about legal theory. For example, about midway through the chapter, the editors seemingly bolster their preference for the remedies-first view by alluding to the Blackstonian formulation that there is no right without a remedy. Near the end, they critique the idea that "law is a forum ... for a confrontation between parties with 'rights-based' claims," which they characterize as a "restricted vision of the nature and scope of the relations that the law governs and supports." They propose alternative views that focus "less on the idea of rights and more on the ideas of mutual duties and good faith," and "less on the limited bounds of the relation created by a contract and more on the expectations that the relation has encouraged." In comments like these, the editors' preference for relational understandings of contract, including the reasonable expectations of the parties, rises to the surface. If these comments serve to undermine the centrality of rights, others undermine other tenets of classical legal thought, arguing for functional considerations over coherence ("If it works, why worry about the doctrinal purity of the law?").[363]

In addition to these more lengthy and explicit passages, the chapter contains comments that reinforce the editors' commitment to their view of law. They refer to the "recurrent theme of the importance of the context of any transaction," invite students to see "the purpose of the law of contract as the protection of the parties' reasonable expectations," highlight functionalism by asking "what values and interests" the law should support, and emphasize the negotiation, planning, drafting, risk management, or counselling activities that the "careful solicitor," who is "professionally concerned to 'foresee' or worry about the consequences of a breach of contract," might undertake.[364] The organization

363 *Ibid* at §§2.266, 2.435, 2.456. *Cf.* William Blackstone, *Commentaries on the Laws of England, Book the Third*, 15th ed, with notes and additions by Edward Christian (London: Cadell & Davies, 1809) at 109 ("it is a settled and invariable principle in the laws of England, that every right when withheld must have a remedy, and every injury [its] proper redress").

364 *Swan* 9th ed, *supra* note 208 at §§2.340, 2.331, 2.376, 2.82, 2.148. On context, see also *ibid* at §§2.27–2.32, 2.33, 2.85, 2.98, 2.122, 2.332–2.334, 2.338, 2.339, 2.340, 2.402. On reasonable expectations, see also *ibid* at §§2.125(a), 2.338, 2.435, 2.449 (a), 115, 140, 233 (reproducing passages from *Bowlay Logging Ltd v Domtar Ltd* (1978), 87 DLR (3d) 179, *Fidler v Sun Life Assurance Co of Canada*, 2006 SCC 30, [2006] 2 SCR 3, and *Bank of America Canada v Mutual Trust Co*, [2002] 2 SCR 601, 211 DLR (4th) 285). On functionalism, see also *ibid* at §§2.63, 2.89, 2.208, 2.389, 2.402, 2.472. On the role of the solicitor, see also ibid at §§2.24 (negotiation); 2.44, 2.114, 2.342, 2.513(2) (drafting); §§2.47, 2.126, 2.141, 2.283, 2.385, 2.490, 2.514(3) (counselling); §§2.84, 2.108 (risk management).

of the chapter, whose main subject headings tend towards practical considerations instead of doctrinal divisions – "The Compensation Principle," "Some Problems in Awarding Damages," "Interest and the Date for Assessing Damages," "Accounting for Gains Arising from Breach" – reinforces the functionalist view. In addition to these views about law, which correspond well with the editors' "practitioner" identities, there is also evidence of a lively intellectual and critical spirit, with more traditional commentary about the cases themselves and academic disagreement with some theoretical views, such as law and economics.[365]

In summary, therefore, both the form of the remedies chapter (its structure and heavy use of commentary) and the substance (the content of the commentaries) align well with the vision of law, legal reasoning, and legal practice propounded in Chapter 1. There is no significant discernible gap between the aspirations expressed in Chapter 1 and the execution of the subject matter in the remedies chapter. This congruence is unique among all three books. Both *Waddams* and *Ben-Ishai & Percy* disclose a much greater contrast between the propositional or underlying attitudes about law and the presentation of remedies.

Waddams: The Remedies Chapter

In the *Waddams* chapter on remedies, we observe a similar tension to that detailed earlier. This is the tension between, on the one hand, a purposive, functionalist, realist vision of law and, on the other, a preoccupation with the adjudicative process and law's internal rationality. Because the chapter is so sparing in its commentary, this tension has to be discerned largely in-between the lines.

Superficially the *Waddams* chapter on remedies presents largely as a conventional anthology of cases. Aside from a short introductory comment on specific performance, a slightly longer one on restitution, and some comments on unjust enrichment, most of the chapter consists of reproductions from cases interspersed with short notes and questions.[366] This lack of extended commentary is probably the most noteworthy difference with *Swan*; the fact that the cases are left to "speak for themselves" gives rise to the inference that a court-centric view – such as the

365 For traditional case commentary, see e.g. *Swan* 9th ed, *supra* note 208 at §§2.13, 2.143, 2.181, 2.204 ("Should the rules for damages differentiate between dogs and stereos?"), 2.239, 2.267, 2.269, 2.292, 2.295, 2.300, 2.304, 2.475. For critiques of law and economics, see e.g. *ibid* at §§2.88, 2.396, 2.398, 2.399, 2.406, 2.428 (efficient breach can have no impact on long-term relational contracts).

366 *Waddams* 6th ed, *supra* note 209 at 115, 144, 149.

one that Macdonald ascribes to Waddams in *Introduction to the Study of Law* – figures prominently. Recall that, unlike in *Milner*, there is no "apology" for the large number of cases and, unlike in *Swan*, there is no introductory framing about the limited usefulness of appellate judgments. The first and primary message communicated by the format is the central and straightforward importance of cases.

Further bolstering this impression is the nature of the notes, questions, and commentary. Not only are they sparse and compact; at times they serve to create an impression that contract law comprises a series of abstract rules, and that legal thinking and practice consist of applying rules to hypothetical fact scenarios. By far the most common formulation in the notes and questions is the provision of facts similar to those in a case just reproduced, with the invocation that the student "advise" a client as to the likely outcome of a legal claim.[367] In some instances, interesting and obvious policy considerations are raised by the facts of a case, but the commentary and questions constrain themselves to the conventional formulation.[368] Many of the questions following cases invite students to focus on rules, whether to clarify, evaluate, or elaborate upon them.[369] The prevalence of such interventions reinforces a traditional view of legal rationality preoccupied with analogical reasoning and discerning relevant differences, very much in line with Waddams's stated views in the Preface to his textbook. The presumed model of the lawyer here looks much more like the courtroom advocate than the solicitor – even when the student is asked to "advise" a client, the implied invitation is to focus on the rules and their application. The themes of relational contracts, the limited usefulness of contract doctrine, and the disjuncture between what judges do and what they say are largely absent from the notes and commentary, even when the excerpts might lend themselves naturally to such discussion.[370]

These observations apply to a large portion of the chapter, and might give rise to the impression, similar to Macdonald's, that a traditional

---

367 See e.g. *ibid* at 32, 36, 44, 51, 76, 106, 114.

368 See e.g. *ibid* at 106 (following a fact pattern about an unwelcome child, in which the question raised is whether the situation should give rise to mitigated damages, the student is asked only to "Advise C," without any further discussion of broader or related issues), 118, 142.

369 See e.g. *ibid* at 35, 43, 58, 118, 161.

370 See e.g. *ibid* at 119 (reproducing an excerpt from *Sky Petroleum v VIP Petroleum Ltd*, [1974] 1 WLR 576, [1974] 1 All ER 954, in which the judge awards only an interim, not a permanent, injunction). Swan had invoked this decision to suggest it resulted from "concerns about ... forcing parties into a continuing relation" (9th ed, *supra* note 208 at §2.444). *Waddams* provides no commentary about continuing relations.

view of law, with its emphasis on rules and courts, predominates. But there is a danger in oversimplifying. Embedded in the chapter – not so much in the commentary as in the choice of excerpts – is material that serves to supplement this vision with an appreciation of the contingency of rules, the importance of context, and pragmatic considerations.

A number of devices highlight the contingency of rules. One is the highly comparative nature of the case law. The first seven cases of the chapter, for example, come from England, Oregon, Ontario, New Hampshire, and Minnesota, with a reference in a note to a Kentucky case. Examples from other jurisdictions are often raised to demonstrate alternative rule formulations.[371] Such a selection disturbs any impression that this "traditional" casebook is concerned with transmitting the doctrinal content of any one place. It communicates a broader intellectual appreciation for legal developments, a sensitivity amplified by the inclusion of historical developments of rules and examples of dissenting or differing opinions. By showing rules as contingent upon place, circumstance, or history, the chapter appears to support Waddams's concern, stated in the Preface to his textbook, with looking beyond the surface of rules to their underlying principles.[372]

Moreover, despite the absence of *Swan*-like commentary which might argue for the importance of context, many of the editorial decisions about what to include demonstrate an appreciation of its value. Indeed, although *Waddams* is sometimes considered to have rather short excerpts, its case excerpts are occasionally longer than those in *Swan* – so although the cases are left to speak for themselves, they sometimes say more. On at least one occasion, the authors use an excerpt from an academic article to provide commentary about a case, achieving an end similar to that which the *Swan* editors accomplish with their commentary. Sometimes the paraphrasing of facts is more detailed and colourful than necessary to situate judicial reasons for decision, and on numerous occasions the editors provide postscript information about what happened after the resolution of the case, continuing the story

371 See e.g. *Waddams* 6th ed, *supra* note 209 at 51 (the US distinction between wilful and non-wilful breach, not adopted in Canada or England), 83 (different jurisdictions decide differently whether the contract as a whole must be for peace of mind in order to award damages for mental distress), 115–16 (examples of specific performance from Scotland and the *Civil Code of Québec*), 148 (the Restatement's theory "remained heterodox in England" until the last decade of the twentieth century).

372 See e.g. *ibid* at 53–4 (nuanced development of ratios in a line of English cases), 149 (how old rules might lose and regain favour at different historical moments); 114, 144 (dissents); Waddams, Preface to 1st ed text, *supra* note 297 at vii–viii.

beyond the courtroom and indirectly communicating the practical reality of the litigation.[373]

The editors also provide historical and intellectual context for many areas of law – for example, a brief history of the distinction between law and equity or the origins of the tort of inducing breach of contract. In the chapter's one lengthy commentary, introducing the section on restitution, the editors place the cases that follow in a broader intellectual framework. Unlike *Swan*, whose editors seem impatient with doctrinal distinctions, the *Waddams* editors provide a more neutral account, indicating some allegiance to the categories of the common law. Yet this treatment cannot be said to indicate a commitment to doctrinal purity. The thrust of the introduction is that Canadian courts would go on to adopt the more functional view of the *Restatement of Contracts*, treating the constructive trust as a widely available remedy. In passages such as this – not to mention that the chapter opens with an excerpt from Fuller & Perdue's reliance interest articles – we see evidence of the editors' functionalist and realist leanings.[374]

The overall impression is that the chapter was compiled by someone with a love of the subject and an appreciation for its nuance and complexity. It would be inaccurate to characterize it as a Langdellian exercise in legal science. But it would be equally inaccurate to say that the chapter, on its face, communicates an unambiguous commitment to the realist values that explicitly appear in Waddams's other writing. The style is too minimalist to make such a claim, the missed opportunities too frequent. Rather, the chapter appears to be designed for students and instructors alike to discover for themselves the emphasis they prefer. The instructor who wishes to treat the law of remedies as a set of judicially constructed rules that might be applied to different hypothetical fact scenarios will have the resources to do so. The instructor who might wish to tease out the policy or practical considerations has

---

373 For longer excerpts, see e.g. *Waddams* 6th ed, *supra* note 209 at 72ff (including Baroness Hale's decision in *Transfield Shipping v Mercator Shipping (The Achilleas)*, [2008] UKHL 48, [2009] 1 AC 61), 137–42 (including many facts not germane to the ratio in *Wroth v Tyler*, [1974] Ch 30), 151–2 (additional facts and context in *Attorney-General v Blake*, [2001] 1 AC 268, [2000] 4 All ER 385). Compare *Swan* 9th ed, *supra* note 208 at §§2.410–2.414 (*Wroth v Tyler* in five paragraphs), 247 (fewer facts and context in *Attorney-General v Blake*). For an academic excerpt, see e.g. *Waddams* 6th ed, *supra* note 209 at 34 (citing AI Ogus, "Damages for Pre-Contract Expenditure" (1972) 35 Mod L Rev 423). For more extensive paraphrasing, see e.g. *Waddams* 6th ed, *supra* note 209 at 106–7, 134. For colourful postscript information on *Groves v John Wunder Co*, 205 Minn 163, 286 NW 235 (1939), see e.g. Waddams 6th ed, *supra* note 209 at 43.

374 *Waddams* 6th ed, *supra* note 209 at 115, 137, 144–6, 51.

the raw material to do so as well – both excerpts and questions raise issues of marital property regimes, abortion, efficient breach, risk, reasonable expectations, and the recovery of profits. The chapter is neither dogmatic nor polemical. Commentary or critique is often indirect, such as via a series of rhetorical questions.[375]

That said, the result of such neutrality, in the end, might be a triumph of the conventional, traditional view. Absent a corrective such as that which Milner or Swan provide to the adjudication-centric model, the dominant message the student likely receives is the importance of judge-made rules. Although the chapter is rich in context, history, and nuance, the objective of such contextualization appears to be to test or push the limits and contours of the rules, not to challenge their relevance or centrality. Indeed, the relevance of what is included is taken for granted, not argued for, leaving the criteria for relevance (as previously observed in Waddams's introduction to his treatise) unstated and implicit.

This silence creates something of a vacuum, and it likely would take a particularly diligent student to follow the chapter's pinpoint references to the Waddams and McCamus textbooks and fill it with nuance. By leaving so much unsaid, the *Waddams* editors curiously vacate the arena in which they have so ardently contested conventional doctrinal thinking in their other writings.[376] Their reticence produces an implied emphasis on the conventional doctrines and categories of contract law, and the impression that the case method and adjudication are the natural (and most important) domains of its study. This naturalness privileges conventional analogical reasoning and the importance of substantive doctrinal rules as the core of the lawyer's (and law student's) work, casting the realist ideas to the peripheral domain of "theory." This marginalization of theory is emblemized by the stand-alone nature of the Perspectives chapter, which, it turns out, a number professors who teach from *Waddams* do not assign at all.[377]

---

375 See e.g. *ibid* at 141–2 (marital property regimes); 106 (abortion or adoption as mitigation of damages); 51, 54, 68–9 (risk); 101, 161 (efficient breach); 68–9, 72–3 (reasonable expectations); 161 (recovery of profits); 151 ("Could it be argued that this anomalous distinction should no longer be applied once the underlying unjust enrichment basis of these claims is recognized?"), 58.

376 See e.g. Michael J Trebilcock, *The Limits of Freedom of Contract* (Cambridge, MA: Harvard University Press, 1993). For references to SM Waddams, *The Law of Contracts*, 6th ed (Aurora, ON: Canada Law Book, 2010) and John D McCamus, *The Law of Contracts*, 2d ed (Toronto: Irwin Law, 2012), see *Waddams* 6th ed, *supra* note 209 at 32, 34, 75, 84, 101, 122, 128, 144, 145–6.

377 See *supra* note 318 and *infra* note 390.

Ben-Ishai & Percy: The Remedies Chapter

Stephanie Ben-Ishai has been the editor of the remedies chapter of *Ben-Ishai & Percy* since the eighth edition. For the purposes of this review, I refer to the chapter as if she is the sole editor responsible, although the chapter represents an accretion of contributions from its previous editors. Since, for eight out of the ten editions of *Ben-Ishai & Percy*, the editor of the remedies chapter has also been an editor of the casebook (aside from David Mullan in the sixth and seventh, all previous editions were edited by David Percy), inferences drawn about the chapter might be more generally applicable to the entire book than might otherwise be the case.

Similar to the tension between the Boyle Introduction and the reception of the book as a whole, the remedies chapter discloses a tension between critical and traditional perspectives. What is *said* in the commentary often resembles a realist or critical framing, while what is *done* pedagogically serves to perpetuate a more traditional view of law and legal reasoning. In addition, the chapter's structure adopts a more conceptual, as opposed to functional, organization, furthering the impression that formalist commitments lurk in the background.

This interpretation requires some justification, for the chapter – which contains a good deal more commentary than *Waddams*, though less than *Swan* – is laced with references to legal realism and other critical perspectives. For example, the very first two excerpts in the chapter are from Holmes, with his invocation that law should be considered from the perspective of the "bad man" who "cares only for ... material consequences," and Posner. They are deployed here in the service of what Ben-Ishai calls the "the dominant position" that "contract breach should be morally neutral."[378] This is a striking treatment of Posner when contrasted with *Swan*'s critical take of concepts such as efficient breach, and even with *Waddams*, which refrains (despite the law and economics expertise of Trebilcock, a lead editor for the first three editions) from praising or arguing for such claims. Indeed, elsewhere in the *Ben-Ishai & Percy* remedies chapter, the economic perspective is deployed rather uncritically, perhaps so that it might function unimpeded as critical of doctrinal presumptions.[379]

378 *Ben-Ishai & Percy* 10th ed, *supra* note 210 at 786–7 (reproducing excerpts from Holmes, "Path of the Law", *supra* note 276 and Richard Posner, *Economic Analysis of Law*, 9th ed (New York: Wolters Kluwer Law & Business, 2014)).

379 See e.g. *Ben-Ishai & Percy* 10th ed, *supra* note 210 at 829 (offering Posner's critique of *Groves v John Wunder Co*, *supra* note 373, without any critical response), 942 (presenting as fact without evidence the idea that economic efficiency accounts for the

Numerous other realist perspectives are offered throughout the chapter. Ben-Ishai alludes to the practical motivations of clients (did the injunction "drive" Bette Davis to perform her contract or merely "tempt" her to?) and the reality of litigation (reliance comes up in the jurisprudence because expectation damages are too difficult to prove).[380] She refers to the policy considerations that are "obscured by verbal formulae," and signals "noteworthy" changes in bench composition.[381] She suggests that judges use the "flexibility" of principles "to impose liability when it seems appropriate," and hints at the consequent practical irrelevance of some legislative interventions.[382] She refers to the importance of values, distributive concerns, and the solicitor's role in drafting, counselling, and structuring transactions.[383] The very first "Learning Objective" listed at the beginning of the chapter is to "[a]rticulate and assess the general policy considerations influencing judicial decisions." The voice of the commentary is fresh, with references to popular culture and accessible everyday examples.[384] All of these references give the impression that the chapter's editor is critically minded, concerned with practical and realistic implications of contract law, and desires to inculcate in readers a broad understanding of the subject that cultivates a diverse array of skills.

If the critical spirit does animate the editorial choices in this chapter, it does so alongside an apparently disparate set of commitments. These commitments presume the pre-eminence of doctrinal rules, the primacy of analogical reasoning, and the marginal role that policy plays in legal reasoning. This other constellation of views lies in stark contrast to the realist messages in the chapter, and parallels the tension observed in the Introduction.

---

preference for damages over specific performance, and relying on the "assum[ption] that most contractual parties will generally act in an economically rational way," without defining "economically rational" or providing empirical support).

380 *Ben-Ishai & Percy*, 10th ed, *supra* note 210 at 956, 799.

381 *Ibid* at 882, 892. For other policy considerations, see *ibid* at 829, 891, 938.

382 See e.g. *ibid* at 892, 950 ("the current availability of the injunction approximates its availability before 'fusion'").

383 See e.g. *ibid* at 785, 939 (values of efficiency, morality, freedom of contract, and protection against oppression or unconscionability), 946 (specific performance in sales of residential property "a consideration that to this point has been favouring the wealthy"), 924 (drafting), 932 (counselling), 938 (structuring sales transactions).

384 *Ibid* at 785, 843 (referring to *The Paper Chase*, *supra* note 2 to introduce *Hawkins v McGee* (1929), 89 NH 114, 146 A 641), 842 ("When I agree with a friend to exchange books that we have each read recently and enjoyed, both sides to this transaction have as their objective the achievement of the pleasure that comes from reading a good novel or biography").

A number of indicia justify this interpretation. There is the obvious point that, of the three commercial casebooks, *Ben-Ishai & Percy* is the only one to place remedies last. The chapter opens with a list of learning objectives; six of the eight use action words that presume a fixed rule or other knowledge base. Four of them hope that students will "[d]escribe and apply" legal rules, one that students will be able to "calculate" damages, and another that students will be able to "explain" what types of losses are compensable. Only two objectives – "[a]rticulate and assess the general policy considerations influencing judicial decisions," and "[p]rovide a critical analysis of the dominance of the expectancy measure of damages" – relate to more critical goals, yet even the latter is closely tied to a narrow doctrinal subject. Only in one place in these objectives are students expected to "critically assess the law."[385]

Moreover, the way in which readings are introduced suggests that many can be distilled into discernible takeaways, often in the form of rules. This process of simplification and transmission of knowledge occurs with respect to cases, scholarly articles, and even to the entire law of remedies. Some passages in the commentary simply set out rules or principles in the same manner as might a conventional treatise. Many of the questions require students to distil rules or tests to demonstrate comprehension.The chapter's highly conceptual and taxonomic organization serves to further the impression that abstract rules and ideas form the intellectual building blocks of the law.[386]

The chapter does not particularly exalt the notion of context. There is the occasional reference to "common" practices of certain types of agreements, but in other instances the editor refers the reader to whole other chapters to discern the factual matrix of the case. Many of the excerpts are shorter than in the other casebooks, and some cases that receive detailed treatment in the others are not reproduced at all (although the inverse is true in some instances). A reference to Danzig's contextual study is so brief as to be perfunctory.[387]

---

385 *Ibid* at 785.

386 See *ibid* at 822 (*Chaplin v Hicks*, [1911] 2 KB 786 (CA) "illustrates that courts are not prevented from awarding expectancy damages just because there is an element of guesswork in assessment"), 789 (outline of three types of damages as a prelude to Fuller & Perdue, "Reliance Interest 1", *supra* note 112), 786 (law of contractual remedies might be broken down into four key general concepts), 885 (What are the two limbs of the remoteness test?), 889 (What is the remoteness test to this point?), 938.

387 See *ibid* at 833 (farm-out agreements), 799 (referring to the fact pattern in another chapter). For cases mentioned but not excerpted, see e.g. *ibid* at 798 (*Wertheim (Sally) v Chicoutimi Pulp Co*, [1911] AC 301 (PC)), 804 (*Anglia Television Ltd v Reed*, [1972] 1 QB 60 (CA)), 829 (*Peevyhouse v Garland Coal & Mining Co*, 382 P (2d) 109

Policy, while ranking first in the list of learning objectives, receives ambiguous treatment. The editor poses a number of questions that invite policy-related thinking, yet on closer inspection many include rather vague and open-ended formulations – "should" X be the case, do you "agree," which choice do you "prefer," "how" should X be justified – with little guidance to the reader (instructor or student) as to what considerations or other information should go into making such determinations. In other places, key policy considerations and other interesting features are either omitted from the discussion or not taken up – for example, discussions of liquidated damages or penalty clauses underplay the policy considerations militating against their enforcement. This treatment is reminiscent of the "anecdotal and speculative" ways that US Contracts teachers incorporate policy.[388]

And while there are references (albeit clustered in one section) about the role of the solicitor, the model of the barrister might be seen to figure equally, if not in greater degree, throughout the chapter. Practice-related questions refer to setting up a claim or cause of action. Of the intellectual tasks most frequently demanded of students, comparing and distinguishing cases figure prominently, as does analysis of hypothetical and counterfactual scenarios.[389]

The number of these examples suggests that the main messages conveyed by the remedies chapter are not the critical, functional, or realist ideas of law, but rather a vision premised on the importance of rules and analogical reasoning. This vision might not be one shared by its editor – indeed, the fact that Ben-Ishai, along with Percy, has assumed authorship of Chapter 1 and that the two have made a number of contemporary additions suggests that her commitments are quite

---

(SC Okla 1962) [*Peevyhouse*]), 832 (*Ruxley Electronics and Construction Ltd v Forsyth*, [1966] 1 AC 344), 865 (*Wallace v United Grain Growers Ltd*, [1997] 3 SCR 701). For shorter excerpts than in *Waddams*, see *ibid* at 889 (*Scyrup v Economy Tractor Parts Ltd* (1963), 43 WWR 49, 40 DLR (2d) 1026 (Man CA)). For longer excerpts than in *Swan*, see *ibid* at 911 (*Southcott Estates Inc v Toronto Catholic District School Board*, 2012 SCC 51, [2012] 2 SCR 675), 873 (*Hodgkinson v Simms*, [1994] 3 SCR 377, 117 DLR (4th) 161). The reference to Danzig appears in *ibid* at 885 (citing Richard Danzig, "*Hadley v Baxendale*: A Study in the Industrialization of the Law" (1975) 4 J Legal Stud 249 [Danzig, *Hadley*]).

388 See e.g. *Ben-Ishai & Percy* 10th ed, *supra* note 210 at 891, 924, 811, 821, 882, 904 (vague policy questions); *ibid* at 920–1, 932, 934 (liquidated damages and penalty clauses). *Cf* Mertz, *Language of Law School*, *supra* note 38 at 77.

389 See e.g. *Ben-Ishai & Percy* 10th ed, *supra* note 210 at 803–4, 961 (barrister-related tasks); *ibid* at 832, 866, 872, 891–2, 932, 934 (comparing and distinguishing cases); *ibid* at 803–4, 807, 872 (asking students to invent hypothetical scenarios); *ibid* at 807–8, 811, 823, 832, 882, 904, 949 (hypotheticals provided by the editors).

decidedly critical. If so, her remedies chapter might stand as yet another example (albeit one complicated by the multiple contributing editors over time) of an apparent contradiction between the scholarly commitments of the editor and the dominant message communicated by the casebook's substance.

CONCLUSION

Each of the leading commercial casebooks takes as a premise the idea that law is more than a system of abstract rules. Each at the very least acknowledges the century of (largely American) legal scholarship that has served to undermine classical legal thought. Each in its own way participates in an intellectual discourse that privileges underlying factors in judicial decisions, functional and purposive thinking, and exogenous critique.

And yet the old guard still stands sentry. The commercial casebooks, *Swan* aside, privilege rules and courts, and model legal reasoning primarily as the judicial technique of reasoning by analogy. The conventional view persists, notwithstanding most lead editors' scholarly commitments to realism. The casebooks therefore disclose a gap between most editors' propositional views about law and the views about law and legal reasoning communicated through their substance and pedagogical direction in notes and questions.

But the picture is not entirely straightforward. Both *Waddams* and *Ben-Ishai & Percy* intersperse propositional statements about realism throughout their remedies chapters as well. So it is not simply a question of stating one thing in an introduction and abandoning those ideas completely in the presentation of "substance." Rather, the principled commitment to American realist and critical thought informs the whole, but manages, nonetheless, to remain apart from the casebooks' core message.

The gap between propositional and executed commitments suggests that, on the whole, the casebooks fail to operationalize their theoretical commitments. Policy and contextual factors figure prominently as a matter of theory, but do not meaningfully inform how legal reasoning is presented. Policy and context become marginalized in the same way that Mertz observed in the US classroom. The uneven tendency of professors actually to assign the introductory chapters is a sign of this marginalization, as is the low market share of *Swan*, the one book that does thoroughly attempt to connect its theory with its practice.[390] All

390 Based on syllabi, three instructors assign the *Waddams* perspectives chapter, whereas six do not. By contrast, seventeen instructors assign the introductory chapter in *Ben-Ishai & Percy*, whereas seven do not.

the casebooks evidence a theoretical eclecticism (even *Swan*, which has a unifying theory, draws on a wide variety of ideas about contract derived from different American authors), but very few of those actually used by teachers and students put these ideas into practice.

This failure to incorporate theory into practice is somewhat ironic given that the editors all, in their own way, seem to *aspire* to do so. This aspiration is most evident in *Swan*, which actually realizes it via the solicitor's approach, and *Milner*, which explicitly embraces both professional and academic virtues. But even *Waddams* and *Ben-Ishai & Percy* evince a similar concern. The assumed professional consensus that appears to operate in the background shows how neither book is a mere academic discursus on law, but is intimately tied to the future training of legal professionals. *Ben-Ishai & Percy*'s Introduction both begins and ends with an emphasis on the "essential skills" students will develop over the course of studying contract law, and the *Waddams* notes and questions frequently invite students to "advise" hypothetical clients.[391] Practice *is* important to all the books – they are meant to be used as teaching tools in a self-consciously *professional* educational environment. But just because the books seem to embody the virtue that a theoretical and practical study of law are mutually reinforcing, that does not mean – and this is crucial – that the particular theories and particular visions of practice correspond.

The reasons for this gap are legion, and I explore them in detail in the concluding chapter. But the most obvious and perhaps most powerful force is the implicit, unstated idea that there is a core body of knowledge and shared professional competence of lawyers that *specifically* requires a focus on courts, rules, and analogical reasoning. *Milner*'s not-so-abject apology, *Ben-Ishai & Percy*'s "confession and avoidance," and Waddams's references to the importance of rationality in his textbook Preface all point in the direction of a powerful *non-dit* operating in the background that implicitly prioritizes a traditional, classical view of law and legal reasoning, despite a century of scholarly developments to the contrary. Notwithstanding the aspiration to translate theory into practice, deeper intellectual commitments seem to get in the way. This, as it turns out, is a pattern we see when speaking to Canadian common law Contracts professors about their own teaching, as the next chapter explores.

391 *Ben-Ishai & Percy* 10th ed, *supra* note 210 at 1, 15.

Chapter Four

Making Better Lawyers: The Aspiration to Translate Theory into Practice

It is now time to hear from the professors in my study. Notwithstanding the fact that conversations about legal education inevitably are conducted in the shadow of the "fierce debate" between the profession and the academy, when professors actually talk or write about their teaching, they overwhelmingly express an aspiration to translate theory into practice. Many vaunt the importance of theory or critique, but when asked why these are important, few answer that they need to be taught for their own sake, out of a desire to uphold the purely academic mission of a university.[392] Instead, and consistently among those with very different theoretical perspectives, most say that theory is important *because it makes better lawyers.* These Contracts professors, moreover, spell out in detail how their specific theories make more proficient, ethical, and socially conscious lawyers. This aspiration confirms the possibility of teaching Contracts for the lawyer as citizen. It also invites us, in the following chapter, to investigate the extent to which the aspiration to translate theory into practice is actually being realized.

Before elucidating this common aspiration, I begin by recounting how these professors talk about the relationship between theory and practice when they are speaking, not about their own teaching, but about the more abstract question of the role of the law school or law professor. In these more abstract discussions, the conventional oppositional trope predominates. The idea that theory and practice should be

---

392 *Cf.* Jules L Coleman, "Legal Theory and Practice" (1995) 83 Geo LJ 2579 ("legal theory is both instrumentally and intrinsically valuable. It is instrumentally valuable insofar as it contributes to or enhances actual legal practice. It is intrinsically valuable in [that it enhances] the integrity of law as a field of study [and] ... the integrity of law as a social practice" at 2579–80) [emphasis omitted].

balanced or integrated is at the moment only an emerging narrative in these higher-order discussions about legal education – much like the integrative visions of Kronman, Carnegie, and Arthurs are but hiccups in the long-standing perennial debates between the academy and the profession. It is therefore all the more striking that, when we get to the more personal, contextual, and detailed discussions of the teaching of Contracts, professors overwhelmingly view theory and practice as mutually reinforcing.

THEORY AND PRACTICE, WORLDS APART: REPRODUCING THE CONVENTIONAL NARRATIVE

In my interviews, the conversation would often drift – sometimes directed by me, sometimes more organically – to the attitudes that professors hold about legal education writ large. These moments never formed the heart of our discussion, but they are useful for highlighting the milieu in which professors imagine themselves to be operating. In this context, the fierce debates about the jurisdiction and control of legal education figure prominently. The prevalence with which professors talk about the conflict between theory and practice, profession and academy, in general terms, highlights just how tenacious this oppositional construct is – especially given that, in discussing their own teaching, most professors appear to reject it.

The Perennial Debate

The tension between the academy and the profession is often portrayed as a given, as a background condition that operates as a matter of fact. Some, like Professor 15, view the tension as relatively harmless in that it serves to highlight two separate objectives, neither mutually exclusive:

> The debates are just the same now as they were forty years ago ... And it's the old debate about to what extent is the academic study of law really just a preparation for practice and to what extent is it a *broader* intellectual discipline. And the answer is – it's both ... Acknowledging that people take this degree ... to get qualified for the Bar ... is *relevant*. And [it] is also what gives law schools their claim to be a distinct discipline.[393]

393 [015], Interview, lines 744–56.

Similarly, Professor 44 self-identifies both with the tension and with having reconciled it:

> [The title of] one the finest articles on law teaching I've ever read ... is ... "The Law Teacher – A Man Divided against Himself"... And the idea is, what are we? Are we academics, or are we people preparing students for practice? Now is it ... purely academic, or is it ... kind of *vocational*? ... I've been in that situation because ... I've always done both![394]

Professor 7 takes a less benign view, arguing that the tension makes it difficult for first-year students to navigate between technical and broader conceptions of law, and "drums out" enthusiasm:

> There's a ... tension between intellectual goals and professional goals that perhaps makes it harder for [students] to ... understand what it is that they're supposed to achieve ... The profession itself has a huge influence on students and [produces] pressure ... to get the highest possible marks immediately ...
>
> The tension between learning what you need to be a lawyer – which sometimes gets reduced down to learning what you need to pass the bar exam – and the ambitions of law schools to teach law as a social phenomenon, is not always easy for the students to navigate ... The pressure from the *profession* – ... as the profession actually exerts it, and also the pressure that comes from students who *think* they know what the profession wants them to learn – makes it hard for them to navigate those two objectives that exist in tension.[395]

A number of professors similarly stake out a position in favour of the law faculty's "academic" role, in part as a reaction against the pressure from the profession that Professor 7 references. Professor 40 rails against the incursion of the local bar into teaching priorities:

> We're *not* embedded in a courthouse ... We're in a university campus ... There is a great deal of pressure upon the faculty of law to see itself as a kind of vocational training ground for the local bar ... [I]t's not unknown for members of the law society ... to come to [faculty] councils and tell us ... what we should be teaching, with a view to producing the kinds of lawyers that they want ... There's always been a certain amount of pushback,

394 [044], Interview, lines 27–37, referring to Thomas F Bergin, "The Law Teacher: A Man Divided against Himself" (1968) U Virginia L Rev 637.

395 [007], Interview, lines 33–89.

> but it's never been thoroughly successful ... I'm not terribly inclined to do some of the things that ... law society folks would want us to do, which is pure drafting skills ... *I won't do that*. And I've been quite *resolute* in that ...
>
> I do think that it's important to maintain a fairly clear divide between the two experiences ... Here, you're being taught the law, but you're also being taught to analyse it, to think about it rigorously, systematically, to see if it makes sense, to see how it can be *improved* when it doesn't make sense ... And the best practitioners *do that*, day in, day out. But ... there should be a divide of some sort. Not an absolute divide, but a divide nonetheless.[396]

Professor 40, like just over a third of the participants, has limited experience practising law. However, we see a similarly oppositional attitude among professors who *do* practise. Professor 2 is very interesting in this regard. Professor 2 has taught law for over thirty years and has maintained an active practice during that time. Professor 2's connections to practice are so deep that former students regularly contact Professor 2 to get advice on active files; Professor 2's course syllabus outlines a list of nine detailed objectives that are heavily weighted to practical objectives, including "negotiation, drafting, and interpretation" and "preparing and presenting claims." But despite this apparent embrace of the practice of law, Professor 2 is among the most oppositional in describing the role of the law professor and law school:

> The intellectual approach is the basic skill. We are first and foremost a faculty of law ...
>
> A university is a place of reflection, a place of critique, a place of social change. That's the role of a faculty of law and the same for faculties of social sciences. To help students reflect on society. A faculty of law is ... not a place where you learn a practice [*une pratique*] or technique. It's not a technical school ... I've worked in offices. I do practice, it's important, but it is easily learned. What you must learn [in a law faculty] is more the theoretical aspect of law, reflection and social critique ...
>
> The day faculties of law stop playing this role, they will no longer belong in a university ... I know there are significant discussions these days in Canada on the role of law faculties to prepare students for practice, but I don't believe it is my role to do that. My role is to enable them to be able to understand the law, and once they have understood it, they will learn the rest.[397]

---

396 [040], Interview, lines 865–905.

397 [002], Interview, lines 925, 225–42, 732–64; [002], Syllabus (2015–16), pp 2–3 [translation from French].

Other professors reference the distinctively academic goals of the law faculty or university in briefer compass. For example, Professor 32 insists on using the term *jurist* instead of *lawyer*:

> This is – frankly, in reality, nowadays, probably a bit of a fiction – but I'm clinging to it anyways ... You argue that you don't necessarily go to law school to be a lawyer ... Even if that is somewhat a fiction, I ... still think it's important that students consider themselves ... to be *jurists* and not only proto-professionals who are learning the tools of the trade ... It goes back ... to the old ... law-school-is-a-trade-school versus part-of-the-academy debate, and just for me it's one of those ... codes or symbols of keeping me grounded in the academic pursuit.[398]

These preceding quotations seem to corroborate an image of hostility on the part of legal academics to the demands of the profession. Yet, among the participants, we see evidence of hostility in the other direction. Professor 12, for example, says that the *Arthurs Report* was "absolutely dreadful" because it "deprecated severely" the "highly practical" work that Professor 12 does in contract law teaching and writing:

> [T]o the extent that the law schools repudiate the obligation to teach their students how to practise law, they're not doing what they should be doing. You would think it *monstrous* if the faculty of medicine said to its students, "We're not going to teach you how to cure people. We're going to teach you the *theory* of medicine." Medicine and law are professions, and the job of a profession is to *do things in the world* ... Law schools should ask themselves the question, "Is what we are teaching, whether individual courses or a *range* of courses, *designed* to give a student the ability to give ... good legal advice?"[399]

Professor 60, hired many years before the *Arthurs Report* came out, stipulated as a condition of employment that Professor 60 "would not write." This professor, who "never" did publish legal scholarship other than a case comment, describes the opposition in similar terms:

> I always valued law school mainly as the way to prepare for a *profession*, where you do the work as opposed to ... an *academic discipline* in itself ... And we're in a somewhat difficult position. We're at a university and ... the idea is you should do what other professors do at the university. You know, make it *academic*. But it's a *professional school*.[400]

398 [032], Interview, lines 138–49.
399 [012], Interview, lines 783–9, 409–18.
400 [060], Interview, lines 583–91, 284–91.

Professor 43, also quite senior, argues that law schools *should* respond to the demands of the profession:

> In the good old days, [firms] could take articling students on ... and charge them out to a company and they didn't mind. They can't do that anymore ... [To] improve their profitability, ... law firms [want students] to be damned good right from the start. They've got to hit the decks running ...
>
> We're busy ... going, "Oh! Come to us!" ... "We're diverse! ... We've got social access to justice! ... We'll get you an internship here, and we'll give you that here" ... We can't do that any longer because the firms, the big client, the buyer, has shown up at the door and said, "That's not what I want ... I want the kid who's ready to go now because I'm worried about my profitability. I can't train anybody anymore."
>
> And so we as law schools have to recognize that and gear up and transition ... We ... have to put them out more prepared.[401]

Each of the above three professors, who advocates strongly for preparing students for practice, is an outlier in one sense or another: one has left the full-time academy, another was hired on condition of specifically avoiding scholarly writing (at a time when such a demand was plausible; it likely no longer is), and a third genuinely stands out in pedagogical approach (as an advocate of problem-based learning). These expressions are much more emphatic, idiosyncratically so, than the views of the majority of the participants in my study, although a number express similar views, albeit more mildly. Professor 49, who compresses the doctrinal material into one semester, and focuses on reading real contracts for another semester, states simply that "I don't see why you *wouldn't* emphasize the practical side of contracts."[402] Professor 26 sees it as an "obligation to students" not to emphasize theory over "a sufficient knowledge ... of core concepts," tied to a "practice-oriented approach ... in emphasizing law as something that is usable as opposed to knowable."[403] Professor 54 tells students the practical benefits of what they are learning in class "all the time" because "[legal reasoning is] really what they'll be doing as articling students, and I think *that's* what we're in large measure training them for in law school."[404]

Sometimes professors assert the importance of professional considerations by reference to their own experience practising law (forty-seven out of seventy-five participants did some sort of legal practice in addition

401 [043], Interview, lines 723–810.
402 [049], Interview, lines 216–17.
403 [026], Interview, lines 238–40, 523–7.
404 [054], Interview, lines 352, 366–8.

to a year of articling). Comments such as "I'm sort of a practitioner; I'm not a theory person"[405] or "I'm trying to teach the course from a practical perspective ... because I'm a practitioner"[406] relate pedagogical choices to a sense of personal role or identity. Using one's practitioner's identity is, moreover, not restricted to adjunct professors: one of those comments was by a full professor, one by a full-time practitioner.

The oppositional narrative, therefore, is alive and well among Canadian common law Contracts professors. However, this statement needs to be qualified in a number of important respects. First, the fact that we see both pro-academy and pro-profession arguments undermines the idea that the legal academy is wholeheartedly at war with the profession; the academy, as judged by this cross-section of Contracts professors, does not speak with one voice. Moreover, as the example of Professor 2 shows, just because someone identifies strongly as a practitioner does not mean that he or she will adopt a pro-practice attitude when it comes to legal education; and vice-versa. And while the oppositionality of the narrative does figure prominently, it does not do so exclusively. As with all stories, there are subplots, and in the next section I identify the instances in which professors articulate – at the more abstract level – the notion that theory and practice can and should be integrated and balanced.

Balance and Integrate: A Secondary Narrative

There are signs that a secondary story is starting to be told – by a small number of professors, for the moment – about the nature and purpose of legal education. In this story, theory and practice should be integrated, and it is natural to do so. The most explicit champion of the integrative approach is Professor 62, a young professor who has published on legal education theory and also maintains an active practice of law.[407] Professor 62 challenges the orthodox view with as much vigour as some of those who advocate for one side or the other:

> I find the distinction ... between theory and practice or skills and theory, an inane, untenable distinction ...
>
> [P]art of the reason I think I was hired is because I'm kind of a hybrid academic/practitioner to begin with ... Before I even began to put together ... my syllabus, there was an expectation that this is what we do [at this particular law school] – we *explode* the distinction between theory and

405 [013], Interview, lines 630–1.
406 [065], Interview, lines 164–7.
407 [062], Interview, lines 509, 524.

> practice ... [I]n many ways, [my institution]'s ... focus on trying to integrate skills and practice ... in some ways grows out of, ... at least intellectually, the article that I [co-authored], ... focusing on law, the teaching of law, the learning of law, the practice of law, as an interpretive practice ...
>
> I'm not just trying to help students become *lawyers*, ... but rather ... how to ... lead a virtuous life as a lawyer. And that's a huge, of course, ambitious undertaking ... and I almost feel embarrassed to say it, and I think that says something about the climate that we're in, politically and ideologically, but I think that has to be the task ... We're not trying to foreground and emphasize skills to the detriment of theory or to the detriment of ideas. It's the opposite. It's trying to bring the two together. And it's trying to use skills and techniques as windows ... into the ideas underneath them and underlying them, and to challenge them, to remake law and legal practice from the inside out.[408]

A number of factors combine to produce such an impassioned articulation: a prior intellectual commitment (evidenced by the co-authored article), the sense that Professor 62 is furthering an institutional mandate, and some desire to resist, or even reframe, a conventional debate (reacting against "the climate we're in"). These conditions combine with Professor 62's dual identity as a scholar and a practitioner to produce a highly refined articulation of legal education's mission at the more abstract level.

The confluence of these conditions and personality is not common, but nor is it necessary to produce expressions of an integrative philosophy or story of legal education. They can appear in more prosaic ways, as when Professor 51, a particularly innovative instructor who, among other things, founded and performed in a contracts dance collective with students, describes the "ideal" as being to "integrate and balance ... doctrine, theory, and some practice."[409] Another example is when Professor 16 describes theory as a "container" or "framework" of law, and aspires to find the "right balance ... connecting that theory to practical real-life examples."[410]

Although it is the rare professor who has the words to characterize the role of the law school or law professor as being to balance or integrate theory and practice, the few who do might reflect a more common understanding. When we descend the high peaks of generality and arrive at the more grounded conversations about what professors actually

408 [062], Interview, lines 455–513, 642–56.

409 [051], Interview, lines 582–4.

410 [016], Interview, lines 467–80.

do in the classroom, the integrative commitment becomes much more apparent. Here, on this contextual, familiar terrain, professors describe their "highly personal" (to recall *Milner*) visions of teaching, discussing what they believe and what they want to accomplish. The image portrayed about theory and practice in these discussions is much different. Almost unanimously, professors express the desire to translate their particular theoretical commitments into making better lawyers.

"BECAUSE IT MAKES BETTER LAWYERS": THE PRACTICAL UTILITY OF THEORY AND CRITICAL PERSPECTIVES

Commitments to academic values flourish among Canadian common law Contracts professors. Most participants in my study express a commitment to some theoretical view of law, informed by research, scholarly training, and reflection. Many say that engendering critical thinking or critical perspectives is an essential goal. These two features are perhaps the hallmark of the academy; seeing them surface among law professors appears to vindicate the victory of universities' control over legal education. What disturbs this narrative is the frequency with which professors answer the question "Why is a particularly theoretical or critical perspective important?" with some variation of "because it makes better lawyers." *When speaking about their own teaching*, at least half of the participants in my study provide a clear, direct, and distinctive answer in this vein. By contrast, only about four express some scepticism about the importance of practical utility. This overwhelming tendency to justify the importance of academic values in practical terms suggests that the aspiration to translate theory into practice is widespread.

Reinforcing the depth of this integrative commitment is the sophistication and diversity of ways in which theory is said to inform practice. No one theory seems to be more, or less, amenable to the instrumental-practical justification that teaching theory makes better lawyers. Moreover, the formulation "because it makes better lawyers" serves to deepen and enrich what it means to practise. Sometimes this occurs when professors specify the particular skills that define or constitute the better lawyer. Other times professors use the term "better lawyer" without disaggregating it into particular attributes. A *particular* theoretical virtue is said to make better lawyers. In both these instances, professors signal their intention to translate their theoretical commitments directly into an eclectic toolkit of lawyerly skills. Moreover, sometimes a "better lawyer" is a lawyer with a more public ethos – and in these instances, we see seeds of an aspiration to cultivate the lawyer as citizen in the broader sense of the word.

Making "Better Lawyers" Generally: A Shared Commitment

The aspiration to translate theory into practice can be seen most directly among those professors who, themselves, are highly theoretical. Professor 4, a formalist legal thinker whose main goal is to show that there is an "internal logic, a set of principles, that anchor contract law," puts the point most directly:

> [Y]ou do theory to help you with practice, right? I'm very theoretically inclined, but theory for the purpose of theory is silly ... We want to know how to act in life and ... do law in life, and when we run into an obstacle, we have to analyse what's going on, and that takes us to theory and philosophy.[411]

Professor 1, also very theoretically inclined, speaks at length about the complex interplay between technicalities and high theory. It would be hard to invent a more potent illustration of the integrative conception of theory and practice:

> It's in the material that we call "technical" that there is a need to bring well elaborated theoretical material ... It's indispensable to show, in teaching, that at the heart of this technical material lies a theoretical content, or theoretical forms, or content borrowed from other disciplines. Put another way, in the technical material there is an interplay between law and the totality of knowledge.

Professor 1, who once taught licensed lawyers as part of continuing professional development, more generally affirms that "theory makes better practitioners." The commitment appears to run deep. In an "argument" section of the course syllabus, Professor 1 writes that the primary objective of the course is

> to reason and work in the law of contracts at a high theoretical level. This is to say, to move from a technical solution according to a certain system of positive law to a concept. And, returning from this concept, [to] be able to understand the technical solutions that flow from it.

For Professor 1, "concepts," variously including "freedom, will, responsibility, patrimony, market, certainty, foreseeability, calculability, et cetera," are more easily "operationalized" than doctrinal law.[412]

---

411 [004], Interview, lines 7, 607–12.

412 [001], Interview, lines 99–113, 284–92, 142–3; [001], Syllabus (2015–16), p 1 [translation from French].

A number of professors simply proclaim that theory makes for "better lawyers" without spelling out the detailed interaction between theory and practice. This tendency surfaces both among professors with formalist leanings and among those who fall more squarely into the realist camp. (In the next chapter, I delve more deeply into how professors' words imbue these labels, realism and formalism, with greater meaning.) For example, Professor 8 takes a highly taxonomic approach to law, reminiscent of Langdellian systematization; such categorization specifically helps students "create a road map," and "helps them to understand the situations they're dealing with."[413] For Professor 15, who "like[s]" the logic of contract law and who is a "believer in rules," learning to "mix ... the logical and the ... quasi-intuitive," fitting "real life into these abstract ... categories" "makes better lawyers."[414]

Another example of a highly categorical approach is Professor 27, who dedicates significant class time to ensuring that students understand the Hohfeldian distinction between rights and freedoms. Without this categorical clarity, Professor 27 says, one is "lost as a lawyer":

> There is a deepening narrative of what contract law ... should be doing. But there's also a grammar, and it does it in a particular way. If you don't understand the grammar, then you're lost as a lawyer. So ... we actually spend time with Hohfeld and ... draw the distinction between rights and freedoms and liberties and immunities ... There is [this] basic ... conceptual bedrock which ... law forces you to come to grips with. Otherwise you're just gassing around in the abstract.[415]

If for Professor 27 a "conceptual bedrock" grounds students in the contextual and practical realities of lawyerly work, then for a number of other more realist professors it is the underlying factors of policy, politics, and context that provide useful clarity on the path to making better lawyers. For example, for Professor 67, "going beyond the obvious makes you a great lawyer." Professor 56 argues that the "realist, policy-driven" question of "what is going on here and do you think that's right" should "always ... stay[] with you as a lawyer." For Professor 29, understanding how doctrine "does in fact have a solid foundation in public policy ... makes you a better lawyer." Professor 16, who

413 [008], Interview, lines 152–7, 163–80.

414 [015], Interview, lines 32, 283, 235, 323–5, 431.

415 [027], Interview, lines 403–12 (referring elsewhere to Wesley Newcomb Hohfeld, "Fundamental Legal Conceptions as Applied in Judicial Reasoning" (1917) 26 Yale LJ 710).

emphasizes the ability to "see law in context," which includes "policy and politics," and the idea that law is "a very integral part of our society that affects and is affected by other societal matters," believes that "it makes you a better lawyer if you understand that there are those things going on." And Professor 28 has seen that those students who "excel" at law firms are

> ones that know that it's just not enough to look at the law on ... paper or ... doctrine ... But ... they search farther – they try and figure out where it came from. Where that particular rule came from, and what the context of that case was, they look at the context of this case – and they're able to do much more.[416]

Just what "more" can a lawyer do, given exposure to diverse theoretical perspectives? A number of professors spell this out quite distinctly.

Specific Skills of the Better Lawyer

Persuasive Argumentation (Advocacy)

The most prominent specific skill is the ability to craft persuasive arguments, usually before a court of law. Consider, for example, this quotation from Professor 3, a self-described Marxist who specifically connects his theoretical commitments to enabling students to make better arguments:

> I try to encourage students to see what I believe is the truth of law, which is it's a battleground of ideology ... It's the basic conflict that we play on politically between our more ... capitalistic tendencies and our socialistic tendencies, and it's a conflict we play on personally between our sense of wanting our individual freedom unencumbered by social constraint and wanting and needing communities to support us and help us understand who we are. It's the human condition, laid out in contract law ...
>
> I tell them you're going to be much better lawyers if you understand that legal argument is about manipulating, rhetorically and analytically, the grand arrogance of our collective culture. That's where you're going to be persuasive. That's where you're going to appeal.[417]

---

416 [067], Handwritten notes of untranscribed, unrecorded interview; [056], Interview, lines 110–14; [029], Interview, lines 217–22; [016], Interview, lines 863, 862, 581–3, 866–7; [028], Interview, lines 363–8.

417 [003], Interview, lines 124–38, 234–8. On Professor 3's commitment to Marxism, see *ibid*, lines 108–9.

And just as Professor 3 connects theoretical commitments, which very much align with the CLS construct of individualism/altruism, with the skill of persuasion, many more professors committed to tenets of realism perform a similar move. Thus, Professor 31 will specifically bring up "realist" comments, emphasizing that "judges know the result they want to reach, and then they have to fit it in the common law doctrine" in order to "signal the importance of ... making persuasive arguments." For Professor 50, highlighting factors that might "play a very persuasive role in the way a judge will jump" is important in order to "get to the heart of the judge." For Professor 16, looking at the law "in a broader context ... makes you a much more powerful advocate." For Professor 11, it is important to understand how the "judge is also concerned with ... policy implications" because "their job as lawyers is going to be to make arguments, and sometimes they're going to be making the tougher argument." Professor 44 focuses on "disagreements in policy between the judges" to help students reflect on their "argument before the final court." And, for Professor 30, who emphasizes relational contracts, "understanding a contractual relationship between parties as an evolving process, which may depart from the strict terms of the contract, is vital to ... students' ability later on to craft arguments on behalf of their ... clients."[418] At the other end of the realist-formalist spectrum, Professor 4 highlights how being able to discover an inner logic generates a persuasive advocacy strategy:

> When they go into court, the judge wants to know, "Put these two cases together for me ... Tell me why I should follow this case as opposed to the other one" ... Every now and then you'll say, "Well, no – they're contradictory" ... That's never the preferred answer ... The judge will always prefer the answer that actually is able to reconcile the materials together.[419]

Professors also emphasize the importance of cultivating argumentative skills, not by connecting them to a *particular* theory, but by exposing students to *multiple* theories. On this "eclecticism" rationale, exposing students to various theories equips them with multiple possible tools for the lawyer's toolkit – reflecting an aspiration that resembles Kennedy and Fisher's characterization. A variant of the theme is that having access to these multiple tools enables students to take on

418 [031], Interview, lines 201, 205–7, 230–2; [050], Interview, lines 135–6, 166; [016], Interview, lines 548–9; [011], Interview, lines 421, 443–4; [044], Interview, lines 684, 699–700; [030], Interview, lines 515–19.

419 [004], Interview, lines 279–92.

both sides of an argument, consider alternative perspectives, and anticipate counterarguments – resembling Kronman's virtue of imaginative sympathy, the ability to "place oneself imaginatively in the position of others" while being simultaneously detached.[420]

Professors from across the theoretical spectrum demonstrate their commitment to this argumentative eclecticism rationale. Both the strongly committed formalist Professor 4 and the realist Professor 28 assert that their job is to "play devil's advocate," and "won't share" their strong views.[421] Professor 50, who speaks about the importance of getting to the heart of the judge, does not "take a clear view on what is good or bad about particular cases," but emphasizes instead that "it is very important in practice that you fully and completely understand where the other side is going to go ... and fully understand the arguments they're going to make." Professor 64, who ascribes to an "element of critical legal theory," tries to "minimize my opinion," describing a "convincing" argument as one that "is going to be some combination of legal impact, policy effect, and values." Professor 33 specifically cultivates the ability to make arguments by randomly assigning positions to students based on themes of class, race, and power. Professor 52 says, "Part of what makes a person a good lawyer is to be able to consider different perspectives."[422]

In addition to theory, the academic virtue of critical thinking – definitions of which vary – is often justified in terms of making persuasive arguments in practice. Professor 37 wants students to "hone their skills of imaginative insight and to think with an agile mind that's able to transcend boundaries" in order (in part) to "be better advocates for their clients ... at a very basic level"; "to question assumptions, to look *beyond* the answers, *behind* the answers – and ultimately to be able to be *creative* enough to think of *new* answers." Why? You can "help your client better if you understand how to think in this much more creative and critical way." For Professor 45, the ability to "critically analyse rules" – to "offer some kind of critique [and] ... not just blindly follow" or apply rules – would help "persuade the court of a particular perspective, or to convince a court to move in a particular direction ... The

420 Kennedy & Fisher, "Introduction", *supra* note 27 at 3; Kronman, *Lost Lawyer*, *supra* note 16 at 72, 98.

421 [004], Interview, lines 427 ("I think my answers to these questions [as to whether law is autonomous] are irrelevant to the course"), 452 ("[s]o they say one thing, I say the opposite. They say something completely radically opposed and I'll say again the opposite"); [028], Interview, line 236.

422 [050], Interview, lines 438–40, 486, 503–6; [064], Interview, lines 743–50; [064], Interview, lines 584–6; [033], Interview, line 480; [052], Interview, lines 167–8.

best lawyers, the great lawyers, are those who can construct the most persuasive legal arguments."[423]

Although courtroom advocacy remains the most frequent practical skill that professors invoke for the relevance of theoretical perspectives and critical thinking, other skills not directly related to advocacy also surface. When professors express an ambition to cultivate these skills – problem solving, planning, and creative lawyering – they reflect the aspiration to translate diverse theories into an even broader array of tools for the lawyer's toolkit, often quite directly outlining the connection between specific theories and these manifestations of practice.

Problem Solving and Planning

Two participants, distinctive in their emphasis on non-state normativity, specifically connect a pluralist focus on the "legal systems" of contracting parties to skills of planning, problem solving, negotiation, and drafting. Professor 42 says:

> I try to persuade students that contract is a dynamic and forward-looking mode of social ordering, and that therefore it's a course about lawyers' involvement in the construction of little legal systems, each time they negotiate a contract. And although it's a planning exercise, a dynamic forward-looking exercise, there are all kinds of really good skills that are grounded in law, but are nonetheless skills. So, negotiation, figuring out how much to say when and where, determining how many of a client's instructions should be acted upon, *and* later on, maybe, having to convert a deliberately ambiguous or informal arrangement into codified form ... The idea is to compare all of these little legal systems that lawyers make for their clients, usually in multifarious and informal ways, ... against the background of some basic contract doctrine ... It also tries to be a course in the kinds of skills that are relevant to that operation.[424]

Professor 36, for whom Stewart Macaulay and Ian Macneil were "formative," connects socio-legal and pluralist theories of law by arguing that the ability to navigate different normative systems trains problem solvers:

> [T]he reality is that if you speak to a client in a particular business environment or particular cultural environment or family environment, you

423 [037], Interview, lines 274–7, 259–61, 318; [045], Interview, lines 135–9, 112–13, 158–60.

424 [042], Interview, lines 79–95.

> quickly become conscious of all of the stuff that constrain[s] their actions which doesn't actually flow from law. It flows from different kinds of pressures, normative or otherwise. And so when people say, "I learned more in [the first month at a law firm] than I learned in law school," actually what they're saying is, "I wish I'd understood earlier on that there was this connection that needed to be made in order to be effective problem solvers. I needed to modulate my understanding of legal norms to fit with the environment" ...
>
> If one is concerned about training professionals who are effective problem solvers in the world, and I am, ... people who are able to understand the aspirations of the individuals who rely [on] them for those skills, then I think the first and most important value should be the ability to navigate different normative systems and the recognition that they exist out there.[425]

Problem solving also appears to be another objective, like making persuasive arguments, that is a feature of more traditional doctrinal teaching. Two instructors, both with over forty years of experience, use doctrine to explore underlying policy ideas, and emphasize the importance of problem solving. Professor 48 says that determining relevance (a core feature of legal reasoning, which I explore in depth in the next chapter) is a skill that students

> can take to any kind of problem solving. What are the facts you've got? What do you have to resolve? How would you go about resolving [it]? What are the options for resolving? How have others resolved it? ... [P]eople who are not lawyers ... [have] no concept that when you've got a problem, [a key thing to determine is] which parts of those problems are key and have to be solved and which parts you can talk about forever but actually they're not key.

Likewise, Professor 29 tries to get students "to see how what they are doing might be relevant to problem solving in the real world." Another senior professor draws from "problems" from Professor 44's own law office files to evaluate students. The desired end is similar: Professor 44 seeks a "confluence" of theory and practice: "I do theory and then switch into, 'Well, here's how we *use* the theory in everyday practice.'"[426]

There is also the example of Professor 43, an early adopter of technology, who has been using some form of screen capture of lectures in order to free up class time for problem-based learning since the mid-1990s.

---

425 [036], Interview, lines 207–16, 247–59.

426 [048], Interview, lines 438–42, 700–15; [029], Interview, lines 663–4; [044], Interview, lines 226–35, 40–2.

Professor 43 believes strongly in the importance of context in providing good legal services: "[Law firms are] saying, 'We need people who understand our clients and our clients' businesses ... we need [lawyers] to have that context ... side of things.'" The desire to emphasize context also motivates the problem-based pedagogy: problem solving is what students "do when they get out of here." It is "the *biggest skill* we give our lawyers."[427]

Creative Lawyering

Finally, professors state that theoretical or critical perspectives on law are important because they help produce creative lawyers capable of effecting change. The contingency or arbitrariness of law, which for some flows from the insights of legal history, might help students participate in changing the law. As Professor 17 says:

> *The rules really do get made* ... They get made by people. They arise in certain circumstances, and if ... circumstances had been different, they might have developed a completely different way ... I say to them: "If you want to change it, if you want it to be different, you ... have to [understand law's arbitrariness and contingency]."[428]

Similarly, Professor 62 tries to "deconstruct" contract doctrine, or "teach the social construction" of contract law doctrine, to show how "law is made and remade and what the constraints are and what the creative opportunities" are. This objective is deeply connected to Professor 62's theoretical commitments as a "critical legal pluralist":

> I think it's really important to *counter* ... [students' inclination to] look for certainty and black letter law ... Even something that seems as dry and as technical as contract law has a socio-cultural construction ...
>
> [A] critical approach to law to me is grounding law as a social and cultural institution with a history, that's both ... temporal and place-based ... *De*construction can only be useful if it leads to *re*construction, and ... remaking legal practice is something I'm really interested in ... I'm trying to help them *critically unmask*, so to speak, contract law doctrine, so that we can then begin the task of thinking collectively ... about how contract law doctrine should be remade, if at all.[429]

427 [043], Interview, lines 1295–300, 1146–52.
428 [017], Interview, lines 332–43.
429 [062], Interview, lines 276–8, 295–301, 350–3, 615–63.

Other professors articulate a similar idea in more prosaic ways. Professor 54 encourages students to "become comfortable with uncertainty ... As long as you can identify what's uncertain, why it's uncertain, and what the potential arguments ... to resolve the uncertainty are, ... that's all you need to do ... as a lawyer." To analogous effect, Professor 33 states that morality and public policy play a large role in the course because "that's where the most creative lawyering takes place."[430]

The Ethos of "Better" Lawyers

> But what do you mean by better lawyers? ... Are better lawyers ... lawyers who are better people and more likely to be ethical? That's one way of being a better lawyer, and then the other way of being a better lawyer is they can manipulate the hell out of the law to win for their clients ... And I think I'm doing both.[431]

When professors describe the importance of teaching theory or critique, they do not simply say that it will help make more proficient lawyers. Instead, a number of them use this occasion to identify the ethos of what it means to be a better lawyer. In these formulations, we see how the translation of theory into practice can also help to serve some broader public objectives. Although the examples are not nearly as numerous as the ones about proficiency, they are frequent enough to suggest that, at least at the level of aspiration, some professors attempt to integrate theory and practice in a way amenable to the broader vision of the lawyer as citizen. Professors describe how theory makes lawyers who are more ethical, who advocate for marginalized communities, who incorporate concerns of social effects, power imbalances, and diversity, and who perform their "moral duty" to represent clients.

Sometimes becoming an ethically better lawyer means incorporating concerns of justice into the lawyer's identity, much as Swan admonishes students never to think that it is "unlawyerly to be passionately concerned for justice." Professor 3, from whom the quote opening the section was taken, espouses such a view, emphasizing the lawyer's "moral role":

> A lot of people come into law school believing in justice ... I want to vindicate that belief rather than destroy it. I want to tell them that they're

430 [054], Interview, lines 733–8; [033], Interview, line 260.
431 [003], Interview, lines 309–16.

> actually reflected in the law ... I think when people feel they can detach themselves from the moral basis of what they're doing and create a sensibility that this is a purely technical enterprise, I think that's a really dangerous place to be ... I try to say, "Actually, your intuition that law is about justice is absolutely right. And I'm going to show you that, in the law, the struggle about what justice is is happening all the time, everywhere, and that, as a lawyer, you are part of that struggle. So you cannot escape that moral role as a lawyer."[432]

Many professors draw on their specific theoretical commitments to articulate how "better" lawyers serve justice. Professor 63 emphasizes both a "realist" and "critical" perspective directly in order to "advocate for change ... for members of marginalized communities or [those] less well represented in the judiciary"; advocates must become proficient at explaining "context" to judges. In this respect, critical thinking is a "professional responsibility." Similarly, Professor 33 exposes students to a "range of theoretical perspectives ... because I don't want them to be – *unknowingly* – participating in perpetuating something that is *harmful* to other people, without any thoughts as to the consequences of their actions."[433] Professor 35, who "takes a light *crit* approach ... tying ... the practical, everyday practice of law to theory," strives to "make visible underlying tensions" to clarify legal doctrine and help with issue spotting, but also to ensure that lawyers are aware of concepts such as "power relationships [and] the way socio-economic resources are distributed":

> It annoys me ... when lawyers are out in the world and not paying attention or not engaging with ... and *not seeing* ... that law can have that effect. Particularly when you're talking about regulating the market. So I just want lawyers to be *conscious* and not stick their heads in the sand.[434]

Professor 15, who focuses largely on doctrinal law, strives to show students that "*even contract law* has this dimension [of social policy] and is part of a social order and ... has certain social effects ... and you *do* have to ask yourself, is this good?" For Professor 15, the good lawyer is able to "master the nuts and bolts ... but also ... be alive to why they're doing it, and whether it's a good thing to be doing it."[435]

---

432 [003], Interview, 269–86. *Cf Swan* 3d ed, *supra* note 208 at xxxiii.

433 [063], Interview, lines 167–73, 153–4, 850–4; [033], Interview, lines 374–7.

434 [035], Interview, lines 771–4, 303–13, 618–29.

435 [015], Interview, lines 677–9, 638–40.

Professor 17 probes the context of a case in part to raise awareness of diversity issues as part of a professional "acculturation":

> It's almost like *ethics issues*, really. You are going to be a lawyer, so you need to know that you have agency, and you are ... going to have power, and you're in control of how you might use that. Also you're going to be entering a profession that has ... this long history of gender inequality and sexism ...
>
> [It] makes me feel like I'm doing something important for *them* – not necessarily in terms of contracts but just in terms of their general acculturation to the profession ... You want people ... out there to be sensitive to diversity issues.[436]

Professor 53, another professor heavily influenced by realism, attempts to help students challenge authority through critical thinking, which Professor 53 describes as the joint ability of being able to "break things down ... in a strictly legal sense" and "see the problem in a human sense":

> Our graduates are legal thinkers. They're the ones that have to protect society from the government, from the police, from big business, from each other ... That's what legal thinkers do, whether they're practising lawyers or academics or anything else. They're the ones that have to say, "The emperor has no clothes."[437]

Even in circumstances where the aim is not to challenge authority, theory still serves to accomplish ends that professors describe in principled terms. Thus Professor 26 describes the moral duty to represent a client in relation to both the principle of perspective taking and an instrumental conception of law:

> I want them to start thinking, right from the moment they get here, that they're in a profession ... That they owe an obligation to clients, that they have both *legal* and *moral* duties to their clients and duties to represent their client's point of view ... I want them to start thinking like this isn't just a game ... There's real lives ... involved here.[438]

Theory and Practice as Mutually Reinforcing

In all the above examples, professors describe how theory endows practice with a robust and principled content. Theoretical commitments

---

436 [017], Interview, lines 202–34.
437 [053], Interview, lines 397, 434–40, 421–2, 398–403.
438 [026], Interview, lines 393–409.

translate into a broader and more comprehensive toolkit for lawyers to deploy in serving their clients, and they also encourage a more social and moral view of the lawyer's role. There is, in other words, a widespread aspiration to translate theory into practice in a way that reflects the lawyer-as-citizen ideal in both the narrower sense of cultivating an eclectic toolkit and the broader sense of incorporating public concerns into the lawyer's role. A more fully integrative vision of theory and practice is also hinted at when professors describe the inverse of translating theory into practice: the belief that practice also informs theory.

An excellent example of this tendency is Professor 33, who, though bristling at the "label" of legal realism, describes how experience practising generated numerous realist insights:

> [M]y experience practising in [a particular area of] law was that you had to be extremely aware of the practical outcome of doctrines being interpreted in different ways. And that if you weren't extremely aware of the on-the-ground *consequences*, and address them in your legal argument, [then] your legal argument was going to be rejected. So – whatever object, whatever label you want to put on that, [my perspective] is very much [grounded] in the trenches experience of judicial decision making.[439]

Similarly, Professor 1 writes in the course syllabus of the complicating insight that actual practice will have on one's theoretical or conceptual view of law, discussing the mutual importance of "praxis" and "critical" thinking to the development of "professional aptitudes":

> A day at a law firm, in the legal department of a business, or in court will suffice to disabuse anyone of the idea that knowledge [*la connaissance*] enables one to master the law *as it is* ... That which can seem to go without saying intellectually might disappear in the violence of a clash of interests. In the entanglement of pro and con arguments. There is also context. There is also all that distinguishes one case from another. Legal practice – one should say *praxis* – disrupts the idea of common law or civil law as *systems*.
>
> A dogmatic jurist loses a part of his or her skills, a part of his or her professional agility. By contrast, the jurist capable of critiquing his or her knowledge augments his or her professional aptitudes. Thus, critical work must accompany conceptual work in the learning of law.[440]

In such passages, where practice is specifically invoked to inform or complicate theoretical understandings, we see the inklings of a view that considers theory and practice as *mutually* reinforcing virtues,

439 [F], Interview, lines 624–31.
440 [001], Syllabus (2015–16), p 2 [translation from French].

analogous to Kronman's idea that the traits of deliberative wisdom and civic-mindedness simultaneously enable the "outstanding" lawyer to serve the interests of private clients and the public.[441]

Thinking as Preparation for Practice

The foregoing sections should not be taken to indicate that all professors unproblematically assert the importance of practice in their teaching. A number of professors speak in a way that suggests that they qualify, or even outrightly reject, the idea that they should be preparing students for practice. On closer look, however, these comments disclose not so much an antipathy towards practice per se, but rather a distinctive vision of what practical preparation means: the ability to "think" like a lawyer. For example, Professor 58 writes in the course syllabus:

> [T]he focus is not on preparing you to write a professional Bar examination in a particular jurisdiction or immediately to write legal opinions on complex contractual matters. Instead, after this course you will be able to do the legal thinking and research necessary to do so.[442]

Similarly, Professor 23 states that first-year Contracts does not prepare students for practice, but "prepare[s] people for thinking about practice." In somewhat stronger terms, Professor 47 states:

> My objective is not to turn out legal *plumbers*. They're not doing contract law *plumbing*. They're saying where the plumbing fits in the big house ... I will gladly teach stuff that is practically *useless* [if I think it will help] ... students to get some idea of the context of law.[443]

Indeed, the idea that, as Professor 64 says, "it's not our obligation to teach everything from a practitioner's perspective" often translates into the distinctive contributions of the "law faculty" as opposed to the law school. Professor 1, for example, distinguishes the "law school" objective of training good legal workers from the "law faculty" objective of participating in the construction of knowledge:

> Once students have left the faculty, one imagines that they will produce better work ... That is a very "law school" answer. But the other answer is

---

441 *Lost Lawyer*, *supra* note 16. See also Sandomierski, "Training Lawyers", *supra* note 21 at 744–7.

442 [058], Syllabus (2007–8), p 2.

443 [023], Interview, lines 516–17; [047], Interview, lines 774–7.

> more "faculty of law," more relating to the university. We don't distribute a knowledge that is considered as complete, but a knowledge in the process of being made. The people who teach are people who, in their way, try to progress this understanding, thus participate in its confection, its creation.[444]

Unlike in the highly oppositional "fierce debate" narrative, when these types of distinctions get made in the context of teaching, academic and practical objectives are not so cleanly defined. As we observed in the *Milner* introduction, the university law faculty has a distinctly academic contribution to make to the preparation of future lawyers. Encouraging students to think *so that they eventually might be able to practice* is, in the end, another variant of using theory to make better lawyers. The revolt against "practice-readiness" that we observe in some of the above comments might be seen, therefore, not as a rejection of the importance of practice, but rather as an assertion about a particular vision of practical preparation for which the university environment is uniquely suited.

One final quotation highlights this point. Professor 22, a highly abstract thinker with formalist leanings – who endeavours to classify concepts according to moral ideas – speaks in a way that sets up the contrast between the academy and practice that, at first glance, is most severe:

> I tend to think the practical implications are not as important ... I think we use classification systems *fundamentally* to understand – and in *theory* they have practical implications, but in *practice* ... I ... think that people reason more from the results backwards to theory ... The fundamental role is understanding, but that's not really going to change the world ... I don't think philosophical reflection changes the world very much ...
>
> I think Marx had it ... *backwards*. He said the point of philosophy is not to understand the world but to change it ... And I think the reality is the opposite of that – philosophy is to understand the world, not to change it. And once you start changing it, you're not doing philosophy. Or you're not being academic.[445]

And yet, despite this strong claim in favour of understanding over "practical implications," earlier in the interview Professor 22 describes

444 [064], Interview, lines 498–9; [001], Interview, lines 685–709 [translation from French].
445 [022], Interview, lines 150, 198–240.

how classification both "preconditions our ... practical implications" and helps students handle hypothetical fact patterns, which in turn enables students to better advise clients or judges by being able to better explain doctrine – "maybe a little more than average I care about those things."[446] Professor 22 describes the specific theoretical construct (in this case, classification) as directly relevant to practical lawyering, even while expressing some scepticism about the purity of the process of theory generation ("people reason ... from the results backwards to theory"). And even taking Professors 22's words about Marx's having it backwards at face value, this quote represents more the exception that proves the overarching rule: most Canadian common law Contracts professors do conceive of theory as significant precisely for the effect it has on the real world.

CONCLUSION

The widespread commitment to using theory to make better lawyers suggests that the oppositional narrative – the perennial fierce debate between universities and law societies – is not the most prevalent idea among Canadian common law Contracts professors. Instead, an emerging story of balance and integration of theory and practice – which at this stage only describes a *minority* viewpoint expressed in the more abstract discussions about legal education – actually captures the *majority* of attitudes about teaching. In a sense, the attitudes and beliefs expressed through these conversations about teaching appear to reverse the relative priority between oppositional and integrative accounts, and suggest that the integrative belief easily outstrips the oppositional belief among Canadian common law Contracts professors. Such an observation disturbs the conventional narrative of institutional conflict, and signals the iconoclastic potential of empirical legal education research.[447]

At the same time, the oppositional narrative does appear to be alive and well among Canadian common law Contracts professors when they speak about the big picture of legal education. The profession and university are described as being at odds with each other, sometimes in hostile terms. Untangling the contrast between integrative views as expressed in teaching discussions and oppositional views expressed in more abstract discussions generates yet additional insights and

446 *Ibid*, lines 408–19.
447 See David Sandomierski, "Theory and Practice, Together at Last: A Heretical, Empirical Account of Canadian Legal Education" in Meera E Deo, Mindie Lazarus-Black, and Elizabeth Mertz, eds, *Power, Legal Education, and Law School Cultures* (Abingdon, Oxon; New York: Routledge, 2019) 1.

questions. For example, it could be that the conventional debates are just so familiar and ingrained that any discussion operating at the higher level of abstraction becomes automatically, almost subconsciously, conditioned by the familiar terms. On this account, the tenacity of the conventional oppositional account results from a kind of discursive inertia: professors reproduce the familiar terms even though they might dissonate with their lived experience, but the very fact of reproducing these terms ensures that they remain predominant. The "perennial" nature of the debate might be driven more by the dynamic of myth telling and retelling and less by the empirical reality of lived experience.

Alternatively, professors' views about teaching might actually be different from their views about their bigger-picture role or the mission of the institution. In describing their role or the mission of the law school, professors might be apt to emphasize their dominant role identity (scholar), which is putatively distinct from the relatively circumscribed role of teacher. In the case of those who espouse a preference for the academy, the practical virtues of producing "better lawyers" might well describe their attitudes as teachers, but they might *relate* more to being scholars, and in that role might perceive threats to scholarly independence posed by professional demands more acutely. In the case of those who express a preference for the profession, the stated views about teaching could be the ones they actually believe, but they might perceive these ideas to run counter to the norms of the university community in which they find themselves. How professors understand the relationship between theory and practice differently in different contexts might signal a dissonance between those areas over which professors experience agency and those about which they feel structured or conditioned by external factors. I explore the relationship between structure and agency in greater detail in Chapter 6.

Yet another characterization is plausible. Upholding the distinctiveness of the university (and the oppositional view between academy and profession) might be perfectly reconcilable with the idea of producing better lawyers. On this view, the university is able to prepare students for the primordial practical task – thinking like a lawyer – in a distinctively broad, heterogeneous, and intellectually ambitious way. Professors appear to imbue the term "practice" with a robust and nuanced understanding – and much of this flows from the *claim* that these professors are translating their diverse theoretical commitments into a heterogeneous vision of what it means to become a "better lawyer." It is at least plausible to think that the university's distinctive role in cultivating theoretical diversity equips it to model – in a way that other legal education or training might not – legal reasoning as an eclectic toolkit.

That, at least, is one possible implication of the widespread, nearly consensus view that theory matters, but not for its own sake. The image portrayed by professors' articulation of the relationship between theory and practice is that diverse theories become operationalized into diverse visions of legal reasoning. The question is – do they? The next chapter answers this question by diving into the details of professors' theoretical commitments and the details of how they describe legal reasoning. To anticipate, I find that, while professors do indeed possess a wide range of theoretical commitments consistent with the intellectually heterogeneous academic environment, the range of theoretical ideas of law *operationalized* by their understandings of legal reasoning – and by selected teaching methods – appears to be much narrower. The aspiration to translate theory directly into practice does not, accordingly, appear to be realized.

Chapter Five

The Failure to Operationalize: Realism and Formalism in Canadian Common Law Contracts Teaching

So far we have a somewhat ambiguous picture of the relationship between theory and practice in legal education. On the one hand, we have the claim, by Kennedy and Fisher, that contemporary legal reasoning is an eclectic practice built up from the methodological sediment produced by a series of realist and critical schools of thought. In their view, legal reasoning today is the exercise of deploying an eclectic toolkit that contains a wide range of strategies appropriate to legal discourse and argumentation. Chief among these are diverse arguments based on policy and social context: theirs is a vision of legal reasoning "operationalizing" the theoretical ideas from the realist and critical schools, which (as outlined in Chapter 2) have been developed and instantiated by the seminal contract law scholarship of the twentieth century. The widespread aspiration among Canadian common law Contracts professors to translate their theories into practice, combined with the theoretical survey of the seminal contract law scholarship, suggests that the vision of legal reasoning in Canadian common law Contracts teaching might well resemble Kennedy and Fisher's eclectic toolkit formulation.

On the other hand, the study by Elizabeth Mertz and my reading of the Canadian common law Contracts casebooks suggest an alternative possibility for the messages communicated by Contracts teaching. Mertz's study of eight Contracts classes shows how Contracts professors tend to *marginalize*, not operationalize, considerations of policy and context in teaching students to think like lawyers. In the Canadian common law Contracts casebooks, likewise, while the editors *espouse* attitudes amenable to the realist and critical schools of the American canon, the image of legal reasoning in the two most frequently assigned books focuses on reasoning by analogy and the primacy of rules and courts – a somewhat far cry from the eclectic toolkit of argumentation. The Canadian casebooks appear to fail to translate their theoretical eclecticism into a methodological pluralism – to put into practice their avowed beliefs about law. These observations suggest that the Canadian experience might resemble Mertz's account more than it does Kennedy and Fisher's.

We now turn to the words of the participants in my study to determine how Canadian common law Contracts teaching as a whole fits into this story. I examine professors' substantive attitudes about law expressed in three different contexts – espoused beliefs, descriptions of legal reasoning, and teaching accounts and materials – to ascertain the extent to which the aspiration to translate theory into practice is realized. As it turns out, the patterns observed in the casebooks appear to recur in the words of my sixty-seven interviewees and in the course materials I reviewed. As with the casebook editors, most Canadian common law Contracts professors espouse strong theoretical commitments to the ideas of American legal realism and its intellectual heirs. Indeterminacy, policy, context, politics, underlying factors, and external critique all figure prominently in professors' propositional statements about law. When we look at how they describe legal reasoning, however, and when we examine their teaching practices and materials for the attitudes of law they reflect, a preoccupation with a narrower conception of "relevance" – one more concerned with internal consistency among judicially formulated rules and the operation of analogical reasoning – predominates. This tendency suggests that realist themes do not figure prominently in the way most professors understand the practice of legal reasoning, and that most professors do not operationalize these realist and critical ideas in how they teach Contracts – which includes both how they teach and evaluate legal reasoning and the other substantive ideas about law they emphasize in the course. The privileged set of attitudes about law reflected in both cases evokes a different set of ideas that only a minority of professors – formalism's "champions" – propositionally proclaim.

In the first part of this chapter, I focus on how professors describe what they believe about law. These beliefs surface both when professors describe their legal philosophy directly and when they talk about their pedagogical goals or the rationales for those goals. In these comments, most professors espouse genuine and deep commitments to the realist ideas that law is indeterminate; that rules are mutable and contingent; that one must look to underlying factors of judicial personality, politics, and policy considerations to explain legal doctrine; that social context and non-state normativity are relevant to law; and that critical perspectives that evaluate law from external normative positions are essential to a complete understanding of law. By contrast, a minority of professors proclaim the idea that law is an autonomous discipline distinct from prudential considerations. For these thinkers, doctrinal rules are not so much contingent expressions of political or policy considerations as they are expressions of an internal, immanent coherence. These professors seek to understand law not by reference to extrinsic contextual concerns, but in pursuit of an internal logic that explains how the rules fit together. This internal coherence is considered important both because it upholds the claim that law possesses a distinctive rationality and because it serves the related virtue of providing equal treatment to all people under the law.

In the second part, I show how the relative weighting of realist and formalist ideas reverses when professors speak about legal reasoning. In these instances, most describe legal reasoning as a distinct form of discourse, take the content of rules and judicial reasoning seriously, believe that legal reasoning primarily consists in drawing lines between what is relevant and irrelevant, and espouse the importance of structure and coherence. Only a minority of professors call into question legal reasoning's distinctiveness or actively try to translate their theoretical realist or critical ideas about law into a corresponding vision of legal reasoning. These professors emphasize cultivating human judgment, thinking critically, training one's gut, incorporating policy, and developing an eclectic range of argument-types. However, not only are these professors largely in the minority, but the rigour and extent to which they attempt to inflect legal reasoning with these other features pale in comparison to the focus in most other accounts of legal reasoning on the ruthless discernment between the relevant and the irrelevant, while treating those categories as neutral.

In the third part of the chapter, I show how the attitudes put into practice through teaching methods and materials are largely the same as those that predominate in professors' descriptions of legal reasoning. In direct expressions about teaching philosophy or course objectives (whether in interviews or course syllabi), in decisions about how to order the course or what readings to assign, and especially in the choice of evaluation, the importance of rules and conventional legal reasoning figures as the privileged message. The prevailing impression communicated by teaching materials and practices is of a much narrower vision of law than that reflected in professors' propositional statements. This trend is by no means absolute – there are examples of custom-designed evaluations, syllabi, and even reading materials that fit with the critical and realist aspirations. I detail these here, too, but the overwhelming impression is that they remain, at least for now, in the minority.

Accordingly, the claim from the previous chapter, that theory and critique are important primarily to make better lawyers, should best be understood as aspirational, rather than as reflecting the true state of common law Contracts teaching in Canada. Although many, if not most, professors might believe that theory serves practice, their own theoretical commitments do not appear to generate targeted and particular conceptions of legal reasoning or to be integrated thoroughly into their teaching practices, materials, and evaluations. There are two profound mismatches between theory and practice. First, although there is an eclecticism of theories about law, spanning the range of theoretical schools canvassed in Chapter 2, there is a relatively homogeneous attitude about what constitutes legal reasoning. Second, the content of legal reasoning coalesces around the skills of discerning the relevant from the irrelevant, a line-drawing exercise that serves to cast the *purportedly* central concerns of policy, context, and politics to the margins of legal epistemology. This line-drawing exercise weaves the whole of the Contracts course together, animating and driving the substantive teaching, and modelling a powerful, but circumscribed, understanding of the "core" of legal professional practice.

REALIST AND FORMALIST ATTITUDES ABOUT LAW AND CONTRACTS

For the purposes of this analysis, I have provisionally categorized ideas about law according to the labels "realist" and "formalist." Such a device is necessarily a heuristic, given the heterogeneity of ideas that each of these two labels encompasses. Realism, on the one hand, has famously been described not as a "movement" at all, but as more an "intellectual mood than a clear body of tenets"; it is much less frequently defined affirmatively than it is described as a "revolt again formalism."[448] For Kennedy and Fisher,

> *legal realism* ... remains in the vernacular to refer to those debates and affinities, and also to denote a series of loose reasoning tendencies – a

448 See Horwitz, *Transformation of American Law*, *supra* note 103 at 169, 184; Llewellyn, "Some Realism about Realism", *supra* note 104 at 1233–4; Gilmore, "Legal Realism", *supra* note 104 at 1038. Canada has had its own major contributions to legal realism. See e.g. RCB Risk, "Volume 1 of the Journal: A Tribute and a Belated Review" (1987) 37 UTLJ 193; RCB Risk, "Lawyers, Courts, and the Rise of the Regulatory State" (1984) 9 Dal LJ 31; RCB Risk, "John Willis – A Tribute" (1985) 9 Dal LJ 521; G Blaine Baker, "Willis on 'Cultured' Public Authorities" (2005) 55 UTLJ 335; RCB Risk, "My Continuing Legal Education" (2005) 55 UTLJ 313; Robert W Gordon, "Willis's American Counterparts: The Legal Realists' Defense of Administration" (2005) 55 UTLJ 405; RCB Risk & Michael Taggart, "The Published Work of John Willis" (2005) 55 UTLJ 887; Eric M Adams, "The Dean Who Went to Law School: Crossing Borders and Searching for Purpose in North American Legal Education, 1930–1950" (2016) 54 Alta L Rev 1.

> heightened awareness of deductive errors in doctrinal analysis, the routine use of criticisms of analytic positivism, enthusiasm for purposive and functional styles of reasoning, and efforts to tolerate and affirm legal pluralism and social custom.[449]

Formalism, on the other hand, is a word that receives deep philosophical treatment and definition. Some, like Brian Leiter, take pains to confine the term to theories of *adjudication*, combining the ideas that "the law is rationally determinate, ... judging is mechanical, ... [and] legal reasoning is *autonomous*." Others, like Ernest Weinrib, use it more broadly to refer to a legal philosophy that "embodies a profound and inescapable truth about law's inner coherence," postulates that "law is intelligible as an internally coherent phenomenon," and "proffer[s] the possibility of an 'immanent moral rationality.'"[450] My purpose here is not to reconcile or even select from among such definitions, but rather to use the general ideas of each school to categorize the views and attitudes expressed by Canadian common law Contracts professors.

This task is necessarily imprecise, but the purpose is not precision. Rather, it is to elucidate the underlying attitudes about law that the participants in my study espouse. Not every professor whose utterance or written word I classify as realist or formalist might identify in one camp or the other, although some do. The fact that some individuals might resist being so categorized does not preclude us, however, from noticing that some of their words have an affinity with ideas associated with realism or formalism. The labels, therefore, are helpful to paint a picture about the general state of ideas about law. Moreover, the act of classifying certain words as realist or formalist enables us to highlight the discrepancies that might appear between what is said in some contexts and what is said in others. The labels thus facilitate the key observation in this chapter: that views about law differ greatly as between when professors assert their views about law and when they describe their views about legal reasoning or their teaching practices. Finally,

---

449 Kennedy & Fisher, "Introduction", *supra* note 27 at 7.

450 Brian Leiter, "Positivism, Realism, Formalism", Book Review of *Legal Positivism in American Jurisprudence* by Anthony Sebok, (1999) 99 Colum L Rev 1138 at 1145 [emphasis in original]; Ernest J Weinrib, "Legal Formalism: On the Immanent Rationality of Law" (1988) 97 Yale LJ 949 at 950, 951, 953–4. See also Grey, *supra* note 96 at 9 ("formalism" describes legal theories that stress the importance of rationally uncontroversial reasoning in legal decisions, whether from highly particular rules or quite abstract principles), 8 ("a legal system is *formal* to the extent that its outcomes are dictated by demonstrative (rationally compelling) reasoning").

by classifying professors' particular words according to the capacious and contested labels of realism and formalism, we can learn something about how these terms manifest in the attitudes of law professors across the board, beyond the subset of those who choose to write about them.

With these qualifications in mind, let us explore the attitudes about law that the professors in my study espouse. These expressions arise, in almost all cases, not in response to direct questions such as "What is your philosophy of law?" but rather by their being asked to expand on something they had mentioned in response to an initial open-ended question. In the first section, I focus on the realist views that professors express about law generally, or about contract law in particular. These include an emphasis on the indeterminacy of law, the importance of underlying policy factors, the idea that the purportedly "external" factors of politics, morality, and context are integral to law, and the importance of exogenous critiques to a complete understanding of law in its social context. The second section highlights ideas expressed by a vociferous minority – the "champions" of formalism – about the distinctiveness of legal rationality and the importance of doctrinal coherence to the rule of law. Elements of these formalist views also appear more subtly among the professors characterized in the first section as realists. What begins as a clean classification thus gives way to a picture of a more complicated relationship between realist and formalist ideas, which leads directly into the starker contrasts revealed in the second part of this chapter.[451]

Realist Views about (Contract) Law

Two interrelated claims about law pervade my interview transcripts. First, there is the widespread belief that law is not a collection of fixed rules whose application yields determinative legal results. In this rejection of

451 Apart from the detailed look at selected quotations of which this chapter is comprised, I have tried to give a global assessment of each professor's interview transcript to determine whether each could be classified as leaning formalist or realist. While I acknowledge that both the exercise of categorization and the particular categorizations might be contestable, the numbers do give a flavour of the relative weighting. Judged primarily on their stated beliefs about law, I identified forty-nine professors who fall squarely in the realist camp and seven in the formalist camp. Eleven professors fall into an "in-between" category, either because they do not express strong views or because their views seem truly mixed. I do not mean to suggest that only these eleven participants labelled as "in-between" exhibit complex or contradictory tendencies; as I discuss, many of the forty-nine "realist" professors exhibit such contradictions.

a mechanical jurisprudence,[452] many Canadian common law Contracts professors insist that rules themselves are indeterminate – contingent on historical and social factors, potentially arbitrary, "made by people," subject to change, and never fixed or revelatory of truth. Accordingly, law is portrayed not as a collection of discrete rules, but as something messy and much more uncertain. Second, many professors take pains to emphasize the underlying factors that help account for this indeterminacy or contingency. Thus, in an apparent rejection of the idea that law is a distinct discipline consisting principally of internal reasoning techniques, many professors show how factors otherwise considered exogenous – policy, politics, justice, morality, behavioural economics, social relations – impact and even constitute law. To tease out these pervasive influences of realism, I divide the discussion below into the indeterminacy of law and "external" factors.

The Indeterminacy of Law

Claims about the Nature of Law

A thread that runs throughout the interview transcripts is the idea that professors want to "disabuse" students of the idea that law is a closed system of rules that are immune to social forces and determinative of legal results. As Professor 27 writes:

> Most people come [with] some set of ideas about law – almost all of which turn out to be good starting points for showing them that's not what's really going to happen, or not what's going on ... [These include the ideas] that law is a bunch of rules, that it's a ... *certainty*, has a certain form. That ... in order to have legal certainty, we must have a number of things in place. So, in contract law ... people believe that contracts should be in writing, or that they *have* to be in writing ... That's a very simple idea that turns out to be *very untrue* ... The classical view of contract law fits perfectly with ... most people's preconceptions.[453]

A host of instructors, in differing ways, attack the idea of law's determinacy. Mostly this takes the form of undermining the very idea that there are fixed rules of law. Thus, Professor 26 wants to "shake" students of the "notion ... [t]hat the law is out there, it just is what it is, and either you know it or you don't." Professor 13 rejects the idea that "contract

---

452 See Roscoe Pound, "Mechanical Jurisprudence" (1908) 8 Colum L Rev 605.

453 [027], Interview, lines 213–32. See also [052], Interview, line 33; [027], Interview, lines 79, 1016; [026], Interview, lines 494–6.

law is just a sort of a puzzle ... and [that] there are ... black and white rules that apply to give you determinate answers." Likewise, Professor 31 tries to "avoid the students taking the legal rules as being some sort of ... data that go into a statistical calculation and you come up with the answer." Professor 44, with almost five decades of experience, describes how this appreciation for indeterminacy dawned gradually:

> [W]hen you get to my age ... what you do realize is how ... *little* you know ... [I]n my first two or three years of teaching, it was a goal – a rule, "Yeah, that's it!" Whereas today, it's just, "Well, yeah, it could be. It might be. Yeah, it could be too." There's just more questions and never answers, at which the kids get a ... bit frustrated. "But surely you must know after all these years." "No, I'm telling you that there's so many different ways to look at this, and there's not *an* answer. There's just answers, and there's just more questions ... So that's the way the law *is* and that's why we litigate, because there's never a rule."[454]

The theme of uncertainty – and students' discomfort with it – comes up frequently. For example, Professor 54 states:

> [T]hey love certainty and clarity [and] ... they don't like indeterminacy ... at the beginning. But I ... tell them, "Look – the reality is that it *is* indeterminate, and you're going to have to become *comfortable* with uncertainty ... As long as you can *identify* what's uncertain, *why* it's uncertain, and what the potential arguments you would bring to bear to resolve the uncertainty *are,* then that's okay ... It's just the reality, so we need to embrace that reality and become comfortable with uncertainty."[455]

Similarly, Professor 26 illustrates a commitment to the same idea by recounting how a colleague (who teaches Property) would

> walk into the room and before he would say anything, ... would write "UNCERTAINTY" in big letters on the chalkboard, and turn around and say, "Get used to it." And students always want to know, "What's the answer? What's the rule? What's *the* outcome?" And often in law it's – there isn't a "*the* answer." There may be wrong answers, but that doesn't mean there's only one right answer.[456]

---

454 [026], Interview, lines 454–5; [013], Interview, lines 73–8; [031], Interview, lines 216–18; [044], Interview, lines 802–29.

455 [054], Interview, lines 730–42.

456 [026], Interview, lines 459–67.

Reinforcing this ontological point about the nature of law, a similar message appears in Professor 26's syllabus. This excerpt also appears in the syllabus of Professor 70, a senior colleague at the same institution, who is likely the original author: "The rules of contract law are not set out in any book or (to any significant degree) any act of any legislature. They cannot simply be looked up. Nor *could* they be. While it is possible to baldly state some fundamental principles of contract law, their meaning and scope is never fixed, since there are always further distinctions to be made."[457]

In addition to the widely held claim that law is indeterminate and uncertain, we see other such ontological claims, related to the ideas that law is "messy," not "God-given" or "static," and that it is a "highly complex product of ... social historical interactions."[458]

Normative Claims and Aspirational Language

Sometimes professors connect these ontological claims to more idealized visions of law and lawyering activity. This occurs, for example, when Professor 63 states that "you probably wouldn't *want* to have law that's a perfectly defined, clear set of rules applicable in every circumstance because we'd have an institution that would be pretty difficult ... to respect at the end of the day." The idea that rules applied "rigidly across ... every case" would undermine the respect due to law[459] corresponds to another widely held idea: that law is a socio-cultural construct – that it is made by people, and can therefore be changed. Numerous professors advocate such a view, connecting it to an aspirational vision of the lawyer or jurist who participates in the "making and remaking" of law.

Thus, Professor 26 "thinks of the law as a human institution ... [that is] constituted anew in each litigation or in each contract negotiation." Professor 11 connects the idea that law graduates are going to try to "change the law" with the idea that law is a "human" and "political construct" – "it ... didn't have to develop this way but it did for various reasons." Similarly, Professor 54 focuses on judicial personalities in order to show students that "law really is a construct," "artificial in the sense that these are just humans that are writing these things."[460]

As a construct, law is often portrayed as something that can be changed by legal actors. Thus Professor 17, who underscores the

---

457 [070], Syllabus, 2015–16, p 1; [026], Syllabus, 2012–13, p 2.

458 [001], Interview, line 596; [027], Interview, lines 723, 695; [002], Interview, lines 551–63; [056], Interview, lines 415–17.

459 [063], Interview, lines 421–6, 411–12.

460 [026], Interview, lines 403–5; [011], Interview, lines 445–8, 474–9; [054], Interview, lines 699–701.

"arbitrariness and contingency" of law, says, "The common law is not just the rules – they're mutable, they've changed over time, they're subject *to change* ... [I]n the future you can change them as a legal actor ... You're going to be one of these *people* at some point either as a lawyer or a judge or whatever."[461] In an analogous fashion, Professor 37 connects the aims of "destabilizing" students and showing them that "the ground beneath [them] isn't firm anymore" to the virtue of becoming "creative" lawyers who think of "new answers":

> I don't think that there *is* one answer in law, and I don't think that the answers, to the extent that they exist, exist for an interminable period of time ... I really want [students] ... to question assumptions, to look *beyond* the answers, *behind* the answers – and ultimately to be able to be *creative* enough to think of *new* answers ... I want them to *hone* their skills of *imaginative insight* and to think with an agile mind that's able to transcend boundaries.[462]

Accordingly, Canadian common law Contracts professors overwhelmingly view their role as trying to undermine the idea that law is a collection of determinate rules or a source of certainty. They demonstrate strong theoretical commitments about the nature of law, and they reinforce the strength of their commitments by making aspirational claims about the role graduates will play as legal actors capable of effecting change. Closely intertwined with this general notion about the nature of law are the more specific ways, outlined below, about the factors that affect law.

Underlying Factors, Policy, and External Perspectives

It is extremely common for Canadian common law Contracts professors to espouse the realist claim that "underlying" factors – whether judicial personality, policy, politics, concerns of justice or morality, or empirical truths about relationships and human behaviour – impact or even constitute law. Most professors portray the legal discipline as porous, and law as the product of these underlying factors.

To begin this part of the analysis, I elucidate the professors' wide and varied claims about the importance of underlying factors, or results-based reasoning. I then explore how this focus on underlying factors, often expressed by a commitment to the importance of policy, can be disaggregated into two quite distinct understandings. One is the idea that the underlying perspectives describe the policy considerations effectively internalized by

461 [017], Interview, lines 148–53.
462 [037], Interview, lines 244–75.

contract law doctrine. "Policy" in this sense refers to the underlying motivations for existing doctrine. Law and policy are interrelated because the latter explains and accounts for the former. The other understanding is the idea that "policy" serves as an external vantage point for evaluating law. Exogenous concerns of politics, morality, justice, economics, historical context, or social relations are essential not so much because they *account* for doctrine, but because they enable a more global understanding of law in its broader social context. This distinction in turn leads to an extended discussion of the importance of external perspectives.

The General Claim: The Importance of Underlying Factors and Results-based Reasoning

Professors frequently assert that it is important to go beyond, or behind, the words of judges to determine the real factors motivating legal decision making. They often express this idea very simply. Professor 67 speaks of going "behind the words" that "disguise differences" or "mask complexity"; Professor 50 aims to "identify below doctrine, what is really *driving* decisions"; Professor 25 tries to elucidate the underlying "problem" that judges as "human beings with pasts" are not "confronting" directly, but rather are addressing indirectly by manipulating legal doctrines. Professor 23 aims to help students "understand what it is that is motivating – influencing – judges in making their decisions *beyond* their words ... Their words are often important but often there's an economic, social, legal, political context that is important to understand." Professor 45 aims to understand "gender biases, racial biases, economic biases" from a "systemic point of view." Professor 54 emphasizes how the "personality" and "inclinations" of a judge affect the law.[463]

In the same way that a focus on underlying factors undermines the importance of the actual words used in preference for some imagined reality, many professors express scepticism towards doctrine by focusing on the importance of results. This can take several forms. Judicial reasoning might be characterized as "reasoning backward from the *just result*," bolstering the scepticism about the importance of particular words used. For example, Professor 53 says:

> [I]t is an ongoing struggle to remind ourselves that often the judge is engaging in result-based reasoning. That is, they've decided what the result that they think is right *is*, and so now they're just reasoning backwards from that result. And although they *say* it's about the words, it really isn't. If you had

463 [067], Handwritten notes of untranscribed, unrecorded interview, pp 4–5; [050], Interview, lines 128–9; [025], Interview, lines 173–85; [023], Interview, lines 97–101; [045], Interview, lines 252–8; [054], Interview, lines 680–4.

> worded it the way the judge suggested, he or she would have just come up with some other reason why they had to come to this same result.[464]

Alternatively, professors might encourage their students to think primarily about how to achieve results, either by considering rules as "powerful tools" for effective argumentation or by prioritizing a consideration of the "demographic" make-up of a decision maker.[465] One professor, expressing an extreme version of the disdain for doctrine, simply states that "black letter law" will "never really help you."[466] Professors occasionally make a more ontological point that what law *is* is deeply tied to results. Some, like Professors 48 and 64, specifically invoke Holmes for this claim: "law is predictions ... [of] what the courts say it will be"; a ratio is "a form of prophesizing."[467] Others emphasize utility to characterize law: "law is something you *use* – not something that *is*"; by looking at a "practical solution, ... you actually see much more clearly what the law actually is."[468]

Occasionally professors might expand on the importance of external perspectives in more extended ways. For example, Professor 7 aims to

> convince [students] that a positivist theory of law, which sees law as ... an autonomous social phenomenon that doesn't take into account other dimensions, is not convincing ... [P]urely positivist thinking, at least in the *extreme* version you sometimes parody, is not possible ... [T]here's positive law that *exists* and there are formal criteria that help us identify what the law *is*. But the fact that the law *is*, is not in itself a justification of that law.[469]

Such a quotation captures the prevailing attitude that the law cannot be understood apart from its underlying factors. The suite of "underlying factors," of course, varies among professors and spans a wide range. The following two subsections attempt to disaggregate these underlying factors to show how the realist attitude contains a number of discrete ideas about law, both immanent in contract law doctrine and drawn from an eclectic range of external perspectives.

Policy: Internal and External Conceptions

Policy can mean a vast range of things – from arguments about function, institutional competence, or the behaviour of market actors to settled and

464 [016], Interview, line 284; [053], Interview, lines 568–75.
465 [016], Interview, line 372; [063], Interview, lines 169–70.
466 [049], Interview, lines 253–9.
467 [048], Interview, lines 193–7; [064], Interview, lines 318–21.
468 [026], Interview, lines 408–9; [012], Interview, lines 282–8.
469 [007], Interview, lines 281–91.

stable formulations that take on a universality akin to "principle" in judicial reasoning.[470] As Stephen Waddams writes, "Policy, as applied to judicial decision-making in English law, has sometimes been a word of approbation, signifying that which it is desirable for judges to do ... but sometimes it has signified the opposite ... where policy considerations [are considered] to be excluded from the proper judicial sphere."[471] These debates about the role of policy in judicial reasoning inform an understanding of how professors invoke policy in describing their views of contract law and law teaching. They signal that policy might be used alternatively to describe internal considerations (the principles or interests internalized by, and thus immanent in, contract law doctrine) or external considerations (factors that contradict or challenge the tenets of existing doctrine). Although the distinction between internal and external might be "difficult to apply to contract law, viewed as a historical phenomenon, because considerations that have effectively influenced the law have, by that very fact, been internalized," it nevertheless serves as a useful organizing logic for understanding the ways that Canadian common law Contracts professors talk about their understandings of law and their objectives.[472]

POLICY AS FACTORS EFFECTIVELY INTERNALIZED INTO DOCTRINE

Many professors assert the importance of underlying policy factors in a way that assimilates policy to factors, considerations, or interests that contract law doctrine has effectively internalized. They might do so while specifically identifying with legal realism. For example, consider the following exchange with Professor 51:

> [R:] Would you say that legal realism influences your approach to teaching the course?
> [PROFESSOR 51:] Yes.
> [R:] ... In what ways?

470 See Kennedy & Fisher, "Introduction", *supra* note 27 at 4–5 ("Fuller, Hart and Sacks, Coase and Calabresi each proposed specific types of policy argument that have become routine methods of judicial reasoning"); Waddams, *Principle and Policy*, *supra* note 303 at 223 ("[P]olicy considerations, when they can be incorporated in a rule that corresponds with past practice, that is likely to be fair to individual parties, that is judged to be likely to have beneficial effects in the future, that can be articulated in a form that is likely to be stable and that is suitable to be applied by judges are apt to be called principles. Thus policy might take the form of principle").

471 Waddams, *Principle and Policy*, *supra* note 303 at 216. Waddams underscores that such a tension exists in modern legal theory as well, citing Ronald Dworkin, *Taking Rights Seriously* (Cambridge, MA: Harvard University Press, 1977) for the proposition that "principle only, and not policy, belong[s] properly to the judicial sphere" (*ibid* at 20).

472 Waddams, *Principle and Policy*, *supra* note 303 at 222.

> [PROFESSOR 51:] ... I tend to get very legal realist ... in terms of ... what the final outcome of any contract cases are, in terms of what the parties' reasonable expectations would be in the commercial context ... I tend not to have a lot of patience for some of the long rambling ... House of Lords decisions where these fine semantic distinctions are made, and ... I tend to focus a lot more on ... *policy factors* in terms of being much more determinative ... I tend to emphasize ... policy factors in terms of ... what is actually going to *drive* the decision in the *end.* And you know, it's got to be things like reliance and reasonable expectations and trade practices and assumption of risk, commercial reasonableness.[473]

These policy factors – "reasonable expectations in the commercial context," "trade practices," "assumption of risk," "commercial reasonableness" – can all be considered internal in at least two senses. They are internal to the demands of the commercial economy in that they serve its smooth functioning and do not fundamentally threaten to challenge or regulate it.[474] They are also internal to the body of contract doctrine, either because these considerations have crystallized into principle or because, on a global analysis, courts appear preoccupied with these underlying factors. The idea that the "reasonable expectations of the parties" – a pillar of the *Swan* casebook – underlie the whole of contract doctrine is one such example; Professor 51 began teaching from *Swan,* and includes this idea and other such "facilitative" policies (that contract law ought to enforce voluntary obligations, avoid imposing obligations or unfair surprise, protect reasonable reliance, and promote commercial certainty) in the course syllabus.[475]

We see similar searches for the "internal" policies of contract law in the words of other professors. Professor 50 cites *Swan* directly in describing the driving decisions "below" the doctrine:

> I talk a lot about what lies at the heart of Swan's book, [the] idea that contract law *essentially* is to fulfil the reasonable expectations of honest people, and the importance of bad faith and good faith, and ... the fulfilment of the *intention* of the parties ... I talk about the reliance ... there are so many cases where I'm able to indicate to them that the court didn't say anything about reliance, but there has been such fundamental reliance by the parties, it *had* to have [had] some degree of influence.[476]

473 [051], Interview, lines 203–33.

474 *Cf.* Friedman, *supra* note 43 at 20 ("The law of contract is ... roughly coextensive with the free market").

475 [051], Syllabus, 2013–14, p 3.

476 [050], Interview, lines 45, 463–76.

Similarly, Professor 24 invokes reliance as a major theme used to get at the "underlying question of liability," a formula to help students "bridge" traditional gaps between conventional private law categories and within contract law itself. Professor 12 asserts "good faith" as a "fundamental" feature of contract law despite courts' traditional reticence. In an interview given before the Supreme Court of Canada's recognition of good faith as an "organizing principle," Professor 12 says:

> A large part of my first-year class here is to *challenge* the idea that good faith in fact *isn't* ... fundamental. Good courts say, there's no good faith in negotiations. Well actually there is because there's many cases which say, "If I know you've made a mistake in your draft, and I don't tell you about it, I can't enforce it. If I make an amendment to the draft you sent me and don't draw it to your attention, I can't enforce it." Now you might not call it good faith, but if you look at it, *it really is good faith.*[477]

Professor 13 similarly aims to identify the "conventional contract law policies that underlie a lot of the basic law of contracts" – that "courts themselves" do not identify. These include "freedom of contract and maximizing personal choice and ... individual liberty, [on the one hand,] and ... fairness on the other."[478]

Taken together, these examples demonstrate how many professors use the idea of the underlying policies of doctrines to better understand what courts are actually doing. There are two distinct intellectual tasks here. One is rendering explicit what is otherwise implicit – showing what is motivating judges, doing what the judges' words do not (indicating what the courts "didn't say" [Professor 50], rejecting "fine semantic distinctions" [Professor 51]). The other task, however, is to show the congruence between these "underlying" policies and the law itself. This goal is to elucidate the "true" content of the law, and in this sense it considers law and policy as indistinguishable. As one professor says, "I certainly tell the students that there there's no real distinction between law and public policy. Law *is* an exercise in developing, implementing, and applying public policy choices to social activity, commercial activity of various kinds."[479]

Accordingly, policy, when used as the underlying interests or factors beneath doctrine, predominantly refers to the range of factors that have

---

477 [024], Interview, lines 216–19, 164–72; [012], Interview, lines 326–33. See *Bhasin v Hrynew*, *supra* note 339.

478 [013], Interview, lines 265–309.

479 [A], Interview, lines 231–3.

been "effectively internalized" by judicial decisions. The fact that many of these factors coincide with realist projects of elucidation – the search for reliance, unconscionability, or good faith as true underlying factors – demonstrates the depth to which realist attitudes have permeated Canadian common law Contracts teaching.[480]

And yet this is only one way in which policy can be understood. Policy can also be used to bundle external perspectives that provide standards against which to measure the suitability of existing doctrines. It is *this* understanding of policy that at times can become marginalized by virtue of its relegation to theory.

POLICY AS EXTERNAL PERSPECTIVES

So-called external perspectives of law can also be translated into policy arguments for use in judicial reasoning. Kennedy and Fisher portray policy as central to their vision of legal reasoning as the methodological sediment of the critical schools: "What should go into reasoning about 'policy' – how much ethics, how much empiricism, how much economics? ... Each new method of professional policy argument was proposed – and continues to be taught – as a corrective to common errors and misunderstandings in the ways lawyers typically reason about policy."[481] In Kennedy and Fisher's account of American legal thought, these external perspectives have become admitted into the range of acceptable legal argumentation by being framed as policy arguments. Accordingly, "each new method of professional policy argument ... has found its way into the background consciousness of today's legal professional."[482]

There are, of course, two distinct steps to this characterization. First is the belief that these external perspectives are valuable for understanding law. Second is the idea that they can be operationalized into legal reasoning. In the next section, I explore how, among Canadian common law Contracts professors, the first belief is alive and well: they overwhelmingly assert the importance of external perspectives for the purposes of understanding and critiquing law. Professors state this proposition at a general level, and also discuss the specific factors of politics, morality, justice, economics, and social context.

---

480 See Fuller & Perdue, "Reliance Interest 1", *supra* note 112; Waddams, "Unconscionability in Contracts", *supra* note 300; Swan & Adamski Student Ed, *supra* note 244 at §8.139 ("It is possible to see expressions of the general concern represented by the concept of good faith in many areas of the law, even though there is no explicit reference to the phrase, 'good faith'").

481 Kennedy & Fisher, "Introduction", *supra* note 27 at 4.

482 *Ibid* at 4.

External Perspectives

THE GENERAL CASE FOR AN ECLECTIC SERIES OF EXTERNAL PERSPECTIVES

Canadian common law Contracts professors very commonly emphasize the importance of exposing students to external perspectives. Most such professors, even those whose own scholarly work is firmly situated in one school, tradition, or perspective, emphasize that their own perspective is "irrelevant," and strive to expose students to a range of perspectives.

One proponent of law and economics makes the general case for the importance of external perspectives. Making reference to Professor 18's own intellectual development, Professor 18 argues that *any* external perspective is important for the "normative reference point" that it provides:

> An economic [perspective] ... requires one to ... justify the legal doctrines by reference to something *outside* the legal doctrine itself ... Without some kind of a normative reference point, I always felt a bit unsatisfied ... You have to have some sort of relevant theory as to what the rules or doctrine are trying to achieve ... I'm not claiming any special vehemence for economics here but rather for ... almost *any* perspective external to the details of the doctrine itself.[483]

In an analogous fashion, Professor 57, in expanding on the idea of teaching "critical perspectives," emphasizes the idea of external "standards of preferability":

> [In] calling it critical ... I'm not trying to sign up to a particular *school*, ... [but] I would anticipate that students ... do *some thinking* about the normative dimension of what we're doing, and ... why some rules of law [or approaches to law] might be preferable to others, considered against a variety of ways that they might consider one thing preferable ...
>
> I started with preferability because I think that can ... open it up to a number of different *ranges* of approaches ... [For example, students may] need to say something about what *makes* something *more or less just* ... [Or] which rule of law is more economically efficient ... [Or] what's the impact of a particular rule on specific groups within society versus the impact of another rule on specific groups within society? What's the impact of one rule on stability of society versus the impact of another law on stability of society? ... I don't try to judge for them which standard of preferability they should use, but ... try to get them to think about a *few* of these.[484]

483 [018], Interview, lines 89–111.
484 [057], Interview, lines 523–69.

Professors often expose students to a range of perspectives in order to produce a "sophisticated appreciation" of the law. Thus, Professor 47, whose intellectual self-description is both eclectic – "I put [Patrick Atiyah, law and economics, and Charles Fried] in a blender" – and "conservative," teaches all of those perspectives, plus "feminist" perspectives, in order to "challenge" students and render them more "critical." Professor 2 includes a range of perspectives – law and economics, critical legal studies, feminism, even Marxism – to show that there are "different ways of conceiving and approaching law. None is perfect. There are different ways of viewing it and questioning it." Professor 58 not only describes the perspectives explored in the course as "eclectic, rather than a single overarching ideology," but begins the course syllabus with these words, which the professor writes were also featured prominently in the "registration materials" for the course: "Facilitator of fruitful exchange, irrelevancy ignored by parties in functioning relationships, or instrument of exploitation? Contract is perhaps all of the above." And, Professor 32 canvasses almost the entire waterfront of theoretical perspectives:

> [I introduce students] to notions of corrective justice and some of the theories of contract – contract as promise for example, and the notion of relational contracting, the notion of contract law in its ... legal pluralist perspective. And then some of the ... more *doctrinally* based theories ... about what kind of interest you're protecting when awarding remedies.[485]

This theoretical eclecticism maps tightly onto the widespread attitude that professors do not aim to proselytize their own favoured perspective. Professors variously state that "my answers to [the question of whether law is autonomous] are irrelevant to the course"; "you can't tell them what to think or believe, but you can at least *show* them that they're *acting* upon a belief, if only an implied one, or an implicit one"; "I try to minimize my own opinion"; "[o]ther than being able to ... *articulate* [and apply] the different ... positions, ... there's no requirement that somebody ... actually *change* their personal beliefs"; "I hope that they understand different alternatives ... but I know they won't share [my strong views]"; "I try to explain to them the various perspectives or views that one might have, rather than *declaring* [mine] ... you need to allow those students to come

485 [018], Interview, lines 424–5; [047], Interview, lines 481–94; [047], Interview, lines 923–4; [047], Interview, lines 859–66; [002], Interview, lines 815–49; [058], Syllabus, 2007–08, p 1; [032], Interview, lines 236–42.

to those conclusions themselves"; "I don't try to advocate for one [worldview] or another"; and "my objective is *never* to have the students to think about contract law the way *I do*." Some emphasize the role of playing "devil's advocate."[486]

The overarching picture, therefore, is of professors who are highly committed to the project of presenting a series of eclectic theoretical perspectives. Their purpose is overwhelmingly to provide external critiques of law and to encourage a deeper understanding of contract law in a broader context. Moreover, the use of external perspectives serves to further the realist rejection of law as a purely internal, self-referential system. Canadian common law Contracts professors very frequently assert that "external" considerations are actually essential to its study. These considerations include politics, morality, justice, economics, social context, race, and gender.

Specific External Perspectives

Politics: Many law professors appear to have internalized the message from critical legal studies that "law is politics." This commitment surfaces in different ways. Frequently law professors make the general claim that law and politics are constituted by each other. We also see instances of professors dissolving the distinction between public and private law, conceiving of law as a battleground between opposing forces of individualism and collectivism, emphasizing the role of power and inequality, and focusing on winners and losers.[487]

The idea that law "is" politics surfaces in many different ways. Sometimes professors will use that formulation directly, referencing legal realism, without further elaboration. When this happens, as it does with Professor 31, the lack of description almost passes for a shorthand, reflecting an obvious, taken-for-granted truth: "We talk about, and this comes back to ... legal realism, ... [how] law *is* politics, and how laws can be deployed to reinforce the position of the *more powerful* and how

---

486 [004], Interview, lines 428–9; [042], Interview, lines 465–7; [064], Interview, lines 745–6; [033], Interview, lines 475–8; [028], Interview, lines 234–7; [050], Interview, lines 438–43; [026], Interview, line 678; [053], Interview, lines 386–7; [004], Interview, lines 452–4.

487 See Mensch, *supra* note 134 at 33; Kennedy, "Politicizing the Classroom", *supra* note 134 at 84; Dalton, *supra* note 128 at 1002, n 14; Kennedy, "Form and Substance", *supra* note 60 at 1712–13, 1723 (altruism/individualism); Feinman, "Critical Approaches to Contract Law", *supra* note 135 at 838, 839–44 (individualism/collectivism); Singer, "Legal Rights Debate", *supra* note 136 at 980 (self-regarding/other regarding).

that might change over time."[488] Similarly, Professor 64 explains how the "political" comes up in class:

> [B]oth the political and law are constituted by one another ... and so ... the law does not exist in the absence of a political context, nor does the political context exist in the absence of law ... That is the philosophical message of trying to teach ratio as prophecy ... you are looking through the lens of a legal thinker who is also incorporating ... the socio-economic and political climate that they're making the decision in.[489]

Professor 21 aims to "*unpack* the political, social, economic value judgments that inform judicial decision making in the realm of contract law," using legislative examples to show how

> judges are in a sense *very unimaginative* and, in fact, *unresponsive* to changing social market norms in contract law ... [An] example of where the legislative dimension actually *is required* ... helps break down the idea that contract law is private law ... I actually ... teach contract law *as a form of public law*. It's a mechanism by which we regulate market norms.[490]

Professor 35 also tries to highlight market regulation and political choices:

> I try to get them into thinking about ... basic ... political principles about regulating the market ...
>
> I do want them to see that the court is making choices ... and that *they* are making choices – and that their clients are making choices about how we organize market relationships ...
>
> [In some cases, like unconscionability, good faith, or economic duress,] the courts have said, "Oh, we can't go here. This is a political *choice* ... that's something for the legislature to step in and deal with" ... And I ... try to say to them, "Well, *that's* the court making a political choice, in and of itself. It's not [that] the legislature is political and the court is *not* ... [M]aking choices about what boundaries they can set on market behaviour is its own political choice" ...
>
> I say there's no *natural* role for the courts ... The courts *have chosen to set boundaries for their behaviour* and we see places where they've come in through the back door. [491]

488 [031], Interview, lines 408–11.
489 [064], Interview, lines 759–68.
490 [021], Interview, lines 35–7, 42–8.
491 [035], Interview, lines 47–8, 386–407, 418–25.

Several other professors similarly emphasize the political role that law plays in regulating the market, reinforcing the idea that the supposedly "private" field of contract law has an important public element. Thus Professor 27 argues how contract law gets to the core of basic political values:

> [C]ontract law is great is because it touches on the central nerve ... about the limits of markets. It's about what are markets good for ... What do we render unto the market and what don't we? ... And this just takes you right to the ... *core values* ... and *limits* of market ordering as ... a way of running things. Which is ... the large political debate that divides [Ontario Progressive Conservative Party leader] Tim Hudak from ... [Ontario New Democratic Party leader Andrea] Horvath, or [Ontario premier and Liberal Party leader Kathleen] Wynne for that matter ... It's *just* the basic debate about the markets, which I think is probably the most sensitive and overpolitical socio-economic sort of set of choices we face.[492]

Other professors similarly describe contract law as a "launching pad to talk about the role of autonomy versus the paternalistic protection of the state ... [and] about the pros and cons of distributive justice in private law," or the product of "choices [that] involve ... not just precedent, but political preferences [and] economic preferences." Professor 42, for whom "every burp and hiccup in law is about ethics and politics," conceives of holding up a mirror to students in class to get them to say, "'Now you're making a choice here. What are the assumptions that you're bringing to bear? And why did you make that choice?'"[493]

Some professors elucidate judges' political and economic preferences by portraying law as the product of a universal battle between individualism and collectivism, a long-standing claim of critical legal studies. A number of professors invoke this binary directly. Professor 3 does so perhaps most explicitly, reproducing at times a "Marxist analysis." Not only does law manifest decisions on either side of the dichotomy; the "myth" of law as neutral is itself political:

> [Contract law] really is an area where ... fundamental moral dilemmas of living in an organized society are palpable in the law ... Are we these self-interested, rapacious, consuming, unconnected-to-others types of individuals who don't need society and don't want [its] constraints ... or

492 [027], Interview, lines 321–35.

493 [037], Interview, lines 113–15; [062], Interview, lines 730–3; [042], Interview, lines 464–5, 719–21.

is our true nature that we are collectively oriented communal beings? ... [L]iberalism versus communitarianism, socialism versus capitalism ... free market versus regulated market – all of those ... lines of political economic social thought ... are so palpably present in contract law ...

I try to encourage students to see what I believe is the truth of law, which is it's a battleground of ideology ...

The myth is that law is this neutral, amoral kind of system that doesn't reflect ideology, that doesn't reflect philosophy, that doesn't reflect any particular politics.

And that myth is itself political because it presents the courts and therefore the state as purely neutral actors, whereas ... the predominant tendency of [classical] contract law ... is to sustain a capitalist market economy... [I]n order to have a particular kind of capitalism that is unrestrained, ... it helps to have a state that says you can do whatever you want ...[I]t also helps to legitimate that – to say that that's not political, that's just normal, that's just natural ... The view that law is somehow ... different from ... new types of normativity – political, moral, social, justice, whatever – ... serves a very profound political purpose. It serves the interests of capital over those of the environment and of the workers and everybody else.[494]

Another professor, who "peppers" the discussion with allusions to Marx, similarly highlights the role of competing ideologies, with specific reference to critical legal studies:

I ... teach the course from, broadly speaking, a legal realist slash critical legal studies perspective ... [I try to] bring to the surface of the discussion questions about *power*. Power relations, asymmetries in power, power dynamics, and *shifts* in power dynamics, and how those have *influenced* and in turn *been influenced* by the law ... You can tell a very interesting story ... of the various power dynamics that have *fashioned* the law, and in turn been constituted at least partly *by* the law ...

I'm *open* about my politics ...When we get to unconscionability, duress, particularly economic duress, undue influence, [I] drop a bit of Marx into those discussions ... in order to show them [how to look] at these cases ... as an attempt to *socialize* the law ... I try to get them, though, to think of themselves as social actors, not simply ... as *neutral, objective specialists* in the law. This doesn't exist, of course. It's a fabrication. It's an abstraction ... They're *always* already embedded in a whole variety of social relations, some of which are playing out behind their backs and of which I want them to be at least somewhat conscious. Similarly with

494 *Ibid*, lines 14–35, 108–9, 124–39, 209–28.

politics, similarly with political economy, the whole bit – *all of this* is bundled up into the law.[495]

Other professors emphasize the role of competing ideologies. Professor 33 describes how the theme of ideology comes up in discussions of reasonableness and commercial efficacy, and how the "notion of neutrality ... is certainly not left unchallenged." Likewise Professor 25 emphasizes the tension between the "will of the parties" and "social judgment" as the "big picture" of contract law. Professor 25 also expands on this theme quite extensively in the course syllabus:

> Often we forget that on the playing-fields of Contract-dom thrilling ideological interests are in contention ...
>
> The legal correlative of laissez-faire economics is freedom of contract; ie, the source of obligation as the will of the individual contracting freely. Hence is the notion that the proper function of a court (ie, the state, society) is not to make or unmake contracts for parties but passively to enforce contracts that the parties themselves made of their own freely-operating will. Historically this idea of free contract was viewed as wonderfully liberating. Freedom of contract was the mechanism that enabled those born poor to die rich if they were sufficiently shrewd bargainers of their talents. Here again, you see, contract is a sort of antithesis of feudalism, where one was classified at birth (as a noble, a serf, &c) more or less for life. Of course, the idea that untrammeled economic/contractual freedom is infinitely liberating and that all status-based relations will and should give way to contract-based relationships underwent such severe scrutiny in the 20th century (1929, social democracy, feminism, &c) that the grand intellectual edifice of 19th-century contract theory sometimes seems to be falling to ruin. That is the story of this course.[496]

The theme of ideological battle sometimes surfaces in professors' desire to elucidate how power imbalances manifest in the law or to highlight distributive consequences (winners and losers) of a particular legal rule. Thus even among professors who might not explicitly self-identify as Marxists or critical legal scholars, the role of politics surfaces. For example, Professor 28 includes "power relations" as an important underlying theme of the course, "touching on it" in "almost every topic" in the course – in more legislated topics such as family, labour, and consumer contexts, but also in traditional doctrinal areas such as

495 [040], Interview, lines 64–88, 381–422.

496 [033], Interview, lines 311–23; [025], Interview, lines 105–16; [025], Syllabus, 2015–16, p 4.

consideration. Professor 35 tries to "draw[] to the surface" "the power relationships between people ... and the way socio-economic resources are distributed." Professor 7 tries to get students to think about "power and inequality," which "traditional contract law tends to suppress."[497]

The concern of fairness, distributive justice, or "winners and losers" also arises periodically. Thus Professor 58 looks at doctrinal rules from the perspective of "design choices," getting students "to think through who wins or who loses" from doctrinal decisions such as the mailbox rule of offer formation, considering it "pretty important" that students "assess the enterprise in terms of justice or its effects ... [by] thinking who was being advantaged or disadvantaged by different things we do." Professor 45 aims to "shed[] light on ... the role that [contracts] play in ... disadvantaging certain groups." Professor 32 emphasizes "practical judicial politics," which relates to "distributive justice" and is "essentially ... about fairness." Professor 4 asks students to think about "who will be the overpowered? Who will be the losers in this – and the winners?" Professor 26 seeks to emphasize how broader "social values," "political objectives," or distributive justice are "encoded" in technical rules, and to show how "contract law is full of apparently neutral rules that actually systematically favour one side or another."[498]

Accordingly, the influence of critical legal studies, and some of its early realist origins, is alive and well in the minds of Canadian common law Contracts professors as they conceptualize and explain the vision of law they attempt to present to their students. Many of them – this section has quoted from twenty professors – dismantle the distinction between law and politics and between public and private law. They view contract law doctrine as a "launching pad" for exploring the battleground of ideologies that constitute human nature. And they insert distributive concerns into the core of the Contracts course.[499]

---

497 [028], Interview, lines 173–209; [035], Interview, lines 618–21; [007], Interview, lines 319–21. Other professors specifically use consideration to explore the grand tension between autonomy and social control. See e.g. [003], Interview, lines 141–59:

> It used to be the case that law and morality were not very separate. And now they're saying consideration is just anything – something of value in the eye of the law – we're not going to judge what it is or whether it's good or what intention was behind it. So right there, it's the whole story – between talking about a law that is animated by moral concern – concerns about justice, and talking about a law that's effectively amoral.

498 [058], Interview, lines 157–9; [058], Interview, lines 194–6; [045], Interview, lines 186–9; [032], Interview, lines 719–23, 740–4; [004], Interview, lines 404–6; [026], Interview, lines 1018–19, 887–8, 1046–7.

499 *Cf.* Hale, "Coercion and Distribution in a Supposedly Noncoercive State", *supra* note 60; Hale, "Bargaining, Duress, and Economic Liberty", *supra* note 128; Dawson, "Economic Duress", *supra* note 128.

Morality and Justice: Another long-standing tenet of classical legal thought is the idea, in its strongest form, that law is a separate domain from morality or justice; or, in a more qualified form, that such considerations are relevant "only so far as they are embodied in principles – abstract yet precise norms that [are] consistent with ... other fundamental principles of the system."[500] Oliver Wendel Holmes Jr attributed the strong form of this idea to Langdell, who famously argued that "substantial justice, and the interest of the contracting parties" were "irrelevant" considerations.[501] Holmes attacked this idea with his memorable claim that "[t]he life of the law has not been logic: it has been experience ... The important phenomenon is the man underneath it, not the coat; the justice and reasonableness of a decision, not its consistency with previously held views." Since then, the extent to which justice or morality should be considered central to, or apart from, law has featured prominently in legal philosophical debates, with realists such as Fuller arguing for their centrality.[502]

A number of professors assert that morality or justice ought to be considered central to law – either explicitly or by implication. Professor 55 articulates a strong version of this philosophy:

> The rules are meant to be ... the realization of what is ... a *just ordering* of things ... The rules ought to *unfold* in that fashion, so we should be examining them and criticizing them in that light ...
>
> I understand law very much in moral terms ... It is an attempt to put in place rules that are just and right and advance human good ... We criticize law when it fails in that enterprise, and rightfully so, and it fails all the time, but then say, "No it's *bad law* and ought to be made better to conform better to what ... any one of us might think is right or just."[503]

Professor 30 articulates an equally strong commitment to morality, but does so in a more autobiographical way, rejecting individualism and instrumentalism as foreign to the way Professor 30 "had been raised and grew up":

> In the world that my mother came from ... she grew up in a village where the *emphasis* in all relations was not on breaching your engagements

500 Grey, *supra* note 96 at 15.

501 *Ibid* at 3–5.

502 Holmes, Review of Langdell, *supra* note 99 at 234. See HLA Hart, "Positivism and the Separation of Morals" (1958) 71 Harv L Rev 593; Lon L Fuller, "Positivism and Fidelity to Law: A Reply to Professor Hart" (1958) 71 Harv L Rev 630.

503 [055], Interview, lines 319–24, 448–68.

> [but] ... on *observing* your relations ... The *law* as I first encountered it in Canada ... seemed to ... infer and imply an autonomy and an individuality that was *foreign* to the way in which I had been raised and grew up.[504]

Professor 43, who decries the loss of an "internal sense of decency," argues: "[Y]ou have to bring your morality to the law *internally*. There's no law and morality separation. There's not a split. I've always been *massively opposed* to that idea."[505] And Professor 3 speaks about "vindicating" students' instinctive belief in justice as a means of warding against the "dangerous" separation between law and morality:

> I have a belief that a lot of people come into law school believing in justice. And part of what I want to do is ... to vindicate that belief rather than destroy it. I want to tell them that they're actually reflected in the law ... Because law is all about trying to create that detachment ... when people feel they can detach themselves from the moral basis of what they're doing and create a sensibility that this is a purely technical enterprise, I think that's a really dangerous place to be.[506]

These strong rejections of the separation between law and morality clearly take as a given the long-standing debates in the legal academy. Occasions to insist on the centrality of justice arise periodically as well, although these are somewhat less elaborate. Rather than strongly rejecting the separation between law and justice, the tendency instead is simply to insist on its importance, making a point of saying the word *justice* because it needs to be said. Thus Professor 56 wants to ensure that students do not get "lost in the doctrine," that conversations are not "eclipsed by the doctrinal discussion," but rather that the doctrine is "*always* relate[d] to ... larger themes of ... *justice*." Professor 58's three-page substantive introduction to the course syllabus concludes with the question "Why is the word *justice* uttered so rarely?" Professors also argue more affirmatively for ideas such as "law isn't just about the rule of law, but it's also about producing justice across communities," or "we put a lot of investment into law now as way to provide ... a way that people can live in harmony with one another in a fair and just society."[507]

---

504 [030], Interview, lines 602–18.

505 [043], Interview, lines 350, 475–7.

506 [003], Interview, lines 269–81.

507 [056], Interview, lines 79–107; [058], Syllabus, 2007–08, p 3; [063], Interview, lines 383–4; [020], Interview, lines 712–14.

Context: The debates in contract law have been caricatured as a disagreement over what judges should be able to consider in adjudicating contract disputes: just the four corners of the contract, or the series of other factors that exist alongside the contract. Much of legal realism sought to show how other contextual factors – for example, judicial preferences and psychology, details of the factual record, and realities of social and business relations – were essential to understanding judicial decisions and the empirical reality of contracting norms.[508] Canadian common law Contracts professors frequently refer to the importance of context. They do so by invoking specific scholarly writings – the case-in-context studies of legal historians such as Simpson and Danzig; relational theorists Macaulay and Macneil; Grant Gilmore; Roderick Macdonald – and by offering their own contextualized interpretations of ideas such as the objective theory of contract. And even when they do not make these specific references, they refer more casually to the importance of social context, complete facts, everyday life, or the real world, suggesting a thoroughgoing commitment to the idea that elements "apart" from the text need to be taken into consideration.

Professor 27 provides an elaborate description of the way in which a richly contextual understanding underlies the whole law of contract, invoking the case-in-context studies of Brian Simpson as a "beautiful" example of using context to determine "objective" intention:

> The objective theory is a theory about figuring out what *you* said to me and how I *know* what you said to me, and in some sense it's the whole of contract law.
>
> So, are you talking to me? Are you talking contract? Are you making me an offer? What are the terms of that offer? Is that *really* a promise or is that idle sales talk? Is that misrepresentation? What does that mean? Was that a promise? What kind of promise? ... *That's* what contract law *is* ... It doesn't matter what you subjectively *think* you're saying to me, it's how I as a reasonable [person would understand what you are saying] ... What is a reasonable [person?] It's not a fly on the wall, it's not some judge sitting on a bench, it's not some ... composite of ... people on the Clapham omnibus. It is, rather, *you*, in this context.

---

508 See Gilmore, *Death of Contract*, *supra* note 90 at 14–17, 43–4; Frank, *supra* note 108; Simpson, "Quackery", *supra* note 195; Simpson, "Beauty", *supra* note 195; Macaulay, "Non-Contractual Relations", *supra* note 60; Macneil, *New Social Contract*, *supra* note 81. Swan uses the Canadian case *Scott v Wawanesa Mutual Insurance Co*, [1989] 1 SCR 1445 to tease out this contrast (9th ed, supra note 208 at 694). *Ben-Ishai & Percy* also includes this case (10th ed, *supra* note 210 at 524), although *Waddams*, 6th ed, *supra* note 209 does not.

So it *deeply* depends on who *you* are, when it comes to you making claims about how I understood what the other person was saying ... It's *deeply* contextualized ... This is why Brian Simpson's articles about contract law are *so beautiful* ... To arrive "ex Peerless" – what does that mean? Well, it turns out it's really difficult to find out what it means. You have to go back and learn a lot about the cotton trade, and Liverpool, and technology, and mercantile practice and it turns out that was a *highly technical meaning*, and when they said "ex Peerless" they actually were saying something about the timing of the arrival of the cotton – and that actually was a term. So, people ... a hundred years later saying, "Oh, that's this – stupid judges! They thought the name of the ship was important – how stupid can they get?" ... It turns out, if you do the work, and you contextualize it, it actually *was*.[509]

Professor 17 likewise uses case-in-context studies to "generate critical distance" from, and to "historicize the uptake" of, rules. For Professor 25, teaching historically is "*my* version of legal realism," teaching "trends in the cases" to point out to students how "law is contingent." Professor 28 specifically says that "the law doesn't matter so much ... [what matters is] *context* and how ... the rules ... are used," reprising themes of case-in-context studies without citing them.[510]

Professor 42, who describes Brian Simpson as a "mentor," uses case-in-context studies to counteract the "pathological" presentation of relationships in case law. These studies can emphasize the "little legal systems" created by the parties, in an approach that bridges historical studies, socio-legal perspectives, and legal pluralism:

The case law [is misleading because it] describes *pathological relationships* ... Our socio-legal friends tell us that that's something like one or two per cent of commercial time, so what kind of lens or telescope or vantage point is this, really? The difficulty is that you can't go on *field trips* inside of law firms to watch the constitution of contracts, the formation of contracts, in action ... The *risk* is that you end up viewing a mode of social ordering contract through unrepresentative lenses of it.

We have a *growing* literature ... courtesy of scholars who have attempted to do case-in-context studies of particular contract cases. My own mentor

509 [027], Interview, lines 850–99.

510 [017], Interview, line 117 (referring to Danzig, *Hadley, supra* note 387); [051], Interview, lines 302–23 (referring to a historical study of *Hadley* and Simpson, "Beauty", *supra* note 195); [017], Interview, lines 449–58, 624–31; [025], Interview, lines 518–30; [028], Interview, lines 111–29.

> Brian Simpson ... has done several of those ... They're not plentiful, but you can work through them. Moreover, if you select judgments ... on the basis of what they tell you about the parties' relationship, and how they set out creating this little legal system for themselves ... you can do some of that too ...
>
> Contract doctrine ... doesn't tell you anything about the content of those legal systems because that's the blank slate that the state provides *facilitatively* ... *That's* the exercise you've got to get your *hands* on. The haggling, the bargaining back and forth, the mediation, the negotiation ... You've got to *march* back through time and start asking, "Well, how did they really perform?" ... Either there's *no* text or there are *multiple* texts of words and conduct. But the key point *is* that the doctrinal part ... only tells you about the *parameters* for constitution making by the parties themselves.[511]

Professor 36 similarly connects legal realism and the influence of Stewart Macaulay to a pluralist focus on "mini-customary environments" in describing intellectual influences on teaching the Contracts course:

> [My teaching of Contracts] was very much influenced by people like ... Rod Macdonald and others, and therefore [there] was a strong emphasis in the course on legal realism, on informal contractual relations ... The *primary* subtext ... was the ways in which contractual relationships operate as ... *mini*-customary environments in which the formal dimensions of the contract are *just one* element in a much larger normative set ...
>
> If you were asking ... "How do you think you can prepare your students *best* for legal practice in a contractual setting?" I would say, "Well, read Stewart Macaulay over and over and over again ... these people *very much* shaped *my* approach to the teaching of contract law.[512]

Similarly Professor 37, who concludes the course every year with a reading of Macneil's "Whither Contracts," says, "The course on Contracts allows us to explore how ... we govern complex personal relationships. And ... that's what law's all about. If you read Fuller and ... Macdonald, ... at the *base* of it, the basic nature of ... law is human interaction. What better example of human interaction *than* contracts?" Professor 62, who also credits Gilmore as a major influence, is also "predisposed to like *most* of Lon Fuller's ideas, because of Rod Macdonald's influence on my thinking."[513]

511 [042], Interview, lines 106–46, 394–433.

512 [036], Interview, lines 37–42, 236–44.

513 [037], Interview, lines 107–12, 365–6 (referring to Macneil, "Whither Contracts", *supra* note 193); [062], Interview, lines 122–3, 255–6.

A number of professors acknowledge or reveal an intellectual debt to Ian Macneil and his theories of relationalism. Professor 12 "admired" Macneil's ideas about relational contracts "early on," and teaches the course as if contractual relations are "more important practical and economic terms" than discrete transactions; Professor 44, a former colleague and "good friend" of Ian Macneil, considers both Macneil and Macaulay as influences, particularly with respect to "ongoing relations." Professor 30 supplements readings with "Macneil and other relational scholars" to counteract the focus on individualism and efficient breach. Professor 32's syllabus opens with an emphasis on themes of contractual relations, and invites students to "be mindful of [contracts'] commercial or social context – in other words, how contract functions in everyday life."[514]

For these scholars, the granular context of "mini-customary environments" disturbs the focus on propositions derived from case law. Understanding contract law becomes a search for the empirical reality of social or business relations, an activity that can be aided by historical research. Although these professors develop this attitude with specific reference to realist and pluralist scholars – Fuller, Gilmore, Macneil, Macaulay, Simpson, Danzig, Macdonald – a number of other professors display a commitment to the importance of context and empirical reality and, implicitly, about the importance of non-state normativity. References to the importance of everyday life and the "real world" communicate a similar commitment to idea of incorporating context.

Professors frequently mention how important it is that what they teach accords with everyday life, or the "real world." These claims rely, however implicitly, on the ideas that context outside of legal doctrine, and indeed entire normative systems outside the state, are essential to a complete understanding of contract law. Thus, although many of these professors might not specifically invoke the scholarly case-in-context studies, or studies that directly connect everyday life to legal pluralism, the widely occurring tendency to seek everyday and real-world examples further disrupts the emphasis on doctrine.[515]

This tendency takes a number of forms. Sometimes professors state that they want to incorporate everyday examples in order to connect with students and to show them how their own lives, experiences, and understandings are relevant to contract law (and vice versa). We see this in the

514 [012], Interview, lines 1024–6, 1004–7; [044], Interview, lines 103–31; [030], Interview, lines 205–14; [032], Syllabus, 2013–14.

515 See e.g. Roderick A Macdonald, *Lessons of Everyday Law* (Montreal; Kingston, ON: McGill-Queen's University Press, 2002) at 13–14 (providing a detailed bibliography on law and everyday life).

frequent attempts to provide everyday examples of contracting, such as buying a cup of coffee, an exercise bicycle, or a computer program, or the desire to choose examples that specifically relate to students.[516] Often, these examples only implicitly suggest how students' own understandings generate contextual and normative information that is relevant to understanding contract law. But sometimes professors are more explicit. Professor 51's course syllabus states, in its Introduction, that "in most cases the parties are oblivious to law and act in response to other interests or norms." Professor 1 specifically aims to "valorize" the intuitions that students bring from their own lives prior to law school; and Professor 62 offers a theoretical connection between law and life, citing again the influence of Roderick Macdonald: "Law is play and therefore is life ... that active interpretive constitutive practice in many ways is play, and ... one of the best ways to do legal pedagogy, is to do *play*."[517]

Some professors refer to "practical" reality, often meaning the pragmatic business or strategic considerations of legal practice. Occasionally they do this by providing examples from their own practice, as when Professor 39 "thinks back to practice" to come up with relatable examples that convey information about strategy. Sometimes professors connect the idea of context to a claim about the "reality" of commercial activity. Professor 12, who believes that casebooks should "tell a story" and give "context to" cases, and who wants to expose "students to *real life contracts*," aims primarily to "situate doctrine ... in the real world." Professor 13 argues that a drafter "need[s] to take into account the ... interchange between [the] client and the other person with whom it interacts in the marketplace to figure out how ... to ensure that [the] provisions will prevail." Professor 11 emphasizes to students that, in a "practical" or "business" context, contracts go "smoothly" "most of the time." And Professor 43 directly connects the idea of context to the task of understanding client needs.[518] In all these ways, teaching

516 See e.g. [008], Interview, lines 605–12 (landlord issue or exercise bike), [041], Interview, lines 181–206 (deposit for hotel room); [016], Interview, lines 38–9 (informal contracts); [009], Interview, lines 129–45, 164–8, 748–53 (bringing in a statement of claim regarding a Marilyn Manson contract); [010], Interview, lines 231–37 (replacing Sandra Bullock for Bette Davis (the subject of *Warner Bros Pictures v Nelson*, [1937] 1 KB 209) because students "don't know who Bette Davis is").

517 [051], Syllabus, 2016–17, p 2; [001], Interview, lines 410–27; [062], Interview, lines 550–3.

518 [039], Interview, lines 766–94; [012], Interview, lines 220–4, 871–3; [013], Interview, lines 388–94; [011], Interview, lines 94–117; [043], Interview, lines 1288–319 ("The law firms [are] saying, 'We need people who understand our clients, and our clients' businesses. We don't need people who just know the law. We need them ... to have that context ... side to things'").

about context not only moves the subject of study beyond the reported facts and legal analysis contained in judicial reasons for decision; it elucidates the normative relevance of everyday experiences, commercial reality, and social relations.

Law and Economics, Feminism, and Race: Whereas many professors provide detailed and committed accounts of the importance of law-and-society scholarship, critical legal studies, and legal pluralism, when it comes to some other seminal schools of thought, such as law and economics or feminist and race critiques, the treatment is somewhat more attenuated. Although most professors do include these schools, they usually do so as part of a grab bag of "alternative perspectives," without demonstrating a deeply developed intellectual commitment to the ideas. There are a few exceptions, but these tend to prove the rule that, in Canada, common law Contracts professors consider law and economics, feminism, and race to be important perspectives to include, but generally not significant enough to frame the central logic of the course. Unlike the role of politics, policy, or context, it is more frequent to see economics, feminism, and race grouped together in a series of perspectives, sprinkled throughout the course or deployed selectively to canvass argumentative techniques – but, as I discuss in the second part of this chapter, without the requisite rigour to truly "operationalize" these perspectives into legal reasoning.

Law and Economics: Most professors in my study include some degree of law and economics in their course, but those who enthusiastically commit to the field are in the minority – only about ten describe law and economic ideas as compelling and important, and a number of these downplay the use of the term "law and economics" for fear of driving students away.[519] Only two volunteer a description of themselves as "law and economics scholars."[520] Another eleven describe their specific commitments to law and economics ideas with somewhat

519 See e.g. [048], Interview, lines 337–9 ("law and economics changed at least *my* thinking about the law of contracts and those kinds of issues that I tried to introduce into class"); [053] ("I'm very interested in it"); [023], Interview, lines 69–73 ("I don't talk about it in that language, usually because as soon as I say "law and economics" people get anxious ... I try to stay away from terminology and just talk about *economic forces*"); [047], Interview, lines 119–49 ("You can tell students [that an example] involves law and economics, but that's a horrible way of teaching it").

520 [018], Interview, lines 45–6 ("my general orientation or perspective on law is a bit of a law and economics scholar"); [061], lines 23–7 ("I teach very much in a law and economics kind of way ... Contracts ... is one of the natural go tos for [a] law and economics scholar").

less conviction, calling the ideas helpful in some instances but not in others, including the concepts in only a minor way, or claiming inadequate knowledge about the subject.[521] Some professors do not expand greatly on the ideas themselves, but include them among a series of perspectives that they aim to include, along with others such as feminism, race, and "critical" perspectives.[522] Ten professors (nine of whom are otherwise realists) either do not include it or are hostile towards it, with reticence ranging from the mild to the severe.[523] This variegated embrace of law and economics differs markedly from the American situation, in which law and economics plays a much more dominant role. Indeed, even among the strongest acolytes in my study, no professor expressed a sentiment similar to the idea that it would be almost impossible to teach Contracts without law and economics,[524] or as one US Contracts professor expressed to me: "there are a number of lessons of law and economics ... that have become [so] completely hard-wired into the modern understanding of contract law [such that] if you didn't understand those lessons you'd be disserving your students."[525] Indicative of the distance between Canada and the United States on this point, one Canadian professor distinguishes Canada by implication,

---

521 See e.g. [026], Interview, lines 1106–11 ("I think law and economics analysis of contract *formation* is *really helpful* ... In what areas is it *efficient* to impose contractual liability and not? But, ... and this is counterintuitive to a lot of people, I feel like the law and economics literature has *not* been so helpful in remedies"); [008], Interview, line 500 (bringing law and economics "occasionally into the syllabus"); [056], Interview, lines 703–8 ("from *my* perspective, the one thing that I'm not doing enough ... is law and economics ... [I]t's because I'm really not good at it. I don't have any ideological *bias* against it, as some people do at [my institution]").

522 See the discussion above under "The General Case for an Eclectic Series of External Perspectives," pages 194–6. See e.g. [002], Interview, lines 817–21; [004], Interview, lines 28–9 ("[I ask] realist [questions] every now and then, economics questions, feminist questions – whatever").

523 See e.g. [011], Interview, lines 365–6 ("it doesn't explicitly play a role. It's not *my* approach to law"); [025], Interview, line 439 ("I don't see the world as a legal economist sees the world"); [040], Interview, lines 280–2 ("law and economics was not something I was sympathetic to ... Seeing a contract as ... being about transaction costs and information asymmetries made no sense to me"); [055], Interview, lines 427–39 ("law and economics as kind of a normative account of moral decisions is ... fundamentally mistaken"); [012], Interview, lines 462–4 ("Basically I think that law and economics is a dead end. Better we never had gone down that [road] because quite frankly, its ability to be useful is almost nil").

524 See e.g. Stephen, *supra* note 159.

525 Douglas Baird, Interview with author (11 April 2013) at 29:20–29:32 [attributed with permission]. Baird is former president of the American Law and Economics Association.

"mentioning [in class that] law and economics [is] ... a *dominant structure* in the American education of contract law."[526]

Feminism and Race: Feminism came up in at least a third of the interviews – at least twenty-three professors volunteered that they seek to incorporate themes of feminism into the course. But as with law and economics, most of the time they simply mention feminism along with a series of other perspectives, usually critical legal studies and economics. Fifteen professors list feminist, gender, or "women's" issues in this way, without significantly expanding on how they seek to incorporate them.[527] This cursory mention does not necessarily imply that these professors treat feminist issues cursorily in the course, but it does suggest that most do not consider feminist issues to be significantly central to their approach as to expand upon them in depth, as they do with the themes of contingency, indeterminacy, policy, politics, and context. About five professors give slightly more expanded examples;[528] only two provide lengthy discussions about the role of feminism.

Professor 17 underlines the "chauvinism" and "patriarch's privilege" revealed in leading cases, and specifically emphasizes the "issue of women in the profession."[529] Professor 9, even more emphatically, teaches

> feminism in contracts expressly ... I teach ... feminisms ... Balfour and Balfour ... [is] the best example [of] ... a strong argument for a misogynist rule that really excludes women from the courtroom when they're trying to enforce a "domestic contract" – in quotation marks ...

526 [020], Interview, lines 421–3.

527 See e.g. [021], Interview, lines 60–2, 290–1 ("I've taken on board feminism, I've taken on board critical disability theory, critical race theory"); [032], Interview, lines 244–6 ("a brief run at times of the feminist critique of contract, ... a racialized perspective on contract and so on").

528 See e.g. [047], Interview, lines 207–12 ("I love doing [*Balfour v Balfour*, [1919] 2 KB 571 (CA)] and the position of women in contracts ... I put up a 1972 Australian textbook by Sutton whose chapter is 'The Drunk and the Insane and Married Women' all in one chapter, 'and contract capacity'"); [051], Interview, lines 291–3 (undue influence and spousal guarantee cases); [010], Interview, lines 62–6 (man standing in place of wife for a loan transaction; [059], Interview, lines 213–33 (critiquing Lord Denning's judgments on domestic agreements); [048], Interview, lines 63–74 (referring to Ayres, *supra* note 328, and to Frug's feminist critique of contract law casebooks, "Re-Reading Contracts", *supra* note 331); [065], Interview, lines 305–8 (women coming back into the work force and engaging with an employer).

529 [017], Interview, lines 189–200, 205–18 (highlighting both Bertha Wilson's career as an example of women in the profession receiving little acknowledgment and the chauvinism in *Jackson v Horizon Holidays Ltd*, [1975] 1 WLR 1468, [1975] 3 All ER 92 (CA), Denning MR).

> There are some people that are opposed to feminism. And being a feminist is a political state. Now I talk about what I say feminism is ... my son was saying, when you say you're a feminist for ... his age group, and that's the age group of many people that I teach – what you're really saying is, "Women should be more equal ... than men." That's what in his age group he says a lot of people [think] feminism is. So, I'm like, "Well that's not what I think feminism is." So I talk about what I think it is.[530]

Such explicit and strong statements are not the norm, however, and while the overall impression is that feminism is widely considered an important perspective to expose students to, only occasionally does this appear to correspond with an agenda of advocating for greater equality. Even firm proponents such as Professor 9 disclaim any desire truly to advocate: "It's not my job to make you feminists."[531]

The situation with race is even more cursory and sporadic. Race is occasionally mentioned on a list of critical perspectives, and a few professors discuss Ian Ayres's study of discrimination in car sales.[532] One difference between law and economics, on the one hand, and feminism and race, on the other, is that no professor in my study expresses hostility to critical race or feminist theoretical projects, although occasionally there is some slight distancing.[533] However, while all three theories do play a role in the teaching of common law Contracts in Canada, none holds the centre of gravity that some of the other realist themes do.

The importance of these schools therefore appears to lie less in the normative reference points they typically offer (such as efficiency or equality), or in their particular methodological or critical techniques (cost-benefit analysis, deconstruction).[534] Rather, they primarily serve as items on a shopping list of possible "critical" perspectives that might assist students in developing a range of argumentative techniques. In other words, the largely cursory ways in which these specific schools are invoked serves only to confirm the preference for a general eclecticism. Moreover, while the occasional professor specifically designs pedagogy

530 [009], Interview, lines 177–200, 630–9 (referring to *Balfour v Balfour*, *supra* note 528).

531 *Ibid*, lines 638–9.

532 See e.g. [033], Interview, lines 352–7 (invoking Ayres, *supra* note 328).

533 See e.g. [040], Interview, lines 299–304 ("I actually try to tell them throughout, 'Well look, you know, a feminist would actually look at this case in this way, and a law and economics scholar would look at it in this way.' And then I'd say, 'Well, they're wrong! ... and here's how I read it'"); [038], Interview, lines 314–19 ("feminine or gender issues ... don't come up"); [046], Interview, lines 519–26 (feminism comes up "not very often").

534 See Coase, *supra* note 161; Dalton, *supra* note 128.

to translate these eclectic perspectives into diverse argumentation,[535] as I expand upon in the second part of this chapter, the overall impression is that most do not mine these schools rigorously for their methodological and argumentative possibilities. Judging by the way professors describe how they use these schools, the impression is closer to that of a loose and casual invocation than to a tight and technical one, recalling Mertz's observation of how policy discussions are often treated less seriously than doctrinal ones.[536]

Indigenous Perspectives: I did not systematically ask participants whether they incorporated Indigenous or Aboriginal perspectives into their Contracts courses. In part, this is because the *Truth and Reconciliation Commission of Canada: Calls to Action* report, which specifically calls on law schools to "take a course in Aboriginal people and the law," and which has since spawned numerous efforts to "indigenize" the core curriculum, only came out partway through this study.[537] Accordingly, references to Indigenous perspectives are sporadic. A study conducted today, in light of the report and greater awareness of this issue, might well bring up more examples.

That said, the issue comes up in a significant way in ten interviews.[538] The professors who raise the issue often articulate the importance of incorporating Indigenous perspectives or subject matter, often specifically in aid of advancing broader realist objectives. Some of the examples, therefore, illuminate possibilities for incorporating Indigenous perspectives into the course, and indicate that there might be a more broad-based willingness to do so. In this sense Indigenous perspectives differ markedly from the treatment of race-based perspectives in that they appear to be more theoretically developed and less likely to be considered important primarily as "one among many perspectives." As

---

535 See e.g. [033], Interview, lines 364–7 ("I get the students to divide up and present responses based on law and economic theorization, feminist theorization, critical race studies"). See also the discussion below under "Operationalizing External Factors," pages 258–62.

536 *Cf.* Mertz, *Language of Law School*, *supra* note 38 at 75–7.

537 Truth and Reconciliation Commission of Canada, *Truth and Reconciliation Commission of Canada: Calls to Action* (Winnipeg, 2015) at 3 (Recommendation # 28). For an example of a crowd-sourced attempt to respond to the Commission, see "reconciliationsyllabus: a TRC-inspired gathering of materials for teaching law", online: https://reconciliationsyllabus.wordpress.com/. For a critical perspective on the term "Indigenizing," see Jeffrey G Hewitt, "Decolonizing and Indigenizing: Some Considerations for Law Schools" (2016) 33 Windsor YB Access Just 65.

538 In addition to these ten interviews, variants of the terms "Aboriginal," "Indigenous," "First Nations," or "Indian" come up in thirteen additional interviews – though in such a passing manner as not to be materially significant.

with race and feminist perspectives, however, there is little evidence that Indigenous perspectives are (or were, at the time of my study) meaningfully or systematically employed in the Contracts course. Even those professors with the greatest exposure to Indigenous issues (through personal experience or scholarly expertise) seem to incorporate them only in a marginal way, however committed they might be to the importance of more thoroughgoing integration in the future.

The relationship between legal realism and Indigenous perspectives surfaces in two distinct ways. More generally, professors occasionally reference the experience of practising Aboriginal law, or particular cases involving Aboriginal persons, as touch points for the idea that legal decision making might be determined by desired outcomes. One professor, for example, says:

> I've been practising in Aboriginal Law ... which is a very creative, dynamic area of law, where ... you're developing the law as you go, because it is so uncertain ... [I]f you weren't extremely aware of the on-the-ground consequences, and address them in your legal argument, [then] your legal argument was going to be rejected.[539]

Similarly Professor 56 specifically uses a contract law case involving an Aboriginal claimant to "switch" to a realist perspective:

> [In] Harry and Kreutziger ... the judge in BC ... talks about the unconscionability of an agreement and is trying to protect an Aboriginal person from an unfair contract, at the same time using kind of [patronizing] language ... [T]hat's a nice case to start a discussion [to the effect that] we feel what the judge is trying to do, [but] are these the right means to do it? You know, is this really serving the interest of this person?[540]

At a deeper level, at least two professors invoke distinct cultural understandings in Indigenous communities to illustrate the contingency of certain conceptions of contract, undermining any sense that the common law rules are universal. One professor refers to "the treaty that my First Nation signed" to illustrate the cultural specificity of contracting rules that require written formality or reciprocal exchange:

> So we'd talk ... about different concepts of contract ... [T]hat the North American or Canadian kind of written document kind of contract is

539 [F], Interview, lines 618–29.

540 [056], Interview, lines 128–40 (referring to *Harry v Kreutziger* (1978), 9 BCLR 166, 95 DLR (3d) 231 (CA)).

> actually amongst huge chunks of the populace in the world not recognized as a contract. And that ... contracts don't all have to be written and they can be solemn and they can be important and the terms can be agreed upon when they're not reduced to writing and that there's different cultural concepts about what a contract is ...
>
> I'm also ... able to talk about ... about the potlatching system and ... the settlers' viewpoint of ... seeing all these people giving away ... all this stuff that ... settler society put[s] value on ... And the giving of that item was complete with all sorts of legal obligations ... that the settler society never saw – or refused to see ...
>
> I ... talk from my own personal perspective on that and ... others are not able to do that but ... if you were ... born and raised in, let's say, rural China or something, you'd have a very different viewpoint of what a contract would mean ... We even have ... rules ... about what contracts mean in families ... [W]hy does a certain society choose to give ... legal force to certain kinds of agreements but not others?[541]

Professor 30 similarly invokes Indigenous perspectives to highlight a vision of contracting at odds with the orthodox common law view – namely, the relational contract. For Professor 30, Indigenous understandings can illustrate a world that "is heavily relational" and expose individualist concepts of contract associated with Holmes and Posner as culturally specific:

> I would hope [the contractual relations model] would create a bridge for those students who may come from a non–Anglo-Saxon background and who may be less comfortable, as I was less comfortable, with a traditional perspective on contract law where everything is assumed to be episodic, and efficiently breached.
>
> For instance, ... in a world that is heavily relational, like ... that of Indigenous people, the idea that you might break or breach a contract would be attended with all sorts of misgiving that somebody like Richard Posner, doesn't [ascribe] to at all. And if I had an Aboriginal student in my class ... I'd want them to at least be able to understand where Anglo-Canadian contract law comes from. And how maybe an Indigenous perspective might be reflected in contract law – because some cases are in fact relational ... I would hope to make the law more ... accessible to students who may come from a more relational background.[542]

541 [G], Interview, lines 177–86, 603–32.

542 [030], Interview, lines 467–502.

A small number of other professors specifically refer to Aboriginal persons, perspectives, or treaties. Professor 63, for example, lists Indigenous persons as one marginalized group discussed in the course, suggesting that uncritically accepting certain common law doctrines might have the effect of contributing further to their marginalization:

> [We discuss] the idea that we shouldn't be looking beyond the four corners of the contract in order to interpret the meaning of the contract [and think] about what that means in the context of communities who have *oral traditions* ... [We discuss] what sort of ... *political* choices we're making if we prefer written evidence over oral evidence, what the impact of that [is] on communities with oral traditions.[543]

Another scholar, whose expertise includes "Aboriginal rights," chose to teach Contracts in part because there were "some analogies with Aboriginal treaties" and wanted to explore how certain contractual issues "transfer over to Aboriginal rights." This professor has published in the field and explores the analogies in class from time to time:

> Undue influence and duress ... have never been applied to Aboriginal treaties in Canada, partly because they say all of these treaties are unique and *sui generis* ... So occasionally [students will] see that kind of analogy. If the Indians are told in southwestern Ontario, a guy named Simcoe, the lieutenant governor, said, "[Since you] can't stop white people from squatting on all of your land and taking it away from you here in southern Ontario, why don't you just give up all of those lands and retreat to the northernmost corner of your traditional territory? People won't bother you there because it's generally infertile." He's talking about Manitoulin Island. So that raised interesting questions about [whether] that [is] consideration if ... what you're allowed to keep in the transaction is ... a small part of what you originally had. So [treatises] can be useful as an analogy – thinking about some of the contract principles.[544]

Notwithstanding these examples, however, at the time of my study the inclusion of Indigenous and Aboriginal perspectives appears largely to be a marginal practice – both because only a relative minority of professors mention them, but also because even those who do mention them emphasize that they are not central. The professor quoted just above,

543 [063], Interview, lines 701–9.

544 [H], Interview, lines 276–93. *Cf* [023], Interview, lines 622–3 ("I talk sometimes about – treaties for Aboriginal peoples as a kind of [contract]").

for example, says: "I don't want to exaggerate this," and "I must admit, it's not something I rely on heavily."[545] Professor 52, who takes pride in the "close connection [between the law faculty and] the First Nations community," candidly states that this close connection does not "really impact ... the law I taught [in] contract law ... I can't think of anything I ... did ... different[ly] with that First Nations angle in mind ... but I'm not precluding that from being something that happens in the future."[546]

The prevailing tendency, among those who mention the issue, like Professor 52, is to identify incorporating Aboriginal, First Nations, or Indigenous perspectives as an important but incompletely realized objective. Professor 63's views might be representative of the character of the commitment among those who share it. A desire to be an "ally" is tempered by a desire to avoid tokenization and a sense of having limited personal capacity to implement the goal:

> It's essential ... We have a tripartite system of law in Canada that we've not recognized. You can't be a law school in a tripartite system that only teaches two ... It's going to challenge ways of thinking, it's going to challenge organization of materials, it's just that it has to be done ... You can't be training people who are professionals with responsibilities to the public and just decide you're not [going to incorporate these ideas] ...
>
> I'm an ally on this. I'm not a person who's informed directly about Indigenous law, but we have expert scholars on our faculty. So I fully intend to ... follow their lead, and give whatever support that I can and ... take on whatever learning that I have to take on ... in order to deliver.
>
> It will be challenging, because I think one of the risks ... [is] taking the established common law paradigm as if it's the baseline and then sort of injecting some comparative examples from Indigenous law ... a sort of tokenization is a risk ... That's something that I'm conscious of ... but it's definitely a plan moving forward.

Accordingly, a number of professors express the hope to incorporate Indigenous and Aboriginal perspectives, whether out of an express commitment to reconciliation or as an instantiation of more generalist realist principles. This aspiration, however genuinely felt, is at the time of writing largely inchoate. For example, as of January 2020, the "reconciliation syllabus" – an online repository for Canadian law professors to share pedagogical resources on incorporating Indigenous law and perspectives – includes no category for contract law examples and very few

545 [H], Interview, lines 625, 294–5.
546 [062], Interview, lines 435, 465–6.

individual examples pertaining to contract law.[547] There are signs, however, that this relatively recent disregard of Indigenous perspectives and law in Contracts teaching might be coming to an end. The University of Victoria, for example, has created a second-year course in "Transsystemic Contract Law" for students in its Joint Degree Program in Canadian Common Law and Indigenous Legal Orders. As that develops, it might provide additional resources for other professors. Moreover, the *Ben-Ishai & Percy* casebook, which, in its eighth edition actually *removed* important references to First Nations issues, has inserted new language into the tenth edition that might signal that the issue will soon be in ascendance:

> At the time of the publication of this edition, a positive development in the legal academy is the renewed interest and urgency around exploring the continuing legacy of settler colonial structures in both the oppression of Canadian Indigenous peoples and the suppression of their laws. Recognizing that Indigenous and Canadian legal structures are co-produced, we encourage students to think about (1) the role of community-based emancipation through contract law and (2) ways in which each of the topics we consider are directly relevant to the Indigenous peoples in Canada.[548]

This optimism reflects the general attitude of support that I heard from the participants who chose to discuss this issue. It also, by its largely future-looking formulation, serves to corroborate the general impression that, at the time of this study (a period that straddled the publication of the Truth and Reconciliation Report), the practices of incorporating Indigenous and Aboriginal law and perspectives into Canadian common law Contracts teaching were relatively marginal.

Summary: Realism at Different Speeds

Legal realism is alive and well in the minds of Canadian common law Contracts teachers. The majority of professors in my study enthusiastically

---

547 "reconciliationsyllabus, By Course", online: https://reconciliationsyllabus.wordpress.com/reconciliationsyllabus-by-course/, accessed 1 January 2020. A blog posting by Julie Tucker and Gemma Smyth on the site makes a brief reference to an activity that asks students to give up their rights to a collective art work for one dollar, an exercise that "recall[s] the way contract law is used in modern and historical contexts to deprive people of their rights – often without knowing exactly what they are giving up" (Julie Tucker & Gemma Smyth, "Art, Law, and Community: Truth and Reconciliation through Art" (28 February 2019), online: https://reconciliationsyllabus.wordpress.com/).

548 *Ben-Ishai & Percy*, 10th ed, *supra* note 210 at 12. On the University of Victoria Transsystemic Contract Law course, see *infra* notes 835, 840 and accompanying text.

describe how they strive to highlight the indeterminacy and contingency of law; how underlying factors, such as policy, politics, and context, play an essential role in understanding contract law; how "external" virtues of morality and justice are legitimate ends for law to pursue, and legitimate standards against which to evaluate law; and how economic, feminist, and race-based analysis and critique are important – at the very least for enabling students to develop a range of different argument types.

Professors articulate these commitments with detailed reference to the scholarship of realist authors and their intellectual heirs, which not only directly influences professors' beliefs, but which they also cite to explain their commitments, and recount how they assign and teach these authors in their classes. American authors predominate, but some British authors (e.g., Atiyah) and some Canadians (e.g., Macdonald) surface as well. The views are thus well informed, well referenced, and well digested; professors intertwine references to the literature with their personal convictions.

I have detailed these genuine commitments at length for at least two reasons. First, these professors' words concretize the catch-all phrase "realism," providing specificity to the generic label I use to roughly categorize their theoretical leanings. Second, the detail provides ample evidence for the claim that legal realist perspectives form a core feature of Canadian common law Contracts professors' attitudes about law. This claim is also important to keep in mind for the rest of this chapter, the bulk of which aims to qualify, attenuate, or even undermine this apparent consensus commitment. We will see, in the next section, how a series of apparently contradictory attitudes about law play an important role in Canadian common law Contracts professors' legal consciousness. There are champions of formalism, and there are instances where the realists canvassed here reveal attitudes associated with formalism. Moreover, as I demonstrate in the second and third parts of the chapter, formalism figures prominently in the descriptions of legal reasoning and in pedagogical practices. Given how complicated the picture is about to become, it is important to remember just how emphatic professors are about their commitments to realism at a theoretical level. The realist professors – the vast majority in my study – espouse strong, genuine commitments to realism; the prevalence of ideas associated with formalism expressed elsewhere reveals the central puzzling contradiction of this study.

Formalist Views about (Contract) Law

Professors who resist or reject the lessons of realism are certainly in the minority, but those who do, do so with eloquence and commitment. Although "formalism," like realism, might capture a range of possible meanings, I use it here to group together those professors who emphasize the idea that law is an autonomous discipline with a distinctive form of reasoning, in which doctrinal rules actually do matter, not as indicators of contingent value choices, but because the rules themselves guide thinking. The understanding of rules as relatively fixed constructs facilitates the pursuit of an internally coherent legal system. This coherence helps realize the rule-of-law ideal of equal treatment, providing legitimacy to law and producing a certain "aesthetic appeal."

The Champions of Formalism: Rehabilitating Law

For some, the sceptical approach of realism, which seeks underlying factors for judicial decisions, undermines the legitimacy of law by portraying it as arbitrary. These professors view their role as "rehabilitating" law by focusing on the distinctive reasoning that makes the legal discipline autonomous and that ensures that everyone is treated equally under the law. Their "negative" attack on realism goes hand in hand with a more "positive" reconstruction of the importance of law. Tightly connected to these claims is the assertion that law and politics are distinct.

Approximately seven professors articulate some version of this rule-of-law justification for law as an autonomous discipline. I call these professors "champions" of formalism, because they are the few who put into words the reasons they believe in the autonomy of law. These champions say explicitly what many other professors appear to believe implicitly. A careful look at how the champions describe their commitments about law serves as an important reference point for the rest of the book, providing a more rich and textured presentation of views for which the label "formalist" will serve as shorthand.

Among the formalists, the champion of champions is Professor 19, who details at length a series of formalist commitments. Consider, in the following extended passage, how an attack on legal realism connects to the goal of rehabilitating law in service of the rule-of-law virtue of equal treatment; how a distinctive and autonomous idea of legal reasoning is the main bulwark against the dangers of arbitrariness; and how the aspiration to rehabilitate law depends on the clean distinction between "law" and "politics," "*juris*" and "*prudence*":

> I find a lot of my course [is] *defending* the common law from claims it's ridiculous ... I think it's *important* that ... when the law comes and *takes* something from [someone] that they think it's being taken for a good reason. When I threaten to throw you in jail, or I threaten to seize your house

and sell it, I think that people would want to know, well, there's a good reason ... and it's not arbitrary ...

Part of the rule of law is treating like cases alike – and so, if we're not treating like cases alike, we're not just breaking the rule of law – we're just arbitrarily taking somebody's house in situation X and *not* taking somebody's house in situation Y to satisfy a judgment, when it's totally arbitrary or ridiculous ... It's very important that the law *tries* to make sense. As Ernie Weinrib would say, [law] tries to show itself working itself pure ... It's trying to show you there's ... some *coherent undertaking* that's involved, and we are trying to treat like cases alike, and if they don't *appear* to be alike, then either they're wrong, or perhaps you don't understand they're alike in a particular way that you can't realize because you're not a lawyer yet ...

[I challenge legal realism because] *any* theory that says you have to understand something by assuming everybody's lying to you all the time ... is probably not a good theory of anything ... That's basically what legal realism is: judges aren't telling you the truth all the time. And I don't think it's true, because I've worked for judges as a clerk and ... I don't think they were lying to me or lying to the people all the time in their judgments ...

[O]ne other academic once called me ... "The Great Rehabilitator" in the sense that ... there's these areas of law ... [that] everybody said didn't make any sense or wouldn't possibly make sense – that I almost always could try to give you some reason why it might not be as *dire* as you thought it was before ... Judges aren't just sitting there ... *flipping coins* or doing things which are ridiculous. They actually have some *reason* why they're doing these things ...

As one professor ... actually said, "There's too much *prudence* and not enough *juris.*" So there's too much policy and not enough law – not enough attempting to *understand* the law ... I think there's too much *prudence* and not enough *juris,* and so I try to give my students a little bit of *juris* because I assume everyone else is giving them the *prudence* part ...

That's the heart of law ... If it's all *prudence,* why don't we just be part of the politics faculty, or economics faculty? Is there *not* some type of particular knowledge that's distinctive to law? *That's* the *juris* part. If we're not doing that, then we don't need law school. Then we're just *applied* mathematicians or *applied* social scientists, or *applied* economists, or *applied* political philosophers or *applied* politicians. Then we're nothing if we don't have a legal method. And unfortunately that seems to be happening in the United States – they've given up ...

In some ways I feel ... that I'm trying to rehabilitate and understand the *law* – that was around at one point in time that ... people have lost focus of ... If you ... show a student today what [a judge] said in 1920, they just won't understand it. They'll think of it as *code* for something else. Everything that they read, even if it's framed in terms of *juris*, will be understood in terms of *prudence*. And that's an effect ... of legal realism and the effect of economic analysis, the effect of policy analysis, the effect of laziness, or lack of instruction [in] *juris* [that] has led to this self-fulfilling prophecy.

If you start off with a casebook ... that says, "Look at this case. Isn't this ridiculous? ... We don't need to know [what previous cases said] because it's just all preference and policy." And those kinds of people then get to be law professors and write books that say, "Oh look, isn't that ridiculous" ... And then those people get taught, and those people then become judges, and you have sort of a *negative reference loop* ... And somebody has to try to break that ...

I have this *hope* ... that if ... we emphasize the *juris*, those same people then will go on to write textbooks, they'll be appointed judges, and then we'll ... have a positive reference loop rather than a negative one.[549]

Professor 20 provides a similarly developed defence of certain formalist ideas, though of a somewhat different variety. Like Professor 19, Professor 20 takes the content of doctrinal rules seriously, is "dismissive" of critical perspectives, which "withdraw legitimacy from law," and believes that law is a distinct discipline from politics. Unlike Professor 19, however, Professor 20 is sceptical of models that aspire to unity, in the way that Professor 19 interprets Weinrib's corrective justice account to do.[550] Nevertheless Professor 20 still aims to construct a model – a "cathedral edifice" for a "secular world" – that provides a "fair normative structure," incorporates ethics and morality, provides for certainty, and leads to a more "fair and just society." Law, as a distinct discipline, is a "legitimate" means to do this, and taking contract doctrine seriously aids in working towards such a model. Professor 20 says:

I'm dismissive of critical perspectives in the sense that ... after *demolishing* the cathedral, I don't actually see what's being put back in ...

---

549 [019], Interview, lines 724–813, 188–209, 585–645, 724–813. One entry point for understanding the reference to Ernest Weinrib's work is *The Idea of Private Law*, *supra* note 102.

550 [020], Interview, lines 340–81 (contract law doctrine is important because it is a "building block" for other courses), 478–83 ("I don't accept the ... corrective justice perspective. I think corrective justice ... provides some *illumination* but I ... see in the law ... so many practices of distributive justice that [I can't accept] ... the categorical perspective of corrective and distributive justice"), 692–4 ("It's when the person building the model espouses that this is the *only* model and [that] ... it explains *all conduct* that I think they fall astray").

> I think a lot of what ... critical perspectives were doing were basically *demolishing* things, ... withdrawing legitimacy from law and from judgment ... It was just *power* and ... society is nothing more than just raw power ...
>
> At the end of the day, it's a ... sort of *cathedral* edifice that we're building ... We want the *certainty* of the rule in its application because people can make determinations on that ...
>
> There is something in law which is inherently different from other disciplines ... There is a certain *ethics* and *morality* to it that the public expects to see ... in law ... [I]n a secular world, these are ... rules to guide conduct and normative behaviour. And that's not just a question of ... who's going to win. It *is* different than politics ...
>
> Can we come to a better model that will reconcile more normative behaviour? ... I hope that we will ... Law is a worthwhile investment in doing that ... You can't travel around Europe without seeing the influence of religion in these magnificent cathedrals and edifices and churches. You think ... what was a society that was able to organize *so much* of people's behaviour or action around building these marvellous edifices? ... Well, ... we abandoned that, and ... rightly so – we put a greater investment in political processes, and we find those political processes wanting, we put a lot of investment into *law* now as way to provide ... a *way* that people can live in harmony with one another in a *fair and just society* ...
>
> At the moment we still sense that people have *free will* and ... that there's a notion of responsibility for one's actions, and so we have to structure a world that's *fair*, and law seems to be a legitimate avenue [to do that] ... Can we create a model that will provide a ... more fair normative structure? ... I wish I could, but I know I can't. But I don't think Duncan Kennedy can either. I don't think Ernie [Weinrib's] model is the way to go either.[551]

For Professors 19 and 20, the rules themselves are important because they provide both the stable, secure footing on which parties can plan their behaviour and the constant, universal guides to normative conduct that apply to everyone equally (and thus further the rule of law). The *judicial formulation* of these rules is important because it demonstrates the distinctive type of legal reasoning that justifies differential treatment. Where they differ is in the possibility of a unitary model to describe how rules fit together. For Professor 19, a "unity" of private law is possible and Weinrib's account is persuasive. Professor 20, on the other hand, thinks no one model can describe all of contract (or private) law; unity is therefore elusive. This difference, for present purposes, might be considered largely a difference in degree. Professor 20

551 *Ibid*, lines 466–96, 586–601, 631–738.

considers it worthwhile to seek a more general account of discrete elements – this is what "building a model" does, analytically. The purer "coherence" of Weinrib's formalism and Professor 20's aspiration to find a model for "normative guides to conduct" are different versions of a similar desire to construct law as a "cathedral": a solid edifice, a legitimate source of authority and power.

The solidity of rules and the idea that they fit together in an internal coherent structure are thus two extremely important ideas for the formalist. Alongside the notion of a distinctive "legal reasoning" – the subject of the second part of this chapter – they contribute to the idea that law is an autonomous discipline.

The Importance of Rules

A number of professors resist the realist idea that rules are nothing but "pretty playthings."[552] They do so both negatively – attacking scepticism – and positively – articulating why rules are important. For example, Professor 15 says:

> I'm a *believer* in the rules ... You don't hear it as often as you used to, but in the seventies and eighties ... people were basically saying, "The rules are just a sham." That is, really they are just after-the-fact rationalizations for ... a decision arrived at along non-legal logical grounds. And, yeah, okay – there's some truth to that. But when you look at the way cases are *actually decided*, the constructs matter! ... You can't just treat them like Silly Putty and ... push them into any shape. *They do guide thinking* ...
>
> It's not a totally unpredictable ... *crapshoot* ... depending on the judge you happen to encounter. You *can* make predictions about how a particular case is going to be decided ... I think it is doing the students a disservice by *overemphasizing* the manipulability of the rules. They are manipulable, and ... fitting an abstract label onto real life ... *is* a very creative process. But it's not a totally random process ... A proper understanding of law ... *does* require a respect for the power of the concepts. With all of their limitations, *they matter*.[553]

Like Professors 19 and 20, some invoke the importance of doctrine specifically in relation to the rule of law. As Professor 56 says:

> I ... try to make them understand ... what the lofty idea of the rule of law can be broken down to. You know, that there's actually a *point* in doing

552 Llewellyn, *Bramble Bush*, *supra* note 108, quoted in Schauer, *supra* note 29 at 131.
553 [015], Interview, lines 283–315.

> this ... There is a path dependency that makes doctrine develop in sometimes curious ways and that it mushrooms, and then you have to invent counterdoctrines to make it work again. But that this is all ... born out of the idea that ... like cases should be decided alike, and ... that judicial arbitrariness should [be] bridled somehow, and ... that it's the rule of law, not of men.[554]

An extension, perhaps, of the idea that the rules matter is the idea that it matters how (and that) they fit together.

Coherence, Logic, Structure

A number of professors believe there is a coherence, "inner logic," or "structure" to the law of contracts and, moreover, argue why this inner logic is an important virtue for students to discover. Professor 46, for example, "think[s] that there is a coherence to contract law," and is sceptical about attempts to foreground ideology in assessing judicial reasoning. Like Professors 19 and 20, Professor 46 asserts that the stated rationales for rules are important, and suggests that doctrinal explanations should precede critique:

> [*Ben-Ishai and*] *Percy* ... spent more time presenting the feminist approaches to law or ... various race theory or whatever other Marxist critique ... in a context that I thought made the critiques look more powerful than they are ... [and] made the mainstream theory look like it was more irrational and more absurd.
>
> I guess I have a prejudice because [although] ... contracts law was developed by men ... to address business needs initially, ... because it's applied *neutrally* to both parties ... in general it [has] developed some rules that ... are somewhat fair ... I think that there *is* a coherence to contract law that is helpful for the students to be able to see, *meanwhile* being able to imagine how the law could be reformed in particular areas ...
>
> [Students should] understand why the principles evolved as they did. *Then* they can more intelligently criticize them ... [T]hey need to at least understand coherence in the sense of why it might originally have been thought fair to have [a] rule of consideration or a rule of privity, et cetera, and *then* move to ... challenge those doctrines as perhaps not always meeting goals of fairness or the parties' expectations. I think the one comes before the other. It's almost like ... it makes some sense to understand Newtonian physics as a context for understanding the small number of

554 [056], Interview, lines 394–409.

> cases where Newtonian rules don't apply and Relativity does ... You need *both* ... the original theory and the revolutionary theory.[555]

Like Professor 19, Professor 46's experience in having been a law clerk has produced a scepticism about ideological critiques of judicial reasoning:

> I can't recall a single time when there's been any substantial discussion [in my Contracts course] based on an ideological critique of a particular set of principles ... That might be informed in part by the fact that I used to clerk for [a high-ranking Canadian judge], and ... I'm not particularly persuaded that ... their judgments were clouded by some deep ideological biases, whether the judges were women or men.[556]

And while Professor 46 is not "trying to get [students] to see a structure that's as clear as a Napoleonic Code," structure is still very important:

> I'm trying to help them see what at least is the *ostensible* rational structure of contract law, while recognizing that there are areas of ambiguity and areas that need clarification ... I would like them to be able to look at it and ... at least understand the structure the judges see when they think of contract law ... The vast bulk of my time is spent trying to help the students understand what the courts have said and be able to play with the principles the courts have set out, to basically see how these different rules interact.[557]

Professor 4 similarly is interested in a "rational structure" of contract law, but inclines somewhat more towards a unitary conception. For Professor 4, there is one "central logic" that "animates the various rules of contract law" – the "equality of the two parties" – and the main pedagogical goal is to "connect various rules together through the set of underlying principles." Similar to the other professors canvassed in this section, understanding this inner logic is important to assure order in the law and to ward off arbitrariness:

> *Only* concepts and principles ... will be able to put some order in the law. Otherwise ... it looks like it's just arbitrary and all over the place ... When

---

555 [046], Interview, lines 171–92.

556 *Ibid*, lines 527–94.

557 *Ibid*, lines 607–28. Professor 15 utters a very similar sentiment: "[I'm] trying to get [students] to understand the conceptual structure ... [and] give them a *decent respect for the value of concepts*" (Interview, lines 217–18).

> you see [two cases on consideration that] look exactly the same but [yield] the opposite conclusion, ... [if] you go back to the initial concept, you can account for the different decisions ... You can see why it is that it was "Yes" in one case and "No" in the other ... It's an act of reconstruction.

For Professor 4, not only does "reconcil[ing] the principles together ... improve on the consistency of the law," it is an activity that Professor 4 finds aesthetically and intellectually gratifying. Taking the doctrine seriously is thus a double virtue:

> I just think [contract law is] beautiful – it's aesthetically pleasing ... It works together. Maybe it's one of the areas of law that is most responsive to this structure, ... the constant return to central principles ... I've been teaching this for twenty years now, and every year I reread the cases from beginning to end. And every year I change my interpretation of the cases. I refine them. There's new things I understand that I didn't understand before ... Fortunately I have to say it's going in the right direction because ... these principles that I think are central do more and more work for me as the years go by ... Every year ... I have a new layer of understanding ... and that's nice.[558]

Other professors characterize the virtues of structure differently. Professor 22 emphasizes the intellectual task of "classification" – it is "basic to knowledge" and "fundamental" to legal reasoning, which largely consists in seeing "how certain cases are alike and other cases are unalike." But unlike Professor 4, who uses the central logic of equality of the parties to reconcile principles, Professor 22 seeks to show how law is "animated" by moral ideas: law is "intimately tied to morality, so it makes sense to classify the law in terms of ... moral things."[559] Despite differences, both professors are ultimately concerned with organizing doctrine along rational and structured grounds that are intrinsic to law. Professor 59, in briefer terms, speaks about a "passion" for building a "framework of understanding" that seeks to show how doctrine at various levels of generality "fits together."[560]

Similarly Professor 8 seeks to show how "contract always tells the same consistent story ... The beauty of contracts ... is that it *ought* to tell a coherent story." Professor 8 strives to remediate "[o]ne of the great failings of legal education" of presenting law as a "series of snapshots"

558 [004], Interview, lines 49–56, 38–9, 254–64, 299, 342–64.
559 [022], Interview, lines 126–57, 65.
560 [059], Interview, lines 155–65, 494–9, 680–1.

by developing a "taxonomy" of private law. The virtues of a taxonomic approach sound very similar to those of doctrinal coherence articulated by the professors quoted above:

> Peter Burke had an idea of legal taxonomy – the idea that you can't understand the natural world unless you have a taxonomy. You have the platypus – you have to do something with it – it can't just be an outlier. And his idea was that you can do the same with law ... It's not just a mass of miscellaneous and disparate instances where we have rules, that it all makes sense – that you can categorize these things and it makes the individual subjects more accessible because you can understand where they are and how they relate to other subjects.[561]

The commitments expressed by these seven champions of formalism exert a powerful counterforce to ideas expressed by the much more numerous realists. Their convictions are equally, if not more, deeply held, and they coalesce into a more consistent message. Doctrine is something to be taken seriously in order to establish and uphold law's distinctiveness and, ultimately, its legitimacy. Specific rules are important both for their content – reflecting principles or moral ideas – and for the method illuminated by their judicial formulation: the distinctively legal reasoning of determining like from "unalike" cases. This reasoning skill forms one basis for the rule of law – the idea that the law treats everyone equally and that any differential treatment is arrived at (and justified) rationally. This requirement of rationality in turn explains why rules are important not only in the particular but also in the aggregate: a big-picture look at how rules fit together helps identify the central logic or structure – derived entirely internally from judicial reasons – that is the foundation for rationality and differential treatment. Thus, rules, legal reasoning, and coherence all support the rule of law; the rule of law is a pre-eminent social good (it ensures a "fair and just society," in the words of Professor 20), and is the moral basis for law's distinctiveness as a discipline.

Juxtaposing the ideas canvassed thus far presents a rather dichotomous view of the ideas underpinning Canadian common law Contracts professors' attitudes about law. Such a dichotomous construct aligns with other accounts of legal thought, as when Kennedy and Fisher describe legal realism as a "wholesale assault on the jurisprudence of forms, concepts, and rules" of classical legal thought, or in Grant

561 [008], Interview, lines 129–31, 185–97, 574–5, 143–51.

Gilmore's account of the Williston-Corbin divide in contract law.[562] As ideal-types, the ideas expressed by the "realists" and "formalists" (as I have labelled them) fit comfortably on opposing poles. However, this crystalline presentation is only a first-level picture of Canadian Contracts professors' attitudes. It is (to evoke Professor 46) akin to the Newtonian model of physics: a basic initial model necessary to understand a subsequently more complex and accurate one.

That complexity is about to unfold. We return for a moment to the words of the realists – and hear in them echoes of the champions of formalism. In off-hand expressions and references, we see how the importance of forms, concepts, and rules permeates the realists' understandings of law. The following *realists* take doctrine seriously, reveal a commitment to law's distinctiveness, and occasionally reinforce the importance of structure.

The Realists as Formalists

A number of the professors that I otherwise characterize as realists, in light of my global assessment of their views, nevertheless imply, in other comments, a commitment to some version of ideas associated with formalism. Many professors, despite their more propositional commitments to the indeterminacy or contingency of rules, nevertheless speak about rules in such a way as to imply their solidity or fixity. When professors speak, for example, of "delivering" content, or when they emphasize precision and accuracy, they evoke the formalist notion of the rules as important constructs that guide thinking. Similarly a number of professors highlight the distinction between law and policy, or between law and politics, reflecting a version of the argument that law is an autonomous discipline. Thus, in these more throwaway comments, a much broader set of professors beyond the formalist champions articulate a commitment to variations on the formalist theme.

Substantive Law: "Delivering" Content

Numerous professors emphasize the importance of the solidity of rules. Often, they do so by referring to the importance of information that must be "delivered," or through an unproblematized reference to law as if that term connotes defined, substantive content. We see this even from those who speak elsewhere of the need to disabuse students of the determinacy of law.

562 Kennedy & Fisher, "Introduction", *supra* note 27 at 10; Gilmore, *Death of Contract*, *supra* note 90 at 42–63.

Thus, Professor 52, who wants students to be "free thinkers" and not "adhere blindly to doctrinal dogma," who likes it when students are "disabused" of the idea that law is a "a static, verifiably correct or incorrect thing," designs the "overall structure of the exam ... to create *maximum* coverage of the content."[563] Frequently, Professor 52 uses the verb "deliver" to describe both Professor 52's role and that of the law school in general.[564] Professor 52 includes the idea of not accepting prevailing contract law "dogmatically" in the course objectives of the syllabus, but it appears at the very end of a half-page-long section that lists a series of detailed doctrinal concepts of which the student is encouraged to develop a "sound" and "solid" understanding.[565]

Similarly Professor 31, quoted above as trying to avoid the idea that law can be treated as "data that go into a statistical calculation and you come up with the answer," and who tries to make the point that "rules are *tools*," nevertheless appears preoccupied with the idea that the "content" of law and its accuracy matter. Professor 31 emphasizes the importance of "correct" answers on exams, and prepares for class largely by updating cases and legislation with the concern not to give students "bad information."[566] Professor 54, who states that the "reality is that [law] *is* indeterminate and [that students must] become *comfortable* with uncertainty," discloses a preference for the idea of "core" substance in discussing the curriculum:

> The real *advantage* at [my school] is that it has a focus on the bread and butter first ... [T]he students are actually getting a fabulous *black letter* doctrinal experience and education ...
>
> [I]f you're going to be a lawyer or have a law degree, I think you *need* to have ... been *introduced* to some of the foundational core zones of law and have some *sense* of the doctrine in all of these areas.

Thus the claims about law's indeterminacy coexist with the putatively more foundational idea that doctrinal substantive knowledge is a key requirement for becoming a lawyer. That implicit commitment might also be revealed in the way Professor 54 describes preparing for class: "I familiarize myself with the material and I have my lecture notes and I go in and I just *deliver*."[567]

---

563 [052], Interview, lines 165, 143–5, 31–3, 268–9.

564 *Ibid*, lines 296–7 ("the way I deliver a particular case or get into a particular discussion"), 338–9 ("[where I studied contract law] was delivered in much the same way as we deliver contract law here").

565 [052], Syllabus, 2015–16, p 2.

566 [031], Interview, lines 217–18, 224, 446–51.

567 [054], Interview, lines 733–4, 845–55, 893–6, 437–9 [emphasis added].

This emphasis on substantive doctrine appears among other professors. Professor 28, who highlights context in part to show "that the law doesn't matter so much," lists substantive knowledge first in discussing course objectives ("I want them to *know* [the] rules").[568] Professor 30, who emphasizes the importance of Macneil and relational contracts, conveys an apparently disparate concern with substantive doctrine and systemization by making "extensive use of the Canadian Encyclopedic Digest because I find that's *most* like the *Restatement* [*of Contracts*], in terms of a kind of clear exposition of what the law *is*."[569] For Professor 57, "a *basic expectation*, if someone says they have a law degree, [is that they] should be able to identify what the law is"; many other realists express similar views.[570] Related to this idea of a fixed content of doctrinal law is the idea (even among the realists) that there is a "proper structure" to thinking about law, or that rules might fit together neatly like a "puzzle."[571]

The point of highlighting these examples is not to imply that a realist concern with underlying factors is inconsistent with a concern for precision or accuracy, but rather to show that these professors *emphasize* precision and accuracy about law in a way that reveals a commitment to the importance of rules. This treatment stands somewhat at odds with their statements elsewhere that other factors (context, policy, relationships, etc.) are more important. Notwithstanding their critical and realist commitments that disaggregate, complicate, and render contextual the place of law in society and law's relationship to justice, many use the word "law" *as if* it is an uncomplicated source of definitive information and normativity.

568 [028], Interview, lines 111–12, 159–68 ("I expect them to know like *ten* basic overshadowing concepts – and then all the subs of that ... I want them to *know* those rules").

569 [030], Interview, lines 202–12, 547–9.

570 [057], Interview, lines 510–12. See also [039], Interview, lines 609–10 ("I don't [want] loosey goosey answers ... I want them to *learn* the law"); [006], Interview, lines 308–9 ("In first year you have to learn how to read the law and understand the law"), 815 (doctrine "actually is the law ... understanding or using case law or statutes [is] ... the fundamental capacity and skill of the lawyer"); [041], Interview, lines 823–5 ("I do short answers, which are basically what I call 'brain dumps.' 'Tell me everything you know about this doctrine'"); [041], Syllabus, 2015–16 (course title is "*The* Law of Contracts" [emphasis added]; learning the "fundamental principles and rules of the law of contracts" is the first learning objective); [056], Interview, line 269 (there's "just so much *law* you have to teach them").

571 See e.g. [037], Interview, lines 211–14; [062], Interview, lines 47–54.

Law as Distinct from Policy and Politics

Closely related to the solidity of doctrinal rules is the notion that law is a distinctive type of discourse, separate from policy or politics. Even among those who express realist attitudes, "law" is treated not only as denoting a core substance, but also as a distinctive way of reasoning that yields a distinctive authority. Some professors, while considering additional factors important for generating legal results or for evaluating or critiquing law, nevertheless assert law's distinctiveness in a way that echoes the formalist champions. Consider some of the explicit ways in which professors articulate this idea, first with respect to policy:

> [R:] Do you think that there's a ... useful distinction between law and policy?
>
> [PROFESSOR 6:] Oh there ... certainly should be. One should keep clear that there is a difference ... To teach more policy would be to give up teaching some of the law. [In first year] there's a lacking in understanding [and] ability and facility with law. I don't think [emphasizing policy is] appropriate.[572]
>
> [PROFESSOR 30:] The question of policy has to be distinguished from questions of law. So law is what's *binding*. Policy is everything that, in my view, is done as a matter of practice.[573]

In these comments, however indeterminate or contextual law might be, "law" is nevertheless its own discipline, its own domain.

With respect to politics, we see a similar divide. Consider Professor 30's attitude: "Politics and law are closely related but they're *absolutely distinct* ... My goal is to make sure that students are absolutely clear in how those things are distinct."[574] Similarly Professor 64, who states that "the political and law are constituted by one another," describes the two as "independent," and refers to factors such as facts and the "socio-economic and political climate" as "non-legal aspects."[575] Professor 54 asserts that "zero" politics appears in the Contracts course, as opposed to "policy," which has a place, recalling the distinction explored above between "internal" and "external" understandings of policy. Asked whether politics enters the classroom, Professor 54 responds:

> I would say just about zero, really, in Contracts ... One of the enjoyable things about teaching [Contracts,] frankly, is that students have almost no

572 [006], Interview, lines 600–10.
573 [030], Interview, lines 335–8.
574 [053], Interview, lines 526–8.
575 *Cf.* [064], Interview, lines 759–68 (reproduced at text accompanying note 489, above).

> understanding or preformed views about the subject matter *at all* when they come in ... I doubt they've ever thought about the doctrine of frustration. Nobody's ever thought about mistake of law ... [or] consideration or promissory estoppel ... Most of this stuff is pretty *apolitical* ... The policy choice that runs through ... every subarea of contract law is really this conflict ... between certainty and flexibility ... We see *that* tension lots in contracts ... but I don't know that that's really a political question.[576]

In this response, not only do internal policy considerations of certainty and flexibility pre-empt any political considerations, but the answer presupposes the importance of doctrinal categories. The considerations proper to law eclipse external considerations. This is from the same professor who insists that the "reality is that law is indeterminate."[577] In an analogous way, Professor 11, who says that "law is political" in the sense that it's "developed by people" – evoking the realist idea that contract law elides the public/private divide – nevertheless reinforces this divide in the course syllabus.[578]

In the next part of this chapter, I show how such articulations are not mere slips of the tongue, but rather a window into the prevalent tendency of most Canadian common law Contracts professors to consider legal reasoning to be a distinctive mode of reasoning, in which rules stand as fixed data points and the analytical task of determining relevance predominates. The realist or critical expressions about law somehow fade into the background when these professors describe what it means to reason or argue like a lawyer.

FORMALIST AND REALIST ATTITUDES ABOUT LAW AS REFLECTED IN UNDERSTANDINGS OF LEGAL REASONING

In this second part of the chapter, we now depart the staging ground of attitudes about law and proceed to the operating theatre of legal reasoning – or at least, how Canadian common law Contracts professors *describe* legal reasoning. Whereas the bulk of explicit attitudes about law tend to decentre doctrinal rules by considering them indeterminate,

---

576 [054], Interview, lines 472–97.

577 *Ibid*, lines 733–4.

578 [011], Interview, lines 381–4; [011], Syllabus, 2014–15, p 1 ("[a]long with Torts, Contracts serves to introduce you to the field of law known as 'private law' or the private law of obligations, which generally governs legal obligations between individuals, in contrast with 'public law', which generally deals with the relationship between individuals and the state").

contingent, or less relevant than external considerations of policy, politics, and context, the overwhelming impression of how Canadian common law Contracts professors describe legal reasoning tends much more to the formalist emphasis on doctrinal coherence and the related rule-of-law concern with formal equal treatment.

Most generally, there is the overarching claim that there *is* a distinctive "legal" reasoning. Most professors take this idea seriously, and describe this distinctiveness in a way that invokes law as an autonomous discipline. No professor directly said to me any serious version of the idea that "legal reasoning is ordinary reasoning applied to legal problems,"[579] and the small minority of professors who question the "legal" in "legal reasoning" do not seem to do so in order to attack the notion of a distinctively legal epistemology. This alone indicates a commitment to law's autonomy in a way that would be amenable to the formalist champions, but is a bit more at odds with the widespread realist idea that politics, policy, and law are intertwined. Thus while professors' ontological claims about the nature of law might portray law as mutually constitutive with other domains and disciplines, epistemological claims about the nature of legal knowledge – that is, the reasoning that derives from and generates legal knowledge – treat law as very much distinct.

The way professors describe how legal reasoning functions also reinforces this separation between law, on the one hand, and policy, politics, or context, on the other. A main structural feature of legal reasoning that emerges from professors' accounts is the ability to discern the relevant from the irrelevant – which facts are relevant to legal analysis, which rules of law are relevant to hypothetical fact scenarios, which judicial words are relevant to determining a rule of law. This preoccupation with relevance reinforces a sense of otherness between law and its surrounding context in a manner consistent with the formalist claims about law's autonomy.

A core skill emerging from this preoccupation with relevance is the ability to make reasonable distinctions between similar fact scenarios – to distinguish and analogize cases. This core skill not only embodies the structural preoccupation with relevance; it directly supports the rule-of-law aspiration that everyone be treated equally under the law. This skill is the formalist's bulwark against arbitrariness, as Professor 19 so eloquently describes above. Distinguishing and analogizing also has the effect of emphasizing the importance of discrete doctrinal rules. The importance of discernible, solid rules and an attendant concern with coherence or structure thus round off the formalist commitments

579 Alexander & Sherwin, *supra* note 29 at 3.

embodied by the vast majority of professors' accounts of legal reasoning. As observed in the casebooks, the overwhelming impression is that Canadian common law Contracts professors do not conceive of legal reasoning as the operationalization of their realist and critical theoretical ideas about law.

Formalist Methodology: Mainstream Legal Reasoning in Canadian Common Law Contracts Teaching

A New Language: Legal Reasoning's Distinctiveness

It is reasonably common for professors to make the general claim that legal reasoning really is a distinctive type of reasoning. Some professors specifically distinguish legal reasoning from other methods of reasoning, which they implicitly criticize as unrigorous, casual, or merely common sense. These other methods are sometimes explicitly labelled "policy reasoning," reflecting Mertz's finding about the marginalization of policy reasoning in the US context; other times, professors simply criticize incoming students' tendency to label outcomes as unfair.[580] Other professors, while not necessarily making comparisons with other modes of reasoning, emphasize the notion of legal reasoning as a lingua franca for the legal profession – they want to equip students with a new language. The status of law's distinctive reasoning, furthermore, is enhanced when professors assert that critique is subordinate to legal reasoning as taught through the case method.

Legal Reasoning as Distinct from Other Reasoning

A number of professors almost echo one another in their common tendency to assert that their role is to teach students that the formulation "that's not fair" is not a legal argument. Professor 6 provides a good example of this tendency: "The type of critique ... that they engage in is very unsophisticated, like, 'That's not fair!' ... That's not a legal argument so we've got to ... recast that into a legal argument."[581] Professor 35 similarly provides critiques of judgments only "periodically," because "sometimes then the students think they're free to *ignore* what

580 *Supra* note 38 at 75–7.

581 [006], Interview, lines 317–20. *Cf.* [019], Interview, lines 845–7 ("I tell my students, 'A lot of the rules aren't fair – but they're just ... [T]here's a difference between fairness and justice, and that's why you study the law'"); [061], Interview, lines 104–10 ("If they say a particular word they're not allowed to finish the sentence. They *have* to spell out what they mean by certain words ... You have to explain *why* it's efficient, *why* it's fair, *why* it's against public policy").

the law is – and just tell you what they think it *should be* – no matter how many times you tell them that ... *'I think that's unfair'* is not a legal argument."[582]

In slightly larger compass, Professor 5 specifically tries to direct students towards the "parameters of appropriate legal reasoning," showing how judicial rules can prevent students from going "too far" in making general arguments based on unfairness:

> There are certain *ways* of approaching legal argument that are ... acceptable in legal circles. [Learning to use] those methods of argument is a lot of what you learn as a lawyer ... [I] go through a case and indicate ... how the judge reasoned the decision and ... relied ... or stepped out [of] the precedent or expanded the concepts a bit ... Students try the same thing and sometimes they go a little bit ... too far, or they miss the point, and so [I try] to model back ... what the appropriate way of reasoning in this context is.[583]

Many other professors outline the "appropriate parameters" of legal reasoning, distinguishing legal from other types of reasoning. Like Professor 5, most professors do not claim that legal reasoning is universally better, but better for specific purposes. Thus Professor 47 tries to get at the "*peculiarity* of the legal way of analysing [a] problem ... without *devaluing* other ways of looking at the same problem ... Our function is to [look] at it from a legal viewpoint."[584]

Similarly Professor 27 says that, while law "is a way of doing politics," it is its "own" way. In this professor's words, a substantive concern with political and economic theory lies side by side with the methodological claim that law has a distinctive "grammar" – which, for Professor 27, relates to understanding Hohfeld's fundamental legal conceptions. Professor 27 describes this relationship with great enthusiasm. Exposing students to law's distinctiveness in first year is "electrifying":

> [First year is] a chance to ... [investigate] whether law is a discipline unto itself – whether it has something to say or if it's just *reducible* to other disciplines, like economics – which I don't believe. I believe that ... there is a *legal* view of the world – a language, a grammar of law ... Law is a way of doing politics, but it *is* its own way ... How common law works is one of the great mysteries of this life ...

582 [035], Interview, lines 464–8.
583 [005], Interview, lines 35–58.
584 [047], Interview, lines 258–65.

> The law imposes its own discipline upon answering ... questions [of political and economic theory] ... There are *ways* of ... determining the limits of a market. You can go into [a] legislature and pass a law. You can go over the ramparts and overthrow a society and establish an autonomous collective ... There's just *lots* of ways of changing the way things work. But law is one way of doing it, and ... law ... carries its own internal discipline [that] imposes itself ... Sometimes I put it this way: ... there is a deepening narrative of what contract law ... should be doing. But there's also a *grammar* and it does it in a particular way. If you don't understand the grammar, then you're lost as a lawyer.[585]

The metaphor of "narrative" and "grammar" might account for why so many professors, who do believe in the role law plays in furthering political or economic ends, nevertheless express that law has "its own way." Though expressed less completely and eloquently than does Professor 27, a good number of professors do explicitly differentiate legal reasoning from policy, economic, political, or even "normative" reasoning.

For example, Professor 53, who insists that "no law is neutral," states that "legal reasoning is completely different from political reasoning." And while students' common sense or intuition might accurately predict legal results, students must, "rather than react with emotional reaction about what should happen in a particular case, ... apply a *legal reasoning structure* to ... problem[s]." Professor 38, whose own research emphasizes the connection between law and policy, refers to incorporating policy in the Contracts classroom as going "offside." Professor 11 aims to reveal policy concerns that are otherwise "hidden," but conceives of that task as distinct from "legal analysis." Professor 14 critiques the casebooks other than *Waddams* for having too much "extraneous" commentary: "a lot of commentary ... detracts from acquiring [the] basic skill [of learning to read cases]." Professor 54 aims to help students move away from the idea that "everything is very normative, [meaning without] reference to authority," and towards the ability to "unbundle ... the compound assertion ... into constituents ... [and] analyse each one independently with reference to authority." And Professor 4 specifically distinguishes between legal and non-legal arguments to provoke students subtly to reflect on the nature of law's autonomy:

> I'll say something like, "Oh, that's all very nice, Counsel, in this policy consideration, but can you give me a legal argument for that?" ... Which a judge

585 [027], Interview, lines 406–12, 445–7, 5–72, 394–406.

> would honestly do ... They have to find a way to wedge into this policy argument ... It's not automatically the case that because you have a strong economic, ... moral, ... political, ... or sociological argument that somehow it's something you can present in a court of law. And why is that? ... To what extent is the legal autonomous? Clearly there's a very close connection, so ... can we still make sense of law as separate from these things? ... I won't say this that explicitly [but] ... just will poke them to reflect on these things.[586]

This focus on law's autonomy is not surprising coming from Professor 4, one of the formalist champions. As the preceding examples show, however, the tendency to articulate law's distinctive way of reasoning transcends professors of all theoretical stripes.

Taking Doctrine Seriously: The Language, Grammar, and Discourse of Law

The professors just canvassed explicitly juxtapose law with other types of reasoning. Yet another group of professors expresses the same idea, implicitly and less directly, by speaking about law as its own "language," "science," or "discourse," or about legal education as a process of "indoctrination," or its role in producing "linguistic competence."[587] In this way they paint a picture of law's distinctiveness by constructing a kind of exclusive epistemological community into which students become initiated. Messages about law's autonomy not only surface in the *existence* of such an exclusive community, but by virtue of the fact that this initiation largely occurs through the specific process of taking doctrine seriously.

For example, Professor 56 speaks of an "initiation" in which doctrinal discourse is to be treated not "cynically," but "seriously on a level of craftsmanship":

> [T]he initiation [is really] the use of legal terminology ... and that ... relates to understanding the role of doctrine as the language you have to speak to partake in a very specific discourse ... You actually need to be able to

586 [053], Interview, lines 544–8, 143–50; [038], Interview, lines 251–69; [011], Interview, lines 413–21; [014], Interview, lines 65–8; [054], Interview, lines 332–41; [004], Interview, lines 410–24.

587 See e.g. [059], Interview, lines 28–34 ("It's almost like teaching someone a new language"); [044], Interview, line 413 ("They're learning a new science"); [036], Interview, lines 26–9 ("I particularly *dislike* [the term 'thinking like a lawyer'] but [my goals do include] understanding legal discourse and becoming *proficient* with legal discourse"); [032], Interview, lines 133–6 ("In addition to the *contracts stuff* ... there's also that sort of general indoctrination into the juristic world, and juristic reasoning"); [062], Interview, lines 195–8 ("Building their sophistication ... and their linguistic competence, was a key goal of mine").

> speak this language ... Even if we're *critical*, we can't be *cynical* about the actual doctrinal discourse because ... we're training ... [students] to *partake* in this discourse ... Even if we find that [a given doctrine is] ridiculous, ... it doesn't spare us from actually being able to handl[e] it ... We still have to master it ... I don't think you're doing students a service if you're not making sure that they understand the importance of taking this seriously on a level of craftsmanship.[588]

Professor 1 elaborately connects the importance of "technical" and "dogmatic" law to the notion of exposing students to the "grammar" of private law, learning the language of law, and developing the "juridical unconscious" (a term that could also be translated as "legal consciousness"):

> I find technical courses – basic, fundamental courses that form the heart of many legal traditions and whose study constitute a rite of passage for jurists – to be absolutely necessary. Teaching Contracts involves both a substantive study of the subject but also teaching a grammar of the private law in general ... The course is dogmatic in the sense that it spontaneously appears in all curricula as representative of the positive law ... [These dogmatic, technical courses are important to teach] because they fix the fundamental vocabulary, the categories or concepts ... It is also in these courses where the juridical unconscious [*l'inconscient juridique*] is formed. And I believe we have to intervene at all costs in this unconscious if we don't want to leave it to develop outside of our control. It's an exigency of justice, of transparency; the value of knowledge is to enlighten rather than to allow things to remain concealed.[589]

Together these attitudes give an impression that the prevailing norm among Canadian common law Contracts professors is to take the idea of doctrinal discourse seriously, not to denigrate it as mere "rhetoric."[590] This prevailing norm appears to lie in stark contrast to the US context,

---

588 [056], Interview, lines 315–62.

589 [001], Interview, lines 25–160 [translation from French].

590 *Cf.* Posner, *Economic Analysis of Law*, *supra* note 160 at 23; *Oxford English Dictionary* (online), *sub vero* "rhetoric," entry 2c ("language characterized by artificial, insincere, or ostentatious expression; inflated or empty verbiage"). Even when participants in my study use the term "rhetoric," its usage appears less derogatory and closer to the OED's first listed definition, "The art of using language effectively so as to persuade or influence others" (*ibid*, entry 1a). See e.g. [026], Interview, lines 215–45 ("[Law is] not really logic at all ... it's a species of rhetoric. It's a formalized and specialized species of rhetoric and it's a tool rather than a thing that exists").

in which advocates of "taking doctrine seriously" articulate it as an outsider claim.[591]

Doctrine First, Critique Second

Another tendency among Canadian common law Contracts professors reinforces the idea that legal reasoning is intimately tied up with the judicial formulations of doctrinal rules. Professors tend to treat critique as a subordinate virtue vis-à-vis the objective of teaching legal reasoning through case law. Placing critique second effects two separate attitudes. First, prioritizing legal reasoning reinforces the idea that it has a comprehensible, identifiable, distinctive core. It is not only something that *can* be taught; it is more important than other virtues. Second, it suggests that subjecting the core to critique is not particularly important, or at least not of equal importance to communicating that core. Thus, the attitude that "critique" is deferrable avoids portraying legal reasoning as contestable or contingent. This in turn reinforces the apparent solidity and impermeability of legal discourse.

One particularly acute expression of this idea lies in the words of Professor 46, one of the formalist champions quoted above. To recall, Professor 46 states that:

> [Students should] understand why the principles evolved as they did. *Then* they can more intelligently criticize them ... [T]hey need to at least understand coherence in the sense of why it might originally have been thought fair to have [a] rule of consideration or a rule of privity et cetera, and *then* move to ... challenge those doctrines as perhaps not always meeting goals of fairness or the parties' expectations. I think the one comes before the other. It's almost like ... it makes some sense to understand Newtonian physics as a context for understanding the small number of cases where Newtonian rules don't apply and Relativity does ... You need *both* ... the original theory and the revolutionary theory.[592]

In the way that the metaphor about physics is used above, the classical ("Newtonian") ideas provide a foundational understanding for

591 See e.g. Markovits, *Contract Law and Legal Methods*, *supra* note 78 at x–xii:

> [C]ontemporary legal education slights doctrine. Although considerations from outside law remain at the margins of even contemporary casebooks, they come quickly to dominate classroom discussion ... And so doctrine is slighted in modern legal education, even as modern teaching texts continue to valorize it ... *Contract Law and Legal Methods* ... takes doctrine seriously – more seriously than other contemporary casebooks.

592 [046], Interview, lines 171–92.

subsequently developed, more complex accounts of phenomena ("Relativity"). The classical model is not superseded by subsequent theorization, but rather retains its importance ("You need both" theories). Such an idea does, indeed, surface among physicists – in the oft-quoted statement by Niels Bohr, the "patriarch of quantum mechanics," that "it would be a misconception to believe that the difficulties of the atomic theory might be evaded by eventually replacing the concepts of classical physics by new conceptual forms," or Werner Heisenberg's claim that "Newtonian mechanics is a kind of a priori for quantum theory ... in the sense that it is the language which enables to say what we observe."[593]

The idea that it is important to emphasize a classical "core" of law is expressed by other metaphors. For example, Professor 41, in recommending a cautious approach to answering examination questions – some of which are designed to be "brain dumps," disclosing another preference for core, substantive knowledge – invokes chess and the well-worn metaphor of "thinking outside the box":

> It's kind of like playing chess ... If you do the traditional things in chess, there's going to be a long game, you're going to win some, and you're going to lose some, but you're not going to look like an idiot ... Sometimes people try something very original, and it doesn't work and then you look kind of like an idiot. And I don't know whether it's because you were trying something original, or because you just *don't know* ... where the box is. Being outside the box is fine, but you also have to show you know where the box is.[594]

Professor 43 sounds an analogous note of caution in describing why questions of fiduciary obligations, which Professor 43 otherwise describes as "crucial" to legal education, are best left to upper-year courses: "You have to be careful with racehorses. You can't just put them in the race right at the start. You have to *train* them ... It's a *staged* process."[595] More prosaically, Professor 30 explains how clarity must come before critique:

> I ... share ... excerpts from the *Restatement of Contracts (Second)*, because the *Restatement* is often a really good distillation of things, almost in the

593 Sergio Chibbaro, Laberton Rondoni & Angelo Vulpiani, *Reductionism, Emergence and Levels of Reality: The Importance of Being Borderline* (Cham, Switzerland: Springer, 2014) at 122; Niels Bohr, *Atomic Theory and the Description of Nature* (New York: Cambridge University Press, 1961), vol 1 at 16; Werner Heisenberg, Oral history interview by Thomas Kuhn, Archive for the History of Quantum Physics, Harvard University (27 February 1963), quoted in Chibbaro et al, *ibid* at 123.

594 [041], Interview, lines 824, 737–47.

595 [043], Interview, lines 40, 1172–80.

> manner of a code. That *clarity* ... is something that we want to try to emphasize to students, *at least* for the purposes of their *debut* in the area. Later on I think it's possible to come at issues in contract law with a critical perspective, but I think that you can *lose* a lot of students by not indicating what the *basis* and most recent expressions of the law *are*.[596]

This quote, like many others in the section, constructs this choice as largely one of pedagogical effectiveness – the concern with not "losing" students. Pedagogy is indeed a powerful explanation for the choices professors make, one that I explore in the third part of this chapter. For present purposes, however, I want to emphasize how the decision to place clarity or core content before critique also reveals a commitment to the solidity of law, a commitment somewhat at odds with the notion of law's indeterminacy. For Professor 30, the desire for clarity brings with it a concern for the "basis" of law.

Numerous other professors express the similar desire to focus on black letter law before critique. Professor 39 draws an analogy with science education to explain why Professor 39 foregrounds "proper analysis," again invoking pedagogical effectiveness but revealing a deep concern with learning "black letter law":

> I want them to *learn* the law ... I want them to do proper analysis ... It's like when you learn *medicine*. You don't learn medicine just by ... learning about generally how people are. You learn very specific information ... about the anatomy, about the physiology ... And *then* you can say, "Maybe there are these environmental factors" ... Same with learning about animals in the environment. You don't learn about the animal just by looking at ... the bear walking around on top of ... the mountain ledge. You need to learn about ... the bear unto itself. And *then* you might look at its environment and then its interactions with other animals ... [My preferred approach is] learning contract law from the minutiae, ... the traditional way, and then ... understanding it in its broader context ...
>
> I know other people would prefer to start analysing/critiquing contract law in the bigger picture and say that this isn't fair and stuff. But I don't know that [first-year] students ... have had ... enough experience to be able to understand those bigger-picture ideas [of] ... the law in context ... [I don't want to] overwhelm or undermine the capacity to learn black letter law by bringing too much information in to critique it when you don't really have the tools to understand what it is that you're looking at in the first place.[597]

596 [030], Interview, lines 119–28 (referring to American Law Institute, *Restatement (Second) of Contracts* (St Paul, MN: American Law Institute Publishers, 1981)).

597 [039], Interview, lines 609–43.

Similarly Professor 59 explains how the decision to abandon the *Swan* casebook flows from the idea that "understanding precedes critique":

> I felt that the Swan and Reiter book was getting so heavily into ... philosophical and social questions ... I just didn't think students were sufficiently well equipped to be able to deal with them ... I was more interested in a book that I thought was a better foundation for establishing ... what ... contract doctrine [is] ... I talk about [uncertainties and contextual issues] ... but they tend to be secondary [and] not primary in the way I teach ... [I] believe that, in order to challenge *any* thought system or belief system, you need to understand what it is very well before you're qualified to evaluate, criticize, [or] really fully understand the implications of it. So, to me, understanding *precedes* critique.[598]

Professor 6, likewise, emphasizes the idea that first year is a "boot camp of doctrinal law," reserving upper years for "sophisticated critique." Reasons of pedagogical effectiveness (students are "not ... realistically capable of critiquing law in the second month of law school") blend into claims about the essence of law as doctrinal and the importance of "using" formal legal sources:

> First year is actually not a bad place to be ... quite doctrinal and very black letter ... Become *fluent* in law. Get the tools. And upper year is where you can then work with it ... [and] engage in sophisticated critique ... A first year ... boot camp of doctrinal law where you get a really strong foundation in the main areas of law is [not] necessarily a bad thing ... It actually is the law ... Even in second and third year, [I see students who are] not good at using ... case law or statutes. And that's the ... fundamental ... capacity and skill of the lawyer.[599]

Other professors express similar attitudes. Professor 54 describes in the course syllabus how underlying premises and policy rationales "animate" the "basic rules," and how the "purpose of this course is to introduce students to the fundamental principles." In interview, Professor 54 jettisons the notion of critique not only from first year but from the entire undergraduate law curriculum:

> All this policy-type criticism and so on and so forth, it's very interesting [at] a graduate level, but I'm not sure at an undergraduate level. I don't

598 [059], Interview, lines 292–326.
599 [006], Interview, lines 311–12, 801–22.

> know how you can set about criticizing something you don't really understand yet. That's my view. So I think you really need to learn the law, and then if you really want to criticize it, go do a master's.[600]

Other professors take a similar approach, though not at the level of curricular order, but within the course itself. Professor 63 describes optimal sequencing as "begin[ning] with a very thorough understanding of what *is*, before moving on to the critique and the plan for what ought to be." Professor 61 speaks of starting first with distilling "the legal rule, ... us[ing] it for reasoning by analogy," and then later asking "what should it be?"[601]

The notion that a knowledge of doctrine necessarily must precede critique contributes to the idea that the content of substantive rules matters. The prevalence of this idea among professors of all theoretical stripes somewhat belies the otherwise majoritarian claim that legal rules are contingent on historical and social factors, and therefore mutable. Rules, as it turns out, are not only essential elements of the legal discourse – a discourse that, for the most part, Canadian common law Contracts professors treat as distinctive – but are portrayed as knowable and important to know, and thus are construed as relatively fixed points within that discourse. The implicit message of "doctrine before critique," therefore, is that the law comprises a set of rules that are determinate and fit together in a certain coherent whole, evoking the image of the formalist's cathedral.[602]

Extracting Rules and Fitting Them Together

Professors in my study frequently state that "extracting" or "distilling" rules is a key feature of legal reasoning. In this light, the attitudes of Canadian common law Contracts professors about legal reasoning seem not far removed from that of Langdell, who wrote that "the shortest and best, if not the only, way of mastering the doctrine effectually is by studying the cases in which it is embodied."[603]

Professor 57, for example, foregrounds the importance of rules in legal reasoning, treating them as having definitive content:

> [Legal reasoning is] being able to arrive at what the legal rule is and to explain why that's the case, or to advocate that the legal materials support a particular legal rule. [It involves] working with case law materials to be

600 [054], Syllabus, 2012–13, p 1; [054], Interview, lines 924–30.
601 [063], Interview, lines 154–6; [061], Interview, lines 269–84.
602 See text accompanying note 551, above.
603 *Selection of Cases* (1879), *supra* note 56 at vii.

> able to extract the ratio, to ... know what to do with *obiter* ... [It's] being able to use the legal materials to interpret the rule of law that's *there*.[604]

Extracting or distilling rules is often the first goal professors say they have for their students. For example, Professor 35 says: "I want [my first-year students] to be able to *read* a case and ... extract the legal principles and reasoning. Which is challenging in contract law because the cases are *old* and there's a lot ... of *imprecision* ... about the doctrine ... That ... is a big goal."[605] Professor 39 emphasizes "developing the skill set for extracting principles and ideas [from cases]." Professor 54 doesn't "think you can *do* law and think like a lawyer unless you can *distil* legal arguments" into a structure of facts, issues, rule, analysis, conclusion ("FIRAC"). Professor 14 wants students to "extract an understanding of the case[, including]... what the issues are, ... what the reasoning of the judge is, and recognize what is important and what is less important or not important at all."[606]

The preference for abstracting general principles might have the effect of reducing appreciation for contextual differences. In the hands of some professors, the idea that the same rules might apply to different situations actually might serve to collapse, not highlight, distinctions: "[What makes someone good in contract law is] the ability to see the commonplace ... in quite extraordinary circumstances ... They can recognize that, 'Hey, this case ... *seems* so very different, [but] once you cut away the frills and look at the facts, it's really *identical* to this other case.'"[607]

The focus on abstract rules can also translate into a concern for the underlying structure or coherence of contract law. Not surprisingly we see this among our formalist champions, who include in the idea of legal reasoning the ability to "articulate ... issue[s] in a more *general* way, or build "a framework and [fill] in the blanks of the framework ... by addressing the elements and subelements within each part of the doctrine"; or the ability to assimilate analytical tasks at different levels of generality, "classifying all the way up and all the way down – ... classifying rules ... [and] classifying the situation."[608] But it surfaces among others, as in Professor 29's commitment that

> aspects of the law of contract form an interlocking or interweaving whole. Students are forced to go through the exercise of assembling the various

604 [057], Interview, lines 452–84.

605 [035], Interview, lines 35–41.

606 [039], Interview, lines 54–5; [054], Interview, lines 314–17, 49–50; [014], Interview, lines 95–8.

607 [060], Interview, lines 31–7.

608 [059], Interview, lines 178–9, 496–8; [022], Interview, lines 472–9.

> pieces of the puzzle and internalizing them and creating the diagnostic tool in their brain ... [Students] have to develop the ability to ... assimilate large bodies of information of this kind and develop those kinds of underlying frameworks ... That's what lawyers do.[609]

Occasionally the focus on rules brings with it a type of narrowness that some professors deprecate, reflecting a humility and awareness of legal reasoning's partiality. Thus, Professor 15 says:

> *[L]egal thinking* ... is in its own way rather blinkered. It's learning to think in a particular way in order to do particular things ... *It lacks a lot of imagination.* There's no poetry in it. And it values certain things a lot more than it values others – simply because of the job that law has to do ... *Lawyers have to learn to think like lawyers* [and] for some [non-lawyers] it is *also* a very good thing. But I wouldn't have thought it's a good thing for everybody.[610]

Professor 7, similarly, says:

> I tell my students all the time, "Law is boring. Law is about detail. It's about learning how to fill in documents. It's about learning how to pay attention to the finest detail of situations and it's not exciting. It's not what you see on TV. It's about being meticulous, and being meticulous isn't exciting."[611]

This recognition of legal reasoning's shortcomings serves, if anything, to highlight and reinforce the idea of law's distinctive reasoning. Moreover, the idea that legal reasoning might be "blinkered" or "boring" implies that legal reasoning gains its distinctiveness from a particular type of authoritativeness: its reference to a discrete set of technical, precise, and formal sources. In this way, the importance of rules constitutes not only a substantive element of legal reasoning, but a foundational source of its distinctiveness and authority.

Determining Relevance: A Structural Feature of Legal Reasoning

Another essential element of legal reasoning – again, among a majority of professors, of all theoretical stripes – is the ability to distinguish the relevant from the irrelevant. This intellectual task transcends the various levels of generality to which legal analysis applies: identifying

609 [029], Interview, lines 55–9, 86–94.
610 [015], Interview, lines 489–92, 545–60.
611 [007], Interview, lines 44–8.

relevant facts, relevant rules, and relevant principles. There is a deep parallelism between the common tendency to distinguish legal reasoning from other forms of reasoning, and the mechanics of that legal reasoning, which obsesses with what is "inside" and "outside" the parameters of relevance.

Drawing a line between what is relevant and irrelevant, and categorizing phenomena as falling on either side of this line, might be considered a structural element of legal reasoning in two senses. First, determining relevance *descriptively* captures the main intellectual task involved in a range of discrete, more particular steps in the reasoning process; transcending many discrete parts, it reveals a deeper structure to what legal reasoning is. Second, it specifically bolsters – provides the supporting structure for – law's claim to legitimacy, and in this sense is a *normative* requirement of the rule of law. To subject some people, and not others, to legal consequences in way that respects the rule-of-law principle of equal treatment under the law requires a coherent, universal, non-arbitrary method of arriving at decisions. The words of the participants in my study suggest that the core of this method is the ability to determine rationally which criteria are relevant to producing differential outcomes.

The examples that follow serve to confirm the descriptive sense in which determining relevance is structural: the notion of relevance indeed appears frequently as both a general virtue and embodied by discrete steps of legal reasoning. But the very fact of its ubiquity also gives the impression of a shared belief in the normative appeal of relevance. The concern for rational argumentation and rule-of-law equal treatment, expressed so eloquently above by Professor 19, the formalist champion of champions, therefore emerges as a shared value among almost all participants in my study.

Determining Relevance: The General Case

In a field in which legal reasoning is so often described using the terms "reasoning by example" or "reasoning by analogy," it is informative to see how frequently professors use a related, but alternative, formulation – "determining relevance" – to describe the crux of legal reasoning.

One very senior professor, Professor 48, describes relevance as being at the centre of the legal method. Consider the following exchange, in which Professor 48 asserts how the ability to determine relevance distinguishes lawyers from non-lawyers:

> [R:] Is what they're learning in the first-year Contracts course important for ... students?
>
> [PROFESSOR 48:] The method part is, yeah.

> [R:] Why?
>
> [PROFESSOR 48:] Because those are skills you can take to *any* kind of problem solving. What are the facts you've got? What do you have to resolve? How would you go about resolving? What are the options for resolving? How have others resolved it? That's *basic* legal method ... The problem I find with people who are not lawyers ... is they have no concept of relevance. They've no concept that when you've got a problem, [it is essential to determine] which parts of those problems are key and have to be solved, and which parts you can talk about forever but actually [are] not *key*. And that's something I think legal education trains you – in *relevance* – in working out a problem, what exactly is important, and getting rid of the non-important parts, interesting though they may be, and deciding it.[612]

Two other very senior professors express similar ideas about lawyers' peculiar ability to discern the relevant from the irrelevant. For example, Professor 15 says:

> The *lawyer* – the person with the *legal* background – has a *huge advantage* in terms of distinguishing the irrelevant from the relevant. And it drives you crazy because everybody else at the table is talking about stuff that you keep saying, *"No – no – no – that's not the issue! The issue is this!"* And that's something law gives you. Which other disciplines, even if you're fabulously gifted at them, [do] not give you.[613]

Professor 44, the most senior professor in my study, assimilates "analysis," the core of what the lawyer does, mostly to discerning relevance:

> [R:] What are the lawyering skills that you're trying to convey?
>
> [PROFESSOR 44:] Analysis, analysis, analysis ... I do say to the students, "You listen to the client speaking, and as you're listening your brain is formulating what's material, what's immaterial, what's relevant, what's irrelevant, what's the cause of action, what strengths have they got, ... what remedy can we go with ... That's all we do for a living! An endless analysis of the story told by the client.[614]

Articulating the word "relevance" is the ambit not only of experienced professors – the three just quoted have a combined 130 years of experience

---

612 [048], Interview, lines 696–715. Elsewhere Professor 48 describes legal method as "how you read and analyse cases and understand what courts are saying and understand what is relevant from one case into another" (*ibid* at 126–33).

613 [015], Interview, lines 601–7.

614 [044], Interview, lines 534–42.

teaching Contracts – some young law professors use that term to describe legal reasoning as well. For example, Professor 58, who had taught Contracts just twice at the time of our interview, says that "excluding the irrelevant" is among a lawyer's "core work ... To be able to really focus on what matters most is important." Professor 26, teaching Contracts for the fifth time at the time of our interview, says, "I want them to learn the skill of reading a case and deciding what in it is relevant." And Professor 54, in the second year of teaching, says, "There's so much in that thinking like a lawyer business ... Part of it is that really heightened sense of relevance."[615]

In addition to these general expressions of the importance of "relevance" are the more specific, and fairly widespread, articulations of the need for students to learn how to discern which facts are relevant to legal analysis and, conversely, which legal issues are relevant to a given fact pattern.

Determining Relevant Facts

Cultivating the skill to determine relevant facts sometimes takes the form of professors' wanting to ensure that students read complete accounts of the facts in cases, as opposed to short excerpts. Professor 50, for example, says:

> I want the students to read the whole case to have a *full* understanding of the facts, and to be able to ... read a full judgment to figure out for themselves what was important and what was not important, what is *obiter*, what were the material facts, why did the court talk about this fact and not that fact?[616]

Other professors make similar claims about wanting to include whole cases, or at least extended excerpts, in order for students to learn to "winnow the irrelevant from the relevant" or develop the skill of "finding" issues, ratio, *obiter*, and analytical reasoning "in an actual case."[617] Sometimes this preference for long cases leads directly to helping students identify how specific facts yield specific results:

> One of the reasons why even reading four pages of a contracts case can be a long, involved process is [that] every sentence could be considered

615 [058], Interview, lines 772–85, 794–800; [026], Interview, line 582; [054], Interview, lines 321–6.

616 [050], Interview, lines 194–9.

617 [047], Interview, lines 354–62 (short excerpts are "*really harder* to teach than ... a ... reasonable ten-page extract"); [064], Interview, lines 481–4. See also [014], Interview, lines 105–10 ("[R:] There's a preference for having *more* case material there because it helps them develop the skill of knowing what is relevant? [Professor 14:] Yes").

important. What's *really important* though? That's an analysis skill. That's a division skill – dividing up the not important at all, kind of important, really important ... The thing that many students don't get, when they read snippets, is they get the "really important because it's the law" part, but they don't get *why*. The facts are sort of summarized, and they don't spend a lot of time going, "Okay, what are *all* the facts?" So then they have to read through and figure out what the important facts are ... If I flip this factor out, does it change things?[618]

Likewise Professor 65 connects determining relevant facts to thinking about how cases might have been different, had the facts been different: "I don't want ... a summary of all of the facts – just what are the important facts ... How do you ... train a lawyer's mind to figure that out? And what are considered quote unquote 'important' facts? Those are the ones that a case turns on ... 'Without this fact, there may have been a different decision.' *That* is an important fact."[619] Similarly Professor 66 gets students to "identify in ... [a] certain key case, what is the *operating fact* of the story?"[620]

Issue Spotting

Another deeply important feature of legal reasoning, as described by the professors in my study, is the ability to identify the relevant legal issues that arise in a complex fact scenario. The shorthand for this skill is "issue spotting," the primary skill examined in a conventional examination question, which consists of a hypothetical fact scenario. As Professor 32 tersely says, "In the hypothetical type case, ... issue spotting is fifty per cent of the battle"; Professor 6 says that "analysis" and "identification of the legal issues" "gets you the ninety-seven marks."[621]

Issue spotting involves determining the relevant legal issues from a mass of factual information. For Professor 51, it is "translating the facts of a human problem into legal categories." For Professor 29, legal analysis involves "pull[ing] apart a factual situation and identify[ing] the issues of ... law that it implicates. For Professor 43, the "biggest skill we give our lawyers" is "the ability to take a complex set of facts, to sift them out and isolate the relevant issues – to find out the rules and principles that you want to apply to solve ... problems." For Professor 59, the focus is on "identifying an issue ... [or] governing principle" – a

618 [041], Interview, lines 595–607.
619 [065], Interview, lines 171–8.
620 [066], Interview, lines 164–5.
621 [032], Interview, lines 482–3; [006], Interview, lines 514–16.

task that directly requires making determinations of what "matters" and what does not:

> [O]ne of the *puzzles* of contract law or any law ... is that it ... kind of puts us in a box where we say, "These are the things that matter inside this box ... There are some other things, like ... how people felt ... or how it impacted their family life or the business ... We're not looking at those things ... I try and make them *conscious* of that difference, between the things that law *recognizes* and the things that it *doesn't*.[622]

Similarly Professor 14 describes the evaluation methods – memo writing and exam writing – as essentially testing students' ability to discern which legal issues are relevant:

> [The memo requires students to] sort through the materials that you dug up and decide which materials you want to include and which ones you feel you can overlook ... [The exam requires students to] appreciate what the problem is. And then to apply the appropriate legal principles to that problem. And ... that means as well to *recognize* the principles or areas that *do not apply* to the problem.[623]

A similar concern with excising the irrelevant occurs when professors emphasize the need to discern the *ratio decidendi* of cases from *obiter dicta*.[624]

Distinguishing and Analogizing

Identifying the relevant facts and the relevant issues (or principles) are the building blocks of analogical reasoning, or reasoning by example. Indeed the determination of "relevant" similarity is often posited as the most important intellectual task.[625] What is important about a set

622 [051], Interview, lines 335–6; [029], Interview, lines 78–9; [043], Interview, lines 1148–51; [059], Interview, lines 168–9, 56–66.

623 [014], Interview, lines 446–9, 488–91.

624 See e.g. [004], Interview, lines 163–6 (The common law emphasizes "the difference between the holding and the *dicta*"); [050], Interview, lines 119–22 ("I want them to understand ... what might be the ratio and what might be the *obiter*"); [057], Interview, lines 455–7 (legal reasoning is "working with case law materials to be able to extract the ratio, to extract *obiter* and know what to do with *obiter*"); [064], Interview, lines 479–81 ("We're trying to teach students *how* to discern what the issues were before a court, what the ratio is, what's *obiter*, and what the analytical reasoning was").

625 See e.g. Edward H Levi, *An Introduction to Legal Reasoning* (Chicago: University of Chicago Press, 1949) at 1–6; Schauer, *supra* note 29 at 94.

of facts and what is not is the analytical task involved in treating "different facts differently."[626] As Professor 22 says, "Working out what's alike and what's different is the *fundamental* thing you're doing in legal reasoning. It's not the only thing you're doing, but it's ... maybe the most fundamental thing to see how certain cases are *alike* and other cases are *unalike*."[627] Closely related to the task of "distinguishing" cases is that of "analogizing" them – the two terms are frequently used hand-in-hand – which involves deciding when and to what extent to "apply" the rule derived from a previous case to a new fact scenario. Making distinctions is essential to this act of application. Professor 70 provides a particularly elaborate description of these interrelated tasks in the course syllabus, invoking Edward Levi's classic account of reasoning by example:

> The study of law is the study of distinctions. Failing to show up for a dinner engagement will rarely attract legal sanction, but the case for imposing legal liability ... is more compelling in some circumstances than in others and the law is, or ought to be, sensitive to these shades of gray. The study of (contract) law is therefore rarely "easy." It is never enough to know the easy cases – that a dinner engagement with a close friend is non-contractual, for example. Only if we are able to say exactly what, if anything, distinguishes this case from that of the restauranteur ... will we be able to fully understand and critically evaluate the legal principle involved in that "easy" case.
>
> The study of law is therefore the study of individual cases. The rules of contract law are not set out in any book or (to any significant degree) any act of any legislature. They cannot simply be looked up. Nor *could* they be. While it is possible to baldly state some fundamental principles of contract law, their meaning and scope is never fixed, since there are *always* further distinctions to be made. The best we can do as students of the law is to learn how to make these distinctions by learning how judges think. And this involves reading a great many decided cases. Legal reasoning is nothing else but reasoning by example, that is, from case to case:
>
> It is a three-step process described by the doctrine of precedent in which a proposition descriptive of the first case is made into a rule of law and then applied to a next similar situation. The steps are these: similarity is seen between cases; next the rule of law inherent in the first case is announced; then the rule of law is made applicable to the second case. (EH Levi, *An Introduction to Legal Reasoning*, 1948.)[628]

626 [004], Interview, line 638.
627 [022], Interview, lines 126–30.
628 [070], Syllabus, 2015–16, pp 1–2.

This long quote demonstrates how "application" – central to both a lay understanding of law ("applying the law") and to my participants' own conceptions of lawyerly tasks[629] – is in fact deeply connected to making distinctions, which is at heart a task of determining relevance. Professor 26, who also happens to reproduce the second paragraph quoted above in Professor 26's own syllabus,[630] highlights how, in contract law, the more difficult task is not the application, but the determinations of relevance that come before the task of application:

> In contracts you have a whole lot of rules, and they apply to very narrow sets of facts. So once you know which rule applies, *applying* it is easy. It's knowing *which* rule that applies – that's the hard part. In ... contracts, it *appears* to be extremely rigid – for each situation, there is a rule. But once you start reading the cases, you realize that it's very easy to characterize the particular factual situation one way or another way in order to invoke a different rule ... It's important for [students] to learn ... the importance of *how* you characterize the facts, and how you analogize to other cases, in order to achieve a result.[631]

Thus, while Levi's three-step description of reasoning by example culminates in "application," it appears to depend importantly on the intellectual task of determining relevant similarities. Treating like cases alike requires determining *which* facts matter; applying rules to a given fact scenario requires deciding *which* rules to apply. Such line drawing emerges as a structural feature of legal reasoning, but also a ubiquitous one, given the prevalence of hypothetical fact scenarios as a pedagogical and evaluative technique: fifty-one out of the sixty-seven professors I interviewed use "hypothetical," "fact pattern," or "fact scenario" to describe their teaching or evaluation practices.

To the extent that line drawing is presented as the fundamental, or structural, feature of what it means to think distinctively like a lawyer, "legal" analysis appears to consist primarily of the act of excluding. In direct contrast to the (realist) propositional claims that policy and context are essential to law, the predominant conception of legal reasoning might lead students to determine that "contextual" factors constitute

629 See e.g. [052], Interview, lines 317–26 ("it's really about application, ... which I think is a big part of what we do as lawyers. It's not ... enough to *know* what the law is or understand what a particular rule provides. We need to know how to *apply* it").

630 Professor 26 reproduces the paragraph that begins with "The study of law is ... the study of individual cases" with only minor modifications (Syllabus, 2011–12, p 1).

631 [026], Interview, lines 270–9.

"irrelevant" facts, and "policy" considerations ought to fall by the wayside in favour of more determinative, doctrinal legal principles.

Focus on Adjudication

Given the prevalence of determining relevance in Canadian common law Contracts professors' accounts of legal reasoning, it is not surprising to find that most professors also highlight the importance of adjudication. Judicial reasoning is, after all, a perfect example of the exercise of legal rationality – recall Waddams's words that the aim of rationality cannot be "otherwise realized than by an impartial tribunal giving reasons subject to appeal."[632] Just as in the casebooks, where the pluralistic legal process ideas of Fuller and Milner ultimately took a back seat to the emphasis on adjudication, among current Contracts teachers we observe a similar emphasis on cases as the primary source material.

For example, Professor 2 likes to focus on the "pure" common law and on the "monologue of the courts" to see how jurisprudence works. Professor 53 speaks of the "incredible importance of judges"; Professor 26 tries to get students to "put themselves ... in the shoes of the judge"; Professor 63 "come[s] at this course like a litigator"; Professor 45 likes to focus on the "big personalities" of certain judges, getting students to imagine themselves as "litigator[s] ... or barrister[s]"; and Professor 57 speaks about the "in-built bias" in favour of focusing on case law.[633] The first-year course at the Schulich School of Law at Dalhousie University is aptly named "Contracts and Judicial Decision-Making."[634] Correlatively, legislative processes (legislation, negotiation, drafting) figure less prominently – examples exist, as detailed below in the third part of this chapter, but these are more exceptions that prove the rule.

To summarize, Canadian common law Contracts professors, when they describe legal reasoning, tend to uphold the idea of a distinctive type of reasoning in which the judicial formulation of doctrinal rules is taken on its face, in which the rules themselves are treated as solid and fixed reference points that fit together with a certain degree of coherence, and in which the intellectual task of line drawing – distinguishing relevant from irrelevant features of fact and law – predominates. In this way, an internal system of rules articulated in judicial decisions gains

632 Waddams, Preface to 1st ed text, *supra* note 297 at vii–viii [emphasis added].

633 [002], Interview, line 635 [translation from French]; [053], Interview, line 244; [026], Interview, lines 386–7; [063], Interview, line 114; [045], Interview, lines 20, 110–11; [057], Interview, lines 273–6.

634 Devlin Syllabus, *supra* note 355.

an eminence that is at odds with the importance placed on external factors – policy, politics, context – that most professors (the realist majority) assert in discussing "law" more generally. Put another way, the vast majority of professors do not seem to put into practice, through their conceptions of legal reasoning, the theories of legal realism and its heirs. The majority picture of legal reasoning not only reflects the importance of rules and how they fit together; it also serves to reinforce and support the preoccupation with the rule of law. Commonly held understandings of legal reasoning constitute and reproduce the idea of a distinctive, reasoned form of argumentation that establishes law's legitimacy by yielding rational justifications for differential treatment.

Realist Methodology: A Minority Position

The next section serves primarily as a foil to this main story. In it I reproduce the instances – not isolated, but by no means pervasive – in which Canadian common law Contracts professors describe legal reasoning in a way that *does* appear to put into practice a commitment to realist ideas. The following are examples of professors' realizing, to a certain extent, the aspiration we saw expressed in Chapter 4, whereby teaching theory is important in order to make better lawyers. In these minority accounts, we see examples of what it might look like to translate certain realist ideas into the practice of legal reasoning – to approach Kennedy and Fisher's vision of legal reasoning as an eclectic toolkit.

Questioning the "Legal" in "Legal Reasoning"

Although falling short of the aggressively realist claim that "legal reasoning is ordinary reasoning applied to legal problems,"[635] a number of professors call into question the extent to which there is a distinctively legal type of thinking or reasoning. Professor 58, for example, questions the term "thinking like a lawyer" by explicitly placing it in "scare quotes."[636] Professor 36 attacks the term more directly, taking issue more with the term "lawyer" than with "thinking":

> "Thinking like a lawyer" ... is a phrase I *never* use. I particularly *dislike* this idea ...

---

635 Alexander & Sherwin, *supra* note 29.

636 [058], Syllabus, 2007–08, p 3 ("What does 'thinking like a lawyer' – these are scare quotes – mean, and what are the advantages and costs of learning to do so?").

> *If* thinking like a lawyer is understood [as Kronman presents it in *The Lost Lawyer*] then I like it. But it's *never* understood that way ... It's understood in reductive terms, as though you can break down the habits of mind of a lawyer in ways that don't connect to any kind of moral duty, or ethical duty, or public duty, and don't relate to a sense of the unique role of lawyers in society ... as problem solvers, but also *leaders,* ... and the *conscience* of a community ... I don't like that phrase anymore. I try not to use it.[637]

This quotation can be read as emphasizing the need for a more contextual and nuanced understanding of the lawyer's task and, by implication, legal reasoning. Professor 36 appears to incorporate realist concerns about law's contingency into a vision of the lawyer's work, emphasizing how the role of the lawyer is "embedded in doubt":

> Years ago, as I was just starting to teach, [a newspaper columnist] wrote something about ... what you should give your children: ... "It comes down to two things – laughter and doubt" ... If I had to summarize what I'm trying to do as a teacher, I would say that's exactly that. I want my students to have *fun* – because law should be *fun* ... And then doubt ... [Doubt is important] because ... students come here ... with a preconceived image of law as *not* based on doubt, ... as pretty much given, fixed, and relatively straightforward. They quickly discover ... that this picture is inaccurate, and it makes them anxious. It's part of the anxiety of being a law student.
>
> But in a sense ... it's such a central dimension of one's life as a lawyer, that you need to *reinvent* yourself, *question* well-established principles, examine every *premise*, every *time,* that you need to develop doubt as a way of life ... I think the role of lawyers is *embedded* in doubt ... You really have to ... accept it as a way of being.[638]

Like Professor 36, who aims to help students become "proficient with legal discourse," other professors do not jettison the idea of a distinctively legal way of speaking or thinking, but nevertheless seek to include broader or more critical attitudes in legal reasoning. Thus, Professor 2 says that law is a "discipline that requires an open and critical spirit." Professor 53, in a longer passage, implicitly critiques conventional legal reasoning as "dehumanizing," but explains how it can

637 [036], Interview, lines 27–8, 382–99.
638 [036], Interview, lines 59–111.

"rehumanize" by integrating human judgment, emotion, and critical thinking. This integrative vision nevertheless upholds the distinction between politics and law:

> [R: How would you] *unpack* what those legal reasoning skills are that you're trying to teach them?
>
> [PROFESSOR 53:] It's sort of a *whole circle*. So what we want to do first of all is ... to *dehumanize* the people ... in the cases. We want to try to break things down to a legal structure ... But then, when we're done, we want to *rehumanize* everybody in the story ... and recognize that ... what we started off discounting, the emotion or the human aspect, really *is* a big part of it, but it's not the *only* part ... We have to be true to the rules because otherwise it's politics, not law. But ... judges *do* have flexibility ... and that means you have to understand the human element as well. But it's a feature that *shapes* how the rules will be applied. It's not a decision-making feature on its own ...
>
> [R:] If I were to ask you to unpack what you mean by critical thinking, how would you do that?
>
> [PROFESSOR 53:] That's sort of the "thinking like a lawyer" question. Which is *really hard* ... Law schools across North America have a horrendous record of damaging students ... Many students feel ... like they have to turn their back on *who* they are and what they *believe*. And then ... we'll sort of fill them up with this "thinking like a lawyer" thing, and that is being dispassionate, dehumanizing the court case, applying legal principles ... The question is always, "What's the test? What's the legal test here?" ... What we're *really* trying to do and *don't* do very well is to say, "But you have to bring *your passion* to this, *your* perspective, *your* life experience, and interpret this in the ways that *you* see" ...
>
> [R:] So ... this humanizing element and the critical thinking element, really go hand in hand?
>
> [PROFESSOR 53:] Absolutely![639]

Like Professor 53's attempts to help students incorporate their own life experiences and perspectives into their legal reasoning, a number of other professors explain how other "external" factors of politics, policy, or even common sense form an integral part of legal reasoning. In these comments lie the seeds of attempts to render operational many of the realist theoretical perspectives.

---

639 [036], Interview, line 29; [002], Interview, lines 551–3; [053], Interview, lines 175–206, 406–43.

Operationalizing External Factors

As detailed in Chapter 4, many Canadian common law Contracts professors argue how a particular theoretical perspective can help students craft persuasive arguments. This tendency is merely a seed of the attempt to operationalize theory, because while in principle it reflects the notion of putting a theoretical perspective into practice, it does not appear to go so far as to redefine what distinctively legal reasoning is. Nevertheless, some of the examples from Chapter 4, if their logic were followed through to full execution, could exemplify the attempt to integrate various factors into legal reasoning.

Sometimes professors make general statements about integrating external factors into legal reasoning. For example, Professor 64 says that the "best lawyers" are able to make convincing arguments that are "some combination of legal impact, policy effect, and values." Professor 74 reproduces a passage from a colleague's syllabus in which students are told that their participation grade in part will reflect the extent to which they "articulate their own positions by reference to basic underlying values." The course syllabus states that "the *operative* values must become explicit." Professor 3, who highlights ideology at the core of Professor 3's legal philosophy, trains students to "evoke those grand themes and the more powerfully you can do that, the more successful you're going to be in persuading people." Also stated somewhat aspirationally, Professor 7 describes how one aim is to show how "the frontier between legal reasons and other kinds of reasons is not impermeable. It's not *fixed*. As you learn to think about problems, you can ... convince a court to incorporate *into* law the certain kinds of reasons that would not otherwise have been acceptable."

Similarly Professor 13 wants students to be able to "marshal[] facts and policy considerations and legal doctrine to create a legal argument." For others, like Professor 31, legal reasoning includes "how courts respond to the *felt* necessities of the day and ... [incorporate] values ... like what is economically efficient, what protects the reasonable expectations of the parties, what is fair, [and] protecting vulnerable parties."[640]

Other times professors specifically invoke the importance of facts and context to suggest that legal reasoning is not just an operation of abstract thought. For example, Professor 27 says that one distinctive feature of legal reasoning, as opposed to philosophy, is the idea that

640 [064], Interview, lines 585–8; [074], Syllabus, 2016–17, p 3 [emphasis added]; [003], Interview, lines 250–61; [007], Interview, lines 365–72; [013], Interview, lines 218–19; [031], Interview, lines 38–53.

"you just *have* to bring it down to the ground." Professor 67 describes legal reasoning as going behind the words that "mask complexity" and "engaging with actual facts," because "that's how law arises – not through generalities." For Professor 15, the "ideal" of the case method is to "bring home" to students the idea that "law ... is not just an intellectual construct [but] an instrument of ... human justice," by demonstrating how things "actually play out for people" in "concrete terms." "Part of what is being a good lawyer is having a good sense of what the law is doing in people's lives." For Professor 43, "you get the context ... [from] the fact patterns."[641]

Just as incorporating context or concrete experience into legal reasoning reflects an attempt to put into practice the importance of everyday reality, some professors seek to include in legal reasoning the notion of common sense or intuition. Professor 33 speaks of the "common sense component that has to always be held onto when you're dealing with a new situation." Professor 1 rejects the conventional idea that it is necessary to "erase" students' consciousness and substitute new concepts in order to be a good jurist: "It's neither necessary nor established that the brutal exercise of erasing students' consciousness and putting in its place a series of concepts, categories, and words makes better jurists, better educated, or better human beings." Professor 58 speaks of the need for students to "train their gut" to counteract the tendency of legal education to alienate students from their sense of common sense.[642]

Other realist attitudes make their way into descriptions of legal reasoning or thinking skills. Some professors specifically try to cultivate the skill of reasoning backwards from results. Professor 16 will take students through the following sequence: "Here's the facts. Here's the decision we want to reach. How do we fill in the middle? ... How would we work backwards?" For Professor 33, the ability to distinguish between ends-based reasoning and understanding when to read a case "on its face" is an "essential lawyering skill." Other professors emphasize the skill of "framing a case," reflecting the realist idea that the development of doctrine is contingent on many factors, including the vicissitudes of advocacy choices. Thus a key legal skill for Professor 62 is the ability to "*frame* problems, ... to identify different ways of framing

---

641 [027], Interview, 283–96; [067], Interview, Handwritten notes of untranscribed, unrecorded interview, pp 4–5; [015], Interview, lines 87–111; [043], Interview, lines 1317–20.

642 [033], Interview, lines 644–6; [001], Interview, lines 512–19 [translation from French]; [058], Interview, lines 463–81 ("of course you will be solving the problem using legal tools, but your fundamental gut instinct about the thing probably should be guiding you to some extent").

a problem, and [to see] ... the really critical connection between how you frame a case and what remedies you try and get." Professor 13 tries to train the ability to "characterize the facts in a way that allows you to make particular arguments. The way in which Swan and Reiter [argue that] you have to give the court a 'peg' ... to hang their result on – in the form of a legal argument."[643]

As illustrated in Chapter 4, some professors aspire to translate their theoretical commitments into a desire to cultivate discrete skills outside the framework of adjudication. The number of examples expanding upon or concretizing this aspiration pales in comparison to the overwhelming emphasis on making better arguments, but they are worth highlighting because they indicate how some professors actively try to resist the "pathological" look at contract law focused on litigation (with its commensurate emphasis on judicial reasoning) and instead focus on various prospective, forward-looking skills. Thus, policy analysis, problem solving, and drafting skills all surface among the various skills that professors aim to develop in their students. Consider the following examples.

Professor 61, a law and economics scholar, takes the opportunity of the small-group format to encourage students to think about policy design by "imagin[ing] there is no law":

> Imagine that ... *you* have to make the law. Like, there's *no* law to start from. *You* have to make an argument ... [I ask them to argue] what the rule should be ... They probably veer towards economics types of arguments because they know I am an economist. [But] I have no problem with them bringing up any ... arguments based on morality or [other considerations].[644]

Professor 42 says that "skills like reading cases, or synthesizing cases, or extracting ratios, or reading statutes, are important skills, but only insofar as a door to exposure to other kinds of skills," such as "negotiation, figuring out how much to say when and where, determining how many of a client's instructions should be acted upon, *and* later on, maybe, having to convert a deliberately ambiguous or informal arrangement into codified form." Similarly Professor 12 gives students cases not to be studied for their ratios but "as examples of solutions to problems." Professor 12 not only says this in the interview, but also articulates it to students in a summary of the course provided to them:

---

643 [016], Interview, lines 281–6; [033], Interview, lines 588–606; [017], Interview, lines 145–59; [062], Interview, lines 591–7; [013], Interview, lines 573–5.

644 [061], Interview, lines 237–94.

> A useful understanding of the Law of Contracts ... regards the cases, not as sources of legal propositions, but as examples, sometimes horrible examples, of problems and of solutions to them. As I said more than once in class, my course is a course focused on problems; the problems that arise when people try to arrange their affairs – where to live, where to work, what to eat and wear, where and how to have fun, who to work with, how to make money – by dealing with other people.

Other professors describe course objectives as including developing "forward-looking transactional skills," or express a desire to one day incorporate drafting exercises in order to add to the students' "toolbox" the ability to "proactively prevent a dispute ... [You need to not only know] the law that's out there [but also] understand ... [what] can go wrong in the future [and] ... predict[] how certain developments will go."[645] And finally, Professor 63 emphasizes empathy, listening skills, and the ability to inhabit and communicate to a judge the perspective of marginalized communities:

> [If students] bring the perspective of being a member of a marginalized community, [I want them to show how] a rule doesn't make sense for them or for their community, or [that] it would have to be understood in [a] different way in order to be meaningful. [If they don't have personal experience, I want them to] start thinking [about] building empathy and listening skills so ... we can nevertheless understand [that] we have obligations as legal professionals ... to work to make sure that law isn't just about the rule of law, but it's also about producing justice – across communities.[646]

The foregoing examples demonstrate that the project of putting critical and realist insights into practice *is* on some Contracts professors' radar. But in contrast to the prevailing model of legal reasoning, the focus on these approaches is somewhat insignificant – in terms of both the number of professors who examine them and the depth to which they do so. The descriptions of conventional legal reasoning are much more elaborate and fiercely defended than the episodic and tentative forays into realist methodology just quoted.

This impression is furthered by a number of instances in which professors fail to operationalize their theoretical viewpoints, and

645 [042], Interview, lines 85–9; [012], Interview, lines 99–101; [012], Review Notes for the Course (30 November 2016), p 1; [051], Interview, lines 340–57; [056], Interview, lines 280–98.

646 [063], Interview, lines 370–84.

reveal an understanding of legal reasoning in which rules and reasoning by example predominate. This leaves the impression, analogous to our discussion above with respect to ideas about law, that formalist conceptions of legal reasoning are truly "core," even among the realists.[647]

The Failure to Operationalize and What Is Really Core

The Failure to Operationalize

Professor 48, in concluding a discussion about the influence of law and economics and socio-legal studies, illustrates almost perfectly the point that, by and large, Contracts teaching fails to translate its theoretical commitments into methodological ones: "I think law and economics and ... social context have been the biggest factors that have influenced not the *method of delivery* of contracts, but the *kinds* of things you talk about in class."[648]

Less directly, a number of other professors suggest that the work of these theories lies outside the practice of legal reasoning. Thus, while Professor 33 views perspectives of class, race, gender, and power to be "integral" to teaching Contracts, these perspectives are addressed primarily at the "beginning and ... end" of the course. Moreover, while in interview Professor 33 is clearly passionate about these perspectives – "dislik[ing]" the traditional focus on the development of doctrine – the course syllabus simply states that students will be "*exposed to* contemporary and historic discourses regarding judicial rule-making and political interventions."[649] Accordingly, rather than thoroughly integrating the critical perspectives, the mainstream vision of what it means to study contract law seems to predominate.

Similarly, in Professor 50's course syllabus, the most active words in a list of learning objectives pertain to conventional legal reasoning – "*analyze*" factual disputes, "*distil* legal rules from judicial opinions," whereas the one reference to underlying factors is comparatively passive – "*identify* factors which influence judicial thinking." Underlying factors are not presented as useful for making persuasive arguments, and the one reference to making arguments is preceded by the goal of

647 Compare the discussion above under "Realists as Formalists", pages 229–33.
648 [048], Interview, lines 346–9.
649 [033], Interview, lines 448–72, 400, 15–24; [033], Syllabus, 2015–16, p 1 [emphasis added].

"applying rules to factual situations" and followed by that of "appreciat[ing] the importance of precision in the use of legal terms." Professor 38 includes policy analysis (which is the subject of Professor 38's own research) in the course, but frames it as pertinent only to students who might become "a judge or a legislator" – "You may not be thinking about this *as a lawyer*." Moreover, in explaining the lack of regrets about discontinuing policy questions in examinations, Professor 38 distinctly separates policy analysis from "legal skills":

> I guess I could have decided to instil in them the love for policy analysis! But I don't perceive that as my job ... [My job is to] giv[e] them the legal skills and the legal training to functionally operate as effective lawyers and provid[e] them a little bit of awareness of basic principles of policy analysis in case they go to these other roles that I have talked about. But I don't think the course should be focused on policy.[650]

What Is Really Core?

Like Professor 38, a number of other professors with strong realist convictions convey the idea that the conventional tasks of legal reasoning are core. For example, Professor 24 in interview expresses a sophisticated and original concern with rethinking the order of the course, and emphasizes critical thinking – yet the first objective Professor 24 lists is to "be able to write a clear answer to a fact pattern." Professor 37 says, "I don't teach by way of doctrine. I teach by way of big questions and big topics" – and yet a paragraph in the course syllabus about the role of human relationships in contract law is immediately followed by the statement, "The aim of this course is to examine basic principles governing these contractual relations." Immediately following is a list of subjects that, however functionally stated, closely resemble conventional doctrinal categories.[651] Professor 45 emphasizes the importance of "critical analysis" in interview – yet the course syllabus describes the course's two "primary objectives" as providing "an understanding of the process of development of the common law through judicial

---

650 [050], Syllabus, 2013–14, p 1 [emphasis added]; [038], Interview, lines 124–34, 303–11 [emphasis added].

651 [024], Interview, lines 333–4; [037], Interview, lines 650–1; [037], Syllabus, 2016–17, p 1 ("the enforceability of contractual undertakings (what constitutes an 'agreement' and what kinds of agreements will the law enforce); justifications for their non-performance (and reasons for setting aside prima facie valid agreements); sanctions for their breach; and an examination of to whom obligations are owed").

decisions" and "a basic knowledge of the doctrines and precepts" of contract law. Examples of this kind proliferate.[652]

A concluding example of the taken-for-granted nature of the conventional case method can be found near the end of my interview with Professor 61, who earlier claimed to feel no constraints whatsoever in how to teach the course:

> [R:] And [if,] hypothetically, you wanted to dispense with case reading [altogether, could you]?
>
> [PROFESSOR 61:] I guess that would be stretching the bounds ... My unmitigated freedom was certainly ... a more local thing than the global freedom ... I mean obviously I have to teach contracts ... Let's hypothetically say I decided to teach contracts by just bringing in a different contract in every week ... If I taught it that way, I don't know who would be stamping down on me ... [But] my guess is that the case method is one of those *core elements* of the first year program that *should* be taught.
>
> [R:] ... Why should the case method be taught?
>
> [PROFESSOR 61:] ... One of the central elements of being a lawyer is being able to ... understand what cases are useful for. Which is: we unpack rules, we discern how the law has evolved, and why it's evolved in this way, and ... cases provide *reasons* ... We also teach reasoning by analogy via these cases ... I teach my students [that] the ... two reasons why a lawyer will use ... cases ... in legal writing [are to] discern rules and for reasoning by analogy ... Now, having said that ... if they got all their case method ... from other courses and then *one* of their courses was more practical and they did contracts? ... I don't know ... My guess is that's *not* the purpose of a law school. Not the purpose of an academic law school, anyway.[653]

This exchange is revealing for several reasons. First, it illustrates how, even for a professor whose scholarly views fall squarely within the "realist" camp – Professor 61 is the law and economics scholar earlier quoted as emphasizing policy thinking[654] – there is a very strong sense

---

652 [045], Interview, lines 121–89; [045], Syllabus, 2015–16, p 1. See also [013], Syllabus, 2013, p 2 (criteria include "(i) comprehensive identification of the issues raised by fact pattern problems; (ii) demonstrated familiarity with related case law ... ; (iii) clear and concise identification and application of the relevant legal test(s) to the fact pattern given"); [017], Interview, line 619 (conceives role as giving students the "black letter plus"); [063], Interview, lines 97–102 ("I try to ... balance ... between ... encouraging mastery of the fundamentals of common law ... and then to help them ... start thinking about the critique").

653 [061], Interview, lines 923–77.

654 See text accompanying note 644, above.

that distilling rules and reasoning by analogy are core. This notion of core, moreover, appears to transcend both academic and practical visions of legal education: conventional legal reasoning is central to both the work of the lawyer and the function of the academic law school.

Second, the exchange raises a number of possible factors to account for this commitment to a "core" methodology. On the one hand, Professor 61 seems to express a personal conviction about the importance of the case method through the possessive formulation, "my students." On the other hand, there is a sense that some external forces operate to impose or condition the use of the case method. These might in part be external, concrete, or institutional – Professor 61 at least contemplates the idea that someone might "stamp[] down on me." But in large part, explicit sanctions do not seem to figure predominantly. Instead the overwhelming impression is that the requirement to teach the case method flows from a collective idea, however ethereal, of what "should" be taught, as well the sense of having inherited a tradition (the common law) that develops its substantive law through cases.

The reasons for formalism's powerful hold on the attitudes of Canadian common law Contracts professors are among the mysteries to be explored in Chapter 6. Before proceeding to that exploration, this chapter concludes by looking at some examples and accounts of pedagogical practices to demonstrate how most of the messages communicated through teaching corroborate the emphasis on formalism illustrated up to this point. Again, realism is not silent, but it is the minority player.

ATTITUDES EXPRESSED THROUGH TEACHING MATERIALS AND PRACTICES

In this third part of the chapter, we look at how ideas about law can be operationalized through teaching. The choices professors make about what content to emphasize, how to frame it to students, and how to evaluate, all put into effect certain visions about law. I investigate here the pedagogical dimension of how theory is translated into practice by looking at course syllabi, examination questions, and other course materials. I also examine professors' descriptions of their teaching practices.

Unlike the methodology used in other studies, such as Mertz's, I did not engage in direct observation of classroom teaching – and so there is a necessary limitation to the data. How someone actually teaches might differ a great deal from how one describes one's teaching in an interview, or how one articulates one's goals in a course syllabus. One advantage of the interview context or a syllabus, however, is that professors are able to express their aspirations freely. So, if we observe a gap between their beliefs about law and their attitudes about law as expressed in their self-description of their teaching, we come one step closer to identifying a gap between theoretical and methodological commitments. And, indeed, the bulk of the examples here seem to corroborate that gap: pedagogical practices illustrating an affinity with certain ideas associated with formalism figure in the majority. Pedagogically operationalized expressions of realism are much less common, but these minority examples do demonstrate the *possibility* of teaching Contracts in a way that cultivates an eclectic toolkit and broader notions of the lawyer as citizen.

Formalist Pedagogy

To reveal the formalist underpinnings of many professors' approach to teaching, this section is organized not around the substantive ideas – as they have already been developed in some detail – but according to the sources analysed. I start by examining the explicit reflections on teaching that teachers offer both in describing their teaching practices and in their syllabi. Then I focus on the key question of "substance." Finally I discuss evaluation methods.

Syllabi and Expressions of Teaching

Course syllabi are a useful source of information because they give professors an untrammelled opportunity to articulate what they believe. Professors take up the opportunity to express themselves explicitly to varying degrees: some syllabi contain only the bare minimum of administrative statements and a reading list, without adornment;[655] others extend to multipage discourses on legal education, law, legal writing, and career advice.[656] Although the minimalist approach to syllabus writing in itself might implicitly communicate the importance of doctrine by making cases effectively the only substantive content in the presentation of the course, I focus here on the affirmative attempts to articulate pedagogical priorities.

The examples that follow are not exhaustive, but rather serve to exemplify how the course syllabi of even strong realists might reinforce the importance of doctrine and the notion of conventional legal reasoning. For example, while Professor 10 includes examining contract law "in its social and political context" as an "aim of the course" in the first sentence of the syllabus, the next sentence states that the "*main*

655 See e.g. [003], Syllabus, 2015–16, [067], Syllabus, 2013–14.
656 See e.g. [025], Syllabus, 2015–16.

objective" of the course is to "enable students to acquire basic legal skills to competently identify, analyze, synthesize and apply the law of contract." Professor 40, who teaches, "broadly speaking, [from] a legal realist slash critical legal studies perspective," includes a wide range of conventional objectives at the very beginning of the course syllabus, stating, "The purpose of this course is to familiarize you with these rules and principles."[657] Other examples are easy to find.[658]

Along with syllabi, professors' accounts of their own teaching are an opportunity to highlight or foreground their priorities. Frequently, in interview professors describe their teaching objectives in similarly conventional terms, notwithstanding commitments elsewhere to realistic attitudes. Indeed, when asked about their goals for teaching the course, almost every professor identifies learning substance and teaching analogical reasoning as the first two goals (in that order), with about a third of professors adding a third goal of incorporating critical perspectives. It is not uncommon to hear expressions such as "I want them to be able to think like a lawyer operating within contract law" or accounts that focus "*primarily* [on] ... cognitive skills and ... the skills of reasoning through analogy."[659] Other examples emphasize the distinction between law and policy or between law and politics.[660]

Decisions regarding Substance

Remedies, First or Last?

Whether remedies should be taught first or last is a long-standing theme in the literature on Contracts teaching.[661] The choice to begin

---

657 [010], Syllabus, 2012–13, p 1; [040], Interview, lines 64–5; [040], Syllabus, 2015–16, p 1.

658 See e.g. [011], Syllabus, 2014–15, p 1 ("The main objective of the course is to introduce you to the core legal principles and concepts of the law of contract"); [002], Syllabus, 2014, pp 2–3 (first listed objective is to "analyse case law in determining the relevant facts, the issues, the ratio, the holding and the rules or principles that flow from it" [translation from French]); [058], Syllabus, 2007–8, pp 1–2 ("By the end of the course, you should be able to translate a factual problem into a legal problem, to express the stakes of a conflict as a function of the fundamental concepts of the law of contract, and to identify the major questions and juridical arguments raised by a contractual dispute").

659 [004], Interview, line 4; [066], Interview, lines 122–4.

660 See e.g. [039], Interview, lines 704–12 (distinguishing "two sets of questions" – "narrow questions" about "ratio[s]" and "questions around policy"); [038], Interview, lines 312–33 ("neither politics broadly defined or narrowly defined" enters the classroom); [059], Interview, line 759 (politics not a significant element).

661 See generally Gerber, *supra* note 357. See also the discussion in Chapter 3 above under "*Swan*: The Remedies Chapter", pages 138–41.

a course with remedies was pioneered by Lon Fuller in his 1947 casebook. According to Karl Klare, this choice signalled "a central realist message [that] it is impossible to understand the nature of legal rights and relationships or to logically deduce remedial conclusions from them without knowing what courts can and actually will do to and for litigants."[662] By contrast, the decision to start a Contracts casebook with issues of formation dates to Langdell, whose first chapter was "Mutual Consent"; Langdell did not include remedies in his casebook at all. Accordingly, in caricatured terms, the decision to foreground issues of formation might suggest a preoccupation with doctrinal categories that evoke the formalist conception of contract law associated with Langdell, whereas the desire to focus on remedies can appear as an attempt to highlight the "real" consequences of legal decisions.

The practices of Canadian common law Contracts professors suggest a preference for putting formation first. Out of the seventy-four professors in my study who taught the full course, fifty of them teach formation first; nineteen teach remedies first, and three use a "hybrid" approach, with a mini remedies section, followed by formation, and with a longer remedies section at the end.[663] Among those who teach formation first, at least six (Professors 7, 19, 22, 25, 51 and 53) have tried it the other way and affirmatively decided to switch. By contrast, only one participant (Professor 18) describes switching the other way around.

More interesting than the numbers are the ways in which some professors describe the preference for the formation-first approach. Perhaps surprisingly, given the historical importance placed on the question of order, a number of professors state they have "no strong feeling" about what order to teach in.[664] Others simply treat the order in which the subjects are presented in the casebook as determinative, and might

662 Klare, "Contracts Jurisprudence and the First-Year Casebook", *supra* note 88 at 882.

663 These numbers refer to the approach taken at the most recent moment for which I have information. For some, this is the date of interview; for those who submitted syllabi, it is the date of the most recent syllabus provided. Two professors teach in a different order altogether, and one participant taught only half-semesters (according to my data). These numbers are simply meant to capture the relative order of formation and remedies. Some of them precede a discussion of one or the other, with a small section on critical or theoretical perspectives, or consideration.

664 See e.g. [005], Interview, lines 357–8 ("I don't actually think it matters that much, to be honest. There's advantages to each"); [031], Interview, lines 361–2 ("[R:] It doesn't sound like you have a strong feeling one way or another. [Professor 31:] I don't"); [018], Interview, line 631 ("Having taught it both ways, I don't have a strong preference").

switch orders depending on the casebook they use.[665] Still others argue that beginning with formation is pedagogically more effective and easier for students, as it provides them with a series of relatively discrete and concrete concepts to confront in the early days of law school.[666] Yet another group says how they prefer to follow the order of the natural life of a contract in the way parties might encounter it.[667] And finally, a number of professors express that beginning with formation is the "proper order," that it just "makes sense," that it enables them to present in a clear way how law is structured, or that including remedies is simply a "mistake."[668]

These different responses have different implications. Some, like the choice of casebook or references to pedagogical effectiveness, highlight the idea that frameworks other than legal theory might be useful for understanding the complex relationship between how realist and formalist themes surface in the teaching of Contracts. The point, for example, about following the order of casebooks raises the question of path

665 [033], Interview, lines 233–5 ("pretty much" follows the order of the casebook (formation first)); [052], Interview, lines 75–6 ("we basically followed the *Percy and Ben-Ishai* casebook"); [044], Interview, lines 85–6 ("I follow the casebook. I take Steve Waddams' volume ... and I just go through it"); [006], Interview, lines 988–9 ("I don't think an outline would be very exciting to you. It's basically just the [*Swan*] casebook").

666 See e.g. [026], Interview, lines 544–7 ("I really appreciate the arguments for starting with remedies – both theoretical and practical – but I think for *teaching* purposes, it's really jarring for the students, and it's better to start with formation"); [051], Interview, lines 99–115 ("Students ... get the idea of offer, acceptance, and ... bargain quite quickly, and ... being immersed in a market-based society, they ... catch on to that quite easily, while ... the concept of expectation damages and lost opportunity ... are ... maybe more complex"); [025], Interview, lines 287–93 ("I start with offer and acceptance. I have surrendered ... As far as the student structuring his or her understanding, *it just makes sense* to begin at the beginning").

667 See e.g. [009], Interview, lines 57–64 ("I'm a big believer in narrative, in a story arc, and the beginning of a contract really is offer and acceptance ... Following this idea of a narrative, I think that thematically, it makes sense"); [032], Interview, lines 416–23 (teaching remedies first is "putting the cart before the horse in some ways. I understand *why* people [do it], but I like to start with the basic building blocks and make my way up to remedies").

668 [055], Interview, lines 401–2; [046], Interview, lines 230–53 ("It doesn't make a lot of sense to spend a couple of months teaching about damages and compensation before the students know what it is the courts are talking about when they say there was a contract here"); [053], Interview, lines 43–54 ("we move slowly ... to make sure that they have a clear concept of how the law is structured ... [and] try to make sure that everybody's got a very clear understanding ... of the *content* particularly"); [022], Interview, lines 315–20 ("I think it's a mistake to focus too much on ... remedies ... Remedies aren't actually part of contract law").

dependence and the extent to which institutional and other material factors might play a role in constructing legal consciousness. The point that it is easier to teach in the classical mould suggests that pedagogy is not only a subject of analysis (as it is in this section), but also a framework for explaining apparent inconsistencies between messages about law. I explore these frameworks in Chapter 6.

At the same time, while the formation-first approach should not necessarily be taken to imply that a formalist vision of law is being advanced (and vice versa) – there are some revealing counterexamples[669] – explanations that focus on clarity and structure *do* reveal an implicit preference for these values. To say that it is easier or it makes more sense to focus on areas of law in which rules can be distilled and made to seem coherent presents this exercise as natural. What might start out as the path of least resistance may implicitly communicate the idea that it is natural, neutral, acceptable, or even preferable to view law in this particular way.

Other Course Materials

The way Canadian common law Contracts professors treat substantive ideas in their slides, handouts, and other study aids occasionally communicates the importance of doctrine and systematization, notwithstanding proclamations about law elsewhere. Professor 30, for example, who speaks about the importance of relational contracting, provides students with self-authored class outlines that resemble a treatise, restatement, or digest.[670] Professor 26, who expresses the instrumental

---

669 The idea that the formation-first approach reflects the way parties themselves encounter contractual issues might suggest more of a preoccupation with empirical behaviour than with doctrinal coherence. Thus Professor 42 likes to "march through the transaction in the same sequence that the parties followed" in a manner that prioritizes the parties' perspective (email correspondence with author, 28 April 2017 [reprinted with permission]). In another counterexample, Professor 59, one of the formalist champions, teaches remedies first in order to bolster the importance of doctrinal categories:

> In order for the students to understand why all [the doctrinal rules matter], you need to know what's the consequence at the end of the road ... Now this sounds like ... results-oriented reasoning, but I like students to be aware that the end of the line can *influence* the way in which we think about those initial issues, like contract formation ... It's important to help students understand the relevance of those *preliminary* issues – contract formation, terms, and enforceability (Interview, lines 109–23).

670 See e.g. [030], Contracts Small Group Outline Class 26, Spring Term 2014:

> Mistake of Identity
>
> 1 An operative mistake as to the identity of one of the contracting parties renders the contract void. Such a conclusion will likely result in the vitiation of any intention to pass property under the contract.

idea that "the law is something you *use* – not something that *is*," reproduces in class slides a sense that legal reasoning is focused on determining relevance, emphasizing the importance of rules:

> [C]oncentrate on the facts that are legally significant ... This can only be reasoned backward once you understand the whole case ... rules are the link between the law and the facts. They are statements of the law relevant to the particular facts of the case ... Rules say: "in situation x the result will be y" (although they usually aren't phrased that way).[671]

Evaluation

Perhaps the most striking evidence of an emphasis on formalist values is the predominant method of evaluation: the final examination. In almost every large section of Contracts, a final examination worth the majority of the grade is the primary mode of evaluation.[672] These examinations, moreover, tend to focus primarily on hypothetical fact-pattern questions that test the knowledge of substantive rules, issue spotting, and the application of rules to fact scenarios through reasoning by analogy. Both the nature of the questions asked and the criteria of evaluation serve to reinforce the importance of these skills and implicitly to prioritize the related formalist ideas about law.

The Questions Asked and Not Asked

The most common type of examination question sets out a long, hypothetical fact scenario, and asks the student to "advise" a hypothetical

---

> 2 Thus, if the contract purports to be one for the sale of goods, no property in the goods will pass to the buyer, and the buyer will be unable to pass good title to an innocent third party purchaser.
> 3 If, however, there is *no* operative mistake of identity, the contract is not void but might be voidable on grounds of some fraud or misrepresentation.
> 4 If a voidable title passes to the buyer, it will be able to pass good title to an innocent third party purchaser, provided it does so before the original seller rescinds the original contract of sale (*Shogun Finance v Hudson*[, [2004] 1 AC 919]).

671 [026], Interview, lines 408–9; [026], Class Slides, January 2017.

672 In small sections, legal writing exercises might form the bulk of a grade, but overall these are in the minority. Moreover the types of legal writing that tend to be encouraged are memos and facta that often reproduce conventional case analysis, albeit in a different format. The most common practice is to have a December "fail safe" examination, whose grade can count towards the student's final grade only if it is equal to or higher than the grade received on the final. A typical allocation is 25 per cent for the December mid-term and 75 per cent or 100 per cent for the final, depending on whether the December examination is counted.

client. Very often the action part of the question is framed in the most generic terms possible. Professor 48's examination script is representative: a page and a half of factual story is followed by "Advise [X] on all the legal issues that arise." Except in the most indirect of ways, the examination does not appear to engage students with the questions of "social context" that, for Professor 48, are so important to the course. Professor 26's examination questions reveal a similar pattern. Although Professor 26 tells students in class slides that "exam questions will require you to ... engage critically with a philosophical or doctrinal issue," all the exam questions from the 2009–12 period appear to emphasize conventional legal analysis: "What recourse ... does [X] have against [Y]?"; "Can [X] obtain a remedy against [Y] or [Z]?"; "Advise [X]"; "Advise [X] with respect to possible legal claims he may have against [Y]"; "Advise [X] about whether he can recover any or all of the remaining [money]"; "Discuss the possible remedies that each party might pursue and assess their chances of success"; "Please advise [X]."[673]

Such a tendency is common, even among those professors who attempt to design their courses to align with their theoretical commitments. Professor 7, for example, one of the few who begins the course with neither formation nor remedies but with a study on the limits on contract, has a "very traditional law school exam" in which students are asked to "identify the issues," "argue for and against ... a specific result," "advise the client," or sometimes pretend to be a "judge."[674] The exams set by Professor 40, who teaches from a legal realist/critical legal studies perspective, focus primarily on issue spotting using cases, and "never" include a policy question. Professor 40 describes the standard practice in the following way:

> My exams ... *always* have the same structure ... Question one, question two – each of them tends to be about two pages long, single-spaced ... Typically I'll have two to three issues or clusters of issues embedded in each question ... I'm interested in seeing that [students] know the general contours of contract law, the basic analytical frameworks that have been worked up in these big issues, that [they] know all the cases that are relevant ... to the contentious issue at hand, that [they're] able to deploy those cases in persuasive ways on behalf of all the relevant parties.
>
> I don't have a policy question ... on any of my exams. And I never have. I *was* sort of told *not* to do that when I first came here, that there was a

673 [048], "Contract Exams – Example A"; [048], Interview, lines 290–8; [026], Class Slides, 2017; [026], Examinations, December 2009, April 2010, December 2010, April 2011, December 2011, April 2012, December 2012.

674 [007], Interview, lines 562–73.

custom of not having policy questions on exams, the reason being there was no way of really grading them accurately ... The thinking [was that] you couldn't ... set up ... a points chart ... It was just sort of everything under the sun ... I'm not persuaded by that argument, but [when I was in law school] ... I actually found generally that policy questions *hurt* people ... *more than they helped* ... I'm not sure [the exam is] the place to ask questions like that.[675]

The idea that exams are not the place to incorporate policy considerations arises elsewhere, coupled with the idea that a focus on conventional legal reasoning is fairer to students. Thus, Professor 38, who does policy analysis "for a living," explains the choice to abandon policy questions on exams:

It's always fact patterns. I never do policy questions on exams ... There were a couple of years in which I had an assignment with policy questions. But that didn't go very well, so I took it out ... The students didn't know what to do! They were completely lost. And the students who had some sort of background in policy analysis did *beautifully*, but then everybody else was at a loss ... So I felt it was very unfair ... Whereas, assignments that are focused on legal skills, nobody has legal skills ... We're levelling the playing field.[676]

Commitments to other considerations also appear to fall by the wayside in evaluation. Professor 23 speaks animatedly about how the breadth of the Contracts course enables students to expand their minds beyond adjudication – but in the next breath acknowledges the limited nature of exam questions:

[Contracts is] such a broad course ... it's an introduction to ... *half of law school* ... One could call it "Contracts: A Selection of Interesting Principles," although ... the way I teach it, it's probably more than that ... [I want to] get [students] thinking about being both a lawyer and a judge and what the difference is between those things ... and how they ... fight back and forth and interact with each other. And to think about *transactional practice* as well. It's sort of difficult because the exam, ... if I have an exam, and even the problems I set when I have them do memos, [is] very ... litigation oriented.[677]

---

675 [040], Interview, lines 766–820.
676 [038], Interview, lines 273, 256–67.
677 [023], Interview, lines 275–92.

Similarly Professor 25 "finds it hard" to put questions about the contingency of law on a "compulsory question," even though it is a theme Professor 25 "approach[es] daily in half a dozen ways." Professor 44 relishes the opportunity to expose students to "pragmatic" factors in class, but never tests this: "that's not fair, because they're not in the office ... the examination is always on the casebook." And Professor 51 – who takes a "very legal realist perspective" focusing on the "outcome of cases" and the "reasonable expectations of parties," who views even questions of formation through a "policy framework," and who endeavours to recast the course to emphasize transaction skills and theory – uses mainly a "standard hypothetical" question with an "issue identification aspect," and has recently stopped using essay exams in order to align with a co-instructor and to save on marking time; a recent final examination consists entirely of issue spotting and application questions.[678]

The Best Answers

Evaluation criteria generally align with the types of hypothetical fact patterns just described: the best answers master substantive doctrine, identify issues "correctly" and comprehensively, apply rules to the hypothetical facts persuasively, and are "concise" and "devoid of fluff." Together these descriptors paint an image of law as a collection of discernible, discrete rules, and legal reasoning as technical, precise, and surgical. The following examples breathe life into this description:

> [The best exam answers] are *concise*. They clearly identify the issues. They don't identify the issues that are *not issues*. They do a very neat and tidy analysis. They are able to pinpoint the authority for ... the principle that they're stating, and apply it really clearly ... I had *one* exam this past year that was just *so phenomenal*. I had never ever seen anything like it, actually. It was almost the *perfect answer*. Which was quite *shocking*, because it really just said, "This is the issue. Here is the analysis. These are the cases." You know? And it was perfect. It was concise. It was brief. And it was *amazing*, actually.[679]

678 [025], Interview, lines 582–613; [044], Interview, lines 515–35; [051], Interview, lines 205–45; [051], Interview, lines 384–413; [051], Interview, lines 465–514; [051], Final Examination, April 2014 ("Did [X] breach its contractual obligations to [Y]?"; "Assuming that the contract does not limit [Y's] liability, what damages can [X] seek from [Y]?"; "Advise Y with respect to the ... contract"; "What legal claims offer [Z] the best chance of success?"; "What damages might be recoverable in this case?").

679 [039], Interview, lines 169–79.

> The best answers will identify the issues in the problem and then provide an analysis of the applicable doctrine – which manifests *absolute mastery* of the material.[680]
>
> [The best answers "correctly"] identif[y] the issues and ... the rules applicable to that issue, and then discuss [the] application of those rules to the issues.[681]
>
> The best answers are devoid of fluff ... [They] identify the issues with some precision, and [give] a *tight* answer that's tailored to the facts at hand. And when you see that, you sort of breathe a sigh of relief.[682]
>
> The best answers ... concisely hit all the issues ... And although it doesn't happen very often ... the *very best* answers come up with a different way of seeing the problem. And they actually throw back some issues at me that I hadn't thought of when I set it.[683]
>
> The best exam answers give *plausible* answers well justified by the *cases* as to why the result is *this* and not *that*.[684]
>
> [The best answers] combine fairly comprehensive coverage with greater depth and application. [They] recognize ... the decisive parts of the story and ... provide safe advice, rather than ... treating it as some exercise in summarizing contract law.[685]

Although these examples provide good evidence that policy-based reasoning typically is excluded from evaluation criteria, occasionally professors make this claim explicitly:

> [In] a traditional hypothetical problem ... essentially ... what I'm looking for is an evaluation of how well they're doing in the first *two* of my goals – that is, their understanding of doctrine and their ability to make legal arguments. I'm *not* particularly interested in *examining* them on whether

680 [029], Interview, lines 404–6.
681 [031], Interview, lines 301–6.
682 [032], Interview, lines 480–6.
683 [053], Interview, lines 85–8.
684 [019], Interview, lines 364–6.
685 [066], Interview, lines 196–200. See also:

[The best answers] demonstrate a capacity to ... employ the skills of legal analysis to solve a problem ... [They identify] the issues ... and what principles are relevant to [the] solution of that issue, [and also] what cases ... those principles derive from ([055], Interview, lines 602–13);

[The best answers demonstrate] the power of analysis ... When you read the papers, you see students who've got the ideas but they're so disorganized ... The more adept ... have got the hang of the legal thing and the organization of your thoughts and your approach and your analysis, and your knowledge of the law, and drawing conclusions ([044], Interview, lines 236–45).

> they think [a] particular contract doctrine or case is ... good, bad, or indifferent ... I'm interested in ... how well they're beginning to understand the rule system and how well they're able to use that rule system to create legal arguments both for the plaintiff and the defendant ...
>
> What *they* think is good contractual policy, or what is *fair*, or what is *just*, or what is *reasonable* in the circumstances, ... I just find that a very difficult thing to evaluate. [What is really important is whether] they have those basic skills and an understanding of doctrinal analysis that [will] send them comfortably on into second year.[686]

Indeed, even when social and policy issues are included explicitly in evaluation criteria, they might appear last after a long list of more conventional criteria. Consider, for example, Professor 63's course syllabus:

> In evaluating each exam we will look for: (i) comprehensive identification of the issues raised by a fact pattern problem; (ii) demonstrated familiarity with related case law, and any relevant statutory provisions; (iii) clear and concise identification and application of the relevant legal test to the fact pattern given, including possible alternative arguments on both sides of the issues; and (iv) identification of any social/policy issues arising from legal adjudication of the fact pattern.[687]

This review suggests that the emphasis on rules and conventional legal reasoning predominates in many of the attitudes and pedagogical practices of Canadian common law Contracts professors. The picture, however, is not a homogeneous one. There are some instances in which realist attitudes appear to have inspired departures from convention in both teaching and evaluation.

Seeds of a Realist Pedagogy

Occasionally professors attempt, through their teaching, their choices regarding substance, in their course syllabi, and in their evaluations, to foreground or put into practice realistic attitudes. These examples demonstrate that it is possible to operationalize realist messages through pedagogical decisions and priorities. They reflect the seeds of an approach that deliberately aims to develop an eclectic set of argumentative techniques, as well as a wider variety of skills that gesture towards a more complete treatment of the lawyer as citizen.

---

686 [050], Interview, lines 388–401, 444–50.
687 [063], Syllabus, 2015–16, p 3.

Teaching Methods

Some professors use various techniques to encourage a different set of skills than conventional legal reasoning. Among these, problem solving and drafting exercises are perhaps the most common.

Problem Solving and Flipped Classrooms

Pedagogical techniques that focus on problem solving can be thought to respond to the functionalist idea that law is a purposive endeavour, and to engage policy analysis in a prospective, pragmatic way. In one sense, problem solving is a feature of all hypothetical fact-pattern exams, as the act of "advising" clients requires solving a legal problem using legal reasoning and conventional doctrine. In this section, however, I focus on the few instances in which professors attempt to take the problem-solving objective further.

One example is when professors record a video of themselves delivering a conventional lecture on substantive areas of the law and have students watch this outside class, reserving class time for small group problem exercises. Some people refer to this as a "flipped" classroom because it reverses the conventional division whereby class time is for lecturing and any group work is to occur outside of class.[688] A few instructors in my study articulate the desire to do this, but, with one exception, the use of flipped classroom remains aspirational. Professor 37 "dream[s] of doing a flipped classroom"; Professor 24 is "trying to progress toward" it in order to use the classroom as "a forum for discussion as opposed to information transfer"; and Professor 31 is "interested" in doing one to increase "active learning," but is waiting for administrative support to do so.[689]

The exception is indeed exceptional. Since 1998 one professor (whom I will identify as Professor X to avoid revealing this person's identity at other points in this book) has been "using technology to bring [students] together into small groups" using a case method based on the "business school model." Professor X videorecords a lecture and develops an elaborate set of case materials around which students, in small groups, submit a discussion document prior to class. In class, one representative of each group serves as discussion leader, and Professor X

688 See e.g. Lakmal Abeysekera & Phillip Dawson, "Motivation and Cognitive Load in the Flipped Classroom: Definition, Rationale and a Call for Research" (2015) 34 Higher Education Research & Development 1 at 1.

689 [037], Interview, line 667; [024], Interview, lines 125, 111–12; [031], Interview, lines 505–20.

coaches the students through comparing their approaches to the problems. Professor X has experimented with different formats over the years, at times bringing in practising lawyers, but these core elements remain the same. Professor X describes one version of it as follows:

> [Students] hand in the response paper, so now I have fifteen papers coming in ... I circulate those fifteen papers to the whole class. So now you all worked on the same problem and you saw your problem and you know it very well, hopefully, because you chatted about it inside your group. Now you see everyone else's solutions ... So now we have fifteen spokespersons in the class, so now I've got a seminar ... I'm no longer running the class ...
>
> [I will say], "You and you came out to a different response. What's going on? Talk to each other ... Why did you go that way? What facts did you focus on? What context did you put this in?" The assignments are always a bogus memo from a principal, coming out saying, "A client just came in the door. This is what they did. This is what they told us ... This is the information we have. What do you think?"[690]

Rather than transmitting substantive information and modelling legal reasoning, the professor acts as coach to draw out the students' own approach to problem solving. This interpretation is consistent with Professor X's high regard for the students: "They love the challenge ... This model ... lets them run."[691]

Another professor, a former student of Professor X, uses a similar method, drawing on the US-based "case file method."[692] And another deploys a similar strategy in assignments, producing extensive case materials around which legal memo exercises are designed.[693]

Drafting

Drafting is prototypically the solicitor's skill. It involves a prospective and planning attitude and, if done at a conceptual (rather than technical) level, develops the ability to think about clients' purposes and anticipate problems. Drafting also might involve understanding and responding to requirements elucidated in case law, but even then the intellectual task, however analytical, has a pragmatic element. It also

---

690 [X], Interview, lines 835–7, 888–913.

691 *Ibid*, lines 1053–60.

692 This professor uses the materials from casefilemethod.com, associating them with Professor X (lines 414–45, "I used them myself when I was in Contracts").

693 [014], Interview, lines 245–306; [014], Research Memorandum Assignment, Fall 2012, pp 9–23.

emphasizes the importance of attention to detail – not just linguistic detail, but the detail of the context in which the drafting problem is situated. For the most part, the professors in my study include few drafting exercises and few examples of actual contracts other than the excerpts that appear in the cases themselves. A few, however, experiment with each of these, and in these instances they tend to communicate the importance of a different set of priorities than the mainstream focus on doctrinal rules and reasoning by analogy.

Professor 12, for example, asks students to redraft an exclusion clause that was at issue in the Supreme Court of Canada *Tercon* case.[694] Professor 47, at the time of our interview, had just assigned an "evaluative drafting assignment" for the first time in forty years, describing it as follows:

> I'm giving a fairly simple problem, an outline of "you must read these five cases before you attempt to solve this problem, from the casebook. What I want you to do is to draft your way around for one side's perspective or the other. Give me a clause of not more than six lines in length, six or eight lines in length, to deal with this issue" ...
>
> The great problem of Contracts is there's a lot of abstract discussion. What we need to do is have a way to find the students solve a concrete problem, or to show them how to solve a concrete problem.[695]

Professor 20 makes some "modest attempts at contract drafting" of sale and purchase agreements, having students "swap" their drafts to "respond to whether they would agree with [the other student's] clause, and how they'd want to change [it]." Professor 32 brings in a practitioner to teach "a class on contract drafting, or contracts in the real world." Professor 30 spends "two or three classes" looking at different types of contract, because it is "important to see a contract from that real-world perspective."[696]

The most extensive use of drafting happens with Professor 49, who dedicates half of the entire course to it: "In the second term, we draft contracts – that's all we do." Students begin with a negotiation exercise developed

694 [012], Interview, lines 503–15, referring to *Tercon Contractors Ltd v British Columbia (Minister of Transportation & Highways)*, 2010 SCC 4, [2010] 1 SCR 69.

695 [047], Interview, lines 677–99.

696 [020], Interview, lines 350–60; [032], Interview, lines 98–104; [030], Interview, lines 225–38 ("The reality is – when students go into practice, ... 99.9 per cent of times, they're either going to ... be *concluding* a contract, or resolving some question arising out of the *application* of a contract, or settling a *dispute* over a contract – but *rarely* will in fact they go to court").

at Harvard on oil price negotiation, and then students "draft a confidentiality agreement, a licensing agreement, and then an outsourcing agreement." Drafting exercises comprise 60 per cent of the final grade, and the third objective of the course underscores and places in bold the goal that students will be able to "apply [contract] principles in practice."[697]

Course Syllabi and Expressions of Teaching

Professors also occasionally discuss their teaching in ways that suggest they are genuinely trying to incorporate certain realist attitudes. For example, Professor 54 starts each section with a discussion of the underlying rationales that the rules are "striving to achieve," and prepares for class by researching policy. Professor 39, who says elsewhere that policy really only comes in at the beginning and end of the course, actually includes a "policy issue" for each case studied. Professor 42 prepares for class not by summarizing "subject matter or ... doctrine," but by seeding and anticipating exchanges with particular students:

> [M]y classroom notes don't say very much about the subject matter or the doctrine. They tell me who to ask which question to and then how to build on it. It's like the script for a play ... [They differ] from one year to the next ... What I *try* to do is make a provocative statement that builds on something or other that Mr Smith had said before, such that he will be *compelled without being named* to come forward.[698]

Professor 28 gets students to think as policy thinkers through classroom discussion, asking students, "What would you do? ... How would you respond to this issue? [Is] there a need for legislation? What would it look like?" There is a policy question on the exam "every time" reflecting the policy questions explored in class. In "skill and comprehension outcomes," Professor 35's course syllabus includes "legal reasoning," which involves both "making an assessment about what the law IS on a given topic" and, "where appropriate, making an argument about what law SHOULD BE, i.e. why the law should change in a given direction." Professor 58, who seems to incorporate backwards reasoning into teaching, "invite[s]" students, in the course syllabus, to "read the materials for this course with a vigilant eye for doctrinal classifications

---

697 [049], Interview, lines 19–32, 110–229; [049], Syllabus, 2012–13, p 2. See Harvard Law School, Program on Negotiation, "Oil Pricing Exercise", online: https://www.pon.harvard.edu/shop/oil-pricing-exercise-3/.

698 [054], Interview, lines 211–15; [039], Interview, lines 726–30; [042], Interview, lines 726–45.

that do violence to the messiness of human interaction." One class's objectives include "identify[ing] the legislative policy objectives in declaring surrogacy agreements unenforceable."[699]

Occasionally a professor's pedagogical philosophy reflects an iconoclasm reminiscent of the realist attack on the "jurisprudence of forms, concepts, and rules," and maps neatly onto the desire, detailed above, to disabuse students of their preconceptions about law. This is the case with Professor 27:

> [O]ne of my [former] colleagues ... who studied with Wittgenstein ... told me that education consists in largely taking furniture out of the mind, not putting furniture in. So it's disabusing people of their preconceptions, trying to get received wisdom, ... the commercial, crass, ... talk-radio view of the world out of people's brains ... No matter how well educated, ... people come with the preconception of law as a bunch of rules ... And it turns out it doesn't work that way at all ...
>
> [Northrop] Frye's got the most *radical* view of education ... that I have believed in deeply for a long time ... The idea is that in some sense ... professors are like *drug pushers* ... People in the modern world ... are ... *locked into* extremely conventional, mass-market, non-critical, conventional, what's-on-TV, what's-popular [attitudes] ... [They have] *never* taken charge of their own thinking [and] don't have the capacity for critical self-engagement with the world. And that's what education is ... He has this wonderful line ... "If governments really knew what I did in class they wouldn't let me do it because I'd be like smuggling kids *dope*!" That is, [education] actually blows their mind. But blows it in the sense that they're taking charge of their own thinking rather than just being a *consumer* of prepackaged goods.[700]

In this excerpt, a critical understanding of education coincides with a desire to critique a prepackaged understanding about law. We see an analogous concern in the choices some professors make about substance.

Decisions regarding Substance

A small number of professors assign readings in Contracts that are critical of legal education more broadly. The most common of these is Duncan Kennedy's famous article on the reproduction of hierarchy. This is

699 [028], Interview, lines 451–68; [035], Syllabus, 2015–16, p 2; [058], Interview, lines 447–9; [058], Syllabus, 2007–8, p 1; [058], Calendar and Learning Objectives, 2007–08, p 12.

700 [027], Interview, lines 71–90, 140–90.

a noteworthy piece to include in a first-year Contracts course because, other than some passing allusions and unlike other of Kennedy's major works, the subject matter is not about contract law per se, but rather about the ideological content of law school as a whole.[701] Including it thus signals a desire for students to critically self-reflect on the broader enterprise of legal education. Professor 25 used to include the article at the end of the course because it might "resonate" with students and help them "see the forest." Professor 64 assigns it at the beginning of the course to help students "start evaluating more critically their legal education ... and start thinking about *what* they would like as legal professionals and how they can construct their education."[702]

In an analogous fashion, Professor 37 concludes the course every year with a discussion of Ian Macneil's article, "Whither Contracts," getting the students to reflect on whether six learning objectives that Macneil outlines were achieved in the course. This is part of a broader critical strategy to get students to ask, "Why do we have a course called Contracts? Is there something we can really put in this box?"[703] Professors commonly assign supplemental readings, often specifically to highlight realist perspectives or to counteract the perceived shortcomings of the casebooks. For example, Professor 33 seeks to supplement the "weak section on the ... explicit role of public policy and morality in *Ben-Ishai & Percy*, and expose students to the themes of sex, race, and power in a more detailed way than the introduction does."[704]

---

701 Kennedy, "Legal Education and the Reproduction of Hierarchy", *supra* note 61 at 594 (exemplifying a "hot case" as one in which "an Appalachian farm family ... rent[s] their land for strip mining, with a promise to restore it to its original condition once the coal has been extracted, and then reneging on the promise"; the reference is almost certainly to *Peevyhouse, supra* note 387). See Kennedy, "Form and Substance", *supra* note 60.

702 [025], Interview, lines 459–73; [064], Interview, lines 208–16.

703 [037], Interview, lines 365–94. See *supra* note 514 and accompanying text for a survey of other professors who include Macneil as a supplement to other readings. The Macneil article is the final chapter of all editions of *Swan*.

704 [033], Interview, lines 240–56, 324–57. See also [006], Interview, lines 67–124 (insufficient problems and exercises in all Canadian casebooks); [009], Interview, lines 106–49 ("I always like to find opportunities to talk about context-based, practice-based application of what we're talking about"); [010], Interview, lines 200–43 (providing more contemporary examples than in *Ben-Ishai & Percy* to appeal to students' sense of relevance); [021], Interview, lines 556–608 (filling in key moments missed when some cases taken out of *Ben-Ishai & Percy*); [017], Interview, lines 109–203 (providing more context, more contemporarily relevant examples, and more gendered material than in *Waddams*); [027], Interview, lines 621–49 (providing extended excerpts to teach the cases more as "parables" in contrast to the editing in *Waddams* that "strip[s] the guts out of cases"); [035], Interview, lines 616–37

Occasionally a professor will choose to switch casebooks to better reflect a realistic attitude:

> [Angela Swan] said to me something that resonated ... based on my experience in practice, which was that the issues that we focus [on] ... in the *Boyle & Percy* approach ... put emphasis on the wrong things ... [T]echnical issues of contract formation, which in the vast majority of cases ... are not issues at all. And that the much more complex and indeed for that reason socially important ... issues are ... related to damages, and remedies more generally ... I decided ... that I would investigate using [*Swan*,] and after looking at it, was convinced that it was a better tool for teaching contracts to students in a way that would allow them to appreciate not only what was important about contracts, but ... would give them a *better sense* of the nature of contract law rules.[705]

Finally, not surprisingly, some professors opine specifically about the importance of teaching remedies, whether that means placing it first or suggesting to students that remedies "drives" analysis.[706] And while in almost every course legislation plays a relatively minor role, a number of professors make the point of including some legislation, often consumer protection legislation, in order to explore the "history and [political] rationale of legislation," provoke a "value discussion," show the "context to [a] case, where it came from, and that more can be done with these issues," avoid "unduly emphasizing case law," or understand how the legislature acts to "level the playing field."[707]

(without a "conscious effort" to include "big picture issues," they would be missed because *Ben-Ishai & Percy* "doesn't really raise those issues at all ... and that would be one of my minor disappointments").

705 [013], Interview, lines 55–78. See also [048], Interview, lines 48–50 ("The reason I switched to [*Swan*] was that the earlier versions of *Milner* and ... *Waddams* ... didn't provide much social context for the subject ... I went back to *Waddams* because it started to do that as well").

706 [013], Interview, lines 73–87 ("the ... problem with teaching offer and acceptance [first] is you communicate to students a sense that ... contract law is just a sort of a puzzle [and that] ... there are ... black and white rules that apply to give you determinate answers. And to the extent that you start by looking at remedies where the issues are complicated and the answers are not obvious, ... you give students a better starting point"); [051], Interview, lines 125–44 ("Even when I start with offer [and] acceptance, I spend ... two classes [first] on remedies [to show how] different contractual analyses will give you a different remedial outcome ... From the legal realist perspective, to what extent is the remedy *driving* the legal analysis?").

707 [053], Interview, lines 469–89 (consumer protection and other legislation); [064], Interview, lines 525–6 (pledge agreement legislation); [028], Interview, lines 219–20

Evaluation

Some professors try to evaluate on some of the realist themes. We see this in selected examples of different types of evaluation, examination questions, and criteria. Nine professors describe having a significant writing assignment outside the final examination. These range from commenting on "proposals for legislative reforms in contract law" to providing commentary and critical thoughts on a scholarly journal about contract law. One professor has "four or five interim assignments that emphasize different kinds of writing or counseling or synthetic skills."[708]

Twelve professors mention in interview that they include an essay question on the exam; these range from "policy questions" to "law reform questions" that ask students to "do a critical assessment of ... an area of law ... in a normative context."[709] Such essay questions might ask students specifically to evaluate the classical theory of contracts, as Professor 56 does with reference to Patrick Atiyah or Grant Gilmore, and as Professor 52 does with relation to Friedrich Hayek.[710]

Some professors articulate the idea that the fact-pattern question *itself* tests students' critical thinking and engagement with policy. Thus Professor 67 tells students that the fact pattern will examine them on "being critical about the law," requiring them to "go behind what's obvious and what you're told, both in terms of theory and in terms of the facts."[711] Professor 48 specifically tries to incorporate policy and social

---

(consumer protection and debt collection legislation); [032], Interview, lines 763–4 (consumer protection legislation); [050], Interview, lines 372–86.

708 [056], Interview, lines 228–9; [024], Interview, lines 577–88; [042], Interview, lines 251–3. See [022], Interview, lines 633–4 ("I've always had an essay assignment. It's just been traditionally required to have that").

709 [028], Interview, line 462; [051], Interview, lines 492–4.

710 [056], Interview, lines 214–23 ("[I] focus on the broader themes ... The kind of *Death of Contract* quotes ... In my last exam [I] had something by Atiyah who describes ... the classic contract theory of the nineteenth century where the courts just follow what parties have written ... [I asked,] 'Is that ... an accurate description of what happened then and what happens now? Please compare'"); [052], Interview, lines 236–46:

> I gave them a quote from Friedrich Hayek which discussed the conditions that exist in the great society, among them freedom of contract. Then I posed them the question ... "Hayek espouses this classical liberal theory of contract law where the purpose of this institution is to allow people to chart their own paths – that they're free to contract as they so choose. But we've ... examined various doctrines and [those] principles that seem to undercut that" ... I ask the students to identify ... doctrines that override or temper ... the predominance of the *pure* classical liberal theory.

711 [067], Handwritten notes of untranscribed, unrecorded interview, p 6.

context into the problems themselves, preferring this method over an essay question: "When you write a paper [from] a feminist analysis of those husband-and-wife cases ... that's not making them think of this as really part of how they should be thinking about contracts all the time. *If you can integrate it into problems*, it's much better."[712] Professor 35 states in the course syllabus that the "critical reflection skills" of "identify[ing] the political and intellectual assumptions that underpin Canadian contract law doctrine, ... critically reflect[ing] on the contradictions and tensions between and amongst them," and "critically engaging with the consequences of those assumptions and tensions for parties ... and for the development of contract law in Canada" are "primarily assessed through the midterm and final exams." In a question that appears to integrate specific examples with a theoretical idea, Professor 58 asks students to "assess [one scholar's] thesis on the normative importance of facts in light of materials covered in the course," specifying that "the objective is not to reproduce the rule in the cases ... [but rather] to identify the role that these factual elements assume."[713]

Occasionally professors describe their assessment criteria as including an engagement with policy or critical thinking. For example, Professor 54 includes "making some reflection on policy" at the end of a long list of factors that make the "best answer." Professor 37 describes how the best answers on a recent exam came up with "imaginative solutions" after having thought in a "creative and critical way." And Professor 58, in a detailed examination grading memo, writes that the "best answers" to a question that asked students to write a "reasoned dissent"

> combined a careful, close reading of the dispute ... and mastery of larger principles ... The most convincing dissent persuades and convinces at the level of the parties to the particular dispute and on bigger ideas: it demonstrates that the majority judges have misunderst[ood] both the facts *and* the key ideas. I think we discussed in class once, in the context of persuasive legal argumentation, the idea that you would make submissions on several different levels for maximum persuasiveness.[714]

---

712 [048], Interview, lines 438–42.

713 [035], Syllabus, 2015–16, p 2; [058], Final Exam, April 2008, p 2.

714 [054], Interview, line 189; [037], Interview, lines 301–15 ("The *best* answers didn't just go along with the kneejerk reaction path of 'Oh! This is the prof trying to see whether I know the law on exclusion of liability clauses. This is a prof trying to make me *think!*' Right? Think outside the obvious boundaries to much more *imaginative* solutions"); [058], Memorandum to Class Re: April Final Examination, May 2008, pp 2–3.

In these examples, we see the seeds of an attempt to internalize theoretical or critical perspectives, or factors such as context or policy, into one definition of the privileged core of the Contracts course: that which is evaluated. Moreover, in the questions that require students to integrate these factors into the exercise of legal argumentation, we also catch a glimpse of how they might be operationalized in legal reasoning. Nevertheless, however illustrative these examples are, they still represent the minority. The overwhelming impression is that most pedagogical choices reinforce a conventional idea of legal reasoning, one that is predicated upon an understanding of rules with a relatively fixed content and that emphasizes the line-drawing exercise of determining relevance through reasoning by analogy.

SUMMARY AND CONCLUSION

When Canadian common law Contracts professors describe and elaborate on their beliefs about law, most espouse a strong commitment to realist and critical attitudes. These include the notion that the rules of contract doctrine do not determine legal results and are the products of numerous contextual factors that ultimately render them mutable and contingent. Professors underscore the importance of broader factors emanating from outside the realm of distinctively legal discourse, such as judicial personality, political preferences, the contextual details of factual scenarios, social relations, and non-state normativity. Moreover, Canadian common law Contracts professors largely consider critical and theoretical perspectives that seek to evaluate law from an external reference point to be integral to a complete understanding of law as a social phenomenon. In the embrace of both underlying factors and external perspectives, Canadian common law Contracts professors seem to have internalized many of the lessons of American legal realism and its heirs, making detailed references to the canonical authors, but also expressing the ideas in their own words and personal ways.

For the most part, however, Canadian common law Contracts professors do not translate these well-developed and internalized attitudes into practice, either in the way they describe legal reasoning or in their pedagogical choices. Instead legal reasoning and pedagogy appear to operationalize a different set of attitudes about law – those that emphasize the solidity of rules and the importance of distinguishing the relevant from the irrelevant with reference to an internally coherent set of rules. The methodological and pedagogical commitments of the majority thus map more cleanly onto the commitments about law that only a minority – the "champions" of formalism – directly articulate.

These commitments emphasize the autonomy of law by insisting on its distinctive grammar, which not only constitutes a descriptive claim about how law speaks in its "own way," but also bolsters law's legitimacy by providing justification for imposing sanctions in some cases but not others. In teaching and evaluating legal reasoning, most Canadian common law Contracts professors take doctrine seriously, both in the sense that the content of the rules matters – rules are no "pretty playthings" – and in that judicially articulated reasons for decision also matter – they are no "mere rhetoric."

The primary story, therefore, is of a disjuncture between the attitudes expressed about law and the attitudes revealed by the practices of legal reasoning and teaching. This disjuncture recalls the tendency Elizabeth Mertz observed in US Contracts classes to marginalize considerations of policy vis-à-vis the "carefully disciplined core focus" of legal reasoning.[715] It also signals a distance from the claims by Kennedy and Fisher that American legal thought is "an eclectic practice built from the methodological sediment laid down in successive projects of wholesale criticism and reform." The methodological sediment of legal reasoning expressed through Canadian common law Contracts teaching does not seem particularly stratified, nor does it seem much to be a product of the realist "assault on the jurisprudence of forms, concepts, and rules."[716] The realist attitudes are alive and well, but they do not appear largely to be operationalized into discrete forms of reasoning and argumentation. Even less frequently do professors thoroughly design the substance of their courses, their teaching methods, or their evaluation techniques to put into practice their realist and critical beliefs about law.

Accordingly the realist and critical perspectives appear to be suspended, rather than dissolved, in the Canadian legal consciousness. The ideas perform a powerful theoretical function in helping professors describe their attitudes about law, but for the most part these theoretical insights remain disembodied from the epistemological acculturation of making lawyers. These ideas do not penetrate the structural grammar of law or displace the conventional categories and practices for teaching Contracts. Indeed, to the extent that the methodological

715 Mertz defines policy as "whether law operates in a just manner, whether certain legal decisions were motivated by class interests or other extralegal concerns, whether particular social conditions caused or resulted from specific legal decisions," and further writes that in her study policy is "marginal not only in terms of discursive structure, but also because these policy discussions never impart any real analytic standards for assessing one story against another ... When social context comes in the door, structure, standards, and rigor exit" (*supra* note 38 at 77–9).

716 Kennedy & Fisher, "Introduction", *supra* note 27 at 3, 10.

and pedagogical choices – the prevalence of hypothetical fact patterns, the "reasoning by analogy" formula, the final exam, the choice to adopt or follow the order of a casebook, to name just a few examples – are experienced and portrayed as natural or obvious, they reveal even more deeply the tenacity of the classical, formalist vision of law – what Thomas Grey describes as "Langdell's secret triumph":

> Categorical schemes have a power that is greatest when it is least noticed. They channel the attention of those who use them, structuring experience into the focal and the peripheral. In doing so, they influence judgment much as the agenda for a meeting influences the results of its deliberations. Heedless of this power of categories, modern legal theorists have not supplanted the classical ordering but have left it to half-survive in the back of lawyers' minds and the front of the law school curriculum, where it can shape our thinking through its unspoken judgments – Langdell's secret triumph ...
>
> [L]egal discourse largely retains its orthodox form. On official occasions, lawyers and judges still mostly talk in terms of rules and principles, presupposing right answers even to hard questions of law and disfavoring explicit arguments of policy ...
>
> [O]ne must recall and try again to feel the pull of the simple tenets of Langdell's creed: law is a science; its materials are all in law books; behind the mass of those materials are a few simple principles; and discovery of those principles will allow us to "master the ever-tangled skein of human affairs."[717]

Replace, in the first paragraph of that quotation, "modern legal theorists" with "Canadian common law Contracts professors," and one arrives at a somewhat caricatured, but by no means wildly inaccurate, account of this chapter's primary story. Canadian common law Contracts teaching appears to rely largely on classical categorical schemes of subject matter and legal reasoning. The result is the perpetuation of a discourse focused on "rules and principles" that "disfavor[s] explicit arguments of policy" by excluding them from legal reasoning proper and by deeming them insufficiently worthy of rigorous cultivation or evaluation.[718]

---

717 Grey, *supra* note 96 at 49–52.

718 The tenacity of these conventional categories, and the force with which they are self-perpetuated within the profession, should not be underestimated. See Robert W Gordon, "The Case For (and Against) Harvard", Review of *Logic and Experience: The Origin of Modern American Legal Education* by William P LaPiana (1995) 93 Mich L Rev 1231 [Gordon, Review of LaPiana] at 1244–5: "Practicing lawyers almost never appreciate new theories when they are proposed, dismissing them scornfully

But Langdell's secret triumph has handed down not only the category of Contracts and its doctrinal subdivisions, but also, crucially, the pedagogical formula of focusing on cases. The emphasis on adjudication in Canadian common law Contracts teaching and casebooks perpetuates a focus on the present, fixed content of rules and on discerning relevance in legal reasoning. It has also spawned the tenacious fact-pattern exam and its concomitant reinforcement of the litigator's and judge's perspectives. The case method, with all of these implications, has become the norm. As Professor 61 says, it is just "one of those *core elements* of the first-year program that *should* be taught."[719]

The picture of a formalist centre of gravity with realist convictions at the periphery would, however, be incomplete. It would give short

---

as airhead speculation. All the same, the new theories soak gradually into the marrow of lawyers' bones, and, in time, lawyers come to rely on them without being aware of it. Lawyers bought the new treatises ... for their encyclopedic collections of cases; but, with the cases, they absorbed the categories and principles as well." Gordon then goes on to cite Grey's formulation of "Langdell's secret triumph" (*supra* note 96).

This tenacity has also been observed in the British context. As David Sugarman wrote a generation ago, summarizing the observations made about the "textbook tradition" in English law teaching in the second half of the nineteenth century ("'A Hatred of Disorder': Legal Science, Liberalism and Imperialism" in Peter Fitzpatrick, ed, *Dangerous Supplements: Resistance and Renewal in Jurisprudence* (Concord, MA: Pluto Press, 1991) 34 at 34):

> The "black letter" tradition continues to overshadow the way we teach, write and think about law. Its categories and assumptions are still the standard diet of most first-year law students and they continue to organize law textbooks and casebooks. Stated baldly it assumes that although law might appear to be irrational, chaotic, and particularistic, if one digs deep enough and knows what one is looking for, then it will soon become evident that the law is an internally coherent and unified body of rules. This coherence and unity stems from the fact that law is grounded in, and logically derived from, a handful of general principles, and that whole subject areas such as contract and torts are distinguished by some common principles or elements which fix the boundaries of the subject. The exposition and systematization of these general principles and the techniques required to find and to apply both them and the rules that they underpin, are largely what legal education and scholarship are all about ...
>
> Despite the variety of producers and consumers of legal discourse, it is what judges say and the supposed needs of the legal profession as narrowly defined, that have had the greatest magnetic pull over the nature and form of legal education and scholarship. Other aspects that are equally important to understanding law, such as legislation, the operation of law in practice, as well as the history, theory, morality and politics of law, are ignored or marginalized.

719 [061], Interview, lines 955–7.

shrift to the genuine and deep commitments to realism outlined in the first part of this chapter and to the attempts, outlined in the second and third parts, by a minority of professors to reconstitute legal reasoning through realist influences and to adapt their pedagogical practices, including evaluation, accordingly. A more accurate picture would admit the coexistence of two powerful forces in the Canadian legal consciousness while also specifying their asymmetry. This observation very closely parallels the analysis of the Canadian common law Contracts casebooks in Chapter 3. Taken together, the views and practices of both editors and teachers lead to the generalization that Canadian legal thought might be characterized by an eclecticism of largely realist theory coexisting with a homogeneous, largely formalist methodology.

In the concluding chapter, I interpret this apparent disjuncture through three different frames. The first is loosely one of legal theory: I explore the extent to which realism and formalism are incompatible theories of law and the extent to which they are bundled up in one another. Is there an account of law that can render the coexistence of these apparently contradictory views coherent? Although this sounds like a philosophical task for the ages, I approach it modestly, using data from the project to explore whether Canadian common law Contracts professors' words shine a light on the compatibility, coexistence, or incoherence of realist and formalist commitments. The second frame explores the "pedagogical effectiveness" rationale – the idea that pedagogical agency might account for the apparent inconsistencies. Finally, I explore how certain structural features of legal education might help explain the gap. Do constraints or cultures within institutions, the profession, or the broader market for legal services condition or explain the apparent disjunction between what Canadian common law Contracts professors say they believe and what their teaching practices and descriptions of legal reasoning reflect?

Chapter Six

Transcending Langdell: Agency, Structure, and Transformation in Contemporary Legal Education

This book has examined two perennial tensions in legal education. In Chapter 4 I explored how the conventional opposition of theory and practice in the discourse on legal education does not align with Canadian common law Contracts professors' accounts of their aspirations for teaching. Although the professors in my study might reproduce elements of the conventional narrative when speaking abstractly about their role or that of the law school in general, when they describe their own teaching objectives and practices, they overwhelmingly express the idea that theory ought directly to inform practice. To a lesser extent, they also express how practice informs theory, and thus they reflect the idea that theory and practice are mutually reinforcing concepts. The near consensus that theory and critical perspectives are valuable because they produce "better lawyers" serves to dismantle the conventional dichotomy between theory and practice, and also suggests that an emerging narrative – that legal education can integrate and balance theory and practice – one day might come to subvert the traditional story.

Chapters 3 and 5 complicated the near consensus that theory translates into making better lawyers. Those chapters delved into the substantive theoretical ideas about law that Contracts professors and casebook editors espouse, and compared these ideas to those conveyed by teaching practices and the presentation of legal reasoning. Those chapters observed how, despite a commitment to an eclectic range of critical and realist theories about law and the strong influence of American authors, Canadian common law Contracts teaching largely privileges a methodology that is homogeneous, purportedly autonomous, and serves ultimately to marginalize the considerations of policy, context, and politics that professors propositionally claim are central to an understanding of law. Professors do not seem to translate these theoretical concerns into their understanding of legal reasoning, and do not appear to privilege them in their teaching materials or practices.

Taking those two chapters together, we begin to see how Canadian common law Contracts teaching reveals a deep gap between aspiration and reality. The aspirations are multiple. One is to convey a vision of law as contingent, grounded in uncertainty, connected to contextual factors, and expansively inclusive of "external" perspectives, including politics and policy. Another is to translate theoretical ideas into an operationalized vision of legal practice. If these two aspirations were jointly met, we would encounter descriptions of legal reasoning that internalize and operationalize the critical and realist ideas. This integration could be achieved both by incorporating the reasoning techniques of other disciplines into an expanded set of argument-types for the lawyer, and by modelling a set of other skills, such as planning, negotiation, problem solving, and policy analysis, that in turn would both cultivate an eclectic toolkit of legal reasoning and model to students a wide range of "law jobs."[720] Instead the primary practice of professional acculturation that we observe – inculcating legal reasoning ("thinking like a lawyer") – implicitly marginalizes the central tenets of the realist and critical theories, emphasizing the determination of relevance largely through a self-referential, internally closed system of rules and precedents as the key reasoning and argumentative technique, and privileges the judge or barrister in the conception of legal professional.

How best to make sense of this tension? One possibility is that Contracts professors and casebook editors conceive a conceptual compatibility between realist and formalist ideas. This compatibility manifests either in a theoretical linkage that connects these ideas under a unified view of law or in intellectual attempts to reconcile the coexistence of two apparently contradictory ideas. To the extent this account is compelling, the apparent failure of the aspirations becomes less acute, because the gap between theoretical convictions and manifestations of practice is either smaller or nonexistent.

Alternatively, deliberate pedagogical choices might account for the apparent disjuncture. On this account, casebook editors emphasize in their treatment of substance only a partial vision of what they assert propositionally in their introductions – and professors emphasize conventional legal reasoning and substance – out of a

720 *Cf.* KN Llewellyn, "The Normative, the Legal and the Law-Jobs: The Problem of Juristic Method" (1940) 49 Yale LJ 1355.

desire for pedagogical effectiveness. This account, while not eradicating or minimizing the gap between aspiration and reality, nevertheless places it in a more positive light by acknowledging that conceptual coherence might have to make way for the pragmatic realities of teaching, and that unless professors teach students to walk before they can run, students might end up being able to do neither.

Both these ideas – explored in each of the first two parts of this chapter – can be thought of as individual "agency" accounts of the gap between aspiration and reality, as they derive from professors' intellectual formulations or pedagogical choices. Yet while each account surfaces in the words of the professors in my study, neither is wholly explanatory. Instead, external factors might explain the discrepancy between aspiration and reality. On this view, structural features of legal education – pressures from within law faculties, including from students, and from outside law faculties, including from the profession and markets – play an integral role in shaping the substance, method, and emphasis of Contracts teaching. I explore this structural account in the third part of this chapter.

THE CONCEPTUAL COMPATIBILITY OF REALIST AND FORMALIST IDEAS

Realist Ideas Serve the Rule of Law?

Some law professors write or speak in a way that suggests that certain realist ideas and some preoccupations of legal formalists might be more compatible than contradictory. In this iteration, we see the idea that the realist concern with identifying underlying factors for legal decision making actually upholds the rule of law by strengthening the capacity for rational decision making.

A chief example of this appears in the preface to Waddams's textbook. There, he writes that "rational decision making is strengthened, not weakened, by open recognition of conflicting values."[721] Put more fully, the rule-of-law value that law ought to treat everyone equally requires that there be rational distinctions to justify differential treatment. Adjudication is the pre-eminent legal process for cultivating this rationality, and thus should be the focus of legal education. Understanding legal rationality requires not only understanding

721 Waddams, Preface to 1st ed text, *supra* note 297 at viii.

what judges say, but *also* (not instead)[722] what they do. As Waddams puts it:

> It is better to recognize competing values, even if that recognition appears to involve a difficult and uncertain balance, than to pursue certainty by adopting a rule that suppresses important countervailing principles. Such pursuit is self-defeating, for important values are rarely permanently suppressed. The rule that is supposed to achieve clarity and certainty becomes riddled with exceptions, judicial and statutory, devised to avoid injustice, and leads in the end to the loss of the very certainty that was supposed to be its chief merit.[723]

In this vision, there is no contradiction between a realistic tendency to understand values underlying judicial decisions and a desire for judicial rule making to attain "certainty." One serves the other.

In a similar vein, John McCamus – a contributing editor to both *Waddams* and *Ben-Ishai & Percy*, as well as the author of the contract law textbook most highly recommended by the participants in my study – emphasizes how realist preoccupations with flexibility and policy can serve to produce a more stable and certain doctrine. McCamus's preface emphasizes the common law's "adaptability to changing social and economic circumstances and its ability to reformulate doctrine in light of evolving professional attitudes and insights as to how the law can be improved." This emphasis on adaptability is clearly intended to further the "main objective" of his textbook, which is "to provide an accurate account of the principles and doctrines of the law of contract as it is currently understood and practiced in the common law provinces of Canada."[724]

Professor McCamus describes his own teaching in a way that more fully explains how policy thinking is beneficial to understanding doctrine:

---

722 Waddams, "Unconscionability in Contracts", *supra* note 300 at 1 ("My view is that the law of contract, when examined for what the judges do, *as well as* for what they say, shows that relief from contractual obligations is in fact widely and frequently given on the ground of unfairness") [emphasis added].

723 Waddams, Preface to 1st ed text, *supra* note 297 at vii–viii [emphasis added].

724 McCamus, *Law of Contracts*, *supra* note 376 at xxiii (Preface to the First Edition). McCamus has edited the chapter on "Representations and Terms; Classification and Consequences" since the first edition of *Boyle & Percy*. He also edits a chapter in *Waddams* and makes contributions on the subject of restitution to a "number of chapters" (John D McCamus, Interview with author, 28 February 2014, lines 527–30) [attributed with permission].

[It is important for students] to consider whether the doctrine does in fact have a solid foundation in public policy. If it doesn't, it's likely to change. If it does, it's *unlikely* to change ...

I certainly tell the students that there's no real distinction between law and public policy. Law *is* an exercise in developing, implementing, and applying public policy choices to social activity, commercial activity, of various kinds... Understanding the ... basic architecture of the doctrine of promissory estoppel ... no doubt *rests* on the analysis of why [we] would give some effect to a promise that's relied upon – and was *intended* to be relied upon ... The two analytical tasks are quite deeply related, and it's never been my view that you could somehow teach the law without thinking about the policy aspects of it.[725]

Accordingly the underlying factors of policy and context ("changing social and economic circumstances") are considered not as a challenge to, but directly in service of, doctrine. As with Waddams, realistic insights serve to buttress the demands of a "solid" doctrine. The baseline commitment is that the rule of law requires that (1) there is a solid body of rules that (2) are applied equally to all people, requiring (3) a well-refined rationality to justify differential treatment in similar circumstances. (4) This rationality is best refined and developed through judicial reasoning; thus, its study should be the predominant activity of legal education. Realistic attitudes are important not because they *challenge* these tenets, but because they serve them: by elucidating and sharpening judicial reasoning and rationality, and by ensuring that the rules are "solidly founded."

This interpretation might very well explain some of the apparently contradictory statements in the casebooks, and it might also capture the attitudes of some Contracts professors. The emphasis on the "internal" policy factors, including those that have crystallized into principles, is another example of how the realist search for underlying factors directly serves the quest for the solidity of doctrine and bolsters the rule of law.[726] Declaring realism as being in the service of tenets championed by the formalists (doctrinal consistency, rule of law) makes it conceptually intelligible for a law professor to express attitudes about both simultaneously.

---

725 McCamus, Interview with author, 28 February 2014, lines 218–45 [attributed with permission].

726 See the discussion in Chapter 5 above under "Policy as Factors Effectively Internalized into Doctrine," pages 190–3 .

Absent, however, a full theorization that explains away the contrast between professed attitudes about law and the attitudes reflected in conceptions of legal reasoning and in teaching practices, there remain two other strategies – at the conceptual level – of accounting for their coexistence. On the one hand, professors are fully aware of their inconsistencies and "own" the contradiction. On the other, some might seek to reconcile their beliefs – not through a unified theory of law, but through a more partial and tentative account.

Owning Intellectual Contradiction

A number of professors do indeed explicitly acknowledge that they hold contradictory attitudes at the same time. Professor 42, for example, describes a "schizophrenic" adherence to divergent sets of ideas – actually labelling them "realist" and "formalist":

> We're in a way *conflicted*, since on the one hand we continue to pay lip service to the rule of law, which is something else that you get out of this conception of legal science. [This includes] the idea that judges doing *de*ductive reasoning from *in*ductively articulated principles are merely making the future like the past ... It's a conservative kind of approach to normativity ... And, at least in after-dinner speeches ... or in initiation rituals, like law school, we continue to [pay] a lot of credence to it. But again, there's a disconnect. Take the field trip to Bay Street, and as often as not you'll find folks engaged in long-term planning exercises, not adjudicative exercises, in respect of which – drafting a will, or incorporating a company, or preparing a trust instrument, or negotiating a contract, or doing tax planning – the role of law is invisible. [Doctrinal law] just doesn't matter with respect to those kinds of activities that constitute a very large proportion of what people do. Moreover, we have come to think that, at the same time as we have this thing called "rule of law," which is sort of a formalistic brake on law reform, ... we can do things with rules: that we can modify rules, adjust rules, and do social engineering. *It's virtually schizophrenic! We are, at one and the same time, formalists and realists!*[727]

Other professors describe their intellectual influences in ways that disclose simultaneous beliefs in very different philosophies of law. This arises most starkly in the interview with Professor 32 – the only other instance in which a professor uses the term "schizophrenic" to

727 [042], Interview, lines 630–52 [emphasis added].

describe his or her attitude. In this conversation, Professor 32 speaks at length about attempts to incorporate social context by inserting a "case in context" class four times throughout the year. Among the course objectives, which Professor 32 quotes aloud from the syllabus, is the goal that students "have ... a contextual understanding of the role and limits of contract in society through a basic familiarity with historical, theoretical, and socio-legal insights." Professor 32, moreover, incorporates Roderick Macdonald's *Lessons of Everyday Law* and Stewart Macaulay's work on relational contract theory into the course; legal pluralism figures prominently in the course and forms part of Professor 32's "theoretical orientation."[728] So, when I asked about Professor 32's theoretical commitments, I was shocked to hear not pluralist or socio-legal theories mentioned first, but rather the thinking of the Canadian formalist theorist, Ernest Weinrib. Consider the following exchange:

> [R:] Would you say your own thinking is ... influenced by any particular theoretical perspective?
>
> [Professor 32:] ... I'll probably be a bit schizophrenic in this regard.
>
> [R:] Why?
>
> [Professor 32:] In the sense that ... I really *get* and have a lot of sympathy for a kind of Weinribian corrective justice type of approach ... I find that very ... compelling intellectually. And so I *probably* find myself there. But ... that can't be the end of the story, and I don't think they argue that it should be the end of the story either.[729]

Perhaps revelatory of this "schizophrenia," Professor 32 is also one of the only professors to recommend both the formalist Fridman and the anti-formalist Swan & Adamski textbooks as "further readings" on the course syllabus.[730]

---

728 [032], Interview, lines 525–8, 106–7 (referring to Macdonald, *Lessons of Everyday Law*, *supra* note 515), 538–53 ("Contracts have various meanings in various places ... There can be different notions of what it means to contract, and ... there are different ways of enforcing a contract or not ... in maintaining a relationship ... It's a question of letting them know the big picture and the realities involved").

729 [032], Interview, lines 694–706.

730 [032], Syllabus, 2013–14, p 2 (recommending, as reference texts, Fridman, *The Law of Contract in Canada*, *supra* note 226 and Angela Swan & Jakub Adamski, eds, *Canadian Contract Law*, 3d ed (Markham, ON: LexisNexis, 2012)). One of the few similar instances is when Professor 14 recommends both *Corbin on Contracts*, *supra* note 117 and Williston, *Selection of Cases on the Law of Contracts*, *supra* note 117 ([014], Syllabus, 2015–16, p 5).

Reconciling Realism and Formalism

In-between owning an outright contradiction and conceiving realist ideas as being in the service of the rule of law is a somewhat milder claim that the opposing attitudes from realism and formalism can be reconciled by finding a middle ground between the two. A number of professors in my study take this approach.

In one particularly well articulated example, Professor 40 speaks about trying to find an "intermediate terrain" between the extremes of "ultra formalism and excessive antiformalism" that can "reconcile" the two polar approaches:

> I think there are two ... radical approaches to understanding law. One is the ultra formalist approach and one is a kind of no-holds-barred, anything goes, extreme, excessively antiformalist approach. And I think real critique, both external and immanent, *inhabits the territory between those two* ... [The] default presumption that a lot of people, including [myself, have is that law is an] internally coherent, immanently rational system ... A lot of people continue to ... retain residual attachments, fetishistic attachments, to this kind of an approach, even when they've been ... intellectually weaned off of it ... It's a sort of comfort food ... Another extreme is the excessively antiformalist approach ... It can manifest itself in the form of legal realism and early critical legal studies. It can manifest itself in the form of rational choice theories of various kinds as well ...
>
> I think *real critique tries to get a handle on the ... conceptually intermediate territory*, by which I mean the following: you've got certain organizing rules and principles, ... some established or semi-established, quasi-established, patterns of reasoning [and] argumentation that can be ... deployed ... But ... those don't actually gel together. They don't fuse in the form of a [gapless] system ... that defers or displaces all contradictions ...
>
> I try to ... teach them that ... there *is* something that is specifically legal, but the law is not wholly autonomous. It's not entirely independent of political economy, of socio-political dynamics, even of culture ... It's embedded in all of those things ... It's nourished by them and it in turn nourishes them as well ...
>
> Law isn't simply *anything* that we want it to be, but it's also not THE LAW in caps lock! It's somewhere in-between ... We need something that ... takes the best from both, and reconciles them in some more adequate account of how law functions.[731]

---

731 [040], Interview, lines 131–3, 311–76 [emphasis added]. See also *ibid*, lines 158–85 ("It's not simply as ... the old legal realists and first ... critical legal scholars would say ... But it's also not Weinribian ... Somewhere between the two").

A number of other professors describe their own attitudes as a mix of realist and formalist beliefs. Professor 56, for example, who takes a "realist, policy-driven" approach to justice, while arguing that "judicial arbitrariness should be bridled somehow and ... it's rule of law, not men," describes Professor 56's own ideas as a "weird concoction" of different traditions:

> I try to describe it at the beginning [as] trying to deal with cases on several levels, [trying] to keep the balls in the air ... Doing one thing, understand why they're doing it and at the same time being able to *critique* ... The culture is a bit different in Canada than it is in the United States ... There's also more attention to doctrinal detail, I would say, because ... the Canadian classroom is still more heavily influenced by *English* ideas of doctrine. It's not ... entirely American in the sense that ... all law is ... ridiculous – it's just policy, ... politics and whatnot. So I just try to strike a balance there ... in terms of intellectual works on contracts in the anglophone world. [I include Atiyah and Geoffrey Samuel] and ... [for a] very clear exposition of what cases say, I always liked McCamus here in Canada. That's ... the book I *love* – I really like best. And ... in terms of ... my *broader philosophy*, I studied with [a leading critical legal studies scholar]. So that ... helps you sometimes switch out of that doctrinal mode ... It's a *weird concoction*.[732]

Another way in which realism and formalism might be reconciled is to consider them as providing alternative perspectives, or sets of arguments, to be deployed selectively depending on the circumstances. Professor 1 does exactly this, aiming to cultivate the virtue of "lucidity" that includes

> the ability to see [realist and formalist] attitudes and ... be aware that [either of] these two points of view may be *determinative* at a given moment ... If one can alternate between these views, integrate them or simply understand them, one has a deeper understanding of law even though the mode of selecting among them may be random and spontaneous and it is not always possible to determine whether you are treating a problem from a realist or formalist perspective.[733]

Professor 1 goes so far as to suggest that the coexistence of realism and formalism expresses a truth about the law; the "ethical" reason for exposing students to both realism and formalism is to ensure that

732 [056], Interview, lines 111, 406–9, 511–41.
733 [001], Interview, lines 561–78 [translation from French].

Professor 1's teaching is not founded on a "lie." Jurists, Professor 1 writes, are trained to "use" realist and formalist points of view about contract: "neither is more or less true."[734]

In these multiple ways – constructing a unified account of the rule of law, entertaining simultaneously contradictory beliefs, or reconciling realism and formalism by finding a middle ground, mixture, or alternation – a conceptual frame might help account for the apparent tension between realist theories about law and formalist practices of reasoning and pedagogy.

These accounts of compatibility between realism and formalism, while grounded in the expressed views of the participants in my study, might nevertheless leave a residual unsatisfactory feeling. The critical project of legal realism, recall, was a "*wholesale* assault" on classical legal thought, part of a wider "generational revolt" against formalism. In its purest form, it serves to destabilize, not solidify, "forms, concepts, and rules."[735] The attempts above to render them compatible, whether the hard rule-of-law explanation or the softer explanations of reconciliation, sit uncomfortably with claims about the polemical and bellicose character of twentieth-century American legal thought. Such a qualification *might* be made somewhat plausible by positing a distinctively Canadian legal sensibility – one that places Canada on the middle ground between US scepticism and UK reverence for judicial reasoning, or, more broadly, that asserts a distinctively Canadian temperament for toleration, grounded in a history of admitting multiple legal traditions.[736] Even these cultural qualifications, however, would not obliterate the apparent incompatibility, at some deep conceptual level, of certain formalist and realist ideas. In the absence of any readily proffered philosophically complete reconciliation, therefore, resources

734 *Ibid*, lines 712–8, 653–67 [translation from French].

735 Kennedy & Fisher, "Introduction", *supra* note 27 at 10 [emphasis added]; Horwitz, *Transformation of American Law*, *supra* note 103 at 184. See also Grey, *supra* note 96 at 39, n 149 (citing Morton White, *Social Thought in America: The Revolt against Formalism* (New York: Viking Press, 1949) for the claim that "the turn against classical orthodoxy was part of that 'revolt against formalism' that characterized much American social thought during the early years of the twentieth century").

736 For an example of the Supreme Court of Canada's common practice of citing diverse common law jurisdictions and the Quebec civil law, even in a common law case, see *Bhasin v Hrynew*, *supra* note 339. On Canada's identity as a "Métis nation," see John Ralston Saul, *A Fair Country: Telling Truths about Canada* (Toronto: Penguin, 2008). For an example of Canada's constitutional embrace of common and civil legal traditions, see *Constitution Act, 1867* (UK), *supra* note 83, s 92 (13); *Quebec Act of 1774* (UK), *supra* note 83. See also Philip Girard, "The Making of the Canadian Legal Profession: A Hybrid Heritage" (2014) 21 IJLP 145.

from other frames and perspectives might be necessary to account fully for the ubiquitous co-presence of realism and formalism in Canadian common law Contracts teaching.

PEDAGOGICAL EFFECTIVENESS

One such idea is that the inconsistencies flow from a deliberate strategy to maximize pedagogical effectiveness. We can explore this possibility with reference to the words of both teachers and casebook editors.

Instructors: The Pedagogical Strategy of Sequencing

Although realist and critical attitudes might reflect law professors' *ideal* beliefs about law, the demands of teaching a first-year course might require provisionally bracketing these ideals. In this sense, the fairly prevalent tendency of professors to insist that "critique" is a secondary objective reflects this prioritization. Recall Professor 46's formulation:

> [Students should] understand why the principles evolved as they did. *Then* they can more intelligently criticize them ... [T]hey need to at least understand coherence ... and *then* move to ... challenge those doctrines as perhaps not always meeting goals of fairness or the parties' expectations. I think the one comes before the other. It's almost like ... it makes some sense to understand Newtonian physics as a context for understanding the small number of cases where Newtonian rules don't apply and Relativity does ... You need *both* ... the original theory and the revolutionary theory.[737]

In the same way that one might teach physics to high school students by first positing a classical description of Newtonian mechanics, only to reveal the inaccuracy of the initial model once quantum physics is introduced, so a classical picture of law might figure as a necessary precursor to more "modern" ideas about law.[738] One can tease out a few possible rationales for this sequencing. One is that the content of the classical substance is a necessary precondition for further study in

737 [046], Interview, lines 171–92. See the discussion in Chapter 5 above under "Doctrine First, Critique Second," pages 240–4 .

738 *Cf.* minutephysics, "Open Letter to the President: Physics Education", online: https://www.youtube.com/watch?v=BGL22PTIOAM (asking why high school physics classes emphasize concepts that date no later than 1865). See *supra* note 593 and accompanying text.

upper years, whether that means engaging in critique or simply acquiring specialized knowledge in upper-year courses. As Professor 26 says:

> So many upper-year courses ... really depend on that kind of knowledge. So ... any course in business associations or securities, there's going to be some contract law underlying it ... Any course in insolvency, ... labour and employment, ... commercial law or international arbitration, ... or remedies or advanced contracts ... There's just a large bulk of classes that you don't necessarily think of as contract law courses, but which depend on those initial concepts ... I see it as an obligation to the students to equip them with a sufficient knowledge of those core concepts [so] that they're not going to feel like they're swimming when they get to an upper-year course.[739]

As noted earlier, these attitudes imply a notion that there is a foundational or core knowledge, so while they might be framed in pedagogical terms, they also reveal commitments about law.

Another idea is simply that the substance of classical ideas matters because it will be useful to the work of the practising lawyer. Thus, in parallel with the idea that theory or critique matters because it makes "better lawyers" lies the idea that "what lawyers do" requires the mastery of certain skills, such as "assembling the various pieces of the puzzle, ... internalizing them, ... [and] assimilat[ing] large bodies of information."[740] Emphasizing substantive doctrine and thinking like a lawyer is thus a pedagogical responsibility because it teaches what graduates pragmatically might need to know. As Professor 56 says:

> If you're graduating from this school and take the bar and you're in the courtroom, you have to be able to speak that language in order to make yourself heard ... There's no point ... in being a scholar in the courtroom ... Even when you have the privilege of criticizing ... we're still, *as a law school*, a place where lawyers are being trained.[741]

In this somewhat dismissive reference to the "scholar," one might be tempted to infer that this law professor inhabits two distinct roles simultaneously, the scholar and the teacher. On this interpretation, critical and realist theories are the domain of the scholar, but in the classroom the scholar's role yields to the domain of the teacher, who

739 [026], Interview, lines 227–41. See also [009], Interview, lines 39–40 (contract law is "just absolutely foundational to upper-year courses").

740 [029], Interview, lines 86–94.

741 [056], Interview, lines 338–45.

must emphasize substance and conventional legal reasoning out of an "obligation to the students."[742] The "schizophrenia" alluded to earlier might not be about concepts, but rather about two mutually exclusive identities simultaneously inhabited.[743]

Tempting as such an interpretation might be, it finds little overall support in my study. Most frequently, when professors refer to being "teachers" or "scholars," they bundle those terms together in a way that suggests the objectives of each role are aligned.[744] Only one professor indicates one to be "primary" over the other, but even that person admits they are "not so exclusive."[745] Most professors do not indicate that their goals, attitudes, or priorities differ substantially depending on whether they inhabit the role of teacher or of scholar. The one exception is when professors suggest that their goals in Contracts differ from those in courses in which they are experts in the field. But this distinction has more to do with the subject matter of those courses than with the fact that, in specialized courses, the identity of "scholar" figures more prominently.[746]

A third pedagogical reason professors might choose deliberately to downplay realist and critical theories is the idea that beginning law students are simply not ready to encounter their complexity. In this sense Professor 46's statement that "one comes before the other" is another way of saying that students need to walk before they can run. Indeed some professors do express variations on this theme. Professor 6, for example, says, "In first year you have to learn how to read the law

742 [026], Interview, line 239.

743 See Sandomierski, "Theory and Practice Together at Last", *supra* note 447.

744 See e.g. [062], Interview, lines 618–21 ("What's important to me, what I try to ... work through – as a law student, and now as a legal academic, a scholar, and teacher, [is] the reconstruction part"); [058], Interview, lines 31–3 ("as a scholar and a teacher, I do constitutional stuff better ... – with increased sensitivity to the private law stakes – [for having taught Contracts]").

745 [061], Interview, lines 1002–11 ("I see my primary role here is not a teacher ... My primary role is a researcher. Having said that, I love teaching and I'm glad it's part of the role, part of the job. And they're not ... so exclusive. A lot of what we talk about in class is helpful for when I'm thinking about research").

746 See e.g. [038], Interview, lines 296–300 (So, for example, Professor 38 does emphasize policy in an upper-year seminar, but feels justified in doing so only because students self-selected into it: "When I teach ... my upper year seminar, it's only policy analysis. Law is instrumental to whatever policy you're making ... These students self-select ... They sign up for the seminar because they're interested in that"); [046], Interview, lines 563–9 ("[My other course is] full of that kind of critique of Marxist and all kinds of other critiques ... and pluralism and various philosophical theories of liberalism, ... et cetera. In that one area, I think it can be quite helpful to be aware of the different prisms ... from which the problems can be analysed and the different perspectives").

and understand the law. Use the principles. And then you can move on when you're a bit more sophisticated, into critiquing them. You're not actually realistically capable of critiquing law in the second month of law school. Not really."[747] Although not many professors make the claim about first-year students' lack of capability explicitly – some, by contrast, emphasize how capable their students are – the tendency to shake students out of their old patterns of reasoning is a more widespread version of the same sentiment. First year is the year to build up the "cathedral edifice" of law, not to tear it down.[748]

Casebooks: Allocation of Pedagogical Competence

One could apply an analogous sequencing rationale to the casebooks. On this view, the casebook editors consider their books simply the raw material to be deployed by instructors. Any failure to incorporate theoretical ideas into the substance and methodology of the rest of the books then would simply reflect the decision of how best to allocate responsibility between editor and instructor. The marginalization of policy and the relegation of critical perspectives to the unoperationalized domain of "theory," then, would not be the end of the story, but would simply reflect the idea that the casebook is but a way station en route to classroom experience.

This interpretation is certainly plausible. At minimum, the editors of both *Ben-Ishai & Percy* and *Waddams* emphasize that the casebooks are designed as teaching tools, meant to serve a wide variety of approaches. As the editors of *Ben-Ishai & Percy* write:

> The book continues to be designed primarily as a teaching tool ... We do not attempt to imbue the reader with a particular philosophy ... Rather we try to note a number of different approaches to contracts throughout and to leave scope for individual teachers to pursue their own themes with these materials as a solid base.[749]

---

747 [006], Interview, lines 299–313. See also [054], Interview, lines 926–7 ("I don't know how you can set about criticizing something you don't really understand yet").

748 [043], Interview, line 1097 ("They're *amazing*"); [005], Interview, lines 35–91 (conveying to students the "appropriate parameters of legal reasoning"); [020], Interview, lines 36–8 ("I'm dismissive of critical perspectives in the sense that ... after demolishing the cathedral, I don't actually see what's being put back in").

749 See *Ben-Ishai & Percy* 10th ed, *supra* note 210 at vi. See also *Waddams* 6th ed, *supra* note 209 at iii ("[W]e have designed it to be suitable for dealing with the material in several different orders ... We hope that all will find the book equally suitable for their purposes").

Moreover, the *Ben-Ishai & Percy* editors specifically highlight the role of the instructor in promoting "critical reflection." The fact that some law professors actually *do* attempt to incorporate the material from the introductory chapters into later substantive areas also suggests that the casebooks might serve this function. Moreover the fact that most of the professors demonstrating realist pedagogy described earlier use these casebooks in part to do so suggests that it can be done.[750]

On the other hand, it is equally plausible that the editors conceive of the casebooks' pedagogical role as emphasizing the "core" status of doctrinal rules and analogical reasoning. On this view, critical perspectives are important to understand, but really secondary to the basics. This attitude surfaces in editors' pedagogically oriented language, which describes the books as "designed to constitute the basis of a core course in contracts" or as a "collection of materials suitable for the basic course in the subject."[751] That many instructors perceive the casebooks to focus on a dogmatic core at the expense of critical perspectives is revealed by the fairly common tendency of Contracts professors to produce their own supplements in order to highlight critical perspectives. Of the fifty-eight professors who assign a commercial casebook, twenty-one assign supplementary materials that include scholarly articles and an additional eleven supplement their materials with extra cases or legislation. These supplements serve to provide additional problems and exercises and contemporarily relevant examples, and to add to the cases historical and factual context, themes of public policy, morality, feminism, "sex, race, and power," and other "big-picture" issues.[752]

Which is the more accurate view? *Swan*'s survival in the marketplace makes any sweeping generalization impossible; many instructors specifically use *Swan* because its overarching argument enables them to

---

750 *Ben-Ishai & Percy* 10th ed, *supra* note 210 at 2 ("Your own instructor will direct you to and discuss with you the writings that he or she feels will best promote critical reflection on the basic material reproduced here"). See e.g. [009], Interview, lines 222–48 (incorporating critical perspectives from *Ben-Ishai & Percy* into class discussion). See generally the discussion in Chapter 5 above under "Seeds of a Realist Pedagogy," pages 276–86 .

751 *Ben-Ishai & Percy* 10th ed, *supra* note 210 at vi; *Waddams* 6th ed, *supra* note 209 at iii.

752 See e.g. [006], Interview, lines 67–124 (problems and exercises); [010], Interview, lines 200–43 (contemporary examples); [017], Interview, lines 109–203 (context and contemporarily relevant examples); [027], Interview, lines 621–49 (extended excerpts); [033], Interview, lines 240–56, 324–57 (public policy, morality, and "sex, race, and power"); [035], Interview, lines 616–37 ("big picture issues").

connect the ideas of legal realism to legal professional practices, including legal reasoning. As Professor 13 says:

> The Swan and Reiter book ... make[s] decisions based on a complex matrix of things including the facts, their ... response to the facts, motivated by concerns about fairness, and then using legal argumentation to support the conclusion ... I think that that is a much more accurate way of describing what courts do and how judges actually do make decisions, and therefore if you're trying as a lawyer to either predict what's going to happen in a case, or you're trying to put together an argument with a view to determining what's going to happen in a case, or you're drafting a contract with a view to trying to achieve a specific legal result, you need to take into account all of those things.[753]

Nevertheless the other two books' majority market share, the fact that their editors come from almost every common law Canadian law school, and the fact that the books have undergone regular restructuring and editing suggest that the dominant messages of the casebooks *do* illustrate a widespread viewpoint or, at the very least, are compatible with many different views or approaches.

But the idea that the casebooks are primarily a launching pad for instructors to realize their own desired ends might be too simplistic, and might disregard the integral role the casebooks play in the construction of legal consciousness. As artefacts, casebooks capture and reflect the attitudes of their editors, who are teachers themselves. As pedagogical tools, they structure and guide the way the instructors teach the course. Their pedagogical assertions therefore cannot be considered in isolation from their role in sustaining and perpetuating classical categories through an exercise of collaborative, ongoing editorial agency.

Each of the pedagogical accounts here relies to some extent on the idea that there is a core substance of law – doctrinal rules of contract law – that it is important to master, or on the idea that there is a distinctively legal mode of reasoning. Accordingly, while pedagogical justifications no doubt figure prominently among Contracts professors, these justifications seem to presuppose certain understandings about law that have an affinity with formalism. It is not entirely possible to decouple pedagogical and conceptual accounts of the interplay between realism and formalism. Like the simultaneous belief in the solidity of doctrine and the contingency of law, pedagogical attitudes seem to alternate between paradigm-building and

753 [013], Interview, lines 55–87, 111–24. See also [023], Interview, lines 315–26. But see [016], Interview, lines 741–7 (feeling the need to supplement *Swan*).

paradigm-busting aspirations. The widespread desire, detailed earlier, to "disabuse" students of their preconceptions, to "take the furniture out of the mind," as Professor 27 says, coexists with the desire to replace the now-empty mind with a new set of furniture: the substance of contract law doctrine and the delineated (and delineating) practice of legal reasoning.[754]

Professors' subjective attitudes about law and pedagogy therefore seem inadequate to account fully for the complex interplay between realism and formalism, theory and practice, in Canadian common law Contracts teaching. I turn, therefore, to an alternative account of some of the phenomena observed.

STRUCTURAL ACCOUNTS

The two accounts offered thus far to explain the apparent disjuncture between propositional statements about law, on the one hand, and attitudes about law reflected in conceptions of legal reasoning and teaching practices, on the other, tend to emphasize Contracts professors' intellectual and pedagogical agency by focusing on their theoretical *inclinations* and pedagogical *choices*. These agency-based accounts, however, are not wholly satisfactory. Accordingly, here I adopt a different frame – from *outside* law professors' personal choices – to understand the disjuncture, focusing on the importance of structural considerations. My data reveal the extent to which professors' choices of what they teach and how they teach, including the vision of legal reasoning they privilege, are influenced by explicit and implicit pressures from students, the profession, and within the law faculty. Identifying these features reminds us of the wisdom in Harry Arthurs's claim that "legal education is not an autonomous regime capable of defining and redefining itself from within," and paints a picture of law professors as agents situated in an environment with its own norms and structures.[755]

Structure and Path Dependence

To understand the complex interplay of explicit and implicit pressures that condition Contracts professors' choices about what they teach and how, I use a chronological device. Stitching together the accounts by various professors, I endeavour to tell a story about how a beginning

754 [027], Interview, lines 71–90. See the discussion in Chapter 5 above on "Course Syllabi and Expressions of Teaching" under "Seeds of a Realist Pedagogy," pages 280–1.

755 Arthurs, "Political Economy of Canadian Legal Education", *supra* note 61 at 14.

professor might come to propagate conventional ideas about legal reasoning, through conventional pedagogy, that reflect a set of beliefs about law that differ from that professor's own theoretical commitments. Although this story might not precisely reflect that of any one individual, and viewed as an individual story might seem somewhat caricatured, it integrates a number of factors whose interconnection might not be as apparent were I simply to classify them. This hypothetical narrative reveals how explicit and implicit pressures might combine to create a path dependence that results in a series of conventional "self-evident" doxa about law that are remarkably resistant to the critical and realist ideas.[756]

The Beginning Teacher

Most professors hired to teach Contracts are not experts in the field: only twenty-six of my sixty-seven participants have published once or more in the field of contract law, and of these only eighteen have published major or multiple works; some faculties have no specialists in contract law at all.[757] Few affirmatively request to teach the course.[758] Most are given a small degree of choice, and express some interest in it, either because they enjoyed it in law school, did some research on contract law in graduate school, practised in the area, or have related primary research interests.[759] But many are simply "told," "required," or "forced" to teach

756 See Pierre Bourdieu, *Outline of a Theory of Practice*, translated by Richard Nice (Cambridge: Cambridge University Press, 1977) at 164.

757 I have not included in the twenty-six those who publish in cognate areas such as labour or family law. See also [048], Interview, lines 659–61 ("we don't have anyone at the law school who is really specializing in contracts. All of our Contracts teachers are people who are specializing in something else and teach Contracts").

758 I did not pose this question systematically in my study, so I must be cautious in making this claim. However, I did ask most participants what led them to teach Contracts and only three (Professors 52, 56, and 61) responded that they affirmatively asked to teach the course. Professor 56's description is unique: "I had ... in the negotiation let go of other important things to get the Contracts course" (Interview, lines 26–7). It is possible that a small number of participants *did* request to teach the course but did not mention this in our interview. Nevertheless I believe the true figure would still be firmly in the minority.

759 A total of thirty professors in my study describe the initial interest they had in teaching the course. Five enjoyed the course while in law school (Professors 23, 26, 31, 40, and 62), seven practised law in an area in which contract law played an important role (Professors 13, 14, 44, 46, 49, and 65), six did graduate work in contract law (Professors 1, 9, 19, 22, 48, and 61), and twelve state that it related to their primary area of research (Professors 10, 16, 18, 20, 26, 28, 30, 35, 45, 46, 50, and 52).

it with minimal input. As Professor 3 says, "When I first got my first teaching job ... I was basically told, 'You have to teach a first-year course in addition to courses in your ... areas of expertise and we need you to teach Contracts.' So I said, 'Fine,' having little choice in the matter."[760]

The combination of a lack of experience and lack of expertise makes deference to existing practices extremely likely. As Professor 38 says:

> Canadian contract law was something that *I had not learned before*. So I think you're less likely to rock the boat, so to speak, when you're in that position, than when you are ... well versed ... I have invested a lot more time redesigning, reconceiving, researching my [upper-year seminar] than the Contracts course, just because I spent most of my time *thinking* about it when I'm outside the classroom.[761]

Starting professors almost never design the Contracts course from scratch; most "inherit" it.[762] As Professor 52 says, "I didn't play a role in ... structuring the table of contents or the syllabus. That all ... came *prepackaged*."[763]

The pressure to use existing materials is even more prevalent and enduring. This pressure not to "buck the trend" might come implicitly from students. As Professor 17 says:

> When I was starting out, I didn't want to use this [casebook]. I wanted to use ... Angela Swan's book ... because that's one I had [been] taught with ... but I felt as a starting person, "No – I can't do that! I have to use the house book" ... Because I have ... no credibility and [students] look at you [as if to say] "You've

760 [003], Interview, lines 7–11. Twenty-one professors indicate they had simply been assigned the course without a meaningful choice in response to faculty needs (Professors 3, 6, 7, 8, 11, 15, 21, 24, 27, 32, 33, 37, 39, 41, 51, 53, 58, 59, 63, 64, and 66). See e.g. [006], Interview, line 3 ("Because I was forced to").

761 [038], Interview, lines 539–42, 712–15. See also [026], Interview, lines 592–600 ("for my commercial law course ... I did design my own syllabus, and it was an enormous amount of work ... but I didn't want to do that for a first-year course for ... I was a totally inexperienced teacher"); [051], Interview, lines 523–8 ("Contracts is not my main area of research interest ... I guess originally, [the impediment to doing exactly what I wanted] was more [that] I didn't feel I had enough experience").

762 See e.g. [058], Interview, line 67 ("the overall structure was ... pretty directly inherited"); [066], Interview, lines 46–9 ("the course is not ... structured very imaginatively ... These syllabi can sometimes be ... inherited or legacy documents"); [021], Interview, lines 720–2 ("I did inherit the basic idea and ... [the] framing"); [045], Interview, lines 382–4 ("a lot of my materials are largely inherited ... Part of it's just ... being a young prof coming in and having not taught Contracts before").

763 [052], Interview, lines 59–61.

got to be kidding me! You look way too young!" ... You're not famous ... So it's very difficult I think when you're first starting out – to buck [the trend].[764]

The pressure to use certain materials might also arise out of the desire to go in "lockstep" with colleagues. Professor 51, for example, describes feeling compelled to use *Swan* when starting out:

[I started teaching with *Swan* because] that was the casebook that [the other Contracts teacher] was using at the time ... I went in lockstep with him then. I was the new guy on the block. I'd never taught Contracts before and ... trying to reinvent the wheel when you're in your first year teaching is, as I've learned from experience, ... not generally a good idea! It's better to ... take ... what's there and then get some experience with it and then decide what you want to change.[765]

Indeed the professors who discussed with me their process of selecting a casebook overwhelmingly adopted the "house book." Of these, nineteen describe their decision as motivated by wanting to have consistency with fellow instructors, to be able to draw on colleagues' experience, or simply to fit in. By contrast, only one (Professor 26) describes reviewing all three casebooks in detail prior to teaching the course the first time.[766] Very occasionally there might even be explicit pressure from the administration to use the house book:

When [another colleague] retired, the dean sort of came to me and said, "Okay, you're the only one who's not [using the house book]. You're the junior person ... You don't want to be seen as being different unless you're really committed to it. So are you really committed to it?" And I said, "No, not particularly."[767]

---

764 [017], Interview, lines 517–62.

765 [051], Interview, lines 190–9.

766 See e.g. [033], Interview, lines 41–2 ("I didn't [select *Ben-Ishai & Percy*;] it was what they were teaching with when I started teaching Contracts here"); [035], Interview, lines 495–6 ("[*Ben-Ishai & Percy*] was the one that most people seemed to be using"); [054], Interview, lines 122–5 ("[The] professor ... who teaches the other section of Contracts was already using [*Ben-Ishai & Percy*] and just by default I thought I'd use the same one, so I actually didn't shop around"); [016], Interview, lines 744–5 ("the Swan and Reiter text was the one that was being used at that particular time); [038], Interview, lines 561–3 ("I asked around, whether people used different casebooks. And what I heard was, "Everybody uses [*Waddams*], except for [one colleague], who has his own materials").

767 [041], Interview, lines 555–9.

In addition, young professors might internalize the authoritativeness of existing materials, as even Professor 62, a strong advocate of critical pedagogy, did:

> [A senior colleague] very generously shared with me the casebook that he had assembled and put together over the years, which was ... about nine hundred pages of cases. And I took those, but he's a true gentleman, and a true scholar, and he said, ... "These are yours. Do with them what you want, and make changes, by all means." Now ... I was *loath* to make any changes. I didn't remove anything because I thought, "Who am I to remove something? If *he* thinks it's relevant, I'm going to keep it."[768]

Those who make an effort to design a course on their own often begin by "pulling" from the course syllabi of colleagues from different law schools, looking for "consensus cases."[769] Some might feel that, for "political and pragmatic" reasons, it might be better not to "reinvent the wheel":

> The ultimate question when you're starting out is how much do you take from what's currently existing within the faculty and how much do you try and design your own thing? And there's both ... political and pragmatic pros and cons that go into that ... [At this institution] there tends to be one senior faculty who quote unquote "owns" the course. Or owns the way the course is being taught ... there's a real pole bend to follow that person's approach ... I certainly felt free to make the course in my own image, but from a practical perspective, also just within how much time it takes to teach a new course ... there's really good logistical reasons for not trying to reinvent the wheel.[770]

And even in the absence of heavily influential senior colleagues, many starting professors follow the lead of their own Contracts teachers or mentors. Professors choose the casebook they studied as a student,

---

768 [062], Interview, lines 807–17. Many professors simply follow the order of the casebook. See the discussion in Chapter 5 above on "Decisions regarding Substance" under "Formalist Pedagogy", pages 267–71.

769 See e.g. [011], Interview, lines 27–8, 32–4 ("I was able to get syllabi from ... my colleagues, which was really helpful ... I basically looked at what other people taught and ... picked the cases that seemed to be the ... consensus cases"); [035], Interview, lines 528–36 ("for the most part I pulled other people's syllabi. So I pulled from these guys who teach it here. I have some by [three professors at two other institutions]").

770 [064], Interview, lines 76–94.

start with remedies or formation because their own Contracts teachers taught it that way, adopt their own teachers' or mentors' general approach, or simply refer to the "huge" influence of graduate supervisors or former teachers – one describing their own student experience studying Contracts as the "best education experience in my life."[771]

When it comes to teaching, many starting professors often take advantage of notes and other guidance provided by colleagues and former teachers. Professor 38 recounts the widespread sharing and borrowing fairly representative of the general attitude among Canadian common law Contracts teachers:

> When I was hired here, [a former professor] was very kind. He asked his assistant to copy all his handwritten notes for that course. And he ... shipped it ... via courier! ...
>
> I contacted everybody here who was teaching Contracts [and] all of them were kind enough to share their syllabus. And ... two of them ... shared their notes with me ... The first year I just got ... a syllabus that looked exactly [like] what most people were doing ... and then, in preparation for class, I would just read the cases, read [my colleagues'] notes, ... try to prepare my own class. Then I would knock on somebody's door.[772]

Conversely professors report being very open to helping their junior colleagues become familiar with new material: "In cases where somebody's new, I think all of us, and I can certainly speak for myself, are

771 [062], Interview, lines 514–23 ("there wouldn't have been any other way for me to go about teaching this course" other than under the influence of a mentor whose (non-Contracts) course was "the most important educational experience in my life"); [028], Interview, lines 290–5 ("my supervisor for my graduate work, she is a phenomenal teacher and ... definitely influenced me – huge"). On casebook selection, see e.g. [041], Interview, lines 533–8 ("the first year that I taught Contracts, I [used] ... *Boyle & Percy* ... the reason I picked it was that it was the same thing that I'd been taught as a student"); [063], Interview, lines 533–6 ("I use *Swan* ... [and] have always used it. Nick Bala was my Contracts professor"). On remedies or formation first, see e.g. [028], Interview, lines 480–1 (teaching remedies first is "the way I learned it ... that's why I started like that"); [064], Interview, lines 622–41 (teaches formation first in part because that is "how I learned myself"). On the general approach, see e.g. [045], Interview, lines 275–7 ("my approach to this class ... was largely shaped by ... the professors that taught me Contracts years ago").

772 [038], Interview, lines 446–83. *Cf.* [051], Interview, lines 171–7 ("when I started teaching ... I was teaching with another professor ... and ... often before class ... we'd meet for half an hour and just talk about ... what we were teaching that day, and I found that, particularly as a new professor who'd never taught contract law ... incredibly useful").

happy to share our teaching materials and notes or anything and to talk about issues relating to teaching the course."[773] This sharing and convergence of materials extends to exams and assignments: some starting professors rely on "other people [to take] complete responsibility for being the lead," simply "responding" to these drafts; others try to "closely mirror what the other small groups professors" are doing, enjoying the "benefit" of a "common exam."[774] This combination of factors – lack of expertise, readily available resources provided by colleagues, and significant time savings – all combine to encourage a fair degree of convergence in the use and presentation of materials and in evaluations.

At the same time, there appear to be few incentives to instigate an original approach to teaching the course. At some institutions, the idea predominates that research is more important than teaching. For example, one senior colleague advises young professors that "tenure and promotion doesn't depend on teaching ... don't spend your life making new teaching materials ... because that's not what they are going to evaluate [you] on." Professors are quick to internalize the lack of incentives. One junior professor says, "We get the message ... a lot that our research is ... more important than our teaching. So I think that people rationally respond to that ... and put ... less effort ... into their teaching."[775]

Beyond the question of incentives, some professors experience implicit pressure from colleagues to conform to the existing approach. As Professor 45 says:

> They don't want radically different approaches being taken ... There's an expectation that you work with other colleagues ... And being somebody who is *new*, ... again, it's not that someone has come to me and said, "You can't do this." But I think as ... a good colleague it makes sense that I don't come in here and *radically ... torch* the current approach to teaching contract law because "it's all wrong, and this is how I would do it." I think that would be *probably not* an appropriate way to do things.[776]

773 [031], Interview, lines 327–31.

774 [033], Interview, lines 735–8; [064], Interview, lines 106–13. See also [035], Interview, lines 189–90 ("I draw [my in-class problems] from [a colleague's] old exams").

775 [048], Interview, lines 724–47; [017], Interview, lines 1008–12. *Cf.* [061], Interview, line 1005 ("I see my primary role here is not a teacher"); [011], Interview, lines 589–90 ("[R:] What would your professional goals be? [Professor 11:] Uh – to get tenure! [Laughs]").

776 [045], Interview, lines 369–80, 450–7.

Some beginning professors also experience this drive towards conformity from the students themselves. One professor says:

> All of our first years want parity – it's extraordinary. Time and time again it's come up that students have pressed the administration to mandate that all first-year courses all teach the exact same thing. So [teaching Contracts in a particular way] would be quite possibly more trouble than it's worth ... just the amount of resistance it might encounter ... in conjunction with the tremendous amount of work, it probably would not be worth it.[777]

Exacerbating the issue of student pushback is the perception among some professors that being more junior, or being female, makes deviating from the norm more difficult. The professor just quoted above continues:

> [Another colleague] ... [teaches Contracts in a] significant departure [from the norm] – but first of all he's very senior, and a male, and ... one shouldn't actually underestimate the importance of that in terms of students' views of faculty ... He's done it – it's excellent for students. But you know what? They do fuss. They do fuss about it.[778]

More prosaically, many beginning professors simply try to stay "one case ahead" of students, and grapple with the overwhelming time pressures to meet the workload demands of the job.[779] As Professor 45 says, putting a "personal imprint" on the course will have to wait until "I have a bit more time ... [I've] got this work *burden* and [I'm] trying to just *survive*."[780] Some consider it simply not a worthwhile investment to redesign a course from scratch – an exercise best left for their courses of substantive expertise:

---

777 See e.g. [B], Interview, lines 889–96.

778 *Ibid* at lines 900–9. See also [017], Interview, lines 748–9 ("you get less pushback as you get more senior, regardless of what you're doing"); [064], Interview, lines 897–9 ("It's also problematic as a part-time, ... non-tenured faculty to do something that is *drastically* different than the rest of your colleagues").

779 [017], Interview, lines 574–5. Being just ahead of students is not always perceived as a weakness. As one senior professor says, "I would probably put all young professors who are keen and engaged into the first-year classes, so the students get the benefit of that intellectual engagement by people who [are], as it always used to be, only a couple pages ahead of the students in preparation" ([048], Interview, lines 545–9).

780 [045], Interview, lines 441–6, 474–5.

> I have other things on my plate that needed my attention. And, you know, it's my first time – what I learned from [designing the course in] Corporations ... [in which] I hand-picked every case in the syllabus ... [was that] you don't really know how it's going to go until you teach it. So there's not a ton of value in putting all that work in ... There's no need for me to reinvent the wheel.[781]

Experienced Teachers

In time the patterns established in the early years might take on a more stable form, as professors at later stages experience a series of factors that impede the inclination to innovate. Professors at all stages of their career are likely to encounter considerable pressure to maintain consistency between sections. This pressure can serve as a general disincentive to switching casebooks, as does the idea that professors have already sunk costs into the decision. The overwhelming impression is that most professors choose one casebook and stick with it. In my interviews, only thirteen professors describe having deliberately switched casebooks (and only two of these had taught from all three commercial books).[782]

In respect of non-commercial materials, a similar tendency arises. In one particularly illustrative example, consider the aspiration expressed by Professor 50, lead editor of an unpublished "house" casebook:

> I'm certainly in favour of *first*-year teachers, and maybe *second*-year teachers, probably using an existing casebook, either an in-house casebook or a commercial one, while they get to understand the subject and understand what they want to do. And then I think they should probably develop their own materials after that.[783]

Now compare that statement to the reality at Professor 50's institution. As it happens, the collection that Professor 50 put together has become

781 [011], Interview, lines 279–89.

782 See e.g. [060], Interview, lines 106–7 ("of course you have to *all* use the same book, because if you don't, questions arise on both sides"); [017], Interview, lines 572–83 ("what I think can sometimes happen, is that, so you've been doing it a certain way – you just keep doing it that way because it's just way easier and you can spend your time on other things"); [065], Interview, lines 136–8 ("to be honest with you, [*Ben-Ishai & Percy*] wasn't my selection, and it's just been more a product of the fact that that is now the casebook that I've used and will going forward").

783 [050], Interview, lines 272–9.

the de facto in-house book – it is this collection that one dean pressured a new professor to adopt, saying, "You don't want to be seen as being different unless you're really committed to it," and about which another beginning professor says, "If *he* thinks it's relevant, I'm going to keep it."[784] Indeed all the professors I interviewed from Professor 50's institution use a version of it. As Professor 50 says, "I think *most* of them have used my materials." At another institution, a different well-developed supplement is shared among most teachers.[785]

The desire for "comity" might incline professors, even experienced ones, to conform to a conventional approach to evaluation. Professor 51, for example, stopped assigning on exams "law-reform-type questions," those that "do a critical assessment of an area of law ... in a normative context": "The reason I've stopped is ... out of ... comity for my ... colleagues ... In most recently working with [a particular colleague], her preference was for ... more *traditional* hypothetical exams. And so ... I was willing to go with that." Professor 33, likewise, sacrifices personal interest for "consistency and collegial support": "we write the exams together, we do grading together, and ... I'd rather have *that*, than get rid of the parts that bore me to tears."[786]

Moreover, there might be an implicit pressure to cover the same material as other instructors. Professor 66, for example, describes "some faculty [as] focused on having ... cohesive delivery of first-year subjects ... When I joined the faculty here, the syllabus was discussed, and it was *exact* between three sections." Professor 35 speaks of "coverage pressure," while Professor 24 feels "obliged" to cite leading cases.[787] Professor 33 actively "dislikes" the approach communicated by the materials, but adopts it to conform with "school tradition" and to work collaboratively with colleagues:

> I dislike the emphasis that's in the course, ... which is very much in the historical development of contract law, because it requires the students to grapple with extremely complex but now obsolete doctrines on their little journey to understand how it operates today ... The amount of effort that they put into understanding how rules operated fifty years ago – which

---

784 See *supra* note 767 and accompanying text.

785 [050], Interview, line 666. For discussions of a common supplement at another institution, see e.g. [C], Interview, lines 364–7 ("there *is* a supplement that we use ... I've also ... *altered* some aspects of the content ... but ... there's also the importance of ... consistency").

786 [051], Interview, lines 491–507; [033], Interview, lines 692–4.

787 [066], Interview, lines 56–80; [035], Interview, lines 806–8; [024], Interview, lines 664–5.

are now really quite irrelevant for practice today – doesn't feel like a very good use of classroom time ...

The major textbooks very much take a historical approach and I use one of the major textbooks, so it would either be that or leave out most of the materials ... And there's a school tradition, ... which I'm a part of. And working with my colleagues, if I'm going to have their support, co-write exams and have them co-read exams and so forth, then it's important that we're teaching very similar materials.[788]

At a deeper level, some express hewing to a more conventional approach out of a desire to fit in with "institutional culture." As Professor 38 says:

Institutions have cultures, right? ... And I think I got the sense from getting the notes from my colleagues that ... there was an institutional culture here that was a little more focused on getting some basic concepts across, and it wasn't so much about ... conveying some sort of broader message about the world. It was more like, ... "These are the cases, this is what you need to understand, and these are the skills you need to get as a lawyer."[789]

Institutional culture, however commonly it might function as a source of pressure or constraint, might be experienced differently by different professors at the same institution. In this regard, Professor 4's words are most interesting. Professors 4 and 38 (quoted immediately above) teach at the same institution. But whereas Professor 38 describes the institutional culture as militating *in favour* of "getting some basic concepts across" – describing a focus on conventional doctrine and skills – Professor 4 experiences the opposite tendency: a bias *against* doctrinal teaching:

I've changed my method over time. I've become more and more and more doctrinal ... In my first years of teaching I was much more ...

788 [033], Interview, lines 15–35.

789 [038], Interview, lines 544–55. *Cf.* John Willis, "Canadian Administrative Law in Retrospect" (1974) 24 UTLJ 225 at 227: "[E]ven I, who am, as I have already said, 'a government man,' 'a legislation man,' and 'a what actually happens man,' and try to talk administrative law with a civil service and political science accent, have always felt constrained by social pressure to put my class materials together in such a way that they can, if necessary, be held out as constituting at least the shadow of a professional course." See also John Willis, *A History of Dalhousie Law School* (Toronto: University of Toronto Press, 1979) at 76, 139 (his putting on a Judicial Review of Administrative Action course, instead of an Administrative Process Course, to satisfy the powers that be).

> directly theoretical. Comparing the feminist approach and law and economics approach and this and that. And using the doctrine more as a pretext to really see the different conceptions and theories ... I think it had to do a little bit with a sense of insecurity at first ... Doctrinal law is looked down on as somehow ... dry and easy ... Black letter law as opposed to all this fancy theory, and when you're in a top school you're supposed to do theory ... The more I gained confidence, the more I personally saw the interest in the doctrine and how interesting the doctrine was.[790]

The power of institutional culture or intellectual frameworks might also manifest in student demands. As Professor 13 says, "The people who ... will fight the rearguard action are the students ... The students do not like change. And if they think that what they're getting is different from what their colleagues are getting in the other sections, they won't be happy."[791] This student pressure combines a desire for consistency across sections with a preference for the traditional substance of the course. Professor 3, for example, describes the disincentive student expectations create for going "against the grain":

> I'd rather [not] ... work ... against the grain because you always confront student expectations ... [Incorporating] collective bargaining and employment law ... and consumer protection and regulation [in Contracts], ... students start to get really nervous because ... their friends are doing doctrine of consideration, mistake and frustration, and my students are like, "When are we going to do that?" [If I say] you're not going to do that because I think this is more important, ... they freak out and they tune out and you lose them.[792]

Student demands constitute, therefore, an additional impediment to venturing beyond the conventional doctrinal categories and pedagogical methods. They might also discourage professors from adopting

790 [004], Interview, lines 586–603.

791 [013], Interview, lines 903–9. See also [057], Interview, lines 287–301 ("If [students] look at the other section and see that the other section is getting more case law than they are ... some of them get concerned"); [006], Interview, lines 888–9 ("all of our first years want parity – it's extraordinary").

792 [003], Interview, lines 522–31. See also [017], Interview, lines 707–11 ("I don't all of a sudden want to put them on notice that [they're] not getting the traditional thing").

decidedly philosophical, conceptual, or policy-based approaches to teaching the subject matter.[793]

These student demands take on additional force when viewed in the context of the financial pressures students experience, in part due to high tuition fees. These concerns might be voiced by students themselves. For example, as Professor 6 reports, "Some of the students broke it down to me that they were paying seventy-three dollars and eighty cents per lecture so they wanted to get their money's worth." Or professors might take on this concern of their own accord: "It's a crucially, crucially important consideration: people pay a lot of money for law school ... So ... I don't want to *screw people over*, to put it bluntly, by not giving them what they're expecting." Either way, the notion that students want (or ought) to "get their money's worth" seems to amplify the demands for consistency, parity, and a traditional approach.[794]

A series of institutional features of the law school also might distort professors' ability to teach the way they like. Some professors might consider the *requirement* of having to assign grades as problematic. As Professor 27 puts it tersely, "Evaluation is a pile of crap." The grade curve might be experienced as a distortion: "I'd rather give students what I think they deserve ... I'm *forced* to take my twelve best and ... put *half* of them into B pluses."[795] Others chafe at the institutional requirement of grading first-year courses by means of a 100 per cent final examination – "probably the worst way ... to evaluate students" – especially in case of semesterized schools, where December grades end up on students' final transcripts.[796]

The curriculum also may impose constraints. Professors 6 and 29 both say that having only one semester to teach the course is insufficient;

793 See e.g. [020], Interview, lines 228–37 ("I team-taught with a philosopher from Philosophy ... The ... law students ... hated the indeterminacy of the philosopher king"); [001], Interview, lines 210–22, 395–500 (refusal on behalf of some students, particularly younger ones, to engage with a conceptual approach). See also [040], Interview, lines 944–54 ("to the extent that I wanted to build in large chunks of theory and policy into ... a mandatory first-year bread and butter course [like Contracts] ... there would be pushback ... from the students, pushback from other faculty as well, pushback from the profession that would be mediated through the faculty and the administration").

794 [006], Interview, lines 420–4; [040], Interview, lines 981–90. See also [043], Interview, lines 525–6 ("So we're pleasing the students. Why? Because they're the bloody source of revenue now").

795 [027], Interview, line 783; [054], Interview, lines 452–64.

796 [053], Interview, lines 260–2; [006], Interview, lines 360–8 ("The Christmas exam was a final and ... these are marks for the transcripts ... [This] disrupts the learning for the students because they're so worried about marks for getting jobs ... [T]hey're focused ... on memorization, not skill-building and understanding and learning").

Professor 59 refrains from incorporating a drafting assignment because of "student load in first year"; Professor 20 considers it unfair to give writing assignments because it would require students to invest "a disproportionate amount of time on my course." Pressures from teaching loads also play into the disinclination for multiple assessments: "[My institution] already has a fairly high teaching load." Professor 58 laments the lack of administrative support to hand back assignments: "I've cut back on feedback I give them because we've cut administrative support here."[797] Professors also cite room layout, scheduling, and class size as barriers to venturing beyond conventional and traditional practices.[798]

Professors frequently cite lack of time; sometimes it is the only constraint that professors acknowledge. For example, Professor 58 suggests that, with more time, different approaches would be possible: "I have a pretty ruthless sense that ... I can't do everything ... because one doesn't have unlimited time ... There are things I don't do that I might do if I had [more time] ... You could have them going out and ... seeing more stuff in the community than we do, but it's time intensive."[799] Similarly, given more time, Professor 30 might include more comparative law materials, Professor 4 might discuss legislation more, and Professor 57 might assign more writing assignments.[800] Lack of time appears to be one complaint that unites professors of different ranks and statuses,

---

797 [006], Interview, lines 27–8, 456–7 ("I have *never* found that in one term ... I can cover even all the [issues] that I think are really crucial"); [029], Interview, line 130 ("not really enough"); [059], Interview, lines 335–7; [020], Interview, lines 260–1; [051], Interview, lines 523–6; [058], Interview, lines 829–31.

798 [053], Interview, lines 840–8 ("one [room] is new and modern and you're very close to the students ... The other is the old lecture theatre ... with rows of horizontal desks going back to the horizon ... [Each provides] a very different teaching experience"); [064], Interview, lines 874–80 ("the first-year program is designed ... as ... four or eight individualized classes, which is not my ideal. [My ideal] would be to see not just more problem-based learning but integrated problem-based learning as multiple legal issues that are raised in ... aspects of what are covered in different classes"); [006], Interview, lines 274–84 ("There are constraints to having a very large lecture class. It can't be that nimble or responsive"); [057], Interview, lines 663–7 ("We don't have small groups anymore. And I think there's something valuable in that ... They were removed as a budgetary measure a few years back").

799 [058], Interview, lines 819–24. See also [051], Interview, line 523; [059], Interview, line 559; [065], Interview, line 485.

800 [030], Interview, lines 540–6 ("Somewhere between three and five hours a week of teaching isn't enough to teach them a Canadian law point, and then some comparison maybe with ... the United States and ... Quebec"); [004], Interview, lines 528–40; [057], Interview, lines 672–5 ("doing more writing assignments ... would be beneficial. But ... that's also always a balance on how much time can I spend reading and giving feedback").

surfacing in the words of a full-time practitioner, a beginning professor, an associate dean, and a sitting dean.[801]

Finally, concerns about time translate into assertions about priorities, which might signal the idea that some institutional cultures or reward systems do not prioritize teaching. For example, Professor 15 would incorporate problems, negotiation, drafting, and other solicitor skills "in a perfect world," but chooses to prioritize more conventional models because "the *payoff* isn't big enough to justify spending the huge amount of time on it." Similarly Professor 13 has not delved into law and economics to elucidate policy because "it's a more complex construction of a set of norms that ... would take us more time in class than ... I would justify." As Professor 43 bluntly states, "We don't have any support. We're not used to having support."[802]

The End Game

The combination of incentives to start teaching in the mould of senior colleagues and lack of incentives to depart significantly from this practice as time moves on results in a state of affairs where change can be very slow to come, if it comes at all. At least three senior professors – each with several decades of experience teaching Contracts – acknowledge that their approaches have not significantly changed over the years.[803] Another says that "after thirty years I have very comprehensive notes," suggesting a strong degree of continuity.[804] At the other

801 [065], Interview, lines 510–12 ("I don't have ... as much time as ... some of the academics ... to really develop a course"); [045], Interview, lines 441–6, 474–5 ("I'm an early faculty, I'm just getting my legs, all this is new to me, I'm finishing up a doctorate ... and that's like two full-time jobs"); [016], Interview, lines 405–10 ("I was ... really shifting in my focus [in] teaching Contracts and became associate dean and had this kind of gap of, 'I'll go back to teaching Contracts when I'm finished being associate dean'"); [E], Interview, lines 117–21 ("I'm probably less effective as a teacher than when I'm *not* dean. I have more time to devote to my teaching, [am] more conscious of the rhythms of the class and the ways in which ... students interact with one another and ... with me").

802 [015], Interview, lines 393–419; [013], Interview, lines 661–3; [043], Interview, lines 1378–9. *Cf.* [020], Interview, lines 222–8 ("to write any of those problem-based learning exercises [takes] a tremendous amount of ... personal time ... I just personally didn't see the payoff to me for the time it was taking me to do that particular exercise").

803 See [029], Interview, lines 680–4 ("I don't think so"); [048], Interview, lines 325–30 ("I don't think so"); [060], Interview, line 156 ("Very, very little") (each in response to the question of whether their approach to teaching the course had changed).

804 [020], Interview, line 111.

end, some younger professors indicate a prospective steady-as-it-goes approach. Professor 66 is "not that ambitious" to contemplate changing the order in which the course is taught; Professor 32 "bid" for Contracts mid-career, "not because I *like* it more, but having prepped a course, it's more efficient." And Professor 52, a starting professor, does not "plan on doing anything a whole lot different than what I've previously done."[805]

The above story recounts how some structural features might produce a degree of path dependence in legal education. Occasionally professors describe this phenomenon. As Professor 17 says:

> What ... can sometimes happen is that ... you've been doing it a certain way [and] you just keep doing it that way because it's ... way easier and you can spend your time on other things ... I really think for a lot of people it takes a fair bit of effort to ... re-engage with [the material] and [ask,] ... "How am I going to make it more my own?"[806]

Added to the many institutional and internal cultural features described here is also the idea that the profession of law is inherently conservative. This characteristic is a factor in the way some professors describe legal education. As Professor 43 says:

> Because we're lawyers, [we have] a couple of personality ... characteristics. One of them is we're risk averse. All good lawyers are risk adverse. Two, we're tremendously sceptical and we hate uncertainty. That ... builds into the risk-averse thing. So we can't take that leap easily. And we are, by and large, in every law faculty I've seen, a bunch of nay-sayers. We have more reasons for "no" than for "yes." So turning the models around is *really hard*.[807]

A powerful set of norms, therefore, operates in the law school. These norms are rarely both formulaic and explicit; as Harry Arthurs once observed with a certain degree of self-evidence, "Of course, pressures from the profession and the university only rarely arrive in the form of explicit prescriptions or even clearly articulated requests."[808]

---

805 [066], Interview, line 599; [032], Interview, lines 476–7; [052], Interview, lines 607–8.

806 [017], Interview, lines 580–5.

807 [043], Interview, lines 1772–81. *Cf.* [064], Interview, lines 943–7 ("[R:] And any resistance that you might ... *perceive* to increasing the amount of problem-based learning, where do you think that comes from? [Professor 64:] Well, as you know, we are a profession [that] doesn't like change").

808 Arthurs, "Political Economy of Canadian Legal Education", *supra* note 61 at 22.

The norms that most powerfully appear to be operating on law professors are implicit and inferential, akin to unwritten general principles, expressed by the term "institutional culture." Other powerful influences include the formulaic but implicit norms resulting from the structures imposed by curriculum design, class size, and layout.[809] Whatever the influence of law professors' conceptions about law, or their pedagogical rationales, there is no denying that professors are heavily influenced by the many and varied norms and structures within which they operate. These norms and structures create a deep channel through which mainstream practices course, undulating and powerful.

Agency

The relationship between structure and agency is, however, dynamic. Professors do not appear to be passive "subjects" of the law school's norms, but rather participate in constituting, constructing, interpreting, and, at times, transcending those norms.[810] In one sense this manifests in the commonplace assertion that professors experience little or no constraints. When asked about what constraints they feel (and I did so ask, directly, forty-five times), most professors mention very minimal constraints, and fully fourteen state they feel "no" constraints whatsoever.[811] Many describe having complete freedom. As Professor 54 says, "I'm free to pick any textbook I want, ... make any syllabus I want, teach any material that I want." Professor 55 even laments the

809 I borrow the classification of norms according to two axes – implicit/explicit and inferential/formulaic – from Roderick Macdonald. See Roderick A Macdonald & David Sandomierski, "Against Nomopolies" (2006) 57 Northern Ireland LQ 610, n 16; Macdonald, "Vieilles Gardes", *supra* note 80. See also Macdonald, "Custom Made", *supra* note 82. For a thorough exploration of the term "institutional culture", especially as it can be deployed to conduct empirical research into legal education, see Habermacher, *supra* note 52.

810 *Cf.* Macdonald & Sandomierski, *supra* note 809 at 614–15 ("Legal norms, in whatever site of law, are imagined by human beings, given expression by human beings, lived by human beings, followed by human beings, modified by human beings, rejected by human beings – in a word, constituted by human beings not primarily as passive legal subjects, but above all as active legal agents").

811 [008], Interview, line 514; [023], Interview, line 773; [011], Interview, line 614; [031], Interview, line 319; [039], Interview, line 936; [066], Interview, line 103; [049], Interview, line 446; [029], Interview, line 690; [032], Interview, line 600; [048], Interview, line 572; [052], Interview, line 522; [050], Interview, line 599; [026], Interview, line 952; [055], Interview, line 826. In addition, Professors 59 and 65 say they have no constraints whatsoever, except time (Interviews, lines 559 and 485, respectively).

"overstated idea of academic freedom which [operates to shut down] ... conversation[s] about coordinating ... different sections."[812]

Such statements could reveal that professors might be blind to the constraining forces around them and that a formal notion of academic freedom describes only one of many normative strata; professors could be constrained without seeing or acknowledging it. Alternatively the subjective reporting about freedom might signal a sense of agency and ownership over the law school's structures and over their own teaching. And indeed there are numerous examples of professors' exercising their agency *as against* some of the structures identified above.

For example, while the tendency is ever-present to adopt a house book, a good number of professors – twenty-one of the fifty-eight who use a commercial casebook – either design their own materials or develop extensive supplements.[813] Professor 1, for example, designed an original set of materials the very first year of teaching the course. Professor 71, another beginning teacher, includes a highly curated and original set of extended readings for almost every class. Numerous mid-career professors have eclectic and custom-designed reading lists, some of which were developed gradually over the years.[814] And other long-standing professors prefer to "construct [their] own curriculum," use "materials which are tailored to *me* and to my course," or produce a custom casebook "put together over time" that is emailed to students for free.[815] Moreover, while many professors do not change casebooks, at least thirteen in my study have done so. Some switched casebooks for strong principled reasons about law; others did so because

812 [054], Interview, lines 396–7; [055], Interview, lines 815–19. See also [061], Interview, lines 911–13 ("I don't have anyone ... looking over my shoulder and seeing what cases I'm teaching at all. I have an enormous amount of freedom"); [026], Interview, lines 624–6 (no pressure from colleagues to choose any particular casebook); [021], Interview, line 785 ("I get pretty much free range here"); [032], Interview, lines 601–2 ("I feel like I've got complete free rein on what kind of material I deliver and how to do it").

813 See *supra* note 752 and accompanying text.

814 [001], Interview, lines 882–909; [071], Syllabus, 2015–16. See e.g. [037], Fall and Winter Term Reading Lists, 2015–16; [017], *Contracts Supplementary Materials*, 2012–13; [017], Interview, lines 175–7 ("I wouldn't say when I first started teaching that I [included a lot of race and gender materials in the supplement], but I have started doing it increasingly"); [016], Interview, lines 746–7 ("[a colleague] and I were getting less and less *satisfied* with [*Swan*] because our supplement every year got bigger and bigger").

815 [002], Interview, lines 125–6; [050], Interview, lines 187–8; [007], Interview, lines 475–80.

of pedagogical considerations.[816] One beginning professor spent the equivalent of two weeks, full time, reading all three commercial casebooks and deciding on them before teaching for the first time.[817]

As powerful an intellectual force as former teachers or mentors might be, a number of professors specifically react against how they were taught. Professor 32 departed from the "'let's get ... down to ... to business' kind of Contracts course" the professor had been taught by specifically injecting four "contracts-in-context" days. Another professor decided to teach Contracts in a more contextual way as a "reaction against" how that person was taught. Professor 48 includes "questions about inequality of bargaining power [and] the role of public policy in contract law," notwithstanding the fact that "as a student [those issues] were never raised because I simply learned the rules."[818]

Similarly many professors demonstrate original thinking or the ability to change their minds. Professor 28 discusses how the conviction to include context comes from within:

> I've always liked when I've taken courses to hear where the instructor's coming from in their work ... In recent years I've been ... particularly influenced by [having] taken a lot of ... creative writing [courses] ... I've been influenced by those teachers the most in their style and the way they've brought their own writing into the class.[819]

Professor 12 freely admits to "changing my mind" about substantive issues in contract law: "I never leave a class without knowing more than I knew when I went in. Which is very exciting! I don't know what I'm going to know more." Similarly Professor 42 says, "I'm more or less self-educated, and I do it the way I like!"[820]

Professors also take original approaches to designing and teaching courses. Professor 24 conducted a "major reorganization" early on in teaching, and aspires to produce an "honest course that [is] my own"; the 2013 and 2015 course syllabi differ markedly, bearing out this

816 See e.g. [013], Interview, lines 55–78 (quotation reproduced at text accompanying note 705, above); [025], Interview, lines 302–3 ("I just think [switching casebooks is] a good thing to do. To some extent it shakes up the students a little"); [031], Interview, lines 349–50 ("usually every few years I like to change the book I use, just to mix it up a bit").

817 [026], Interview, lines 587–608.

818 [032], Interview, lines 434–43; [D], Interview, lines 93–100; [048], Interview, lines 177–81.

819 [028], Interview, lines 319–26.

820 [012], Interview, lines 172–6; [042], Interview, lines 75–6.

aspiration.[821] Professor 35, who borrowed many course syllabi from colleagues when starting out, has now drafted a very original one.[822] Professor 39 "read all the cases and made my own notes" on them in the first year of teaching. Professor 51 switched the order in which remedies appears in the course after having read an article about pedagogical effectiveness, does "not want to become complacent," and switches the cases assigned so that "you can't rely on your same notes from the previous year" and in order to "keep *engaged* with the material."[823]

As for any disinclination to depart from standard practices, some, like Professor 43, disregard student resistance entirely: "I have no resistance because I don't care ... My job isn't to listen to the kids. My job is to *teach* ... I'm not in the crowd-pleasing mode."[824] And whatever the perceived resistance, many professors do articulate plans to make changes in the future, whether to omit seminal readings, change the order of topics, design new materials, or even, as is the case with Professor 62, to alter radically the mode of evaluation on the basis of self-reflection and assessment:

> One of the ways that I'm going to try to *resist* [student pressures about grades] ... is to try ... a mode of evaluation... [that] I'd call *transvaluation* ... They're going to get grades for doing ... [what] they actually *want* to do when they come in the first place, and [that] better matches and tailors their *actual aspirations*, without being adulterated by ... the instrumentality of how to get particular grades to get particular jobs ... I'm glad you asked that question because I felt one of the biggest *failures* that I committed this year was sticking with this instrumental form of evaluation that didn't *match at all* or ... *not nearly as well* as it could have – the integration ... of theory and practice.[825]

---

821 [024], Interview, lines 94–106; [024], Syllabus, 2013–14; [024], Syllabus, 2015–16.

822 [035], Syllabus, 2015–16, p 1:

> Contract law is one of the foundational building blocks of the common law, the core of market regulation, and a legal relationship that underpins a myriad of statutory and specialized common law regimes. The common law presents contractual relationships as voluntary agreements between parties, and defines a contract as an exchange of promises, the breach of which gives rise to a legal remedy. But a contract can also be thought of as a social relationship, as an institution that facilitates transactions on the market, as a problem solving tool, and/or as grounding political philosophies concerning liberal, market-based democracy.

823 [039], Interview, lines 704–9; [051], Interview, lines 88–123, 613–29.

824 [043], Interview, lines 1103–13.

825 [062], Interview, lines 1096–124. See also [035], Interview, lines 521–3 ("I'm not sure I'm going to" [teach *Ron Engineering & Construction Eastern Ltd v Ontario*, [1981]

CONCLUSION: TRANSCENDING LANGDELL?

Canadian common law Contracts professors, accordingly, appear to inhabit a complex relationship between agency and structure. On the one hand, agency-based accounts that might explain the apparent failure to operationalize realist and critical theories are somewhat unsatisfactory. Attempts to conceptually reconcile realism and formalism seem destined to succeed incompletely, if at all, given the revolutionary character of realism and the widely acknowledged idea that realism constituted a "wholesale assault" on formalist and classical ideas. At the same time, accounts of pedagogical effectiveness seem irremediably tied up in an understanding of "core" knowledge and skills, an idea that cannot be decoupled completely from attitudes about law. Claims that students need to learn the basics for future courses or need to walk before they can run appear to rely on taken-for-granted conceptual categories, reflecting "Langdell's secret triumph." Pedagogical rationales do not seem to extricate us from the apparent tension between realist and formalist commitments about law.

On the other hand, the institutional and structural features of legal education do not account completely for the tension: however powerful the forces of incentives and institutional culture, these factors do not entirely determine outcomes or inhibit innovation. Although professors' starting choices do appear to be in some practical senses constrained, and the forces in favour of path dependency seem acute, there are nonetheless numerous examples of professors' transcending conventional approaches – foregrounding realist ideas in syllabi, experimenting with diverse evaluations, and (in the case of Angela Swan) even producing an entire casebook around the "solicitor's perspective." The multiple seeds of a possible realistic methodology suggest that, notwithstanding powerful external forces, there is a significant degree of experimentation and innovation.

Moreover the structural influences themselves do not appear to be exclusively externally imposed. Rarely are constraints formal and explicit; much more common are the implicit and inferential norms of institutional culture. This institutional culture, moreover, is not a monolithic, top-down disciplining power to which professors are subjected.

---

1 SCR 111, 119 DLR (3d)] again"); [052], Interview, lines 103–7 ("in future years ... I *might* monkey around with it and do ... a mini lecture on damages right at the beginning of the course, and then ... follow the Percy and Ben Ishai text from that point forward"); [064], Interview, lines 450–1 ("I *may* use one assignment from last year as [a problem set], but I'll probably design them myself").

Rather, in possessing academic freedom, intellectual strength, good job security, high social status, and so on, law professors participate affirmatively in reproducing the structures that condition them.[826] The enthusiastic and well-elaborated descriptions of legal reasoning are perhaps the best example of this expression of agency in reproducing conventional institutional structures; so is the tendency to talk about theory and practice in oppositional terms when describing the role or mission of the law school. These descriptions are every bit as genuine and authentic as the articulations of realist or critical theories or of the aspiration to integrate theory and practice. And none of this is to forget the seven "champions of formalism," who own and celebrate a vision of law that, it seems, many more professors relate to at some level. Indeed one of the possible reasons professors describe so few constraints might be that they experience many of the structural features that surround them, in part, as practices to which they themselves are genuinely committed.[827]

The active participation of Canadian common law Contracts professors in the structures that condition and delimit their exercise of intellectual and pedagogical agency implies that legal education reform projects, to be effective, ought to function at various levels simultaneously. Institutional reform can play an important role in signalling (or reshifting) priorities. For example, university teaching support centres provide inspiration and resources for refiguring approaches to teaching law; initiatives for strategic review enable administrators and faculty to work together to refashion the explicit norms and value statements of the faculty, and can direct investments in particular initiatives. Curricular reform initiatives might function as the "law school's primary heuristic device," providing a vehicle

826 In Bourdieu's terms, these last features can be thought of as elements of the law professor's capital, which, combined with the structural conditioning in a given field of activity, constitute a practice. See Pierre Bourdieu, *Distinction: A Social Critique of the Judgement of Taste*, translated by Richard Nice (Cambridge, MA: Harvard University Press, 1984) at 101. Other potential theoretical framings of the interplay between structure and agency would include the recursive and mutually constitutive relationship between structure and agency in Anthony Giddens's structuration theory, and a relational concept of autonomy that views social structures as a necessary condition for autonomy. See Anthony Giddens, *The Constitution of Society: Outline of a Theory of Structuration* (Cambridge: Polity Press, 1984); Jennifer Nedelsky, *Law's Relations: A Relational Theory of Self, Autonomy, and Law* (Oxford: Oxford University Press, 2011).

827 I am grateful to Mark Antaki for eliciting this reflection in a conversation about the distinction between "constraints" and "commitments."

through which contested visions of legal education can be debated and put into practice.[828]

Beyond these initiatives, law schools can experiment with initiatives to combat some of the institutional factors that otherwise might inhibit innovation. For example, incentives could be made available to instructors who wish to redesign a course or produce a new set of teaching materials – these could take the form of "negative" incentives such as reduced teaching loads or fewer administrative responsibilities, or more "affirmative" incentives such as pay raises or formal recognition.[829] Law faculties could strive to encourage a climate of deliberation about teaching innovation by bringing in speakers, funding teaching assistants or research fellows, and supporting technological experimentation. Law faculties could also seek to marshal existing norms of institutional culture to develop new practices – for example, a norm in favour of "comity" could inspire, instead of shared evaluations and consistent coverage, novel collaborative teaching initiatives. Faculty and administrators could try to shift institutional culture by championing innovative teaching efforts or convening faculty workshops focused on pedagogy.

Addressing the more substantive gap – that between the ideas about law and how they are operationalized in legal reasoning and

828 Macdonald, "Curricular Development", *supra* note 61 at 569. See also [032], Interview, lines 880–9 ("Our centre for teaching [and] learning here is ... very active and good. We're [also] undergoing curricular reform right now ... so I suspect there will be some things that come out of there. I suspect we're going to go ... more into the area of experiential learning ... You might ask the associate dean or the dean for ... our strategic vision ... document"). For examples of consultative strategic initiatives, see e.g. University of British Columbia, Allard School of Law, *Allard School of Law Strategic Plan (2016 to 2021)*, online: http://www.allard.ubc.ca/allard-school-law-strategic-plan-2016–2021-1, Teaching and Learning ("Engage committed teachers and students in an active learning environment informed by research and effective approaches to pedagogy"); Osgoode Hall Law School, *Experience Osgoode: Strategic Plan 2011–2016*, online: https://www.osgoode.yorku.ca/wp-content/uploads/2014/07/2011-16_Lorne_Sossin_double.pdf at 3 ("Osgoode's commitment to ambitious curricular innovation, to active learning, and to excellence in legal pedagogy ... will continue in our new Plan"); Dalhousie University, Schulich School of Law, *Strategic Directions 2017–2021*, online: https://www.dal.ca/faculty/law/about/strategic-directions-2017–2021.html (resulting from "enthusiastic engagement and thoughtful contributions" over the course of a "series of facilitated consultation sessions with faculty, staff, alumni, and partners").

829 Teaching fellowships are one way of providing financial and other support for innovations. See e.g. Western University, Western Law, "Teaching Fellowship to Promote Mental Health and Mindfulness" (2018), online: https://law.uwo.ca/news/2018/teaching_fellowship_to_promote_mental_health_and_mindfulness.html.

practice – poses a greater challenge, but conceivably it could be targeted through macro initiatives such as curricular and program design. For example, the current trend towards increasing experiential education at least posits the ideal of "*deploying* substantive knowledge" and critical analysis.[830] In a more declarative mode, Ontario's two newest law schools signal their intention to integrate theory and practice as a foundational, distinctive pillar of their curricula. The Bora Laskin Faculty of Law at Lakehead University, with its Integrated Practice Curriculum (graduation from the faculty also satisfies the Law Society of Ontario's licensing requirements), claims to be a place that "fuses the theory of law with the practice of law; where students not only learn law, but learn the necessary practice skills to use that law effectively." Ryerson University's proposal for its new law school, which has since been approved to offer its own Integrated Practice Curriculum, endorsed the "need to blend theory and practice."[831] An optimistic and broad interpretation of these declarations could see them encouraging educators to think carefully about the relationship between the particular theories they espouse and the visions of legal practice they convey. And even if these declarations were intended in a narrower sense, they signal the possibility that an explicit institutional mission *could* function to address the substantive gap between theory and practice identified in this study. Finally, legal publishers could play a role in reducing this gap by designing new pedagogical materials (teaching manuals or new formats altogether) that guide instructors in how to incorporate the theoretical ideas canvassed in their introductions into the substance matter of the course.[832]

---

830 See e.g. Sossin, *supra* note 26 at 851 ("experiential learning transforms legal education from a focus on conveying specialized knowledge about law (and, in its best incarnations, critical analysis of law) to a problem-solving model, in which the goal of [the] law school curriculum is *deploying* legal knowledge (and, ideally, critical analysis) in order to advance our understanding of law and its contexts").

831 Lakehead University, Bora Laskin Faculty of Law, "Integrated Practice Curriculum", online: https://www.lakeheadu.ca/academics/departments/law/curriculum/ipc; Ryerson University, Academic Standards Committee, *Proposal for a Juris Doctor Program* (Report #W2017–4, June 2017), online: http://www.ryerson.ca/content/dam/senate/ASCReports/2016–2017/ASC_Report_W2017_4_June_5_2017.pdf at s 1.3 (foregrounding the "Key Elements" of the proposed program with a positive reference to a 2012 Report by the Federation of Law Societies of Canada that "stresses the need to blend theory and practice"); Ryerson University, Faculty of Law, "Integrated Practice Curriculum", online: https://www.ryerson.ca/law/about/integrated-practice-curriculum/.

832 For an example of a well-developed teaching manual, see e.g. Stewart Macaulay et al, *Contracts: Law in Action, Volume One: The Introductory Course Teacher's Manual,*

Such macro, top-down, or programmatic initiatives, however, risk missing one important stratum of legal education: professors' own choices within the classroom. One important insight of this study is that, despite the powerful protections of academic independence and the heterogeneity of ideas, many professors nevertheless choose to exercise their pedagogic and intellectual agency in remarkably homogeneous ways. Getting to the heart of this dynamic is a vexing puzzle, and might strain the limits of institutional reform initiatives. Truly operationalizing diverse theories about law into diverse visions of what it means to think like a lawyer – and, by extension, cultivating a vision of the lawyer as citizen – might require a more thoroughgoing introspection process. It might require instructors to ask intellectually honest questions of themselves about a series of interconnected questions: What do I believe about law? What do I believe about legal education? How do I imagine my teaching to contribute to students' understandings of how they ought to contribute to society? Each of these questions is difficult and, with the possible exception of the first, rarely a first-order question in the contemporary social and political economy of the law school. But any possibility of actually translating theory into practice would require a full reckoning of these three questions as a prior exercise.

As a subsequent exercise, Contracts teachers would need to contend with Langdell's "secret triumph" – the perpetuation of classical conceptual categories despite a century and a half of scholarly and empirical development in the ideas around contract law.[833] Why, for example, does the discrete contract continue to provide the architecture for the Contracts course, despite the widespread acknowledgment of the importance of the relational contract? Why does the question of whether to teach remedies first continue to function as a meaningful dividing line as to how the course is organized, even though the controversy is over seven decades old and many experienced teachers downplay its significance? Why does the paradigm of adjudication – a focus on appellate-style argumentation and taking judicial language seriously – continue to predominate, even though most lawyerly activity happens outside of court? Why does "legal reasoning" receive such a homogeneous definition among so many different instructors, even

---

4th ed (Durham, NC: Carolina Academic Press, 2016). For an example of a new book designed to integrate substantive teaching and pedagogy being offered as an "'all-in-one' course package," see Stephanie Ben-Ishai & Thomas GW Telfer, eds, *Bankruptcy and Insolvency Law in Canada: Cases, Materials, and Problems* (Toronto: Irwin Law, 2019). For its companion picture-book, see Wela Quan, *Bankruptcy Law Picture Book* (Toronto: Irwin Law, 2019).

833 Grey, *supra* note 96 at 50.

though lawyers do drastically different types of work that engage in so many more types of thinking than discerning relevance? Asking these questions, generating others, and attempting to answer them, can help disrupt the idea that any of the forms, conventions, or concepts of teaching Contracts are natural, neutral, or to be taken for granted. Such questions are the thin edge of a wedge that could pry open the barrier between the capacious aspirations for law teaching and the daily reality of the Contracts classroom.

A prospective vision of teaching Contracts for the lawyer as citizen might posit a reorganization of the course not around doctrinal categories, but according to categories that each instructor chooses for him- or herself. One could, for example, organize the course around different ways in which law school graduates might contribute to society and their corresponding functions. One could give more equal billing to the planning function of the solicitor, the advocacy work of the litigator, the analytical and rhetorical work of the judge, the policy-design function of the law reformer, the critical work of the scholar or activist, the journalist's contribution to social advocacy and commentary, the engineering function of the drafter, and the value-maximizing work of the negotiator. Each of these lawyerly functions could be taught so as to acquaint students with some aspect of the "substance" of the law of contracts – "law of contracts" read broadly to include doctrine, legislation, and the written and unwritten law of the parties.

My point here is not to develop a specific vision of what it might mean to teach Contracts for the lawyer as citizen, but to suggest that radically reimagining the categories within a course in Contracts is a useful (and potentially requisite) heuristic for more closely aligning one's attitudes about law with the messages one communicates about legal practice and social contribution. The problem with the conventional categories is not so much the categories themselves as their conventional nature, which might pre-empt the intellectually and pedagogically demanding work of truly customizing a course to one's own vision of law and learning. By accepting these categories without question, the instructor with an otherwise blank slate and deep personal convictions foregoes the opportunity to put into practice his or her beliefs to the fullest extent. Granted, there are innumerable sensible reasons one might choose to proceed in this way. But the collective outcome of multiple such individually sensible decisions is an inhibiting homogeneity in the image of how lawyers are portrayed as thinking and acting in the world. The alternative – each Contracts teacher establishing a rationale for the course's organization according to his or her own beliefs and inspiration – would go a long way towards producing, in the aggregate, a diverse and capacious vision of the lawyer and of law.

This exercise in radical (in the sense of going to the roots) agency in course design might have broader implications for the scope and ambit of legal education. Organizing a course according to one's first principles might have knock-off effects for the structure of legal education as a whole. Once familiar categories within a course become treated as contingent expressions of particular pedagogical or theoretical desiderata, the door opens for more original curricular structures. Inviting instructors to exercise "categorical agency" might help break apart the homogeneity of the curriculum and put a lie to Grey's pessimistic claim that legal scholars "will probably never supply a scheme of categories and concepts that actually shape legal argument and judgment," and instead open new horizons for the foundational structure of legal education and law.[834]

In Canada today, a number of curricular initiatives promise to up-end the conventional offerings and to imagine possible variants of the typical law school staples. For example, the University of Victoria's Joint Degree Program in Canadian Common Law and Indigenous Legal Orders (JD/JID) reconfigures many of the conventional offerings into "Transsystemic" courses, while making mandatory courses such as Coast Salish Legal Studies and Language, and Indigenous Field Study.[835] This approach reflects a double-barrelled attempt to incorporate Indigenous law and perspectives into the "core" of what is taught, targeting both the curriculum and individual courses.

Another prospective example is the future law school at Ryerson, which aims to "address[] the societal need for a law school of a different kind." Core elements of the proposal include a series of "bootcamps," the abandonment of semesterized courses in second year in favour of short intensive courses complemented by practical experience, and a semester-long work placement in third year.[836] Although Ryerson's claims to be truly "different" were vigorously challenged by the Canadian Council of Law Deans on the grounds that the proposal underrepresented the state of innovation in existing Canadian

---

834 *Ibid* at 53.

835 See University of Victoria, "Joint Degree Program in Canadian Common Law and Indigineous Legal Orders JD/JID", online: https://www.uvic.ca/law/about/indigenous/jid/index.php.

836 Ryerson University, *Proposal for a Juris Doctor Program, supra* note 831. See also Ryerson University, Faculty of Law, "Program Information", online: https://www.ryerson.ca/law/program/.

law schools, subsequent attempts to articulate a vision for the new school disclose an attempt to define the law school's mission in apparently novel terms.[837] Sari Graben, associate professor in Ryerson's new Faculty of Law, who played an important role in the initial proposal, has suggested that Ryerson will distinguish itself by positioning technology at the centre of its mission. This vision is arguably distinctive not only because it posits a concept – technology – purportedly external to law as the stable reference point for the legal curriculum, but also because it uses that reference point to inform the notion of legal practice:

> Ryerson has operationalized an understanding that technology is deeply implicated in the practice of law … [The program] places systemic thinking about legal technologies at the centre of professional education … What has been disrupted is the essential role that lawyers play in understanding and designing legal technologies and what those technologies do to the interpretation, application, delivery, and transformation of law.
>
> [I]nnovation based learning in Ryerson's program … teaches students to create new processes, forms, digital systems, and computational methodologies for legal practice.[838]

It remains to be seen whether Graben's curricular vision takes hold. But the presence of a new law school in Ontario is at the very least an opportunity to imagine anew legal education and its conceptual categories.

As potentially disruptive and transformative as these initiatives might prove to be, however, they still appear circumscribed by convention. Both continue to use the categories of Contracts, Torts, Property, Criminal, and Constitutional Law as the main organizational features of their core programs. In this, they are reminiscent of the structure

---

837 Dean Camille Cameron, Chair, Canadian Council of Law Deans, letter to Dr Christopher H Evans, Interim Provost and Vice President Academic, Ryerson University, 24 November 2016 at 1–2, online: https://s3.amazonaws.com/tld-documents.llnassets.com/0005000/5463/ccld%20response%20to%20ryerson%20proposal.pdf ("Ryerson's LOI declares it is a different kind of law school, but describes its differentiation based on a caricature of law schools a generation ago ... Had they taken a closer look at contemporary legal education, those behind the proposal might have realized that [the three grounds of social need on which the proposal is based] are, in fact, the values that animate most Law Schools throughout Ontario and Canada").

838 Sari Graben, "A Systemic Approach to Law and Technology at Ryerson University", draft paper on file with author (2019) at 10, 20.

of teaching law of a century ago.[839] This is by no means to say that they will fail at their missions. A major premise of this study is that it is *possible* to put into practice a wide range of visions about law and legal practice within the confines of a conventionally labelled course such as Contracts. And, on this score, both the University of Victoria and Ryerson programs do hold out the promise of operationalizing certain theories on which the programs themselves are founded. At Victoria, Transsystemic Contracts might very likely succeed at incorporating Indigenous legal orders throughout both the materials and the pedagogical approach. This would not only concretize the principled aims of the program, but also might serve as model or resource for other Contracts instructors across the country who wish to incorporate Indigenous law and perspectives but have not yet done so.[840] In the Ryerson proposal, Contracts receives its own distinctive treatment,

839 See Ryerson University, *Proposal for a Juris Doctor Program*, *supra* note 831, ss 1.4, 2.8 (first-year required courses proposed as Contract Law, Torts Law, Property Law, Criminal Law, Constitutional Law, Administrative and Regulatory Law, Legal Research and Writing, Ethics and Professionalism, Foundations of Law and Legal Method, Indigenous Law in Canada, and a one-week Technology and Innovation Bootcamp). *Cf* Reed, *supra* note 54 (detailing law school curricula in North America in the 1920s). The proposed law school at Memorial University adopts similar categories, including Contracts, Tort Law, Real Property Law, Criminal Law, Public Law, Legal Research and Writing, and a Dispute Resolution module in its proposed first-year curriculum – notwithstanding the claim to have a distinctive focus on northern resource development, social justice, and indigenous issues. See Memorial University of Newfoundland, "Memorial University Faculty of Law Proposal" (August 2018), online: https://www.mun.ca/vpacademic/law_proposal_Senate_Nov_13_18.pdf, Appendix 1; Juanita Mercer, "Memorial University one step closer to getting law faculty", *Western Star*, 23 November 2018, online: https://www.thewesternstar.com/news/local/memorial-university-one-step-closer-to-getting-law-faculty-262355/.

840 See the discussion in Chapter 5 above under "Indigenous Perspectives," pages 213–18. The Fall Term Reading Schedule for Transsystemic Contracts for the 2019-20 year, taught by Professor Alan Hanna, includes readings from *Ben-Ishai & Percy* 10th ed, *supra* note 210 and from diverse Indigenous sources. Professor Hanna's goal is to "teach students from three separate, but interconnected, perspectives: 1) common law contracts; 2) contracts that arise within Aboriginal law (Canadian law applied to Indigenous peoples and groups); 3) Indigenous legal perspectives about obligations and agreements." He aims to establish a sense of "different Indigenous worldviews early in the course. These ways of knowing the world should be running in the background of students' minds as we work our way through common law contracts so they can conceptualize different ways of understanding legal relationships and the obligations that flow from them." The approaches used include "1) providing readings from outsiders to a First Nation (anthropologists, ethnographers, other historical works); 2) internal perspectives from people within a First Nation who have written on their society; 3) the oral tradition itself" (Alan

with a focus on "working with real contracts," "reviewing and drafting contract clauses," and the critical assessment of "emerging topics such as electronic, 'smart' and self-executing contracts." Graben, moreover, advocates for a "transactional" approach to teaching contracts, which includes "the use of emerging technologies that are foundational to transactions" as a way of meeting Ryerson's aspirations.[841] It is entirely possible that the Contracts course might function as an important vector for a genuinely distinctive vision of legal education focused on innovation and technology.

Nevertheless it remains striking that even these two innovations retain the conventional model. To some extent, the approaches might be responding to external forces. In the case of the University of Victoria, there is probably a desire, if not an institutional requirement, to align with the JD program in order to award a "joint" JD/JID degree. In the case of Ryerson, the choice might reflect a pragmatic attempt to maximize the chances of a favourable assessment by the regulators charged with granting its approval. The Federation of Law Societies of Canada has mandated certain competencies that map onto the conventional curriculum, and Ryerson, requiring the approval of both the Federation and the Law Society of Ontario, perhaps wanted to propose a model that transparently delivers on these competencies.[842] Yet, as with the choices of individual professors, structure (in the sense of external forces) might not be the only thing in play. The imposition – or perceived imposition – of these categories on law schools by the regulators might itself reflect a certain inertia of ideas. There might be an extent

---

Hanna, email correspondence with author, 24 September 2019). Selected titles for class readings include "Law in Stories: Ilru Method", "Indigenous Responses to Breakdown of Relations", "Formation of the Agreement: Offer and Acceptance", "Formation of the Agreement: Authority of First Nation Bands to Contract", "Treaties of Contracts?", and "Parties to a Contract" (Alan Hanna, "Law 105I – Transsystemic Contracts Fall Term Reading Schedule" (University of Victoria Faculty of Law, 2019-20)).

841 Ryerson University, *Proposal for a Juris Doctor Program*, *supra* note 831, s 2.9; Sari Graben, email correspondence with author, 17 December 2018. On teaching Contracts from a transactional perspective, see Graben, *supra* note 838 at 15; Michael Hunter Schwartz et al, "All About the First Year of Law School" (2011) 12 Transactions: The Tennessee Journal of Business Law 77; Avery W Katz, "Contractual Incompleteness: A Transactional Perspective" (2005) 56 Case Western Reserve L Rev 169; Erin O'Hara, "Contracts Roundtable: Contracts as a Transactional Course", *Conglomerate* (8 July 2011), online: https://www.theconglomerate.org/2011/07/contracts-roundtable-contracts-as-a-transactional-course.html.

842 *FLSC Report*, *supra* note 5 at 47–8.

to which the mandated competencies derive, however remotely, from the categories the regulating lawyers themselves experienced in law school and that have since "soaked into the marrow of [their] bones."[843] Also, one ought not disregard the possibility that the architects of the new programs themselves hold a genuine commitment to these familiar categories.

Indeed, in the retention of familiar categories, neither Ryerson nor Victoria would appear to go as far as the Georgetown Law School has with its "Curriculum B" – an alternative, optional curriculum that does away with the conventional course titles in favour of courses like Bargain, Exchange, and Liability; Democracy and Coercion; Government Processes; Legal Justice; Legal Practice: Writing and Analysis; Legal Process and Society; and Property In Time. Although the conventional antecedents remain vestigial, the Georgetown example reflects an attempt to put into practice, at the curricular level, a vision of law with a "public" focus that extends beyond adjudication:

> A [traditional] curriculum ... takes little account of the disruption in the common law system caused by the emergence of the regulatory state in the first part of the last century. Today, it is widely understood that adjudication amounts to much more than a retrospective sorting out of the rights of the particular parties before the court. Legal rules govern the conduct of large classes of people and provide appropriate incentives for how they should act in the future. Most of our law comes not from judges deciding individual cases, but from complex statutory schemes written by legislative bodies and from detailed regulations authored by government agencies. Law has a public focus. It allocates power and distributes resources.[844]

Such an approach illustrates both the scope of possibility in curricular design and, by contrary inference, the implicit boundaries of the conventional approach.

---

843 Gordon, Review of LaPiana, *supra* note 718 at 1244–5 ("Practicing lawyers almost never appreciate new theories when they are proposed, dismissing them scornfully as airhead speculation. All the same, the new theories soak gradually into the marrow of lawyers' bones, and, in time, lawyers come to rely on them without being aware of it. Lawyers bought the new treatises ... for their encyclopedic collections of cases; but, with the cases, they absorbed the categories and principles as well").

844 Georgetown Law School, "Curriculum B (Section 3): Introduction", online: https://curriculum.law.georgetown.edu/jd/curriculum-b-section-3/.

Even more radically, one could envision a first-year curriculum restructured around one functional subject, in the spirit of early, but ultimately commercially unsuccessful, realist casebooks that organized materials around subject matter.[845] As Kim Brooks recounts of a conversation with the late Rod Macdonald:

> One day while I was laying there staring at the ceiling he announced: "I think we should teach all of our first year through the lens of some regular object. Cars. Forget obligations and property. Imagine that we taught all of first year through something rooted in everyday life. Something that centred the real people for whom law is made" ...
>
> The idea was so outrageous that I laughed. More than that, imagine teaching at a law school that had already made massive, fundamental change to the curriculum, and being willing to think about another way of revisioning it, yet again, from the ground up.[846]

In these musings, we observe the seeds (ultimately not germinated) of a radically different vision of legal education, one that starts from an entirely different premise: everyday life. Such a vision of legal education not only would *look* completely different, in its course offerings, materials, and pedagogy; all of these distinctive elements would serve to operationalize a distinctive underlying theoretical understanding about law.[847] By contrast, to the extent that curricular structures remain conventional and familiar, the underlying theories of law on which they are based remain unchallenged. Thus, just as a Contracts professor might convey, through teaching, a vision of law potentially at odds with his or her convictions, the broader curriculum might embody a vision of law not explicitly or deliberately intended. The gap between theoretical conviction and practical implementation, between scholarly belief and educational delivery, between aspiration and reality, is therefore a pervasive phenomenon in legal education, spanning the micro and the macro scales.

---

845 See e.g. Harold C Havighurst, *A Selection of Contract Cases and Related Quasi-Contract Cases* (Rochester, NY: Lawyers Co-operative, 1934); Harold C Havighurst, *Cases and Materials on the Law of Contracts*, 2d ed (Chicago: Callaghan & Company, 1950).

846 Kim Brooks, "The World Needs More Rod Macdonald" (2014) 51 Alta L Rev 871 at 872.

847 In Macdonald's case, the theoretical commitment could be labelled "critical legal pluralism." See e.g. Macdonald, "Custom Made", *supra* note 82. For examples of concrete exercises that might contribute to such a curriculum, see Macdonald, *Lessons of Everyday Law*, *supra* note 515.

What stands in the way of reimagining legal education – a classroom, a curriculum, or an institution – from the ground up? On the one hand, this study suggests there is much in the way. Powerful forces from both within and without the law school encourage the replication and merely evolutionary development of the conventional categories and forms of legal education that have predominated since the days of Langdell. Moreover, many law professors are, to put it simply, somewhat divided in their own legal consciousness, propositionally believing in one vision of law while revealing a commitment to very different views of law through their accounts of legal reasoning and in their teaching practices. The impediments to revolutionary thinking in legal education – even in a Contracts class over which the instructor ostensibly has complete control – result from a curious alchemy of explicit constraints, implicit pressures, conscious attitudes, and subconscious beliefs. In light of this, it is no surprising that Brooks found Macdonald's musings so outrageous.

And yet, on the other hand, this study also sheds light on the counterpoint. Most professors in my study are iconoclastic in at least one sense: when speaking about their teaching, they envision theory as serving the preparation for practice, in that theory and critical thinking skills are important to making better lawyers. Such an impetus shows a certain rejection of the determinism that typifies the conventional debate between the academy and the profession, suggesting that conventional structures – in this case, the common bias in favour of the oppositional narrative – are not so definitive as they might appear. Moreover, that such counterstructural attitudes occur with reference to *teaching* suggests that pedagogy is a likely site for the exercise of agency. Rod Macdonald's invitation to think truly outside the bounds of convention might appear less outrageous if viewed as a natural extension of the teacher's inclination to spontaneously articulate ambitious aspirations – as the professors in my study do, over and again, when prompted to speak about their own convictions and first principles. Inasmuch as this study has revealed the indicia and causes of the *failure* to translate theory into practice, it also has highlighted the widespread shared intention to do so. It is this commonly held aspiration that holds the most optimistic promise for inculcating a broad image of the lawyer as citizen.

Legal educators, however, are unlikely to live up to this promise absent a thorough revisiting of the notion of "thinking like a lawyer." This is the primary mechanism by which the idea of legal practice manifests in the Contracts classroom: it is the lingua franca, the primordial task, of the functioning lawyer. And yet, as this study has shown, what it means to "think like a lawyer" is largely presented as the limited task of determining relevance through analogical reasoning and issue spotting. To be sure, these are extremely important intellectual tasks that lawyers often use to ensure, in various contexts, that rules are applied fairly and that differential outcomes are rationally justified – a cornerstone of the rule of law. Other qualities, however, are at play when lawyers think and practise. Teasing out these diverse elements of human thinking and judging – the affective qualities, the attention to social context and reality, the impact of distributional preferences (however implicit), the ability to listen empathetically, the purposive, facilitative, and prospective modes of problem solving, to name just a few – allows a more complete and more accurate picture to emerge of what it means to think like a lawyer. If these diverse human qualities can be internalized into the dominant motif of "legal reasoning," legal educators are likely to move much closer to their stated aspiration of translating their theoretical beliefs into making better lawyers. These lawyers will be "better" not only in their command of an eclectic range of skills and strategies, but also in the scope of their outlook on what it means to contribute to society.

By elucidating the full slate of human qualities that are properly considered the domain of the thinking lawyer, legal educators would strengthen their claim to making a distinctive contribution to the legal profession and to society at large. Although this aspiration remains, for now, unrealized, the requisite theoretical and pedagogical resources are already within contemplation. They just need to be put into practice.

Works Cited

Legislation

Civil Code of Québec.
Constitution Act, 1867 (UK), 30 & 31 Vict, c 3, reprinted in RSC 1985, Appendix II, No 5.
Quebec Act, 1774 (UK), 14 Geo III, c 83.

Jurisprudence

Anglia Television Ltd v Reed, [1972] 1 QB 60 (CA).
Attorney-General v Blake, [2001] 1 AC 268, [2000] 4 All ER 385.
Balfour v Balfour, [1919] 2 KB 571 (CA).
Bank of America Canada v Mutual Trust Co, [2002] 2 SCR 601, 211 DLR (4th) 285.
Bhasin v Hrynew, 2014 SCC 71, [2014] 3 SCR 494.
Bowlay Logging Ltd v Domtar Ltd (1978), 87 DLR (3d) 179, [1978] 4 WWR 105 (BCSC).
Carlill v Carbolic Smoke Ball Co, [1892] 2 QB 484.
Central Trust Co v Rafuse, [1986] 2 SCR 147, 31 DLR (4th) 481.
Chaplin v Hicks, [1911] 2 KB 786 (CA).
Fidler v Sun Life Assurance Co of Canada, 2006 SCC 30, [2006] 2 SCR 3.
Groves v John Wunder Co, 205 Minn 163, 286 NW 235 (1939).
Hadley v Baxendale (1854), 9 Ex 341, 156 ER 145.
Harry v Kreutziger (1978), 9 BCLR 166, 95 DLR (3d) 231 (CA).
Hawkins v McGee, 89 NH 114, 146 A 641 (1929).
Hodgkinson v Simms, [1994] 3 SCR 377, 117 DLR (4th) 161.
Jackson v Horizon Holidays Ltd, [1975] 1 WLR 1468, [1975] 3 All ER 92 (CA).
J Nunes Diamonds v Dominion Electric Protection Company, [1972] SCR 769.
Law Society of British Columbia v Trinity Western University and Brayden Volkenant, 2018 SCC 32, [2018] 2 SCR 293.

Omychund v Barker (1744), 1 Atk 21 at 33, 27 ER 15.
Peevyhouse v Garland Coal & Mining Co, 382 P (2d) 109 (SC Okla 1962).
Raffles v Wichelhaus (1864), 2 H & C 906, 159 ER 375.
Ron Engineering & Construction Eastern Ltd v Ontario, [1981] 1 SCR 111, 119 DLR (3d) 267.
Ruxley Electronics and Construction Ltd v Forsyth, [1966] 1 AC 344.
Scott v Wawanesa Mutual Insurance Co, [1989] 1 SCR 1445.
Scyrup v Economy Tractor Parts Ltd (1963), 43 WWR 49, 40 DLR (2d) 1026 (Man CA).
Shogun Finance v Hudson, [2004] 1 AC 919.
Sky Petroleum v VIP Petroleum Ltd, [1974] 1 WLR 576, [1974] 1 All ER 954.
Southcott Estates Inc v Toronto Catholic District School Board, 2012 SCC 51, [2012] 2 SCR 675.
Tercon Contractors Ltd v British Columbia (Minister of Transportation & Highways), 2010 SCC 4, [2010] 1 SCR 69.
Transfield Shipping v Mercator Shipping (The Achilleas), [2008] UKHL 48, [2009] 1 AC 61.
Trinity Western University and Brayden Volkenant v Law Society of Upper Canada, 2018 SCC 33, [2018] 2 SCR 453.
United Steel Workers, Local 1330 v US Steel Corp, 492 F Supp 1 (ND Ohio 1980), aff'd in part, vacated and remanded in part, 631 F (2d) 1264 (6th Cir 1980).
Wallace v United Grain Growers Ltd, [1997] 3 SCR 701.
Warner Bros Pictures v Nelson, [1937] 1 KB 209.
Wertheim (Sally) v Chicoutimi Pulp Co, [1911] AC 301 (PC).
Wroth v Tyler, [1974] Ch 30.

Secondary Materials: Monographs

Alexander, Larry & Emily Sherwin. *Demystifying Legal Reasoning*. New York: Cambridge University Press, 2008.
American Law Institute. *Restatement (Second) of Contracts*. St. Paul, MN: American Law Institute Publishers, 1981.
Aristotle. *Politics*, translated by CDC Reeve. Indianapolis; Cambridge: Hackett, 2017, Book III.
Atiyah, PS. *Essays on Contract*. Oxford: Clarendon Press, 1986.
Atiyah, PS. *The Rise and Fall of Freedom of Contract*. Oxford: Clarendon Press, 1979.
Bailey, Carol A. *A Guide to Qualitative Field Research*, 2d ed. Thousand Oaks, CA: Pine Forge Press, 2007.
Blackstone, William. *Commentaries on the Laws of England, Book The Third*, 15th ed, with notes and additions by Edward Christian. London: Cadell & Davies, 1809.

Bohr, Niels. *Atomic Theory and the Description of Nature*, vol 1. New York: Cambridge University Press, 1961.

Bourdieu, Pierre. *Distinction: A Social Critique of the Judgement of Taste*, translated by Richard Nice. Cambridge, MA: Harvard University Press, 1984.

Bourdieu, Pierre. *Outline of a Theory of Practice*, translated by Richard Nice. Cambridge: Cambridge University Press, 1977.

Cardozo, Benjamin N. *The Nature of the Judicial Process*. New Haven, CT: Yale University Press, 1921.

Chibbaro, Sergio, Laberton Rondoni & Angelo Vulpiani. *Reductionism, Emergence and Levels of Reality: The Importance of Being Borderline*. Cham, Switzerland: Springer, 2014.

Cohen, Felix. *Ethical Systems and Legal Ideals: An Essay on the Foundations of Legal Criticisms*. New York: Harcourt, Brace, 1933.

Consultative Group on Research and Education in Law. *Law and Learning* (Report to the Social Sciences and Humanities Research Council of Canada, Chairman Harry Arthurs). Ottawa: Social Sciences and Humanities Research Council of Canada, 1983.

Cooter, Robert & Thomas Ulen. *Law and Economics*, 6th ed. Boston: Pearson Education, 2012.

Côté, JE. *An Introduction to the Law of Contract*. Edmonton: Juriliber, 1974.

Danzig, Richard. *The Capability Problem in Contracts*. Mineola, NY: Foundation Press, 1978.

Dworkin, Ronald. *Taking Rights Seriously*. Cambridge, MA: Harvard University Press, 1977.

Fernandez, Angela. *Spreading the Word: From the Litchfield Law School to the Harvard Case Method*. JSD Thesis, Yale University, 2007.

Fernandez, Angela & Markus Dirk Dubber, eds. *Law Books in Action: Essays on the Anglo-American Legal Treatise*. Oxford: Hart, 2012.

Frank, Jerome. *Law and the Modern Mind*. New York: Coward-McCann, 1949.

Fridman, GHL. *The Law of Contract in Canada*, 6th ed. Toronto: Carswell, 2011.

Fried, Charles. *Contract as Promise: A Theory of Contractual Obligation*. Cambridge, MA: Harvard University Press, 1981.

Friedman, Lawrence. *Contract Law in America*. New Orleans: Quid Pro Books, 2011.

Fuller, Lon L. *The Morality of Law*, rev ed. New Haven, CT: Yale University Press, 1969.

Giddens, Anthony. *The Constitution of Society: Outline of a Theory of Structuration*. Cambridge: Polity Press, 1984.

Gilmore, Grant. *The Death of Contract*. Columbus: Ohio State University Press, 1974.

Gordley, James. *Philosophical Origins of Modern Contract Doctrine*. Oxford: Oxford University Press, 2011.

Habermacher, Adrien. *Institutional Cultures and Legal Education at Select Canadian Law Faculties*. DCL Thesis, McGill University Faculty of Law, 2019 [unpublished].

Hall, Geoff R. *Canadian Contractual Interpretation Law*. Markham: LexisNexis Canada, 2016.

Hart, HLA. *The Concept of Law*, 3d ed. Oxford: Oxford University Press, 2012.

Honohan, Iseult. *Civic Republicanism*. New York: Routledge, 2002.

Horwitz, Morton. *Transformation of American Law, 1870–1960*. New York: Oxford University Press, 1992.

Kalman, Laura. *Legal Realism at Yale: 1927–1960*. Chapel Hill: University of North Carolina Press, 1986.

Kaplow, Louis & Steven Shavell. *Fairness Versus Welfare*. Cambridge, MA: Harvard University Press, 2002.

Kelsen, Hans. *Introduction to the Problems of Legal Theory: A Translation of the First Edition of the Reine Rechtslehre or Pure Theory of Law*, translated by Bonnie Litschewski Paulson & Stanley I Paulson. New York: Oxford University Press, 1997.

Kennedy, David & William W Fisher III. *The Canon of American Legal Thought*. Princeton, NJ: Princeton University Press, 2006.

Korzybski, Alfred. *Science and Sanity: An Introduction to Non-Aristotelian Systems and General Semantics*, 5th ed. Brooklyn, NY: Institute of General Semantics, 1994.

Kronman, Anthony T. *The Lost Lawyer: Failing Ideals of the Legal Profession*. Cambridge, MA: Belknap Press, 1993.

Kronman, Anthony T & Richard A Posner, eds. *The Economics of Contract Law*. Boston: Little, Brown, 1979.

Kyer, C Ian & Jerome E Bickenbach. *The Fiercest Debate: Cecil A Wright, the Benchers, and Legal Education in Ontario*. Toronto: Osgoode Society, 1987.

Levi, Edward H. *An Introduction to Legal Reasoning*. Chicago: University of Chicago Press, 1949.

Llewellyn, Karl N. *The Bramble Bush: On Our Law and Its Study*. New York: Oceana, 1989.

Macdonald, Roderick A. *Lessons of Everyday Law*. Montreal; Kingston, ON: McGill-Queen's University Press, 2002.

Macdonald, Roderick Alexander. *Prolegomena to a Theory of Legal Relevance*. LLM Thesis, Faculty of Law, University of Toronto, 1975 [unpublished].

Macneil, Ian R. *The New Social Contract: An Inquiry into Modern Contractual Relations*. New Haven, CT: Yale University Press, 1980.

Maharg, Paul. *Transforming Legal Education: Learning and Teaching Law in the Early Twenty-First Century*. Burlington, VT: Ashgate, 2007.

McCamus, John D. *The Law of Contracts*, 2d ed. Toronto: Irwin Law, 2012.

Mertz, Elizabeth. *The Language of Law School: Learning to "Think Like a Lawyer."* New York: Oxford University Press, 2007.

Morse, J et al. *Developing Grounded Theory: The Second Generation*. Walnut Creek, CA: Left Coast Press, 2009.

Nedelsky, Jennifer. *Law's Relations: A Relational Theory of Self, Autonomy, and Law*. Oxford: Oxford University Press, 2011.

Nelson Espeland, Wendy & Michael Sauder. *Engines of Anxiety: Academic Rankings, Reputation, and Accountability*. New York: Russell Sage Foundation, 2016.

Oktay, Julianne S. *Grounded Theory*. New York: Oxford University Press, 2012.

Polinsky, A Mitchell. *An Introduction to Law and Economics*. Boston: Little, Brown, 1989.

Posner, Richard A. *Economic Analysis of Law*, 4th ed. Boston: Little, Brown, 1992.

Posner, Richard A. *Economic Analysis of Law*, 6th ed. Boston: Little, Brown, 2003.

Posner, Richard A. *Economic Analysis of Law*, 9th ed. New York: Wolters Kluwer Law & Business, 2014.

Radin, Margaret Jane. *Boilerplate: The Fine Print, Vanishing Rights, and the Rule of Law*. Princeton, NJ: Princeton University Press, 2013.

Reed, Alfred Z. *Present-Day Law Schools in the United States and Canada*, Carnegie Foundation Bulletin No. 21. Boston: Merrymount Press, 1928.

Reiter, Barry J & John Swan, eds. *Studies in Contract Law*. Toronto: Butterworth, 1980.

Rochette, Annie. *Teaching and Learning in Canadian Legal Education: An Empirical Exploration*. DCL Thesis, McGill University Faculty of Law, 2010 [unpublished].

Saul, John Ralston. *A Fair Country: Telling Truths about Canada*. Toronto: Penguin, 2008.

Schauer, Frederick. *Thinking Like a Lawyer: A New Introduction to Legal Reasoning*. Cambridge, MA: Harvard University Press, 2009.

Schlegel, John Henry. *American Legal Realism and Empirical Social Science*. Chapel Hill: University of North Carolina Press, 1995.

Schwartz, Michael Hunter, Gerald F Hess & Sophie M Sparrow. *What the Best Law Teachers Do*. Cambridge, MA: Harvard University Press, 2013.

Shachar, Ayelet. *The Birthright Lottery: Citizenship and Global Inequality*. Cambridge, MA: Harvard University Press, 2009.

Simpson, AWB. *A History of the Common Law of Contract: The Rise of the Action of Assumpsit*. Oxford: Clarendon Press, 1975.

Smith, Stephen. *Contract Theory*. New York: Oxford University Press, 2004.

Stephen, Frank H. *The Economics of the Law*. Brighton, UK: Wheatsheaf Books, 1988.

Strauss, Anselm & Juliet Corbin. *Basics of Qualitative Research: Techniques and Procedures for Developing Grounded Theory*. Thousand Oaks, CA: Sage, 1998.

Sullivan, William M et al. *Educating Lawyers: Preparation for the Profession of Law*. San Francisco: Jossey-Bass, 2007.

Summers, Robert. *Lon L Fuller*. Stanford, CA: Stanford University Press, 1984.

Swan, Angela & Jakub Adamski. *Canadian Contract Law*, 3d ed. Markham, ON: LexisNexis, 2012.

Swan, Angela & Jakub Adamski. *Canadian Contract Law*, 3d student ed. Toronto: LexisNexis, 2012.

Swan, John. *Canadian Contract Law*. Markham, ON: LexisNexis, 2006.

Tamanaha, Brian Z. *Failing Law Schools*. Chicago: University of Chicago Press, 2012.

Thaler, Richard H & Cass R Sunstein. *Nudge: Improving Decisions About Health, Wealth, and Happiness*. New Haven, CT: Yale University Press, 2008.

Trebilcock, Michael J. *The Common Law of Restraint of Trade: A Legal and Economic Analysis*. Toronto: Carswell, 1986.

Trebilcock, Michael J. *The Limits of Freedom of Contract*. Cambridge, MA: Harvard University Press, 1993.

Turow, Scott. *One L: The Turbulent True Story of a First Year at Harvard Law School*. New York: Penguin, 1978.

Valverde, Mariana. *Chronotopes of Law: Jurisdiction, Scale and Governance*. Abingdon, UK: Routledge, 2015.

Waddams, SM. *Dimensions of Private Law*. Cambridge: Cambridge University Press, 2003.

Waddams, SM. *Introduction to the Study of Law*. Toronto: Carswell, 1979.

Waddams, SM. *The Law of Contracts*. Toronto: Canada Law Book, 1977.

Waddams, SM. *The Law of Contracts*, 6th ed. Aurora, ON: Canada Law Book, 2010.

Waddams, SM. *The Law of Contracts*, 6th student ed. Toronto: Canada Law Book, 2010.

Waddams, SM. *Principle and Policy in Contract Law: Competing or Complementary Concepts?* Cambridge: Cambridge University Press, 2011.

Weinrib, Ernest. *The Idea of Private Law*, rev ed. Oxford: Oxford University Press, 2012.

White, James Boyd. *Acts of Hope: Creating Authority in Literature, Law, and Politics*. Chicago: University of Chicago Press, 1994.

White, James Boyd. *Living Speech*. Princeton, NJ: Princeton University Press, 2006.

White, Morton. *Social Thought in America: The Revolt Against Formalism*. New York: Viking Press, 1949.

Williamson, OE. *Economic Organization: Firms, Markets and Policy Controls*. Brighton, UK: Harvester Wheatsheaf, 1986.

Willis, John. *A History of Dalhousie Law School*. Toronto: University of Toronto Press, 1979.

Winston, Kenneth I, ed. *The Principles of Social Order: Selected Essays of Lon L Fuller*, rev ed. Portland, OR: Hart, 2001.

Secondary Materials: Articles and Book Chapters

Abeysekera, Lakmal & Phillip Dawson. "Motivation and Cognitive Load in the Flipped Classroom: Definition, Rationale and a Call for Research" (2015) 34 Higher Education Research & Development 1.

Adams, Eric M. "The Dean Who Went to Law School: Crossing Borders and Searching for Purpose in North American Legal Education, 1930–1950" (2016) 54 Alta L Rev 1.

Ainsworth, Janet. "Law in (Case)books, Law (School) in Action: The Case for Casebook Reviews (1997) 20 Seattle UL Rev 270.

Åkerlind, G et al. "A Threshold Concepts Focus to First Year Law Curriculum Design: Supporting Student Learning Using Variation Theory" in *13th Pacific Rim First Year in Higher Education Conference*. Adelaide, Australia, June 2010.

Arthurs, Harry. "Madly Off in One Direction: McGill's New Integrated, Polyjural, Transsystemic Law Programme" (2005) 50 McGill LJ 707.

Arthurs, Harry W. "Poor Canadian Legal Education: So Near to Wall Street, So Far from God" (2000) 38 Osgoode Hall LJ 381.

Arthurs, Harry & Annie Bunting. "Socio-legal Scholarship in Canada: A Review of the Field" (2014) 41 JL & Soc'y 487.

Arthurs, HW. "The Political Economy of Canadian Legal Education" (1998) 25 JL & Soc 14.

Arthurs, HW. "The Tree of Knowledge, The Axe of Power: Le Dain and the Transformation of Canadian Legal Education" in G Blaine Baker & Richard Janda, eds, *Tracings of Gerald Le Dain's Life in the Law*. Montreal; Kingston, ON: McGill-Queen's University Press, 2019, 106.

Ashley, Stephen S. "The Economic Implications of the Doctrine of Impossibility" (1975) 26 Hastings LJ 1251.

Atiyah, PS. "Executory Contracts, Expectation Damages, and the Economic Analysis of Contract" in PS Atiyah, *Essays on Contract*. Oxford: Clarendon Press, 1986.

Ayres, Ian. "Fair Driving: Gender and Race Discrimination in Retail Car Negotiations" (1991) 104 Harv L Rev 817.

Baker, C Edwin. "The Ideology of the Economic Analysis of Law" (1975) 5 Phil & Pub Affairs 3.

Baker, G Blaine. "Introduction: Quebec and the Canadas, 1760–1867: A Legal Historiography" in G Blaine Baker & Donald Fyson, eds, *Quebec and the Canadas*. Toronto: University of Toronto Press, 2013, 3.

Baker, G Blaine. "Willis on 'Cultured' Public Authorities" (2005) 55 UTLJ 335.

Baker, JH. "From Sanctity of Contract to Reasonable Expectation?" (1979) 32 Current Legal Problems 17.

Bakht, Natasha et al. "Counting Outsiders: A Critical Exploration of Outsider Course Enrollment in Canadian Legal Education" (2007) 45 Osgoode Hall LJ 667.

Bala, Nicholas. "Domestic Contracts and the Supreme Court Trilogy: A Deal Is a Deal" (1988) 13 Queen's LJ 1.

Bala, Nicholas. "Recognizing Spousal Contributions to the Acquisition of Degrees, Licences, and Other Career Assets towards Compensatory Support" (1989) 8 Can J Fam L 23.

Belley, Jean-Guy. "L'entreprise, l'approvisionnement et le droit: vers un théorie pluraliste du contract" (1991) 32 Cahiers de Droit 253.

Ben-Ishai, Stephanie. "Thinking about Technology in Canadian Law Schools: A Literature Review" (2007) 1 Canadian Legal Education Annual Review 37.

Ben-Ishai, Stephanie & Saul Schwartz, "The Role of Governments in the Overindebtedness of the Economically Disadvantaged" (2010) 35 Queen's LJ 539.

Bergin, Thomas F. "The Law Teacher: A Man Divided Against Himself" (1968) U Virginia L Rev 637.

Bhabha, Faisal. "Towards a Pedagogy of Diversity in Legal Education" (2015) 52 Osgoode Hall LJ 59.

Bliss, John. "Divided Selves: Professional Role Distancing among Law Students and New Lawyers in a Period of Market Crisis" (2017) 42 Law & Soc Inq 855.

Bridgeman, Curtis & Karen Sandrik. "Bullshit Promises" (2008), FSU College of Law, Public Law Research Paper No 314.

Brooks, Kim. "The World Needs More Rod Macdonald" (2014) 51 Alta L Rev 871.

Campbell, David. "Ian Macneil and the Relational Theory of Contract" in Ian R Macneil, *The Relational Theory of Contract: Selected Works of Ian Macneil*, edited by David Campbell. London: Sweet & Maxwell, 2001, 3.

Christensen, Craig W. "Legal Ordering of Family Values: The Case of Gay and Lesbian Families" (1997) 18 Cardozo LR 1299.

Coase, RH. "The Problem of Social Cost" (1960) 3 J L & Econ 1.

Cohen, Felix S. "Transcendental Nonsense and the Functional Approach" (1935) 35 Colum L Rev 809.

Cohen, Morris R. "The Basis of Contract" (1933) 46 Harv L Rev 553.

Coleman, Jules L. "Legal Theory and Practice" (1995) 83 Geo LJ 2579.

Coquillette, Daniel R & Bruce A Kimball. "The Republic of Merit: Harvard Law School, the First Century (1817-1910) in *The Bicentennial History of the Harvard Law School*, vol 1. Cambridge, MA: Harvard University Press, 2015.

Corbin, Arthur. "Offer and Acceptance, and Some of the Resulting Legal Relations" (1917) 26 Yale LJ 169.

Cownie, Fiona. "Legal Education and the Legal Academy" in Peter Crane & Herbert M Kritzer, eds, *Oxford Handbook of Empirical Legal Research*. Oxford: Oxford University Press, 2010, 854.

Dalton, Clare. "An Essay in the Deconstruction of Contract Doctrine" (1985) 94 Yale LJ 997.

Danzig, Richard. "*Hadley v Baxendale*: A Study in the Industrialization of the Law" (1975) 4 J Legal Stud 249.

Dawson, John P. "Economic Duress – An Essay in Perspective" (1947) 45 Mich L Rev 253.

de Sousa Santos, Boaventura. "Law: A Map of Misreading. Toward a Post-modern Conception of Law" (1987) 14 J Law and Society 279.

Devlin, Richard, Anthony Duggan & Louise Langevin. "Doing Theory in First Year Contracts: The Iceberg Method" (2007) 1 Canadian Legal Education Annual Review 1.

Dewees, Donald N & Michael J Trebilcock. "Judicial Control of Standard Form Contracts" in Paul Burrows & Cento G Veljanovski, eds, *The Economic Approach to Law*. London: Butterworth, 1981.

DiPippa, John MA. "Lon Fuller, The Model Code, and the Model Rules" (1996) 37 S Tex L Rev 303.

Donson, Fiona & Catherine O'Sullivan. "Building Block Or Stumbling Block? Teaching *Actus Reus* and *Mens Rea* in Criminal Law" in Kris Gledhill & Ben Livings, eds, *The Teaching of Criminal Law: The Pedagogical Imperatives*. Milton Park, UK: Routledge, 2017.

Eisenberg, Melvin A. "Why There Is No Law of Relational Contracts" (2000) 94 Nw UL Rev 805.

Epstein, Richard A. "Unconscionability: A Critical Reappraisal" (1975) 18 J Law & Econ 293.

Erlanger, Howard S et al. "Law Student Idealism and Job Choice: Some New Data On an Old Question" (1996) 30 Law & Soc Rev 851.

Eskridge, William N Jr & Philip P Frickey. "The Making of *The Legal Process*" (1994) 107 Harv L Rev 2031.

Farnsworth, E Allan. "Contracts Scholarship in the Age of the Anthology" (1987) 85 Mich L Rev 1390.

Feinman, Jay M. "Critical Approaches to Contract Law" (1983) 30 UCLA L Rev 829.

Feinman, Jay M. "Good Faith and Reasonable Expectations" (2014) 67 Ark L Rev 524.

Feinman, Jay M. "The Reception of Ian Macneil's Work on Contract in the USA" in Ian R Macneil, *The Relational Theory of Contract: Selected Works of Ian Macneil*, edited by David Campbell. London: Sweet & Maxwell, 2001, 59.

Feinman, Jay M. "The Significance of Contract Theory" (1990) 58 U Cinn L Rev 1283.

Feinman, Jay M & Peter Gabel. "Contract Law as Ideology" in David Kairys, ed, *The Politics of Law: A Progressive Critique*, rev ed. New York: Pantheon Books, 1990, 373.

Fernandez, Angela. "An Object Lesson in Speculation: Multiple Views of the Cathedral In *Leaf v International Galleries*" (2008) 58 UTLJ 481.

Fernandez, Angela & Markus D Dubber. "Introduction: Putting the Legal Treatise in Its Place" in Angela Fernandez & Markus Dirk Dubber, eds, *Law Books in Action: Essays on the Anglo-American Legal Treatise*. Oxford: Hart, 2012.

Forcese, Craig. "The Law Professor as Public Citizen: Measuring Public Engagement in Canadian Common Law Schools" (2016) 36 Windsor YB Access Just 66.

Friedman, Lawrence M & Stewart Macaulay, "Contracts and Contract Teaching: Past, Present, and Future" [1967] Wis L Rev 805.

Frug, Mary Joe. "Re-Reading Contracts: A Feminist Analysis of a Contracts Casebook" (1985) 34 Am U L Rev 1065.

Fuller, LL & William R Perdue, Jr. "The Reliance Interest in Contract Damages: 1" (1936) 46 Yale LJ 52.

Fuller, LL & William R Perdue, Jr. "The Reliance Interest in Contract Damages: 2" (1937) 46 Yale LJ 373.

Fuller, Lon L. "Consideration and Form" (1941) 41 Colum L Rev 799.

Fuller, Lon L. "The Lawyer as Architect of Social Structures" in Kenneth I Winston, ed, *The Principles of Social Order: Selected Essays of Lon L Fuller*, rev ed. Oxford; Portland, OR: Hart, 2001, 285.

Fuller, Lon L. "Means and Ends" in Kenneth I Winston, ed, *The Principles of Social Order: Selected Essays of Lon L Fuller*, rev ed. Oxford; Portland, OR: Hart, 2001, 61.

Fuller, Lon L. "Positivism and Fidelity to Law: A Reply to Professor Hart" (1958) 71 Harv L Rev 630.

Fuller, Lon L. "The Forms and Limits of Adjudication" (1978) 92 Harv L Rev 353.

Fuller, Lon L. "What the Law Schools Can Contribute to the Making of Lawyers" (1948) 1 J Legal Ed 189.

Gabel, Peter & Duncan Kennedy. "Roll Over Beethoven" (1984) 36 Stan L Rev 1.

Galanter, M. "Justice in Many Rooms: Courts, Private Ordering, and Indigenous Law" (1981) 19 J Legal Pluralism & Unofficial Law 1.

Gerber, Scott D. "*Corbin and Fuller's Cases on Contracts* (1942?): The Casebook That Never Was" (2003) 72 Fordham L Rev 595.

Gilmore, Grant. "Legal Realism: Its Cause and Cure" (1961) 70 Yale LJ 1037.

Girard, Philip. "The Making of the Canadian Legal Profession: A Hybrid Heritage" (2014) 21 IJLP 145.

Girard, Philip. "Who's Afraid of Canadian Legal History?" (2007) 57 UTLJ 727.

Gordon, Robert W. "Is the World of Contracting Relations One of Spontaneous Order or Pervasive State Action? Stewart Macaulay Scrambles the

Public-Private Distinction" in Jean Braucher, John Kidwell & William C Whitford, eds, *Revisiting the Contract Law Scholarship of Stewart Macaulay: On the Empirical and the Lyrical*. Portland, OR: Hart, 2013, 49.
Gordon, Robert W. "Macaulay, Macneil, and the Discovery of Solidarity and Power in Contracts" [1985] Wisc L Rev 565.
Gordon, Robert W. "Willis's American Counterparts: The Legal Realists' Defense of Administration" (2005) 55 UTLJ 405.
Graben, Sari. "A Systemic Approach to Law and Technology at Ryerson University," draft paper on file with author (2019).
Grammond, Sébastien. "Reasonable Expectations and the Interpretation of Contracts Across Legal Traditions" (2010) 48 Can Bus LJ 345.
Granfield, Robert. "Cynicism and the Law: The Emergence of Legal Consciousness In Law School" (1994) 25 J Soc Phil 188.
Green, Leslie. "Introduction" in HLA Hart, *The Concept of Law*, 3d ed. Oxford: Oxford University Press, 2012, xv.
Green, Leslie. "Preface to the Third Edition" in HLA Hart, *The Concept of Law*, 3d ed. Oxford: Oxford University Press, 2012, xi.
Grey, Thomas C. "Langdell's Orthodoxy" (1983) 45 U Pitt L Rev 1.
Hadfield, Gillian K. "An Expressive Theory of Contract: From Feminist Dilemmas to a Reconceptualization of Rational Choice in Contracts" (1998) 146 U Pa L Rev 1235.
Hadfield, Gillian K & Iva Bozovic. "Scaffolding: Using Formal Contracts to Support Informal Relations in Support of Innovation [2016] Wisc L Rev 981.
Hale, Robert L. "Bargaining, Duress, and Economic Liberty" (1943) 43 Colum L Rev 603.
Hale, Robert L. "Coercion and Distribution in a Supposedly Noncoercive State" (1923) 38 Political Science Quarterly 470.
Hansmann, Henry. "The Current State of Law-and-Economics Scholarship" (1983) 33 J Legal Educ 217.
Hart, HLA. "Positivism and the Separation of Morals" (1958) 71 Harv L Rev 593.
Hewitt, Jeffrey G. "Decolonizing and Indigenizing: Some Considerations for Law Schools" (2016) 33 Windsor YB Access Just 65.
Hohfeld, Wesley Newcomb. "Fundamental Legal Conceptions as Applied in Judicial Reasoning" (1917) 26 Yale LJ 710.
Holloway, Ian & Steven I Friedland. "The Double Life of Law Schools" (2017) 68 Case Western Reserve L Rev 397.
Holmes, OW. "The Path of the Law" (1897) 10 Harv L Rev 457.
Horwitz, Morton. "The Rise of Legal Formalism" (1975) Am J Legal Hist 251.
Hume, David. "Of the Original Contract," reprinted in *Social Contract: Essays by Locke, Hume, and Rousseau With an Introduction by Sir Ernest Barker*. Westport, CT: Greenwood Press, 1980, 148.
Jutras, Daniel. "The Legal Dimensions of Everyday Life" (2001) 16 CJLS 45.

Kairys, David. "Introduction" in David Kairys, ed, *The Politics of Law: A Progressive Critique*, rev ed. New York: Pantheon Books, 1990, 1.

Kaplow, Louis & Steven Shavell. "Why the Legal System Is Less Efficient than the Income Tax in Redistributing Income" (1994) 23 J Legal Studies 667.

Katz, Avery W. "Contractual Incompleteness: A Transactional Perspective" (2005) 56 Case Western Reserve L Rev 169.

Keener, William A. "The Inductive Method in Legal Education" (1894) 17 Ann Rep ABA 473.

Kennedy, David & William W Fisher III. "Introduction" in David Kennedy & William W Fisher III, *The Canon of American Legal Thought*. Princeton, NJ: Princeton University Press, 2006, 1.

Kennedy, Duncan. "Cost-Benefit Analysis of Entitlement Problems: A Critique" (1981) 33 Stan L Rev 387.

Kennedy, Duncan. "Form and Substance in Private Law Adjudication" (1976) 88 Harv L Rev 1685.

Kennedy, Duncan. "From the Will Theory to the Principle of Private Autonomy: Lon Fuller's 'Consideration and Form'" (2000) 100 Colum L Rev 94.

Kennedy, Duncan. "Legal Education and the Reproduction of Hierarchy" (1982) 32 J Legal Ed 591.

Kennedy, Duncan. "Politicizing the Classroom" (1995) 4 Rev L Women's Stud 81.

Kennedy, Duncan. "Toward an Historical Understanding of Legal Consciousness: The Case of Classical Legal Thought in America, 1850–1940" (1980) 3 Research in Law and Sociology 3.

Kessler, Friedrich. "Contracts of Adhesion – Some Thoughts about Freedom of Contract" (1943) 43 Colum L Rev 629.

Kimball, Bruce. "Langdell on Contracts and Legal Reasoning: Correcting the Holmesian Caricature" (2007) 25 Law & Hist Rev 345.

Klare, Karl. "Teaching *Local 1330* – Reflections on Critical Pedagogy" (2001) 7 Unbound: Harvard Journal of the Legal Left 58.

Koshan, Jennifer et al. "Rewriting Equality: The Pedagogical Use of Women's Court of Canada Judgments" (2010) 4 Canadian Legal Education Annual Review 1.

Kronman, Anthony T. "Mistake, Disclosure, Information, and the Law of Contracts" (1978) J Legal Studies 1.

Kronman, Anthony T. "Specific Performance" (1978) 45 U Chi L Rev 351.

Leering, Michelle. "Conceptualizing Reflective Practice for Legal Professionals" (2014) 23 J L Soc Policy 1.

Llewellyn, KN. "The Normative, the Legal and the Law-Jobs: The Problem of Juristic Method" (1940) 49 Yale LJ 1355.

Llewellyn, Karl N. "Some Realism about Realism – Responding to Dean Pound" (1931) 44 Harv L Rev 1222.

Locke, John. "An Essay Concerning the True Original, Extent and End of Civil Government," Part VIII, reprinted in *Social Contract: Essays by Locke,*

Hume, and Rousseau With an Introduction by Sir Ernest Barker. Westport, CT: Greenwood Press, 1980, 56.

Macaulay, Stewart. "Elegant Models, Empirical Pictures and the Complexities of Contract" (1977) 11 Law & Soc Rev 507.

Macaulay, Stewart. "Non-Contractual Relations in Business: A Preliminary Study" (1963) 28 Am Soc Rev 55.

Macaulay, Stewart. "Private Legislation and the Duty to Read – Business Run by IBM Machine, the Law of Contracts and Credit Cards" (1966) 19 Vanderbilt L Rev 1051.

Macaulay, Stewart. "The Real Deal and the Paper Deal: Empirical Pictures of Relationships" (2003) 66 Mod L Rev 44.

Macaulay, Stewart et al. "What Contract Study Should Be" in Stewart Macaulay et al, *Contracts: Law in Action*. Charlottesville, VI: Michie, 1995, vol 1, 17.

Macdonald, Rod. "Legal Education on the Threshold of the 1980s: Whatever Happened to the Great Ideas of the 60s" (1979) 44 Sask L Rev 39.

Macdonald, Roderick A. "Curricular Development in the 1980s: A Perspective" (1982) 32 J Legal Ed 569.

Macdonald, Roderick A. "Custom Made – for a Non-Chirographic Critical Legal Pluralism" (2011) 27 CJLS 301.

Macdonald, Roderick A. "Here, There ... and Everywhere: Theorizing Legal Pluralism; Theorizing Jacques Vanderlinden" in N Kasirer, ed, *Étudier et enseigner le droit: hier, aujourd'hui et demain – Études offertes à Jacques Vanderlinden*. Montreal: Éditions Yvon Blais, 2006, 381.

Macdonald, Roderick A. "Les Vieilles Gardes: hypothèses sur l'émergence des normes, l'internormativité et le désordre à travers une typologie des institutions normatives" in Jean-Guy Belley, ed, *Le droit soluble: Contributions québécoises à l'étude de l'internormativité*. Paris: Librairie générale de droit et de jurisprudence, 1996, 233.

Macdonald, Roderick A. "Pour la reconnaissance d'une normativité juridique implicite et inférentielle" (1986) 18 Sociologie et Sociétés 47.

Macdonald, Roderick A & David Sandomierski. "Against Nomopolies" (2006) 57 Northern Ireland LQ 610.

Macdonald, Roderick A & Jason Maclean. "No Toilets in Park" (2005) 50 McGill LJ 721.

Macneil, Ian R. "Contracts: Adjustment of Long-Term Economic Relations under Classical, Neoclassical and Relational Contracts" (1978) 72 Nw U L Rev 854.

Macneil, Ian R. "Economic Analysis of Contractual Relations: Its Shortfalls and Its Need for a 'Rich Classificatory Apparatus'" (1981) 75 Nw U L Rev 1018.

Macneil, Ian R. "Relational Contract Theory: Challenges and Queries" (2000) 94 Nw UL Rev 877.

Macneil, Ian R. "The Many Futures of Contract" (1974) 47 S Cal L Rev 691.

Macneil, Ian R. "Whither Contracts" (1969) 21 J Legal Ed 403.

Manderson, Desmond & Sarah Turner. "Coffee House: *Habitus* and Performance Among Law Students" (2006) 31 L & Soc Inq 649.

Marisco, Richard D. "The Higher Cost of Being African-American or Latino: Subprime Home Mortgage Lending in New York City 2004–2005" (2007), NYLS Legal Studies Research Paper No. 07/08-12.

Mensch, Elizabeth. "The History of Mainstream Legal Thought" in David Kairys, ed, *The Politics of Law: A Progressive Critique*, rev ed. New York: Pantheon Books, 1990, 13.

Michelman, Frank I. "A Comment on *Some Uses and Abuses of Economics in Law*" (1979) 46 U Chi L Rev 307.

Minow, Martha. "Foreword: Justice Engendered" (1987) 101 Harv L Rev 10.

Mnookin, Robert H & Lewis Kornhauser. "Bargaining in the Shadow of the Law: The Case of Divorce" (1979) 88 Yale LJ 950.

Moore, S. "Law and Social Change: The Semi-Autonomous Social Field as an Appropriate Object of Study" (1973) 7 Law & Soc Rev.

Morag-Levine, Noga. "Facts, Formalism, and the Brandeis Brief: The Origins of a Myth" [2013] U Ill L Rev 59.

Noreau, Pierre & Pierre-Olivier Bonin, "Faire droit ... devenir juriste: Trajectoire des étudiants en faculté: une étude en contexte québécois" (2017) 22 Lex Electronica 169.

Note. (1891) 5 Harv L Rev 89.

Ogus, AI. "Damages for Pre-Contract Expenditure" (1972) 35 Mod L Rev 423.

Posner, Richard A. "Gratuitous Promises in Economics and Law" (1977) 6 J Legal Studies 411.

Posner, Richard A & Andrew M Rosenfield. "Impossibility and Related Doctrines in Contracts: An Economic Analysis" (1977) 6 J Legal Studies 83.

Pound, Roscoe. "Mechanical Jurisprudence" (1908) 8 Colum L Rev 605.

Priest, George. "Social Science Theory and Legal Education: The Law School as a University" (1983) 33 J Legal Ed 437.

Pue, W Wesley. "Common Law Legal Education in Canada's Age of Light, Soap and Water" (1995) 23 Man LJ 654.

Pue, W Wesley. "Educating the Total Jurist?" (2005) 8 Legal Ethics 208.

Raso, Jennifer. "Unity in the Eye of the Beholder? Reasons for Decision in Theory and Practice in the Ontario Works Program" (2020) 70 UTLJ 1.

Reiter, Barry J. "A Study in Reasonable Expectations: A Rebuttal to Geoff Hall" (2008) 46 Can Bus LJ 95.

Richards, Tom. "An Intellectual History of NUD*IST and NVivo" (2002) 5 J Social Research Methodology 199.

Risk, RCB. "John Willis – A Tribute" (1985) 9 Dal LJ 521.

Risk, RCB. "Lawyers, Courts, and the Rise of the Regulatory State" (1984) 9 Dal LJ 31.

Risk, RCB. "My Continuing Legal Education" (2005) 55 UTLJ 313.
Risk, RCB. "Volume 1 of the Journal: A Tribute and a Belated Review" (1987) 37 UTLJ 193.
Risk, RCB & Michael Taggart. "The Published Work of John Willis" (2005) 55 UTLJ 887.
Rochette, Annie & W Wesley Pue. "'Back to Basics'? University Legal Education and 21st Century Professionalism" (2001) 20 Windsor YB Access Just 167.
Rousseau, JJ. "The Social Contract," Parts V and VI, reprinted in *Social Contract: Essays by Locke, Hume, and Rousseau With an Introduction by Sir Ernest Barker*. Westport, CT: Greenwood Press, 1980, 178.
Sanchirico, Chris. "Deconstructing the New Efficiency Rationale" (2001) Cornell L Rev 1005.
Sandomierski, David. "Theory and Practice, Together At Last: A Heretical, Empirical Account of Canadian Legal Education" in Meera E Deo, Mindie Lazarus-Black & Elizabeth Mertz, eds, *Power, Legal Education, and Law School Cultures*. Abingdon, Oxon; New York: Routledge, 2019, 1.
Sandomierski, David. "Training Lawyers, Cultivating Citizens, and Re-Enchanting the Legal Professional" (2014) 51 Alta L Rev 739.
Schwartz, Michael Hunter et al. "All About the First Year of Law School" (2011) 12 Transactions: The Tennessee Journal of Business Law 77.
Scott, Robert E. "Conflict and Cooperation in Long-Term Contracts" (1987) 75 Cal L Rev 2005.
Scott, Robert E. "The Promise and the Peril of Relational Contract Theory" in Jean Braucher, John Kidwell & William C Whitford, eds, *Revisiting the Contract Law Scholarship of Stewart Macaulay: On the Empirical and the Lyrical*. Portland, OR: Hart, 2013, 105.
Shapiro, F. "The Most-Cited Law Review Articles Revisited" (1996) 71 Chicago-Kent L Rev 751.
Simpson, AW Brian. "Quackery and Contracts, *Carlill v Carbolic Smoke Ball Company* (1893)" in AW Brian Simpson, *Leading Cases in the Common Law*. Oxford: Clarendon Press, 1995, 259.
Simpson, AW Brian. "The Beauty of Obscurity: *Raffles v Wichelhaus* and *Busch* (1864)" in AW Brian Simpson, *Leading Cases in the Common Law*. Oxford: Clarendon Press, 1995, 135.
Singer, Joseph. "The Legal Rights Debate in Analytical Jurisprudence from Bentham to Hohfeld" [1982] Wisc L Rev 975.
Smith, Stephen A. "The Reasonable Expectations of the Parties: An Unhelpful Concept" (2009) 48 Can Bus LJ 366.
Sossin, Lorne. "Experience the Future of Legal Education" (2014) 51 Alta L Rev 849.
Sugarman, David. "'A Hatred of Disorder': Legal Science, Liberalism and Imperialism" in Peter Fitzpatrick, ed, *Dangerous Supplements: Resistance and Renewal in Jurisprudence*. Concord, MA: Pluto Press, 1991, 34.

Sullivan, Barbara. "It's All In the Contract: Rethinking Feminist Critiques of Contract" (2001) 18 Law in Context 112.
Tallin, GPR. "Legal Education in Manitoba" 15 (1964) UTLJ 433.
Tidwell, Patricia A & Peter Linzer. "The Flesh-Colored Band Aid – Contracts, Feminism, Dialogue, and Norms" (1991) 28 Hous LR 791.
Trebilcock, MJ. "The Doctrine of Inequality of Bargaining Power: Post-Benthamite Economics in the House of Lords" (1976) 26 UTLJ 359.
Valverde, Mariana. "Jurisdiction and Scale: Legal 'Technicalities' as Resources for Theory" (2009) 18 Social & Legal Studies 139.
Veljanovski, C. "The Coase Theorems and the Economic Theory of Markets and Law" (1982) 35 Kyklos 66.
Waddams, SM. "Nineteenth-Century Treatises on English Contracts" in Angela Fernandez & Markus Dirk Dubber, eds, *Law Books In Action: Essays on the Anglo-American Legal Treatise*. Oxford: Hart, 2012, 127.
Waddams, SM. "Unconscionability in Contracts" (1976) 39 Mod L Rev 1.
Webb, Julian. "The 'Ambitious Modesty' of Harry Arthurs' Humane Professionalism" (2006) 44 Osgoode Hall LJ 119.
Weinrib, Ernest J. "Can Law Survive Legal Education?" (2007) 60 Vanderbilt L Rev 401.
Weinrib, Ernest J. "Legal Formalism: On the Immanent Rationality of Law" (1988) 97 Yale LJ 949.
Weresh, MH. "Stargate: Malleability as a Threshold Concept in Legal Education" (2014) 63 J Legal Ed 689.
Williams, EK. "Legal Education in Manitoba: 1913-1950 (1950) 28 Can Bar Rev 759.
Williams, EK. "Legal Education in Manitoba: 1913-1950 (1950) 28 Can Bar Rev 880.
Williams, Patricia J. "Alchemical Notes: Reconstructing Ideals from Deconstructed Rights" (1987) 22 Harv CR-CL L Rev 401.
Willis, John. "Canadian Administrative Law in Retrospect" (1974) 24 UTLJ 225.

Secondary Materials: Reviews

Atiyah, Patrick. Book Review of *Studies in Contract Law* by Barry J Reiter & John Swan, eds, (1981) 5 Can Bus LJ 245.
Beale, Hugh. Book Review of *The Law of Contracts* by SM Waddams, (1980) 15 J Soc't Pub Tchrs L ns 139.
Bigfoot, Rick. Book Review of *Canadian Contract Law*, 3d ed by Angela Swan & Jakub Adamski, (2014) 55 Can Bus LJ 313.
Bilodeau, Roger. Book Review of *Introduction to the Study of Law*, 3d ed by SM Waddams, (1988) 67 Can Bar Rev 394.
Brazier, Rodney. Book Review of *Contracts: Cases, Notes & Materials* by John Swan & Barry J Reiter, (1980) 43 Mod L Rev 235.

Brownsword, Roger. Book Review of *Contracts: Cases, Notes & Materials* by John Swan & Barry J Reiter, (1979) 42 Mod L Rev 479.

Carr, Christopher. Book Review of *Milner's Cases and Materials on Contracts*, 2d ed by SM Waddams, ed, (1971) 6 UBC L Rev 451.

Coote, Brian. Book Review of *Studies in Contract Law* by Barry J Reiter & John Swan, eds, (1981) 19 UWO L Rev 357.

Devlin, Richard F. Book Review of *Contracts: Cases and Commentaries*, 5th ed by Christine Boyle & David R Percy, eds, (1996) 27 Can Bus LJ 144.

Farber, Daniel A. "What (If Anything) Can Economics Say About Equity?", Book Review of *Fairness Versus Welfare* by Louis Kaplow and Steven Shavell, (2003) 101 Mich L Rev 1791.

Fridman, GHL. Book Review of *Milner's Cases and Materials on Contract Law*, 3d ed by SM Waddams, ed, (1977) UWO L Rev 256.

Fridman, GHL. Book Review of *Studies in Contract Law* by Barry J Reiter & John Swan, eds, (1981) 26 McGill LJ 408.

Fuller, Lon L. "American Legal Philosophy at Mid-Century", Book Review of *Jurisprudence, Men and Ideas of the Law* by Edwin W Patterson, (1954) 6 J Legal Ed 457.

Gordon, Robert W. "American Law through English Eyes: A Century of Nightmares and Noble Dreams", Book Review of *Patterns of American Jurisprudence* by Neil Duxbury, (1996) 84 Geo LJ.

Gordon, Robert W. "The Case For (and Against) Harvard", Review of *Logic and Experience: The Origin of Modern American Legal Education* by William P LaPiana, (1995) 93 Mich L Rev 1231.

Granger, C. Book Review of *Milner's Cases and Materials on Contracts*, 2d ed by SM Waddams, ed, (1971) 5 Ottawa L Rev 268.

Hall, Geoff R. "A Study In Reasonable Expectations", Book Review of *Canadian Contract Law* by John Swan, (2007) 45 Can Bus LJ 150.

Hatherly, Mary. Book Review of *Studies in Contract Law* by Barry J Reiter & John Swan, eds, (1981) 30 UNBLJ 265.

Higgins, PFP. Book Review of *The Law of Contracts* by SM Waddams, (1979) 42 Mod L Rev 239.

Holmes, Oliver Wendel. Review of *A Selection of Cases on the Law of Contracts, With a Summary of the Topics Covered by the Cases* by Christopher Columbus Langdell, (1880) 14 Am L Rev 233 at 234.

Horwitz, Morton. Book Review of *Death of Contract* by Grant Gilmore, (1975) 42 U Chi L Rev 787.

Kaplan, Benjamin. Book Review of *Contracts: Cases and Materials* by Friedrich Kessler & Malcolm Pitman Sharp, (1954) 63 Yale LJ 1039.

Klare, Karl E. "Contracts Jurisprudence and the First-Year Casebook", Book Review of *Problems in Contract Law: Cases and Materials* by Charles L Knapp, (1979) 54 NYU L Rev 876.

Kyer, Clifford Ian. Book Review of *Milner's Cases and Materials on Contracts*, 3d ed by SM Waddams, ed and *Contracts: Cases, Notes & Materials* by John Swan & Barry J Reiter, (1978) 37 U Toronto Fac L Rev 152.

Leiter, Brian. "Positivism, Realism, Formalism", Book Review of *Legal Positivism in American Jurisprudence* by Anthony Sebok, (1999) 99 Colum L Rev 1138.

Macdonald, RA. Book Review of *Introduction to the Study of Law* by SM Waddams, (1981) 31 UTLJ 436.

Manwaring, JA. Book Review of *Contracts: Cases and Commentaries*, 2d ed by Christine Boyle & David R Percy, eds, (1982) Can Bar Rev 781.

McLellan, A Anne. Book Review of *Contracts: Cases, Notes & Materials* by John Swan & Barry J Reiter and *Contracts: Cases and Commentaries* by Christine Boyle & David R Percy, eds, (1979) 28 UNB LJ 257.

Menon, Anne. Book Review of *Canadian Contract Law* by John Swan, (2007) 32 Can L Libr Rev 33.

Norman, Ken. Book Review of *Introduction to the Study of Law* by SM Waddams, (1980) 45 Sask L Rev 171.

Nozick, RS. Book Review of *Milner's Cases and Materials on Contracts*, 3d ed by SM Waddams, ed, (1978) 16 Alta L Rev 544.

Percy, David. Book Review of *Studies in Contract Law* by Barry J Reiter & John Swan, eds, (1981) 59 Can Bar Rev 853.

Porwancher, Andrew. Book Review of *On the Battlefield of Merit: Harvard Law School, the First Century* by Daniel R Coquillette & Bruce A Kimball, (2016) 34 Law & Hist Rev 819.

Pratt, Alan. Book Review of *Introduction to the Study of Law* by SM Waddams, (1979) 37 U Toronto Fac L Rev 270.

Scaleta, Dean I. Book Review of *Studies in Contract Law by* Barry J Reiter & John Swan, eds, (1981) 11 Man LJ 117.

Schwartz, Saul. Book Review of *Studies in Contract Law* by Barry J Reiter & John Swan, eds, (1981) 15 UBC L Rev 519.

Sharp, Malcolm. Book Review of *Basic Contract Law* by Lon L Fuller, (1948) 15 U Chi L Rev 79.

Singer, Joseph William. "Legal Realism Now", Review Essay of *Legal Realism at Yale: 1927–1960* by Laura Kalman, (1988) 76 Cal L Rev 465.

Soberman, DA. Book Review of *The Law of Contracts* by SM Waddams, (1979) 17 UWO L Rev 314.

Turriff, Gordon. Book Review of *Contracts: Cases, Notes & Materials* by John Swan & Barry J Reiter, [1979-80] 4 Can Bus LJ 489.

Vaver, David. Book Review of *Contracts: Cases and Commentaries* by Christine Boyle & David R Percy, eds, (1979) 17 Alta L Rev 567.

Vincent, Linda. Book Review of *Contracts: Cases, Notes & Materials* by John Swan & Barry J Reiter, (1979) 9 Man LJ 347.

Secondary Materials: Casebooks

Ben-Ishai, Stephanie & David R Percy, eds. *Contracts: Cases and Commentaries*, 8th ed. Toronto: Carswell, 2009.
Ben-Ishai, Stephanie & David R Percy, eds. *Contracts: Cases and Commentaries*, 9th ed. Toronto: Carswell, 2014.
Ben-Ishai, Stephanie & David R Percy, eds. *Contracts: Cases and Commentaries*, 10th ed. Toronto: Carswell, 2018.
Ben-Ishai, Stephanie & Thomas GW Telfer, eds. *Bankruptcy and Insolvency Law in Canada: Cases, Materials, and Problems*. Toronto: Irwin Law, 2019.
Boyle, Christine & David R Percy, eds. *Contracts: Cases and Commentaries*. Toronto: Carswell, 1978.
Boyle, Christine & David R Percy, eds. *Contracts: Cases and Commentaries*, 2d ed. Toronto: Carswell, 1981.
Boyle, Christine & David R Percy, eds. *Contracts: Cases and Commentaries*, 3d ed. Toronto: Carswell, 1985.
Boyle, Christine & David R Percy, eds. *Contracts: Cases and Commentaries*, 4th ed. Toronto: Carswell, 1989.
Boyle, Christine & David R Percy, eds. *Contracts: Cases and Commentaries*, 5th ed. Toronto: Carswell, 1994.
Boyle, Christine & David R Percy, eds. *Contracts: Cases and Commentaries*, 6th ed. Toronto: Carswell, 1999.
Boyle, Christine & David R Percy, eds. *Contracts: Cases and Commentaries*, 7th ed. Toronto: Thomson Carswell, 2004.
Corbin, Arthur Linton. *Corbin on Contracts: A Comprehensive Treatise on the Rules of Contracts*. St. Paul, MN: West, 1950.
Dawson, John P, William Burnett Harvey & Stanley D Henderson. *Contracts: Cases and Comment*, 8th ed. Mineola, NY: Foundation Press, 2003.
Fuller, Lon L. *Basic Contract Law*. St Paul, MN: West, 1947.
Havighurst, Harold C. *A Selection of Contract Cases and Related Quasi-Contract Cases*. Rochester, NY: Lawyers Co-operative, 1934.
Havighurst, Harold C. *Cases and Materials on the Law of Contracts*, 2d ed. Chicago: Callaghan, 1950.
Kessler, Friedrich & Malcolm Pitman Sharp. *Contracts: Cases and Materials*. New York: Prentice-Hall, 1953.
Knapp, Charles L. *Problems in Contract Law: Cases and Materials*. Boston: Little, Brown, 1976.
Langdell, Christopher Columbus. *A Selection of Cases on the Law of Contracts: With a Summary of the Topics Covered by the Cases: Prepared for Use as a Text-Book in Harvard Law*, 2d ed. Boston: Little, Brown, 1879.
Macaulay, Stewart et al. *Contracts: Law in Action*, vol 1. Charlottesville, VI: Michie, 1995.

Macaulay, Stewart et al. *Contracts: Law in Action, Volume One: The Introductory Course Teacher's Manual*, 4th ed. Durham, NC: Carolina Academic Press, 2016.

Macneil, Ian R. *Cases and Materials on Contracts: Exchange Transactions and Relationships.* Mineola, NY: Foundation Press, 1971.

Macneil, Ian R. *Contracts: Exchange Transactions and Relations: Cases and Materials*, 2d ed. Mineola, NY: Foundation Press, 1978.

Markovits, Daniel. *Contract Law and Legal Methods*. New York: Foundation Press, 2012.

Milner, JB, ed. *Cases and Materials on Contracts*. Toronto: University of Toronto Press, 1963.

Swan, Angela, Barry J Reiter & Nicholas C Bala. *Contracts: Cases, Notes & Materials*, 8th ed. Toronto: LexisNexis Canada, 2010.

Swan, Angela, Nicholas C Bala & Jakub Adamski. *Contracts: Cases, Notes & Materials*, 9th ed. Toronto: LexisNexis Canada, 2015.

Swan, John & Barry J Reiter. *Contracts: Cases, Notes & Materials*. Toronto: Butterworth, 1978.

Swan, John & Barry J Reiter. *Contracts: Cases, Notes & Materials*, 2d ed. Toronto: Butterworth, 1982.

Swan, John & Barry J Reiter. *Contracts: Cases, Notes, and Materials*, 3d ed. Toronto: Emond Montgomery, 1985.

Swan, John & Barry J Reiter. *Contracts: Cases, Notes and Materials*, 4th ed. Toronto: Emond Montgomery, 1991.

Swan, John, Barry J Reiter & Nicholas C Bala, *Contracts: Cases, Notes & Materials*, 5th ed. Toronto: Butterworths, 1997.

Swan, John, Barry J Reiter & Nicholas C Bala. *Contracts: Cases, Notes & Materials*, 6th ed. Toronto: Butterworths, 2002.

Swan, John, Barry J Reiter & Nicholas C Bala. *Contracts: Cases, Notes & Materials*, 7th ed. Toronto: LexisNexis Canada, 2006.

Waddams, SM, ed. *Milner's Cases and Materials on Contracts*, 2d ed. Toronto: University of Toronto Press, 1971.

Waddams, SM, ed. *Milner's Cases and Materials on Contracts*, 3d ed. Toronto: University of Toronto Press, 1977.

Waddams, SM, ed. *Milner's Cases and Materials on Contracts*, 4th ed. Toronto: Emond Montgomery, 1985.

Waddams, SM et al. *Cases and Materials on Contracts*, 3d ed. Toronto: Emond Montgomery, 2005.

Waddams, SM et al. *Cases and Materials on Contracts*, 4th ed. Toronto: Emond Montgomery, 2010.

Waddams, SM et al. *Cases and Materials on Contracts*, 5th ed. Toronto: Emond Montgomery, 2014.

Waddams, SM et al. *Cases and Materials on Contracts*, 6th ed. Toronto: Emond Montgomery, 2018.

Waddams, SM, M Trebilcock & MA Waldron. *Cases and Materials on Contracts.* Toronto: Emond Montgomery, 1994.

Waddams, SM, M Trebilcock & MA Waldron. *Cases and Materials on Contracts,* 2d ed. Toronto: Emond Montgomery, 2000.

Williston, Samuel, ed. *A Selection of Cases on the Law of Contracts,* vol 1. Boston: Little, Brown, 1903.

Secondary Materials: Other Materials

American Bar Association, Task Force on the Future of Legal Education. "Working Paper" (1 August 2013), online: http://www.americanbar.org/content/dam/aba/administrative/professional_responsibility/taskforcecomments/aba_task_force_working_paper_august_2013.authcheckdam.pdf).

Baird, Douglas. Interview with author (11 April 2013).

Balakrishnan, Anita. "Memorial University senate approves law school proposal" *Canadian Lawyer* (27 November 2018), online: https://www.canadianlawyermag.com/legalfeeds/author/anita-balakrishnan/memorial-university-senate-approves-law-school-proposal-16547/.

Berger, Benjamin et al. "A Submission to the LSUC Dialogue on Licensing: A Response from Some Ontario Law Professors" (2017), online: https://lsodialogue.ca/wp-content/uploads/2018/07/Written-Submissions-Dialogue-on-Licensing-D2_2018jul6-red.pdf.

Cameron, Camille. Letter to Dr Christopher H Evans, Interim Provost and Vice President Academic, Ryerson University (24 November 2016), online: https://s3.amazonaws.com/tld-documents.llnassets.com/0005000/5463/ccld%20response%20to%20ryerson%20proposal.pdf.

Dalhousie University, Schulich School of Law. *Strategic Directions 2017–2021,* online: https://www.dal.ca/faculty/law/about/strategic-directions-2017-2021.html.

Devlin, Richard & Sarah Berger Richardson. "Laws 1000X Contracts and Judicial Decision-making." Syllabus (Schulich School of Law at Dalhousie University, 2018-19), online: https://cdn.dal.ca/content/dam/dalhousie/pdf/law/Academic%20Information%20Syllabi%20Moots%20Regulations/Syllabi/LAWS%201000%20Contracts%20Syllabus%202018-2019%20Devlin.pdf.

Federation of Law Societies of Canada, Common Law Degree Implementation Committee. *Final Report* (August 2011), online: http://docs.flsc.ca/Implementation-Report-ECC-Aug-2011-R.pdf.

Fuller, Lon L. Letter to Arthur L Corbin (7 October 1940), reproduced in Scott D Gerber, "*Corbin and Fuller's Cases on Contracts* (1942?): The Casebook that Never Was" (2003) 72 Fordham L Rev 595.

Fuller, Lon L. Letter to Arthur L Corbin (10 November 1941), reproduced in Scott D Gerber, "*Corbin and Fuller's Cases on Contracts* (1942?): The Casebook that Never Was" (2003) 72 Fordham L Rev 595.

Fuller, Lon L. Letter to Arthur L Corbin (24 November 1941), reproduced in Scott D Gerber, "*Corbin and Fuller's Cases on Contracts* (1942?): The Casebook that Never Was" (2003) 72 Fordham L Rev 595.

Georgetown Law School. "Curriculum B (Section 3): Introduction", online: https://curriculum.law.georgetown.edu/jd/curriculum-b-section-3/.

Graben, Sari. Email correspondence with author (17 December 2018).

Hanna, Alan. Email correspondence with author (24 September 2019).

Hanna, Alan. "Law 105I - Transsystemic Contracts Fall Term Reading Schedule" (University of Victoria Faculty of Law, 2019–20).

Harvard Law School. *Alumni Directory of the Harvard Law School 1963: The Quinquennial Catalogue.* Cambridge, MA: Harvard Law School, 1963.

Harvard Law School. Examination Record of James Bryce Milner, June 1950, York University Libraries, Clara Thomas Archives & Special Collections, James B Milner fonds, 1992-014/005(161).

Harvard Law School, Program on Negotiation. "Oil Pricing Exercise," online: https://www.pon.harvard.edu/shop/oil-pricing-exercise-3/.

Heisenberg, Werner. Oral history interview by Thomas Kuhn, Archive for the History of Quantum Physics, Harvard University (27 February 1963), quoted in Sergio, Chibbaro, Laberton Rondoni & Angelo Vulpiani, *Reductionism, Emergence and Levels of Reality: The Importance of Being Borderline.* Cham, Switzerland: Springer, 2014.

Kennedy, Duncan & Karl E Klare. "A Bibliography of Critical Legal Studies" (1984) 94 Yale LJ 461.

Kerrins, Keeley. Email correspondence with author (15 June 2017).

Lakehead University, Bora Laskin Faculty of Law. "Integrated Practice Curriculum," online: https://www.lakeheadu.ca/academics/departments/law/curriculum/ipc.

Langdell, Christopher Columbus. Speech to the Harvard Law School Association, 1886, reprinted in Grant Gilmore, *Death of Contract*. Columbus, OH: Ohio State University Press, 1974.

Laskin, Bora. Letter to Lon L Fuller, 28 January 1959, Harvard Law School Historical and Special Collections, box 4, folder 16.

Law Society of Upper Canada. *Dialogue on Licensing: Discussing the Realities, Challenges and Opportunities of Lawyer Licensing in Ontario* (Law Society of Upper Canada, 2017), online: https://lsodialogue.ca/wp-content/uploads/2017/03/Dialogue-Topic-1-EN.pdf.

Law Student Survey of Student Engagement, online: http://lssse.indiana.edu/.

McCamus, John D. Interview with author (28 February 2014).

Memorial University of Newfoundland. "Memorial University Faculty of Law Proposal" (August 2018), online: https://www.mun.ca/vpacademic/law_proposal_Senate_Nov_13_18.pdf.

Mercer, Juanita. "Memorial University one step closer to getting law faculty" *Western Star* (23 November 2018), online: https://www.thewesternstar.com/news/local/memorial-university-one-step-closer-to-getting-law-faculty-262355/.

Milner, James. Letter to Caesar Wright, 4 May 1950, York University Libraries, Clara Thomas Archives & Special Collections, James B Milner fonds, 1992-014/005(161).

Milner, James. Letter to Justice JL McLennan, 19 Dec 1956, York University Libraries, Clara Thomas Archives & Special Collections, James B Milner fonds, 1992-014/005 (149).

Milner, James. Letter to Lon L Fuller, 3 March 1959, York University Libraries, Clara Thomas Archives & Special Collections, James B Milner fonds, 1992-014/005 (149).

Milner, James. Memorandum to "Fellow Graduate Students", 28 November 1949, York University Libraries, Clara Thomas Archives & Special Collections, James B Milner fonds, 1992–014/005(161).

minutephysics. "Open Letter to the President: Physics Education", online: https://www.youtube.com/watch?v=BGL22PTIOAM.

Nelson, Robert et al. *After the JD, Wave 3: A Longitudinal Study of Careers in Transition, 2012–2013, United States (ICPSR 35480)*, online: http://doi.org/10.3886/ICPSR35480.v1.

Nussbaum, Martha. "Crossing the Midway, By and By" (7 February 2013), *The Record* (Alumni Magazine of the University of Chicago Law School), online: http://www.law.uchicago.edu/alumni/magazine/spring13/crossing.

O'Hara, Erin. "Contracts Roundtable: Contracts as a Transactional Course", The Conglomerate (8 July 2011), online: https://www.theconglomerate.org/2011/07/contracts-roundtable-contracts-as-a-transactional-course.html.

Osgoode Hall Law School. "Admissions Survey: Fall Call of 2021 Entering Class", online: https://www.osgoode.yorku.ca/admissions-survey/.

Osgoode Hall Law School. *Experience Osgoode: Strategic Plan 2011–2016*, online: https://www.osgoode.yorku.ca/wp-content/uploads/2014/07/2011–16_Lorne_Sossin_double.pdf.

Quan, Wela. *Bankruptcy Law Picture Book.* Toronto: Irwin Law, 2019.

reconciliationsyllabus: A TRC-inspired gathering of materials for teaching law, online: https://reconciliationsyllabus.wordpress.com/.

The Oxford English Dictionary (online).

The Paper Chase, 1973, DVD. Beverly Hills, Cal: 20th Century Fox Home Entertainment, 2003.

Rushowy, Kristin. "Ryerson's law school gets some provincial support, students now eligible for OSAP," *Toronto Star* (6 September 2019), online: https://www.thestar.com/politics/provincial/2019/09/06

/ryersons-law-school-gets-some-provincial-support-students-now-eligible-for-osap.html.

Ryerson University, Academic Standards Committee. *Proposal for a Juris Doctor Program* (Report #W2017-4, June 2017), online: http://www.ryerson.ca/content/dam/senate/ASCReports/2016-2017/ASC_Report_W2017_4_June_5_2017.pdf.

Ryerson University, Faculty of Law. "Integrated Practice Curriculum", online: https://www.ryerson.ca/law/about/integrated-practice-curriculum/.

Ryerson University, Faculty of Law. "Program Information", online: https://www.ryerson.ca/law/program/.

Segal, David. "What They Don't Teach Law Students: Lawyering" *New York Times* (19 November 2011), online: http://www.nytimes.com/2011/11/20/business/after-law-school-associates-learn-to-be-lawyers.html.

Stueck, Wendy & Sunny Dhillon. "B.C.'s Trinity Western University drops mandatory covenant forbidding sex outside heterosexual marriage" *Globe and Mail* (14 August 2018), online: https://www.theglobeandmail.com/canada/british-columbia/article-bcs-trinity-western-university-drops-mandatory-covenant-forbidding/.

Swan, Angela. Email correspondence with author (19 October 2016).

Tucker, Julie & Gemma Smyth. "Art, Law, and Community: Truth and Reconciliation through Art" (28 February 2019), online: https://reconciliationsyllabus.wordpress.com.

University of British Columbia, Allard School of Law. *Allard School of Law Strategic Plan (2016 to 2021)*, online: http://www.allard.ubc.ca/allard-school-law-strategic-plan-2016-2021-1.

University of Victoria. "Joint Degree Program in Canadian Common Law and Indigenous Legal Orders JD/JID", online: https://www.uvic.ca/law/about/indigenous/jid/index.php.

University of Windsor, Windsor Law. *Summary Report: Diversity Survey 2017*, online: https://www.uwindsor.ca/law/sites/uwindsor.ca.law/files/diversity_summary_report_2017.pdf.

Weinrib, Ernest. Email correspondence with author (4 June 2017).

Western University, Western Law. "Teaching Fellowship to Promote Mental Health and Mindfulness" (2018), online: https://law.uwo.ca/news/2018/teaching_fellowship_to_promote_mental_health_and_mindfulness.html.

Willis, John. Letter to Lon L Fuller, 24 February 1961, Lon Fuller Papers, Harvard Law School Historical and Special Collections, box 8, folder 11.

Index

Aboriginal perspectives. *See* Indigenous perspectives

academy. *See* law schools; legal education; research study; universities

Adamski, Jakub, 93–5, 97–8, 297

adjudication: about, 102, 254–5; avoidance of, 88–90, 98; in *Ben-Ishai & Percy*, 111–12, 131, 136, 149; in case method, 88–9, 101–2, 104, 254–5, 331; centrality of, 98, 111, 142, 145, 254–5; formalist assumptions, 254–5, 293–4, 298; vs. forward-looking skills, 260–1; Fullerian legal processes, 101–4, 108–11; in *Milner*, 100–1, 107–12; in *Swan*, 84, 88–9, 98, 111–12; in *Waddams*, 123, 141–2, 145. *See also* judicial decision making

affective qualities, 165, 261, 340

agency of professors. *See* law schools and institutional culture

Ainsworth, Janet, 78–9

alternative perspectives. *See* external perspectives

arbitrariness of law, 220–1. *See also* indeterminacy and contingency

Aristotle and civic virtue, 5n4, 29

Arthurs, Harry, 8, 10–12, 307, 322

Arthurs Report (*Law and Learning*), 10–12, 103, 156

Atiyah, Patrick, 87n231, 195, 219, 284, 299

Attorney-General v Blake (2001), 144n373

Ayres, Ian, 126, 212

backwards reasoning, 187–9, 259–60, 270n669, 271. *See also* legal reasoning

Baird, Douglas, 210n525

Bala, Nicholas C, 83, 91–8

Balfour v Balfour (1919), 211, 212n530

basic legal knowledge. *See* core knowledge

Belley, Jean-Guy, 70n181

Ben-Ishai, Stephanie, 80n210, 124–5, 130, 146, 149–50. See also *Ben-Ishai & Percy*

Ben-Ishai & Percy (Stephanie Ben-Ishai and David Percy, eds, *Contracts: Cases and Commentaries*) (later editions of *Boyle & Percy*): about, 36, 123–36, 150–1; 8th & 9th eds (2009, 2014), 124–5, 129, 146, 218; 10th ed (2018), 124n320, 129–31, 146, 218; commentary, 124–5, 129–32, 135–6, 146, 148–9,

151; core knowledge, 148–9, 151; editors, 80n210, 86, 123–5, 129, 146, 149–51, 294, 306; market share, 81, 82n212, 123, 306; operationalizing of theory, 81, 135–6, 141, 146, 150–1; pedagogical use of, 150n390, 304–6; publication information, 80n210, 123–4; research study analysis of, 36, 79–81; use of "*Ben-Ishai & Percy*" in this book, 80n210. See also *Boyle & Percy*

Ben-Ishai & Percy, topics: adjudication, 111–12, 131, 136, 149; context, 148; economics, 146; feminism, 127, 129; formalism vs. realism, 81, 124, 129, 131, 135–6, 146–51, 282; freedom of contract, 129–31; frustration, 134n351; Indigenous perspectives, 129, 218; legal reasoning, 131, 149; policy, 131, 149; remedies, 132–3, 146–51, 283; solicitor's role, 149; substantive equality, 130–1; technology, 129; values, 130–1. See also *Boyle & Percy*, topics

Bergin, Thomas F, 154n394

better lawyers. *See* legal education "to make better lawyers"

Bhasin v Hrynew (2014), 130n339, 192n477, 300n736

Bickenbach, Jerome E, 9, 103

Bigfoot, Rick, 95

black letter tradition, 230, 288–9n718. *See also* formalism

Blackstone, William, 9, 86, 140n363

Blake, Attorney-General v (2001), 144n373

Bourdieu, Pierre, 328n826

Boyle, Christine, 80n210, 124–9

Boyle & Percy (Christine Boyle & David R Percy, eds, *Contracts: Cases and Commentaries*) (earlier editions of *Ben-Ishai & Percy*): about, 36, 150–1; 1st & 2d eds (1978, 1981), 124n320, 128, 132–3; 3d and 4th eds (1985, 1989), 127n331; 5th ed (1994), 127n331, 128, 133–5; 6th ed (1999), 124–5, 127n331, 128, 134n351, 146; 7th ed (2004), 124–9, 130, 135, 146; commentary, 128–9, 132; core knowledge, 151; editors, 80n210, 86, 124n320, 125, 130–1, 134n351, 146; introduction, 124–9, 135–6; market share, 82n212; operationalizing of theory, 81, 135–6, 141, 146, 150–1; publication information, 80n210; research study analysis of, 36, 79–81; reviews of, 132–5; use of "*Boyle & Percy*" in this book, 80n210; US influences on, 80–1, 125, 129. See also *Ben-Ishai & Percy*

Boyle & Percy, topics: adjudication, 128, 131; context, 125, 134; critical legal studies, 126–7; economics, 126–7; feminism, 127, 129, 134; formalism vs. realism, 124, 129, 132–3, 135–6; freedom of contract, 125–6; frustration, 134n351; good faith, 126; Indigenous perspectives, 128, 129; legal reasoning, 124–5; race, 126, 130, 134; relational contracts, 127; remedies, 126, 132–3, 146–50, 283; skills, 125; values, 125–6. See also *Ben-Ishai & Percy*, topics

Bridgeman, Curtis, 130

Brooks, Kim, 338, 339

Burke, Peter, 228

Calabresi, Guido, 18

Canadian Association of Law Teachers, 124

Canadian Encyclopedic Digest, 231

Canon of American Legal Thought. *See* Kennedy, David & William W Fisher III, *The Canon of American Legal Thought* (2006)
capitalism. *See* law and economics
Carbolic Smoke Ball Company, Carlill v (1892), 73n195
Cardozo, Benjamin, 104–5
Carlill v Carbolic Smoke Ball Company (1892), 73n195
Carnegie Report (2007), 12, 103
casebooks: about, 26–8, 37, 78–82, 150–1, 304–7; chapter assignments, 122n318, 145, 150; as course materials, 26–8, 35–6, 82n212, 309–11; editors, 151, 306; historical background, 41–4, 78–82, 99n257; key questions on, 38; market share, 36, 82n212; operationalizing of theory, 37–9, 78, 81, 120–1, 136, 141, 150–1, 178–9, 304–7; research study analysis of, 25–7, 30–1, 35–6, 79–81, 290; scholarship and reviews, 36, 79–80, 82; selection by professors, 39, 82n212, 309–16, 324–5; teaching manuals, 330; US influences on, 42, 78–81, 83, 150–1, 299. See also *Ben-Ishai & Percy*; *Boyle & Percy*; course materials; *Milner*; remedies, sequence in course; *Swan*; United States, casebooks; *Waddams*
case method: about, 43–4, 252–4, 264–5; adjudication as focus, 88–9, 101–2, 254–5, 331; apologies for use of, 108–11; case-in-context studies, 73, 204–6, 259, 297, 325; commentary and questions, 106–8; consensus cases, 311; core knowledge, 28, 151, 263–5, 289; everyday examples, 147, 259, 297, 338–9; excerpts vs. full case, 249–50; formalism, 37, 81–2, 150–1, 289–90; institutional culture, 264–5, 269–70, 311; vs. legal process school, 111–12; legal reasoning, 43–4, 47, 48, 244–6, 251–4, 264; objectives, 26, 304–7; operationalizing of theory, 26, 37–9, 81, 111–12, 136, 141, 150–1, 264–5, 304–7; realism, 37, 81–2, 104–8, 150–1, 289–90; self-designed courses, 180, 287, 311, 314–16, 324, 325–7, 329, 332–3. *See also* adjudication; pedagogy; pedagogy, strategies
Cases and Materials on Contracts. See *Milner* (James Bryce Milner, ed, *Cases and Materials on Contracts* and Stephen Waddams, ed, *Milner's Cases and Materials on Contracts*); *Waddams* (Stephen Waddams et al, *Cases and Materials on Contracts*)
Cases and Materials on Contracts: Exchange Transactions and Relationships (1971) (Macneil), 73–4
citizen, lawyer as. *See* lawyer as citizen
Civil Code of Québec, 41n83, 92, 143n371, 300n736
classical legal theory, 43–5. *See also* formalism; legal science
CLS. *See* critical legal studies (CLS)
Coase, Ronald, 18, 62
Coase theorem, 62–3, 64
Cohen, Felix, 46, 52
Coleman, Jules L, 152n392
commercial casebooks. *See* casebooks
common sense, 237, 257, 259. *See also* legal reasoning
consciousness, legal. *See* legal consciousness
"Consideration and Form" (Fuller), 29n60, 48, 60n151

consideration doctrine: about, 48, 57–9; bargain theory, 73; in *Boyle & Percy*, 126; "conflicting considerations" paradigm, 48n114; and doctrinal categories, 233; form and substance, 57–9; functions of, 48; indeterminacy of, 57–9; Indigenous perspectives, 216; and morality, 201n497, 202; pedagogy, 138n360, 201, 225, 227, 240, 268n663, 318; private autonomy, 48, 201n497

consumer protection legislation, 112, 130–1, 200, 283, 318

context: about, 46, 51–3, 68–9, 204–9, 218–19, 298; in *Ben-Ishai & Percy*, 125, 134, 148; case-in-context studies, 73, 204–6, 259, 297; everyday life examples, 147, 204, 207–9, 259, 297, 338–9; legal pluralism, 68–70, 205, 207–9, 297–9, 303n746; marginalization of, 20–3, 150–1, 291–2; norms in, 71–4, 207; objective theory of contract, 204–5; operationalizing of theory into teaching, 26, 37–9, 81, 291–5, 298, 338–40; policy, 187–9; relational contracts, 71–4; relevance, determination of, 253–4; results-based reasoning, 187–9, 259–60, 270n669, 271; socio-legal approach, 68–76, 134, 205; in *Swan*, 84, 91, 92, 105, 140–1; thick descriptions, 68, 205; in *Waddams*, 143–5. *See also* critical legal studies (CLS); external perspectives; indeterminacy and contingency; law and economics; policy; politics; realism; relational contracts; values

contingency. *See* indeterminacy and contingency

Contract Law and Legal Methods (Markovits), 37n78, 240n591

contract law: about, 40–3; categories of law, 50, 96–7, 332, 334–7; contract, defined, 71; cost-benefit analysis, 68; discrete contracts, 68, 71–2, 95, 331; norms in, 68, 71–4; as private law, 41, 50–1, 54–8, 196–8, 233; as public law, 50–1; relational contracts, 68–76, 95; scholarship on, 29–30, 41–2; situation types, 49–50, 53n132; state role, 50–1, 68, 72, 74, 110. *See also* formalism; law; realism; relational contracts

Contracts courses: about, 4–7, 27–31, 308–9; canon, 76–7; categories of law, 332–7; as core knowledge, 28–9, 239; in first-year programs, 28; key questions on, 331; legal theory in, 6–7, 29; reforms in legal education, 333–40; research study on, 4–7, 23–5, 27–31; research study professors, 308–9. *See also* casebooks; core knowledge; course materials; operationalizing of theory into teaching; pedagogy; pedagogy, strategies; professors in research study; research study

Contracts: Cases and Commentaries. See *Ben-Ishai & Percy* (Stephanie Ben-Ishai and David Percy, eds, *Contracts: Cases and Commentaries*) (later editions of *Boyle & Percy*); *Boyle & Percy* (Christine Boyle & David R Percy, eds, *Contracts: Cases and Commentaries*) (earlier editions of *Ben-Ishai & Percy*)

Contracts: Exchange Transactions and Relations: Cases and Materials (2d ed) (1978) (Macneil), 73–6, 78, 83, 88

Contracts: Law in Action. *See* Macaulay, Stewart et al, *Contracts: Law in Action* (1995, 2016)

Coote, Brian, 86–7

Corbin, Arthur Linton, *Corbin on Contracts* (1950), 48–9, 80, 94, 137–8, 229, 297n730
core knowledge: about, 24, 151, 229–31, 262–5, 301–2; analogical reasoning, 24, 150–1, 164, 234, 251–4, 264–5; case method, 28, 145, 148–9, 151, 263–5, 289; Contracts as "core" course, 28–9, 239, 317–18; distinctiveness of law, 16–17, 180, 232–8, 244; examinations and evaluation, 24, 154, 230, 241; FLSC competencies, 9, 330n831, 336; formalist assumptions, 24–5, 229–31, 240–5, 262–5, 287–8, 298; Indigenous law, 333; legal discourse, 238–44; legal reasoning, 16–17, 157, 160–1, 263–5, 339–40; marginalization of realism, 24–5; operationalizing of theory, barrier to, 151, 262–5; pedagogical effectiveness, 39, 242–3, 292–3, 306–7, 327; relevance, determination of, 179–81, 246–55; research study results, 23–5; sequencing of content, 240–4, 301–4, 316–17; substantive law, 229–31, 240–4. *See also* legal reasoning; relevance, determination of; skills
course materials: about, 25–6, 270–1; class outlines, 270–1; core knowledge, 24, 135, 148–9, 151; course objectives, 24, 155, 161, 173, 243, 261, 262–4, 267, 282, 297; course summary, 260–1; institutional culture, 309–13, 323–7; operationalizing of theory into teaching, 78, 81–2, 98, 120–1, 134; pedagogy and formalism, 270–1; research study analysis of, 25–7, 30–1, 34–6; self-designed courses, 180, 287, 311, 314–16, 324, 325–7, 329, 332–3; sequencing of content, 240–4, 301–4, 316–17; study aids, 26, 270–1; supplementary readings, 135, 281–2, 297, 305, 324; teaching manuals, 330. *See also* casebooks; case method; examinations and evaluation; pedagogy; pedagogy, strategies; remedies, sequence in course; syllabi; syllabi, topics
courts. *See* adjudication; judicial decision making
Cownie, Fiona, 20n37, 27n52
critical legal studies (CLS): about, 46, 53–61; creative lawyering, 60–1, 168–9, 187; dialectical analysis, 54–7; economic distribution, 62–3; ideology and legal reasoning, 53–7, 60, 199–201; indeterminacy and contingency, 53–4, 57–61; individualism vs. altruism & collectivism, 54–7, 65, 126, 163–4, 196, 198–9, 202–3; lawyer as citizen, 54, 60–1; operationalizing of theory into teaching, 26, 37–9, 81, 291–3, 338–40; politics, 49–50, 53–4, 60–1, 196; power relations, 199–200; situation types, 49–50, 53n132; utopian vision, 53–5, 60–1; values, 50, 54–62. *See also* deconstruction; feminism; gender; indeterminacy and contingency; law and economics; politics; race and ethnicity; realism

Dalhousie University, 31n64, 254, 317n789, 329n828
Dalton, Clare, 56, 57–61, 127n331
damages. *See* remedies; remedies, sequence in course
Danzig, Richard, 148, 204, 207
Davis, Bette, 208n516
deconstruction: about, 57–61; dichotomies, 57–9; feminism,

knowledge, and power, 57–60, 127n331; law as social construct, 47–9, 168–9, 184–7. *See also* indeterminacy and contingency
Derrida, Jacques, 57
Devlin, Richard, 133–5
dignity, 89. *See also* values
diversity: of research participants, 31–2; of students, 32n68
Dworkin, Ronald, 190n471

economics. *See* law and economics
Educating Lawyers (*Carnegie Report*), 12, 103
efficiency standard, 62–7. *See also* law and economics
Eisenberg, Melvin, 83, 138n360
empathy, 165, 261, 340
enforcement. *See* remedies; remedies, sequence in course
"An Essay on the Deconstruction of Contracts Doctrine" (Dalton), 57–61
ethics of better lawyers, 169–71. *See also* justice; lawyer as citizen; legal education "to make better lawyers"; values
ethnicity. *See* race and ethnicity
evaluation. *See* examinations and evaluation
everyday life examples, 147, 204, 207–9, 259, 297, 338–9. *See also* context
examinations and evaluation: about, 271–6, 284–6; collaboration with colleagues, 274, 313, 316–17, 329; essay exams, 274, 284–5; evaluation, 284–6; final exams, 271, 284, 288, 319; formalist vs. realist approach, 24, 271–6, 284–6, 288, 316; and institutional culture, 272–3, 284n708, 316–17; marks, 258, 271n672, 319, 326; operationalizing of theory, 272–4; questions and best answers, 271–6, 285; research study analysis of, 25–7, 36, 284; writing exercises, 251, 271n672, 273–4, 278–80, 284, 320–1. *See also* course materials; pedagogy
examinations and evaluation, content: core knowledge, 24, 154, 230, 241; critical thinking, 284–5; fact patterns, 271–3, 284–5, 289; indeterminacy and contingency, 274; issue spotting, 250–1, 271–2, 274–5; legal reasoning, 271–3, 284–6; policy, 263, 272–3, 275–6, 280, 284–5; relevance, determination of, 24, 250–1, 253
expectations. *See* reasonable expectations
external perspectives: about, 46–7, 187–96, 218–19; good faith, 191–3; in indeterminacy of law, 184; in legal reasoning, 193, 254–5; norms in, 194, 199; operationalizing of theory into teaching, 26, 37–9, 258–62, 291–3, 338–40; policy as, 187–93; range of perspectives, 194–6; results-based reasoning, 187–9; as underlying factors, 57–60, 184, 187–93, 293. *See also* context; feminism; good faith; indeterminacy and contingency; Indigenous perspectives; justice; law and economics; morality; policy; politics; race and ethnicity; realism; reasonable expectations; values

fairness, 89, 91–3, 98, 235–6. *See also* values
Federation of Law Societies of Canada (FLSC), 9, 330n831, 336
Feinman, Jay M, 54n135, 56–7, 61, 126
feminism: about, 209, 211–13, 218–19; in casebooks, 127, 129,

134; images of women, 59, 60; indeterminacy of law, 57–60; knowledge and power, 57–60, 211–12; marginalization of, 209, 211–14; relational contracts, 59, 127, 129. *See also* gender
Fernandez, Angela, 106
fiduciary principle, 128, 130, 241
The Fiercest Debate (Kyer and Bickenbach), 9, 103
First Nations. *See* Indigenous perspectives
Fisher, William. *See* Kennedy, David & William W Fisher III, *The Canon of American Legal Thought* (2006)
flipped classroom, 277–8. *See also* pedagogy, strategies
FLSC (Federation of Law Societies of Canada), 9, 330n831, 336
formalism: about, 43–5, 181–3, 219–33; attacks on formalism by realists, 18, 42–3, 46–51, 76, 181–7, 228–9, 300, 327; attacks on realism by formalists, 220–5; autonomy of law, 16n28, 42, 118–19, 202, 220–1, 229, 234, 237–8, 287; in casebooks, 37, 81–2, 150–1, 289–90; categories of law, 288–90; champions of, 220–4, 286; classification as formalism, 181–3; coherent system of rules, 16n28, 23–4, 42–5, 180, 182–3, 220–9, 240–5, 288–9n718; as core knowledge, 24–5, 229–31, 240–4, 262–5, 287–8; defined, 182; distinctiveness of law, 16n28, 180, 183–4, 220–2, 228–9, 232–8; equal treatment under law, 17, 39, 220–1, 225–6, 228, 234–5, 247, 293–5; individualism and legal reasoning, 54–6; inductive/deductive reasoning, 43–4, 47, 48; legal reasoning, 21–2, 43–4, 47–8, 180, 220–1, 224, 227–8; norms in law, 222–3, 323nn809, 810; operationalizing of theory into teaching, 23–4, 37–9, 81, 265–6, 286–92; pedagogy, 240–4, 265–76, 301–7; vs. policy and politics, 220–1, 229, 232–3, 234; professors' categorization as, 179–83, 219–24; realists as formalists, 229–33; reconciliation of realism with, 298–301; rule of law, 81, 183, 224–6, 228, 247, 255, 293–6, 298–9; substantive law, 229–31. *See also* Langdell, Christopher Columbus, *A Selection of Cases* (1879); legal theory; legal theory and formalism/realism relationship
"Form and Substance" (Duncan Kennedy), 54–7
freedom of contract, 125–6, 129–31, 192, 200. *See also* law and economics; values
freedoms vs. rights, 162
free will, 223
Fridman, Gerald, 86–7, 112–13, 297
Friedman, Lawrence, 21n43, 43, 50n125, 133, 191n474
Fuller, Lon L: adjudication, 101–4; *Basic Contract Law* (1947), 78, 83, 137–8; career, 101–3, 119, 137; case method, 104; "Consideration and Form," 29n60, 48, 60n151; ethics, 104, 202; functionalism, 47–8, 109; influence on casebooks, 80, 83, 86; influence on Milner, 102–3, 108–12, 119; influence on professors, 206, 207; legal processes, 101–4, 108–11, 119; pedagogy, 137–8; reliance interest, 47–9, 59–60, 115, 136–7; remedies, 137–8, 268; social architects, 110–11, 119; "What the Law Schools Can Contribute to

the Making of Lawyers," 101–2, 104n275, 108
functionalism and underlying factors: about, 46–9; in casebooks, 98, 112, 144; judicial decision making, 46–9, 57–60, 187–92, 220, 293; purposiveness of law, 48–9, 277; remedies, 47–8, 137, 139–41; situation types, 49–50, 53n132; underlying interests, 57–60, 184, 187–93, 293. *See also* realism

Galanter, M, 18–19
gender: law students, 32n68; marginalization of, 134, 135, 211–13, 262; operationalizing of theory into teaching, 26, 37–9, 262, 291–3; patriarchy, 211; professors in research study, 32; sexism and legal profession, 171. *See also* feminism; LGBTQ
Georgetown Law School, 337
Giddens, Anthony, 328n826
Gilmore, Grant, 48, 80, 86, 125, 204, 206, 207, 229, 284
good faith, 126, 128, 130, 191–3
good lawyers. *See* core knowledge; lawyer as citizen; legal education "to make better lawyers"; values
Gordon, Robert W, 70, 76n202, 288–9n718, 337n843
Graben, Sari, 334, 336
Grey, Thomas, 182n450, 288, 300n735, 333
Groves v John Wunder Co (1939), 144n373, 146n379

Hadley v Baxendale (1854), 100n260, 149n387, 205n510
Hale, Robert L, 51
Hall, Geoff, 93, 94
Handerson, Stanley, 137
Hanna, Alan, 335–6n840
Harry v Kreutziger (1978), 214
Hart, Henry M, 18, 102, 111n289
Hart, HLA, *The Concept of Law*, 117n304
Harvard Law School, 9–10, 28nn55, 56, 44n90, 101–3, 107n280, 280n697. *See also* Langdell, Christopher Columbus, *A Selection of Cases* (1879)
Hatherly, Mary, 85nn219, 220, 221, 86
Hawkins v McGee (1929), 147n384
Hayek, Friedrich, 284
Hodgkinson v Simms (1994), 130n339, 149n387
Hohfeld, Wesley Newcomb, 162, 236
Holmes, Oliver Wendell, Jr: casebook citations, 105, 112–13, 146; contract theory, 48, 58, 59, 215; influence on professors, 189, 215; review of Langdell's casebook, 45, 137, 202
Horwitz, Morton, 46, 48, 50
Hutchison, Allan, 126

indeterminacy and contingency: about, 57–60, 184–7, 218–19; analytical messiness of law, 96–7; in casebooks, 96–7, 98, 105, 143–4; CLS approach, 53–4, 57–61; contingency of law, 143–4, 184, 187, 211, 214–15; deconstruction, 57–61, 127n331; exam questions, 230, 274; and feminism, 57–60; form and substance, 57–9; Indigenous perspectives, 214–15; law as social construct, 47–9, 168–9, 184–7; operationalizing of theory into teaching, 26, 37–9, 233–4, 291–3; public vs. private law, 57–8; realism, 76, 184–7, 218–19, 256, 259; remedies, 143–4;

student discomfort with, 185–7, 230, 256; uncertainty, 185–6, 230, 256; underlying factors, 57–60, 184; unwritten contracts, 214–15, 216. *See also* context; external perspectives; realism
Indigenous perspectives: about, 128, 213–19; in casebooks, 128, 129, 218; contingency, 214–15; distinctiveness of, 213–15; fiduciary duty, 128; key questions on, 128; and legal realism, 214–15; marginalization of, 213–18; online resources, 217–18; oral traditions, 214–15, 216; reforms to legal education, 213, 333, 335–6; relational worldview, 215; research study interviews, 213; transsystemic courses, 218, 333, 335; treaties and rights, 128, 214–15, 216
institutional culture. *See* law schools; law schools and institutional culture
interviews with professors, 6, 26, 30–4, 36, 179, 213, 265–6. *See also* professors in research study; research study
Introduction to the Study of Law. See Waddams, Stephen, *Introduction to the Study of Law* (1979, textbook)

Jackson v Horizon Holidays (1975), 211
judicial decision making: about, 47, 56, 254–5, 293–5; analogical reasoning, 150–1, 164, 221; argumentation by lawyers, 163–6; Charter's influence, 92; CLS legal reasoning, 55–7; economic approach, 64, 67; feminism, 57–60; formalist approach, 45, 47, 55–6, 254–5, 293–5; functionalist approach, 46–9; individualism and formalism, 55–6; judicial reasoning, 52, 114–17, 187–90, 293–5; personalities of judges, 186–7, 188, 254; policy, 192–3; precedent, 252–3; realist approach, 51–3; results-based reasoning, 187–9, 259–60, 270n669, 271; rule of law, 293–5; underlying factors, 57–60, 187–92, 220, 293; values, 52, 197, 293–4; what judges do vs. say, 47, 93–4, 113, 120, 142, 192, 294. *See also* adjudication
jurist, as term, 156
justice: about, 169–70, 202–3, 218–19; altruism, 54–7; vs. autonomy of law, 202–3; competing values, 52, 114, 293–4; distributive justice, 62–3, 198, 201, 222n550; empathy for marginalized people, 261, 340; lawyer as citizen, 75, 169–70; in *Milner*, 100, 104–5; purposiveness of law, 48–9, 100; realist visions, 52, 55; relational contracts, 75; social justice, 61, 75, 90, 169–70; in *Swan*, 89–93, 98, 105, 114, 169. *See also* lawyer as citizen; morality; values

Kalman, Laura, 46, 49
Keener, William A, 107n280
Kennedy, David & William W Fisher III, *The Canon of American Legal Thought* (2006): eclectic toolkit of skills, 18–23, 29, 42, 76, 164, 178–9, 193, 255, 287; legal consciousness, 18–19, 193; legal realism, 18–19, 181–2, 193, 228–9
Kennedy, Duncan, 29n60, 30n61, 44n95, 48n114, 53n133, 54–7, 223, 281–2
Kessler, Friedrich & Malcolm Sharp, *Contracts: Cases and Materials* (1953), 78
Klare, Karl, 19n35, 61, 137n356, 268

Knapp, Charles L, *Problems in Contract Law: Cases and Materials* (1976), 78
Kronman, Anthony, 11–12, 65, 103, 165, 173, 256
Kyer, Clifford Ian, 9, 103, 106

Lakehead University, 31n64, 330
Langdell, Christopher Columbus, *A Selection of Cases* (1879): about, 43–5, 78; autonomy of law, 202; case method, 9, 28, 43–4, 244; categories of theory, 288, 333; formation-first approach, 137, 268; Holmes's review of, 45, 137, 202; law as science, 9; legal realist critiques of formalism, 49; theory of contract law, 44. *See also* formalism
The Language of Law School (Mertz). *See* Mertz, Elizabeth
law: about, 3–7, 40–1; Canadian sensibility, 299–301; categories of, 162, 174–5, 181–3, 288–90, 334–7, 339; *juris* and *prudence*, 220–2; multiple traditions, 300; norms in, 222–3, 323nn809, 810; private law, 41, 50–1, 54–8, 196–8, 233; purposiveness of, 48–9; as social construct, 47–9, 168–9, 184–7; state role, 50–1, 68, 72, 74, 110, 337; unitary model, 226. *See also* purposiveness of law; rule of law
law and economics: about, 46, 62–7, 209–12, 218–19; Coase theorem, 62–3, 64; cost-benefit analyses, 62, 70, 212; distribution of resources, 17, 62–3, 67, 170; efficiency standard, 62–7, 194; freedom of contract, 125–6, 129–31, 192, 200; ideology and legal reasoning, 55–7, 163, 199–201; interdisciplinary approach, 66–7; laissez-faire capitalism, 50, 55–6, 125; legal reasoning, 65–7; liability, 64; marginalization of, 209–13; market system, 50–1, 90, 170, 197–8; norms in, 194, 199, 212; planning skills, 63–4, 67, 296; policy emphasis, 62–5, 188; politics marginalized, 62–3, 67; power relations, 199–201; private law, 50–1, 65–7, 196–8; relational contracts, 68–9; remedies, 64; substantive equality, 130–1; values, 66n175, 170, 198. *See also* policy; realism
law and everyday life, 204, 207–9, 259, 338–9. *See also* context
Law and Learning (*Arthurs Report*), 10–12, 103, 156
law and society. *See* context; realism; socio-legal studies
The Law of Contract (Fridman), 113, 297
The Law of Contracts. *See* Waddams, Stephen, *The Law of Contracts* (1977, textbook)
law professors. *See* operationalizing of theory into teaching; professors in research study; professors in research study, careers; professors in research study, quotations; research study
law schools: about, 152–3, 307; academic freedom, 324; categories of law and curriculum, 288–90, 334–7; Contracts courses, rationale for research study, 28–9; curricular reforms, 328–40; curricular sequencing, 240–4, 301–4; diversity in, 32n68; faculties in research study, 31; funding, 4; historical background, 8–14; Indigenous perspectives, 213–18; intellectual vs. professional goals, 38–9, 153–60, 175–7, 302–3; jurisdiction

over legal education, 4, 8–14, 103; new law schools, 4n1, 13–14, 330, 333–6; publication expectations, 156–7; roles of scholars and teachers, 302–3, 313; semestered courses, 319–20; supplementary readings on, 281–2; tension with the profession, 8–14, 38, 153–8, 175–7; tenure and promotion, 313; theory/practice relationship, 8–14. *See also* Contracts courses; legal education; legal theory and practice; operationalizing of theory into teaching; professors in research study; research study; students

law schools and institutional culture: about, 39, 293, 307–8, 317, 322–8; agency of professors, 39, 293, 307, 323–8, 333; career paths, 31–2, 33(f), 307–9; case method, 264–5, 269–70, 311; collaboration with colleagues, 310–17; Contracts as "core" course, 28–9, 317–18; course materials, 269–70, 309–13, 323–7; examinations and evaluation, 272–3, 284n708, 316–17; legal practitioners, 157–9; norms, 322–4, 327–9; path dependency, 307–10, 322–3, 327; reform in, 328–40; workload of professors, 314–15, 320–1. *See also* professors in research study; professors in research study, careers; students

"Law Schools" (Fuller), 101–2, 104n275, 108

law societies: about, 8; bar exams, 154; FLSC on competencies, 9, 330n831, 336; integrated practice, 330, 333–4; jurisdiction over legal education, 4, 8–14, 103; tension with the academy, 8–14, 38, 153–8, 175–7; *Trinity Western* cases, 4n1, 13–14. *See also* law schools; legal education; universities

Law Society of BC v Trinity Western University (2018), 4n1, 13–14

Law Society of Ontario, 336

Law Society of Upper Canada (LSUC), 4n, 13–14, 103

law students. *See* students

lawyer as citizen: about, 3–7, 11–16, 76–7, 332–3, 339–40; affective qualities, 165, 261, 340; citizen, as aspiration, 5–7, 11–16, 160; in CLS approach, 54; eclectic toolkit of skills, 5–7, 15–20; everyday consequences, 172, 259; historical background, 8–14; ideal qualities, 11–12, 159; identity and legal reasoning, 16; Kronman's *Lost Lawyer*, 11–12, 103, 165, 173, 256; moral duties, 171; mutual reinforcement of theory and practice, 152–3, 171–3, 291; reforms in legal education, 15, 328–40; research study on, 4–7, 160; as social actors, 5, 75, 110–11, 119, 152, 187, 199–200. *See also* justice; legal consciousness; legal education "to make better lawyers"; legal theory and practice; research study; values

legal consciousness: about, 239–40, 287–8, 339–40; casebooks and formation of, 82–3; categories in, 288–90, 332–7; common sense, 259; contradictory attitudes, 219, 287–8; new theories, 288–9n718; role of casebooks, 306. *See also* formalism; legal theory; operationalizing of theory into teaching; realism

legal discourse, 238–40

legal education: about, 8–12, 153–8; conservatism in, 322–3; core knowledge, 28–9, 151, 263–5; curriculum, 28–9, 328–30, 333–40; FLSC competencies, 9, 330n831, 336; Fullerian legal processes, 101–4, 108–11; funding for, 4; goals of, 24, 37, 153–8, 238, 267; historical background, 8–14; Indigenous perspectives, 213–18; integrated practice, 330, 333–4; intellectual vs. professional goals, 38–9, 153–60, 175–7, 302–3; interdisciplinary approach, 66–7; introductory texts, 117n304; jurisdiction over, 8–14, 103; key questions on, 331; in legal terminology, 238–40; legislative processes, 101; operationalizing of theory into teaching, 23–5, 37–9, 81; reforms to, 15, 328–40; relationalism in, 72–6; research on, 25, 27–30; stated vs. implied ideas, 288–90; student preconceptions, 184–7, 203, 230, 235–6, 280–1; tension between academy and profession, 8–14, 38, 153–8, 175–7; transsystemic approaches, 92, 218, 333, 335. *See also* core knowledge; law schools; lawyer as citizen; legal consciousness; legal processes; legal theory and practice; research study; students; universities

legal education, materials and strategies. *See* casebooks; case method; Contracts courses; core knowledge; course materials; examinations and evaluation; operationalizing of theory into teaching; pedagogy; pedagogy, strategies; remedies, sequence in course

legal education "to make better lawyers": about, 7, 153–63, 169–71, 175–7, 291, 339–40; affective qualities, 165, 261, 340; ethics, 169–71; gap between aspiration and teaching, 291–2; historical background, 8–14; legal reasoning, 169–71; legal theory's role, 7, 160–2, 291; professors' aspirations, 7, 38, 160–3; research study results, 38, 160, 169–71. *See also* lawyer as citizen; legal consciousness; legal reasoning; skills

"Legal Education and the Reproduction of Hierarchy" (Duncan Kennedy), 281–2

legal formalism. *See* formalism; legal theory; legal theory and formalism/realism relationship

legal practice. *See* law societies; legal theory and practice

legal processes: about, 100–2; adjudication, 101, 254–5; drafting, 155, 261, 278–80; legislation, 101, 283; and Lon Fuller, 101–4, 108–11, 119; marginalization of, 254; negotiation, 101, 279–80; politics, 197–8

legal process school, 101–3, 108–11, 119

legal realism. *See* context; critical legal studies (CLS); external perspectives; feminism; Indigenous perspectives; law and economics; politics; race and ethnicity; socio-legal studies; values

legal reasoning: about, 7, 15–23, 40–3, 233–8, 254–5, 339–40; affective qualities, 261, 340; analogical reasoning, 98, 114, 142, 150–1, 164, 178, 227–8, 234, 251–4, 264–5, 340; autonomy of law, 16n28, 118–19, 202, 229, 234, 237–8, 287; backwards reasoning, 187–9, 259–60, 270n669, 271; basic method, 247–8; combining of rules, 244–6; common sense, 237, 257, 259; Contracts courses, 29, 76–7; core knowledge, 16–17, 28–9, 151, 262–5, 339–40; creative thinking, 57–61, 168–9, 187, 260; critical thinking, 170–2, 257; dehumanization/rehumanization process, 256–7, 339–40; distinctiveness of, 16–17, 180, 232–8, 255–7; eclectic toolkit of skills, 5–7, 15–20, 42–3, 52–3, 164–6, 176–9; equal treatment, 17, 39, 220–1, 226, 228, 247, 293–5; extraction of rules, 244–6; formalist approach, 43–5, 54–7, 180, 220–1, 233–5, 254–5; ideological spectrum, 53–7, 60, 199–201; inductive/deductive reasoning, 43–4, 47, 48, 296; issue spotting, 250–1, 271–2, 274–5; key questions on, 331–2; legal consciousness, 18–19, 23, 82–3, 132–3, 193, 239–40, 287, 339; legal discourse, 238–40; marginalization of policy and context, 20–3, 150–1, 178–9, 211–13, 291–2; Mertz's research on, 20–3, 178–9; operationalizing of theory into teaching, 7, 15–17, 23–5, 37–9, 81, 286–90; as a practice, 16–17; precedent, 252–3; professors' categorization as realists or formalists, 179–83; realist approach, 51–7, 180, 233–5, 255–62; relevance, determination of, 179–81, 234, 246–54; results-based reasoning, 187–9, 259–60, 270n669, 271; sequencing doctrine and critique, 240–4, 301–4, 316–17; single-theory reasoning, 19n35; source of law, 23; terminology, 16–17, 18; thinking as preparation for practice, 173–5; "thinking like a lawyer," 255–7; values in, 54–7, 258, 293–4. *See also* adjudication; external perspectives; indeterminacy and contingency; judicial decision making; lawyer as citizen; operationalizing of theory into teaching; relevance, determination of; skills

legal science, 9, 43–5, 48, 65, 76, 289n. *See also* formalism; Langdell, Christopher Columbus

legal skills. *See* skills

legal theory: about, 288–90; categories of, 162, 174–5, 181–3, 227–8, 288–90; in Contracts courses, 6–7; eclectic toolkit of skills, 5–7, 15–20, 52–3, 164–6, 176–9; external perspectives, 194–7; historical background, 44; new theories, 288–9n718; realist critiques of formalism, 46–51. *See also* external perspectives; formalism; operationalizing of theory into teaching; realism; rule of law

legal theory and formalism/realism relationship: about, 288–301, 327; agency of professors, 39, 307, 323–7, 331, 333; Canadian sensibility, 299–301; compatibility of formalism and realism, 293–301; contradictory attitudes, 219, 296–300; core knowledge, 327; eclecticism of realist theory, 289; institutional influences, 307–23, 327–8; integration and reconciliation, 39, 291, 298–301, 330; key questions on, 331; legal education reforms, 15, 328–40; operationalizing of theory into teaching, 26, 37–9, 81, 179, 265–6, 286–301, 338–40; path dependency, 307–10, 322–3, 327; pedagogical

effectiveness, 39, 242–3, 293, 301–7, 327; reflection on personal goals, 331; rule of law, 293–5. *See also* operationalizing of theory into teaching; rule of law
legal theory and practice: about, 7–16, 152–3, 173–7, 291–3; better lawyers as goal, 7, 38, 161–3, 291; core knowledge, 151; eclectic toolkit of skills, 5–7, 15–20, 164–6; goals of, 152–3, 173–5, 267, 291; historical background, 8–14; integrated practice, 330, 333–4; integration of, 7, 38, 105, 153, 158–61, 175–7, 291, 330; intellectual vs. professional goals, 38–9, 153–60, 175–7, 302–3; lawyer as citizen, 11–16; legal reasoning, 16–17, 151, 173–5; mutual reinforcement of, 7, 10–14, 152–3, 171–3, 291; operationalizing of theory into teaching, 37–9, 338–40; opposition of, 8–10, 175–7, 298; practice, as term, 7, 16n28; research study results, 7, 23–5, 38, 291–3. *See also* core knowledge; lawyer as citizen; legal education "to make better lawyers"
Leiter, Brian, 182
Lessons of Everyday Law (Macdonald), 297, 338–9
Levi, Edward, 252–3
LGBTQ: diversity of students, 32n68; relational contracts, 127; *Trinity Western* cases, 4n, 13–14. *See also* gender
liability and Coase theorem, 62–3, 64
lived experience. *See* context; everyday life examples
Llewellyn, Karl, 47, 69, 85n220, 224n552, 292n720
Local 1330 v US Steel Corp (1980), 19n35, 28n58, 60n154, 61
The Lost Lawyer (Kronman), 11–12, 54n136, 103, 165, 173, 256
LSBC (Law Society of British Columbia), 4n, 13–14
LSUC (Law Society of Upper Canada), 4n, 13–14, 103

Macaulay, Stewart: "Elegant Models," 126; "Non-Contractual Relations," 29n60, 68–70, 133n349, 204n508; policy arguments, 18–19; "Real Deal and the Paper Deal," 69n178, 73n195; socio-legal studies, 68–70
Macaulay, Stewart et al, *Contracts: Law in Action* (1995, 2016): about, 73–4, 78; 4th ed, teacher's manual (2016), 330n832; casebook references to, 133; influence on professors, 166, 206, 207, 297; relational contracts, 73–4; settlement strategies, 73n195, 126
Macdonald, Roderick Alexander: "Against Nomopolies," 323nn809, 810; career, 119; influence on professors, 204, 206, 207, 208, 219, 297; *Lessons of Everyday Law*, 297, 338–9; *Prolegomena to a Theory of Relevance*, 119n311; review of Waddams's *Introduction*, 117–23, 142
Macneil, Ian R: about, 70–5; casebook references to, 80, 83, 84–7, 134; *Cases and Materials on Contracts: Exchange Transactions and Relationships* (1971), 73–4; *Contracts: Exchange Transactions and Relations: Cases and Materials* (2d ed) (1978), 73–6, 78, 83, 88; discrete vs. relational contracts, 68, 71–2, 95; influence on professors, 166, 206–7, 231; *The New Social Contract* (1980), 40n81, 71–2, 84, 95, 125n323,

127n332, 204n508; relational contracts, 70–4, 84, 127, 204, 206–7; socio-legal studies, 68; "Whither Contracts," 83n216, 206, 282
Manwaring, John, 132–4
markets. *See* law and economics
Markovits, Daniel, 37n78, 240n591
Marxism, 163, 175, 198–9, 303n746
McCamus, John, *The Law of Contracts*, 145, 294–5, 299
McGill University, 31n64, 91–2
Memorial University of Newfoundland, 4n, 335n839
men and patriarchy, 211. *See also* gender
Mertz, Elizabeth: about, 20–3; formalist analysis, 20–3, 43, 287; marginalization of policy and context, 20–3, 42, 76, 150, 178–9, 213, 235, 287; policy, defined, 287n715; research study by, 20–3, 25, 28, 39, 178–9, 265
method, case. *See* case method
methodology in research study, 25–36. *See also* research study
Métis. *See* Indigenous perspectives
Milner, James Bryce, 99, 100, 101–3, 106, 108, 111
Milner (James Bryce Milner, ed, *Cases and Materials on Contracts* and Stephen Waddams, ed, *Milner's Cases and Materials on Contracts*): about, 36, 99–112; 1st ed (1963), 99–108; 2d & 3d & 4th eds (1971, 1977, 1985, Waddams, ed), 99, 106n279, 108–10, 112–13, 116n302; commentary, 106–8; core knowledge, 151; editors, 99, 108, 111, 113, 119–20, 124, 151; historical background, 99, 101–3; integration of theory and practice, 103, 105–6, 108, 110–11, 174; introduction, 99–108, 113; market share, 82n212; operationalizing of theory, 81, 150–1; publication information, 79n207, 113; research study analysis of, 36, 79–81; reviews of, 106, 112–13; US influences on, 101–5, 108–9
Milner, topics: adjudication, 100–1, 107–12, 114–15; case method, 99, 104–12, 128–9, 151; client-focused practice, 103–5; critique of formalism, 99, 105; Fullerian legal processes, 101–4, 108–11, 119; indeterminacy of law, 105; justice, 100, 104–5; legal reasoning, 114; private arrangements, 109–10; purposiveness of law, 100, 105, 110; rational decision making, 116n302; remedies, 100, 112; state's role, 110; values, 104
morality: about, 202–3, 218–19, 222–3; vs. autonomy of law, 201n497, 202–3; formalist approach, 222, 227, 228; ideology and legal reasoning, 55–7, 198–9; marginalization of, 20; myth of law as neutral, 198–9, 201n497; norms in law, 222–3; realism and situation types, 49–50, 53n132. *See also* justice; realism; values
Mullan, David, 146

The New Social Contract (Macneil), 40n81, 71–2, 84, 95, 125n323, 127n332, 204n508
"Non-Contractual Relations in Business" (Macaulay), 29n60, 68–70, 133n349, 204n508

objective theory of contract, 204–5. *See also* context
operationalizing of theory into teaching: about, 17–19, 23–5, 37–9, 120–1, 150–3, 178–81, 262–6,

286–92; agency of professors, 323–8; barriers to, 151, 262–3, 290; contradictory attitudes, 219–20; core knowledge, 151, 262–5; in course materials, 78, 81–2, 98, 120–1, 134, 150–1, 178–9; curricular reforms, 15, 328–30, 333–40; eclectic toolkit to use in, 18–19; external factors, 258–62; formalist vs. realist approach, 23–5, 219–20, 266, 286–90, 292; gap between aspiration and teaching, 26, 37–9, 286–92, 296, 338–40; key questions on, 331; legal reasoning's role, 17, 180–1, 286–7; marginalization of realism, 20–3, 37–9, 81, 150–1, 179, 265–6, 288–93, 338–40; pedagogical choices, 242, 265–6, 286, 288, 301–7, 331; research study results, 23–5, 37–9, 77, 81, 177–81, 266, 288–92; self-designed courses, 287; tensions in casebooks, 150–1; values, 258–62. *See also* course materials; legal reasoning; legal theory and formalism/realism relationship; pedagogy; pedagogy, strategies

Osgoode Hall Law School, 8, 31n64, 329n828

participants in research study. *See* professors in research study; professors in research study, careers; professors in research study, quotations; research study

patriarchy, 211. *See also* gender

pedagogy: about, 24–5, 242, 265–6, 286–90; administrative support, 320–1, 328, 329n828; agency of professors, 39, 293, 307, 323–7, 333, 339; categorical approach, 162; collaboration with colleagues, 310–17, 329; core knowledge, 24, 28–9, 151, 241–2, 262–5, 327; critical legal pedagogy, 19n35; curricular reforms, 15, 328–30, 333–40; empathy, 165, 261, 340; formalist approach, 240–4, 265–76; Mertz's research on, 20–3; operationalizing of theory, 276, 280, 286–7, 301–7; pedagogical effectiveness, 39, 242–3, 293, 301–7; realist approach, 276–86; research study scope and results, 27, 34, 38–9, 266; self-designed courses, 180, 287, 311, 314–16, 324, 325–7, 329, 332–3; substantive law, 229–31. *See also* casebooks; case method; course materials; examinations and evaluation; legal education; operationalizing of theory into teaching; syllabi

pedagogy, strategies: categories of knowledge, 332–7; creative thinking, 260, 285; everyday life examples, 147, 204, 207–9, 259, 279, 297, 338–9; experiential learning, 15, 329n828, 330, 334, 336; flipped classrooms, 277–8; integrated practice, 330, 333–4; marginalized perspectives, 213n535, 213n537, 217–18; online resources, 213n537, 217–18; policy issues, 277, 280–1; problem-based learning, 157, 167–8, 277–8, 320n798, 320n802, 322n807; sequencing of content, 225–6, 240–4, 301–4, 316–17; sequencing of remedies, 267–70, 283, 331; small groups, 260, 277–8, 320n798; teaching manuals, 330; technologies, 167–8, 277, 336; writing exercises, 251, 271n672, 273–4, 278–80, 320–1. *See also* casebooks; case method; course materials; syllabi

Peevyhouse v Garland Coal & Mining Co (1962), 148–9n387, 282n701
Percy, David, 80n210, 86–7, 124–5, 146, 149–50. See also *Ben-Ishai & Percy; Boyle & Percy*
Perdue, William R, Jr, 47–9, 136–7
policy: about, 46, 51–3, 187–93, 218–19; context, 187–9; creative lawyering, 169; defined, 188, 189–90, 287n715; distinctiveness of law, 220–1, 232–8; economic analysis, 63–6; efficiency standard, 62–7; ethics of better lawyers, 170; exams and evaluation, 263, 272–3, 275–7, 284–5; external perspectives, 187–96; formalist approach, 220–1, 229, 232–3, 234, 295; functionalist approach, 47–8; good faith, 191–3; judicial decision making, 192–3; legal reasoning, 17–19, 51–3, 63–4; marginalization of, 20–3, 142n368, 147–9, 150, 213, 263, 287, 291–2; market system, 170; norms in, 194, 199; operationalizing of theory into teaching, 37–9, 263, 294–5; pedagogical strategies, 280–1; reasonable expectations, 191; relational contracts, 74; and remedies, 48, 149; situation types, 53n132; as underlying factors, 187–93, 219. *See also* law and economics; operationalizing of theory into teaching; realism
politics: about, 46, 49–53, 196–201, 218–19; CLS legal reasoning, 53–4, 60–1, 196; collectivism vs. individualism, 56, 65, 196, 198–9; distinctiveness of law, 220–1, 232–8; formalist approach, 220–1, 229, 232–3, 234; ideology and legal reasoning, 55–7, 60, 198–201; "law is politics," 60–1, 196–7, 236–7; legal reasoning, 17, 50–7, 60–1, 236–7, 294–5; legislative process, 197–8; marginalization of, 291–2; market system, 197–8; Marxism, 163, 175, 198–9; myth of law as neutral, 198–9; norms in, 199; operationalizing of theory into teaching, 37–9; power relations, 196–7, 199–201; as underlying factors, 219; utopian visions, 53–4, 60–1; values, 49–50, 60–1, 163, 196–201; winners and losers, 196, 200–1. *See also* critical legal studies (CLS); law and economics; operationalizing of theory into teaching; policy
Posner, Richard A, 65–6, 86, 146, 215, 239n590
power relations: about, 59–60, 199–201; competing values, 57–8, 163, 199–201; ethics of better lawyers, 170; feminism, 57–60, 211–12; formalist approach, 57–8, 223; ideologies, 199–201; legal reasoning, 57–8, 199–200; marginalization of, 20, 262; operationalizing of theory into teaching, 262; pedagogy, 165; politics, 196–7, 199–201; relational contracts, 70, 74. *See also* realism
practice of law: practice, defined (OED), 16n28; terminology, 16–17. *See also* law schools; law societies; legal education "to make better lawyers"; legal theory and practice
precedent, 252–3, 292. *See also* legal reasoning
private law, 41, 50–1, 54–8, 196–8, 233. *See also* contract law
professors in research study: about, 6–7, 23–7, 31–2; agency, 39, 307–9,

323–7; authors of publications, 26, 308; beliefs as realists or formalists, 23–5, 165, 179–83, 195–6; categories, statistics, 183n451; categorization as realists or formalists, 23, 181–3, 220; Contracts courses, 27–32, 308–9; course materials, 24–6, 30–1, 34–6, 82n212; diversity, 32; eclectic toolkit of skills, 5–7, 15–20, 164–6; interviews, 6, 26, 30–4, 36, 179, 213, 265–6; key questions on, 23, 331; law faculties, participating, 31; legal consciousness, 339–40; operationalizing of theory into teaching, 23–5, 37–9, 178–81, 339–40; pedagogy, 265–6; practitioners, 157–9; role or mission of, 38; US influences on, 76–7; workload, 314–15, 320–1. *See also* research study

professors in research study, careers: about, 31–2, 33(f), 307–9; beginning teachers, 31–2, 308–15; mid-career teachers, 31–2, 315–21; practitioners, 157–9; senior teachers, 31–2, 321–3; tenure and promotion, 313; years of experience, 31–2, 33(f). *See also* law schools and institutional culture; research study

professors in research study, quotations: about, 36, 152–3, 178–81; categorization as realists or formalists, 181–3, 220; #1, 161, 172, 173–4, 208, 239, 259, 299–300, 308n759, 319n793, 324; #2, 155, 158, 195, 254, 256, 267n658; #3, 163–4, 169–70, 198–9, 201n497, 203, 258, 309, 318; #4, 161, 164–5, 201, 210n522, 226–7, 237–8, 251n624, 317–18, 320; #5, 236, 268n664, 304n748; #6, 231n570, 232, 235, 243, 250, 269n665, 303–4, 319, 320n797, 320n798; #7, 154, 189, 201, 246, 258, 268, 272; #8, 162, 227–8; #9, 211–12, 269n667, 282n704, 308n759; #10, 266–7, 282n704, 308n759; #11, 164, 186, 208, 210n523, 233, 237, 267n658, 313n775, 315n781; #12, 156–7, 192, 207, 208, 210n523, 260–1, 279, 325; #13, 158n405, 184–5, 192, 208, 258, 260, 264n652, 283n706, 306, 308n759, 318, 321; #14, 237, 245, 249n617, 251, 297n730, 308n759; #15, 153, 162, 170, 224, 226n557, 246, 248, 259, 321; #16, 159, 162–3, 164, 259, 308n759, 310n766, 321n801, 324n814; #17, 168, 171, 186–7, 205, 211, 282n704, 309, 314nn778, 779, 314nn778, 779, 315n782, 318n792, 322, 324n814; #18, 194, 209, 268, 308n759; #19, 220–3, 234, 235n581, 247, 268, 275n684, 308n759; #20, 222–4, 228, 279, 304n748, 308n759, 319n793, 320, 321n802; #21, 197, 211n527, 282n704, 309n762, 324n812; #22, 174–5, 227, 252, 268, 269n668, 284n708, 308n759; #23, 173, 188, 209, 216n544, 273, 308n759; #24, 192, 263, 277, 316, 325–6; #25, 122n318, 188, 200, 205, 210n523, 268, 269n666, 274, 282, 325n816; #26, 157, 171, 184, 185–6, 201, 210n521, 239n590, 249, 253, 254, 269n666, 270–2, 302, 308n759, 309n761, 310, 324n812; #27, 162, 184, 198, 204, 236–7, 258–9, 281, 282n704, 307, 319; #28, 163, 165, 200, 205, 231, 280, 308n759, 312n771, 325; #29, 162, 167, 245–6, 250, 275n680, 302n740, 319; #30, 164, 202–3, 207, 215, 231, 232, 241–2, 270, 279, 308n759, 320, 320n800; #31, 164, 185, 196, 230, 258, 268n664, 275n681, 277, 308n759, 325n816; #32, 156, 195, 201, 207,

211n527, 238n587, 250, 269n667, 275n682, 279, 296–7, 322, 324n812, 325, 329n828; #33, 165, 169, 170, 172, 200, 213n535, 259, 262, 269n665, 282, 310n766, 316–17; #35, 170, 197, 201, 235–6, 245, 280, 285, 308n759, 310n766, 313n774, 316, 326; #36, 166–7, 206, 238n587, 255–6; #37, 165, 187, 206, 263, 277, 282, 285; #38, 237, 263, 273, 303n746, 309, 310n766, 312, 317; #39, 208, 242, 245, 274n679, 280, 326; #40, 154–5, 199–200, 210n523, 267, 272–3, 298, 308n759, 319n793; #41, 231n570, 241, 250n618, 312n771; #42, 166, 198, 205, 206n511, 260, 270n669, 280, 296, 325; #43, 157, 167–8, 203, 208, 241, 250, 259, 319n794, 321, 322, 326; #44, 154, 164, 167, 185, 207, 238n587, 248–9, 269n665, 274, 275n685, 308n759; #45, 165–6, 188, 201, 254, 263, 308n759, 309n762, 312n771, 313–14, 321n801; #46, 225–6, 229, 240, 269n668, 301, 303, 308n759; #47, 173, 209, 211n528, 236, 249n617, 279; #48, 122n318, 167, 189, 209, 247–8, 262, 272, 283n705, 284–5, 308n757, 308n759, 325; #49, 157, 279–80, 308n759; #50, 164, 165, 188, 191, 192, 249, 251n624, 262, 276n686, 308n759, 315–16; #51, 159, 190–1, 192, 208, 250, 268, 269n666, 274, 283n706, 309n761, 310, 316, 326; #52, 165, 217, 230, 253n629, 269n665, 284, 308nn758, 759, 309, 322, 327n825; #53, 171, 188, 189, 209, 237, 254, 256–7, 268, 269n668, 275n683, 320n798; #54, 157, 169, 185, 186, 188, 230, 232–3, 237, 243–4, 245, 249, 280, 285, 304n747, 310n766, 323; #55, 202, 210n523, 323–4; #56, 162, 203, 210n521, 214, 224–5, 231n570, 238–9, 284, 299, 302, 308n758; #57, 194, 231, 244–5, 251n624, 254, 318n791, 320; #58, 173, 195, 201, 203, 249, 255, 259, 267n658, 280–1, 285, 303n744, 309n762, 320; #59, 227, 238n587, 243, 250, 270n669, 275n685, 320; #60, 156–7, 315n782; #61, 209, 235n581, 244, 260, 264–5, 289, 303n745, 308nn758, 759, 313n775, 324n812; #62, 158–9, 168, 206, 208, 217, 238n587, 259–60, 303n744, 308n759, 311, 312n771, 326; #63, 170, 186, 216, 217, 244, 254, 261, 276, 312n771; #64, 165, 173, 189, 197, 232, 251n624, 258, 282, 312n771, 314n778, 320n798, 322n807, 327n825; #65, 250, 308n759, 315n782, 321n801; #66, 250, 309n762, 316, 322; #67, 36, 162, 188, 259, 284; #70, 186, 252; #71, 36, 324; #74, 258; #A, 192n479; #B, 314n777; #C, 316n785; #D, 325n818; #E, 321n801; #F, 172n439, 214n539; #G, 215n541; #H, 216n544; #X, 277–8. *See also* professors in research study; research study

"pure" legal reasoning, 21–2, 43. *See also* formalism

purposiveness of law: about, 48–9, 100; functionalist approach, 48–9, 277; justice, 100; legal reasoning, 48–9; in *Milner*, 100, 105, 110; pedagogical strategies, 277; reasonable expectations, 84–8; remedies in casebooks, 137, 141; in *Swan*, 85–7, 96–7. *See also* realism

Quebec: *Civil Code of Québec*, 41n83, 92, 143n371, 300n736; continuing business (Alcan), 70n181

quotations. *See* professors in research study, quotations

race and ethnicity: about, 209, 211, 212–14, 218–19; in casebooks, 126, 130, 134; cultural specificity of contracts, 215; discrimination, 130; diversity of students, 32n68; marginalization of, 135, 212–14; operationalizing of theory into teaching, 37–9, 262; pedagogy, 165; substantive equality, 130–1. *See also* Indigenous perspectives
Raffles v Wichelhaus (1864), 73n195
"Real Deal and the Paper Deal" (Macaulay), 69n178, 73n195
realism: about, 46–53, 181–3, 218–19; attacks by formalists on realism, 220–2, 224–5; attacks on formalism by realists, 18, 42–3, 46–51, 76, 181–7, 228–9, 300, 327; in casebooks, 81–3, 137, 150–1; classification as, 181–2; defined, 181–2; distinctiveness of law, 180, 232–8, 255–7; eclectic toolkit of skills, 18–20, 52–3; empathy, 261, 340; functionalism, 46–9, 98; historical background, 46–9; ideology and legal reasoning, 54–7, 60, 198–201; indeterminacy of law, 76, 184–7, 218–19; law as social construct, 47–9, 168–9, 184–7; law vs. policy and politics, 229, 234; legal reasoning, 17–20, 51–3, 164, 180, 255–62; operationalizing of theory into teaching, 37–9, 81, 179, 265–6, 286–93, 338–40; pedagogy, 276–86, 301–7; professors' categorization as, 179–83; realists as formalists, 229–33, 295; reconciliation of formalism with, 298–301; results-based reasoning, 187–9; rule of law, 293–6, 298–9; situation types, 49–50, 53n132; student resistance to, 135, 154; underlying factors, 57–60, 188–9, 293, 295; values, 49–52, 84, 202–3, 293–4. *See also* context; external perspectives; functionalism and underlying factors; indeterminacy and contingency; justice; legal theory; legal theory and formalism/realism relationship; morality; policy; politics; purposiveness of law; values
real world. *See* context; everyday life examples
reasonable expectations: about, 84–8, 190–1; competing values, 200–1; critique of, 93–4, 96n252; historical background, 94n247; ideologies, 200–1; indeterminacy and contingency, 94; policy factor, 191; in remedies, 140; in *Swan*, 84–8, 95, 98, 191
reasoning. *See* legal reasoning
Reiter, Barry J, 83, 88
Reiter, Barry J & John Swan, eds, *Studies in Contract Law* (companion to *Swan*): about, 84–8; purposiveness of law, 85, 116n301; reasonable expectations, 84–5, 87, 93; reviews of, 85–7, 93, 112–13, 116. See also *Swan*
relational contracts: about, 68–76; vs. discrete contracts, 68, 71–2, 95, 331; domestic contracts, 91; external perspectives, 195; feminist analyses, 59, 127, 129; formal contracts as scaffolding, 69; Indigenous perspectives, 215; influence on professors, 206–7; informal relationships, 69–70; key questions on, 331–2; legal pluralism, 68–70, 73; Macaulay's theory, 68–70, 133n349; Macneil's theory, 70–2, 127, 206–7; marginalization of, 331;

non-legal aspects, 70–1; norms in, 68–70, 71–4, 110; parol evidence rule, 69; planning skills, 74–5; remedies, 139–40; state role, 68, 72, 74, 110; in syllabi, 326n822. *See also* context; contract law; Macaulay, Stewart; Macneil, Ian R
relevance, determination of: about, 23–5, 179, 234, 246–55; analogical reasoning, 179, 234, 251–4; case excerpts vs. full case, 249–50; case study method, 44; contextual factors, 253–4; as core knowledge, 179–81, 246–54; distinctiveness of law, 180, 234; equal treatment, 247; ethical inquiry, 51; fact patterns, 249–50, 253, 259; formalist approach, 23–4, 44–5; importance of, 247–8; issue spotting, 250–1, 271–2, 274–5; precedent, 252–3; problem solving, 167–8; realist approach, 51. *See also* legal reasoning; skills
reliance, 47–9, 59–60, 115, 136–7, 191–3
"Reliance Interest" articles (Fuller & Perdue), 47–9, 59–60, 116n300, 136–7
remedies: economic analysis, 64; formalism vs. realism, 48, 137; functionalist approach, 47–9, 98, 137, 139–41; policy, 48, 149; range of possibilities, 139; reasonable expectations, 140; risks in, 139; solicitor's role, 138–40; state role, 50–1
remedies, sequence in course: about, 36, 37, 136–8, 150–1, 267–70, 331; in *Ben-Ishai & Percy*, 132–3, 146–51, 283; first vs. last, 121, 132–3, 136–40, 148, 267–70, 283, 331; formalism vs. realism, 37, 136–8; institutional culture, 269–70; Langdell's casebook, 137, 268; learning objectives, 148–9; in *Milner*, 100; operationalizing of theory, 37, 136, 141, 148, 150–1; research study results, 37, 268–70; in *Swan*, 98, 138–41, 150–1, 283; in *Waddams*, 121, 141–5, 150–1
research study: about, 4–7, 25–36; Contracts professors, 27–32; course materials, 24–6, 30–1, 34–6, 82n212; data collection and analysis, 25–7, 33–6, 265; eclectic toolkit of skills, 5–7, 15–20, 23; empirical research, review of, 20–3, 27–8, 35; formalism and realism, as categories, 181–3, 220; interviews with professors, 6, 26, 30–4, 36, 179, 213, 265–6; key questions on, 5, 23, 38, 331–2; law faculties, participating, 31; limitations, 25, 265; marginalization of context, 23; methodology, 25–36; operationalizing of theory into teaching, 6–7, 23–31, 37–9, 81, 265–6, 286–92, 338–40; overview of this book, 37–9; on pedagogy, 265–6; qualitative research, 33–6; results of, 7, 23–5, 77; syllabus, as term, 36; theory/practice relationship, 7; time period, 31, 34. *See also* operationalizing of theory into teaching; professors in research study; professors in research study, careers; professors in research study, quotations
research study, casebooks: analysis of, 25–7, 30–1, 35–6, 79–81, 290; key questions on, 38; selection by professors, 39, 82n212, 309–16, 324–5. See also *Ben-Ishai & Percy*; *Boyle & Percy*; casebooks; case method; *Milner*; *Swan*; *Waddams*

Restatement of Contracts and *Restatement (Second) of Contracts*, 48, 49, 58, 94, 143n371, 144, 231, 241–2
results-based reasoning, 187–9, 259–60, 270n669, 271. *See also* external perspectives; legal reasoning
rhetoric, as term, 239n590
rights, 92, 162
Ron Engineering & Construction Eastern Ltd v Ontario (1981), 326n825
rule of law: about, 220–1, 228, 293–6; distinctiveness of law, 228, 234; equal treatment, 17, 39, 220–1, 225–6, 228, 234–5, 247, 293–5; formalist approach, 81, 183, 224–6, 293–6, 298–9; and justice, 261; realist approach, 293–6, 298–9. *See also* formalism; legal reasoning; realism
Ryerson University, 4n1, 330, 333–6

Sacks, Albert, 18, 102n270, 111n289
Sandomierski, David: "Against Nomopolies," 323nn809, 810; "Training Lawyers," 13n21
Sandrik, Karen, 130
science, legal, 9, 43–5, 48, 65, 76, 289n. *See also* formalism; Langdell, Christopher Columbus, *A Selection of Cases* (1879)
Scott v Wawanesa (1989), 204n508
A Selection of Cases on the Law of Contracts (Langdell). *See* Langdell, Christopher Columbus, *A Selection of Cases* (1879)
A Selection of Cases on the Law of Contracts (Williston): (1903), 48, 49, 94, 229, 297n730
sexuality: *Trinity Western* cases, 4n, 13–14
Sharp, Malcolm Sharp, 78
Simpson, Brian, 29n59, 73n195, 204–7
Singer, Joseph William, 42n86, 46nn105, 106, 47n108, 47n110, 50–3, 54n136, 196n487
skills: about, 5–7, 163–71, 175–7, 292; advocacy and argumentation, 163–6; analogical reasoning, 114, 150–1, 164, 178, 179, 234, 251–4, 264–5; classification, 162, 174–5, 227–8; combining of rules, 244–6; as core knowledge, 302; creative lawyering, 60–1, 166, 168–9, 187, 260; critical thinking, 165–6, 170–2, 257, 281–2; detail, 246, 279; drafting, 155, 261, 278–80; eclectic toolkit of, 5–7, 15–20, 52–3, 60, 164–6, 176–9; empathy, 165, 261, 340; ethos of better lawyers, 169–71; extraction of rules, 244–6; framing cases, 259–60; issue spotting, 250–1, 271–2, 274–5; narratives, 73; negotiation, 74, 101–2, 139–40, 155, 166, 206, 254, 260, 279–80, 292, 321; planning, 63–4, 67, 74–5, 166–8, 260, 278–80, 296; problem solving, 84, 166–8; relational contracts, 73–4, 164; relevance, determination of, 167, 179–81, 246–55; toolkit for lawyer as citizen, 164–5, 173–5. *See also* core knowledge; lawyer as citizen; legal education "to make better lawyers"; legal reasoning; relevance, determination of
Smith, Stephen, 94, 96
social class: marginalization of, 135, 262; operationalizing of theory into teaching, 262; pedagogy, 165. *See also* context
socio-legal studies, 46, 68–76, 134, 205. *See also* context
sociological relationalism, 69

structural factors in teaching. *See* law schools and institutional culture
students: articling students, 157; bar exam pressure, 154; changes in first-year students, 22–3, 303–4; critical thinking by, 257, 281–2; discomfort with uncertainty, 185–6, 230, 256; diversity of, 32n68; financial pressures on, 319; gifts of "laughter and doubt," 256; influence on professors, 307, 309–10, 314, 318–19, 326; institutional culture, 293, 317–19; intellectual vs. professional goals, 153–60; legal consciousness, 22, 239–40; parity across courses, 314, 318–19; preconceptions about law, 184–7, 203, 230, 235–6, 280–1; resistance to realism, 135, 154
Studies in Contract Law (companion to *Swan*). *See* Reiter, Barry J & John Swan, eds, *Studies in Contract Law* (companion to *Swan*)
study, research. *See* research study
substantive equality, 130–1
Sugarman, David, 288–9n718
Supreme Court of Canada: multiple legal traditions, 300n736; *Trinity Western* cases, 4n1, 13–14
Swan, Angela (was John): career, 83, 88, 91–2, 96, 98, 100, 119, 124n320; on remedies, 283. *See also* Reiter, Barry J & John Swan, eds, *Studies in Contract Law* (companion to *Swan*)
Swan, Angela & Jakub Adamski, *Canadian Contract Law* (textbook): 1st ed (2006, John Swan), 93; 3d ed (2012, Angela Swan with Adamski), 93–5, 97, 297; reasonable expectations, 93–5
Swan (Angela Swan et al, *Contracts: Cases, Notes & Materials*): about, 36, 82–4, 98, 150–1; commentary, 138; core knowledge, 151; market share, 77, 82, 150, 305–6; operationalizing of theory, 77, 81–2, 98, 136, 141, 150–1; publication information, 79n208; realist approach, 77, 82–3, 90, 243, 305–6; research study analysis of, 36, 79–81; reviews of, 82, 85–7, 106; social and historical context, 84; US influences on, 80–1, 83, 84, 86, 111, 151. *See also* Reiter, Barry J & John Swan, eds, *Studies in Contract Law* (companion to *Swan*)
Swan (Angela Swan et al, *Contracts: Cases, Notes & Materials*), editions: editors, 79n208, 83, 88, 91, 97, 98, 124, 151; 1st ed (1978, John Swan with Barry Reiter), 83–4, 106; 2d ed (1982, John Swan with Barry Reiter), 84–7, 89, 95; 3d and 4th eds (1985, 1991, John Swan with Barry Reiter), 87–90, 95; 5th and 6th eds (1997, 2002, John Swan with Barry Reiter & Nicholas Bala), 91–3, 95; 7th ed (2006, John Swan with Barry Reiter & Nicholas Bala), 93–8; 8th ed (2010, Angela Swan with Barry Reiter & Nicholas Bala), 83, 97; 9th ed (2015, Angela Swan with Nicholas Bala & Jakub Adamski), 83, 97–8, 139–41
Swan, topics: about, 98; academic/practical divide, 105–6; adjudication, 84, 88–90, 98, 111–12; context, 84, 91, 92, 105, 140–1; contract law as category, 96; critiques of formalism, 90; facts, 100; feminism, 127n331; formalism vs. realism, 81; functionalism, 90, 96, 98, 138, 139–41; indeterminacy of law, 96–7, 98; instrumentalism, 90; justice, 105; legal process school, 111; multiple

jurisdictions, 92; planning, 88, 89; policy, 88; problem solving, 84; purposiveness of law, 85–7, 96–7; reasonable expectations, 84–8, 95, 98, 191; relational contracts, 91, 95, 98, 139–41; remedies, 81, 98, 138–41, 150–1, 283; solicitor's role, 82–3, 87–9, 91, 97, 138–41, 327; values, 84–5, 88–93, 98, 105, 114
syllabi: about, 266–7, 280–1; collaboration with colleagues, 310–17, 329; formalist pedagogy, 266–7; institutional materials, 309–12, 316–17; realist pedagogy, 266–7, 280; research study analysis of, 25–7, 34–6; self-designed courses, 180, 287, 311, 314–16, 325–7, 329, 332–3; supplementary readings, 135, 281–2, 297, 305, 324. *See also* course materials
syllabi, topics: analogical reasoning, 252–3; competing values, 200–1; core knowledge, 267; course objectives, 155, 161, 173, 243, 262–4, 267, 297; critical thinking, 172, 285; distinctiveness of law, 255; evaluation, 276; external perspectives, 195, 207–8, 262–3; law vs. justice, 203; legal reasoning, 252–3, 262–3, 264n652, 267, 280; morality, 203; public vs. private law, 233; relational contracts, 326; uncertainty in law, 186. *See also* course materials

teachers. *See* professors in research study; professors in research study, careers; professors in research study, quotations
teaching methods. *See* case method; course materials; examinations and evaluation; pedagogy; pedagogy, strategies; syllabi
technology: in *Ben-Ishai & Percy*, 129; curricular reforms, 334, 336; professors' use of, 167–8
Tercon Contractors v British Columbia (2010), 279
theory, legal. *See* legal theory; legal theory and formalism/realism relationship; legal theory and practice
thinking like a lawyer. *See* legal education "to make better lawyers"; legal reasoning
toolkit of legal reasoning, overview of, 15–20. *See also* legal reasoning; skills
treaties, 128. *See also* Indigenous perspectives
Trebilcock, Michael, 84, 126, 146. See also *Waddams* (Stephen Waddams et al, *Cases and Materials on Contracts*)
Trinity Western University v Law Society of Upper Canada (2018), 4n1, 13–14
Truth and Reconciliation Commission (TRC), 213, 218. *See also* Indigenous perspectives

uncertainty of law, 185–6, 230, 256. *See also* indeterminacy and contingency
unconscionability: economic analysis, 64; inconsistency of doctrine (Dalton), 58; underlying factors, 193; unfairness, 115–16n300, 294; Waddams on, 115–16, 120, 123, 294n722; what judges do vs. say, 120, 294
underlying factors, 57–60, 187–8. *See also* external perspectives; policy

United States: attacks on formalism, 42, 76, 300n735; vs. Canadian sensibility, 299–301; contract law, 41–2; Contracts courses, 28–9, 31n65; formalism, 42; history of law schools, 9–10; law and economics, 210–11; legal education and curriculum, 28n54, 101, 337; legal reasoning, 18–20; Mertz's research, 20–3, 42; research in legal education, 27n52. *See also* Kennedy, David & William W Fisher III, *The Canon of American Legal Thought* (2006)
United States, casebooks: about, 78–81; historical background, 9, 41–2; influences on Canadian casebooks, 78–81, 83, 86, 101–5; legal realism, 150; remedies, 138n360. *See also* Corbin, Arthur Linton, *Corbin on Contracts* (1950); Fuller, Lon L; Langdell, Christopher Columbus, *A Selection of Cases* (1879); Macaulay, Stewart; Macneil, Ian R; Markovits, Daniel
United Steel Workers, Local 1330 v US Steel Corp (1980), 19n35, 28n58, 60n154, 61
universities: curricular reforms, 15, 328–40; jurisdiction over legal education, 8–14, 103; teaching supports, 328, 329n828. *See also* law schools; legal education; legal education "to make better lawyers"
University of British Columbia, 31n64, 329n828
University of Manitoba, 10, 31n64
University of Toronto, 8, 31n64, 102–3, 111
University of Victoria, 31n64, 218, 333, 335–6
utopian visions, 53–4, 60–1. *See also* critical legal studies (CLS)

values: about, 22, 114, 198, 218–19, 293–4; altruism, 54–7, 65, 164, 196, 198–9, 202–3; Aristotelian virtues, 5n4, 29; civic virtue, 5n4, 29; clarification of, 66n175; competing values, 54, 65, 84, 114, 163, 196, 198–9, 202–3, 293–4; duties as lawyer, 171; efficiency standard, 62–7; ethics of better lawyers, 169–71; fairness, 89, 91–3, 98, 235–6; formalist approach, 81, 222; freedom, 29, 125–6, 129–31; human dignity, 89; ideology and legal reasoning, 54–7; individualism, 29, 54–7, 65, 196, 198–9, 202–3; legislative examples, 197–8; myth of law as neutral, 198–9; normative standards, 194, 199; operationalizing in legal reasoning, 258–62; and policy, 188; in politics, 49–50, 196–9; realist approach, 22, 49–54, 84, 114, 188, 202–3; substantive equality, 130–1; in *Swan*, 84, 89–93, 98, 114. *See also* justice; lawyer as citizen; morality
Vaver, David, 132
virtues. *See* values

Waddams, Stephen: career, 84, 96, 99, 124n320; on competing values, 293–4; overview of approach, 117–23; *Principle and Policy in Contract Law* (2011), 120, 190; "Unconscionability in Contracts," 115–16, 120, 123, 294n722
Waddams, Stephen, ed, *Milner's Cases and Materials on Contracts*. See *Milner* (James Bryce Milner, ed, *Cases and Materials on Contracts*

and Stephen Waddams, ed, *Milner's Cases and Materials on Contracts*)

Waddams, Stephen, *Introduction to the Study of Law* (1979, textbook): adjudication, 117–18; autonomy of law, 118–19; Macdonald's review of, 117–22, 142; tensions within, 120–1, 123

Waddams, Stephen, *The Law of Contracts* (1977, textbook): about, 99, 113–17; adjudication, 114; competing values, 114–15, 293–4; legal reasoning, 114–17, 254; preface, 113–17; realist textbook, 81–2, 113–15; reliance, 115–16; research study analysis of, 36; reviews of, 113; tensions within, 114–15, 123; unconscionability, 115–16

Waddams (Stephen Waddams et al, *Cases and Materials on Contracts*): about, 36, 99, 121–3, 150–1; 1st & 2d ed (1994, 2000, with Michael Trebilcock & Mary Anne Waldron), 99; 3d ed (2005, et al), 99, 121n316, 122; 4th & 5th ed (2010, 2014, et al), 99, 121n316, 122; 6th ed (2018, et al), 99, 121n316, 122, 141–5; assignment of chapters, 122n318, 145, 150n390; commentary, 121–3, 141–5, 151, 237, 293–4; editors, 99, 121n316, 124, 151, 294, 306; market share, 81, 82n212, 306; Milner's influence, 99; operationalizing of theory, 81, 120–3, 136, 141, 143, 150–1; pedagogical use of, 122n318, 304–6; publication information, 79n209, 146; research study analysis of, 79–81; US influences on, 80–1, 122–3

Waddams, topics: adjudication, 123, 141–2, 145; case method, 81; context, 143–5; contingency of law, 143–4; core knowledge, 145, 151; feminism, 127n331; formalism vs. realism, 81, 123, 141–2, 144, 150–1; functionalism, 123, 144; perspectives chapter, 80; purposiveness of law, 122–3; realism, 122–3, 143–4; remedies, 121–2, 141–5, 150; rule of law, 293–5; theory chapter, 122–3

Waldron, Mary Anne, 79n209, 99, 121n316. See also *Waddams* (Stephen Waddams et al, *Cases and Materials on Contracts*)

Warner Bros Pictures v Nelson (1937), 208n516

Weinrib, Ernest: autonomy of law, 16n29; career, 83n214, 96n253; formalist theorist, 45n102, 182; influence on professors, 221–4, 297, 298n731; and *Swan*, 83, 96n253

Western, Trinity. See *Trinity Western University*

Western University, 31n64

"What the Law Schools Can Contribute to the Making of Lawyers" (Fuller), 101–2, 104n275, 108

Williston, Samuel, ed, *A Selection of Cases on the Law of Contracts*: (1903), 48, 49, 94, 229, 297n730

women's issues. *See* feminism

Wright, Cecil Augustus, 99n257, 103

writing and drafting, 251, 271n672, 273–4, 278–80, 284, 320–1. *See also* examinations and evaluation; skills

York University, 8

www.ingramcontent.com/pod-product-compliance
Lightning Source LLC
LaVergne TN
LVHW090146080826
844660LV00013B/695/J

* 9 7 8 1 4 8 7 5 0 5 9 4 3 *